AF906084

Reimagining Curriculum and Assessment in the Age of Generative AI

Aras Bozkurt
https://orcid.org/0000-0002-4520-642X
Anadolu University, Turkey

IGI Global
Scientific Publishing
Publishing Tomorrow's Research Today

Vice President of Editorial Melissa Wagner
Director of Acquisitions Mikaela Felty
Director of Book Development Jocelynn Hessler
Production Manager Mike Brehm
Cover Design Jose Rosado

Published in the United States of America by
IGI Global Scientific Publishing
701 East Chocolate Avenue
Hershey, PA, 17033, USA
Tel: 717-533-8845 | Fax: 717-533-7115
Website: https://www.igi-global.com E-mail: cust@igi-global.com

Copyright © 2026 by IGI Global Scientific Publishing. All rights reserved. No part of this publication may be reproduced, stored or distributed in any form or by any means, electronic or mechanical, including photocopying, without written permission from the publisher. Use of this publication to train generative artificial intelligence (AI) technologies is expressly prohibited. The publisher reserves all rights to license its use for generative AI training and machine learning model development.

Product or company names used in this set are for identification purposes only. Inclusion of the names of the products or companies does not indicate a claim of ownership by IGI Global Scientific Publishing of the trademark or registered trademark.

Library of Congress Cataloging-in-Publication Data

CIP Data Pending
ISBN13: 979-8-3373-7579-3
Isbn13Softcover: 979-8-3373-7580-9
EISBN13: 979-8-3373-7581-6

British Cataloguing in Publication Data
A Cataloguing in Publication record for this book is available from the British Library.

All work contributed to this book is new, previously-unpublished material.
The views expressed in this book are those of the authors, but not necessarily of the publisher.
This book contains information sourced from authentic and highly regarded references, with reasonable efforts made to ensure the reliability of the data and information presented. The authors, editors, and publisher believe the information in this book to be accurate and true as of the date of publication. Every effort has been made to trace and credit the copyright holders of all materials included. However, the authors, editors, and publisher cannot assume responsibility for the validity of all materials or the consequences of their use. Should any copyright material be found unacknowledged, please inform the publisher so that corrections may be made in future reprints.

Table of Contents

Detailed Table of Contents

This chapter explores the integration of humanizing pedagogy in online and distance learning environments in an era shaped by digital transformation and artificial intelligence. Drawing on Paulo Freire's critical education pedagogy, Moore's Transactional Distance Theory, and Pacansky-Brock's humanizing online teaching framework, the chapter explores how relational, inclusive, and equity-focused teaching can target learner disengagement, digital inequity, and psychological isolation in online and distance education. The chapter also presents Pacansky-Brock's eight practical strategies for humanizing instructional design in online and distance education. The chapter also questions the paradoxical role of artificial intelligence in education and advocates for active engagement that fosters critical thinking. The study, which offers applicable strategies and theoretical insights, is expected to contribute to efforts to redesign online pedagogy as a humanized, inclusive, and transformative educational practice.

This chapter examines how generative artificial intelligence (GenAI) equips educators with advanced tools to enhance teaching effectiveness and student outcomes. In particular, it emphasizes the role of these tools in streamlining curriculum design, defining clear learning objectives, and creating adaptive, personalized learning environments. By analyzing platforms like ChatGPT, Claude, Copilot, Gemini, Eduaide.Ai, and MagicSchool, the study shows how GenAI automates administrative tasks, generates dynamic content, and supports individualized learning pathways. While acknowledging significant benefits including improved efficiency and enhanced accessibility, the study critically addresses challenges such as academic integrity concerns, algorithmic bias, and the need for human oversight. Real-world examples offer a practical framework for educators to understand and implement GenAI tools strategically. Ultimately, GenAI is positioned not as a replacement for

Creativity has become increasingly important in all fields. The emergence of generative artificial intelligence (GenAI) technology has sparked debate on the idea that this skill can be emulated by machines. GenAI is used in fields such as architecture, graphic design, game design, fashion, art, sports, advertising and marketing, and medicine. Its impact on education is also under intense scrutiny. This chapter explores the GenAI-human collaboration that is transforming creativity in fields ranging from science and technology to education and the arts. The use of GenAI in creative processes in education is discussed in the context of its opportunities and potential limitations. There are discussions on how it redefines ethical issues related to creativity. Furthermore, the implications for copyright and originality are evaluated, and the situation that these technologies create in relation to ownership is discussed.

This book chapter introduces the McFlai Model, which aims to shape the future of distance education by integrating micro-credentials, flipped learning models, and artificial intelligence. The model proposes employing various language models for distinct purposes throughout the learning process, from enrolment to assessment stages. Consequently, it envisages designing highly personalised, flexible, and interactive learning experiences. The model is supported by dynamic content tailored to learners' individual needs and proficiency levels, learning analytics, and guidance systems powered by generative artificial intelligence. Furthermore, it recommends utilising large language models to convert instructional materials into micro-credential formats and to monitor learner progress, thereby supporting educators. Artificial intelligence systems, overseen by human experts at every step, aim to enhance learner success while enabling educators to subtly contribute to content design and guidance. McFlai offers a sustainable, practical, and scalable solution for distance education systems.

The integration of generative AI into higher education is reshaping traditional teaching, learning, and assessment practices. This paper examines the opportunities AI offers for personalized learning, engagement, and administrative efficiency, while also addressing critical challenges, such as ethical risks, digital literacy gaps, and legal implications, including data protection and copyright issues. It highlights the evolving student profile shaped by digital technologies and the need for balanced educational strategies that integrate AI tools without compromising critical thinking and social interaction. Emphasizing a middle-path approach, the study advocates for legally compliant, pedagogically sound, and socially just AI use in universities, calling for enhanced teacher training, updated academic policies, and the promotion of AI literacy among students to ensure responsible and equitable technological integration.

A wide range of traditional approaches to education continue to be challenged by the development of generative artificial intelligence (Gen AI). These developments and emerging technologies has the potential to provide alternative solutions to assessment problems that have not been adequately addressed in the past. Gen AI has the potential to increase efficiency in diverse areas, which have annually been performed with intensive human labor. Could this "hype" concerning the strengths and potential of Gen AI be concealing its weaknesses? The development of Gen AI is already causing significant problems concerning academic integrity. Second, Gen AI tools are prone to incorporating the biases, since they incorporate almost all human made data. Furthermore, recent studies show that Gen AI algorithms can "hallucinate" or "fabricate". The purpose of this study is to review the opportunities and challenges of Gen AI-based assessments in higher education, as well as make recommendations regarding its effective and fair use within the context of recent studies and policy guidelines.

Preface

The rapid evolution of generative artificial intelligence (GenAI) has brought both opportunities and challenges to the fields of curriculum design, pedagogy, and assessment. While the educational community has long engaged in debates about digital transformation, the scale and speed of GenAI's impact marks a profound turning point. As editors of this volume, we recognize that educators, policymakers, and researchers face an urgent need to critically reflect on how education systems can adapt—not just to the presence of new technologies, but to the ways these technologies reshape knowledge, skills, and learning itself.

This book brings together leading scholars and practitioners who examine these issues from diverse angles, grounded in both theory and practice. Their collective contributions highlight the necessity of balancing innovation with critical caution. We cannot afford to treat GenAI as a simple add-on to existing systems; rather, it demands a rethinking of the very structures of curriculum, pedagogy, and assessment. What emerges from these chapters is a shared recognition: while technology can augment teaching and learning, the human dimension of education must remain at the center.

Our intention is not to present a definitive roadmap, but to curate a scholarly dialogue that offers conceptual clarity, practical insights, and critical questions. By doing so, we aim to equip educators and institutions with tools to navigate this era of uncertainty with confidence and imagination. We hope this collection will serve as both a reference and a provocation, inspiring the educational community to chart futures where human agency, equity, and creativity flourish alongside technological innovation.

CHAPTER OVERVIEW

- **Chapter 1** (Hasan Ucar) explores humanizing pedagogy in online and distance education, framing inclusivity and engagement as antidotes to digital inequities and psychological isolation.
- **Chapter 2** (Baris Avci) examines how GenAI tools streamline curriculum design and content creation, emphasizing both potential efficiencies and ethical challenges.
- **Chapter 3** (Nick Baker, William Evans, and Tom Farrelly) considers curriculum-level approaches, proposing the Constraints-Led Approach and Spiral Curriculum as models for integrating GenAI in higher education.
- **Chapter 4** (Yesim Nalkesen Akin and Betul Yildizhan Bora) focuses on cognitive load and scaffolding, analyzing AI-powered pathways that balance theory and practice in instructional design.
- **Chapter 5** (Yasemin Karal) interrogates the intersection of creativity and GenAI, weighing its role in reimagining originality, ethics, and ownership in education.
- **Chapter 6** (Sefa Emre Öncü) introduces the McFlai Model, a framework blending micro-credentials, flipped learning, and AI for scalable distance education.
- **Chapter 7** (Dana Volosevici, Simona Eftimie, and Iulia Ghita) examines challenges, opportunities, and regulatory issues tied to integrating GenAI into higher education institutions.
- **Chapter 8** (Hayri Suna and Mahmut Özer) highlights both the opportunities and risks of GenAI in assessment, particularly with respect to integrity and algorithmic reliability.
- **Chapter 9** (Jésica Alhelí Cortés Ruiz, María Elena Zepeda Hurtado, and Edgar Cardoso Espinosa) explores systemic challenges in educational evaluation, emphasizing collaboration between educators, researchers, and policymakers.
- **Chapter 10** (Wissal EL Fougour and Mohamed Erradi) looks at formative assessment, proposing adaptive feedback systems powered by AI while cautioning against over-reliance.
- **Chapter 11** (Seval Kemal, Dila Süzan, Ali Öztüfekçi, and Sezin Esfer) presents a framework for AI-supported writing feedback in EFL contexts, stressing ethics, usability, and the preservation of students' voices.

CONCLUSION

The chapters in this book demonstrate that the integration of generative AI into education is not a linear process but a contested and evolving terrain. On the one hand, GenAI offers remarkable potential to enhance learning, personalize assessment, and support educators in their professional roles. On the other hand, it raises complex questions of ethics, equity, and epistemology—questions that educators must confront with both rigor and imagination.

What becomes evident across the contributions is the necessity of maintaining a human-centered approach. Technologies may evolve at a rapid pace, but the enduring goals of education—critical thinking, social responsibility, and creativity—remain constant. If GenAI is to serve as a meaningful partner in learning, its adoption must be shaped by values as much as by technical capacities. This requires collaborative effort across disciplines, institutions, and societies.

We close this preface with a reminder that the future of education is not predetermined by algorithms or platforms. It will be determined by the choices educators, researchers, and policymakers make today. May this volume serve as both a resource and an invitation: to critically engage, to innovate responsibly, and to reimagine curriculum and assessment in ways that affirm the best of what education can be in the age of generative AI.

— *Aras Bozkurt, Editor*

Chapter 1
Humanizing Pedagogy for Online and Distance Education:
Towards a More Inclusive and Engaging Learning Milieus

Hasan Ucar
https://orcid.org/0000-0001-9174-4299
Anadolu University, Turkey

ABSTRACT

This chapter explores the integration of humanizing pedagogy in online and distance learning environments in an era shaped by digital transformation and artificial intelligence. Drawing on Paulo Freire's critical education pedagogy, Moore's Transactional Distance Theory, and Pacansky-Brock's humanizing online teaching framework, the chapter explores how relational, inclusive, and equity-focused teaching can target learner disengagement, digital inequity, and psychological isolation in online and distance education. The chapter also presents Pacansky-Brock's eight practical strategies for humanizing instructional design in online and distance education. The chapter also questions the paradoxical role of artificial intelligence in education and advocates for active engagement that fosters critical thinking. The study, which offers applicable strategies and theoretical insights, is expected to contribute to efforts to redesign online pedagogy as a humanized, inclusive, and transformative educational practice.

DOI: 10.4018/979-8-3373-7579-3.ch001

ght © 2026, IGI Global Scientific Publishing. Copying or distributing in print or electronic forms without written permission of IGI Global Scientific Publishing is prohibited. Use of this chapter to generative artificial intelligence (AI) technologies is expressly prohibited. The publisher reserves all rights to license its use for generative AI training and machine learning model development.

INTRODUCTION

The integration of humanizing pedagogy within online and distance education has moved from a progressive ideal to a critical necessity (Peercy et al., 2022; Razak et al., 2025). This shift has been profoundly accelerated by the global transition to remote learning during the COVID-19 pandemic, a period that cast a harsh light on the limitations of purely technology-centric models. The crisis exposed and exacerbated deep-seated issues of student isolation, digital inequity, and profound disengagement, making clear that effective online education requires more than content delivery systems; it demands human connection (Boz & Uçar, 2025; Pacansky-Brock, 2020). Humanizing pedagogy, a framework rooted in the critical educational theories of Paulo Freire (2020), provides a powerful antidote, advocating for a dialogic, inclusive, and participatory approach to teaching and learning.

In this contemporary landscape, the rapid emergence of generative and agentic Artificial Intelligence (AI) introduces a new and complex dimension (Bozkurt et al., 2024). AI presents a dual potential: it can be leveraged to create more personalized and efficient learning pathways, yet it also risks amplifying the very dehumanizing tendencies it purports to solve by standardizing interaction and potentially perpetuating algorithmic bias (Bozkurt, 2024; Zawacki-Richter et al., 2019). This makes the call for humanizing pedagogy more urgent than ever. Recent research consistently underscores this imperative, offering practical strategies to guide educators in creating supportive virtual environments that foster strong interpersonal connections and trust (Gleason, 2021; Li et al., 2022; Pacansky-Brock et al., 2023; Stewart, 2023).

Engagement is widely recognized as foundational to academic achievement in online settings (Lu et al., 2024). Empirical findings demonstrate that humanizing strategies are positively associated with learner engagement, motivation, and the development of social presence, the feeling of being "real" and connected to others in a virtual space (Garrison, 2017; Ita Olszewska et al., 2023; Kim et al., 2023). By prioritizing empathy and communication, these strategies strengthen the relational and affective dimensions of learning (Pacansky-Brock et al., 2020). Yet, as Li et al. (2022) observe, a significant gap remains in research that systematically examines these strategies in the context of an increasingly AI-mediated educational ecosystem (Razak et al., 2025).

This chapter aims to address this gap. It will first define the core tenets of Freire's humanizing pedagogy, contrasting it with the "banking" model of education. It will then explore how these principles are operationalized online through Pacansky-Brock et al.'s (2023) framework, linking them to Moore's (2019) Transactional Distance Theory. Crucially, it will critically examine the role of generative AI within each dimension. Following this, a new discussion section will analyze the paradox of AI as both a tool for and a threat to humanization, exploring the concept of fostering both human and AI agentic engagement. Finally, the chapter will offer concrete strategies for educators to create inclusive, engaging, and genuinely humanized online experiences in the age of AI.

BACKGROUND

Humanizing Pedagogy: A Human-Centered Inclusive Approach

Humanizing pedagogy originates from the work of Paulo Freire (2020), whose philosophy was forged in his efforts to promote literacy among oppressed communities. Freire vehemently critiqued what he termed the "banking" concept of education, where the instructor is the depositor of knowledge and learners are passive receptacles. This model, he argued, is inherently dehumanizing because it negates learners' own knowledge, experiences, and capacity for critical thought. In online education, the banking model can manifest through static, content-heavy courses with limited interaction, where learners are expected to passively consume pre-recorded lectures and complete automated quizzes, a structure that can be easily replicated and scaled by impersonal AI-driven platforms (Gleason, 2021).

In stark contrast, Freire proposed a "problem-posing" education, a dialogic process where instructors and learners are co-investigators of the world. This approach is central to humanizing pedagogy. It emphasizes that education must be grounded in the lived realities of learners, fostering critical consciousness, the ability to analyze and act upon the social and political forces shaping one's life. This pedagogical orientation provides a vital link between culturally responsive theories and instructional practices aimed at creating equitable and socially just learning environments (Del Carmen Salazar, 2013). While not prescriptive, humanizing pedagogy is guided by core principles that inform reflective teaching. These include: (1) cultivating compassionate and authentic relationships; (2) actively mitigating deficit-oriented thinking; (3) facilitating learners' progression toward critical consciousness; (4) applying this consciousness to enact transformation; and (5) utilizing pedagogical models that embody a holistic philosophy (Czop Assaf et al., 2019).

Four Strands of Humanized Online Distance Education in the AI Era

The principles of humanizing pedagogy find a strong theoretical counterpart in Moore's (2019) Transactional Distance Theory. Moore posited that in distance education, a psychological and communication gap, the "transactional distance", separates learners and instructors. The magnitude of this distance is determined by the interplay of three key variables: Structure (the rigidity or flexibility of the course), Dialogue (the quality and frequency of meaningful interaction), and Learner Autonomy. High structure and low dialogue result in high transactional distance, creating an impersonal and often alienating experience, particularly for learners with less autonomy (Falloon, 2011).

The framework of humanized online teaching by Pacansky-Brock et al. (2023) offers a practical model for reducing this distance, even amidst the complexities introduced by AI. Their model integrates four interconnected strands: equity mindset, culturally responsive teaching, psychologically inclusive course design, and digital fluency. According to Pacansky-Brock et al. (2023) the cultivation of a sense of belonging is a cornerstone of humanized online teaching and necessitates the assurance of identity safety for all learners. Educators committed to humanizing their pedagogical practice must be equipped with the requisite knowledge, dispositions, and competencies to navigate digital environments effectively. This includes developing digital fluency to support an equity-oriented mindset, designing inclusive online learning experiences, implementing culturally responsive instructional strategies, and fostering meaningful relationships in virtual contexts. Given the inherently complex and integrated nature of professional development in this domain, these four dimensions, equity, inclusion, cultural responsiveness, and digital fluency, should not be treated as discrete areas (Figure 1). Rather, they are deeply interconnected and must be approached holistically, as each dimension informs, reinforces, and enhances the others in the creation of humane and effective online learning environments.

Figure 1. Four strands of humanized online distance education

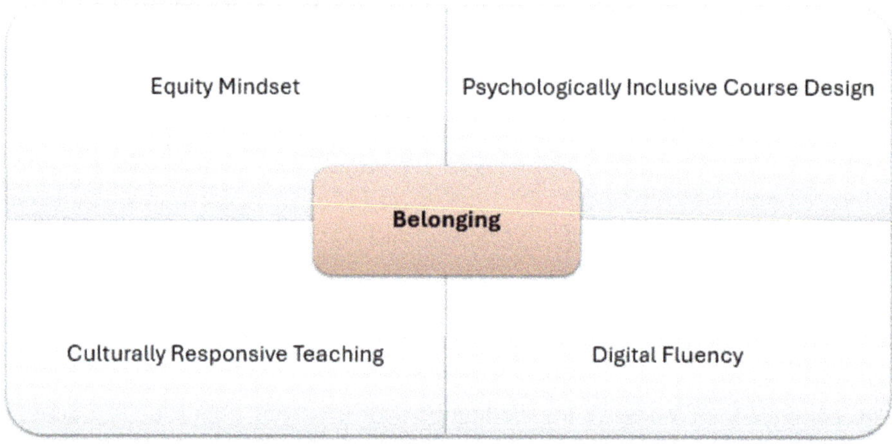

Source: Pacansky-Brock et al., 2023, p. 44

Humanized online teaching is built upon a holistic pedagogical approach that integrates an equity mindset, culturally responsive teaching, psychologically inclusive course design, and digital fluency (Pacansky-Brock et al., 2023; Paguyo et al., 2022). Developing an equity mindset is fundamental to humanized online teaching, particularly where delivery-based instruction remains dominant. While increased student-instructor interaction is a hallmark of humanized pedagogy, research indicates that interaction alone does not guarantee equitable outcomes for all learners. Equity-minded educators engage in ongoing self-reflection concerning their identities, biases, and teaching practices (Dewsbury & Brame, 2019; Kim et al., 2023). Central to this approach is the recognition that fostering a sense of belonging and identity safety for all learners necessitates educators critically examining their own biases and adopting an equity-oriented perspective. This involves instructors critically examining their own biases and committing to addressing systemic disparities in student outcomes. In the AI era, this extends to a critical awareness of algorithmic bias. An equity mindset involves not only self-reflection and race-conscious awareness but also a commitment to tracking and addressing systemic disparities in student outcomes.

Humanized online pedagogy is informed by a rich body of scholarship on culturally responsive teaching, which advocates for affirming learners' racial, cultural, and linguistic identities while ensuring intellectual rigor (Gay, 2018). This framework emphasizes the importance of recognizing learners' diverse cultural and linguistic backgrounds, validating their lived experiences, and ensuring that all learners are intellectually challenged. This strand emphasizes validating learners' diverse cultural backgrounds and lived experiences. While AI can generate culturally generic content, a humanizing approach uses technology to amplify diverse voices, for instance, by creating assignments where learners use digital storytelling tools to share their unique perspectives (Woodley et al., 2017).

A psychologically inclusive design is essential for fostering belonging in online education, where learners often navigate courses remotely. This involves intentionally shaping the course structure with affirming language, supportive visuals, and a warm instructor presence to make the environment feel safe and welcoming. Human oversight is essential here, as AI-generated communication can lack the genuine warmth and empathy needed to create true psychological safety. Consequently, humanized pedagogy calls for the intentional design of psychologically inclusive online environments, where learners perceive dignity and safety through carefully embedded verbal and non-verbal cues (Paguyo et al., 2022). These include affirming language, supportive visuals, and a warm instructor presence, which are particularly critical in asynchronous settings where physical cues are often absent.

Digital fluency is a critical skill for instructors aiming to implement humanized pedagogy in online learning environments. Traditionally, digital fluency meant skillfully using digital tools. Today, it must be expanded to include critical AI literacy, the ability to understand, evaluate, and ethically apply generative AI. It involves teaching learners not just how to use AI, but when and why, and to critically assess its outputs rather than accepting them as objective truth. Effective humanization requires instructors to communicate effectively across culturally diverse student populations. As such, digital fluency is not merely technical competence but a pedagogical imperative in inclusive online teaching. Achieving digital fluency in online and distance learning environments requires instructors to possess a high degree of digital proficiency. This includes the ability to communicate through both high-context and low-context modes, leverage multimedia tools to enhance social presence, and ensure mobile-friendly, inclusive course access. Together, these interrelated dimensions form the foundation of an inclusive and humanizing online learning experience that promotes equity, engagement, and academic success for all learners.

Foundational Principles of Humanized Online Distance Teaching

Humanized online teaching rests on four core principles: trust, presence, awareness, and empathy (Pacansky-Brock et al., 2020; Pacansky-Brock et al., 2023). These form a pedagogical framework for creating inclusive and supportive virtual learning environments.

Trust is the first principle and cultivating student trust is crucial. This involves selective vulnerability (Hammond, 2014), where instructors share personal aspects that reveal them as authentic individuals, for instance, a story of overcoming a struggle or a brief video from their daily life. Such disclosures humanize the instructor, making them more relatable and approachable. The second principle is presence. Establishing presence means projecting one's authentic self, often through brief, unpolished videos (Costa, 2021). These visual and auditory cues confirm the instructor's active participation in the learning journey. Verbal and nonverbal cues are especially important for providing context, which greatly benefits culturally diverse learners.

The third principle, awareness, is achieved by actively understanding learners' unique identities, backgrounds, and needs. Gathering information on their prior knowledge, preferences, and real-life situations allows instructors to tailor their teaching and provide targeted support throughout the course. The fourth principle of online and distance education, empathy, requires instructors to view the learning experience from the learners' perspective, without judgment. This involves flexibility in course design and delivery, and proactively supporting learners in reaching their academic and personal goals. Empathetic instruction acknowledges diverse challenges and opportunities, fostering an environment where learners feel understood and supported.

THE EIGHT HUMANIZING STRATEGIES FOR ONLINE DISTANCE EDUCATION

The integration of humanizing elements into online course design and facilitation represents a deliberate pedagogical shift aimed at fostering an inclusive and equitable learning experience. Pacansky-Brock et al. (2023) proposes eight humanizing strategies for online distance learning environments. The humanizing elements, comprising eight distinct yet interconnected strategies, seeks to cultivate a profound sense of belonging by proactively addressing potential psychological barriers and enhancing interpersonal connections within the online modality (Figure 2). The strategic implementation of these elements, especially during the initial phases of an online course, is posited as crucial for establishing an environment conducive to psychological safety and academic success.

Figure 2. The eight humanizing strategies for online distance education

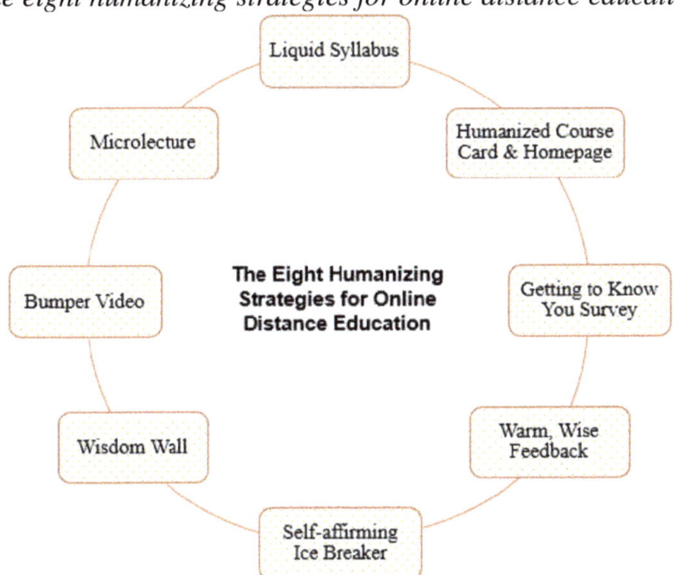

Source: Pacansky-Brock et al., 2023, p. 44

The following section outlines the eight humanizing strategies and provides illustrative examples of their implementation within online distance learning environments.

The Liquid Syllabus: This element involves the creation and dissemination of a public, mobile-friendly website to prospective learners prior to the official commencement of the course. This tool fosters transparency, reduces anxiety, and affirms learners' belonging from the outset. The Liquid Syllabus aims to establish a positive inaugural impression of both the instructor and the course, thereby fostering an early sense of support and clarity. This strategy can be used in online distance learning environments as follows, for example. An instructor can create an online site with sections for course objectives, communication expectations, student support services, and a brief welcome video. The site can be shared via email and learning management system (LMS) announcement one week before the course start to reduce student anxiety and establish early trust.
Humanized Course Card and Homepage: This strategy leverages visual and multimedia elements to convey an inviting and inclusive atmosphere from the outset. Visually warm and inclusive course entry points, often featuring instructor photos, diverse imagery, and approachable language that shape first impressions and set a tone of relational trust and accessibility. Key components include a visually appealing banner, a brief instructor welcome video, and a clearly demarcated "start here" link, collectively working to establish positive student-instructor relationships and a welcoming digital space. This strategy can be used in online distance learning environments as follows, for example. The homepage includes a banner featuring diverse learners, a "Start Here" button, a short bio and welcome message from the instructor, and navigation links with friendly labels like "Let's Get Started" and "Need Help?" to create a positive and intuitive starting point.
Getting to Know You Survey: A survey used at the beginning of a course that invites learners to share their goals, concerns, learning preferences, and identities facilitates the collection of data pertaining to individual learner needs and real-life circumstances. This element positions learners as active co-constructors of the learning environment and informs instructors' inclusive practices. This strategy can be used in online distance learning environments as follows, for example. Using an online form, the instructor can ask learners about their preferred name, time zone, prior experience with online courses, and how they best learn. The instructor can use this information to offer flexible assignment deadlines and to tailor examples during lectures.
Warm, Wise Feedback: Giving constructive, affirming feedback that communicates both high expectations and belief in learners' potential would be helpful

for humanizing course. This approach to feedback delivery is rooted in the "wise" feedback model, which is empirically demonstrated to ameliorate the detrimental cognitive effects of identity threat. By delivering feedback through voice or video recordings, the potential for misinterpretation is minimized, social presence is enhanced, and emotional well-being may be supported. This strategy can be used in online distance learning environments as follows, for example. Instead of only marking errors or giving negative feedback on a learners' writing, the instructor can write, "You've presented a strong argument here, and I can see your effort." or "I believe you're capable of pushing this homework to a better level."

Self-affirming Ice Breaker: Adapting the concept of values affirmation, a social belonging intervention, into an asynchronous format, this ice breaker is particularly beneficial for improving learning outcomes among minoritized student populations. Learners engage in self-reflection through asynchronous videos, articulating their core values and providing concrete examples of how these values manifest in their lives. This strategy can be used in online distance learning environments as follows, for example. The instructor can ask learners to post a short video or written post in the discussion forum titled "What Matters Most to Me!" sharing a personal value (e.g., motivation, creativity) and how it has shaped their learning journey. The instructor replies to each post to validate and connect to learners.

Wisdom Wall: This is a digital space where mostly former learners and present learners offer advice to future learners, fostering a sense of intergenerational community, peer affirmation, and collective success. This element utilizes an asynchronous video tool towards the conclusion of a course, prompting learners to reflect on their learning journey and identify insights they wish they had possessed at the course's inception. These reflections are subsequently shared as advice for future cohorts. This strategy can be used in online distance learning environments as follows, for example. At the end of the online course, learners respond to a discussion in LMS: "What's one thing you wish you had known when starting this course?" The learners' responses are compiled into a shared Padlet or discussion archive, available to the next cohort of learners.

Bumper Videos: Adding brief, low-barrier videos that introduce the course week would be helpful for learners. These help to humanize instruction, reduce ambiguity, and support emotional engagement through instructor presence and vocal tone. This strategy can be used in online distance learning environments as follows, for example. At the start of each course week, the instructor posts a 2-minute video recorded via a mobile phone, summarizing the week's objectives, highlighting key assignments, and offering words of encouragement such as: "Don't forget, you can always reach out to me if you're need help!"

Microlectures: These are instructional videos equipped with accurate captions that guide learners through the assimilation of intricate concepts. The lectures are short, focused instructional videos that combine cognitive clarity with relational warmth. Microlectures model inclusive communication and scaffold learning in an accessible, multimodal format. Such concise instructional videos are widely regarded as beneficial in online learning environments, potentially augmenting student participation in discussions and accommodating diverse learning rhythms by providing consistent access to instruction. This strategy can be used in online distance learning environments as follows, for example. The instructor can record a 5-minute screencast to explain a complex subject using visual slides and voice narration. During the slides the instructor can pause periodically to pose reflective questions like, "Have you seen this in your own experience?" and follow up with a related discussion post.

Navigating the Paradox of AI in Humanized Education

The integration of generative and agentic AI into education presents a fundamental paradox (Bozkurt, 2024). On one hand, AI offers the potential to automate administrative tasks, personalize learning paths, and provide instant support, theoretically freeing human educators to focus on the deeply relational aspects of teaching. On the other hand, its uncritical implementation threatens to erect a new, more sophisticated form of the "banking" model, creating a sterile, standardized, and inequitable educational experience. Navigating this paradox requires a deliberate and critical application of humanizing principles.

A key challenge lies in fostering what can be termed agentic engagement for both humans and AI. Human agency, in the Freirean sense, involves critical consciousness and the power to act upon one's world. Student agency in the AI era means developing the capacity to use these powerful tools critically and ethically as partners in inquiry, rather than becoming passive recipients of AI-generated content. An agentic learner does not ask AI to "write an essay," but rather engages it in a dialogue: "Challenge my thesis," "Offer alternative perspectives," or "Explain this concept in a different way." This is the essence of problem-posing education applied to human-AI interaction.

This approach stands in direct opposition to the risk of AI-induced passivity. If learners use AI simply to get answers, their own critical thinking and creative capacities may atrophy. Therefore, a primary goal of humanizing pedagogy today must be to design learning experiences that demand learners' critical engagement with the AI, forcing them to question, verify, and synthesize, thereby strengthening their own intellectual autonomy. As AI becomes more capable, the core tenets of humanizing pedagogy-empathy, trust, cultural understanding, and authentic relationship-building, become more, not less, important (Bozkurt, 2024). An AI can simulate empathy, but it cannot genuinely care. It can process vast datasets, but it cannot understand the lived experience of a student struggling with personal challenges. The human connection provided by an instructor is the essential anchor that ensures technology serves pedagogy, not the other way around.

CONCLUSION

This chapter has explored the evolving role of humanizing pedagogy within the rapidly changing landscape of online and distance education. Anchored in Freire's critical pedagogy and framed by Moore's Transactional Distance Theory, the chapter has emphasized the urgent need for inclusive, relational, and equity-driven instructional practices in an era increasingly shaped by AI. The conceptual and practical frameworks outlined, particularly Pacansky-Brock et al.'s (2023) four-strand model and eight humanizing design strategies, offer educators actionable pathways to foster belonging, psychological safety, and critical engagement in virtual learning environments.

Through the integration of an equity mindset, culturally responsive teaching, psychologically inclusive course design, and advanced digital fluency, the chapter has demonstrated that effective online education transcends mere content delivery. It involves designing learning environments where diverse learners feel seen, heard, and valued. These strands, when taken together, form a comprehensive pedagogical framework that reduces transactional distance and cultivates meaningful student–instructor relationships, which are essential for engagement and academic success. As AI technologies continue to permeate educational contexts, the foundational values of humanizing pedagogy, trust, presence, awareness, and empathy, are not only relevant but indispensable. Only by intentionally designing for human connection can we ensure that technology serves the needs of all learners and supports inclusive, equitable futures in online and distance education.

ACKNOWLEDGMENT

Based on Academic Integrity and Transparency in AI-assisted Research and Specification Framework, the author of this paper acknowledge that the paper was proofread and edited with the assistance of OpenAI's ChatGPT (Versions as of April 2025), and Google Gemini 2.5 complementing the human editorial process. The human authors critically assessed and validated the content to maintain academic rigor. The authors also assessed and addressed potential biases inherent in the AI-generated content. The final version of the paper is the sole responsibility of the human authors.

REFERENCES

Bozkurt, A. (2024). Why generative AI literacy, why now and why it matters in the educational landscape? Kings, queens and GenAI dragons. *Open Praxis*, *16*(3), 283–290. DOI: 10.55982/openpraxis.16.3.739

Bozkurt, A., Xıao, J., Farrow, R., Baı, J. Y. H., Nerantzı, C., Moore, S., & Dron, J. (2024). The Manifesto for Teaching and Learning in a Time of Generative AI: A Critical Collective Stance to Better Navigate the Future. *Open Praxis*, *16*(4), 1–27. DOI: 10.55982/openpraxis.16.1.654

Costa, K., Castranova, K., & Tumminia, M. (2021). Need to connect: How to build and sustain a faculty community of practice for online teaching. To Improve the Academy: *A Journal of Educational Development, 40*(1). DOI: 10.3998/tia.954

Czop Assaf, L., O'Donnell Lussier, K., Furness, S., & Hoff, M. (2019). Exploring How a Study Abroad and International Service-Learning Project Shaped Preservice Teachers' Understanding of Humanizing Pedagogy. *Teacher Educator*, *54*(2), 105–124. DOI: 10.1080/08878730.2018.1520376

Del Carmen Salazar, M. (2013). A humanizing pedagogy: Reinventing the principles and practice of education as a journey toward liberation. *Review of Research in Education*, *37*(1), 121–148. DOI: 10.3102/0091732X12464032

Falloon, G. (2011). Making the connection: Moore's theory of transactional distance and its relevance to the use of a virtual classroom in postgraduate online teacher education. *Journal of Research on Technology in Education*, *43*(3), 187–209. DOI: 10.1080/15391523.2011.10782569

Freire, P. (2020). *Pedagogy of the oppressed.* Bloomsbury publishing. DOI: 10.4324/9781003060635-5

Garrison, D. R. (2017). *E-learning in the 21st century: A community of inquiry framework for research and practice* (3rd ed.). Routledge.

Gleason, B. (2021). Expanding interaction in online courses: Integrating critical humanizing pedagogy for learner success. *Educational Technology Research and Development*, *69*(1), 51–54. DOI: 10.1007/s11423-020-09888-w

Ita Olszewska, A., Bondy, E., Hagler, N., & Jinna Kim, H. (2023). A humanizing pedagogy of engagement: Beliefs and practices of award-winning instructors at a U.S. university. *Teaching in Higher Education*, *28*(7), 1671–1687. DOI: 10.1080/13562517.2021.1920575

Kim, H. J., Kong, Y., Hernandez, C., & Soban, M. (2023). Student Emotions and Engagement: Enacting Humanizing Pedagogy in Higher Education. *IAFOR Journal of Education*, *11*(3), 185–206. DOI: 10.22492/ije.11.3.09

Li, Q., Bañuelos, M., Liu, Y., & Xu, D. (2022). Online instruction for a humanized learning experience: Techniques used by college instructors. *Computers & Education*, *189*, 104595. Advance online publication. DOI: 10.1016/j.compedu.2022.104595

Moore, M. G. (2019). The theory of transactional distance. In Moore, M. G., & Diehl, W. C. (Eds.), *Handbook of distance education* (4th ed., pp. 22–38). Routledge.

Pacansky-Brock, M. (2020). How to humanize your online class, version 2.0. Retrieved from https://humanizeol.org/infographic/

Pacansky-Brock, M., Smedshammer, M., & Vincent-Layton, K. (2020). Humanizing online teaching to equitably engage students. *Current Issues in Education (Tempe, Ariz.)*, *21*(2), 1–20. https://cie.asu.edu/ojs/index.php/cieatasu/article/view/1905

Pacansky-Brock, M., Smedshammer, M., & Vincent-Layton, K. (2023). In search of belonging online: Achieving equity through transformative professional development. *Journal of Educational Research and Practice*, *12*(0), 39–64. DOI: 10.5590/JERAP.2022.12.0.04

Paguyo, C. H., Sponsler, L. E., & Iturbe-LaGrave, V. (2022). Centering theories of learning to design humanizing pedagogies and inclusive assessments. *New Directions for Student Services*, *2022*(178-179), 175–183. DOI: 10.1002/ss.20438

Peercy, M. M., Tigert, J., Fredricks, D., Kidwell, T., Feagin, K., Hall, W., & Lawyer, M. D. (2022). From humanizing principles to humanizing practices: Exploring core practices as a bridge to enacting humanizing pedagogy with multilingual students. *Teaching and Teacher Education*, *113*, 103653. Advance online publication. DOI: 10.1016/j.tate.2022.103653

Razak, N. A., Zulkifli, C. Z., Abdullah, Y., Khairuddin, A. Z., Misron, A., Somasundram, P., & Shakirdjanovna, A. G. (2025). Bridging technology and humanity: Humanizing online pedagogy in digital environments. *International Journal of Evaluation and Research in Education, 14*(3), 2207–2223. DOI: 10.11591/ijere.v14i3.31937

Stewart, O. G. (2023). Understanding what works in humanizing higher education online courses: Connecting through videos, feedback, multimodal assignments, and social media. *Issues and Trends in Learning Technologies., 11*(2), 2–26. DOI: 10.2458/itlt.5566

Woodley, X., Hernandez, C., Parra, J., & Negash, B. (2017). Celebrating difference: Best practices in culturally responsive teaching online. *TechTrends, 61*(5), 470–478. DOI: 10.1007/s11528-017-0207-z

Zawacki-Richter, O., Marín, V. I., Bond, M., & Gouverneur, F. (2019). Systematic review of research on artificial intelligence applications in higher education – where are the educators? *International Journal of Educational Technology in Higher Education, 16*(1), 2–27. DOI: 10.1186/s41239-019-0171-0

KEY TERMS AND DEFINITIONS

Culturally Responsive Teaching: An instructional approach that recognizes and affirms learners' cultural backgrounds, experiences, and identities, while maintaining high academic expectations and fostering inclusive learning environments.

Digital Fluency: The ability to confidently and critically use digital tools and platforms to communicate, collaborate, and create learning experiences that are inclusive, accessible, and pedagogically sound.

Equity Mindset: A reflective and action-oriented stance taken by educators who acknowledge systemic inequities and actively seek to close achievement gaps by redesigning their practices to support all learners fairly.

Generative Artificial Intelligence: A class of AI technologies capable of producing content such as text, images, or video, often used in educational settings for personalized support, yet requiring ethical scrutiny due to risks of bias and depersonalization.

Humanizing Pedagogy: A learner-centered educational philosophy rooted in empathy, dialogue, and relational trust, aiming to affirm learners' full humanity and promote critical consciousness within learning environments.

Microlecture: A brief, focused instructional video designed to clarify a specific concept while enhancing student engagement through the instructor's presence, tone, and informal delivery.

Psychologically Inclusive Design: The intentional structuring of online learning environments to foster safety, dignity, and belonging, using supportive language, welcoming visuals, and emotionally intelligent instructor interactions.

Social Presence: The sense of being seen, heard, and connected in a virtual learning environment, often facilitated through multimedia communication, instructor engagement, and peer interaction.

Transactional Distance: A theoretical construct referring to the psychological and communicative gap between learners and instructors in distance education, influenced by course structure, dialogue, and learner autonomy.

Chapter 2
GenAI As a Tool for Curriculum Design and Content Creation

Barış Avcı
https://orcid.org/0000-0002-7584-7113
Republic of Türkiye Ministry of National Education, Turkey

ABSTRACT

This chapter examines how generative artificial intelligence (GenAI) equips educators with advanced tools to enhance teaching effectiveness and student outcomes. In particular, it emphasizes the role of these tools in streamlining curriculum design, defining clear learning objectives, and creating adaptive, personalized learning environments. By analyzing platforms like ChatGPT, Claude, Copilot, Gemini, Eduaide.Ai, and MagicSchool, the study shows how GenAI automates administrative tasks, generates dynamic content, and supports individualized learning pathways. While acknowledging significant benefits including improved efficiency and enhanced accessibility, the study critically addresses challenges such as academic integrity concerns, algorithmic bias, and the need for human oversight. Real-world examples offer a practical framework for educators to understand and implement GenAI tools strategically. Ultimately, GenAI is positioned not as a replacement for human instruction but as a collaborative partner that enhances pedagogical practice and supports ongoing professional growth.

CURRICULUM DEVELOPMENT

Curriculum development is the process of determining educational goals, offering appropriate learning experiences, organizing these experiences, and evaluating

DOI: 10.4018/979-8-3373-7579-3.ch002

ght © 2026, IGI Global Scientific Publishing. Copying or distributing in print or electronic forms without written permission of IGI Global Scientific Publishing is prohibited. Use of this chapter to generative artificial intelligence (AI) technologies is expressly prohibited. The publisher reserves all rights to license its use for generative AI training and machine learning model development.

their effectiveness (Tyler, 1949). It also encompasses the content, methods, and materials used to achieve these educational goals (Ornstein & Hunkins, 2018). As Taba (1962) noted, the curriculum is not static but a living entity that "...not only reflects but is also a product of its time" (Oliva & Gordon, 2012). In light of this dynamic nature, curriculum development must continuously evolve, particularly by embracing technological innovations, to remain effective and forward-thinking.

In this context, generative artificial intelligence (GenAI) enhances curriculum and instructional design by helping educators create engaging and effective learning experiences. By analyzing student data, such as performance, behavior, and learning preferences, GenAI identifies common academic challenges and provides insights for refining curriculum to address these gaps. This data-driven approach enables the analysis of existing curriculum and tailoring of the curriculum to address these gaps effectively, ultimately enhancing student learning outcomes. With its efficiency, GenAI empowers educators to design more targeted and impactful learning experiences, transforming lesson plan creation from a time-consuming process into a task accomplished in minutes.

By strategically utilizing GenAI to refine curriculum and address academic challenges, educators can lead the way in the thoughtful integration of AI in education. Rather than resisting this technological shift, they should proactively explore how AI tools can improve teaching practices and boost learning outcomes (Parsons & Curry, 2024). Successfully navigating this transformation requires teachers to develop competencies in evaluating the ethical, pedagogical, and human-centered applications of AI in classrooms. As GenAI technologies evolve rapidly, educators must remain flexible and open to innovation, continuously adapting their practice in alignment with emerging capabilities and best practices.

A strong foundational understanding of AI empowers educators to integrate it more confidently and responsibly. Ongoing professional development is essential in this regard, helping educators deepen their expertise and stay current with both technological advancements and pedagogical implications (UNESCO, 2024a).

However, despite the growing awareness of GenAI's potential, many education systems lack structured teacher training programs focused on AI. A UNESCO survey on governmental AI adoption in education revealed that only a limited number of countries, specifically China, Finland, Georgia, Qatar, Spain, Thailand, and Türkiye had initiated the development or implementation of frameworks or training programs specifically designed to equip teachers with AI literacy (UNESCO, 2023 cited in UNESCO, 2024b). This finding is further supported by many teachers who reported a lack of confidence in using AI, attributing this to insufficient guidance and training. Instead, most of their knowledge about AI is acquired through informal sources and independent research. When asked what would encourage them to utilize AI in their teaching, 57% of teachers indicated a need for training on AI tools, while 49% expressed a desire to see real-world examples of how other educators are successfully integrating AI into their classrooms (Kirkham, 2023).

While the potential benefits of AI in education are considerable, a thoughtful and nuanced approach is required to address the inherent challenges and ethical considerations. Key priorities include ensuring equitable access to AI-powered learning tools, addressing biases in AI algorithms, and preserving the human element in education. Recognizing these critical factors, educators must exercise professional judgment and adhere to school policies when integrating GenAI into educational settings. By prioritizing responsible use and inclusivity, educators can create safe, ethical, and supportive environments that benefit all learners.

Ultimately, GenAI holds a significant promise in addressing some of the most pressing challenges in education. It can revolutionize instructional practices, foster more personalized learning, and accelerate progress toward global education goals, particularly Sustainable Development Goal 4: Quality Education for All (UNESCO, 2019). By integrating GenAI thoughtfully and ethically into curriculum development, educators can ensure that learners are equipped with the skills, knowledge, and critical thinking needed to thrive in a rapidly changing world.

To fully harness the potential of GenAI in education, it is essential to examine how it intersects with the core components of curriculum development. These components, stating learning objectives, creating content, designing teaching and learning situations, personalizing learning experiences, implementing effective evaluation and assessment strategies, and fostering innovative teaching methodologies, form the foundation of any meaningful educational program. By integrating GenAI thoughtfully into each of these elements, educators can enhance the precision, adaptability, and effectiveness of their curriculum design. The following sections explore how GenAI can support and transform these key areas, offering both theoretical insights and practical applications for future-ready education.

Crafting Learning Objectives

Learning objectives are concise statements outlining the knowledge, skills, and attitudes students are expected to acquire or demonstrate upon completing a course or lesson. They play a critical role in shaping teaching strategies and assessment methods, ensuring that educational experiences are effective and focused. By providing clear guidance, well-crafted learning objectives are essential for aligning educational activities with the intended learning outcomes.

In this pursuit, the emergence of GenAI represents a significant advancement in educational planning and development. Through training on vast amounts of educational content and diverse pedagogical approaches, GenAI systems can generate comprehensive ranges of potential learning objectives tailored to specific contexts.

This capability positions GenAI as a valuable resource for instructors who need assistance with curriculum development and course design. Specifically, tools such as OpenAI's ChatGPT, Anthropic's Claude, Microsoft's Copilot (formerly Bing), and Google's Gemini (formerly Bard) are particularly effective for crafting specific, measurable, and achievable objectives that align with course content. The following section presents examples demonstrating the practical applications of these advanced AI capabilities in generating and refining learning objectives across diverse educational contexts.

Effective learning objective development requires a systematic approach that ensures clarity and precision. A widely employed template follows this structure: *By the end of this [course/lesson/unit], learners will be able to [action verb] [specific task] [with measurable criteria] [within a certain timeframe].* This framework provides clear delineation of expectations and facilitates both instruction and assessment.

To further enhance the effectiveness of learning objectives, The SMART framework (Specific, Measurable, Achievable, Relevant, and Time-bound) provides a foundational strategy for crafting precise and quantifiable goals. When combined with established learning taxonomies, e.g. Bloom's revised taxonomy or the SOLO (Structure of Observed Learning Outcomes) taxonomy, this approach ensures that objectives are cognitively appropriate and progressively challenging.

Building on this structured approach, Microsoft Copilot or other tools can utilize AI to generate well-structured learning objectives when given the command: *Create learning objectives for a 3D Printing course using Bloom's Taxonomy and the SMART framework.* These objectives systematically align with all levels of Bloom's Taxonomy while adhering to the SMART framework's criteria, ensuring specificity, measurability, achievability, relevance, and time-bound goals. This integration of AI streamlines the development process, supporting educators in crafting effective and targeted learning experiences. Building upon these principles of clear and specific prompts, educators can effectively leverage GenAI to craft compelling and precise learning objectives:

1. Be specific and clear: subject/topic, target audience, and learning objectives, content type (short story, multiple questions), desired output (video, short story)
2. Provide Context and Constraints: Time limit, learning styles, accessibility
3. Encourage Creativity and Engagement (If possible): e.g. board games, riddles
4. Refine and Iterate: After the first draft, provide feedback to refine it

To maximize the effectiveness of GenAI tools in creating educational materials like lecture notes, presentations, quizzes, exams, assignments, projects, study guides, syllabi, interactive activities, or videos, educators need clear and specific prompts. With well-defined learning objectives as their foundation, educators can then leverage GenAI to develop high-quality, engaging, and effective content that aligns with instructional goals and addresses diverse learning needs. This innovative approach enhances content quality, personalizes learning experiences, and streamlines curriculum design.

Creating Content

As technology continues to evolve, educators are increasingly expected to leverage AI tools for generating educational content across various formats, text, audio, and video. This shift facilitates the collaborative development of national or school-based textbooks, curricular resources, and digital learning materials (UNESCO, 2024a, p.41). However, this transformation also requires a significant pedagogical shift, compelling educators to critically examine both the capabilities and limitations of AI-powered tools in educational contexts.

In examining this transition, Ch'ng's (2023) comparative study between traditional content creation methods and those assisted by Generative AI (GenAI) reveals valuable insights. While traditional methods tend to yield more original content, they are often time-intensive. In contrast, AI-assisted tools can generate content rapidly across a wide range of subjects, even in areas where educators may lack specialized expertise, but raise concerns regarding copyright, authorship, and originality. These findings illustrate the double-edged nature of GenAI, it offers efficiency and versatility while also introducing ethical and legal challenges. This tension has sparked ongoing debates and shifting perceptions around the use of AI in education.

Among the most immediate concerns has been the potential for GenAI tools, such as ChatGPT, to undermine academic integrity, particularly through the generation of essays and written assignments. The initial reaction from educators was one of widespread concern. However, a growing consensus, including among leading universities, now acknowledges the reality that, as many have noted, "the genie is out of the bottle" (UNESCO, 2024b, p.28) or, more precisely "GenAI is out of the bottle" (Kanbach, 2024, p.1). This growing consensus suggests a shift in focus: rather than rejecting these tools, educators must learn to harness them ethically and effectively to enhance teaching and learning.

GenAI is rapidly transforming course development by automating the creation of high-quality learning materials, quizzes, assessments, and simulations. Educators and instructional designers can use concise prompts aligned with learning outcomes to generate content at scale (Gibson, 2023). Tools such as Copilot, Claude, Gemini, and ChatGPT support the development of rich text-based resources, while AI-powered platforms like Craiyon, DALL-E 2, Midjourney, and Photosonic facilitate the generation of custom images. Meanwhile, video production tools such as Elai,

Pictory, Runway, and GliaCloud, as well as AI music tools like Aiva and Boomy, further expand the creative toolkit available to educators, enabling them to design more engaging and multimodal learning environments (UNESCO, 2024b).

However, this technological potential is not without significant challenges. AI-generated content can occasionally reflect biases, misinformation, or discriminatory language, raising concerns about the reliability and ethical integrity of educational materials (Bozkurt et al., 2024; UNESCO, 2024b). Kirschenbaum (2023) warns of a looming *textpocalypse*, in which an overwhelming influx of AI-generated content could flood the web with inaccurate or misleading information. This reality places increased responsibility on educators to critically evaluate and verify AI-generated materials to maintain academic standards. The principle of *garbage in, garbage out* aptly captures this concern, the quality of educational outputs is only as strong as the quality of the input and the rigor of the content validation process.

Further complicating matters, some GenAI systems have been criticized for producing superficial content that prioritizes surface-level features, such as sentence length, over substance. This vulnerability to "gibberish", as Miao et al. (2021, p.16) put it, emphasizes the importance of human oversight and careful content review. The opaque nature of GenAI systems, often described as "black boxes", makes it difficult to trace or justify the reasoning behind specific outputs (UNESCO, 2024a, 2024b). This lack of transparency necessitates editorial scrutiny to ensure alignment with curriculum objectives, cultural appropriateness, and instructional relevance.

Biases embedded within training data also present a risk. For example, while GenAI tools like ChatGPT offer multilingual functionality, they often reflect English-language training and US-centric cultural values, leading to monocultural bias (Rettberg, 2022). Choi et al. (2024) further identified several shortcomings of GenAI in education, including poor contextual understanding, low reliability, unclear activity instructions, repetitive tasks, shallow assessments, and unpredictable content quality, all of which can undermine instructional effectiveness.

Given the spectrum of opinions, AI's integration into education can be perceived as either "opening Pandora's box" (Chen & Feng, 2024, p.1) or "unleashing a treasure chest" (Walther, 2024). Ultimately, how GenAI is perceived and adopted in educational contexts depends largely on user intention, critical awareness, and the broader institutional framework guiding its use.

Despite these complexities, the transformative potential of GenAI is undeniable. The true potential of GenAI lies in its capacity to process vast datasets at unprecedented speeds and scales, surpassing human capabilities. This empowers educators to leverage GenAI tools to refine their pedagogical approaches, fostering a more efficient and effective learning environment. By automating routine tasks, GenAI liberates educators to concentrate on more creative and innovative aspects of instruction, such as developing personalized learning pathways and cultivating deeper student engagement. Moreover, AI facilitates the creation of interactive and immersive learning experiences, such as virtual reality (VR) and augmented reality (AR) simulations, which enhance student engagement and comprehension. It also significantly accelerates the course development process. Traditionally, course creation has been a time-consuming and resource-intensive endeavor for educators and subject matter experts. However, AI streamlines this process, enabling the creation of more rapid, adaptable, and potentially higher-quality learning environments (Gibson, 2023).

Teaching/Learning Situations

GenAI tools facilitate the creation of unit plans and lesson plans aligned with diverse pedagogical frameworks, including the 5E model, Montessori approach, and Gagné's nine events of instruction. Moreover, these tools empower educators to personalize lesson plans, fostering independent learning, collaborative learning, and the integration of gamification elements. While the quality of the output is contingent upon the complexity of the prompt and the capabilities of the specific GenAI model employed, these prompts serve as a valuable guide for developing effective lesson-planning procedures:

1. Begin with clear objectives
2. Provide context and parameters
3. Structure your request
4. Request specific features
5. Ask for detailed timing
6. Include assessment requirements
7. Request modifications and alternatives

These structured guidelines lay the foundation for effective lesson planning with GenAI, ensuring alignment with instructional goals and pedagogical frameworks. Table 1 illustrates how Claude Sonnet 4 applies these procedures, showcasing its capabilities in generating well-structured and adaptable lesson plans.

Table 1. Lesson Planning Procedures for Claude Sonnet 4

Prompt: I need assistance creating a detailed lesson plan with the following specifications: **Topic:** Introduction to Basic Algebraic Expressions **Grade Level:** 7 h Grade Mathematics **Duration:** 60-minute class period **Student Context:** Mixed-ability classroom of 25 students, including 3 English language learners and 2 students with IEPs (Individualized Education Program) Develop a complete lesson plan that includes: **Core Elements:** Three specific learning objectives aligned with Common Core Math Standards. Essential materials and technology requirements. A 5-minute warm-up activity to activate prior knowledge. Main instructional components with time allocations. Formative assessment strategies throughout the lesson. A closing activity that checks for understanding. Extension activities for advanced learners **Differentiation Requirements:** Modifications for English language learners. Accommodation for students with processing speed challenges. Challenge opportunities for advanced students **Assessment Components:** Entry ticket to check prior knowledge. Mid-lesson check for understanding. Exit ticket aligned with learning objectives. "Include transition times between activities and suggest classroom management strategies for group work portions. Additionally, provide a contingency plan if the technology becomes unavailable."

As illustrated in Table 1, Claude Sonnet 4 can generate comprehensive instructional packages, including all necessary teaching materials for each component. Unlike Copilot and Gemini, ChatGPT and Claude allow users to upload entire curricula or educational plans in various formats (e.g., PDF, DOC). Lesson plans and resources are then derived exclusively from the uploaded materials, ensuring precise alignment with the intended curriculum and instructional goals. This method avoids reliance on external web-based content, preserving curriculum integrity and preventing the inclusion of irrelevant or potentially inaccurate information. The generated resources can be seamlessly integrated into Learning Management Systems (LMS) such as Canvas.

According to The Open Innovation Team and Department for Education (2024), educators reported using a range of non-specialized GenAI tools, including ChatGPT, Google Bard (now Gemini), and Bing (now Copilot) Concurrent with the emergence of general-purpose GenAI tools such as ChatGPT, a surge in the development of specialized platforms tailored to the unique needs of educators has become apparent.

Teachers primarily utilize GenAI to support school-related tasks (Teacher Tapp, 2023), particularly in lesson creation, curriculum development, and instructional planning (IFF Research, 2023; Kirkham, 2023). The growing reliance on AI for these functions underscores the importance of integrating GenAI into Learning Management Systems (LMS), enabling efficient management of course materials, student progress tracking, and assignment facilitation.

By integrating AI into LMS platforms, educators can streamline administrative processes while enhancing the quality and adaptability of instructional content. In this context, Vergara et al. (2024), in their bibliometric review of 256 documents published between 2004-2023, investigated the integration of AI into LMSs. The findings highlight that AI-enhanced LMS offers adaptive and personalized learning, promote active and self-regulated learning, and improve student outcomes, engagement, and motivation in various learning environments. Furthermore, these systems enhance accessibility and equity in education by supporting the utilization of open educational resources.

Despite robust research on AI in e-learning, practical guidance for integrating AI into LMSs remains limited. Fırat (2023) addresses this gap by offering real-world examples and detailed steps, including the use of GPT plugins for Moodle. However, a persistent challenge is the requirement for access to application programming interfaces (APIs), which can hinder seamless implementation.

Although, ChatGPT is a versatile tool for tasks such as question answering and text generation, its application in education has limitations. Teachers often need to significantly adapt or reorganize AI-generated content to ensure it meets classroom-specific needs, increasing their workload.

Fortunately, the landscape of AI tools for education is evolving, with free GenAI tools specifically designed for educators now available. Platforms such as Eduaide.Ai and MagicSchool offer a significant advantage over general-purpose AI like ChatGPT. They combine a library of pre-aligned educational resources with user-friendly interfaces, enabling teachers to streamline lesson planning, personalize instruction, and enhance student learning outcomes more efficiently. Rather than requiring educators to start from scratch or spend time adjusting generic materials, Eduaide.Ai provides resources already aligned with classroom requirements. This dedicated tool for educators, which utilizes both OpenAI and Anthropic, integrates evidence-based instructional strategies (Eduaide.Ai, 2025). Ultimately, these specialized platforms empower educators to quickly create, adapt, and evaluate resources that are directly aligned with their learning objectives.

While MagicSchool has not developed its own proprietary model, it is built on a diverse ecosystem of AI engines, including ChatGPT, Claude, and Gemini, with each of its 80+ tools powered by the model best suited for a given task (MagicSchool, 2025). From content generation to classroom engagement features such as image creation and teacher humor tools, this model-matching approach ensures consistently high-quality outputs. Like Eduaide.Ai, MagicSchool facilitates the efficient creation, customization, and assessment of learning activities, enabling educators to align instruction with specific learning objectives more effectively and with reduced effort.

The education sector stands to significantly benefit from the transformative potential of GenAI. Recognizing its capacity to disrupt and innovate within education, a thorough investigation and evaluation of its effectiveness within educational contexts is imperative (Parsons & Curry, 2024). While extensive research examined its role in education, a notable gap exists in studies specifically exploring its application as a tool for supporting instructional design (e.g., Chng, 2023; Parsons & Curry, 2024).

Given the limited research on the potential of GenAI as an instructional design aid, a comprehensive assessment of its strengths and weaknesses in course development is crucial for its effective integration into educational practices. Choi et al. (2024) identified several potential strengths of using GenAI in instructional design. Potential strengths are (1) developing and aligning learning outcomes, (2) proposing suitable resources and tools, (3) formulating discussion questions that stimulate critical reflection in both students and the instructor, (4) creating comprehensive rubrics, (5) offering a wide array of teaching strategies and tasks and (6) conducting cross-comparisons between assessments, curricula, and learning materials to ensure consistency. Furthermore, educators have reported that GenAI significantly boosts their efficiency and creativity. Key benefits highlighted include substantial time savings on tasks, which help improve work-life balance by reducing after-hours work (The Open Innovation Team and Department for Education, 2024). Nevertheless, over-reliance on GenAI poses a threat to critical thinking and problem-solving skills among both students and educators.

This over-reliance can lead to a decline in essential cognitive abilities, making it crucial to maintain a balanced approach that prioritizes independent thought and traditional educational practices (Kurtz et al., 2024). Moreover, educators' failure to establish this balance can significantly impact their professional credibility. According to Milner (2013), deprofessionalization may lead to pressure on teachers, cheating, low expectations, variations in what teachers are expected to know, lack of pedagogical training, teacher attrition, the perception of teaching as technical work that anyone can do, lack of autonomy in curriculum decision-making, an emphasis on subject matter knowledge rather than pedagogical knowledge, and damage the academic and professional reputation of teachers and affect public perception. Smyth and Kum (2010, p.503) stress the "use it or lose it" principle, underscoring teachers' imperative to continuously develop and update their pedagogical expertise to avoid negative professional judgments.

Furthermore, the rapid integration of GenAI into education has the potential to exacerbate technostress among teachers. Also, the lack of clear guidelines, inadequate training, and unrealistic expectations, as highlighted by Kohnke (2024), are likely to create significant stress for educators, potentially contributing to burnout. This is particularly concerning given the absence of adequate research specifically examining the impact of GenAI on teacher burnout levels. Recognizing this, educational institutions must prioritize teacher well-being alongside the technical implementation of GenAI. This necessitates a comprehensive approach that encompasses robust training, realistic expectations, and a supportive environment. By proactively addressing these concerns, institutions can empower teachers to navigate the challenges posed by GenAI, mitigate potential negative impacts, and foster positive and fulfilling professional experiences/techno-eustress (Tarafdar et al., 2024). This ensures that AI serves as an enhancement rather than a hindrance to both teacher satisfaction and the quality of education they provide.

Finally, the absence of national GenAI regulations creates further complexity. Although ChatGPT reached 100 million monthly active users in January 2023, the lack of national regulations on GenAI in most countries leaves users' data privacy unprotected and educational institutions largely unprepared to validate the tools (UNESCO, 2024b). Given this regulatory gap, educational institutions must prioritize data privacy by proactively adapting to the evolving technological landscape. This requires continuous monitoring of emerging technologies and regular policy updates. By fostering a culture of data security awareness and prioritizing responsible data handling practices, institutions can effectively navigate the challenges and opportunities presented by AI while safeguarding sensitive information (Akpan et al., 2025; Yang & Beil, 2024).

PERSONALIZED LEARNING EXPERIENCES

GenAI holds immense potential to enhance education by delivering personalized learning experiences tailored to the unique needs of each student. Through adaptive learning algorithms, GenAI can modify content, pace, and difficulty based on individual learner profiles, ensuring that students remain appropriately challenged and engaged. Intelligent tutoring systems provide around-the-clock support, real-time feedback, and dynamically generated questions, allowing students to receive consistent guidance. Moreover, GenAI can analyze student performance data to predict outcomes, track progress, and create individualized learning pathways, enabling educators to proactively address learning gaps and deliver targeted support.

GenAI also fosters accessibility and inclusivity by offering tools and accommodations for diverse learners, such as text-to-speech, language translation, and adaptive formatting. These capabilities contribute to a more equitable and engaging learning environment. According to Dillig et al. (2024), a growing body of literature underscores GenAI's capacity to support and personalize learning processes. For example, Pesovsky et al. (2024) developed a GenAI-integrated LMS tool capable of autonomously generating instructional materials, ranging from traditional to pop culture-infused resources, aligned with instructor-defined learning outcomes. The tool also creates self-assessment opportunities via auto-generated multiple-choice questions, significantly reducing teacher workload while enhancing instructional effectiveness.

Adaptive learning not only enhances student agency but also significantly improves teacher effectiveness. In this respect, Singh (2023) reported that students utilizing technology-driven learning platforms become more self-directed and actively engage in self-assessment through automated feedback mechanisms. Simultaneously, teachers benefit from reduced workloads as these systems provide timely and relevant feedback, fostering more constructive student-teacher interactions. Building upon this foundation, GenAI is revolutionizing education by personalizing the learning experience. By analyzing individual progress and identifying areas of strength and weakness, AI tailors learning pathways with specific resources. Continuous monitoring and real-time feedback enable dynamic adjustments, ensuring that the learning process remains relevant and effective. This personalized approach maximizes learning potential and cultivates a more inclusive and engaging educational environments for all learners (Li et al., 2024).

Educators also benefit from GenAI's natural language processing and on-demand availability. Tools such as ChatGPT support teachers by providing timely information and feedback, allowing them to address student needs more effectively (Kohnke et al., 2023). By leveraging these capabilities, educators conserve valuable time and energy while maintaining instructional quality. GenAI thus serves as both a learning partner for students and an instructional assistant for teachers, enhancing the efficiency and personalization of feedback delivery. It also supports collaborative learning and research, as highlighted by Hsu and Ching (2023).

Further reinforcing GenAI's value, Jerusha and Rajakumari's (2024) longitudinal study found a positive correlation between AI-assisted learning and improved student outcomes. Students expressed high satisfaction with personalized feedback and AI-enhanced materials. However, educator oversight remains essential, particularly in tracking factors such as time on task, goal alignment, and support needs. Crompton and Burke (2022) emphasize that AI tools offer insights into student learning trajectories often inaccessible through traditional assessment methods.

As argued by Trabelsi et al. (2023), effective teaching hinges on monitoring student engagement. AI-powered behavior recognition, employing deep learning techniques, can analyze student attention and emotions in real-time, providing valuable insights into student behavior, including attention levels, emotions, attendance, and progress. This system empowers educators with real-time and offline data to enhance classroom instruction and make more informed decisions. While the integration of AI into student performance tracking has significant potential to transform education, it also presents notable challenges.

Critical concerns include data privacy, algorithmic bias, transparency, and resistance to change. Ethical implementation and continuous professional development are crucial to align educational practices with emerging technologies. As Allam et al. (2023) point out, deploying GenAI tools for monitoring or instructional purposes requires a high level of educator expertise and preparation.

One practical and time-saving application of GenAI is automated grading, which allows teachers to provide quicker feedback and redirect their efforts toward more in-depth evaluation and instructional refinement. When used thoughtfully, GenAI has the potential to transform education, not by replacing educators, but by amplifying their effectiveness and creating more personalized, equitable, and student-centered learning environments.

Evaluation & Assessment

GenAI has emerged as a powerful tool in educational evaluation and assessment, enhancing both the efficiency and effectiveness of these processes. It can automate the generation of diverse assessment components, such as questions, rubrics, and scenario-based tasks, enabling educators to focus on higher-order instructional goals. By generating assessment items targeting various cognitive levels, crafting open-ended prompts that promote critical thinking, and developing detailed rubrics, GenAI supports more comprehensive and equitable evaluations. Its capacity to design realistic, context-rich scenarios also fosters the application of knowledge in authentic learning environments. Automated grading powered by LLMs further reduces educator workload and provides timely, objective feedback to students, facilitating prompt error correction and learning reinforcement (Yousef et al., 2024).

The effective integration of GenAI in education requires a comprehensive assessment of students' prerequisite knowledge. Recent research by Chiu (2023) indicates that educational institutions must fundamentally reconsider and modify their assessment methodologies to properly evaluate student learning outcomes in this new technological context. Educators must facilitate explicit discussions about GenAI usage, establishing clear parameters for appropriate implementation while encouraging critical analysis of its societal impact. This framework should include practical demonstrations of proper GenAI utilization through well-designed assignments that showcase best practices. Therefore, future research should investigate the multifaceted impact of AI on these practices, encompassing teachers' understanding of student histories, group dynamics, classroom environments, and broader community contexts (Zhai & Nehm, 2023).

Advanced LLMs such as ChatGPT, Claude, and Copilot have demonstrated sophisticated capabilities in assessment generation and evaluation, leveraging vast datasets and natural language processing to produce a wide range of pedagogically aligned tools. While general-purpose models are powerful, educator-specific platforms such as Eduaide.Ai and MagicSchool provide more targeted and accessible solutions. The utilization of GenAI tools specifically designed for educators, such as Eduaide.Ai (2025), empowers educators across all educational levels, from preschool to post-secondary institutions. These applications include independent practice, collaborative learning, gamification, formative and summative assessment, question generation, and rubric development, as illustrated in Table 2.

Table 2. Eduaide.Ai Assessment/Evaluation Tools

Categories	Tools
Independent Practice	Extension worksheets, comprehension assignments, research projects, choice board assignments and portfolio assignments etc.
Cooperative Learning	Debate, project-based learning activities, STEM projects etc.
Gamification	Escape room, quests, this or that, jeopardy etc.
Assessments	Exams quiz, test, project-based assessment, self-assessment etc.
Questions	Multiple choice, true/false, fill in the blanks, scenario-based questions, taxonomy scaffolding etc.
Rubrics	Analytic, holistic, single-point, and developmental rubrics

In addition, Eduaide.Ai can refine prompts *How can we help achieve SDG4?*, into focused inquiries such as *Explore and analyze strategies to promote equitable and inclusive quality education, aligning with SDG4.* This tool then generates comprehensive Project-Based Assessments (PBA), including detailed project outlines with phases like research proposal, data collection/analysis, strategy development and final presentation/reflection. The PBA also includes a rubric with five criteria evaluated on a five-point scale, providing clear assessment guidelines for educators.

Similarly, MagicSchool (2025) offers innovative tools for generating AI-resistant questions and supports seamless integration with YouTube content. Educators can input video links or transcripts to automatically generate customized question sets in diverse formats, such as multiple-choice, short answer, or discussion prompts, tailored to students' learning needs and levels. This functionality promotes differentiated instruction and personalized learning, enabling teachers to more effectively engage diverse learners and assess understanding in dynamic ways.

Building upon the capabilities of educator-specific tools e.g. MagicSchool, advanced language models such as ChatGPT-4 have demonstrated significant potential in automating aspects of the assessment process. Jauhiainen and Garagorry Guerra (2024a) examined ChatGPT-4's capacity to evaluate university students' written exam responses. The model effectively assessed responses across varying lengths via a six-point grading scale. Using a verification-based chain-of-thought prompting approach, ChatGPT-4 accurately recalled responses and aligned with the university's grading rubric. While minor discrepancies with human grader assessments were observed, the overall consistency was promising. These findings indicate the significant potential of LLMs in automating the evaluation of students' written work. LLMs such as GPT-4, Claude-3, and Mistral-Large can be used to assess and grade students' open-ended responses effectively, particularly when the retrieval-augmented generation framework is utilized (Jauhiainen & Garagorry Guerra, 2024b). Furthermore, In Grévisse's study (2024), both Gemini and ChatGPT

LLMs demonstrated moderate agreement with human grades, with GPT-4 showing high precision for fully correct answers in the context of LLM-based automatic short answer grading in undergraduate medical education.

The promising potential of LLMs extends beyond student assignments, as demonstrated by their successful application to various educational contexts, including the analysis of educational surveys. These surveys, crucial for identifying curriculum gaps or evaluating teaching effectiveness, frequently involve laborious manual processing of responses. And, LLMs present a promising alternative, offering flexibility without the need for specialized models or extensive fine-tuning. Therefore, Parker et al. (2024) investigated the application of LLM workflows to a dataset of 2,500 end-of-course survey comments from biomedical science courses. Their findings demonstrated that by utilizing carefully crafted prompts, GPT-4 achieved performance comparable to human analysts, enabling efficient workflows to address common survey analysis objectives.

While GPT-4's efficiency in survey analysis is noteworthy, Kanık (2024) highlights the model's limitations in creating multiple-choice questions, emphasizing the need for further refinement. Further emphasizing this point, Whalen et al. (2024) identified a concerning knowledge gap among educators regarding their ability to detect content generated by large language models (GenAI). Their study revealed that only 20% of educators expressed confidence in identifying such work without relying on specialized tools. Moreover, despite the availability of detection tools, over half of the educators reported never using them. This highlights a critical lack of preparedness for managing student submissions potentially generated by AI in academic environments.

In response to the growing need to identify GenAI content, educators now have a fortunate array of tools at their disposal. These tools cater to various content types, including text (originality.ai, undetectable.ai and copyleaks.com), images (illuminarty.ai and brandwell.ai), and music (aiornot.com). For a comprehensive solution, Detectortools.ai offers a unified platform that can analyze text, voice, images, code, and video content. Moreover, as GenAI tools become more accessible, their potential to generate *deepfakes*, including manipulated text, images, and audio, raises critical concerns (Shoaib, 2023) for assessing and evaluating student work.

Just as these tools make it increasingly difficult to distinguish between fact and fiction in the broader context of mis/disinformation, they also blur the line between authentic student output and GenAI content in academic settings. This has further intensified issues surrounding plagiarism, as students may misuse these tools to produce work that is not their own (Moorhouse, Yeo & Wan, 2023). This trend challenges traditional evaluation methods, as educators may find it harder to verify the originality and integrity of submissions. Without effective mechanisms to identify and address the use of GenAI inappropriately, the reliability of academic assessments and the trustworthiness of educational achievements could be significantly undermined. Moreover, Perkins et al. (2024) identified various straightforward methods to bypass GenAI text detection systems. These include introducing spelling errors, altering text complexity, varying levels of burstiness, adopting writing styles characteristic of non-native English speakers, and employing paraphrasing techniques.

Addressing the risks to academic assessments' reliability, Ardito (2024) argues that reliance on AI detection mechanisms may not align with modern educational practices. Detectors lack sufficient accuracy, are vulnerable to manipulation, and cannot differentiate between compliant and noncompliant AI use. Furthermore, their results are inherently unfalsifiable, limiting their reliability and academic utility. Supporting this, Farrelly and Baker (2023) & Khalil and Er (2023) emphasize how GenAI fundamentally changes education, particularly with respect to its impact on student assessment and academic integrity. A key concern highlighted is the unreliability of AI detection tools, which could lead to *potential false accusations* against students.

Beyond these technical challenges, while undoubtedly spurring productivity, also presents unique challenges. One such challenge is the potential exacerbation of *impostor syndrome*. This persistent self-doubt stems from the apprehension that achievements are primarily attributed to AI rather than individual effort, leading to a fleeting sense of inflated accomplishment. This can also manifest as a temporary state of exaggerated success, akin to feeling like *king for a day,* driven by the perceived power of AI tools. Moreover, streamlining decision-making processes and adhering to the principle of *less is more* can mitigate *decision fatigue*, a phenomenon characterized by a decline in decision quality after extended periods of deliberation. This approach is particularly advantageous in minimizing the cognitive load associated with evaluating student work.

Fostering Innovative Teaching Methodologies

GenAI can be a powerful tool for fostering innovative teaching methodologies by augmenting educators' capabilities and providing new avenues for student engagement. AI-powered tools can automate administrative tasks, freeing valuable time for teachers to focus on creative lesson planning and personalized instruction. Additionally, AI can analyze student data to identify individual learning styles and paces, enabling teachers to tailor instruction and provide differentiated learning experiences. This can involve using AI-powered tutoring systems to provide personalized support or employing adaptive learning platforms that adjust the difficulty and content of lessons based on student progress. Furthermore, it can facilitate interactive and engaging learning experiences through VR and AR simulations, personalized feedback mechanisms, and the creation of AI-generated/powered content like stories, poems, and music. By embracing GenAI, educators can unlock new possibilities for innovative teaching and create more dynamic and effective learning environments for their students. Therefore, the use of both general GenAI platforms and specialized educational tools should aim to enrich teachers' subject knowledge and enhance their understanding of teaching methodologies including collaborative efforts such as the teacher-AI co-design of lesson plans, course materials, or entire curricula (UNESCO, 2024b).

The transformative potential of GenAI in fostering innovative teaching methodologies is further amplified through GenAI-powered assistants and generative twins of teaching assistants (UNESCO, 2024b, p.31). As proposed by Miao et al. (2021, p.18), the future of education presents immense promise for AI-human collaboration, encompassing models such as the AI-human "dual teacher" model, AI-powered "teaching assistants", and AI-driven "lifelong learning companions." These collaborative frameworks represent a paradigm shift in educational delivery and support systems.

The dual teacher model combines human empathy, critical thinking, and relationship-building with GenAI's capabilities. It can assist teachers by providing collaboration opportunities, and performance monitoring. However, the responsibility of teaching decisions remains with the teacher. The role of AI is to ease the teacher's workload and promote a collaborative environment. In addition, by leveraging AI-powered teaching assistants, educators can significantly reduce the burden of administrative tasks like grading assignments and creating lesson plans. This enables them to dedicate more time and energy to addressing the unique needs of each student. Numerous technological solutions are designed to mitigate the time demands placed upon educators, specifically those associated with attendance tracking, assignment assessment, and responding to frequently asked questions.

Moreover, AI-driven lifelong learning companions can empower individuals to continue their education throughout their lives. In addition, GenAI has the potential to serve as a valuable *study buddy*, offering more than just information. It can facilitate learning by posing insightful questions, promoting critical thinking and reflection, aiding in problem-solving, and enhancing the understanding of complex concepts. Additionally, it can provide diverse perspectives, encouraging students to consider alternative viewpoints and broadening their knowledge. (Kurtz et al., 2024). This companion builds on each student's unique interests and goals, guiding them in deciding what, where, and how to learn. These AI systems curate personalized learning pathways, recommend relevant resources, and offer ongoing support and motivation. They help individuals develop new skills, adapt to changing career demands, and stay informed about the latest developments in their fields of interest.

Because GenAI models like Gemini represent a transformative technological paradigm with unprecedented capabilities, developing robust GenAI literacy has become an essential competency for modern professionals. Bozkurt (2024) conceptualizes GenAI literacy as a comprehensive framework of skills and competencies critical for responsible and effective human-machine interaction:

1. Knowledge (What) - Understanding the fundamentals of AI, including its definition, functionality, capabilities, limitations, and ability to recognize AI-generated content.
2. Application (How) - Practical skills for working with AI, including prompt engineering, evaluating outputs, customizing models, and implementing AI solutions across different contexts.
3. Critical Thinking (Why) - Ethical considerations and broader implications, focusing on responsible use, transparency, privacy, equity, and the human role in AI development and oversight.

As Bozkurt emphasizes the importance of GenAI literacy for responsible human-machine interaction, fostering this competency is crucial to addressing the potential benefits of GenAI in academia. While the ethical implications of GenAI in academia present significant challenges, GenAI also offers potential benefits for academic writing by assisting with tasks such as text structuring and information summarization (Rentier, 2024). Furthermore, Hamerman, Aggarwal and Martin (2024) reported that students were more likely to use GenAI when they believed it improved their learning. Social norms also play a significant role, with students being more likely to use GenAI if they perceive it as acceptable within their academic community. The study further revealed that students preferred institutional policies that allowed GenAI use while providing clear guidelines. Notably, assignments that explicitly integrated GenAI were generally viewed as enriching the learning experience. In contrast to the student perspective, Cooper and Tang (2024) investigated how DALL-E 3 and ChatGPT portray science classrooms and educators, uncovering a mix of stereotypical and diverse representations. While these tools offer exciting educational possibilities, they raise concerns about bias and equity that require careful consideration in implementation.

Beyond image creation, GenAI can prepare interactive simulations that enhance learning engagement and effectiveness. These systems generate realistic and immersive simulations replicating real-world scenarios, allowing students to experiment, explore, and learn from interactions in risk-free environments. For instance, virtual chemistry laboratories enable students to mix chemicals and observe reactions without physical hazards, providing hands-on experiences that reinforce theoretical knowledge and enhance understanding.

Beyond risk-free learning experiences in virtual labs, GenAI demonstrates its versatility by simulating job interviews and supporting students with writer's block, showcasing its multifaceted role in education. Ding, Dong, and Grewal (2024) demonstrated the effectiveness of GenAI in simulating job interviews for marketing students, where the AI adopts the roles of various company executives. This innovative approach allows students to experience diverse interview scenarios, enhancing their preparation and confidence. Similarly, GenAI can be a valuable tool for overcoming writer's block, offering assistance in generating story ideas, suggesting intriguing plot twists, and even exploring alternative narrative directions. Furthermore, conversational AI tutors/assistants can provide students with real-time support, answer questions, clarify doubts, and guide them through the learning process. This personalized support, combined with the potential of enhanced VR simulations, offers significant potential for immersive and interactive language learning experiences.

VR simulations such as VirtualSpeech offer significant potential for English language learners. By creating immersive environments that replicate real-life scenarios and integrating GenAI to enable dynamic, two-way conversations with AI-driven characters, these simulations provide a safe and controlled space for practicing English communication skills (Healy, 2024). This immersive experience allows students to overcome communication anxieties, build confidence, and improve their fluency in realistic yet low-pressure environments. Furthermore, GenAI can be used to create immersive VR and AR experiences that bring learning to life, with AI-powered language translation integrated into AR applications to provide real-time translation of text and speech, breaking down language barriers and enabling seamless communication (Koumpouros, 2024). Moreover, GenAI enhances VR/AR experiences by incorporating interactive storytelling elements. In history lessons, students can visit historical sites virtually and interact with AI-generated historical figures. These AI-driven characters can respond to inquiries, provide historical context, and offer immersive narratives, bringing history to life.

Extending beyond student learning, GenAI-enhanced VR simulations demonstrate significant potential in teacher education. Hwang et al. (2024) developed a VR simulation integrated with GenAI agents, providing pre-service teachers with a platform for practicing and refining their instructional techniques and skills, ultimately enhancing their teaching competence.

Furthermore, building upon the engaging nature of game-based learning, Generative AI (GenAI) can significantly enhance educational simulations by integrating gamification elements. Features such as scoring systems, leaderboards, badges, and rewards can increase student motivation and engagement, driving them to pursue and achieve specific learning objectives. These gamified experiences not only make learning more interactive and enjoyable but also support cross-disciplinary exploration. By dynamically adapting content, GenAI can highlight the interconnectedness of knowledge domains, helping students grasp the interdisciplinary nature of real-world challenges. This approach fosters creativity, critical thinking, and holistic understanding, encouraging learners to synthesize information across academic fields.

In addition to its pedagogical benefits, GenAI also holds promise in advancing educational inclusivity. As an assistive technology, it can generate accessible resources tailored to the needs of students with disabilities. This includes audio descriptions, real-time captions, text simplification, and alternative formats that support diverse learning preferences and abilities (Fu, Hadid & Damer, 2025). By offering such personalized accommodations, GenAI contributes to more equitable learning environments that recognize and address the varied needs of all learners.

CONCLUSION

The integration of generative artificial intelligence (GenAI) into curriculum design and content creation marks a transformative shift in educational practice, offering unprecedented opportunities to enhance teaching effectiveness and address the evolving needs of 21st century learners. GenAI serves not as a replacement for human educators but as a powerful collaborative partner that amplifies pedagogical capabilities and streamlines educational processes.

A comprehensive examination of GenAI's applications across core components of curriculum development reveals its multifaceted potential. This includes crafting precise learning objectives, generating diverse and adaptive content tailored to individual student needs, creating comprehensive lesson plans, developing sophisticated assessment tools, and fostering innovative teaching methodologies. GenAI's capacity to personalize learning experiences at scale through adaptive algorithms and intelligent tutoring systems is particularly significant, enabling individualized pathways that accommodate diverse learning styles, paces, and needs. This personalization extends to accessibility, with GenAI supporting inclusive learning environments by breaking down language barriers, providing real-time translation, and creating accessible formats, thus advancing educational equity.

The rapid evolution of AI-powered educational resources is evident in specialized platforms like Eduaide.Ai and MagicSchool, alongside general-purpose tools such as ChatGPT, Claude, Copilot and Gemini. These platforms offer educators streamlined access to evidence-based instructional strategies and pre-aligned educational content, significantly reducing development time while maintaining pedagogical rigor.

However, this technological advancement presents challenges. Concerns surrounding academic integrity, data privacy, algorithmic bias, and the potential for over-reliance on AI tools necessitate careful consideration and proactive management. The reliability issues of AI detection tools and the risk of generating superficial or biased content underscore the critical importance of human oversight and professional judgment. Furthermore, the potential for technostress and professional deprofessionalization highlights the need for comprehensive training programs and supportive institutional frameworks. The fragmented regulatory landscape, with most countries lacking specific frameworks for GenAI in education, requires institutional leadership to develop policies that protect data privacy while fostering innovation.

Looking toward the future, GenAI literacy, encompassing knowledge, application, and critical thinking skills, emerge as an essential competency for modern educators. This framework provides a roadmap for professional development, enabling responsible and effective human-machine interaction. As GenAI technologies evolve, educators must embrace continuous learning and adaptation to remain effective while maintaining their essential human contributions.

The transformative potential of GenAI extends beyond individual classrooms to address broader educational challenges. Its capacity to support Sustainable Development Goal-4 through improved access to quality education, enhanced personalization, and reduced administrative burden positions as a valuable tool for advancing global educational equity. Technology's ability to facilitate cross-disciplinary learning, support lifelong learning initiatives, and create immersive educational experiences through VR and AR integration points toward a future where learning becomes more engaging, accessible, and effective.

Ultimately, the successful integration of GenAI into curriculum design and content creation requires a balanced approach that leverages technological capabilities while preserving the irreplaceable elements of human instruction. The emphasis on collaboration ensures that the unique qualities of human educators, empathy, creativity, critical thinking, and relationship-building remain central to the educational experience. GenAI serves to amplify these qualities by handling routine tasks, providing data-driven insights, and creating opportunities for more meaningful student-teacher interactions.

As educational institutions navigate this technological transformation, success hinges on thoughtful implementation guided by pedagogical principles, ethical considerations, and student-centered goals. By embracing GenAI as a collaborative tool while maintaining focus on educational excellence and human values, educators can harness its potential to create more effective, inclusive, and engaging learning environments that prepare students for success in an increasingly complex and interconnected world.

When strategically integrated, GenAI can empower educators to streamline instructional design, foster dynamic and interactive learning environments, and ultimately enhance student outcomes. However, realizing these benefits requires a nuanced and ethically informed approach that addresses critical challenges such as equitable access, data privacy, and algorithmic bias. To fully harness the promise of GenAI, it is essential to promote responsible adoption, underpinned by ongoing professional development and institutional support, ensuring educators are equipped with both technical competencies and pedagogical frameworks for meaningful and sustainable implementation. By prioritizing inclusive and ethical practices, GenAI can contribute to building a more equitable, effective, and future-ready education system.

Despite growing interest and extensive research into the technical capabilities of GenAI, there remains a notable gap in empirical studies exploring its pedagogical integration in both traditional and digital learning contexts. Furthermore, systematic investigations into the psychological and professional impacts of sustained GenAI use on educators are critically needed. Such research would offer valuable insights into the long-term implications of these technologies on teacher agency, professional identity, and instructional efficacy, ultimately serving the fundamental goal of education, empowering learners to reach their full potential and contribute meaningfully to society.

REFERENCES

Akpan, I. J., Kobara, Y. M., Owolabi, J., Akpan, A. A., & Offodile, O. F. (2025). Conversational and generative artificial intelligence and human–chatbot interaction in education and research. *International Transactions in Operational Research*, *32*(3), 1251–1281. DOI: 10.1111/itor.13522

Allam, H., Khan, Z., Letsholo, K., Pandya, B., Shah, K., & Ahamed, J. (2023, 24-25 May). *A proposed AI method for tracking college students' academic progress* [Conference presentation]. *International Conference on Information Technology Trends (ITT),* Dubai, United Arab Emirates, DOI: 10.1109/ITT59889.2023.10184256

Ardito, C. G. (2024). Generative AI detection in higher education assessments. *New Directions for Teaching and Learning*, •••, 1–18. DOI: 10.1002/tl.20624

Bozkurt, A. (2024). Why generative AI literacy, why now and why it matters in the educational landscape? Kings, queens and GenAI dragons. *Open Praxis*, *16*(3), 283–290. DOI: 10.55982/openpraxis.16.3.739

Bozkurt, A., Xiao, J., Farrow, R., Bai, J. Y. H., Nerantzi, C., Moore, S., Dron, J., Stracke, C. M., Singh, L., Crompton, H., Koutropoulos, A., Terentev, E., Pazurek, A., Nichols, M., Sidorkin, A. M., Costello, E., Watson, S., Mulligan, D., Honeychurch, S., & Asino, T. I. (2024). The manifesto for teaching and learning in a time of generative AI: A critical collective stance to better navigate the future. *Open Praxis*, *16*(4), 487–513. DOI: 10.55982/openpraxis.16.4.777

Ch'ng, L. K. (2023). How AI makes its mark on instructional design. *Asian Journal of Distance Education*, *18*(2), 32–41. DOI: 10.5281/zenodo.8188576

Chen, H., & Feng, Y. (2024). Breaking new ground or opening pandora's box? insights from the special issue on ai and social media advertising. *Journal of Interactive Advertising*, *24*(4), 424–427. DOI: 10.1080/15252019.2024.2428580

Chiu, T. K. F. (2023). The impact of Generative AI (GenAI) on practices, policies and research direction in education: A case of ChatGPT and Midjourney. *Interactive Learning Environments*, *32*(10), 6187–6203. DOI: 10.1080/10494820.2023.2253861

Choi, G. W., Kim, S. H., Lee, D., & Moon, J. (2024). Utilizing generative AI for instructional design: Exploring strengths, weaknesses, opportunities, and threats. *TechTrends*, *68*(4), 1–13. DOI: 10.1007/s11528-024-00967-w

Cooper, G., & Tang, K. S. (2024). Pixels and Pedagogy: Examining Science Education Imagery by Generative Artificial Intelligence. *Journal of Science Education and Technology*, *33*(4), 556–568. DOI: 10.1007/s10956-024-10104-0

Crompton, H., & Burke, D. (2022). Artificial intelligence in K-12 education. *SN Social Sciences*, *2*(7), 1–14. DOI: 10.1007/s43545-022-00425-5

Dillig, M., Böhmer, A., Mason, J., Bolaji, S., Isso, I., Stănescu, M. H., Sahin, H., & Kuraner, A. (2024). A segue from search to dialogue: leveraging GenAI for pre-service teacher training. In Sharma, R., & Bozkurt, A. (Eds.), *Transforming education with generative ai: prompt engineering and synthetic content creation* (pp. 1–34). IGI Global Scientific Publishing., DOI: 10.4018/979-8-3693-1351-0.ch002

Ding, M., Dong, S., & Grewal, R. (2024). Generative AI and usage in marketing classroom. *Customer Needs and Solutions*, *11*(5), 1–15. DOI: 10.1007/s40547-024-00145-2

Eduaide.Ai. (2024). *About us: created by teachers, for teachers* https://www.eduaide.ai/about

Farrelly, T., & Baker, N. (2023). Generative artificial intelligence: Implications and considerations for higher education practice. *Education Sciences*, *13*(11), 1–14. DOI: 10.3390/educsci13111109

Fırat, M. (2023). Integrating AI applications into learning management systems to enhance e-learning. *Instructional Technology and Lifelong Learning*, *4*(1), 1–14. DOI: 10.52911/itall.1244453

Fu, B., Hadid, A., & Damer, N. (2025). Generative AI in the context of assistive technologies: Trends, limitations and future directions. *Image and Vision Computing*, *154*, 1–15. DOI: 10.1016/j.imavis.2024.105347

Gibson, R. (2023, August 14). *10 ways artificial intelligence is transforming instructional design.* https://er.educause.edu/articles/2023/8/10-ways-artificial-intelligence-is-transforming-instructional-design#fn4

Grévisse, C. (2024). LLM-based automatic short answer grading in undergraduate medical education. *BMC Medical Education*, *24*(1), 1–16. DOI: 10.1186/s12909-024-06026-5

Hamerman, E. J., Aggarwal, A., & Martins, C. (2024). An investigation of generative AI in the classroom and its implications for university policy. *Quality Assurance in Education*. Advance online publication. DOI: 10.1108/QAE-08-2024-0149

Healy, V. (2024, October 17). *Gen AI and VR – Changing the way we learn soft skills.* https://virtualspeech.com/blog/chatgpt-vr-learning

Hsu, Y. C., & Ching, Y. H. (2023). Generative artificial intelligence in education, part one: The dynamic frontier. *TechTrends*, *67*(4), 603–607. DOI: 10.1007/s11528-023-00863-9

Hwang, J., Hong, S., Eom, T., & Lim, C. (2024, June 10-14). *Enhancing pre-service teachers' competence with a generative artificial intelligence-enhanced virtual reality simulation* [Conference presentation]. International Society of the Learning Sciences, Buffalo, New York, USA.

Jauhiainen, J. S., & Garagorry Guerra, A. (2024a). Generative AI in education: ChatGPT-4 in evaluating students' written responses. *Innovations in Education and Teaching International*, •••, 1–18. DOI: 10.1080/14703297.2024.2422337

Jauhiainen, J. S., & Garagorry Guerra, A. (2024b). Evaluating students' open-ended written responses with LLMS: Using the RAG Framework for GPT-3.5, GPT-4, Claude-3, and Mistral-Large. *Advances in Artificial Intelligence and Machine Learning.*, *4*(4), 3097–3113. DOI: 10.54364/AAIML.2024.44177

Jerusha, J. A., & Rajakumari, R. (2024). *Longitudinal analysis of student progress in AI-integrated English language courses* [Conference presentation]. International Conference on Knowledge Engineering and Communication Systems (ICKECS), Chikkaballapur, India. DOI: 10.1109/ICKECS61492.2024.10616489

Kanbach, D. K., Heiduk, L., Blueher, G., Schreiter, M., & Lahmann, A. (2024). The GenAI is out of the bottle: Generative artificial intelligence from a business model innovation perspective. *Review of Managerial Science*, *18*(1), 1189–1220. DOI: 10.1007/s11846-023-00696-z

Kanık, M. (2024). The use of ChatGPT in assessment. *International Journal of Assessment Tools in Education*, *11*(3), 608–621. DOI: 10.21449/ijate.1379647

Khalil, M., & Er, E. (2023). Will ChatGPT get you caught? rethinking of plagiarism detection. In: Zaphiris, P., Ioannou, A. (eds) *Learning and Collaboration Technologies.* HCII 2023. Lecture Notes in Computer Science, *14040.* https://doi.org/DOI: 10.1007/978-3-031-34411-4_32

Kirkham, H. (2023). *The rise of AI in education? research report on teacher usage, teacher wishes and teacher concerns. education intelligence AI in education,* Oriel Square, https://www.orielsquare.co.uk/wp-content/uploads/2023/10/education-intelligence_report_summer-2023_digital-1.pdf

Kirschenbaum, M. (2023, March 8). *Prepare for the Textpocalypse.* The Atlantic, https://www.theatlantic.com/technology/archive/2023/03/ai-chatgpt-writing-language-models/673318/

Kohnke, L. (2024). *How GenAI impacts technostress among secondary school English teachers* [Conference presentation]. International CALL Research Conference, Waseda University, Tokyo, Japan. https://doi.org/DOI: 10.29140/9780648184485-17

Koumpouros, Y. (2024). Revealing the true potential and prospects of augmented reality in education. *Smart Learn. Environ.*, *11*(2), 1–62. DOI: 10.1186/s40561-023-00288-0

Kurtz, G., Salmon, G., Watkins, R., Kalz, M., & Buchem, I. (2024). Special Issue: The integration of generative AI in teaching and learning. *European Journal of Open. Distance and E-Learning*, *26*(1), 1–4. DOI: 10.2478/eurodl-2024-0010

Li, H., Xu, T., Zhang, C., Chen, E., Liang, J., Fan, X., . . . Wen, Q. (2024). Bringing generative AI to adaptive learning in education. *arXiv:2402.14601*. https://doi.org// arXiv.2402.14601DOI: 10.48550

MagicSchool. (2025). *Mainpage*. https://app.magicschool.ai/tools

Miao, F., Holmes, W., Huang, R., & Zhang, H. (2021). *AI and education: guidance for policy-makers*. UNESCO, https://unesdoc.unesco.org/ark:/48223/pf0000376709

Milner, H. R. (2013, February 28). *Policy reforms and de-professionalization of teaching*. National Education Policy Center. https://nepc.colorado.edu/publication/policy-reforms-deprofessionalization

Moorhouse, B. L., Yeo, M. A., & Wan, Y. (2023). Generative AI tools and assessment: Guidelines of the world's top-ranking universities. *Computers and Education Open*, *5*, 1–10. DOI: 10.1016/j.caeo.2023.100151

Oliva, P. F., & Gordon, W. R. (2012). *Developing the curriculum* (8th ed.). Pearson.

Open, A. I. (2025, January). *What is the canvas feature in ChatGPT and how do I use it?* https://help.openai.com/en/articles/9930697-what-is-the-canvas-feature-in -chatgpt-and-how-do-i-use-it

Ornstein, A. C., & Hunkins, F. P. (2018). *Curriculum: Foundations, principles, and issues*. Pearson.

Parker, M.J., Anderson, C., & Stone, C., & YeaRim, O. (. (2024). A large language model approach to educational survey feedback analysis. *International Journal of Artificial Intelligence in Education*. Advance online publication. DOI: 10.1007/ s40593-024-00414-0

Parsons, B., & Curry, J. H. (2024). Can ChatGPT pass graduate-level instructional design assignments? potential implications of artificial intelligence in education and a call to action. *TechTrends*, *68*(1), 67–78. DOI: 10.1007/s11528-023-00912-3

Perkins, M., Roe, J., Vu, B., Postma, D., Hickerson, D., McGaughran, J., & Khuat, H. Q. (2024). Simple techniques to bypass GenAI text detectors: Implications for inclusive education. *International Journal of Educational Technology in Higher Education, 21*(53), 1–25. DOI: 10.1186/s41239-024-00487-w

Rentier, E. S. (2024). To use or not to use: Exploring the ethical implications of using generative AI in academic writing. *AI and Ethics*. Advance online publication. DOI: 10.1007/s43681-024-00649-6

Research, I. F. F. (2023). *School and college panel* https://assets.publishing.service.gov.uk/media/652ea669d86b1b000d3a513e/School_and_college_panel_April_2023.pdf UK Department for Education.

Rettberg, J. (2022, December 6). *ChatGPT is multilingual but monocultural, and it's learning your values.* https://jilltxt.net/right-now-chatgpt-is-multilingual-but-monocultural-but-its-learning-your-values/

Shoaib, M. R., Wang, Z., Ahvanooey, M. T., & Zhao, J. (2023, November 28-30). *Deepfakes, misinformation, and disinformation in the era of frontier AI, generative AI, and large AI models* [Conference presentation]. International Conference on Computer and Applications (ICCA) Cairo, Egypt. DOI: 10.1109/ICCA59364.2023.10401723

Singh, S. V. (2023, January). *The prospects for advancing adaptive learning technology through AI methods. In 2023 Future of Educational Innovation-Workshop Series Data in Action.*, DOI: 10.1109/IEEECONF56852.2023.10105111

Smyth, G., & Kum, H. (2010). 'When they don't use it they will lose it': professionals, deprofessionalization and reprofessionalization: the case of refugee teachers in Scotland. *Journal of Refugee Studies, 23*(4), 503–522. DOI: 10.1093/jrs/feq041

Taba, H. (1962). *Curriculum development: Theory and practice*. Harcourt, Brace & World.

Tarafdar, M., Stich, J.-F., Maier, C., & Laumer, S. (2024). Techno-eustress creators: Conceptualization and empirical validation. *Information Systems Journal, 34*(6), 2097–2131. DOI: 10.1111/isj.12515

Teacher Tapp. (2023, November 28). *How to improve behaviour and wellbeing, and how you're using AI in schools* https://teachertapp.com/uk/articles/how-to-improve-behaviour-wellbeing-and-how-youre-using-ai-in-schools/

The Open Innovation Team & Department for Education. (2024). *Generative AI in education, educator and expert views.* https://assets.publishing.service.gov.uk/media/65b8cd41b5cb6e000d8bb74e/dfe_genai_in_education_-_educator_and_expert_views_report.pdf

Trabelsi, Z., Alnajjar, F., Parambil, M. M. A., Gochoo, M., & Ali, L. (2023). Real-time attention monitoring system for classroom: A deep learning approach for student's behavior recognition. *Big Data and Cognitive Computing*, *7*(1), 1–17. DOI: 10.3390/bdcc7010048

Tyler, R. W. (1949). *Basic principles of curriculum and instruction*. University of Chicago Press.

UNESCO. (2019). *Artificial intelligence in education: challenges and opportunities for sustainable development.* UNESCO, https://unesdoc.unesco.org/ark:/48223/pf0000366994

UNESCO. (2024a). *AI competency framework for teachers* https://unesdoc.unesco.org/ark:/48223/pf0000391104

UNESCO. (2024b). *Guidance for generative AI in education and research* https://unesdoc.unesco.org/ark:/48223/pf0000386693

Vergara, D., Lampropoulos, G., Antón-Sancho, Á., & Fernández-Arias, P. (2024). Impact of artificial intelligence on learning management systems: A bibliometric review. *Multimodal Technologies and Interaction*, *8*(9), 75. DOI: 10.3390/mti8090075

Walther, C. (2024, October 9). *Are we unleashing a treasure chest or pandora's box onto humanity?* https://www.forbes.com/sites/corneliawalther/2024/10/09/are-we-unleashing-a-treasure-chest-or-pandoras-box-onto-humanity/

Whalen, J., Grube, W., Xu, C., & Trust, T. (2024). K-12 educators' reactions and responses to ChatGPT and GenAI during the 2022–2023 school year. *TechTrends*, •••, 1–13. DOI: 10.1007/s11528-024-01028-y

Yang, E., & Beil, C. (2024). Ensuring data privacy in AI/ML implementation. *New Directions for Higher Education*, *2024*(207), 63–78. DOI: 10.1002/he.20509

Yousef, M., Mohamed, K., Medhat, W., Muhammed, E. H., Khoriba, G., & Arafa, T. (2024). BeGrading: large language models for enhanced feedback in programming education. *Neural Comput & Applic.*, 1-14. https://doi.org/DOI: 10.1007/s00521-024-10449-y

Zhai, X. (2024). Transforming teachers' roles and agencies in the era of generative AI: Perceptions, acceptance, knowledge, and practices. *Journal of Science Education and Technology*, 1–11. DOI: 10.1007/s10956-024-10174-0

Zhai, X., & Nehm, R. H. (2023). AI and formative assessment: The train has left the station. *Journal of Research in Science Teaching*, *60*(6), 1390–1398. DOI: 10.1002/tea.21885

KEY TERMS AND DEFINITIONS

Artificial intelligence (AI): Is a branch of computer science that focuses on creating systems capable of performing tasks that typically require human intelligence.

Augmented reality (AR): Is an interactive experience that merges the real world with computer-generated 3D content, creating a blended and engaging environment.

Curriculum development: Is a purposeful, strategic process aimed at enhancing the quality and effectiveness of the learning experience. It involves stating clear objectives, creating content, structuring teaching and learning situations, and implementing evaluation methods to assess both student progress and curriculum effectiveness. As a continuous and iterative cycle, curriculum development ensures educational programs remain relevant, responsive, and adaptable to evolving learner needs and societal demands.

Generative artificial intelligence (GenAI): Is a type of artificial intelligence that can create new content such as text, images, and music based on patterns it learns from existing data.

Large language model (LLM): Is advanced artificial intelligence systems that use deep learning to understand and generate human-like language. Trained on massive text datasets, they excel at tasks like answering questions, creating content, translating, and holding conversations.

Learning management systems (LMS): Is a software application designed to establish a comprehensive framework for the creation, management, delivery, and tracking of educational courses, training programs, learning and development initiatives.

Virtual reality (VR): Is a technology that enables users to fully immerse themselves in a computer-generated, artificial environment and interact with it in real-time.

Chapter 3
Potential Curriculum Models for Intentionally Incorporating Generative AI in Higher Education

Nick Baker
https://orcid.org/0000-0003-1326-9060
University of Windsor, Canada

William Evans
https://orcid.org/0000-0001-5722-1259
Munster Technological University, Ireland

Tom Farrelly
https://orcid.org/0000-0002-1986-4154
Munster Technological University, Ireland

ABSTRACT

This chapter examines the challenges educators face in adapting higher education curricula to responsibly incorporate generative Artificial Intelligence (GenAI). While much has been written about changes that can be made to pedagogy at the course or unit level, much less concrete guidance exists at the curriculum or programme level. This chapter explores examples of curriculum approaches that show promise in moving from individual educators adapting their pedagogies, towards a more holistic approach considering the whole curriculum. Drawing from coaching and ecological theories of learning, the authors propose a novel use of the Constraints-Led Approach (CLA), coupled with the Spiral Curriculum model as a promising approach to addressing the challenges and opportunities presented by GenAI in

DOI: 10.4018/979-8-3373-7579-3.ch003

ght © 2026, IGI Global Scientific Publishing. Copying or distributing in print or electronic forms without written permission of IGI Global Scientific Publishing is prohibited. Use of this chapter to generative artificial intelligence (AI) technologies is expressly prohibited. The publisher reserves all rights to license its use for generative AI training and machine learning model development.

teaching and learning. CLA focuses on the dynamic interactions between task, learner, and environmental constraints, providing a flexible and adaptive framework for developing both domain and AI competencies. CLA examples are provided from multiple disciplines.

Introduction

Although AI has been around in various forms for many years, the release of ChatGPT in November 2022 is widely considered "a breakthrough for the acceleration of AI technology"(Kanbach et al., 2024, p. 1189). In the intervening time, educators around the world have been trying to understand what this new and powerful technology means for the traditions and established approaches to education. This has been particularly challenging in higher education, where most educators have minimal if any pedagogical training to draw on in support of the significant curricular changes that are needed, and a significant level of autonomy, meaning that they can often choose to ignore such developments with little consequence.

In professional and regulated programs, where there are prescribed standards and competencies that must be met to ensure the safe practice of graduates, it is critical that we can reliably evaluate those characteristics in learners. In programs that prepare students for careers in education, engineering, law, accounting, and health care professions for example, there is an urgent need for universities and regulating bodies to work together in developing curricular guidance and approaches that recognise the impact of AI on their fields, and prepare students for the world they are about to practice in. In programmes that don't lead directly to specific careers, there is no less urgency to engage and understand what these new technologies mean for our disciplines, but the source of motivation for change must come from within, rather than the spectre of an accrediting body's disapproval.

We have seen educators move relatively quickly through the grief cycle (Kübler-Ross, 1969) as they come to realise that artificial intelligence (AI), and particularly generative AI, is not only here to stay, but that it will have a transformative influence on education at all levels. While some may still choose not to engage, many have begun the journey from shock and denial to anger, bargaining, depression, and eventually acceptance (perhaps even hope and exploration!) (Kearney & Hyle, 2003; Romadona & Setiawan, 2021). The cycle may revert to an earlier state at any time though, especially with a technology evolving as quickly as AI where a development could be released at any moment that negates all the planning and adaptation work one has done to date. The challenge is that university systems were created for another era and are ill-equipped to deal with rapid and widespread disruptive forces.

Understandably, early institutional advice on how to address generative AI in higher education focused on immediate challenges universities were facing. These institutional responses included policy development (Luo, 2024), ensuring assessment security (Foltynek et al., 2023; Moya et al., 2023), banning GenAI all together (de Fine Licht, 2024; Xiao et al., 2023), restricting access to GenAI tools on campus networks, and so on. In the next stage of development, universities started providing advice on syllabus statements, redesigning assessments, the design of possible AI-infused activities, considerations of ethics and bias, and reliability (McDonald et al., 2024). One critical component missing from these early conversations, and largely still limited today, is the student voice and considerations of access, accessibility, and equity.

At an individual level, educators need to wrestle with their own understanding, fears, biases, concerns, and self-efficacy with the technology. Given the rapidity of change, there is clearly a long way yet to go in developing and supporting individual educators to reach at least a baseline of AI competence. However, continuing to focus more on the level of the individual rather than at the broader programme or discipline level may ultimately prove to be less effective at encouraging or facilitating meaningful change that truly addresses the impact of generative AI on education. It is becoming clear that academics need space and permission to explore generative AI through disciplinary lenses (preferably as cohorts of disciplinary colleagues), coupled with practical frameworks for addressing the impact of these technologies at the discipline or programme level, with an eye to the broader social and environmental impacts (McDonald et al., 2024; Xiao et al., 2023). Engaging students as partners in that process is likely to provide rich insights that can help to transform pedagogies for the era we find ourselves in, proactively address challenges, and ensure that improving outcomes for students is at the centre of any changes we make (e.g. Chan, 2023; Fatima et al., 2024; Williams & Ingle, 2025).

Bozkurt et al. (2024) recognise the myriad of potential opportunities for using generative AI in higher education curricula, including developing content, supporting assessment practices (drafting questions, assignments, rubrics, feedback, and even grading), and supporting accessibility. Additional possibilities, include curricular elements (readings, activities, topics), mapping programme curriculums against learning outcomes or external requirements, acting as a tutor trained on the content of a course or module, and a personal learning assistant for students.

Along with the potential positive outcomes however, the same authors recognise that there are also good reasons to be cautious and aware of the potential negative outcomes from utilising GenAI in educational settings, including exacerbating existing biases and inequality, the impact on critical thinking and cognition, loss of human values and agency, environmental impact and sustainability, lack of transparency and explainability, and many others that have and should be explored (Bozkurt et al.,

2024). Universities need to actively engage in this debate and offer critical voices at this time of rapid technological expansion.

Critical voices and cautions

While there are many proponents and advocates of GenAI in universities, there are, of course, voices that urge caution regarding its use. Helen Beetham (2024) critiques the common ways AI is discussed in education, highlighting the need for more careful and nuanced language. She argues that AI is often described as a co-author, thinker, or collaborator, but in her estimation, these characterisations are misleading and fail to capture the complexity of the technology. Beetham suggests that framing AI as a tool that augments human capabilities is more accurate, as it lacks true autonomy or intelligence, though this framing seems to underestimate the capabilities of current and future AI systems, and how quickly those are changing.

Beetham also questions the portrayal of AI as an intelligent entity, a concept rooted in problematic historical ideas of intelligence, which are often tied to eugenics and bias. She cautions against attributing human-like qualities to AI, arguing that it should be understood as a socio-technical project with implications for education, not as a form of intelligence. This of course, remains a highly contested debate with considerable nuance, passion, and emotion embedded, as it should be because it strikes at the very heart of what it means to be human, to learn, and to know things. For the first time, we are truly being challenged by a technology to define our unique humanness (Mollick, 2024; Vallor, 2024), and that is a highly uncomfortable space for many people to be in.

Selwyn (2022, 2024a, 2024b) offers a critical but pragmatic approach to recognising the risks and challenges of AI in education (AIED), as well as potential benefits. He advocates for a slowing down and reframing of the hyperbole associated with AIED (both extremely optimistic and pessimistic ends of the spectrum) and suggests taking a de-growth approach wherever possible. Selwyn suggests that it is important to understand the various interests and agendas that exist beneath the debates over whether technology in education is positive or negative, with critics and proponents of AIED spread across social, technical, educational, and corporate dimensions all becoming more polarised. An important consideration is that too often, both criticisms and hype of AIED lack specificity (i.e. are not referring to a specific application of AI), leaving the proponent open to justified push-back as being misinformed or outdated. For example, critics often rightfully point to the harms caused by biased algorithms, particularly those that automate or inform decision making, as reasons for caution or exclusion of these tools. The same arguments are often inappropriately applied to other forms of AI, which have a different set of risks that must be understood in the context of how those systems are trained, their safety features, and how they are used.

Selwyn also points to the need for grace in the conversation, noting that while AI-enabled products might be used to exacerbate existing inequality or other challenges in the education system, such uses were not likely the intention of the developers. Likewise, he calls on technology developers to consider more carefully the political context in which their technology will be applied and realistically assess the potential that the tool could be used inappropriately. This argument is echoed by Holmes (2024), who points out that since there is an expectation that those developing technologies such as AI that are capable of or designed to change the future of humanity should bear some responsibility for the outcomes of these developments. Openly and explicitly examining the underpinning values and ideologies surrounding AIED should be a starting point for determining how we engage with (or choose not to) AI.

Eryk Salvaggio (2024) also challenges us to address what he considers "pervasive myths" about generative AI; most notably the "control" and "productivity" myths. He argues that there is often an oversimplification of the technology's capabilities, framing it as a tool for effortless control and time-saving productivity, when in reality, AI systems are still often unpredictable and require considerable effort to use effectively. He also critiques the "prompt myth" as it suggests users can easily control AI outputs with minimal input, while in fact, prompt engineering requires skill and practice and can still lead to inaccurate results.

Beetham (2024) argues that narratives surrounding AI often focus too heavily on productivity and speed, overlooking values such as critical thinking and the development of students' own intellectual capacities. She calls for a shift in focus towards a more balanced discussion of AI's potential impact on education and the world of work. Shannon Vallor (2024) also points to the need for balance and perspective, arguing that AI can be either used to strengthen human virtues, or disable them in favour of efficiency and personal gain, but that ultimately it is our choice. This points to the urgent need for critical AI literacy in graduates who will be faced with making those decisions for the long-term future of humans.

Salvaggio also addresses the "intelligence myths" surrounding AI, particularly what he sees as the misleading use of terms like "learning" and "understanding," which are drawn from human cognition but which he argues do not accurately reflect AI processes. These misconceptions, he suggests, contribute to unrealistic expectations about AI's capabilities and influence policy decisions. By recognising these myths, Salvaggio argues that a more accurate understanding of AI can be developed, helping society to navigate its impact in a more informed and balanced manner.

Fawns (2024) argues that the focus on trying to define human and AI boundaries and capabilities misses the fundamental entanglement of human-technology collectives. He calls for a "discursive shift away from framing humans and technologies as separate entities, toward a holistic framing of collective, dynamic, entangled social, material, and digital activity" (Fawns, 2024, p. 1). He further suggests that thinking of AI as a set of technologies that are integrated into collective thinking helps to resist the hype of AI discourse and better understand the risks and possibilities within a holistic context.

Socio-technological limitations

While the broader socio-technological context of AI in higher education is largely beyond the scope of this chapter, it is important to acknowledge that these factors will inevitably play a role in how AI is, and can be, used in education. We acknowledge that most of this chapter assumes that students will have access to some form of generative AI during their studies, either provided by their institution, or personally acquired. It is also reasonable to assume that by the time those students graduate, they will enter a world of work that is shaped by AI capabilities, with employers who will expect them to have some level of AI proficiency (Mollick, 2024; Pratschke, 2024).

Universities around the world in both the Global North and South are currently grappling with the demand from students and instructors to provide access to reliable, safe, and ethical AI tools. While some large, well-resourced universities, particularly in the US and UK, have signed massive deals with commercial AI companies to provide access to powerful tools for their entire campuses (Ascione, 2024), commercially provided enterprise level access to frontier models has largely remained out of reach of most institutions. There have been concerns raised that this 'digital divide' that has historically separated institutions and learners that have access to resources from those who don't may be exacerbated by AI, where those institutions (or individuals) that can afford the best tools might see greater productivity gains and outcomes for their community than those who are resource-constrained (Bozkurt et al., 2024; Davidoff, 2024; R. F. Smith, 2025). That is changing rapidly though with significant improvements in efficiency of models, the release of open access models that perform at or near frontier levels, and small models that can be run locally on personal devices or institutional servers.

Similarly, while the world's most capable generative AI models were initially only available in the US and possibly the UK, they are now generally available to the public globally, and open models that are not geographically bounded are also widely available. Concerns about who has access to which models still exist (for example, a frontier reasoning model will outperform standard public GPT models for many tasks and mostly requires a paid subscription for access, and likewise, an autonomous agent capable of completing tasks for humans generally requires a paid account), but the landscape is rapidly changing, with access to relatively powerful tools becoming more viable. Of course though, 1/3 of the world's population still does not have reliable access to the internet, and this challenge persists in both wealthy and poorer nations (R. F. Smith, 2025). Despite these potential access challenges though, multiple large-scale studies around the world now show that AI use by students is both critical, and becoming universal, indicating that despite concerns, cost, and other barriers, students are finding ways to access and use AI (e.g. Attewell, 2025; Chung et al., 2024; Digital Education Council, 2024).

That is not to suggest though that the other well-recognised AI-related problems such as bias, inequitable treatment, confabulation, cost, environmental stressors, exploitative work, and more recently, unethical behaviour of GenAI tools (Wiggers, 2025) are not important considerations, but institutions can limit exposure of their community to those risks by taking ownership of the challenge. Provisioning AI tools locally no longer requires the massive computing resources it did just a few short years ago (capable AI models are rapidly becoming small enough to run on local servers or even individual laptops, and new approaches to processing data have significantly improved computational efficiency), making it possible to develop an AI ecosystem specifically for the needs of the institution.

For example, the Nigerian government recently announced plans to develop an AI-focused university to address the AI needs of the country and the African continent, seeing it as a catalyst for transformation and prosperity (Israni, 2025). This follows the successful launch of the world's first AI university in Qatar (Mohamed Bin Zayed University of Artificial Intelligence) in 2019 with its first undergraduate programs launching in 2025, and India's Universal AI University, which launched in 2023. Universities in the Global North, such as York University in Canada and the University of Sydney in Australia have also developed and openly shared efficient, adaptable AI architectures that can be modified to local needs in a safe, affordable, and scalable way. These trends are likely to continue as institutional AI maturity, and the demands of students, governments, industry, and society continue to develop and put pressure on universities to engage more robustly with the AI juggernaut. Interestingly, a recent systematic review found that the majority of formally evaluated AI implementations in higher education reported in the academic literature were from outside of North America, with a particular focus in Europe, Asia and Oceania (Belkina et al., 2025).

AI capabilities at this moment (early 2025)

Advances in generative AI are progressing at such a rapid pace that it is almost impossible for universities, let alone individual educators, to keep up with, and adapt to, the latest developments, especially if they see these technologies as completely separate from their daily lives. Higher education institutions are not generally designed for rapid adaptation, making the AI juggernaut even more difficult for them to deal with than for other sectors. It is critical however, perhaps more so than in other knowledge work, that higher education institutions come to grips with the capabilities of generative AI, as these technologies are squarely focused on the work that until very recently was considered only possible by highly skilled humans.

Since the release of GPT4-level GenAI, we have seen rapid advances in AI performance on all human knowledge and capability benchmarks, with the outcome that by early 2025, most major models are now performing at or above human benchmarks in most domains, including math and symbolic disciplines (Maslej et al., 2024; Wilkins, 2024). In fact, these models have blown past human abilities so quickly that they have prompted the creation of a new benchmark known as "Humanity's Last Exam", a multimodal benchmark of the frontiers of human knowledge designed to be the last such closed-ended benchmark for AI (Phan et al., 2025).

At the time of writing, a wave of new and updated tools from established and emerging players in the field have just been released, representing the next step change in the AI space. These developments include significant advances: reasoning models, computer use agents (CUAs), and multi-agent autonomous frameworks capable of generating and managing other AI agents to complete tasks independently in the cloud.

Reasoning models, including Open AI's ChatGPT-o series, Google's Gemini Flash 2, Anthropic's Claude 4, and the DeepSeek R1 model, take an approach that essentially causes the bot to slow down and check its work, leading to better outcomes in complex tasks (although interestingly, poorer outcomes in many other tasks such as creative writing) (Shao et al., 2024; Wang, 2025). The reasoning models more closely approximate human reasoning, and importantly, make that work visible to the end user, literally showing the chain of reasoning that it goes through to arrive at an answer. This goes some way towards addressing concerns about the lack of transparency and explainability of generative AI outputs. For complex, multi-step, interdisciplinary or ambiguous tasks, these reasoning models perform more consistently and some have claimed, move us a step closer to generalised artificial intelligence.

Along with reasoning models, the major AI companies are all scrambling to release a form of semi-autonomous assistants known as deep research models (what you might think of as proto-agents) which, given a task, are able to search the internet and provide a detailed, structured report summarising the evidence around one's question. OpenAI, Google, and Perplexity have all released models (confusingly each named "Deep Research") that are capable of almost expert level research, reasoning, and synthesis of a vast array of information, competently automating many research tasks (OpenAI, 2025; Perplexity Team, 2025).

Autonomous AI agents and embedded AI

Taking this one step further, computer use agents (often referred to as CUAs or just agents), such as Anthropic's Claude Computer Use, Google's Gemini 2.0, and OpenAI's Operator are another breakthrough released to the public in late 2024 that significantly shift the capabilities of generative AI closer to human. These tools are able to take over and interact with a user's computer, effectively taking control and autonomously using the device in the same way a human would; clicking on links, typing in search and content boxes, responding to surveys, quizzes, and assignments, and many more tasks (Hu et al., 2024; Roose, 2025). When the agent encounters something it is unsure of or can't figure out, it can ask for help, search the internet for a solution, or even call on another AI tool to provide answers. Beyond CUAs though are the new multi-agent systems (such as Manus.AI) where one agent controls many others in a virtual cloud environment (outside the user's browser so it can continue to do work when you close your computer) to autonomously tackle complex problems (C. S. Smith, 2025). These tools have the potential to automate typical human tasks from end-to-end.

On top of the software capabilities of generative AI, recent releases of AI-enabled hardware, such as the RayBan Meta glasses, Even Realities smart glasses, AI enabled projection glasses, Rabbit R1 action agent, AI enabled pens, and AI earpieces all change the relationship between humans and AI. These devices represent an early embodied AI experience, but more practically, mean that AI is embedded in everyday devices, ready to assist when called upon.

What all these tools collectively mean for higher education is that we can no longer guarantee that *any* form of assessment is secure against unauthorized AI assistance (e.g. Corbin et al., 2025; Cotton et al., 2024). Instead, we need to develop a range of assessment approaches that exist on a spectrum from less to more secure, and consider carefully what really requires a high level of security, and what can be treated as formative.

AI and assessment

Assessment and concerns about student 'cheating' have been the focus of much of the recent AI-driven angst in higher education. Considerable energy and ink have been devoted to trying to invent 'AI proof' assessments, often through attempts at increasing security of the same assessment approaches that have been used in higher education for centuries, without considering whether the assessment is now, or ever was, fit for purpose. A disproportional focus on cheating also reinforces problematic power dynamics in higher education and drives an unhealthy culture of mistrust, perpetuating the infantilization of adult learners who should be trusted to make their own decisions and mistakes. It also disproportionately targets marginalised students who may be more frequently accused of AI misuse, who may not have access to the best paid models to support their work, and for whom some of the more extreme suggestions for enhanced assessment security will be inaccessible and inequitable (Farrelly & Baker, 2023).

While there has been a disproportionate level of focus on online courses and unsupervised assessments as those where students will inevitably use AI to support or even complete assessment on their behalf, the availability of relatively cheap everyday devices (such as glasses) that allow almost undetectable streaming and communication with other humans and AI assistants indicates that even assessments that have been held up as 'AI proof,' such as pen and paper written exams, or in-person oral Vivas and presentations are now vulnerable to external assistance, and there is little we can do to prevent these uses. Even holding assessment in an internet free environment will soon no longer provide any more security, as highly functional models become small enough to be loaded to a personal device and used locally without the need for internet access.

Given these limitations then, a practical focus on assessment security across a spectrum, with some activities and check points in the curriculum requiring more effort to secure than others is important, especially in disciplines and jurisdictions that require graduates to meet defined learning outcomes and competencies. Importantly, this offers an opportunity to re-examine assessment practice reliability and validity, with realistic adjustments for this new era (Dawson et al., 2024a). Dawson et al. (2024b) consider the use of generative AI not as cheating (a moral judgement), but as an issue of quality assurance (an assessment design issue). They note that many assessment practices that rely on students not using generative AI, but which can't prevent students from using it, are simply not suitable for high stakes assessment – they have a validity flaw, and the problem is not in the use of the AI technology, but in the design of the assessment. Educators need to identify the skills, knowledge, and competencies that must be demonstrated independently (e.g. without the assistance of AI) over the course of a programme. It's also important to recognise that not every assessment needs to be fully secure in order to be valid – there is still great value in formative assessment that may allow the use of AI but not count towards a grade (Dawson et al., 2024b; J. Lodge et al., 2023).

Therefore, instead of focusing on a narrow conception of AI use as 'cheating', and attempts to block use or 'catch' those who use these tools, we should instead turn that energy towards curriculum redesign to intentionally incorporate and scaffold use of AI, building trust with learners, and developing their AI literacy so they have the tools they need to know when to use AI in their work, and when to avoid or minimise it. One of Eaton's (2023) core tenets of Postplagiarism is that "Hybrid Human-AI Writing Will Become Normal." She asserts that trying to discern where human work ends and AI begins is "pointless and futile" drawing on the notion of AI use simply as 'cheating' is unhelpful. If hybrid writing is the new norm, then education must adapt to teach students how to navigate this reality, rather than pretend it doesn't exist (Pratschke, 2024). Employers are now looking for AI literacy (often ill or undefined at this point) as a critical competency in a wide array of jobs, with a recent survey of employers showing 71% would hire a less experienced candidate with AI skills over an experienced candidate without them and two-thirds of employers said they would not hire someone without AI skills now (Wells, 2024); clearly employers are expecting higher education to step up and develop these skills and knowledge in their graduates.

While the not unreasonable initial reaction of many may be to want to return to in-person pen and paper exams as the only way to secure assessment of learning, the lack of authenticity and validity of most exam settings means this may exacerbate concerns about assessment by using an unreliable measure. A more nuanced approach is needed that recognises that students also need to be proficient in demonstrating their skills and knowledge with the tools available to them in their lives outside academia.

Impact on students

A notable trend in the early responses to the emergence of AI in higher education is the tendency to make assumptions about how students are experiencing and using AI in their learning (including assuming that they are, and will want to use, these tools). As suggested in the previous section, there has been a significant focus in both the popular media and academic writing on preventing student academic misconduct, with much written about deploying surveillance technologies and other methods to 'catch' cheaters, designing assessment to 'prevent' use of AI, and returning to pen and paper in-class assessment as the only solution (e.g. Dawson et al., 2024b; Leaton Gray et al., 2025; Nikolic et al., 2024; Westfall, 2023).

Each of these approaches and assumptions about student behaviour has the potential to impact the student experience, including creating a narrative of mistrust and criminalisation of students that is corrosive and the antithesis of good teaching practice, significant equity issues, and reducing accessibility of the learning environment. There is a risk of further marginalization of already vulnerable populations, particularly racialized and international students who already more frequently experience disproportionate accusations of plagiarism (Farrelly & Baker, 2023; Moya et al., 2023), and students with disabilities, for whom AI assistants can provide life changing equity improvements (Dieker & Zaugg, 2024; Gibson, 2024) Fortunately, there are also many reasonable, human-centred and pragmatic approaches that are emerging in the literature as well (e.g. Bearman & Ajjawi, 2023; Curtis, 2025; L. Eaton, 2024; J. M. Lodge et al., 2023). Rather than a one-size-fits-all approach, universities need to recognise that students are diverse and messy (mostly) adult humans with agency who should be involved in the conversation about AI in their education.

Large scale surveys of student use of AI consistently show that they are not only increasingly using AI, but also that they share many of the same concerns that educators do about the potential impact on learning; overreliance leading to reduced creativity, communication, and critical thinking; data privacy and misinformation (particularly public malicious misuse of AI); anxiety about the pace of AI development and potential global impacts; and equity, with unequal access exacerbating the digital divide (e.g. Attewell, 2025; Chung et al., 2024; Digital Education Council, 2024). Rather than seeing AI as a tool to circumvent academic integrity rules, students use it in highly nuanced ways, supporting their writing, research, note taking, summarisation, studying, life organisation, and even increasingly as a personal psychological support and companion.

These large surveys of thousands of students around the world also reveal that they are increasingly concerned about the impact of AI on their future working lives, and particularly their employability if the programmes they are studying don't adequately prepare them for the AI-enabled workforce, with a majority of students feeling that their degrees don't prepare them for the world of AI, or that they are receiving adequate guidance from their institutions (Attewell, 2025; Chung et al., 2024; Digital Education Council, 2024). It is also clear from these studies that students are becoming increasingly frustrated with universities not treating them as partners in the process of addressing AI. As Attewell (2025) summarises the sentiment, "Students want to be partners, not passengers: they don't just want to be taught about AI, they want to help shape how AI is integrated into education and how it prepares them for the future."

Higher education has a significant role to play in helping students develop the skills they need to navigate the complexity of the AI infused world, but needs to act quickly to redesign the learning experience to intentionally incorporate AI. Operationalising AI competency frameworks in all areas of higher education will be key to achieving this.

AI competency and literacy frameworks

Several AI competency and literacy frameworks have been developed recently, emphasising a range of different aspects of the broader interactions between AI, society, and the environment, including sustainability concerns, individual skill development, institutional policy-making, curriculum design, and more. Examples include Chan (2023); Hillier (2023); Farrelly & Baker (2023); Kassoria, Georgieva & Papini (2024),Ng et al. (2021), and the Digital Education Council (2025). These frameworks build on and represent the complex interplay between digital and information literacy (e.g. Long & Magerko, 2020; Yi, 2021). The challenge that these approaches face however is that with this particular technology developing and improving so rapidly, it is difficult to forecast the competencies that such a framework will need to remain relevant even for a relatively short period.

For example, most of the current literacy frameworks consider a scenario where a user of AI has to intentionally interact with a particular AI tool, which uses a particular set of skills like choosing the right model, framing an appropriate prompt and so on. However, with more and more deep embedding of AI in workflows of everyday tools, seeking out a specific AI bot will become less common. Similarly, most frameworks did not anticipate the release of powerful reasoning models, for which the prompting strategies employed with older models are no longer as effective, or agentic models that are able to act autonomously and for which appropriate literacies are quite different as the machine becomes a collaborator or employee, rather than a simple tool.

Elements of literacy development need to be embedded in each module/unit within a programme, as literacies are a set of skills and competencies that develop over time, rather than as a one-shot that could be facilitated in a single unit. Therefore, by their nature, AI literacies need to be considered at the *programme* level to allow for effective development in graduates. The question is, what frameworks can be applied at the curriculum or programme level to enable the development of both domain knowledge and competencies, *and* embedded development of AI literacy within the context of the specific knowledge domain?

Pedagogical responses to AI

The initial response by most higher education institutions to the emergence of widely available generative AI in late 2022 was similar to that used in the transition to online teaching during the COVID-19 pandemic – lots of helpful, rapidly constructed and crowd-sourced advice was generated and shared. This advice was most often targeted at individuals – instructors and students – and the ways in which they had to adapt their behaviour to address this emerging challenge. In some cases, the same advice offered during COVID held true in this new context – rethinking assessment to be more authentic, more meaningful, more focused on process than product, less pressure on one or two points of assessment, and so on. These have been validated in the literature for decades (George, 2023), but they also suffer from the same weakness as an approach that they did in the COVID era – individual action from educators by itself, while an important part of the puzzle, is not enough to effect the systemic changes needed to truly address the scale and magnitude of disruption that generative AI brings to higher education.

As educators become more aware of, and perhaps more comfortable with AI in education, they will inevitably adapt their pedagogical approaches to account for this. There are questions emerging about whether there is such a thing as an 'AI pedagogy' that is distinct from other pedagogies, but there does not yet appear to be any consensus about what those distinct features might be. Bearman and Ajjawi (2023 p. 1047) argue that "…a pedagogy for an AI-mediated world involves learning to work with opaque, partial and ambiguous situations, which reflect the entangled relationships between people and technologies."

Jamieson (2022) argues that pedagogy for an AI world should acknowledge and incorporate AI in the work of learning the discipline (in her case, writing composition), and should be founded on trust and relationality with students. George (2023) suggests that many of the pedagogical approaches already known to be effective – active learning, problem-based learning, collaboration and interdisciplinary project teams – are still fit for purpose in the AI era, with the recognition that skills like creativity, critical thinking, and adaptability will be augmented and extended by AI tools.

Perhaps one place to start understanding what AI pedagogies might look like is to return to the widely accepted Technological, Pedagogical and Content (TPACK) framework (Koehler & Mishra, 2005), which has been used for two decades to describe the relationship between teaching and technology, and which has recently been updated to try and account for the impact of AI in education.

Updating the TPACK model

Building on the works of several educators, scholars and researchers, the Technological Pedagogical Content or TPACK Framework (Koehler & Mishra, 2005; Schmidt et al., 2009; Thompson, 2007) sought to identify the types of knowledge needed by teachers to create engaging and meaningful learning environments that fully utilise the affordances of educational technology. This approach requires a "dynamic amalgam of all three...[existing in a state of] 'creative tension' with each other where changes in in one affect the other two" (Mishra et al., 2023, p. 1). Coinciding with very strong growth in the use of technology in education over the past two decades, the TPACK framework has been utilised in multiple settings globally to understand the interplay of technology and pedagogical content knowledge (Mishra et al., 2023; Ning et al., 2024). Advanced generative AI has the potential to profoundly change what we know about that relationship, and suggests the need to revisit the TPACK framework to ensure it captures the emerging relationship between education, educators, and this transformative technology.

Ning et al. (2024 p.4) consider that "in this context, the pressing issue is whether the existing TPACK model remains applicable to the evolving demands of teaching and the professional development requirements of educators." In the context of increasingly deep integration of GenAI in education, the current TPACK framework does have some limitations, particularly that it did not (understandably) anticipate a technology that is effectively acting as a collaborator in both teaching and learning. Several researchers including Mishra et al. (2023), Lorenz and Romeike (2023), Ning (2024), and Celik (2023) have responded by adapting and modifying the framework to take into account the requisite knowledge and competencies required to effectively incorporate AI into pedagogical practices, thus creating a number of AI-TPACK frameworks that offer insight to how the relationship between technology, pedagogy, and content is being altered (Karataş & Ataç, 2024).

Mishra et al. (2023) note that while the original TPACK model is technology-agnostic, GenAI exhibits properties never before seen in a technology – generativity and sociality, which makes it difficult for humans not to anthropomorphize these systems, and is leading to many examples where AI output and interactions are judged by humans to be more human than the average human (e.g. Ovsyannikova et al., 2025)! Arguing that GenAI is a fundamentally relational technology, they added what they term 'XK' to TPACK – Contextual Knowledge, which recognises that these systems can co-create with humans, shaping and being shaped by that relationship.

Celik (2023) identifies what he calls Intelligent-TPACK as a teacher's core knowledge to select and use the most suitable AI tool for their teaching strategy within their disciplinary domain. He also adds AI ethics as a separate and necessary domain.

Ning et al. (2024) take a slightly different approach, suggesting a new domain of AI-TPACK, which they describe as the cognitive aspects of AI education. Karatas and Atac (2024) developed a scale to measure AI-TPACK, with their contribution adding an AI dimension to *each* of the TPACK domains. What is clear from all these authors is an understanding that how we work at the intersection of technology, pedagogy and content knowledge is fundamentally different with GenAI, calling into question many of the established pedagogical practices that educators have used for centuries in higher education.

The scale of the shift needed in pedagogy suggests that it cannot be achieved by dedicated individuals working alone on adapting their own individual pedagogies to the niche courses they teach. Making those changes in isolation and without close consideration for curriculum level outcomes is likely to have unintended consequences for other parts of the curriculum. The only sensible way forward is to collaboratively redesign the curriculum to embed and scaffold disciplinary use of GenAI in meaningful ways, with appropriate guardrails at each level of learning throughout the programme so that AI fluency in the context of discipline can be developed, while protecting the core traits of the discipline.

Generativism: A new pedagogical approach for the AI world

While many academics and institutions oppose the rise of GenAI, others recognise the evolving landscape and explore ways to integrate this new reality into teaching, learning and curriculum design. Mairéad Pratschke's (2023, 2024) concept of "Generativism", which draws on and extends two well-known digital learning frameworks (the Community of Inquiry and Conversational Frameworks) is a pedagogical framework that reimagines the role of GenAI in education, positioning it as an active collaborator in the learning process, rather than a mere tool for content delivery. Therefore, "students need to be able to work with GAI, not just as a tool for workplace efficiency but as a vehicle for the exploration and generation of knowledge in their field of study." (Pratschke, 2024, p. 58).

Rooted in constructivist and socio-cultural learning theories, Generativism emphasises co-construction of knowledge through dynamic interactions between students, educators, and AI systems. In this approach, AI can serve multiple roles, including that of an expert, mentor, or peer, facilitating personalised, adaptive learning experiences tailored to individual needs. Cox et al. (2024) offer a case study from the Global South that applies the elements of Pratschke's Generativism. In their case, students, instructors, and AI worked together to co-create open educational resources (OERs) to support medical education. They note that this approach has the potential to support scaling up of OER development in the Global South, while also developing critical AI literacy in learners.

A key aspect of Generativism is its focus on critical engagement with AI-generated content, encouraging learners to question, refine, and integrate AI outputs, rather than passively accepting them. This aligns with the broader shift in education towards fostering higher-order thinking skills, creativity, and digital literacy. By embedding AI into pedagogical design, Generativism promotes an iterative learning process in which students and teachers collaborate with AI to generate, evaluate, and refine knowledge.

Pratschke's framework also highlights the ethical and epistemological challenges posed by AI in education. It calls for the development of new digital competencies that enable both educators and students to critically assess the reliability, biases, and limitations of AI-generated outputs. This requires an awareness of how AI systems operate, including their data sources and underlying algorithms, to ensure responsible and informed use.

Ultimately, Generativism represents a shift from a knowledge-transfer model of education towards a participatory, inquiry-driven approach that leverages AI as a creative and intellectual partner (Pratschke, 2024). This has significant implications for curriculum design, assessment methods, and teacher training, as it necessitates a rethinking of traditional pedagogical practices to fully harness the potential of AI in learning and knowledge creation (Pratschke, 2023). This shift in pedagogical practices is further explored by Leon Furze and his collaborators (Furze, 2024b; Perkins et al., 2024), who provide practical recommendations for integrating Generative AI (GenAI) into education, focusing on its responsible and effective use in teaching and assessment.

The AI Assessment Scale (AIAS) and Design Refine Create (DRC) Framework

Furze et al. (2024) provide practical recommendations for integrating Generative AI into education, focusing on its responsible and effective use in teaching and assessment. They emphasise the need for educators to develop foundational AI literacy, advocating for professional development in AI concepts, ethics, and applications before incorporating AI into their teaching practice. Their *Practical AI Strategies* offer structured guidance, including best practices for prompting AI, evaluating AI-generated content, and designing AI-assisted learning activities that enhance student engagement. Furze et al. (2024) encourage educators to use AI as a tool to support, rather than replace, critical thinking and creativity.

A key aspect of Furze and Furze et al.'s (2024a; 2024) recommendations are the development of rigorous and authentic assessment strategies that acknowledge AI's role in student learning. They introduced the *AI Assessment Scale* (AIAS), a tool that helps educators determine the extent to which AI contributes to student work and adjust assessment methods accordingly. The AIAS framework consists of five levels, ranging from *Level 1: No AI*, where all work must be completed without AI assistance, to *Level 5: Full AI*, where AI is fully integrated into the learning and assessment process, with students required to demonstrate critical engagement with AI outputs. Intermediate levels—*Level 2: AI Detection*, *Level 3: AI-Supported*, and *Level 4: AI-Assisted* — allow for varying degrees of AI use, with increasing expectations for students to acknowledge, critique, and refine AI-generated content.

Rather than prohibiting AI, Furze et al. (2024) suggest designing assignments that integrate AI in ways that require students to engage critically, demonstrate originality, and articulate their reasoning process. They also advise educators to implement transparency measures, such as AI-use disclosure statements, and to engage students in discussions about AI ethics, misinformation, and bias.

While these strategies can be used at the individual level, they can also be applied at a programme level to inform the assessments that need to be secured against AI use, and other assessment tools that either have limited or prescribed AI uses. The model has recently been updated to recognise a shift from task-focused to more transformative uses of AI, including as a collaborator, and for exploration of the edges of knowledge (Furze, 2024b).

Additionally, Furze's (2024a) '*Design Refine Create*' framework offers a step-by-step approach for integrating AI into curriculum design, ensuring that AI is utilised meaningfully within structured learning objectives, rather than as an ad-hoc supplement. This approach encourages educators to refine their teaching methods iteratively, allowing for continuous adaptation and improvement in line with the evolving capabilities of AI tools.

Promising curriculum level responses to gen AI

Several early approaches to addressing GenAI within a curriculum have begun to emerge. While they represent emerging approaches to transforming disciplinary practice at the curriculum level, most of the approaches so far have had a strong focus on addressing the challenge of assessment validity and security in the AI era, with less focus on high level educational strategies that need to be employed *across* a curriculum to facilitate the development of both disciplinary and GenAI literacies.

There are also few attempts so far to describe in practical terms what an AI-enabled curriculum looks like at the discipline level.

Institutional responses include the Artificial Intelligence Assessment Scale, University of Sydney's 2-lane assessment approach, a multi-lane student functional approach from the University of New South Wales (UNSW), and the Culture, Rules, Access, Familiarity, Trust (CRAFT) model which developed from the University of Sydney's approach (Liu & Bates, 2025). The Australian Government's Tertiary Education Quality and Standards Agency (TEQSA) has collected examples of institutional responses to AI from every university in the country and published a summary of them, including an interesting assessment uplift model from Griffith University that outlines practical AI integration to the curriculum across a degree programme (Tertiary Education Quality and Standards Agency (TEQSA), 2024), essentially scaffolding access to AI over the course of the degree, and recognising that at the programme level, there needs to be a balance of assessment *for* learning, and assessment *of* learning. This scaffolded approach is reminiscent of other models, such as the Spiral Curriculum Model, that contemplates development of knowledge from novice to expert with multiple points of introduction and reinforcement of concepts, as well as constraints along the way.

The Spiral Curriculum Model

One long-standing model that shows promise for developing AI-enabled curricula is the Spiral Curriculum Model, which has been used in medical, technical and music education (Hanke, 2022; e.g. Harden, 1999; Ireland & Mouthaan, 2020; Maltagliati et al., 2023). The model, originally developed by Jerome Bruner in 1960 for the physical sciences, considers a curriculum as a series of concepts that become increasingly more complex as the spiral loops upwards. As each turn of the spiral is completed, learning is reinforced with additional objectives and more challenging concepts, building on the foundational knowledge of the discipline. In medical education, students learn foundational concepts each year of their programme, and are expected to be able to synthesise prior learning as the curriculum broadens out, until they are required to apply it in clinical practice (Harden, 1999).

In the context of an AI-embedded curriculum, we can envisage a spiral curriculum that includes not only the domain knowledge spiralling upwards, but a connected, contextualised set of AI literacies that sit around the spiral. For example, in a student's first year, the breadth of the spiral would be narrow as they learn the foundational concepts of their chosen domain and possible applications of those concepts. At this level, AI use is likely to be minimal, restricted to developing foundational knowledge *about* AI and using general AI tools in prescribed and supported ways. As the curriculum spirals upward, the domain knowledge broadens and students are also able to take on more complex, AI enabled tasks as they become competent to detect errors and confabulations for example. The tools they have access to also become more specialised to their disciplines as students move towards practice where they will use a range of AI assistants in their work.

While this approach seems like it may be successful and could be applied by many disciplines, the spiral curriculum theory has been criticized by some as being poorly suited to disciplines where learning may be non-linear, like fine arts, or indeed for a world where complexity and uncertainty are the norm. Curricular approaches that are suited to rapidly changing and uncertain fields are relatively rare in higher education, so looking to models in other fields, such as skill acquisition coaching, that are designed to develop competencies to deal with dynamic environments may offer additional insights and opportunities for higher education to adapt to GenAI.

The Constraints-Led Approach (CLA): A promising approach adapted from coaching and ecological-dynamics theory

Thinking outside the traditional theories and boundaries of curriculum development, there are emerging models that draw from contemporary coaching theory and ecological theory, which may be more suited to the complex and rapidly changing AI capabilities becoming embedded in disciplinary knowledge. The Constraints Led Approach (CLA) (Newell, 1986) has been used in coaching, as well as some areas of education, and considers learning happening in a complex environment with interactions between the task, the learner, and the environment (Figure 1) driving outcomes (Renshaw & Chow, 2019). The CLA has been used by some disciplines, particularly those focusing on skill acquisition, including nursing (Renden & Dikken, 2023; William, 2022) and medicine (Taraporewalla et al., 2024). CLA has also been explored in developing skills for law students in preparation for law clinics (Sluijs et al., 2023). In the CLA, skill acquisition is viewed not as an entity, but rather as "the emergence of an adaptive, functional relationship between an organism and its environment" (Renshaw & Chow, 2019, p. 105), with learning a process of continuous adaptation to changing environmental conditions.

Figure 1. Generalised representation of the Constraints Led Approach (CLA) applied to teaching (adapted from Renshaw et al. (2010))

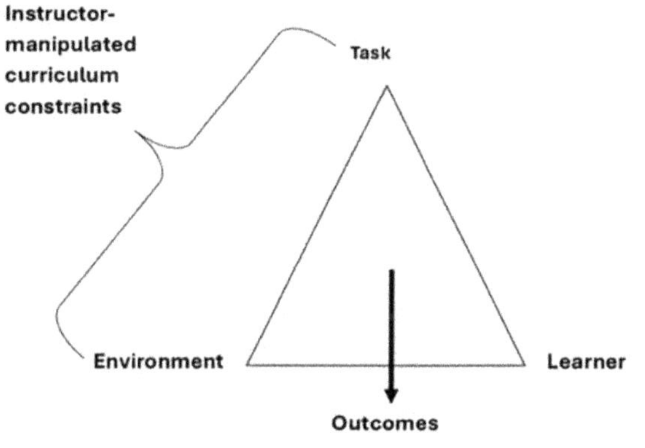

The 'person-environment relationship', the focus of ecological psychologist James Gibson's theoretical insights (1979/1986) is what Renshaw et al. (2019) describes as 'the appropriate scale of analysis' when employing a CLA (p.18). The performance environment in which coaches and athletes are located has many commonalities with the current AI environment that students, educators, and workers find themselves inhabiting. Phrases that describe the evolving AI environment include: 'uncertain, unpredictable and essentially unknowable' (Selwyn, 2022, p. 620), 'evolving' (Baker Stein & Jones-Schenk, 2024; Le Lagadec et al., 2024) where regulatory, professional, legal and ethical factors also have to be considered. AI-enabled environments are also considered complex (Hassija et al., 2024), dynamic (Hamilton, 2024) and require agility (Palaniappan et al., 2024). There are therefore many similarities between the sport performance and AI-enabled learning environments, which suggests that adopting a CLA for the development of curriculums in AI era is a reasonable approach.

In CLA, the environment provides affordances – physical, technological, social and so on – which the learner interacts with in a dynamic interplay of information and energy. In this thinking, the learning environment provides opportunities for action and signals that indicate important information to pay attention to. Araújo, Brito and Carrilho (2023) describe it as follows: 'Perceiving an affordance is to perceive how one can act in a particular set of environmental conditions' (p. 25). Learning to identify those signals and adapt to what they are telling one comes about from exposure to the environment and coaching assistance. Orth, van der Kamp & Button, (2019, p. 154) argue that the 'coach can be considered as a component of the learners' environment where the learner and coach constitute a learning system'.

In the case of learning how to use AI in a domain, learners need to experience examples of the technology in action, with educators playing a coaching role in helping them navigate the accuracy of outputs, exploring nuanced connections between pieces of domain knowledge, including what might be missed or misrepresented. At the same time, the ecosystem in which the AI and domain knowledge interacts is also influenced by ethics, concerns for equity, and environmental sustainability considerations that go beyond the domain knowledge, but which responsible citizens in an AI-enabled world would need to be aware of and factor into their decisions.

Consider a young student walking on a treadmill. Initially, the student is focused on learning how to walk on a moving platform while holding onto the railing and concentrating on not falling off the back of the treadmill – aligning their walking speed with the speed of the treadmill. The teacher can manipulate the constraint the student experiences by increasing the speed of the treadmill. The student will be able to compensate with faster steps to a point, but eventually the speed necessitates that the student start running as the higher speed causes their walking pattern to become unstable and unsuitable for the conditions. To achieve stability again, a new more functional pattern has to emerge (Renshaw & Chow, 2019). Figuring out the fixed constraints (such as learning outcomes, accreditation rules, institutional policies, and available technology), as opposed to the variable constraints within a programme may offer a helpful way for educators to conceptualise the development of AI and domain competencies over time.

Renshaw et al (2019) reinforces the need for practice environments that underpin CLA to strongly reflect the performance environment, or as Seifert et al. (2018) describes it, the 'representative of the richness and the ecological context of the competitive performance environment' (p. 7). Students moving through a degree must be exposed to realistic/authentic and contextually valid practice environments that fully and accurately capture AI capabilities in the workplace. Ethical, regulatory, and legal realities for example, how AI will be part of the decision-making process in practice, must form part of the constraints employed in teaching and assessment.

CLA conceptualises and acknowledges that learners occupy environments that are increasingly complex adaptive systems, where skill development emerges from the dynamic interaction between task, environmental, and learner constraints (Woods et al. 2022). Skill development (in this case, both AI competency and domain knowledge) occurs as the coach manipulates constraints leading to learning (Orth et al., 2019).

Recent CLA theorising by Wood et al (2023) and the focus on coaches' behaviours as emerging under constraints suggests that the coaching framework has great potential within an AI pedagogical context, where the coach/educator imposes constraints that support safe and responsible use, while protecting space for the development of disciplinary knowledge and competencies. Orth et al. (2019) do recognise that this view of the coach as gatekeeper to variability in constraints and behaviour could be problematic in educational contexts. It has the potential to reinforce existing power imbalances in the classroom, and may imply a level of control by the coach that is neither desirable, nor possible in the context of AI. The inclusion of the 'Explore, Discover, Exploit' steps underpinned by CLA (Wood et al., 2023) offers a useful heuristic to guide educators on how AI can be engaged within a supportive and enriching teaching and learning context.

CLA also has potential to be applied to assessment methodologies and in particular to the AIAS framework (Furze et al 2024) discussed earlier; the scale for example, has implicit and explicit constraints embedded throughout the continuum from 'No AI' (level 1) to 'Full AI' (level 5). Such constraints create affordances that influence students' decision-making capacity to act within certain assessment conditions related to their disciplinary area.

Applying CLA as a curriculum model

What we have presented thus far with respect to the CLA is a theoretical adaptation of a model, but our goal is to offer insights to how CLA may be applied in practice as a curriculum model. The following three examples demonstrate how the CLA concepts of learner, environmental, and task constraints can be understood and addressed practically to support the use of GenAI within a curriculum. We offer a series of suggested strategies and considerations for how this might be conceptualised in various disciplines.

(1) Learner Constraints

Individual differences among learners necessitate flexible approaches to GenAI skill development. With the focus on learner constraint, coaches must monitor individual skill development and adjust constraints as the learner progresses.

Practical Examples: In the same way that swimming coaches modify training based on individual capabilities, educators can offer differentiated GenAI learning activities where students with limited AI literacy might start with basic prompt engineering tasks, while advanced users engage in more complex evaluations of output quality.

Adaptive Strategies:

- Recognition of diverse technological literacy levels
- Customisation of learning pathways
- Facilitation of peer learning opportunities
- Implementation of differentiated instruction methods

(2) Environmental Constraints

Environmental constraints encompass the broader context in which GenAI learning occurs, including institutional policies, ethical frameworks, and real-world applications.

Practical Examples: Just as soccer players adapt their techniques to different playing conditions and opposition formations, students learn to navigate various GenAI platforms and contexts such as ChatGPT, Claude, Perplexity etc. and explore how different tools interpret the same prompt or handle context shifts.

Key Considerations:

- Integration of institutional policies on academic integrity and responsible AI use
- Implementation within discipline-specific contexts
- Adaptation to varying technological infrastructures
- Consideration of ethical and professional standards

(3) Task Constraints

Task constraints shape how learners engage with GenAI tools through structured activities and challenges. These constraints guide skill development through carefully designed learning experiences.

Practical Examples: Similar to how young basketball players develop skills by practising with modified equipment or conditions, GenAI learners can progress from basic tool exploration to sophisticated content evaluation through incrementally more challenging tasks. These progressively complex activities could include such tasks as summarising texts of varying lengths, co-creating creative writing outputs, or solving complex problems using multiple AI models.

Possible Implementation Strategies:

- Design progressive learning activities requiring GenAI tool engagement for specific purposes (e.g. research summaries, ideation, writing enhancement)
- Create scaffolded tasks with increasing complexity levels
- Develop structured evaluation exercises for AI-generated content

Acknowledging the need for applying varying constraints at different points in the curriculum is clearly an important step in the adoption of the CLA, so what might programme level strategies look like if an institution were to use CLA to help re/design its curriculum? We offer the following three characteristics as a guide to a curriculum informed by CLA.

- **Progressive Complexity:** Introduce GenAI tools progressively across courses, moving from foundational literacy to advanced critical engagement.
- **Collaboration with Faculty:** Train educators on CLA principles and how to design constraints-driven activities for their courses.
- **Feedback Loops:** Implement continuous feedback mechanisms where students receive formative feedback on their GenAI use and ethical considerations.

Examples: CLA application to specific disciplinary curricula

As noted earlier, CLA has been applied to some disciplines including law (Sluijs et al., 2023), nursing (Renden & Dikken, 2023; William, 2022), and medicine (Taraporewalla et al., 2024), with a particular focus on skill development, rather than curriculum design, and we are not aware of any institutions that have attempted to use this approach yet as the basis for designing an AI-responsive curriculum. Nevertheless, we argue that the approach shows great potential as a strategy for dealing with the uncertainty that AI introduces to curriculum needs.

In the following section, we offer concrete, hypothetical examples of how a CLA may be applied to curriculum design at the programme level, from our own disciplinary fields. This is a simplified format that considers students at a novice, intermediate, and advanced level, and presents examples of CLA applied to different levels throughout a programme. Table 1 provides an example of developing a specific skill at the level of a learning activity. Table 2 looks at the application of a CLA to specific learning outcomes at the programme level across an undergraduate programme. And Table 3 provides insight to ways in which AI can be incorporated at various levels throughout a programme. These three examples come from different disciplines – nursing, environmental studies, and social services – to demonstrate the potential wide applicability of the CLA to any field of study, and from micro to macro curriculum approaches.

For each example, we show how the constraints and environmental conditions can be manipulated by educators, taking into account the development stage and skills of the learners themselves, to achieve scaffolded progress towards competence in meeting learning outcomes. While in its original use the CLA does not typically consider the learners as a constraint, in the context of a learner's development over the course of a programme there are inherently differences in the abilities and skill level of learners that must be considered in the development of a CLA. We also recognise that institutions and their learners will vary considerably in access and technical capacity for AI, so the examples provided are flexible and AI technology agnostic.

Table 1 presents a CLA in teaching Clinical Decision Support Systems (CDSS) underpinned by AI in a Bachelor in Nursing Studies programme. In this example, CLA with AI is employed as a pedagogical tool to promote the knowledge and skills of students at three different levels in relation to clinical decision-making. As part of teaching and learning student workshops, the three groups of students receive a CDSS scaffolded clinical scenario, commensurate to their year of study, with a time completion constraint. In addition, there are several CLA environmental constraints many of which are linked to AI related considerations. (1) Access to resources to support decision making; (2) the scale of AI available to students; (3) Professional ethical and legal AI considerations; (4) Collaboration with other team members; (5) AI coaching input available to the student. The constraints will influence the student to make decisions based on the environmental conditions available to them while receiving guided AI-related coaching. Students are challenged to critically analyse information from many sources, including AI, and arrive at a decision based on the best available evidence. The constraints will nudge the learner in a specified direction offering graduated and controlled opportunities to navigate AI and disciplinary knowledge simultaneously.

Table 1. Example of integrating AI using CLA and Clinical Decision Support System within Nursing studies programme.

Learner Level **CDSS scenario** **CDSS Time Constraint**	**Learner Level - Novice** **Low e.g. patient presenting with a minor alteration in their vital signs.** **15 minutes**	**Learner Level - Intermediate** **Medium e.g. patient presenting with a minor alternation in vital signs and neurological status.** **10 minutes**	**Learner Level - Advanced** **High e.g. patient presenting with a significant alternation in vital signs (fever, tachycardia and tachypnea and alteration in neurological status, oliguria/anuria and cyanosis)** **5 minutes**
Access to resources to support decision-making *(Environment Constraint)*	Nursing Care book on clinical patient care.	Nursing Care book on clinical patient care, hospital policies e.g. Early warning scoring (e.g. Irish National Early Warning Score (INEWS)	Multiple Online Nursing support books on clinical patient care and hospital policies. e.g. Early warning scoring (e.g. Irish National Early Warning Score (INEWS)
Access to AI *(Environment Constraint)*	Access to a single non subscription public AI package	Access to a single Premium (paid) AI tool	Access to multiple Premium (paid) AI tools
Professional, Ethical, Legal AI Considerations *(Environment Constraint)*	Low level e.g. Consideration to ensure no data sharing with any AI technology	Medium Level e.g. All data linked to decision-making to be fully transparent.	High Level All legal and ethical/environmental considerations associated with AI input addressed. e.g. principle of informed consent, algorithmic bias, data privacy (Mohammed et al., 2025).
Collaboration with others on the decision *(Environment Constraint)*	None	One other student from nursing discipline.	Five other students from nursing discipline. One other professional discipline
Coaching Input *(Environment Constraint)*	High. Learner has full coaching support.	Medium. Learner has moderate coaching support.	Low. Learner has limited coaching support.

Table 2 shows an example of a curricular design intended to achieve programme-level learning outcomes in a Bachelor of Environmental Studies programme. The example addresses two learning outcomes; one focused on information literacy in the discipline, and the other on communication approaches. Both these skill sets are highly susceptible to use of AI as a shortcut to learning, so the goal is to develop an understanding of disciplinary knowledge and knowledge sources, and the risks and benefits of different AI tools within the context of the discipline. Use is scaffolded from limited use of generalist AI tools to more extensive use of specialist AI technologies appropriate to the field. Named AI tools are a suggestion only, and focus is on tools that have limited free access.

Table 2. Example of integration of AI using CLA targeting selected learning outcomes across the curriculum for an environmental studies programme

Programme level Learning outcome:	*LO1: Gather, summarize, synthesize and criticize the state of the socio-environmental literature* *LO2: Strategically communicate complex messages to a range of audiences using diverse written, oral and mixed media formats.*		
Learner Constraints			
Knowledge, skill level, competency	**Novice:** Limited disciplinary knowledge and AI competency. Constraints designed to encourage student primary focus on developing non-AI literacies in the discipline.	**Intermediate:** Growing disciplinary knowledge, research and communication skills; improved audience analysis. Constraints designed to encourage student focus on building a critical lens towards AI uses assisting the developing disciplinary skills and knowledge.	**Advanced:** Strong disciplinary foundation; independent research capability; sophisticated communication skills; strategic mindset. Constraints designed to encourage applied and evaluative lens towards AI use in complex co-creation in the disciplinary context.
Environmental Constraints			
LO1. Responsible use of digital technologies for searching disciplinary literature	Structured learning environment; introduction to library catalogue and relevant databases; effectively use library search, librarian support, and general search tools e.g. Google, Google Scholar, Google with AI summaries, plus general AI model e.g. ChatGPT for comparison	Semi-structured environment; moderate guidance; use general library search plus disciplinary literature search tools, databases; use generalist AI assisted research tools (e.g. Perplexity, DeepResearch, AI reasoning models) as an additional check; AI suggests possible additional literature, related topics	Complex research questions; use advanced disciplinary knowledge tools, databases, repositories, open science sources; critically use specialised AI academic research tools e.g. Elicit, Keenious, Consensus, AI Scientist; AI recommends novel connections within and across disciplines
LO2. Communicating complex concepts to diverse audiences	Single audience; simplified messages; templates provided; creating stories, content in multiple short formats e.g. blog posts, physical posters, lab reports with minimal AI assistance	More autonomy; fewer templates; communicating more complex concepts in multiple ways with basic AI assistance e.g. digital posters, complex lab reports, digital images, short videos; simulated work environment	Creating early professional level multimedia explanations of complex environmental concepts and data for multiple audiences in collaboration with AI tools; AI helps adapt message to different audiences from student drafts; practice skills within Work Integrated Learning (WIL) environment
Task Constraints			

continued on following page

Table 2. Continued

Programme level Learning outcome:	*LO1: Gather, summarize, synthesize and criticize the state of the socio-environmental literature* *LO2: Strategically communicate complex messages to a range of audiences using diverse written, oral and mixed media formats.*		
LO1. Search strategy	Simple, focused searches with clear outcomes; focus on efficient use of library catalogue; use general AI tool for the same topic (e.g. ChatGPT) and compare/ critique outcomes; minimise use of AI for research; students must manually verify all AI output	Use library databases in tandem with generalist AI research tools; critically reflect on differences in outcomes – what sources are missed in each? What biases are apparent? Experiment with building own research bot; articulate and consider environmental cost of different search strategies and models	Students fluidly use all available digital research assistants and identify when to deploy each for the best outcomes; design sophisticated prompts for analyzing complex environmental literature; use AI assistants to identify novel connections between disciplinary domains and across disciplines; choose and articulate most sustainable search strategy for the task
LO2. Content creation strategy	Students use mostly analogue and traditional digital content creation tools; limit AI use to in-built suggestions and reflect on the suggestions made; AI helps with grammar/ spelling/ accessibility after students complete drafts; practice identifying AI-generated vs. human content for quality assessment	Students use combination of traditional digital content tools and generalist AI tools to explain complex concepts e.g. summarise, suggest outlines, suggest alternative communication formats; use AI to generate visualizations of environmental data they've analyzed; collaborative AI-human content creation with clear delineation of contributions of each	Fluidly use traditional and AI technologies to create content in multiple formats, using AI as a collaborator, critical reviewer, simulated audience member; students direct AI to help create integrated media campaigns (written, visual, social) for environmental advocacy; clear delineation of AI and human contributions

Table 3 outlines a series of examples demonstrating how the CLA can be integrated across three stages of a social care degree programme. These examples illustrate how students can progressively develop their ability to use GenAI, while simultaneously strengthening their professional capacity, ethical awareness, and critical thinking skills.

As social care professionals work with a diverse range of client groups, the examples provided are indicative rather than prescriptive. They highlight potential applications of AI within different practice areas, but these approaches can be adapted and applied to various social care settings as appropriate. The increasing mastery of AI tools must be accompanied by a parallel development of professional competencies, ensuring that students not only harness AI effectively, but also apply it ethically and responsibly in real-world practice.

While mastery of GenAI is a valuable additional skill for contemporary practice, it is essential to recognise that, as in nursing and other care professions, the core focus of social care remains the wellbeing and support of clients/patients. AI can enhance practice, but it does not replace the fundamental human-centred skills required in the profession—such as empathy, communication, ethical decision-making, and safeguarding.

Table 3. Example of integrating AI using CLA in practice across a Social Care Programme

Level	CLA Elements			Examples of GenAI Use in Social Care
	Task Constraints	**Environmental Constraints**	**Learner Constraints**	
Novice (AI as an assistant): Limited disciplinary knowledge and AI competency	Simple documentation and summarisation. Ethical considerations and responsible AI use.	Limited access to advanced AI tools in early studies. Institutional and/ or registration body policies on AI use may restrict applications.	Limited AI literacy and critical evaluation skills. Need for structured tasks with clear guidance.	1. **Summarising** Case Studies for Foster Care Support – AI summarises case reports of children entering the foster system; students evaluate key concerns such as trauma indicators. 2. **Drafting** Professional Emails & Reports for Adult Social Work – AI structures reports on elderly clients' needs for care home placements; students refine for clarity and sensitivity. 3. **Exploring** Ethical Dilemmas in Disability Support – AI generates scenarios about balancing independence and safeguarding for adults with learning disabilities; students discuss ethical decision-making.

continued on following page

Table 3. Continued

Level	CLA Elements			Examples of GenAI Use in Social Care
	Task Constraints	Environmental Constraints	Learner Constraints	
Intermediate (AI as a co-creator): Growing disciplinary knowledge, research and communication skills; improved audience analysis	More complex case assessments and intervention planning. AI provides structured insights, but students apply human judgement.	Real-world constraints such as confidentiality compliance limit AI's use in handling sensitive data.	Growing ability to critically assess AI outputs. Developing professional judgement in ethical and practical decision-making.	**1. Creating** Personalised Care Plans for Dementia Patients – AI suggests intervention strategies for clients with early-stage dementia; students compare with best practices and adapt for individual needs. **2. Simulating** Service User Interactions for Youth Homelessness Support – AI plays the role of a homeless youth expressing concerns about accessing services; students practise engagement and active listening. **3. Analysing** Policies & Legislation on Domestic Abuse Support – AI summarises legal frameworks related to domestic violence interventions; students assess practical implications for supporting survivors.

continued on following page

Table 3. Continued

Level	CLA Elements			Examples of GenAI Use in Social Care
	Task Constraints	**Environmental Constraints**	**Learner Constraints**	
Advanced (AI as an independent agent): Strong disciplinary foundation; independent research capability; sophisticated communication skills; strategic mindset	AI as a tool for creative and critical thinking. Students apply AI dynamically in complex real-world problems.	Social care settings may not widely adopt AI tools yet, creating implementation barriers. Ethical concerns about bias and accountability when using AI in decision-making.	High level of AI literacy and ability to critically adapt AI-generated insights. Confidence in integrating AI responsibly into professional practice.	1. **Predictive** Analysis for Mental Health Crisis Prevention – AI analyses anonymised data from mental health services to predict risk factors for self-harm; students critique ethical implications and practical applications. 2. **Training** AI for Culturally Competent Support for Refugees – Students customise AI-generated responses to ensure cultural and linguistic sensitivity in refugee social services. 3. **Developing** AI-Assisted Public Awareness Campaigns on Substance Abuse – AI generates outreach materials for drug harm reduction programmes; students refine messages to align with public health guidelines and community needs.

These three practical examples demonstrate the potential application of the CLA to diverse disciplinary and teaching settings. They offer insight to how different educators may use the CLA framework to conceptualise curriculum design in their field at various levels, from individual activities to a whole curriculum approach. The CLA is likely unfamiliar to most educators in higher education and may take some time and practice to be effectively implemented. Combining the strengths of the CLA with a more familiar and traditional pedagogical model such as the Spiral Curriculum may make this curriculum design strategy more accessible to a wider audience of educators.

Coaching students to climb the AI Spiral

Employing CLA and aligning it alongside a spiral curriculum model potentially offers a coherent architecture to successfully embed AI pedagogy across a curriculum (see Figure 2). While the Spiral Curriculum promotes a structured and cumulative learning experience, the Constraints-Led Approach emphasizes adaptability and responsiveness to environmental factors. This approach recognises the need to place reasonable constraints on the ways that GenAI is used in a programme of learning (Curtis, 2025), with those constraints being extensive in the early part of the programme, and decreasing considerably towards the end as domain knowledge grows and the need to use more specialised tools in preparation for the future world of work is apparent.

Figure 2. Conceptualisation of a Constraints-Led Approach to AI in the context of a spiral curriculum

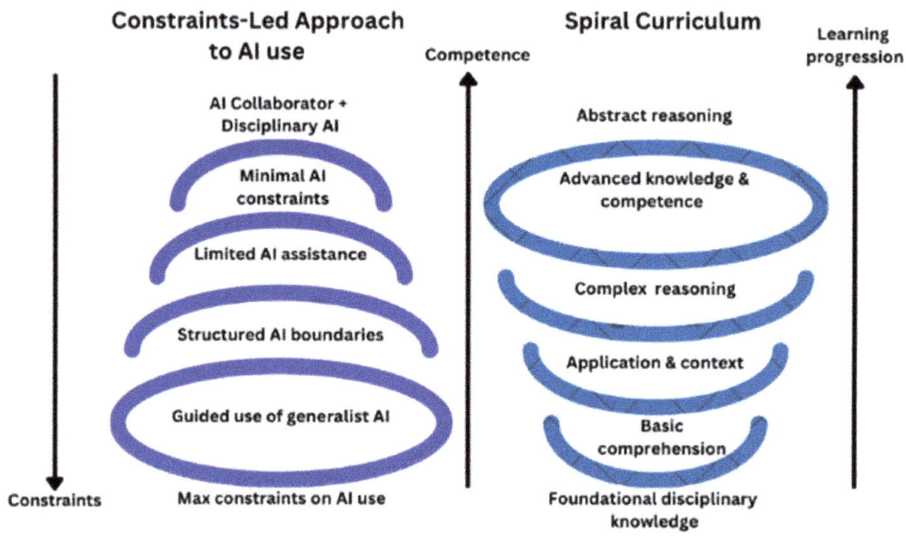

Table 4 summarises the intersection of CLA and the Spiral Curriculum models in more detail, paving the way towards a practical application of the concepts. This combined strategy illustrates how the Constraints-Led Approach and Spiral Curriculum models intersect and can be operationalized in curriculum design. This integrated approach allows curricula to leverage the systematic progression of the spiral curriculum approach, building foundational and increasingly complex and specialized skills and knowledge, while maintaining the adaptive, exploratory nature of CLA. This creates an environment where AI literacy can develop organically alongside domain expertise through learning experiences that expose students to the embedded potential for AI within their developing domain knowledge. This table can be used as a practical guide for educators to design curricula that seamlessly integrates AI literacy with specialized domain knowledge

Table 4. Intersection of the Constraints-Led Approach and Spiral Curriculum models illustrating how they can be operationalized in curriculum design

Dimension	Spiral Curriculum	Constraints-Led Approach	Integrated Application of CLA and Spiral Models to Curriculum for Developing AI and Domain Competencies
Core Philosophy	Knowledge builds progressively through revisiting concepts as complexity and knowledge depth / breadth increases	Learning emerges through manipulation of constraints that shape behavior and skill / knowledge acquisition	Students encounter AI concepts repeatedly within domain-specific contexts, with constraints evolving to promote deeper understanding and skill/knowledge development. Emphasis is on safe and responsible usage
Learning Progression	Linear progression towards mastery with expanding depth and breadth	Non-linear exploration within constraint boundaries	Cyclical engagement where AI tools and domain problems co-evolve at graduated levels of complexity; Responsive cycles based on student readiness and technological evolution
Knowledge Structure	Hierarchical scaffolding from simple to complex; Built through repeated exposure and application in new contexts	Dynamic systems thinking with interacting variables; Emerges from constraint variation and the student level	AI literacy develops as interconnected capability rather than isolated skill set, and is applied to domain specific problems/ contexts
Curriculum Design Process	Map key concepts → Sequence by complexity → Plan revisitation and evaluation cycles	Identify task/ environmental constraints → Design constraint manipulations and subsequent affordances → Create exploration opportunities	Map domain-AI intersections → Design constraints → Sequence for emergent complexity
Assessment Approach	Evaluate progress towards mastery periodically at each spiral level	Assess adaptation and problem-solving within constraints; may be continuous; of/for learning	Evaluate ability to leverage AI appropriately within evolving domain challenges

continued on following page

Table 4. Continued

Dimension	Spiral Curriculum	Constraints-Led Approach	Integrated Application of CLA and Spiral Models to Curriculum for Developing AI and Domain Competencies
Instructor Role	Guide through predetermined sequences and assessment	Facilitate learning by adjusting constraints and having a coaching role effect in facilitating their learning using exploration and adaptation	Orchestrate task and environmental constraints that organically integrate AI with domain learning, facilitating development of foundational and advanced domain knowledge/ competence over time
Student Agency	Structured progression with some choice	High autonomy within the constraint boundaries provided	Self-directed exploration of AI applications within predefined domain and constraint parameters
Error/Failure Treatment	Remediation and re-evaluation (another circuit of the spiral)	Natural part of exploration and adaptation where learning is achieved both from the process and assessment output that emerges.	Productive failure informs domain understanding; incorrect application of AI contributes to higher order learning.
Basic Practical Implementation	Year 1: Basic concepts → Year 2: Applications → Year 3: Synthesis	Introductory constraints (high) → Progressive relaxation → Open-ended challenges	Early courses: AI tools within tight domain problems → Later courses: Student-designed AI solutions for complex domain challenges

The skills of the educator/coach are key in the contexts outlined here. Being adaptable and flexible are crucial traits of coaching when utilising CLA; these become all the more relevant in an AI coaching context and having 'the capacity to change and flow with the dynamics of task and environmental constraints, which vary on different occasions' (Wood et al., 2023, p. 613). The human component of coaching relationships is also crucial to achieving these goals. Learning is hard, and there are many tempting reasons to cut corners, but ultimately, those shortcuts are likely to impair learning in the long term.

Approaching teaching with a coaching mentality means seeking to find ways to move individual learners from one achievement and skill level to the next, striving to help them become the best version of themselves. Coaches will encourage students to do the heavy work of learning the foundational concepts of their discipline, despite having wide access to the performance enhancing drug of generative AI. Developing a performance (learning) environment that supports mutual trust, and respect might just be key to ensuring that human intelligence, learning, and agency are maintained against the odds in an AI-infused world.

Limitations of the CLA

While the Constraints-Led Approach (CLA) provides a robust framework for fostering adaptability across different environments, it is not without limitations. In the context of promoting learners' GenAI literacy, applying CLA can be challenging due to the complexity of designing constraints that appropriately guide exploration without overwhelming or frustrating learners. Moreover, practitioners may struggle to balance the open-ended nature of CLA with the familiar structured learning outcomes common in many educational contexts (Renshaw et al., 2019). The approach also demands significant expertise in the nuanced interactions between task, individual, and environmental constraints, making it potentially less accessible to educators new to the method or to teaching in general (Davids et al., 2023). Many common Western teaching practices are less compatible with a coaching framework than for example some Indigenous pedagogies that are by their nature experiential, relational, developmental and not time bound (Antoine et al., 2018; Bone, 2022).

Another challenge worth noting that is particularly problematic for massified higher education systems, is the potential to scale this approach to large classes. It requires educators to have a personal relationship with each learner in order to monitor development and adjust constraints as necessary. While this approach is obviously a preferable educational scenario that has been advocated for in education for decades, it is very challenging in low-contact large lecture-based courses that are often the norm across programmes. It is particularly challenging - and important to address – in the early stages of any programme when classes are largest and learners need the most support, and when the constraints on AI use need to be at their most restrictive.

Future Research Directions

This chapter provides an overview of a proposed AI curriculum delivery framework as a first conceptual step on the road to addressing AI across the curriculum, which is a complex and nascent idea at present with most institutions yet to begin this work in earnest. We recognise that the work we present here, like most curriculum level planning for AI at this moment, is currently conceptual and has not yet been empirically tested, representing a knowledge and practice gap that urgently needs addressing. It is possible that the proposed approach will work better in some disciplines, institutional cultures, or education systems than others. Next steps must explore pilots within our own context.

With this chapter, we offer a call to move beyond the generic and individually focused advice that has thus far been useful in helping academics and learners navigate the emerging phenomenon of AI. What we need now is a focus on how we can collaborate within and across programmes, institutions, and educational systems to explore and test ideas for curriculum design thinking. Exploratory as well as longitudinal studies are necessary next steps in establishing whether combining a CLA and spiral curriculum models provides a successful framework for intentionally incorporating GenAI across diverse disciplinary curricula and institutional contexts.

There remain many unanswered questions as AI becomes rapidly and increasingly more embedded in teaching and learning practice, and much of the literature on implementation of AI in higher ed suffers from similar methodological challenges – small sample sizes, narrow scopes, short time frames, inappropriate experimental design, over-stating results, and underrepresentation of some geographical areas (Belkina et al., 2025). There are concerns about the potential long-term impacts of AI use (or overuse) on human cognition, critical thinking capacity, creativity, communication, and relationships. Indeed, one of the key reasons for choosing the CLA as a model is that it offers a potential approach to developing disciplinary knowledge alongside AI literacy, with reasonable constraints that attempt to prevent outsourcing of skill development by novice learners. Longitudinal tracking of learner competencies across a programme and into their application in the workforce will be necessary in order to determine whether AI-enabled curricula are still able to adequately prepare learners for their post-graduation lives.

Conclusion

The emergence of generative AI in higher education since ChatGPT's November 2022 public release has sparked the need for a fundamental rethinking of curriculum design. While institutions initially focused on policies, academic integrity and assessment security, the deeper challenge lies in nurturing meaningful connections between students and their learning environment. Although technology integration is inevitable, good curriculum design remains fundamentally about human relationships and interaction quality. The frameworks explored in this chapter, and in particular, the constraints-led approach, recognise that effective education isn't just about acquiring technological proficiency; it's about creating adaptive learning spaces where students can authentically engage with both tools and concepts. Ultimately, success depends not on technology alone, but on fostering robust connections between students, educators, and the systems they navigate.

References

Antoine, A.-N.-H., Mason, R., Mason, R., Palahicky, S., & De France, C. R. (2018). *Pulling Together: A Guide for Curriculum Developers*. BCcampus.

Araújo, D., Brito, H., & Carrilho, D. (2023). Team decision-making behavior: An ecological dynamics approach. *Asian Journal of Sport and Exercise Psychology, 3*(1), 24–29. DOI: 10.1016/j.ajsep.2022.09.005

Ascione, L. (2024, March 6). ASU, OpenAI look to AI's future in higher ed. *eCampus News*. https://www.ecampusnews.com/featured/2024/03/06/asu-openai-ai-future-higher-ed/

Attewell, S. (2025). *Student perceptions of AI 2025.* Joint Information Systems Committee (JISC). https://www.jisc.ac.uk/reports/student-perceptions-of-ai-2025

Baker Stein, M., & Jones-Schenk, J. (2024). The Future of Nursing: Navigating the AI Revolution Through Education and Training. *Journal of Continuing Education in Nursing, 55*(3), 108–109. DOI: 10.3928/00220124-20240221-03

Bearman, M., & Ajjawi, R. (2023). Learning to work with the black box: Pedagogy for a world with artificial intelligence. *British Journal of Educational Technology, 54*(5), 1160–1173. DOI: 10.1111/bjet.13337

Beetham, H. (2024, March 28). How not to talk about AI in education—LSE Higher Education. *LSE Higher Education - Enabling Dialogue and Sharing Different Perspectives in a Changing HE Landscape*. https://blogs.lse.ac.uk/highereducation/2024/03/28/how-not-to-talk-about-ai-in-education/

Belkina, M., Daniel, S., Nikolic, S., Haque, R., Lyden, S., Neal, P., Grundy, S., & Hassan, G. M. (2025). Implementing generative AI (GenAI) in higher education: A systematic review of case studies. *Computers and Education: Artificial Intelligence, 8*, 100407. DOI: 10.1016/j.caeai.2025.100407

Bone, T. (2022). *Key Components of Indigenous Pedagogies Literature Review*. Indspire.

Bozkurt, A., Xiao, J., Farrow, R., Bai, J. Y. H., Nerantzi, C., Moore, S., Dron, J., Stracke, C. M., Singh, L., Crompton, H., Koutropoulos, A., Terentev, E., Pazurek, A., Nichols, M., Sidorkin, A. M., Costello, E., Watson, S., Mulligan, D., Honeychurch, S., & Asino, T. I. (2024). The Manifesto for Teaching and Learning in a Time of Generative AI: A Critical Collective Stance to Better Navigate the Future. *Open Praxis, 16*(4), 487–513. DOI: 10.55982/openpraxis.16.4.777

Celik, I. (2023). Towards Intelligent-TPACK: An empirical study on teachers' professional knowledge to ethically integrate artificial intelligence (AI)-based tools into education. *Computers in Human Behavior, 138*, 107468. DOI: 10.1016/j.chb.2022.107468

Chan, C. K. Y. (2023). A comprehensive AI policy education framework for university teaching and learning. *International Journal of Educational Technology in Higher Education, 20*(1), 38. DOI: 10.1186/s41239-023-00408-3

Chung, J., Henderson, M., Pepperell, N., Slade, C., & Liang, Y. (2024). *Student perspectives on AI in Higher Education: Student Survey*. Student Perspectives on AI in Higher Education Project. DOI: 10.26180/27915930

Corbin, T., Dawson, P., Nicola-Richmond, K., & Partridge, H. (2025). 'Where's the line? It's an absurd line': Towards a framework for acceptable uses of AI in assessment. *Assessment & Evaluation in Higher Education, 0*(0), 1–13. DOI: 10.1080/02602938.2025.2456207

Cotton, D. R. E., Cotton, P. A., & Shipway, J. R. (2024). Chatting and cheating: Ensuring academic integrity in the era of ChatGPT. *Innovations in Education and Teaching International, 61*(2), 228–239. DOI: 10.1080/14703297.2023.2190148

Cox, G., Willmers, M., Brown, R., & Held, M. (2024). Learning along the Way: A Case Study on a Pedagogically Innovative Approach to Engage Medical Students in the Creation of Open Educational Resources Using ChatGPT. *Mousaion: South African Journal of Information Studies, 42*(1), 1. Advance online publication. DOI: 10.25159/2663-659X/15331

Curtis, G. J. (2025). The two-lane road to hell is paved with good intentions: Why an all-or-none approach to generative AI, integrity, and assessment is insupportable. *Higher Education Research & Development, 0*(0), 1–8. DOI: 10.1080/07294360.2025.2476516

Davidoff, M. (2024, November 11). How Broadening AI Access Can Help Bridge the Digital Divide. *EDUCAUSE Review*. https://er.educause.edu/articles/2024/11/how-broadening-ai-access-can-help-bridge-the-digital-divide

Davids, K., Rothwell, M., Hydes, S., Robinson, T., & Davids, C. (2023). Enriching Athlete—Environment Interactions in Youth Sport: The Role of a Department of Methodology. *Children (Basel, Switzerland), 10*(4), 4. Advance online publication. DOI: 10.3390/children10040752

Dawson, P., Bearman, M., Dollinger, M., & Boud, D. (2024a). Validity matters more than cheating. *Assessment & Evaluation in Higher Education, 49*(7), 1005–1016. DOI: 10.1080/02602938.2024.2386662

Dawson, P., Bearman, M., Dollinger, M., & Boud, D. (2024b). Validity matters more than cheating. *Assessment & Evaluation in Higher Education, 49*(7), 1005–1016. DOI: 10.1080/02602938.2024.2386662

de Fine Licht, K. (2024). Generative Artificial Intelligence in Higher Education: Why the 'Banning Approach' to Student use is Sometimes Morally Justified. *Philosophy & Technology, 37*(3), 113. DOI: 10.1007/s13347-024-00799-9

Dieker, L., & Zaugg, T. (2024). Artificial Intelligence and the Intersectionality of Disability. In Bennett, G., & Goodall, E. (Eds.), *The Palgrave Encyclopedia of Disability* (pp. 1–8). Springer Nature Switzerland., DOI: 10.1007/978-3-031-40858-8_121-1

Digital Education Council. (2024). *Digital Education Council Global AI Student Survey 2024*. Digital Education Council.

Digital Education Council. (2025). *DEC AI Literacy Framework*. The Digital Education Council.

Eaton, L. (2024, April 17). On Building a AI Policy for Teaching & Learning [Substack newsletter]. *AI + Education = Simplified*. https://aiedusimplified.substack.com/p/on-building-a-ai-policy-for-teaching?utm_campaign=post&triedRedirect=true

Eaton, S. E. (2023, February 25). 6 Tenets of Postplagiarism: Writing in the Age of Artificial Intelligence | Learning, Teaching and Leadership. *Learning, Teaching, and Leadership*. https://drsaraheaton.com/2023/02/25/6-tenets-of-postplagiarism-writing-in-the-age-of-artificial-intelligence/

Farrelly, T., & Baker, N. (2023). Generative Artificial Intelligence: Implications and Considerations for Higher Education Practice. *Education Sciences, 13*(11), 11. Advance online publication. DOI: 10.3390/educsci13111109

Fatima, S. S., Sheikh, N. A., & Osama, A. (2024). Authentic assessment in medical education: Exploring AI integration and student-as-partners collaboration. *Postgraduate Medical Journal, 100*(1190), 959–967. DOI: 10.1093/postmj/qgae088

Fawns, T. (2024). *Discursive principles for human-technology collectives*. First International Symposium on Educating for Collective Intelligence, University of Technology, Sydney. https://cic.uts.edu.au/wp-content/uploads/2024/06/Fawns_CI.edu2024.pdf

Foltynek, T., Bjelobaba, S., Glendinning, I., Khan, Z. R., Santos, R., Pavletic, P., & Kravjar, J. (2023). ENAI Recommendations on the ethical use of Artificial Intelligence in Education. *International Journal for Educational Integrity, 19*(1), 12, s40979-023-00133–00134. DOI: 10.1007/s40979-023-00133-4

Furze, L. (2024a, August 18). Design Refine Create: A Framework for GenAI Curriculum Design. *Leon Furze*. https://leonfurze.com/2024/08/19/design-refine-create-a-framework-for-genai-curriculum-design/

Furze, L. (2024b, August 28). Updating the AI Assessment Scale. *Leon Furze.Com*. https://leonfurze.com/2024/08/28/updating-the-ai-assessment-scale/

Furze, L., Perkins, M., Roe, J., & MacVaugh, J. (2024). The AI Assessment Scale (AIAS) in action: A pilot implementation of GenAI-supported assessment. *Australasian Journal of Educational Technology*, *40*(4), 4. Advance online publication. DOI: 10.14742/ajet.9434

George, A. S. (2023). Preparing Students for an AI-Driven World: Rethinking Curriculum and Pedagogy in the Age of Artificial Intelligence. *Partners Universal Innovative Research Publication*, *1*(2), 2. Advance online publication. DOI: 10.5281/zenodo.10245675

Gibson, R. (2024, September 10). The Impact of AI in Advancing Accessibility for Learners with Disabilities. *EDUCAUSE Review*. https://er.educause.edu/articles/2024/9/the-impact-of-ai-in-advancing-accessibility-for-learners-with-disabilities

Hamilton, A. (2024). Artificial Intelligence and Healthcare Simulation: The Shifting Landscape of Medical Education. *Cureus*, *16*(5). Advance online publication. DOI: 10.7759/cureus.59747

Hanke, M. (2022). Living the spiral curriculum: Using the Swanwick/Tillman sequence of musical development to support music in primary schools in the 1980s. *British Journal of Music Education*, *39*(1), 115–119. DOI: 10.1017/S0265051721000267

Harden, R. M. (1999). What is a spiral curriculum? *Medical Teacher*, *21*(2), 141–143. DOI: 10.1080/01421599979752

Hassija, V., Chamola, V., Mahapatra, A., Singal, A., Goel, D., Huang, K., Scardapane, S., Spinelli, I., Mahmud, M., & Hussain, A. (2024). Interpreting Black-Box Models: A Review on Explainable Artificial Intelligence. *Cognitive Computation*, *16*(1), 45–74. DOI: 10.1007/s12559-023-10179-8

Hillier, M. (2023, March 30). A proposed AI literacy framework. *TECHE*. https://teche.mq.edu.au/2023/03/a-proposed-ai-literacy-framework/

Holmes, W. (2024). AIED—Coming of Age? | International Journal of Artificial Intelligence in Education. *International Journal of Artificial Intelligence in Education, 34*(1), 1–11. DOI: 10.1007/s40593-023-00352-3

Hu, S., Ouyang, M., Gao, D., & Shou, M. Z. (2024). *The Dawn of GUI Agent: A Preliminary Case Study with Claude 3.5 Computer Use* (No. arXiv:2411.10323). arXiv. https://doi.org//arXiv.2411.10323DOI: 10.48550

Ireland, J., & Mouthaan, M. (2020). Perspectives on curriculum design: Comparing the spiral and the network models. *Research Matters, 30*, 7–12. DOI: 10.17863/CAM.100405

Israni, S. (2025, January 24). Nigeria's AI University: A Revolution for Africa. *CIO Africa*. https://cioafrica.co/nigerias-ai-university-a-revolution-for-africa/

Jamieson, S. (2022). The AI "Crisis" and A (Re)turn To Pedagogy. *Composition Studies, 50*(3), 153–157.

Kanbach, D. K., Heiduk, L., Blueher, G., Schreiter, M., & Lahmann, A. (2024). The GenAI is out of the bottle: Generative artificial intelligence from a business model innovation perspective. *Review of Managerial Science, 18*(4), 1189–1220. DOI: 10.1007/s11846-023-00696-z

Karataş, F., & Ataç, B. A. (2024). When TPACK meets artificial intelligence: Analyzing TPACK and AI-TPACK components through structural equation modelling. *Education and Information Technologies*. Advance online publication. DOI: 10.1007/s10639-024-13164-2

Kearney, K., & Hyle, A. (2003). The Grief Cycle and Educational Change: The Kubler-Ross Contribution. *Planning and Changing, 34*(1 and 2), 32–57.

Koehler, M. J., & Mishra, P. (2005). What Happens When Teachers Design Educational Technology? The Development of Technological Pedagogical Content Knowledge. *Journal of Educational Computing Research, 32*(2), 131–152. DOI: 10.2190/0EW7-01WB-BKHL-QDYV

Le Lagadec, D., Jackson, D., & Cleary, M. (2024). Artificial intelligence in nursing education: Prospects and pitfalls. *Journal of Advanced Nursing, 80*(10), 3883–3885. DOI: 10.1111/jan.16276

Leaton Gray, S., Edsall, D., & Parapadakis, D. (2025). AI-Based Digital Cheating At University, and the Case for New Ethical Pedagogies. *Journal of Academic Ethics, 23*(4), 2069–2086. Advance online publication. DOI: 10.1007/s10805-025-09642-y

Liu, D. Y. T., & Bates, S. (2025). *Generative AI in Higher Education: Current Practices and Ways Forward*. The Association of Pacific Rim Universities. https://www.apru.org/resources_report/whitepaper-generative-ai-in-higher-education-current-practices-and-ways-forward/

Lodge, J., Howard, S., & Bearman, M. (2023). *Assessment reform for the age of artificial intelligence*. Tertiary Education Quality and Standards Agency. https://www.teqsa.gov.au/sites/default/files/2023-09/assessment-reform-age-artificial-intelligence-discussion-paper.pdf

Lodge, J. M., de Barba, P., & Broadbent, J. (2023). Learning with Generative Artificial Intelligence Within a Network of Co-Regulation. *Journal of University Teaching & Learning Practice*, *20*(7), 7. Advance online publication. DOI: 10.53761/1.20.7.02

Long, D., & Magerko, B. (2020). What is AI Literacy? Competencies and Design Considerations. *Proceedings of the 2020 CHI Conference on Human Factors in Computing Systems*, 1–16. DOI: 10.1145/3313831.3376727

Lorenz, U., & Romeike, R. (2023). What Is AI-PACK? – Outline of AI Competencies for Teaching with DPACK. In J.-P. Pellet & G. Parriaux (Eds.), *Informatics in Schools. Beyond Bits and Bytes: Nurturing Informatics Intelligence in Education* (pp. 13–25). Springer Nature Switzerland. DOI: 10.1007/978-3-031-44900-0_2

Luo, J. (2024). A critical review of GenAI policies in higher education assessment: A call to reconsider the "originality" of students' work. *Assessment & Evaluation in Higher Education*, *49*(5), 651–664. DOI: 10.1080/02602938.2024.2309963

Maltagliati, A. J., Paree, J. H., McIntosh, K. L., Moynahan, K. F., & Vanderah, T. W. (2023). Development and evaluation of a pre-clerkship spiral curriculum: Data from three medical school classes. *Medical Education Online*, *28*(1), 2167258. Advance online publication. DOI: 10.1080/10872981.2023.2167258

Maslej, N., Fattorini, L., Perrault, R., Parli, V., Reuel, A., Brynjolfsson, E., Etchemendy, J., Ligett, K., Lyons, T., Manyika, J., Niebles, J. C., Shoham, Y., Wald, R., & Clark, J. (2024). *AI Index Report 2024 – Artificial Intelligence Index*. Stanford University Institute for Human-Centred Artificial Intelligence. https://aiindex.stanford.edu/report/

McDonald, N., Johri, A., Ali, A., & Hingle, A. (2024). *Generative Artificial Intelligence in Higher Education: Evidence from an Analysis of Institutional Policies and Guidelines* (2 citation(s); No. arXiv:2402.01659). arXiv. https://doi.org//arXiv.2402.01659DOI: 10.48550

Mishra, P., Warr, M., & Islam, R. (2023). TPACK in the age of ChatGPT and Generative AI. *Journal of Digital Learning in Teacher Education, 39*(4), 235–251. DOI: 10.1080/21532974.2023.2247480

Mohammed, S. A. A. Q., Osman, Y. M. M., Ibrahim, A. M., & Shaban, M. (2025). Ethical and regulatory considerations in the use of AI and machine learning in nursing: A systematic review. *International Nursing Review, 72*(1), e70010. DOI: 10.1111/inr.70010

Mollick, E. (2024). *Co-Intelligence: Living and working with AI.* Portfolio Penguin.

Moya, B., Eaton, S., Pethrick, H., Hayden, K., Brennan, R., Wiens, J., Mcdermott, B., & Lesage, J. (2023). Academic integrity and artificial intelligence in higher education contexts: A rapid scoping review protocol. *Canadian Perspectives on Academic Integrity, 5*(2), 59–75. https://doi.org/DOI: 10.11575/cpai.75990

Newell, K. M. (1986). Constraints on the Development of Coordination. In Wade, M. G., & Whiting, H. T. A. (Eds.), *Motor Skill Acquisition in Children: Aspects of Coordination and Control* (pp. 314–360). Martinus Nijhoff. DOI: 10.1007/978-94-009-4460-2_19

Ng, D. T. K., Leung, J. K. L., Chu, S. K. W., & Qiao, M. S. (2021). Conceptualizing AI literacy: An exploratory review. *Computers and Education: Artificial Intelligence, 2*, 100041. DOI: 10.1016/j.caeai.2021.100041

Nikolic, S., Sandison, C., Haque, R., Daniel, S., Grundy, S., Belkina, M., Lyden, S., Hassan, G. M., & Neal, P. (2024). ChatGPT, Copilot, Gemini, SciSpace and Wolfram versus higher education assessments: An updated multi-institutional study of the academic integrity impacts of Generative Artificial Intelligence (GenAI) on assessment, teaching and learning in engineering. *Australasian Journal of Engineering Education, 29*(2), 126–153. DOI: 10.1080/22054952.2024.2372154

Ning, Y., Zhang, C., Xu, B., Zhou, Y., & Wijaya, T. T. (2024). Teachers' AI-TPACK: Exploring the Relationship between Knowledge Elements. *Sustainability (Basel), 16*(3), 3. Advance online publication. DOI: 10.3390/su16030978

Open, A. I. (2025, February 2). Introducing deep research. *OpenAI News*. https://openai.com/index/introducing-deep-research/

Orth, D., van der Kamp, J., & Button, C. (2019). Learning to be adaptive as a distributed process across the coach–athlete system: Situating the coach in the constraints-led approach. *Physical Education and Sport Pedagogy, 24*(2), 146–161. DOI: 10.1080/17408989.2018.1557132

Ovsyannikova, D., de Mello, V. O., & Inzlicht, M. (2025). Third-party evaluators perceive AI as more compassionate than expert humans. *Communications Psychology*, *3*(1), 1–11. DOI: 10.1038/s44271-024-00182-6

Palaniappan, K., Lin, E. Y. T., & Vogel, S. (2024). Global Regulatory Frameworks for the Use of Artificial Intelligence (AI) in the Healthcare Services Sector. *Healthcare (Basel)*, *12*(5), 5. Advance online publication. DOI: 10.3390/healthcare12050562

Perkins, M., Furze, L., Roe, J., & MacVaugh, J. (2024). The Artificial Intelligence Assessment Scale (AIAS): A Framework for Ethical Integration of Generative AI in Educational Assessment. *Journal of University Teaching & Learning Practice*, *21*(06), 06. Advance online publication. DOI: 10.53761/q3azde36

Perplexity Team. (2025, February 14). Introducing Perplexity Deep Research. *Perplexity Blog*. https://www.perplexity.ai/hub/blog/introducing-perplexity-deep-research

Phan, L., Gatti, A., Han, Z., Li, N., Hu, J., Zhang, H., Zhang, C. B. C., Shaaban, M., Ling, J., Shi, S., Choi, M., Agrawal, A., Chopra, A., Khoja, A., Kim, R., Ren, R., Hausenloy, J., Zhang, O., Mazeika, M., . . . Hendrycks, D. (2025). *Humanity's Last Exam* (No. arXiv:2501.14249). arXiv. https://doi.org//arXiv.2501.14249DOI: 10.48550

Pratschke, B. M. (2023). *Generativism: The new hybrid* (No. arXiv:2309.12468). arXiv. https://doi.org//arXiv.2309.12468DOI: 10.48550

Pratschke, B. M. (2024). *Generative AI and Education: Digital Pedagogies, Teaching Innovation and Learning Design*. Springer Nature Switzerland., DOI: 10.1007/978-3-031-67991-9

Renden, P. G., & Dikken, J. (2023). Introducing the constraints-led approach in nurse education: An innovative perspective on skill acquisition. *Nurse Education Today*, *121*, 105672. DOI: 10.1016/j.nedt.2022.105672

Renshaw, I., & Chow, J.-Y. (2019). A constraint-led approach to sport and physical education pedagogy. *Physical Education and Sport Pedagogy*, *24*(2), 103–116. DOI: 10.1080/17408989.2018.1552676

Renshaw, I., Chow, J. Y., Davids, K., & Hammond, J. (2010). A constraints-led perspective to understanding skill acquisition and game play: A basis for integration of motor learning theory and physical education praxis? *Physical Education and Sport Pedagogy*, *15*(2), 117–137. DOI: 10.1080/17408980902791586

Renshaw, I., Davids, K., Newcombe, D., & Roberts, W. (2019). *The Constraints-Led Approach: Principles for Sports Coaching and Practice Design*. Routledge., DOI: 10.4324/9781315102351

Romadona, M. R., & Setiawan, S. (2021). Researchers' View on R&D Organizational Change Using the Grief Cycle. *Journal of STI Policy and Management*, *6*(2), 157–171. DOI: 10.14203/STIPM.2021.313

Roose, K. (2025, February 1). How Helpful Is Operator, OpenAI's New A.I. Agent? *The New York Times*. https://www.nytimes.com/2025/02/01/technology/openai-operator-agent.html

Salvaggio, E. (2024, August 29). Challenging The Myths of Generative AI | Tech-Policy.Press. *Tech Policy Press*. https://www.techpolicy.press/challenging-the-myths-of-generative-ai

Schmidt, D. A., Baran, E., Thompson, A. D., Mishra, P., Koehler, M. J., & Shin, T. S. (2009). Technological pedagogical content knowledge (TPACK): The development and validation of an assessment instrument for preservice teachers. *Journal of Research on Technology in Education*, *42*(2), 123–149. DOI: 10.1080/15391523.2009.10782544

Seifert, L., Papet, V., Strafford, B. W., Coughlan, E. K., & Davids, K. (2018). Skill transfer, expertise and talent development: An ecological dynamics perspective. *Movement & Sport Sciences - Science & Motricité*, *102*, Article 102. DOI: 10.1051/sm/2019010

Selwyn, N. (2022). The future of AI and education: Some cautionary notes. *European Journal of Education*, *57*(4), 620–631. DOI: 10.1111/ejed.12532

Selwyn, N. (2024a). Constructive Criticism? Working with (Rather than Against) the AIED Back-Lash. *International Journal of Artificial Intelligence in Education*, *34*(1), 84–91. DOI: 10.1007/s40593-023-00344-3

Selwyn, N. (2024b). On the Limits of Artificial Intelligence (AI) in Education. *Nordisk Tidsskrift for Pedagogikk Og Kritikk*, *10*(1), 1. Advance online publication. DOI: 10.23865/ntpk.v10.6062

Shao, Z., Wang, P., Zhu, Q., Xu, R., Song, J., Bi, X., Zhang, H., Zhang, M., Li, Y. K., Wu, Y., & Guo, D. (2024). *DeepSeekMath: Pushing the Limits of Mathematical Reasoning in Open Language Models* (No. arXiv:2402.03300). arXiv. https://doi.org//arXiv.2402.03300DOI: 10.48550

Sluijs, J. P., Gilissen, H. K., & van Look, K. C. J. (2023). Training law students like athletes: Experimenting with the constraints-led approach in law clinics. *The Law Teacher*, *57*(4), 458–477. DOI: 10.1080/03069400.2023.2275495

Smith, C. S. (2025, March 8). *China's Autonomous Agent, Manus, Changes Everything*. https://www.forbes.com/sites/craigsmith/2025/03/08/chinas-autonomous-agent-manus-changes-everything/

Smith, R. F. (2025, January 20). Closing the digital divide as we enter the Intelligent Age. *World Economic Forum*. https://www.weforum.org/stories/2025/01/digital-divide-intelligent-age-how-everyone-can-benefit-ai/

Taraporewalla, K., Barach, P., Lipman, J., & Van Zundert, A. (2024). The Effectiveness of the Constraint-Led Approach in Developing Medical Procedural Skills. *Universal Library of Medical and Health Sciences*, *02*(02), 11–18. DOI: 10.70315/uloap.ulmhs.2024.0202003

Tertiary Education Quality and Standards Agency (TEQSA). (2024). *GenAI strategies for Australian higher education: Emerging practice*. TEQSA, Australian Government. https://www.teqsa.gov.au/guides-resources/resources/corporate-publications/gen-ai-strategies-australian-higher-education-emerging-practice

Thompson, A. D. (2007). Editor's Remarks: TPCK:A New Direction for Technology in Teacher Education Programs. *Journal of Computing in Teacher Education*, *23*(3), 78–104. DOI: 10.1080/10402454.2007.10784564

Vallor, S. (2024). *The AI Mirror: How to reclaim our humanity in an age of machine thinking*. Oxford University Press. DOI: 10.1093/oso/9780197759066.001.0001

Wang, J. (2025). *A Tutorial on LLM Reasoning: Relevant Methods behind ChatGPT o1* (No. arXiv:2502.10867). arXiv. https://doi.org//arXiv.2502.10867DOI: 10.48550

Wells, R. (2024, November 5). 71% Of Employers Prefer AI Skills Above Experience In 2024. *Forbes*. https://www.forbes.com/sites/rachelwells/2024/11/05/71-of-employers-prefer-ai-skills-above-experience-in-2024/

Westfall, C. (2023, January 28). Educators Battle Plagiarism As 89% Of Students Admit To Using OpenAI's ChatGPT For Homework. *Forbes*. https://www.forbes.com/sites/chriswestfall/2023/01/28/educators-battle-plagiarism-as-89-of-students-admit-to-using-open-ais-chatgpt-for-homework/?sh=221930a3750d

Wiggers, K. (2025, May 22). A safety institute advised against releasing an early version of Anthropic's Claude Opus 4 AI model. *TechCrunch*. https://techcrunch.com/2025/05/22/a-safety-institute-advised-against-releasing-an-early-version-of-anthropics-claude-opus-4-ai-model/

Wilkins, A. (2024, July 25). DeepMind AI gets silver medal at International Mathematical Olympiad. *New Scientist*. https://www.newscientist.com/article/2441450-deepmind-ai-gets-silver-medal-at-international-mathematical-olympiad/

William, C. (2022). The constraints-led approach in nursing education is being introduced as a novel viewpoint on skill acquisition. *Journal of Nursing Research and Practice*, *6*(12), 192–193. https://doi.org/DOI. DOI: 10.37532/ Puljnrp. 22.6(12).192-193

Williams, A., & Ingle, E. (2025). Assessment design through co-creation: Student-staff partnership in evaluating the impact of artificial intelligence. *International Journal for Students as Partners*, *9*(1), 1. Advance online publication. DOI: 10.15173/ ijsap.v9i1.5802

Wood, M. A., Mellalieu, S. D., Araújo, D., Woods, C. T., & Davids, K. (2023). Learning to coach: An ecological dynamics perspective. *International Journal of Sports Science & Coaching*, *18*(2), 609–620. DOI: 10.1177/17479541221138680

Xiao, P., Chen, Y., & Bao, W. (2023). *Waiting, Banning, and Embracing: An Empirical Analysis of Adapting Policies for Generative AI in Higher Education* (No. arXiv:2305.18617). arXiv. https://doi.org//arXiv.2305.18617DOI: 10.48550

Yi, Y. (2021). Establishing the concept of AI literacy. *Jahr – European. Journal of Bioethics*, *12*(2), 2.

KEY TERMS AND DEFINITIONS

Assessment Validity: The concept that an assessment accurately reflects a learner's performance in relation to a skill, knowledge, or ability. A valid assessment is able to identify whether a learner has met the standards of a course to a required performance level.

Constraints-Led Approach: A theory of skill development applied within the context of the ecological-dynamics framework that recognises the development of skills are constrained by and a result of the interactions between the learner's characteristics, the environment, and a given task.

Environmental Constraints: Skill development constraints provided by the context of the environment in which the skill will be performed.

Generative Artificial Intelligence: A form of artificial intelligence capable of creating human-like content across multiple media, including text, images, video, and audio.

Generativism: A symbiotic approach to teaching and learning with generative AI that builds on and applies constructivist and collectivist pedagogies.

Learner Constraints: Skill development constraints that relate to the characteristics of the learner.

Spiral Curriculum Model: A curriculum model developed by Jerome Bruner in which learners are exposed to a task, topic, or theme at multiple points throughout their education, with each encounter reinforcing prior learning and introducing more complexity and deeper application of the concept.

Task Constraints: Specific constraints associated with a task, for example, a rule or procedure that is required to be followed in a particular practice context.

TPAIK/AI-TPACK: An extension of the Technological Pedagogical Content Knowledge (TPACK) framework that recognises the synergistic relationship between AI and the elements of the TPACK model.

Chapter 4
The Role of Artificial Intelligence in Scaffolding Learning and Managing Cognitive Load

Yesim Nalkesen Akin
https://orcid.org/0000-0002-5628-7093
Özyeğin University, Turkey

Betul Yıldızhan Bora
https://orcid.org/0000-0002-4774-3907
Bingol University, Turkey

ABSTRACT

This chapter offers a foundation for designing educational environments that integrate scaffolding and manage cognitive load to optimise learning. It introduces principles of memory and cognitive load theory, including its subtypes, and explores how they apply to educational platforms through empirical studies. Taking a two-way approach, it highlights the reciprocal link between theory and practice (Mayer, 2008). Grounded in current research, the chapter presents four AI-integrated pathways: AI-powered systems, conversational agents, instructional material design, and gamification. These support scaffolding and cognitive balance, promote self-regulated learning, and highlight the role of instructional design in enhancing autonomy, engagement, and knowledge construction. Ethical and cultural considerations are addressed through recent research, supporting a view of education that is human-centred, values-driven, and critically engaged.

DOI: 10.4018/979-8-3373-7579-3.ch004

ight © 2026, IGI Global Scientific Publishing. Copying or distributing in print or electronic forms without written permission of IGI Global Scientific Publishing is prohibited. Use of this chapter to 1 generative artificial intelligence (AI) technologies is expressly prohibited. The publisher reserves all rights to license its use for generative AI training and machine learning model development.

INTRODUCTION

This chapter aims to examine how AI tools and systems can be utilised to scaffold students and manage cognitive load within instructional design (ID) processes. It explores their pedagogical applications and roles in enhancing learning across diverse educational contexts. Drawing on relevant theories, research, and case studies, the chapter critically investigates how AI can be integrated into curricula to support cognitive load management, scaffold learning, and foster cognitive engagement both within and beyond the classroom.

Building on the framework, the principles of *The Manifesto for Teaching and Learning in a Time of Generative AI* (Bozkurt et al., 2024) is embedded in the chapter to discuss the phenomenon of artificial intelligence integration into education in depth with particular emphasis on fostering human agency, resisting techno-centrism and reimagining teaching as a relational, values-driven practice in an age of intelligent machines.

In line with this pedagogical perspective, the chapter also aligns with these principles, which frames generative AI as a socially constructed and ethically complex phenomenon. The present chapter is grounded in this stance by positioning AI systems and tools not as neutral mechanisms, but rather as systems embedded with cultural and ideological assumptions without true reasoning. Equally, having a high level of literacy or a strong foundation in educational approaches may not be enough on its own. Understanding how AI systems function and operate (i.e., how they may reproduce bias embedded in their training data) is essential to utilising these tools effectively. Therefore, the present chapter aims not only to explore how AI can be integrated to scaffold learning and manage cognitive load, but also to draw a scientific frame on building informed and critically reflective approaches to their integration in diverse educational contexts.

The Role of Artificial Intelligence in Scaffolding Learning and Managing Cognitive Load

Recent advances in computing have led to an influx of standalone artificial intelligence systems, AI-integrated systems and custom AI systems in the field of education (AlAli & Wardat, 2024; Alasadi & Baiz, 2023). The unprecedented increase in digital educational resources highlights the importance of managing cognitive load (CL) and the affordances of scaffolding in learning environments. Since CL refers to the allocation of working memory resources for the completion of cognitive tasks, the interaction between information structures, a thorough integration of instructional design (ID) elements and a comprehensive understanding of learners' cognitive traits is critical to optimising learning efficacy and improving learning experiences.

1. SCAFFOLDING, COLLABORATIVE LEARNING, AND AI ASSISTED INTERACTION

Lev Vygotsky's sociocultural learning theory emphasises that individuals' learning capacities can be developed through support (Vygotsky, 1978). Scaffolding, a central concept within the zone of proximal development (ZPD) theory, refers to the gradual support aimed at enhancing an individual's existing knowledge and skills. This support is gradually withdrawn as the individual becomes capable of learning independently and transferring their knowledge. Research highlights that supportive instructional methods consistently improve learners' achievement in both academic and non-academic domains, regardless of whether they have documented learning needs (CAST, 2024; Goddard et al., 2015; Malik et al., 2024). Scaffolding, which plays a critical role in maximising learning potential (Wood, Bruner & Ross, 1976), has the capacity to enhance the impact and extent of the concept of scaffolding through modern technologies (Kim, 2024; Krishna, Prasad & Anjali S., 2024; Sætra, 2022).

AI enhances the learning process by providing personalised, dynamic support mechanisms. AI-driven systems analyse individuals' knowledge levels, learning pace, and learning preferences to deliver tailored guidance (Adiguzel et al., 2023). Furthermore, these systems make learning processes more effective through immediate feedback and opportunities for error correction. This kind of dynamic support is customised to meet learners' specific needs and can be gradually reduced as their capacity grows. AI technologies offer an innovative approach to both cognitive load management and education by integrating the concept of scaffolding to support personalised learning experiences.

Studies focusing on AI-supported scaffolding in collaborative learning environments have shown that such interventions can have positive impacts. An example of this is a recent experimental study by Ge, Lu, and Hao (2025), which focused on the role of GenAI-based scaffolding mechanisms in supporting knowledge construction. In the study, university students were divided into 18 groups. Nine groups participated in collaborative learning processes supported by GenAI-based scaffolding, while the remaining nine engaged in learning activities in conventionally technology-supported environments. The results revealed that students who received GenAI scaffolding demonstrated significant improvements in their cognitive and metacognitive knowledge construction. Echoing these findings, a study by Silva and Tarouco (2022), conducted in an online collaborative learning environment, demonstrated that scaffolding strategies designed with flexibility enhance student participation and support the co-construction of knowledge.

As noted in the manifesto by Bozkurt and colleagues (2024) addressing the theme of collaborative learning and AI-assisted interaction, AI-supported communication has the potential to enrich peer support and collaborative learning by introducing diverse perspectives. However, for this potential to be realised effectively, it is important to find a balance within the socio-emotional aspects of communication by prioritising human interaction while still recognising the role of technological efficiency. For this reason, students should be supported in ways that address both technological skills and social interaction. Likewise, educators must design learning processes that consider both the technical and human dimensions of these learning experiences (Hutson & Plate, 2023).

In conclusion, scaffolding helps personalise learning processes and contributes to more effective outcomes when integrated with AI technologies. AI-supported scaffolding improves cognitive development through individualised support and promotes active participation in collaborative learning. Nevertheless, it is essential to maintain a balanced approach that considers both technological efficiency and human-centred interaction.

Developing Learners' Cognitive Capacity through Ethical and Pedagogical Integration of Artificial Intelligence in Education

The use of artificial intelligence in education does more than transform teaching; it also has the potential to influence learners' cognitive development. Ethical and pedagogical responsibilities are central to guiding how technology is used in educational contexts. While AI can stimulate creativity and encourage the generation of diverse ideas, its overuse may lead to homogenisation, which can limit the depth of learning (Bozkurt et al., 2024; Garcia et al., 2025). For this reason, AI technologies should be applied in ways that support learners in developing creative thinking and the ability to express their ideas clearly. The collaboration between humans and AI should be designed to promote intellectual growth. Bozkurt and colleagues (2024) addressed this in their manifesto by emphasising AI's potential to reduce CL and support schematic learning, as part of a broader focus on developing cognitive capacity. At the same time, they emphasised that integrating AI into education requires careful planning and a strong pedagogical foundation. It is therefore essential to approach its use with balance, evaluating both the opportunities it presents and the potential risks through a process of thoughtful, evidence-informed analysis.

This view is also reflected in recent research. For instance, Gkintoni et al. (2025) suggest that traditional cognitive load theory should be reconsidered in light of developments in educational neuroscience and artificial intelligence. They point out that extraneous cognitive load tends to increase, particularly in digital learning environments that lack rigorous instructional design. In such cases, learning outcomes often fail to achieve intended outcomes, indicating a need to redesign these technologies in line with pedagogical aims. Common issues include poorly structured interfaces, cognitively overwhelming content, and systems that lack meaningful interaction. Building on this, Lademann et al. (2025) conducted an experimental study exploring the effects of AI-supported chatbots on learning performance, affective variables, and particularly cognitive load. Their results show that well-designed systems can improve the overall learning experience and contribute positively to learners' cognitive engagement. Similarly, Feng (2025) demonstrated that in the context of language learning, AI-supported strategies can improve learning outcomes by helping learners manage their cognitive load more effectively.

Adiguzel et al. (2023) emphasised that artificial intelligence tools should be used within a pedagogical framework and noted that educators continue to express concerns about their use. In a related study, Garcia et al. (2025) found that when students use AI technologies intensively, their anxiety levels increase during tasks that demand problem-solving and higher-order cognitive skills. These findings are supported by recent research in the field. It has been suggested that educators may lack the capacity to fully integrate AI into educational processes, which could lead to a range of ethical challenges. As a result, there is growing recognition of the need to prioritise ethical principles in educational contexts (Kamali, Alpat and Bozkurt, 2024). In their qualitative study, Kamali et al. (2024) highlighted a lack of awareness around AI ethics and pointed to inconsistencies in how ethical principles are applied in practice. Furthermore, the use of AI tools can sometimes produce unintended negative outcomes. When applied without pedagogical grounding, these tools risk oversimplifying cognitive processes and restricting learners' ability to think critically (Bozkurt et al., 2024; Stanislaw, 2024). This highlights the importance of managing AI integration in ways that preserve and support learners' cognitive and intellectual development. Within this context, it is essential that pedagogical and ethical considerations are embedded throughout the design and implementation of AI in education. In order to support learners' cognitive capacity, AI tools must be aligned with pedagogical principles and used to optimise cognitive load in a balanced and meaningful way. Meanwhile, Khasawneh and Khasawneh (2024) found that when adaptive AI systems are not appropriately designed for special education settings, they may increase undesirable cognitive load and negatively impact the learning process.

Artificial intelligence tools often reflect the cultural norms in which they are developed (Bozkurt et al., 2024). For this reason, these tools need to be revisited and reinterpreted to ensure they are responsive to the characteristics of different cultural contexts. This highlights the importance of evaluating AI systems used in education not only in terms of technical functionality but also with regard to cultural relevance and ethical responsibility. When AI applications are designed without cultural awareness, they may fail to offer meaningful learning opportunities and instead increase learners' cognitive load, ultimately disrupting the learning process. This view is supported by the findings of Kopecka et al. (2024), who showed that users' expectations of AI differ significantly based on their cognitive tendencies and socio-cultural backgrounds. Similarly, an experimental study by Hong and Guo (2025) found that AI-supported language learning systems that use multiple screens had a positive effect on motivation and cognitive load management when designed in alignment with the learner's cultural context. Ivanović (2025) also reported that instructional systems developed with cultural alignment, whether traditional or AI-supported, led to improved learning performance. In a related study, Shokoohifar (2024) found that while AI-assisted translation tools generally had a positive effect on the translation process and quality, the absence of contextual awareness could lead to an increase in cognitive load. These findings suggest that AI-supported learning materials should be designed not only with individual differences in mind but also with sensitivity to learners' cultural environments. When cultural contexts are ignored, AI-powered systems risk marginalising diverse perspectives and limiting meaningful engagement with learning (Bozkurt et al., 2024).

In this context, the ethical and pedagogical integration of artificial intelligence in education requires more than technological competence; it calls for a learner-centred approach to instructional design that is culturally aware, critically informed, and pedagogically sensitive. When educators and designers align the affordances of AI with sound pedagogical goals, it becomes possible to turn technology into a meaningful tool that supports cognitive development.

2. COGNITIVE LOAD THEORY AND MULTIMEDIA LEARNING

Rooted in the works of Paivio (1986), Mayer (2010), and Sweller (2005), the foundational principles for multimedia learning include: a dual-channel structure (visual and auditory), a limited processing capacity, and five cognitive processes (selecting relevant words and images, forming verbal and pictorial models, and integrating them with each other and with prior knowledge). Cognitive load theory (CLT) distinguishes three types of cognitive load: *intrinsic*, *extraneous*, and *germane*. These loads are typically additive, with their sum representing the total cognitive load. Cognitive overload occurs when the total cognitive load exceeds the learner's working memory capacity. As the interplay of CL affects learning outcomes and processes, it is crucial for instructors and instructional designers to consider the characteristics and the nature of these subtypes in mind when designing and developing materials. Yet, a common pitfall among multimedia instructional designers is allowing technology to dictate the instructional design, rather than tailoring it to the learner's needs and cognitive limitations, which can exacerbate undesirable cognitive overload (Sorden, 2013).

2.1. Differentiating Intrinsic, Extraneous, and Germane Load

Overall, CLT posits that intrinsic cognitive load is determined by the inherent complexity of the material being learned and its interaction with learners' prior knowledge. This type of load is usually considered an unavoidable aspect of the learning process, as it stems directly from the task itself and cannot be altered (Sweller, Van Merrienboer, & Paas, 1998). Extraneous cognitive load, on the other hand, arises from external factors unrelated to the core material, such as ineffective presentation methods or distractions that divide attention between multiple information sources. This type of load is unnecessary and should be minimised to optimise learning. Mayer (2009) emphasises that ID can reduce extraneous load, by adhering to multimedia principles that align with instructional purposes. Likewise, Sweller et al. (1998) highlight the importance of aligning ID with CLT by avoiding unnecessary complexity and focusing on schema acquisition and meaningful learning.

Having mentioned these two types of CL, it is important to note that not all forms of CL are undesirable; on the contrary, it has been increasingly recognised that cognitive load is not solely a hindrance to learning but also plays a crucial role in facilitating it. Meaningful, complex learning is unlikely to occur without engaging in effortful cognitive processing that places demands on working memory (Sweller, Van Merrienboer, & Paas, 1998, p. 3). Germane load, essential for meaningful learning, encompasses the cognitive effort dedicated to processing relevant information aligned with instructional goals through the effortful construction and automation of organised knowledge structures or schemas (Korbach et al., 2018; Sweller et al., 1998).

2.2. Theory-Driven Strategies for Managing Cognitive Load in Instructional Design

This section explores educational research studies that integrate AI into the curriculum or instructional design to provide scaffolding and balance cognitive load (CL) for optimal learning experiences. The chapter aims to provide theory-driven yet practical examples to balance the different subtypes of cognitive load. It adopts a two-way approach, highlighting the reciprocal relationship between learning theory and educational practice (Mayer, 2008). This approach emphasises expanding the science of learning to better explain how learning occurs in real-world contexts, while also refining the science of instruction to address the conditions under which instructional principles are most effective, informed by an understanding of how the human mind processes information. Accordingly, it guides readers through practical steps, illustrating how specific methods can be thoughtfully applied to scaffold learners and manage cognitive load in instructional design (ID) processes using AI tools and systems.

AI-POWERED SYSTEMS TO ENHANCE LEARNING EXPERIENCES

As AI tools become increasingly *invisible* yet integral within educational settings, exploring how they align with established frameworks can offer valuable insights. Research studies show that AI-powered systems can balance cognitive load through adaptive support based on evidence-based strategies (Kim et al., 2024). One framework that exemplifies this alignment is the SAMR Framework (Substitution, Augmentation, Modification, Redefinition), which illustrates the integration of technology in education through progressive categories. AI-powered systems have the potential to further support learners by balancing cognitive load and providing scaffolding opportunities through adaptive feedback, personalised guidance, and dynamic learning pathways (Halkiopoulos & Gkintoni, 2024; Yaseen et al., 2025). Moreover, they facilitate the creation of seamless, immersive, and globally connected learning environments that transcend the *traditional* boundaries of contemporary educational systems. This relationship can be illustrated through Table 1, which presents examples of how AI technologies align with the SAMR model to support instructional practices and learning environments.

Table 1. Example of AI Integration in Education to Offer Scaffolding and/or Balance CL

Stage	Extent	Example
Substitution	Technology is a direct substitute for traditional tools, with no functional change.	Utilising AI-powered technologies to convert audio materials to text (to facilitate note-taking).
Augmentation	The technology serves as a substitute for traditional learning activities, but with functional improvements.	Utilising AI-powered feedback mechanisms that provide immediate feedback.
Modification	The technology enables the redesign of the learning activity.	Utilising sentiment analysis to adapt feedback and support strategies to create a personalised learning environment.
Redefinition	The technology enables the creation of tasks that may not have been possible without its use.	Utilising AI-driven translations and communication platforms among learners from diverse backgrounds to foster projects that overcome language and geographical barriers.

CONVERSATIONAL AGENTS

In the current education system, addressing each learner's unique needs can be a demanding task. Tailoring instruction to accommodate diverse learning preferences presents challenges, potentially leading to some students feeling overwhelmed, while others become disengaged (Qadir, 2022). However, AI-driven systems hold significant potential for enhancing the learning experience (Gkintoni et al., 2025), by providing adaptive feedback mechanisms, scaffolding techniques, and assessment methods. As a result, individualised instruction enables learners to progress at their own pace and focus on areas that require further improvement (Limo et al., 2023).

A chatbot, derived from the term "*chat robot*", refers to an AI-powered conversational agent designed to mimic human interaction. With advancements in AI models such as ChatGPT-4o and DeepSeek, conversational agents are becoming increasingly effective in addressing the challenges of personalised instruction. Advancements in natural language processing (NLP) and multimodal capabilities enable learners to engage in more personalised and immersive learning experiences. These features allow them to interact with AI-generated systems in ways that are authentic, social and effective, similar to a real conversation (Khosrawi-Rad et al., 2022; Lin et al., 2020; Wang et al., 2023). This supports Vygotsky's (1978) sociocultural theory, which emphasises learning through social participation, interaction and negotiation of meaning (Malik et al., 2025). Within this framework, conversational agents can support learning processes by encouraging learners to participate in dialogue, express their ideas, reflect on their understanding, and access scaffolded support that promotes their cognitive growth (Naznin et al., 2025).

Jensen at al. (2024) conducted a study exploring the impact of ChatGPT to scaffold learning and support constructive alignment in higher education. The study revealed that chatbot integration helped students clarify concepts, structure arguments, and deepen engagement with academic tasks. Alongside the positive findings, participating students raised concerns about overreliance, the opacity of AI responses, and the risk of losing ownership over their thinking. This is an important consideration since it may put the learners at risk for reduced meaningful engagement (Bozkurt et al., 2024). Building on this stance, the study concludes by emphasising the role of teachers in guiding AI use intentionally within a critical frame of reference to ensure that technology augments rather than replaces reflective and critical learning.

Similarly, the integration of AI systems and tools into curriculum can be effective to determine the cognitive load of students. Jin et al. (2025) conducted a study to explore the effectiveness of a teachable agent "Chat Melody" powered by LLM in music education. The findings revealed that students, who have high levels of engagement with the agent, were reported to have higher achievement scores as well as lower levels of cognitive load. The agent's capability to provide real time, adaptive feedback served as a cognitive scaffold for students facilitating their mental schemas. In addition, the agent served as an interactive learning companion; the integration, design, and application of these AI tools and systems positioned students as active learners who explain, justify, and refine their understanding through structured dialogue. This framing of AI tools not as content providers or task-doers but rather as active facilitators and challengers aligns with Bozkurt et al.'s (2024) stance on balancing support with opportunities for intellectual growth. While scaffolding can be effective, over-scaffolding in the design that reduces students' cognitive challenge should be avoided. Resonating with the manifesto, the study offers an important nuance in this regard and demonstrates the key role of intentional instructional design that positions AI not as a content delivery tool but as a cognitive partner supporting meaningful learning processes beyond what AI alone can provide.

Multimodal AI systems, capable of integrating and processing diverse input types (i.e., text, audio, video, and visual input), such as GPT-4V and KOSMOS-2, can simulate human-like perception, as they are able to interpret spoken language, visual content, and textual information. This integrative and holistic approach to educational contexts allows AI to support diverse learner needs and pedagogical strategies, while also enhancing adaptive learning through real-time feedback, step-by-step guidance, and the generation of open-ended questions (Alshaik et al., 2024; Bulathwela et al., 2023; Doughty et al., 2024; Elkins et al., 2024; Jury et al., 2024; Malik et al., 2025; Prihar et al., 2023; Rodriguez-Torrealba et al., 2022; Shimmei et al., 2023; Wang et al., 2023). However, along with the manifesto's caution against over-scaffolding that impedes cognitive growth, the design and implementation stages must reflect thoughtful planning, as its outputs can encourage surface-level engagement if not paired with reflective, critical inquiry (Bozkurt et al., 2024)

Conversational agents promote autonomy (Kostka & Toncelli, 2023) by providing immediate feedback and personalised support, thereby enabling learners to develop higher-order skills such as critical thinking, problem-solving, and research autonomy, and to serve as a personalised assistant (Bozkurt et al., 2024; Dowling & Lucey, 2023; Ilkou, Linzbach, & Wallat, 2024). Conversational agents may reduce extraneous cognitive load by presenting information in a well-structured manner, enabling learners to focus on the targeted content itself rather than navigating poorly organised information (Patac & Patac, 2025). As highlighted by Li, Wang, and Li (2024), this augments learning experiences and minimises cognitive strain due to the accuracy and relevance of the responses. As learners naturally engage with conversational agents to critically evaluate AI-generated information by comparing responses against credible sources, they foster deeper cognitive processing through questioning, analysis, and integrating new knowledge with prior understanding. The nature of this engagement facilitates germane cognitive load, as it promotes schema construction and deeper learning, echoing Mhlanga's (2023) observation that access to rich and relevant information encourages learners to engage cognitively and become more self-directed in their learning. Conversational agents may also balance intrinsic cognitive load by breaking down complex tasks into smaller steps, offering clear and structured explanations, and providing strategic guidance to support learners as they apply self-regulated learning (SRL) skills such as planning, monitoring, and reflection (Patac & Patac, 2025).

The analogy of a "*steering mechanism*" (Cain, 2024, p. 5) illustrates the importance of crafting effective prompts in GenAI to enhance the accuracy and relevance of interactions and outputs. Prompting is a skill that can be developed as learners engage with the interfaces (Hocky & White, 2022). As AI becomes more prevalent in higher education, strategic prompt engineering skills can boost student performance and critical thinking (Heston & Kuhn, 2023; Walter, 2024). Prompt engineering is inherently dynamic, developing through trial and error. Adding elements to prompts that align with how AI systems function, such as including phrases like "do it step by step", can improve output effectiveness and may be considered addendums to a "universal and transferable prompt suffix" (Zou et al., 2023). Techniques such as Chain-of-Thought, Expert Prompting, and Tree-of-Thought improve outcomes by enhancing AI's reasoning, precision, and problem-solving strategies. For instance, *Chain-of-Thought* adopts a step-by-step logic, *Expert Prompting* encourages specialised roles for precision, and *Tree-of-Thought* facilitates discussions among multiple experts in specific scenarios (Walter, 2024). However, considering the rapid advances in AI technologies, it is critical for learners to take agile and strategic turns based on their interactions with these systems, rather than relying solely on predetermined approaches to generating effective outputs. Thus, creating opportunities for collaborative scenarios to hone such skills could further scaffold learners in navigating the ill-structured challenges they are likely to encounter in their future professional and instructional practices. Within a pedagogical framework and through rigorous planning, prompt engineering may contribute to the development of cognitive frames that encourage reflective engagement with AI systems, rather than passive acceptance of AI-generated outputs. This kind of reflective reasoning may help mitigate the risk of intellectual distance (Bozkurt et al., 2024). It is important to remember that the goal is not for students to rely on fixed prompt templates, but to cultivate the cognitive flexibility and strategic capacity, analogous to developing *intellectual muscles*, needed to navigate meaningfully in an ever-evolving landscape.

Echoing the notion of reflective engagement, it is important to build a solid foundation for integrating conversational agents into learners' study routines. It is equally important to create pathways that support the development of SRL skills. AI-powered platforms such as LEAP utilise Large Language Models (LLMs) and present unique opportunities by providing personalised feedback that encourages multifaceted thinking and reflection. Such platforms enable instructors to tailor prompts to foster cognitive, metacognitive, and motivational aspects, guiding students through higher-level (i.e., *i+1*) learning tasks. Meanwhile, learners also gain literacy and autonomy in monitoring and revising their learning strategies (Steinert et al., 2024). Similarly, EduChat exemplifies how conversational agents may promote SRL by leveraging LLMs to provide personalised support, helping students with the micro-level steps of the SRL cycle (i.e., setting goals and tracking progress) to develop effective study strategies (Zhang et al., 2024). Expanding on the role of LLMs in supporting SRL and higher-order thinking (i.e., analysis and evaluation stages on Bloom's taxonomy), Ilkou, Linzbach, and Wallat (2024) propose a hybrid Socratic dialogue system that integrates LLMs with Knowledge Engineering (KE) and Hybrid Human-Artificial Intelligence (HHAI) to address the complexities of learner inquiries and ensure personalised, adaptive guidance. AI systems are advancing towards Artificial General Intelligence (AGI), which may reduce the need for hybrid approaches in the future. However, adopting a hybrid approach to address the current limitations of LLMs and the challenges of handling complex, inquiry-based, and/or ill-structured scenarios remains crucial.

Alongside the positive aspects of using conversational agents in educational contexts, it is important to maintain a careful balance between teaching the capabilities of conversational agents and fostering critical thinking skills and domain-specific knowledge (Holmes et al., 2023; Zawacki-Richter et al., 2023). Equally important is the integration of information literacy, digital ethics, and critical thinking skills within the curriculum to ensure learners develop the necessary skill set to engage with AI responsibly and effectively, while safeguarding against bias, misinformation, and over-reliance (Naznin et al., 2025). AI literacy holds a key role in modern education, encompassing technical know-how, ethical awareness, and an understanding of AI's societal impacts and implications (Walter, 2024). Bozkurt et al. (2024) emphasise that AI literacy should not be confined to technical skills, but should also encompass ethical awareness and the ability to critically evaluate AI-generated information. While integrating chatbots into curricula offers valuable scaffolding opportunities, it is equally important to scaffold learners in these areas to help them take charge of their own learning. Thus, a horizontal and consistent approach that equips learners with the knowledge and skills to understand the nature and capabilities of AI technologies is essential to ensure ethical, responsible and effective engagement with these tools in learning environments and beyond.

AI POWERED LEARNING PLATFORMS

AI-powered adaptive learning (AL) platforms refer to systems that dynamically adjust instructional content, feedback, and learning pathways in real time based on data pertaining to learners' cognitive profiles, patterns of learning, and progress. These platforms help manage cognitive load and support learners in performing at their best by adjusting the amount and level of support, regulating task difficulty, providing scaffolding cues, and enhancing knowledge retention (Gkintoni et al., 2025). By adjusting instruction and task complexity to match learners' cognitive capacity, these systems help maintain an optimal challenge within the learners' Zone of Proximal Development (ZPD).

AI-powered adaptive learning platforms have demonstrated effectiveness in sophisticated learning contexts such as STEM disciplines, medical education, and technical training (El Fathi et al., 2025; Rehman et al., 2024), where balancing cognitive load is crucial to achieving instructional goals. In addition, research studies indicate that personalised learning systems can enhance learning efficacy by minimising extraneous demands and reducing unnecessary CL. Therefore, the design of AI-powered adaptive learning platforms may enable learners to shift their focus towards germane processing for the construction of meaningful knowledge structures.

Research studies indicate that physiological monitoring (i.e., tracking learner engagement and/or emotional levels), cognitive profile analysis (i.e., tailoring content based on learners' preferences, strengths, and/or areas for improvement), dynamic scaffolding (i.e., providing guidance towards designated goals), spaced repetition optimisation (i.e., strategically timing reviews), visual learning analytics (i.e., visualising complex learning data to enhance comprehension and decision-making in challenging material), and adaptive assessment (i.e., monitoring progress and providing tailored, targeted feedback) all contribute to the effectiveness of AI-powered adaptive learning platforms (Yan et al., 2024; Gkintoni et al., 2025).

By managing cognitive load through well-structured guidance and tailored explanations, these systems facilitate deeper understanding and better retention of information (Kay, 2023; Lim et al., 2023). This cognitive scaffold is particularly important in educational contexts, where balancing students' cognitive capacity with the extensive content of school curricula and a wide array of different subjects can be challenging (Olugbade et al., 2024). AI-powered systems can help mitigate systemic challenges (i.e., dropout and stopout rates, and poor academic performance), which often result from CL (Oyekan et al., 2023). Integration of AI-powered systems into curricula helps learners effectively guide the responses, make sense of the targeted material, and optimise cognitive resources (Ko´c-Januchta et al., 2022; Mayer, 2021; Taub & Azevedo, 2023). Building on this foundation, gamification could be considered a valuable strategy for minimising CL by improving learner engagement and motivation, especially in tasks that are cognitively demanding or less intrinsically motivating by nature (Chen & Chang, 2024). Likewise, microlearning, which involves delivering educational content in short, focused segments, has demonstrated potential for reducing extraneous CL and improving learning efficiency in digital learning environments (Lopez, 2024; Susilana et al., 2022).

Yan et al., (2024) found that AI-powered platforms can significantly improve students' understanding and engagement with high-level content, visual learning analytics (VLA), particularly when designed with proactive scaffolding mechanisms. The proactive agents that provided dynamic scaffolding were integrated into a structured learning environment, going beyond the role of simple conversational agents. In addition to showing the positive impact of AI-powered learning platforms on comprehension compared to conventional standalone scaffolding, the study also offered valuable insights into the importance of instructor presence, especially in relation to planning, as well as the need for careful instructional design and effective implementation when integrating AI systems into the curriculum. These strategies include monitoring students' progress through analytics dashboards and providing timely support when needed. These findings reflect the manifesto's emphasis on thoughtful planning and highlights that AI is most effective when it works with the teacher's guidance; as students should be encouraged to think more deeply and take greater ownership of their learning (Bozkurt et al., 2024).

Within a similar framework, Ardimento et al. (2024) aimed to enhance students' understanding of software modeling by integrating AI-powered scaffolding into a structured learning environment focused on Unified Modeling Language (UML) diagrams. The study demonstrated that real-time, adaptive feedback from the AI system significantly supported learners in identifying and correcting misconceptions and helped them improve their modeling proficiency. This highlights the importance of managing a dialogic relationship between learners and AI through ongoing, collaborative exchange. This aligns with the manifesto's emphasis on structured, intentional design in the integration of GenA, where the goal is to complement or thoughtfully create new learning pathways that support connection and interaction. While GenAI may support collaborative learning by acting as a virtual peer, offering diverse perspectives, and generating feedback, these interactions must ultimately strengthen rather than replace authentic human engagement (Bozkurt et al., 2024).

Drawing on the key role of structured, intentional design in AI integration, Khasawneh and Khasawneh (2024) conducted a quantitative study to assess the cognitive load associated with different adaptive learning technologies, including AI-based platforms, virtual reality, and gamification, in special education classrooms. Their findings revealed that AI-powered platforms resulted in a higher cognitive burden compared to VR and Gamification tools. These insights highlight the critical role of adaptive scaffolding in managing cognitive load effectively, conducting a thorough planning for a deeper exploration of cognitive load considerations in AI-assisted learning environments. This echoes the emphasis on designing AI systems that respond to learners' needs rather than impose rigid automation. It is critical for educators to ensure that the technology serves to support thoughtful engagement rather than overwhelm it (Bozkurt et al., 2024).

Despite these challenges, several research studies highlight the potential of well-designed, adaptive AI systems to alleviate cognitive load and support more effective learning experiences. However, the effectiveness of these approaches may depend on unique learning contexts and individual learner characteristics (Olugbade et al., 2024). For instance, CL has been shown to be significantly influenced by learners' collaborative problem-solving (CPS) abilities and their knowledge of the subject matter (Du et al., 2023). This highlights the significance of tailoring scaffolding to align with learners' prior competencies — a domain in which AI has already begun to play a significant role, and is likely to do so even more as adaptive technologies advance. Dhillon et al. (2024) advocate for a flexible, user-centred approach to the incorporation of AI into curricula. While less experienced writers benefit from more structured (high-level) assistance, writers with greater experience may prefer lower levels of scaffolding. This aligns with the expertise reversal effect (Kalyuga, 2009), which suggests that the level of instructional support must be adjusted as learners gain proficiency, in order to avoid CL and ensure that scaffolding remains pedagogically effective and non-redundant.

Accordingly, the algorithms behind AI-powered systems should incorporate learner adaptivity, enhancing engagement and ownership rather than undermining learners' unique qualities and preferences. Thus, thoughtful instructional design remains essential in determining the appropriate degree and nature of AI-driven scaffolding that supports and facilitates meaningful schema construction across diverse learning environments.

INTEGRATING ARTIFICIAL INTELLIGENCE INTO INSTRUCTIONAL MATERIAL DESIGN

Effectively managing CL in instructional material design is critical for facilitating meaningful learning, which highlights the significance of integrating AI-supported teaching applications into the design process (Klepsch et al., 2017; Paas et al., 2004; Sweller, 2019). A key starting point is to develop a comprehensive understanding of the conceptual framework in relation to the multimedia principles. Multimedia instructional messages are defined as a form of communication that supports and complements the learning process through written, spoken, and visual elements (Mayer, 2014; Yılmaz Soylu & Akkoyunlu, 2020). Written content may be presented in either print or digital formats, while spoken explanations can take the form of narration or dialogue. Visuals encompass a wide range, from static graphics to interactive animations, all of which serve to enhance the learning experience (Mayer, 2014). These materials can be structured in a variety of formats, ranging from academic publications to interactive online courses (Mayer, 2014; Yılmaz Soylu & Akkoyunlu, 2020). A substantial number of experimental studies have demonstrated that instructional materials developed according to these principles contribute to meaningful learning outcomes across diverse learning environments (Mayer, 2024; Sayma, 2022).

AI-powered systems have brought significant advancements to the design of instructional materials in recent years (Alexander & Belloni, 2024; Fox & Vitor, 2024; Xu et al., 2024). LLMs in particular, are now widely employed across different educational applications, including the development of course content and assessment tools (Diwan et al., 2023; Leiker et al., 2023). Recent studies indicate that over 50% of educators have used ChatGPT at least once (Impact Research, 2024). This highlights the potential of LLMs to act as effective tools in the creation of teaching resources, enabling teachers to save time and effort in producing materials tailored to individual learners (Malik et al., 2025).

These tools deliver content by adapting to learners' individual differences and learning paces, contributing to the regulation of cognitive load. AI-based materials, supported by scaffolding, facilitate a gradual transition to complex concepts while also enhancing the learning process through immediate feedback (Du et al., 2022; Gkintoni et al., 2025; Souchet et al., 2022). These features help reduce undesirable levels of cognitive load by offering personalised learning experiences. Among the examples of adaptive learning, AI-powered systems such as Smart Sparrow and

Learnosity stand out for providing content tailored to students' performance (Firat, 2023). Similarly, the Personalised Study Guide (PSG) plugin, integrated into the Moodle LMS platform, customises learning by sequencing content based on users' interests (Moodle, 2024). As a result of these capabilities, such systems also offer self-regulated learning environments. With the aid of these technologies, students can set their own learning goals, monitor their performance, and restructure their learning strategies, supported by data-driven insights from learner analytics (Tapalova & Zhiyenbayeva, 2022).

One of the most important parameters educators must consider during the design of instructional materials is learner characteristics. Factors such as individual differences, prior knowledge, and the nature of the learning environment need to be taken into account (Kalyuga et al., 1998; Mayer, 2005; Park et al., 2015; Shangguan et al., 2020). CLT highlights that instructional materials can enhance learning performance by optimising the information processing load (Sweller, 2010; Gkintoni et al., 2025). In their work on educational technology, Sweller and colleagues (2019) refined the broader set of principles and identified seven core principles: worked example, split attention, modality, transience, redundancy, expertise reversal and element interactivity, and working memory depletion. For instance, the expertise reversal effect suggests that as learners become more proficient, instructional methods that are effective for novices may become redundant or even detrimental for more advanced (expert) learners (Sweller et al., 2019). Critically, AI-supported systems contribute to more efficient processing of intrinsic cognitive load by offering personalised and adaptive learning materials that eliminate undesirable extraneous load. In Mayer's (2024) recent work on principles for digital learning environments, only the modality principle (the use of both visual and auditory channels to enhance learning) is explicitly aligned with Sweller and colleagues' (2019) cognitive load framework, while the other principles — such as coherence, signalling, dual channel, spatial contiguity, and temporal contiguity — are more closely associated with the broader framework of multimedia learning theory, which builds upon and complements Cognitive Load Theory.

In this regard, considering Mayer's Spatial Contiguity Principle (2009, 2017, 2021, 2024), which emphasises that related visuals and texts should be placed in close proximity to facilitate learning, there is growing evidence of research focusing on AI-generated instructional materials. Sayma's (2023) study, for example, highlights the pedagogical potential of AI-generated multimedia materials in education, emphasising the value of placing text close to relevant graphics, providing feedback in parallel with questions, and the presentation of instructions on the same screen as the activity are key elements that support the learning process. The study also argues, in line with the Multimedia Principle, that students learn more effectively from materials that integrate text and visuals compared to those that present information through text alone (Mayer, 2009). AI-powered visualisation platforms such as DALL·E 2 and Midjourney are reported to facilitate the creation of original visuals by educators, enrich instructional materials, and enhance conceptual clarity (Sayma, 2022). Furthermore, the optimal arrangement of visual and textual elements is found to support learners' cognitive integration processes and to improve the overall effectiveness of learning (Gkintoni et al., 2025; Sayma, 2023).

Moreover, the Gamma App organises content automatically and generates AI-powered visuals aligned with the accompanying text. These tools are consistent with Mayer's (2009) multimedia principles, presenting information in both verbal and visual forms to capture learners' attention and support meaningful acquisition. The Signalling Principle, which involves emphasising critical information to facilitate learning, is another key component of multimedia learning (Mayer, 2009, 2024). Tools such as ChatGPT, Claude, Consensus, and Elicit can support the application of the Signalling Principle by helping users identify key concepts more efficiently through features such as summarisation, highlighting, or formatting. The use of bold and italic formatting draws attention to important points, enhances selective attention, and supports comprehension-based learning. A recent study by AlShaikh, Al-Malki, and Almasre (2024) demonstrated that the integration of OpenAI's Whisper ASR (Automatic Speech Recognition) model with Gemini (formerly Google Bard) can support the implementation of Mayer's principles from the Cognitive Theory of Multimedia Learning (CTML), with findings that align with prior empirical research.

In their study on second language acquisition, Xu et al. (2024) compared the effects of AI-generated instructional videos (AIIVs), created automatically from slide and text content, with traditional recorded videos (RVs) on learning performance. The findings revealed that AI-based videos optimised cognitive load and made the learning process more efficient. More specifically, AIIVs were found to reduce cognitive load by delivering more structured content and improving the alignment between visual and verbal elements. Participants reported that AIIVs felt less cognitively demanding; however, traditional videos provided a greater sense of social presence. In addition, short AI-supported videos were shown to contribute to the faster acquisition of learning outcomes compared to traditional printed materials. These results suggest that AI-enhanced content may offer more effective learning than conventional methods by improving access without increasing undesirable levels of cognitive load.

A recent study conducted in China found that animations and virtual characters used to guide students in computer-assisted learning environments may increase extraneous cognitive load and hinder the learning process. This was particularly the case when the characters featured human-like facial expressions and synchronised speech movements (Lin et al., 2020). This highlights the importance of designing visual and auditory elements in a balanced manner. On the other hand, rapidly advancing AI technologies offer significant advantages in cognitive load management. The Worked Example Principle aims to reduce cognitive load by minimising interaction and providing direct guidance, especially for novice learners (Kirschner et al., 2006; Sweller et al., 2007; Sweller et al., 2019). In this context, AI-supported learning systems can strengthen the impact of worked examples by offering scaffolding through dynamic guidance mechanisms based on student feedback, ultimately enabling more personalised learning experiences.

Recent studies have demonstrated the positive effects of AI tools in managing cognitive load (Gkintoni et al., 2024; Hong & Guo, 2024). For instance, Chen and Wu (2024) developed a system for poetry instruction that integrates AI-based modules for text comprehension, visual generation, and video production. The system was found to reduce extraneous cognitive load. In a different instructional context, Appiah Twumasi (2024) reported that the use of scaffolding in teaching nuclear physics reduced extraneous cognitive load and resulted in statistically significant improvements in the experimental group. Extending this line of research, Sola et al. (2024) employed eye-tracking technology to analyse students' levels of focus and cognitive load, with findings indicating that increased attention was associated with a reduction in extraneous load.

In parallel with these pedagogical developments, AI models developed since 2022 have enabled the generation of human-like, contextually appropriate, and coherent speech (Li et al., 2023; Liao et al., 2024). In this context, tools such as Synthesia convert written texts into videos with talking avatars, offering natural speech with different accents and tones, thus making teacher explanations more engaging (Synthesia.io, 2025). These applications align well with Mayer's (2017) Personalisation and Voice Principles. In particular, the use of human voice, as opposed to synthetic or mechanical speech, has been shown to positively influence learning. In this framework, it is essential to reduce extraneous cognitive load, manage intrinsic cognitive load effectively, and optimise germane cognitive load during instructional design (Sweller et al., 2019). When designed in alignment with sound instructional principles, AI tools not only support cognitive load management but also have the potential to improve learning outcomes.

GAMIFICATION, COGNITIVE LOAD AND SCAFFOLDING

In the post-pandemic context, learners' struggles to achieve academic success in digital learning environments have further highlighted the pressing need for structured and sustained support (Malik et al., 2025). In this context, the integration of game-based learning approaches into learning processes has been shown to enhance cognitive engagement, foster motivation, and improve task persistence, particularly for learners interacting with digital tools (Liu, 2024). As this generation grows up immersed in digital technologies, it is essential that pedagogical approaches are responsive to the realities of the time and designed to provide meaningful, adaptive learning experiences (Bozkurt et. al., 2024; Yıldızhan Bora, 2024). Their tendency towards engaging and interactive stimuli plays a pivotal role in managing cognitive load and improving learning efficiency (Agarwal & Tayal, 2022; Hong & Guo, 2024). Notably, research shows that nearly half of students perform below grade level in at least one subject, clearly highlighting the need for embedded and systematic scaffolding in digital learning environments (Irwin et al., 2023).

Gamification is an innovative learning design that is applied across all levels of education, from early childhood to higher education. It contributes to the development of learners' cognitive and affective outcomes, such as attention, motivation and engagement (Oliveira et al., 2023). This approach involves the integration of game elements such as points, badges, avatars, and task completion into non-game contexts (Zichermann & Cunningham, 2011). When incorporated into instructional strategies, gamification has the potential to transform scaffolding processes in digital environments into more engaging, dynamic and learner-centred experiences. Features such as badges, progression systems, task completion, leaderboards and virtual rewards have been found to boost learning motivation (Lee & Kim, 2025; Li et al., 2024; Jack et al., 2024).

However, many gamification designs offer uniform stimuli to all learners, often overlooking individual differences. This "one-size-fits-all" approach may impede the development of meaningful and lasting learning outcomes (Suresh Babu & Dhakshina, 2023). It is therefore essential to design gamification in ways that address individual learners' needs and preferences. Yet, when these elements are not optimised appropriately, particularly for individuals who are less familiar with digital tools, they may result in distraction, cognitive fatigue and disengagement from the learning process (Ng & Lo, 2022).

AI-supported learning environments offer opportunities to personalise the learning process by adapting content difficulty and pacing to individual needs. Through capabilities such as optimised resource selection, these systems aim to enhance learning efficiency and improve the quality of outcomes (Gupta, 2024). In addition, artificial intelligence can serve as an effective tool for tailoring gamification and scaffolding approaches to individual learners. By analysing students' learning pathways, these systems provide adaptive task suggestions, real-time feedback and personalised support, helping to create more interactive and motivating experiences (Hong & Guo, 2025; Kaswan et al., 2024). As a result, content and its delivery are tailored to individual learners, promoting deeper understanding and greater motivation (Ejjami, 2024). Multilayered support strategies such as the use of prompts, modelling techniques, graphic organisers, visual representations and in-depth questioning can be effectively integrated into digital environments and complemented by gamification elements to construct personalised learning pathways (Drew, 2022). These structures help balance CL while supporting students' task effort, metacognitive awareness and independent learning (Chen et al., 2023; Şahin Kölemen & Yıldızhan Bora, 2025; Zuo et al., 2023).

Recent studies highlight promising developments in the integration of gamification and AI-driven personalisation. Naseer et al. (2025) developed an online learning framework that combines gamification elements with AI-supported personalisation features. Conducted over eight weeks with 250 students (experimental = 125, control = 125), the experimental study revealed a statistically significant difference in post-test scores in favour of the experimental group. These findings suggest that the integration of gamification and artificial intelligence can be considered an effective approach in digital learning environments. In this context, AI-supported personalised learning and gamified components function as scaffolding mechanisms within the framework of Vygotsky's Zone of Proximal Development, positively influencing learners. Gkintoni et al. (2025) demonstrated that the integration of artificial intelligence with neuroadaptive systems enables the continuous monitoring of CL and the provision of dynamic support mechanisms accordingly. Similarly, Chen and Chang (2024) examined the effectiveness of AI-integrated game-based learning environments. In their experimental study, Year 7 students were divided into three groups: (1) game only, (2) AI-supported game, and (3) AI-supported game enriched with examples. Their findings revealed that both AI-supported groups exhibited lower CL and higher motivation, lending further support to the claim that AI integration, particularly when combined with example-based approaches, can enhance learning outcomes. This is consistent with the worked examples approach proposed by Sweller et al. (2019).

Beyond AI integration, recent studies have also explored the impact of gamified design within multimedia learning environments. In an experimental study conducted by Lee and Kim (2024), a practical implementation was carried out with a total of 48 participants divided into control and experimental groups. As part of the research, a gamified video-based learning environment was designed by integrating various game elements into an instructional video, including objectives, sub-tasks, rules, progress indicators, time constraints, and real-time feedback. The findings revealed that the gamified video had a positive impact on students' germane CL, intrinsic motivation, learning satisfaction, and academic achievement. Qualitative results supported these findings, indicating that the gamified video reduced extraneous CL and provided a more effective and engaging learning experience by increasing students' cognitive effort toward learning goals.

Recent studies have highlighted the importance of designing gamified and AI-supported learning environments that not only engage learners but also support the cognitive architecture of learning. In an experimental study conducted by Hong and Guo (2025), the impact of AI-supported multi-screen language learning systems on higher education students was investigated, with particular attention given to the dimension of cognitive load management. The findings showed that students in the experimental group managed their CL more effectively than those in the control group, indicating that such technological systems contribute meaningfully to the learning process. In a separate study, Topu (2023) found that gamification-based course designs led to differences in students' learning attitudes depending on their levels of CL. The study particularly emphasised that gamified content designed with low extraneous load enhanced students' motivation and engagement. Collectively, these studies suggest that both AI-supported systems and cognitively optimised gamification practices improve the effectiveness of the learning process. These findings align with Sweller's Cognitive Load Theory. The theoretical framework developed after Sweller et al. (2019) not only highlights the limits of cognitive capacity but also illustrates how these limits can be balanced through technology-enhanced pedagogical tools. In this context, it becomes clear that gamification should not only include attention-grabbing elements, but also provide coherent content and structural integrity that supports the cognitive foundations of learning and reflects its underlying architecture (Lee & Hughes, 2019).

CLT has recently gained renewed attention, particularly regarding its application in digital learning environments and AI-supported systems. Sweller (2023) describes the theory as dynamic and continuously evolving in response to technological advances and emerging research. Sweller et al. (2019) also emphasise the growing relevance of CLT in the context of digital education. Supporting this perspective, recent research suggests that narrative-based e-learning systems may reduce extraneous cognitive load and promote germane processing, particularly for novice learners (Darejeh et al., 2021).

In this context, gamification elements, which are widely used in AI-supported learning environments, should be carefully considered from a cognitive load perspective. Research suggests that features such as badges, tasks and level progression can promote germane load when they are visually salient and aligned with instructional goals (Baah et al., 2024; Skulmowski & Xu, 2022). However, when such elements are overly complex, distracting or unrelated to learning objectives, they may increase extraneous cognitive load and negatively affect the learning process. Accordingly, AI-based gamification designs should take into account factors such as task relevance, alignment with cognitive demands, and their contribution to information processing. Such considerations are essential to ensuring that gamified learning environments support, rather than hinder, cognitive efficiency.

REFERENCES

Adiguzel, T., Kaya, M. H., & Cansu, F. K. (2023). Revolutionizing education with AI: Exploring the transformative potential of ChatGPT. *Contemporary Educational Technology, 15*(3), ep429. DOI: 10.30935/cedtech/13152

Agarwal, N., & Tayal, D. K. (2022). FFT-based ensembled model to predict ranks of higher educational institutions. *Multimedia Tools and Applications, 81*(23), 34129–34162. DOI: 10.1007/s11042-022-13180-9

Al-Shaikh, R., Al-Malki, N., & Almasre, M. (2024). The implementation of the cognitive theory of multimedia learning in the design and evaluation of an AI educational video assistant utilizing large language models. *Heliyon*, 10. https://doi.org/10.1016/j.heliyon.2024.e25361 PMID: 38352730

Alali, R., & Wardat, Y. (2024). Opportunities and Challenges of Integrating Generative Artificial Intelligence in Education. *International Journal of Religion, 5*(7), 784–793. DOI: 10.61707/8y29gv34

Alasadi, E., & Baiz, C. (2023). Generative AI in education and research: Opportunities, concerns, and solutions. *Journal of Chemical Education, 100*(8), 2965–2971. DOI: 10.1021/acs.jchemed.3c00323

Alexander, W. R. J., & Belloni, R. (2024). Artificial Intelligence and the Sustainability of the Signaling and Human Capital Roles of Higher Education. *Sustainability (Basel), 16*(20), 8802. DOI: 10.3390/su16208802

Appiah-Twumasi, E. (2024). Scaffolding as a cognitive load reduction strategy for teaching atomic and nuclear physics. *Momentum: Physics Education Journal, 8*(2), 194–209. DOI: 10.21067/mpej.v8i2.9580

Ardimento, P., Bernardi, M. L., Cimitile, M., & Scalera, M. (2024, September). Enhancing Software Modeling Learning with AI-Powered Scaffolding. In *Proceedings of the ACM/IEEE 27th International Conference on Model Driven Engineering Languages and Systems* (pp. 103-106).https://doi.org/DOI: 10.1145/3652620.3687776

Bozkurt, A., Xiao, J., Farrow, R., Bai, J. Y. H., Nerantzi, C., Moore, S., Dron, J., Stracke, C. M., Singh, L., Crompton, H., Koutropoulos, A., Terentev, E., Pazurek, A., Nichols, M., Sidorkin, A. M., Costello, E., Watson, S., Mulligan, D., Honeychurch, S., & Asino, T. I. (2024). The Manifesto for Teaching and Learning in a Time of Generative AI: A Critical Collective Stance to Better Navigate the Future. *Open Praxis, 16*(4), 487–513. DOI: 10.55982/openpraxis.16.4.777

Bulathwela, S., Muse, H., & Yilmaz, E. (2023). Scalable Educational Question Generation with Pre-trained Language Models. In Wang, N., Rebolledo-Mendez, G., Matsuda, N., Santos, O. C., & Dimitrova, V. (Eds.), Lecture Notes in Computer Science: Vol. 13916. *Artificial Intelligence in Education. AIED 2023*. Springer., DOI: 10.1007/978-3-031-36272-9_27

Cain, W. (2024). Prompting Change: Exploring Prompt Engineering in Large Language Model AI and Its Potential to Transform Education. *TechTrends*, *68*(1), 47–57. DOI: 10.1007/s11528-023-00896-0

CAST. (2024). *Universal design for learning guidelines*. https://udlguidelines.cast .org/

Chen, C. H., & Chang, C. L. (2024). Effectiveness of AI-assisted game-based learning on science learning outcomes, intrinsic motivation, cognitive load, and learning behavior. *Education and Information Technologies, 29*(14), 18621-18642https://doi .org/DOI: 10.1007/s10639-024-12553-x

Chen, M. F., Chen, Y. C., Zuo, P. Y., & Hou, H. T. (2023). Design and evaluation of a remote synchronous gamified mathematics teaching activity that integrates multi-representational scaffolding and a mind tool for gamified learning. *Education and Information Technologies*, *28*(10), 13207–13233. DOI: 10.1007/s10639-023-11708-6 PMID: 37361748

Chen, X., & Wu, D. (2024). Automatic generation of multimedia teaching materials based on generative AI: Taking Tang poetry as an example. *IEEE transactions on learning technologies*.https://ieeexplore.ieee.org/abstract/document/10474169

da Silva, P. F., & Rockenbach Tarouco, L. M. (2022, September). A Scaffolding Strategy to Organize Collaborative Learning. In *International Conference on Interactive Collaborative Learning*(pp. 171-182). Cham: Springer International Publishing.https://doi.org/DOI: 10.1007/978-3-031-26876-2_16

Darejeh, A., Marcus, N., & Sweller, J. (2021). The effect of narrative-based E-learning systems on novice users' cognitive load while learning software applications. *Educational Technology Research and Development*, *69*(5), 2451–2473. DOI: 10.1007/s11423-021-10024-5

Dhillon, P. S., Molaei, S., Li, J., Golub, M., Zheng, S., & Robert, L. P. (2024). Shaping Human-AI Collaboration: Varied Scaffolding Levels in Co-writing with Language Models. *Proceedings of the CHI Conference on Human Factors in Computing Systems*. https://doi.org/DOI: 10.1145/3613904.3642134

Diwan, C., Srinivasa, S., Suri, G., Agarwal, S., & Ram, P. (2023). AI- based learning content generation and learning pathway augmentation to increase learner engagement. *Computers & Education*, *4*, 100110. DOI: 10.1016/j.caeai.2022.100110

Doughty, J., Wan, Z., Bompelli, A., Qayum, J., Wang, T., Zhang, J., Zheng, Y., Doyle, A., Sridhar, P., Agarwal, A., Bogart, C., Keylor, E., Kultur, C., Savelka, J., & Sakr, M. (2024). *A comparative study of AI-generated (GPT-4) and human-crafted MCQs in programming education*. In *Proceedings of the 26th Australasian Computing Education Conference* (pp. 114–123). Association for Computing Machinery. https://doi.org/DOI: 10.1145/3636243.3636256

Dowling, M., & Lucey, B. (2023). ChatGPT for (finance) research: The Bananarama conjecture. *Finance Research Letters*, *53*, 103662. DOI: 10.1016/j.frl.2023.103662

Drew, C. (2022). 18 scaffolding examples in education. Helpful Professor. Retrieved from https://helpfulprofessor.com/scaffolding-examples-in-education

Du, X., Dai, M., Tang, H., Hung, J. L., Li, H., & Zheng, J. (2023). A multimodal analysis of college students' collaborative problem solving in virtual experimentation activities: A perspective of cognitive load. *Journal of Computing in Higher Education*, *35*(2), 272–295. DOI: 10.1007/s12528-022-09311-8 PMID: 35370382

Ejjami, R. (2024). The Adaptive Personalization Theory of Learning: Revolutionizing Education with AI. *Journal of Next-Generation Research 5.0*. https://doi.org/DOI: 10.70792/jngr5.0.v1i1.8

El Fathi, T., Saad, A., Larhzil, H., Lamri, D., & Al Ibrahmi, E. M. (2025). Integrating generative AI into STEM education: Enhancing conceptual understanding, addressing misconceptions, and assessing student acceptance. *Disciplinary and Interdisciplinary Science Education Research*, *7*(1), 6. DOI: 10.1186/s43031-025-00125-z

Elkins, S., Kochmar, E., Cheung, J. C. K., & Serban, I. (2024). How Teachers Can Use Large Language Models and Bloom's Taxonomy to Create Educational Quizzes. *Proceedings of the AAAI Conference on Artificial Intelligence*, *38*(21), 23084–23091. DOI: 10.1609/aaai.v38i21.30353

Fırat, M. (2023). Integrating AI Applications into Learning Management Systems to Enhance e-Learning. *Instructional Technology and Lifelong Learning*, *4*(1), 1–14. DOI: 10.52911/itall.1244453

Fox, S., & Vitor, F. R. (2024). A cognitive load theory (CLT) analysis of machine learning explainability, transparency, interpretability, and shared interpretability. *Machine Learning and Knowledge Extraction*, *6*(3), 1494–1509. DOI: 10.3390/make6030071

Garcia, M. B., Rosak-Szyrocka, J., Yilmaz, R., Metwally, A. H. S., Acut, D. P., Ofosu-Ampong, K., Erdoğdu, F., Fung, C. Y., & Bozkurt, A. (2025). *Rethinking educational assessment in the age of generative AI: Actionable strategies to mitigate academic dishonesty*. In *Pitfalls of AI Integration in Education: Skill Obsolescence, Misuse, and Bias* (pp. 1–24). IGI Global. https://doi.org/DOI: 10.4018/979-8-3373-0122-8.ch001

Ge, R., Lu, J., & Hao, X. (2025). Exploring the impact of generative artificial intelligence scaffolding on university students' collaborative knowledge building. *Journal of Higher Education Research*, *5*(6), 570–578. https://en.front-sci.com/index.php/jher/article/view/3391/3685. DOI: 10.32629/jher.v5i6.3391

Gkintoni, E., Antonopoulou, H., Sortwell, A., & Halkiopoulos, C. (2025). Challenging Cognitive Load Theory: The Role of Educational Neuroscience and Artificial Intelligence in Redefining Learning Efficacy. *Brain Sciences*, *15*(2), 203. DOI: 10.3390/brainsci15020203 PMID: 40002535

Goddard, Y., Goddard, R., & Kim, M. (2015). School instructional climate and student achievement: An examination of group norms for differentiated instruction. *American Journal of Education*, *122*(1), 111–131. DOI: 10.1086/683293

Gupta, T. (2024). Adaptive learning systems: Harnessing AI to personalize educational outcomes. *International Journal for Research in Applied Science and Engineering Technology*, *12*(11), 458–464. DOI: 10.22214/ijraset.2024.65088

Halkiopoulos, C., & Gkintoni, E. (2024). Leveraging AI in e-learning: Personalized learning and adaptive assessment through cognitive neuropsychology—A systematic analysis. *Electronics (Basel)*, *13*(18), 3762. DOI: 10.3390/electronics13183762

Heston, T. F., & Khun, C. (2023). Prompt Engineering in Medical Education. *International Medical Education*, *2*(3), 198–205. DOI: 10.3390/ime2030019

Hocky, G. M., & White, A. D. (2022). Natural language processing models that automate programming will transform chemistry research and teaching. *Digital Discovery*, *1*(2), 79–83. DOI: 10.1039/D1DD00009H PMID: 35515080

Holmes, W., Bialik, M. and Fadel, C. (2023) Artificial Intelligence in Education. Globethics Publications, 621-653. https://doi.org/DOI: 10.58863/20.500.12424/4276068

Hong, X., & Guo, L. (2025). Effects of AI-enhanced multi-display language teaching systems on learning motivation, cognitive load management, and learner autonomy. *Education and Information Technologies*, *30*(12), 17155–17189. Advance online publication. DOI: 10.1007/s10639-025-13472-1

Hutson, J., & Plate, D. (2023). *Human-AI Collaboration for Smart Education: Reframing Applied Learning to Support Metacognition*. IntechOpen., DOI: 10.5772/intechopen.1001832

Ilkou, E., Linzbach, S., & Wallat, J. (2024). *Hybrid Evaluation of Socratic Questioning for Teaching*. In *Proceedings of the 23rd International Semantic Web Conference (ISWC'24)*, Baltimore, USA. Retrieved fromhttps://www.researchgate.net/publication/385516268

Impact Research. (2024). *AI chatbots in schools: Findings from a poll of K–12 teachers, students, parents, and college undergraduates*. https://8ce82b94a8c4fdc3ea6d-b1d233e3bc3cb10858bea65ff05e18f2.ssl.cf2.rackcdn.com/bf/24/cd3646584af89e7c668c7705a006/deck-impact-analysis-national-schools-tech-tracker-may-2024-1.pdf

Irwin, V., Wang, K., Tezil, T., Zhang, J., Filbey, A., Jung, J., & Parker, S. (2023). Report on the condition of education 2023. NCES 2023- 144 (Tech. Rep.). National Center for Education Statistics. https://nces.ed.gov/use-work/resource-library/report/compendium/condition-education-2023?pubid=2023144

Ivanović, I. (2025). Cognitive load in AI-assisted vs traditional foreign language classroom: Mixed methods research. Disputatio Philosophica. *International Journal for Philosophy of Religion*, *6*, 361–380. DOI: 10.18485/dpls_plucast.2025.6.ch22

Jack, E., Alexander, C., & Jones, E. M. (2024). Levelling up learning: Exploring the impact of gamification in flipped classrooms. *University of Glasgow*. https://arxiv.org/html/2402.18313v1

Jensen, C. G., Dau, S., & Gade, P. (2024). *The role of AI chatbots in scaffolding: Linking learning outcomes with assessment*. Learning Tech – Tidsskrift for læremidler, didaktik og teknologi, (14), 73–97. https://tidsskrift.dk/learningtech/article/view/141213

Jin, L., Lin, B., Hong, M., Zhang, K., & So, H.-J. (2025). *Exploring the impact of an LLM-powered teachable agent on learning gains and cognitive load in music education*. arXiv. https://arxiv.org/abs/2504.00636

Jury, B., Lorusso, A., Leinonen, J., & Denny, P., & Luxton- Reilly, A. (2024). Evaluating LLM- generated worked examples in an introductory programming course. In *Proceedings of the 26th Australasian Computing Education Conference* (pp. 77–86). Association for Computing Machinery. . DOI: 10.1145/3636243.3636252

Kalyuga, S. (2009). The expertise reversal effect. In *Managing cognitive load in adaptive multimedia learning* (pp. 58–80). IGI Global., DOI: 10.4018/978-1-60566-048-6.ch003

Kalyuga, S., Chandler, P., & Sweller, J. (1998). Levels of Expertise and Instructional Design. *Human Factors, 40*(1), 1–17. DOI: 10.1518/001872098779480587

Kamali, J., Alpat, M. F., & Bozkurt, A. (2024). AI ethics as a complex and multifaceted challenge: Decoding educators' AI ethics alignment through the lens of activity theory. *International Journal of Educational Technology in Higher Education, 21*(1), 62. DOI: 10.1186/s41239-024-00496-9

Kaswan, K. S., Dhatterwal, J. S., & Ojha, R. P. (2024). AI in personalized learning. In *Advances in technological innovations in higher education* (pp. 103–117). CRC Press. DOI: 10.1201/9781003376699-9

Khasawneh, Y. J. A., & Khasawneh, M. A. S. (2024). Cognitive load analysis of adaptive learning technologies in special education classrooms: A quantitative approach. *International Journal of Advanced and Applied Sciences, 11*(12), 34–41. https://www.science-gate.com/IJAAS/2024/V11I12/1021833ijaas202412004.html. DOI: 10.21833/ijaas.2024.12.004

Khosrawi-Rad, B., Rinn, H., Schlimbach, R., Gebbing, P., Yang, X., Lattemann, C., ... & Robra-Bissantz, S. (2022). Conversational agents in education–a systematic literature review. https://www.researchgate.net/publication/361039365_Conversational_Agents_in_Education_-_A_Systematic_Literature_Review

Kim, J., Yu, S., Detrick, R., & Li, N. (2024). Exploring students' perspectives on generative AI-assisted academic writing. *Education and Information Technologies, 30*(1), 1265–1300. DOI: 10.1007/s10639-024-12878-7

Kim, P. W. (2024). Fog Computing for Artificial Intelligence Digital Textbooks: Educational Scaffolding and Security and Privacy Challenges. *Expert Systems: International Journal of Knowledge Engineering and Neural Networks, 13801*. Advance online publication. DOI: 10.1111/exsy.13801

Kirschner, P., Sweller, J., & Clark, R. (2006). Why minimal guidance during instruction does not work: An analysis of the failure of constructivist, discovery, problem-based, experiential and inquiry based teaching. *Educational Psychologist, 41*(2), 75–86. DOI: 10.1207/s15326985ep4102_1

Klepsch, M., Schmitz, F., & Seufert, T. (2017). Development and Validation of Two Instruments Measuring Intrinsic, Extraneous, and Germane Cognitive Load. *Frontiers in Psychology, 8*, 1997. DOI: 10.3389/fpsyg.2017.01997 PMID: 29201011

Ko'c-Januchta, M. M., Schonborn, ̈. K. J., Roehrig, C., Chaudhri, V. K., Tibell, L. A., & Heller, H. C. (2022). "Connecting concepts helps put main ideas together": Cognitive load and usability in learning biology with an AI-enriched textbook. *International Journal of Educational Technology in Higher Education, 19*(1), 11. DOI: 10.1186/s41239-021-00317-3

Korbach, A., Brünken, R., & Park, B. (2018). Differentiating different types of cognitive load: A comparison of different measures. *Educational Psychology Review, 30*(2), 503–529. DOI: 10.1007/s10648-017-9404-8

Krishna, L., Prasad, J., & Anjali, S. (2024). The Impact of Artificial Intelligence in Reshaping Education: An Analysis Based on Learning Theories. In *ITM Web of Conferences* (Vol. 68, p. 01008). EDP Sciences.DOI: 10.1051/itmconf/20246801008

Lademann, J., Henze, J., & Becker-Genschow, S. (2025). Augmenting learning environments using AI custom chatbots: Effects on learning performance, cognitive load, and affective variables. *Physical Review. Physics Education Research, 21*(1), 010147. DOI: 10.1103/PhysRevPhysEducRes.21.010147

Lee, C. S., & Hughes, J. H. (2019). Refocusing on cognitive load design through a meta-analysis on learnability, goal-based intentions and extensibility: towards personalized cognitive-social-affective engagement among seniors. In *Advancing Technology Industrialization Through Intelligent Software Methodologies, Tools and Techniques* (pp. 456-469). IOS Press.

Lee, J., & Kim, D. (2025). Levelling up learning in higher education: Gamification of in-video components to supercharge student learning and achievement in video-based learning. *British Journal of Educational Technology.* Advance online publication. https://bera-journals.onlinelibrary.wiley.com/doi/abs/10.1111/bjet.13564

Leiker, D., Finnigan, S., Gyllen, A. R., & Cukurova, M. (2023). Prototyping the use of Large Language Models (LLMs) for adult learning content creation at scale. arXiv preprint. https://arxiv.org/abs/2306.01815

Li, C., Liang, L., Fryer, L. K., & Shum, A. (2024). The use of leaderboards in education: A systematic review of empirical evidence in higher education. *Journal of Computer Assisted Learning.* Advance online publication. https://onlinelibrary.wiley.com/doi/abs/10.1111/jcal.13077

Li, Y., Sha, L., Yan, L., Lin, J., Raković, M., Galbraith, K., Lyons, K., Gašević, D., & Chen, G. (2023). Can large language models write reflectively. *Computers and Education: Artificial Intelligence, 4*, 100140. DOI: 10.1016/j.caeai.2023.100140

Liao, J., Zhong, L., Zhe, L., Xu, H., Liu, M., & Xie, T. (2024). Scaffolding computational thinking with ChatGPT. *IEEE Transactions on Learning Technologies*, *17*, 1628–1642. DOI: 10.1109/TLT.2024.3392896

Limo, F. A. F., Tiza, D. R. H., Roque, M. M., Herrera, E. E., Murillo, J. P. M., Huallpa, J. J., Flores, V. A. A., Castillo, A. G. R., Peña, P. F. P., Carranza, C. P. M., & Gonzáles, J. L. A. (2023). Personalized tutoring: ChatGPT as a virtual tutor for personalized learning experiences. *Przestrzen Spoleczna*, *23*(1), 292–312.

Lin, L., Ginns, P., Wang, T., & Zhang, P. (2020). Using a pedagogical agent to deliver conversational style instruction: What benefits can you obtain? *Computers & Education*, *143*, 103658. DOI: 10.1016/j.compedu.2019.103658

Liu, L. (2024). Impact of AI gamification on EFL learning outcomes and nonlinear dynamic motivation: Comparing adaptive learning paths, conversational agents, and storytelling. *Education and Information Technologies*. Advance online publication. DOI: 10.1007/s10639-024-13296-5

Lopez, S. (2024). The Impact of Cognitive Load Theory on the Effectiveness of Microlearning Modules. *European Journal of Education and Pedagogy*, *5*(2), 29–35. DOI: 10.24018/ejedu.2024.5.2.799

Malik, R., Abdi, D., Wang, R., & Demszky, D. (2025). Scaffolding middle school mathematics curricula with large language models. *British Journal of Educational Technology*, *56*(3), 999–1027. Advance online publication. DOI: 10.1111/bjet.13571

Mayer, R. E. (Ed.). (2005). *The Cambridge handbook of multimedia learning*. Cambridge University Press., DOI: 10.1017/CBO9780511816819

Mayer, R. E. (2008). Applying the science of learning: Evidence-based principles for the design of multimedia instruction. *The American Psychologist*, *63*(8), 760–769. DOI: 10.1037/0003-066X.63.8.760 PMID: 19014238

Mayer, R. E. (2009). *Multimedia Learning* (2nd ed.). Cambridge University Press. DOI: 10.1017/CBO9780511811678

Mayer, R. E. (2010). Applying the Science of Learning to Medical Education. *Medical Education*, *39*(6), 169–175. DOI: 10.1111/j.1365-2923.2010.03624.x PMID: 20604850

Mayer, R. E. (2014). Cognitive theory of multimedia learning. In Mayer, R. E. (Ed.), *The Cambridge handbook of multimedia learning* (2nd ed., pp. 43–71). Cambridge University Press., DOI: 10.1017/CBO9781139547369.005

Mayer, R. E. (2017). Using multimedia for e-learning. *Journal of Computer Assisted Learning*, *33*(5), 403–423. DOI: 10.1111/jcal.12197

Mayer, R. E. (2021). *Multimedia learning* (3rd ed.). Cambridge University Press.

Mayer, R. E. (2024). Increasing the Effectiveness of Digital Learning. In Gegenfurtner, A., & Kollar, I. (Eds.), *Designing Effective Digital Learning Environments* (pp. 279–288). Routledge. DOI: 10.4324/9781003386131-26

Mhlanga, D. (2023). Open AI in education, the responsible and ethical use of ChatGPT: Towards lifelong learning. https://doi.org/DOI: 10.1007/978-3-031-37776-1_17

Moodle. (2024, February 15). *Personalised Study Guide format.* https://moodle.org/plugins/format_psg

Naseer, F., Khan, M. N., Addas, A., Awais, Q., & Ayub, N. (2025). Game Mechanics and Artificial Intelligence Personalization: A Framework for Adaptive Learning Systems. *Education Sciences*, *15*(3), 301. DOI: 10.3390/educsci15030301

Naznin, K., Al Mahmud, A., Nguyen, M. T., & Chua, C. (2025). ChatGPT Integration in Higher Education for Personalized Learning, Academic Writing, and Coding Tasks: A Systematic Review. *Computers*, *14*(2), 53. DOI: 10.3390/computers14020053

Ng, L.-K., & Lo, C.-K. (2022). Online Flipped and Gamification Classroom: Risks and Opportunities for the Academic Achievement of Adult Sustainable Learning during COVID-19 Pandemic. *Sustainability (Basel)*, *14*(19), 12396. DOI: 10.3390/su141912396

Oliveira, W., Hamari, J., Shi, L., Toda, A. M., Rodrigues, L., Palomino, P. T., & Isotani, S. (2023). Tailored gamification in education: A literature review and future agenda. *Education and Information Technologies*, *28*(1), 373–406. DOI: 10.1007/s10639-022-11122-4

Olugbade, D., Edwards, B. I., & Ojo, O. A. (2024). Facilitating cognitive load management and improved learning outcomes and attitudes in middle school technology and vocational education through AI chatbot. *Journal of Technical Education and Training*, *16*(3), 114–131. https://doibet.org/10.30880/jtet.2024.16.03.009. DOI: 10.30880/jtet.2024.16.03.009

Oyekan, K., Ayorinde, A., & Adenuga, O. (2023). The problem of out-of-school children in Nigeria. *RISE Insights*, *58*(1). Advance online publication. DOI: 10.35489/BSG-RISE-RI_2023/058

Paas, F., Renkl, A., & Sweller, J. (2004). Cognitive Load Theory: Instructional Implications of the Interaction between Information Structures and Cognitive Architecture. *Instructional Science, 32*(1/2), 1–8. http://www.jstor.org/stable/41953634. DOI: 10.1023/B:TRUC.0000021806.17516.d0

Paivio, A. (1986). *Mental representations: A dual coding approach.* Oxford University Press.

Park, B., Knörzer, L., Plass, J. L., & Brünken, R. (2015). Emotional design and positive emotions in multimedia learning: An eyetracking study on the use of anthropomorphisms. *Computers & Education, 86*, 30–42. DOI: 10.1016/j.compedu.2015.02.016

Patac, L. P., & Patac, A. V.Jr. (2025). Using ChatGPT for academic support: Managing cognitive load and enhancing learning efficiency – A phenomenological approach. *Social Sciences & Humanities Open, 11*, 101301. DOI: 10.1016/j.ssaho.2025.101301

Prihar, E., Lee, M., Hopman, M., Kalai, A. T., Vempala, S., Wang, A., & Heffernan, N. (2023). Comparing different approaches to generating mathematics explanations using large language models. In N. Wang, G. Rebolledo- Mendez, V. Dimitrova, N. Matsuda, & O. C. Santos (Eds.), *Artificial intelligence in education. Posters and late breaking results, workshops and tutorials, industry and innovation tracks, practitioners, doctoral consortium and blue sky* (pp. 290–295). Springer Nature Switzerland DOI: 10.1007/978-3-031-36336-8_45

Qadir, J. (2022). Engineering education in the era of ChatGPT: Promise and pitfalls of generative AI for education. *TechRxiv*. Preprint. https://doi.org/DOI: 10.36227/techrxiv.21789434.v1

Rehman, A., Mehfooz, Q., Saleem, Q., Ikram, N., Sadiq, M. S., Javaid, N., & Tahir, F. N. (2024). Artificial intelligence-assisted learning in medical education: A randomized study on its effectiveness. *African Journal of Biological Sciences, 6*(2), 4209–4215. DOI: 10.48047/AFJBS.6.16.2024.4209-4215

Rodriguez- Torrealba, R., Garcia- Lopez, E., & Garcia- Cabot, A. (2022). End- to-end generation of multiple- choice questions using text- to- text transfer transformer models. *Expert Systems with Applications, 208*(118), 258. https://www.sciencedirect.com/science/article/pii/S0957417422014014?via%3Dihub

Sætra, H. S. (2022). Scaffolding human champions: AI as a more competent other. *Human Arenas*, 1-23.https://hdl.handle.net/11250/3015827

Şahin Kölemen, C., & Yıldızhan Bora, B. (2025). Oyunlaştırılmış eğitim platformlarının bilişsel yükü azaltmadaki rolü [The role of gamified educational platforms in reducing cognitive load]. *15th International Congress on Social, Humanities, Administrative, and Educational Sciences in a Changing World Full Text Proceedings Book*. Akademik Platform Yayınları. https://doi.org/DOI: 10.30546/19023.978-9952-8545-8-9.2025.601

Sayma, S. R. (2023). *Creating effective multimedia learning material with AI for K12*. https://edtechbooks.s3.us-west-2.amazonaws.com/pdfs/713/13501.pdf

Shangguan, C., Gong, S., Guo, Y., Wang, X., & Lu, J. (2020). The effects of emotional design on middle school students' multimedia learning: The role of learners' prior knowledge. *Educational Psychology*, *40*(9), 1076–1093. DOI: 10.1080/01443410.2020.1714548

Shimmei, M., Bier, N., & Matsuda, N. (2023). Machine- generated questions attract instructors when acquainted with learning objectives. In N. Wang, G. Rebolledo-Mendez, N. Matsuda, O. C. Santos, & V. Dimitrova (Eds.), *Artificial intelligence in education* (pp. 3–15). Springer Nature Switzerland. https://doi.org/10.1007/978-3-031-36272-9_1

Shokoohifar, M. (2024). *Artificial Intelligence-Assisted Translation: A Study of Cognitive Load and Time Through EEG*(Doctoral dissertation, Allameh Tabataba'i University).

Skulmowski, A., & Xu, K. M. (2022). Understanding cognitive load in digital and online learning: A new perspective on extraneous cognitive load. *Educational Psychology Review*, *34*(1), 171–196. DOI: 10.1007/s10648-021-09624-7

Sorden, S. D. (2013). The cognitive theory of multimedia learning. In B. J. Irby, G. Brown, R. Lara-Alecio, & S. Jackson (Eds.), *The handbook of educational theories* (pp. 155–167). IAP Information Age Publishing.

Souchet, A. D., Philippe, S., Lourdeaux, D., & Leroy, L. (2022). Measuring visual fatigue and cognitive load via eye tracking while learning with virtual reality head-mounted displays: A review. *International Journal of Human-Computer Interaction*, *38*(9), 801–824. DOI: 10.1080/10447318.2021.1976509

Stanislaw, P. (2024). Solving the global STEM educational crisis using Cognitive Load Optimization and Artificial Intelligence–A preliminary comparative analysis. *Eurasia Journal of Mathematics, Science and Technology Education*, *20*(5), em2436. Advance online publication. DOI: 10.29333/ejmste/14448

Steinert, S., Avila, K. E., Ruzika, S., Kuhn, J., & Küchemann, S. (2024). Harnessing large language models to develop research-based learning assistants for formative feedback. *Smart Learning Environments*, *11*(1), 62. DOI: 10.1186/s40561-024-00354-1

Suresh Babu, S., & Dhakshina Moorthy, A. (2024). Application of artificial intelligence in adaptation of gamification in education: A literature review. *Computer Applications in Engineering Education*, *32*(1), e22683. DOI: 10.1002/cae.22683

Susilana, R., Dewi, L., Rullyana, G., Hadiapurwa, A., & Khaerunnisa, N. (2022). Can microlearning strategy assist students' online learning? *Jurnal Cakrawala Pendidikan*, *41*(2), 437–451. DOI: 10.21831/cp.v41i2.43387

Sweller, J. (2005). Implications of Cognitive Load Theory for Multimedia Learning. In Mayer, R. E. (Ed.), *The Cambridge handbook of multimedia learning* (pp. 19–30). Cambridge University Press., DOI: 10.1017/CBO9780511816819.003

Sweller, J. (2010). Cognitive Load Theory: Recent Theoretical Advances. In J. L. Plass, R. Moreno, & R. Brünken (Eds.), *Cognitive Load Theory* (pp. 29–47). chapter, Cambridge: Cambridge University Press.

Sweller, J. (2023). The development of cognitive load theory: Replication crises and incorporation of other theories can lead to theory expansion. *Educational Psychology Review*, *35*(4), 95. Advance online publication. DOI: 10.1007/s10648-023-09817-2

Sweller, J., Kirschner, P., & Clark, R. E. (2007). Why minimally guided teaching techniques do not work: A reply to commentaries. *Educational Psychologist*, *42*(2), 115–121. DOI: 10.1080/00461520701263426

Sweller, J., van Merriënboer, J. J. G., & Paas, F. (2019). Cognitive architecture and instructional design: 20 years later. *Educational Psychology Review*, *31*(2), 261–292. DOI: 10.1007/s10648-019-09465-5

Sweller, J., Van Merrienboer, J. J. G., & Paas, F. G. W. C. (1998). Cognitive architecture and instructional design. *Educational Psychology Review*, *10*(3), 251–29. DOI: 10.1023/A:1022193728205

Synthesia. (2025). *Turn text the video in minutes.* https://www.synthesia.io/

Tapalova, O., & Zhiyenbayeva, N. (2022). Artificial Intelligence in Education: AIEd for Personalised Learning Pathways. *Electronic Journal of e-Learning*, *20*(5), 639–653. DOI: 10.34190/ejel.20.5.2597

Taub, M., & Azevedo, R. (2023). Teachers as self-regulated learners: The role of multimodal data analytics for instructional decision making. *New Directions for Teaching and Learning, 2023*(174), 25–32. DOI: 10.1002/tl.20545

Topu, F. B. (2023). Effects of Cognitive Load Level on Students' Attitude towards the Gamified Course. *Journal of Learning and Teaching in Digital Age, 8*(1), 93–112. DOI: 10.53850/joltida.1147246

Vygotsky, L. S. (1978). *Mind in Society: The Development of Higher Psychological Processes.* Harvard University Press.

Walter, Y. (2024). Embracing the future of Artificial Intelligence in the classroom: The relevance of AI literacy, prompt engineering, and critical thinking in modern education. *International Journal of Educational Technology in Higher Education, 21*(1), 15. DOI: 10.1186/s41239-024-00448-3

Wang, T., Lund, B. D., Marengo, A., Pagano, A., Mannuru, N. R., Teel, Z. A., & Pange, J. (2023). Exploring the Potential Impact of Artificial Intelligence (AI) on International Students in Higher Education: Generative AI, Chatbots, Analytics, and International Student Success. *Applied Sciences (Basel, Switzerland), 13*(11), 6716. DOI: 10.3390/app13116716

Wood, D. J., Bruner, J. S., & Ross, G. (1976). The Role of Tutoring in Problem Solving. *Journal of Child Psychology and Psychiatry, and Allied Disciplines, 17*(2), 89–100. DOI: 10.1111/j.1469-7610.1976.tb00381.x PMID: 932126

Xu, T., Liu, Y., Jin, Y., Qu, Y., Bai, J., Zhang, W., & Zhou, Y. (2024). From recorded to AI-generated instructional videos: A comparison of learning performance and experience. *British Journal of Educational Technology, 00*, 1–25. DOI: 10.1111/bjet.13530

Yan, L., Martinez-Maldonado, R., Jin, Y., Echeverria, V., Milesi, M., Fan, J., . . . Gašević, D. (2024). From Data Stories to Dialogues: A Randomised Controlled Trial of Generative AI Agents and Data Storytelling in Enhancing Data Visualisation Comprehension. *arXiv preprint arXiv:2409.11645.* https://arxiv.org/abs/2409.11645

Yaseen, H., Mohammad, A. S., Ashal, N., Abusaimeh, H., Ali, A., & Sharabati, A.-A. A. (2025). The Impact of Adaptive Learning Technologies, Personalized Feedback, and Interactive AI Tools on Student Engagement: The Moderating Role of Digital Literacy. *Sustainability (Basel), 17*(3), 1133. DOI: 10.3390/su17031133

Yıldızhan-Bora, B. (2024). *Alfa kuşağına atfedilen dört becerinin erken çocukluk dönemi kapsamında araştırılması: Dijital okuryazarlık, problem çözme ve eleştirel düşünme, yaratıcılık, iş birliği* [*An investigation of four skills attributed to Generation Alpha in early childhood: Digital literacy, problem-solving and critical thinking, creativity, collaboration*] (Doctoral dissertation, Bahçeşehir Üniversitesi, Eğitim Bilimleri Enstitüsü). Council of Higher Education Thesis Center. https://tez.yok.gov.tr

Yılmaz Soylu, M., & Akkoyunlu, B. (2020). Bilişötesi Düşünme. D*ijital Teknoloji Aracılı Düşünme Öğretimi Düşünme - Akıl Yürütme Dijital Teknoloji Öğretim Teknolojisi* .DOI: 10.14527/9786257880992.15

Zawacki-Richter, O., Marín, V. I., Bond, M., & Gouverneur, F. (2023). Systematic review of research on artificial intelligence applications in higher education – where are the educators? *International Journal of Educational Technology in Higher Education, 16*(1), 1–27. DOI: 10.1186/s41239-019-0171-0

Zhang, Y., Lucas, M., Bem-haja, P., & Pedro, L. (2024). The effect of student acceptance on learning outcomes: AI-generated short videos versus paper materials. *Computers and Education: Artificial Intelligence, 7*, 100286. DOI: 10.1016/j.caeai.2024.100286

Zichermann, G., & Cunningham, C. (2011). *Gamification by Design: Implementing Game Mechanics in Web and Mobile Apps*. O'Reilly Media.

Zou, A., Wang, Z., Carlini, N., Nasr, M., Kolter, J. Z., & Fredrikson, M. (2023). Universal and transferable adversarial attacks on aligned language models. *arXiv preprint arXiv:2307.15043*. https://doi.org//arXiv.2307.15043DOI: 10.48550

Zuo, M., Kong, S., Ma, Y., Hu, Y., & Xiao, M. (2023). The Effects of Using Scaffolding in Online Learning: A Meta-Analysis. *Education Sciences, 13*(7), 705. DOI: 10.3390/educsci13070705

KEY TERMS AND DEFINITIONS

Adaptivity: The capability of a learning environment to respond to individual learners in real time by adjusting content, pace, or feedback based on their needs, performance, learning characteristics or preferences.

Extraneous Load: A type of cognitive load that arises from ineffective instructional design, rather than from the inherent complexity of the learning task. This type of cognitive load consumes working memory resources and should be minimised to support meaningful learning.

Germane Load: A type of cognitive load related to the construction and development of knowledge and mental models. This load is beneficial for learning and should therefore be supported through thoughtful instructional design.

Instructional Design: A systemic and systematic process for planning, developing, and delivering learning experiences based on principles of how individuals learn. While instructional design models may vary in structure and terminology, they share core features such as goal setting, learner analysis, sequencing of content, and evaluation. The overarching aim is to create learning environments that support and enhance engagement, understanding, and performance.

Intrinsic Load: A type of cognitive load that stems from the inherent complexity of the learning task and the nature of the content. While it cannot be eliminated, it can be managed through strategies such as scaffolding, sequencing, and aligning content with learners' prior knowledge.

Large Language Models: Advanced AI systems trained on extensive datasets to recognise and generate human-like language. Built on transformer architectures, they learn patterns in language by predicting missing or next words during training. These models can generate text, respond to prompts, and adapt to a wide range of tasks.

Prompt Engineering: The process of formulating effective prompts to guide language-based AI models in producing accurate and contextually appropriate responses. This skill requires an understanding of how AI systems work and the ability to adjust the wording, structure, objective, and context of the prompt to influence the desired output. It is particularly important in complex tasks involving ill-structured scenarios.

Working Memory: A temporary processing centre that allows us to hold and manipulate a limited amount of information while performing cognitive tasks. It is one of the three main components of human memory, along with sensory memory and long-term memory. Because it can be easily overwhelmed, instructional materials should be designed in ways that reduce unnecessary mental load and support focus on essential content.

Zone of Proximal Development: A concept derived from Vygotsky's theory of learning, referring to the space between what a learner can accomplish independently and what they can achieve with guidance. This zone represents the learner's developmental potential; effective scaffolding supports progress by targeting tasks within this range.

Chapter 5
Generative AI Technology and Creativity in Education:
Technology and Creativity in Education

Yasemin Karal
https://orcid.org/0000-0003-4744-4541
Trabzon University, Turkey

ABSTRACT

Creativity has become increasingly important in all fields. The emergence of generative artificial intelligence (GenAI) technology has sparked debate on the idea that this skill can be emulated by machines. GenAI is used in fields such as architecture, graphic design, game design, fashion, art, sports, advertising and marketing, and medicine. Its impact on education is also under intense scrutiny. This chapter explores the GenAI-human collaboration that is transforming creativity in fields ranging from science and technology to education and the arts. The use of GenAI in creative processes in education is discussed in the context of its opportunities and potential limitations. There are discussions on how it redefines ethical issues related to creativity. Furthermore, the implications for copyright and originality are evaluated, and the situation that these technologies create in relation to ownership is discussed.

DOI: 10.4018/979-8-3373-7579-3.ch005

ght © 2026, IGI Global Scientific Publishing. Copying or distributing in print or electronic forms without written permission of IGI Global Scientific Publishing is prohibited. Use of this chapter to generative artificial intelligence (AI) technologies is expressly prohibited. The publisher reserves all rights to license its use for generative AI training and machine learning model development.

1. INTRODUCTION

The world needs more and more innovative and creative thoughts, processes and products. For this reason, it seems that creativity is becoming a subject of research more than before. Sawyer & Henriksen (2024) state that creativity research began in the 1950s and is divided into two major research traditions: individual and sociocultural approaches. According to the individual definition, creativity is a combination and is defined as "combinational, where ideas must fuse to create something new from what already exists." The sociocultural approach considers creativity as "the production of a new, appropriate, useful and valuable product by a social group" and argues that it should live in the world in objects that can be seen and touched, in processes created in shared ideas, in products or artifacts. Researchers usually investigate creativity by associating it with the four P frameworks: person, process, product and place. The creative development of individuals occurs through the combination of their personal factors, including characteristics, knowledge, skills, dispositions, and the physical, social and pedagogical environment surrounding them (Bereczki, & Kárpáti, 2021).

Creativity is considered a complex and multifaceted concept. It is affected by various cognitive, personality, motivational and environmental components. In this context, it is seen that many theories have been put forward to understand the nature of creativity, to explain how creative thinking, behaviors and products emerge, to evaluate them and to ensure development. Kozbelt, Beghetto & Runco (2010), who made a classification such as developmental, cognitive, psychometric, economic, problem-solving and expertise-based, problem-finding, evolutionary, typological, emphasize the importance of distinguishing between smaller c (usually more subjective) and larger C (more objective) levels of creativity when comparing creativity theories. They argued that the tendency of creativity studies to focus on genius/larger C levels of creativity causes an important distinction between creative product and creative experience to be overlooked. Creative experience represents subjective/small c forms of creativity that do not result in any product, are not subject to external evaluation and do not go beyond the individual's own personal insights and interpretations. Small c, which usually focuses on the creativity of daily life, can represent qualitatively different levels of creativity. Therefore, it is recommended that creativity be brought together by taking into consideration factors such as personality traits, biological basis, techniques for developing creativity, and cultural differences.

Vygotsky deeply examines the role of imagination and reality, reproduction and creativity, emotions and thoughts in the creative process. According to him, imagination is based on elements taken from reality, it takes pieces from reality, transforms them and these new pieces take shape and return to reality. Vygotsky creates a basis for interpreting a dynamic relationship between consciousness and the world, emphasizing that future education should be concerned with the ability to approach problems that do not currently exist, and the importance of assimilating traditional knowledge and the intellectual tools associated with this knowledge (Lindqvist, 2003). Glăveanu (2020) argues that the sociocultural approach to creativity has ancient roots in names such as Dewey (1934), Mead (1934) and Vygotsky (1930/2004) and puts forward a specific theory of the creative process based on the concepts of difference, position, perspective, dialogue and possibility. The theory suggests that individual creativity is possible through sociocultural relationships and interactions, arguing that shifting positions and perspectives within and between individuals will stimulate creative processes and that often, it is the possibilities of material objects or unique combinations of ideas that guide the development of new perspectives in creative work.

Amabile (1983, 1988, 1996, 2016) creativity theory has an important place in creativity research, especially in terms of bringing together cognitive, emotional and environmental factors. Componential theory of creativity is introduced as the oldest theory of creativity and innovation and is one of the well-established theories that does comprehensively explain both the individual creativity process and the organizational innovation process and the interaction of the two (Amabile& Pratt, 2016). According to the model, individual creativity is a function of three main components: Domain-relevant skills, creativity-relevant skills and intrinsic motivation. It is defined as an individual's knowledge, technical skills and abilities in a specific field or the 'raw materials' that an individual must have for performance. Creativity-related skills include creative results, producing flexible solutions, taking risks, cognitive style and personality traits that are suitable for bringing new perspectives, a disciplined working style and idea generation skills. Intrinsic motivation is the desire of an individual to do a task because they see it as interesting, enjoyable, satisfying or a personal challenge. The theory argues that individuals are most creative when they are motivated by the intrinsic pleasure of the work itself (Amabile,1988 & Amabile, 1993). Amabile (2016) suggested that external factors as well as internal factors will significantly affect individual creativity and defined the impact of organizational factors affecting individual creativity and explained the basic stages of the organizational innovation process. Organizations and managers that provide individuals with the freedom to decide how to do the job, provide the necessary money, personnel time and equipment, encourage risk-taking, support the sharing of different ideas and collaboration, and give individuals challenging tasks that are appropriate to their skills and interests as well as sufficient time for creative thinking and exploration encourage creativity. On the other hand, excessive bureaucracy, rigid rules, lack of resources, time and flexibility, poor team management and an environment of competition within the organization can also negatively affect the creative potential of individuals (Amabile, 1988).

The model examines in detail the relationship between the domain-specific skills, creative skills and motivation components in the problem presentation, preparation, idea generation and idea validation stages of the creativity process. Motivation is associated with the problem presentation and idea generation stages. The determination of the problem by the individual or its presentation from the outside affects the degree to which the individual approaches the task or problem with intrinsic interest. In a problem that the individual approaches with intrinsic interest or motivation, the willingness to take risks increases and the individual becomes more open to noticing and exploring aspects of the problem that are not directly related to the problem in order to reach a creative or innovative solution. When the connection between GenAI and creativity is examined within the framework of the model, the following question can be examined regarding motivation: (i) What effect does the use of GenAI technologies have on the task motivation of the individual/student?

Domain-specific skills are associated with the preparation and idea validation stages. If the individual's prior knowledge or knowledge accumulation about the problem is sufficient, reaching a solution becomes fast and easy, but if it is weak, this stage can turn into a very long stage where a lot of learning takes place. In addition, the relationship between the idea validation stage and domain-specific skills is critical. The accuracy or appropriateness of the idea generated is evaluated in line with the analysis techniques and criteria of the field based on these skills. In cases where GenAI is used, the following questions can be addressed in the context of domain-specific skills and creativity: (ii) What is the effect of GenAI's use in the processes of completing the user/student's deficiencies in domain-specific skills? (iii) How does GenAI affect creative solution generation in the processes of evaluating the validity of the idea or solution generated?

Creative skills are associated with the idea generation stage because these skills increase the individual's flexibility in thinking, exploring environmental cues, and the possibility of producing a large number of answers by postponing judgment (Amabile, 1988). In terms of creative skills and the use of GenAI, the following question may be worth addressing: (iv) Can GenAI help the individual/student think flexibly, diversify their perspective, make unusual connections and produce a large number of original ideas during the idea generation process, or vice versa?

The sense of progress played a central role in the reformulation of the model; it is associated with individuals making small progress in meaningful work, increasing intrinsic motivation and supporting the continuity of the creative process, and with the production of meaningful work and, especially in a work environment with a high level of psychological safety, even failures can nourish creative efforts. Meaningful work, the individual's perception that the work they do is positive and important, sustains the creative process by feeding intrinsic motivation, strengthens the progress cycle and contributes to the individual's persistence in creative efforts.

Negative emotion, although generally less beneficial, can support creativity in the preparation and idea validation stages by triggering deeper, more analytical thinking. Extrinsic motivation that supports intrinsic motivation positively affects creativity, and synergistic extrinsic motivations are particularly beneficial in the preparation and validation stages of the creative process. Intrinsic motivation and extrinsic rewards are not opposites, but they can reduce the effects of intrinsic motivation when extrinsic rewards are perceived as controlling (Amabile & Pratt, 2016). In this context, GenAI's ability to foster creativity can be addressed by the following question: (v) How can GenAI foster a sense of meaningful progress by enabling individuals/students to develop their domain expertise and creative skills?

2. RETHINKING CREATIVITY IN THE AGE OF GENERATIVE AI

Henriksen, Creely, Henderson, & Mishra (2021) state that creativity has become an established component of 21st century knowledge and skill discourses and is positioned together with technology. They argue that this is not surprising in an era when technology is rapidly transforming work, life, and production styles. The emergence of GenAI technology, especially in the last 1-2 years, has accelerated this transformation. This technology, which has the ability to produce content like humans, is used to create text, images, videos, codes, and musical compositions. While it is discussed that the use of GenAI in creative industries can increase human performance (Kalpokienė, 2024), there are also those who argue that the use of GenAI is a double-edged sword (Erickson, 2024). Candelon, Krayer, Rajendran, & Martinez (2023) draw attention to the importance of task definition in establishing GenAI-human collaboration and suggest that while results that support human performance can be obtained in task definitions that are in line with the competence of GenAI, this collaboration may decrease performance for tasks outside the competence limit for now. On the other hand, GenAI systems continue to develop at an astonishing pace, and the leaps in GPT models indicate that the limits of competence may expand unpredictably in the near future. Here, what individuals, institutions or organizations in various sectors or industries need to anticipate for success will be to develop and implement a GenAI-human collaboration model that is capable of learning and changing faster than ever before.

This chapter examines GenAI-human collaborations that are transforming creativity in fields ranging from science to technology, education to the arts. After discussing the opportunities and potential limitations for creative uses of GenAI in education, it discusses how this technology is redefining ethical issues related to creativity. It addresses the implications for copyright and intellectual property, and the question of ownership in content production.

3. CREATIVITY THROUGH GENAI-HUMAN COLLABORATION

GenAI holds promise for increasing human productivity (Peng, Kalliamvakou, Cihon & Demirer, 2023). Peschl (2024) states that creativity is related to our interaction with the real world and that the main issue to be addressed is how future interaction or collaboration with intelligent machines should be shaped. He emphasizes that turning creativity into action depends on strengthening people's creative capacities, beyond recombining existing knowledge. Examining how human creativity can be supported with GenAI, Geyer & Rosignoli (2024) identified three key factors that create and reveal a synergistic creative front end: enhanced idea generation, enhanced perspective diversity, and enhanced creative autonomy. GenAI's ability to present a variety of perspectives, meticulously tailored to specific use cases, delve deep into comprehensive data sets, and extract hidden patterns and points that human cognition cannot access, enables the emergence of new perspectives and unconventional approaches. The combination of human creativity with GenAI's outputs leads to a more diverse idea generation process and complements creativity. In addition, GenAI supports faster idea generation by automating processes, so more options can be examined. The opportunity to examine different approaches, strategies, pros, cons and the underlying logic in more depth makes the development of innovative solutions more possible, and functionality and efficiency increase. GenAI has the capacity to empower individuals in decision-making processes by providing the user with the opportunity to choose from more information, ideas and even opposing views, since they already have a perspective or idea. GenAI's ability to personalize content has led many researchers to define it as an assistant. The personalized content, output or solutions it produces depending on user requests allow the user to reach creative limits that they could not reach individually before. In addition, it can also take on the role of an assistant to whom repetitive tasks can be delegated, thus allowing individuals to focus on higher-value activities such as strategic decision-making, creative thinking and innovation development.

In order to ensure quality, satisfaction, and creative diversity in human-GenAI collaboration, the importance of preserving the human creative role is emphasized (Hosanagar & Ahn (2024; Jia, Luo, Fang, & Liao, 2024). How the collaboration is designed is important. In the design of the collaboration, GenAI is included in the process as a collaborative partner for purposes such as idea generation, facilitating routine tasks, and drafting, and as a productivity enhancer that allows people to focus on more creative tasks. It shortens the time to produce work. When human creativity is ignored, satisfaction and work quality have the potential to be negatively affected. Users with higher job skills may be more likely to produce innovative outputs, while less skilled users may have limited improvements in their outputs (Jia, Luo, Fang, & Liao, 2024).

Examining the role of GenAI as a collaborator or co-creator, Figoli et al. (2022) point out that the nature of these systems is gradually evolving towards the nature of a teammate, and thus, it is necessary to focus on how a human-machine relationship similar to the human-human relationship can be established. Pointing out that collaboration between humans and artificial intelligence reaches its highest efficiency in tasks where artificial intelligence is more effective than humans, the researchers presented three main conclusions: (i) simple and repetitive tasks such as data scanning and image creation can be delegated to these systems, and humans can focus on more strategic and creative tasks; (ii) attention should be paid to the distribution of tasks considering the different abilities of artificial intelligence and humans; (iii) it should be used with caution, considering that the potential of low-performing users to increase the quality of work and compensate for their deficiencies may not be valid for high-performing users. Educators have important responsibilities in ensuring that people enrich GenAI with original thoughts and expressions, that GenAI enhances human cognitive and creative efforts, and that human-GenAI collaborations that support innovation are established (Bozkurt et al., 2024).

4. EDUCATION, GENAI AND CREATIVITY

The opportunities and risks that generative AI technology will provide to learning environments are discussed. Ease of use, time saving, personalized learning experiences, innovative and creative production opportunities have increased the pace of adoption of this technology. GenAI has been used in areas such as architecture, graphic design, game design, fashion, art, sports, advertising and marketing, medicine, and education (Hughes, Zhu, & Bednarz, 2021; Sengar, Hasan, Kumar, & Carroll, 2024; Kshetri, Dwivedi, Davenport, & Panteli, 2024). In general, creative applications are employed for five basic purposes, such as content production, information analysis, content development and post-production workflows, information extraction and development, and data compression (Anantrasirichai & Bull, 2022). In this section, the use of creative GenAI in education will be evaluated in the context of risks and opportunities. The implications of generative AI in education continue to be a topic of interest for a broader community, and Bozkurt (2023) emphasizes the importance of adopting a forward-looking perspective that reassesses the contributions of both technology and human educators to the educational process. On the other hand, Shahzad, Xu & Zahid (2024) point out the positive relationship between Gen AI and students' self-efficacy, justice and ethics, creativity and learning performance, and emphasize that in addition to numerous opportunities to enhance learning performance, integrations should be carefully managed to overcome challenges and fully realize their potential. So how should this integration be achieved? What kind of structuring and planning processes are required to employ GenAI technology to increase students' potential in creative processes, considering their knowledge, field, expertise and creative skills, and motivation? How to pedagogically position GenAI in learning environments to encourage creativity remains an important question.

4.1. Creative Use of Generative AI in Education

GenAI has attracted attention in improving the creativity process in the field of education. It takes into account the existing data, situation, user needs and can create a suitable and sufficient content for them. The methods and strategies used by this technology are constantly evolving and increasing the content production capacity. Innovative approaches make it possible to create more flexible and original content in creative processes (Geetha, Hariharan, Jeevanprasanth & Sanjay, 2024). It is becoming increasingly important to strike a balance between human creativity and GenAI's capabilities. Creely, & Blannin (2025) examine the possibilities for a creative partnership between generative AI and humans and suggest that AI in various educational settings can increase creative output by providing new perspectives and ideas and increasing the efficiency of generative processes, as evidenced in both story and poetry examples. Doshi & Hauser (2024) investigated the impact of GenAI-generated ideas on writers' short story production and found that GenAI helped overcome writer's block by providing new ideas and supported individual creativity by providing different starting points. It was shown that stories of writers with access to GenAI were rated as more creative, better written, and more enjoyable. In particular, less creative writers benefited more from the technology. Using a dataset of over 4 million artworks from over 50 thousand unique users, Zhou and Lee (2024) found that text-to-image AI increased human creative productivity by 25% and increased the value measured by the probability of favorites per view by 50%.

According to Divya & Mirza (2024), GenAI is positioned as a transformative force in education. Educators can leverage the power of AI algorithms to create and improve educational materials, ensuring they remain up-to-date, relevant, and engaging. This technology holds great promise for providing personalized feedback and support to students by providing educational materials, quizzes, simulations, and personalized explanations, tips, and corrections, allowing the learning experience to remain dynamic and adaptable to students' ever-changing needs. Yao et al. (2024), who examined the content creation competition between human creators and GenAI, reported that the average utility and content output per human creator has improved and may even exceed that of GenAI creators. This scenario highlights the fact that the widespread adoption of GenAI could sustain the existence of a small and professional group of human creators, replacing less efficient content creators, and even producing more and higher quality content. As a result, it is emphasized that the widespread use of GenAI in content production can direct human creativity to areas that cannot be easily imitated by GenAI, thus contributing to the formation of a more specialized and diversified content ecosystem.

According to Singha & Singha (2024), integrating GenAI into education will significantly change the methods of creating teaching materials and developing curriculum. Tanweer & Ismail (2024) point out that the inclusion of GenAI in curriculum development represents a fundamental shift towards an educational model that prioritizes the needs and preferences of the student. Optimizing personalized, customized and adaptable learning environments is an ongoing endeavor in today's education landscape, and GenAI can play a significant role in this endeavor. According to the researchers, GenAI has the necessary capabilities to analyze comprehensive data, identify learning gaps and create materials that successfully fill these gaps.

On the other hand, the potential of GenAI to support creative processes and outcomes has shifted researchers to the focus of integration into curricula. Fleischmann (2024) investigated how design educators can leverage the power of GenAI without compromising the foundations of design education and jeopardizing the creative process. Pointing out that the integration of GenAI into higher education design curricula should be considered as an important component of the creative design process, the researcher proposed 3 categories as a structured approach to integrating GenAI: theory and context, practice, and reflective practice. The theory and context category was explained as the history of AI, GenAI, designing projects with GenAI, promises and risks of GenAI, ethical issues, determining institutional policies for the use of GenAI, comparing GenAI platforms and selecting appropriate tools, designing collaborations with GenAI, and evaluating the originality of designs produced through GenAI collaboration. The practice category was explained as discussing the pros and cons of GenAI in training/workshops, prompt writing training, idea generation exercises, and clearly defining the GenAI source. The reflective practice category was described as individual critical reflection on experiences and results (e.g., keeping a journal) and critiquing results as a group.

Arguing for the necessity of a collaborative and critical approach to AI in education, Creely et al. (2024) have addressed the role of GenAI in education and the balance between its benefits and risks from three different perspectives: Circumspect, Daring and Cautiously Optimistic persons, voices of characters. Circumspect emphasizes that the primary function of teaching remains entirely in the hands of the teacher and the importance of preserving the human element. Arguing that teaching is an inherently creative and contextual process, this nuanced process cannot be reproduced by machines. Daring argues that AI can complement human teachers and enhance creativity and should be adopted boldly. It starts from the question "What will be the role of human teachers when AI combines the roles of teacher, empathizer and ethical referee?" Education can be personalized with GenAI, learning can be adapted to individual needs, thus eliminating the inadequacies of traditional education and ensuring equality of opportunity in terms of both access and scope. Cautiously Optimistic recognizes the potential of GenAI to support creativity, but emphasizes the importance of approaching its integration into education from a critical perspective. According to this view, GenAI can take on the role of a partner that enhances human creative endeavor. It is argued that the use of these tools democratizes access to creative processes and allows students with different abilities to actively participate (Duran & Alejandro, 2024). Omran Zailuddin et al. (2024), who studied the integration of GenAI into creative design courses, emphasize that GenAI's features such as personalized feedback, encouraging iterative improvement, and providing a better understanding of basic design principles expand the boundaries of what is artistically possible. The researchers emphasized that in an age of collective production, the responsibility for ensuring a balanced integration of GenAI into education falls on educators, and human guidance should continue to be the most important element in nurturing creativity and supporting critical thinking.

GenAI is used for brainstorming, generating innovative ideas, and creative problem solving in individual and group work. GenAI can displace multiple independent idea generators or problem solvers with diverse knowledge and alternative methods in the process of generating innovations or searching for solutions; it can offer cost-effective and efficient ways to generate creative ideas (Boussioux et al., 2024). According to Heigl (2025), it is a complementary technology to human creativity, offering new ways to inspire and generate ideas, but remaining dependent on human original creative outputs and inputs as a collaborative partner. The researcher points out that it offers unique discovery and learning opportunities that can accelerate human development and expand their creative horizons. Fleischmann (2024) examined the experiences of visual communication design students who were given the opportunity to use GenAI platforms in their creative design processes. In the traditional design process, he describes an environment where students are encouraged to experiment freely with their ideas in a safe social environment where creativity develops through trial and error and experience becomes a source of learning. He writes that the process progresses by following the stages of receiving a creative brief, conducting research, brainstorming (idea generation), and iterating and testing ideas. He particularly emphasizes the importance of dialogue and underlines that it enables students to push their boundaries, develop creativity, thought processes, and techniques. The findings of the study confirmed that human experts outperform GenAI in creative tasks. It has been determined that students have ethical concerns against GenAI, which is attributed a collaborative partner role with its features such as being a source of inspiration, saving time, enabling rapid production, and creating an idea spark, and that they are torn between its usefulness and limitations. So how can GenAI become a supportive part of this process? The researcher suggests that while utilizing the potential of GenAI, the core values of traditional design pedagogy should be preserved, and procedures should be carefully planned to ensure that students use GenAI critically, understand ethical challenges, and develop their own creative skills. Beghetto & Zamana, (2025) argue that ignoring, underusing, and misusing GenAI can undermine the co-creative process, and that it is critical to maximize the potential benefits of GenAI in Human x AI co-creative processes in education.

It is important to understand the effect of using GenAI in learning processes on student motivation. Cubillos et al. (2025) investigates the effect of using GenAI on undergraduate programming learning, motivation, and learning environments. An experiment involving 40 computer engineering students compared the use of GenAI with video-based learning. The findings of the study showed that while no significant difference was found between the groups in terms of learning, GenAI increased the perception of autonomy and reduced effort and pressure. In contrast, video-based learning improved the perception of competence. It has been observed that both methods can be effective for teaching programming, but affect motivational and emotional aspects through different mechanisms. The reduction of perceived effort by GenAI may reduce the optimal level of challenge required for deep learning while reducing cognitive load. This led to a sense of relief for students, which, while reducing cognitive load, may potentially lead to excessive AI dependence and a decrease in the development of independent problem-solving skills. Hmoud et al (2024) provide initial findings that ChatGPT can be a powerful tool for increasing task motivation among higher education students. Students who performed a specific task using ChatGPT reported that they enjoyed, were satisfied, and were intrigued by the tool. According to students, the tool facilitates quick access to information and task completion, and is useful for verifying information and evaluating results. It helps students achieve their personal goals. Conversational interaction and immediate feedback make the learning experience more engaging. On the other hand, providing false information and security concerns have revealed that students need to have information verification and critical thinking skills.

Studies on how to make GenAI-human collaboration more effective are ongoing. In general, GenAI, which is prominent in the role of conversation or teammate in collaboration processes, also tool or superintelligence roles (Cheng & Zhang (2024). In the collaboration model where the tool role is carried out by GenAI, its capacity to scan and summarize large amounts of information and produce effective and fast results in the performance of a certain task is emphasized. In the model where GenAI assumes the role of a teammate, its potential to stimulate discussions and increase team motivation by generating ideas, making suggestions and adapting to the team climate is emphasized. In the model where a superintelligence role above human intelligence is assumed, GenAI's rich knowledge, different thinking processes from humans and the ability to offer an analytical perspective can improve individuals' thinking skills such as independent thinking, categorization and conclusion-making during the collaboration process. Of course, these collaboration models may have handicaps. Concerns about becoming addicted to this technology, whose capabilities are expanding every day, what it can do is wondered about every day and which limits our time to generate ideas on how to adapt, continue to maintain their first place. Individuals who begin to feel inadequate in the face of GenAI's capabilities may lose motivation and the collaboration process may be negatively affected. Over-confidence in the information, solutions or ideas offered by GenAI may eventually hinder the creation of new and creative information, solutions or ideas. While the tendency for face-to-face communication to be an option that individuals will prefer less is listed among the risks of this technology, the fact that it requires qualified prompts for creative outputs, problems understanding prompts and giving irrelevant answers, and users repeatedly creating new prompts are considered among the risks in terms of time efficiency. The risks and limitations that GenAI's use in education may pose in the context of creativity will be discussed in the next section.

4.2. Limitations of GenAI to Creativity

In many sectors such as education, health, and art, the transition from Industry 4.0 to 5.0 has begun. Industry 4.0 has been described as a revolution that aims to make production efficient, fast, and autonomous, and even leaves the human factor in the background if possible. In Industry 5.0, it is seen that the place of humans is once again taken to the center. It has been understood over time that systems that exclude humans or simply increase productivity and production power are not sufficient for social good or welfare. Technology is positioned as an auxiliary tool that works in harmony with humans rather than as an element that can replace them. The emergence of GenAI technology at this point is no coincidence. It offers the opportunity to produce by including the human element in the process, taking advantage of the creative power of humans, and allowing them to contribute to decision-making processes. In this way, it seems likely that the transition process will accelerate. Habib, Vogel, Anli, & Thorne (2024) underline the need to be thoughtful about how GenAI is brought into classrooms, just like the core assumption of Industry 5.0, emphasizing a symbiotic relationship between human creativity and AI and the need for pedagogical strategies that enhance each other in this relationship.

Discussions on the effects of GenAI on creativity underscore the need to preserve human creativity. It has the ability to model the learning process, collaborate with users by imitating certain personality traits or engage in discussions, and provide personalized feedback by taking on the role of a tutor. In order to continue to develop critical thinking, problem solving, self-regulation, and reflective thinking skills while educating ourselves with GenAI, and thus preserve human autonomy or creativity, the questions that need to be asked, according to Yan, Greiff, Teuber, & Gašević (2024), are as follows: (i) How can we design human-GenAI collaboration to increase learner agency? (ii) What are the behavioral indicators that will effectively capture cognitive and metacognitive processes during GenAI-assisted learning? (iii) How can we assess learning outcomes to ensure that they reflect the actual human knowledge and skill development? (iii) What strategies can be implemented to ensure that humans continue to lead in critical thinking and problem solving rather than GenAI?" It is clear that educators and educational organizations will need to examine and redefine their current practices. Moreover, with the developing technology, it has become necessary to deeply question how the role of educators, which has long been a subject of debate, will be shaped in the future, and to discuss their unique positions and intersectional identities in curricula, learning and assessment processes in more depth (Bozkurt et all, 2024). On the other hand, it is suggested that new strategies should be employed for the assessment of student development in the GenAI era. New assessment strategies should be intellectually challenging, personally meaningful, resistant to shortcuts created by GenAI, and should reinforce the irreplaceable value of the human element (Pahi, Hawlader, Hicks, Zaman & Phan, 2024).

It is important for students of today to be prepared to use the evolving GenAI technology and tools ethically and efficiently in their academic and daily lives, and to graduate as job-ready graduates. It is clear that students and instructors need more practice in order to gain awareness of the possibilities and limitations of this technology, to encourage constructive use of GenAI, and to integrate GenAI into assessment activities (Foung, Lin & Chen, 2024). However, traditional assessments include tasks and responsibilities that can be easily produced by GenAI. When using GenAI tools, students need to ensure that they truly learn the subject material and maintain academic integrity (Kadel et al, 2024). Tasks that include higher-order thinking skills, reasoning tasks, questions or prompts based on personal experience and current knowledge are indicated as GenAI-resistant assessments. In addition, it is essential to equip both educators and students to use this technology responsibly and safely, and to critically evaluate the outputs produced in terms of accuracy, relevance and bias. In addition to professional development for educators, clear, step-by-step institutional guidelines, strategies, and policies on the ethical use of GenAI are recommended. However, the long-term effects of integrating GenAI into assessment practices and how it impacts knowledge and skill development in the long term remain to be elucidated (Zhao, Chapman, & Sabet, 2024).

Maintaining academic integrity is considered a serious handicap. During the education process, students are expected to comply with values such as honesty, trust, justice, respect, responsibility, and courage, and GenAI has been questioned as a technology that facilitates academic misconduct (Perkins, Furze, Roe, MacVaugh, 2024). On the one hand, it is argued that reasons such as personality traits, cultural values, desire to achieve success, and peer pressure can lead students to unethical behaviors in order to complete their tasks (Rodriges, Silva, Borges, Franco, & Oliveira, 2025). The focus needs to be on establishing a balance between using GenAI to improve learning and not undermining academic integrity. GenAI's capabilities such as monitoring user behavior in real time, analyzing large amounts of academic performance data, and making recommendations based on interests and academic performance can contribute to the process of establishing this balance. While algorithms that detect content produced with GenAI, advanced plagiarism detection software, and the development of artificial intelligence-supported surveillance systems are introduced as possible technical solutions, it is envisaged that increasing the awareness of students and education stakeholders and determining institutional policies and strategies will facilitate the pedagogical adaptation of this technology to education (Bittle & El-Gayar, 2025).

Optimization of assessment activities can be a preventive way to ensure academic integrity. Some frameworks have been proposed in this context. Perkins, Furze, Roe & MacVaugh (2024) present the "Artificial Intelligence Assessment Tool" for educators to determine the appropriate level of GenAI use in assessments according to learning outcomes. It is expressed as a tool that helps educators determine how to organize their assessments, accepts situations where GenAI may not be pedagogically appropriate or necessary, and supports students to complete assessments in accordance with academic integrity principles. The tool, which addresses the use of artificial intelligence in assessment processes, defines 5 levels of usage options, from not using AI at any stage of the assessment to using AI throughout the assessment. GenAI can perform idea generation, editing, task completion, and creative collaboration, but at some levels, content is not allowed to be included in the final product, while at others it is allowed. Again, citing the content produced by GenAI may or may not be used as a criterion.

4.3. Between Creativity and Ethics: Reflections on Using GenAI in Education

Developments in AI raise many ethical concerns. The emergence of GenAI has deepened these concerns. Various principles for AI ethics have been put forward in the literature. These principles have been detailed by Ryan and Stahl (2020) in order to enable AI developers and users to understand and be prepared for AI ethics: transparency, justice and fairness, non-maleficence, responsibility, privacy, beneficence, freedom and autonomy, trust, sustainability, dignity and solidarity. Addressing these ethical principles in educational environments has now become a necessity.

Considering the speed of development and unpredictable future of GenAI, it can be said that educators have an ethical duty to prepare students for an AI-supported working world after graduation (Furze, Perkins, Roe & MacVaugh, (2024). In the context of creativity, one of the main problems is the issue of copyright, originality and ownership.

Hacohen & Elkin-Koren (2024) consider originality as the internalization and reconstruction of ideas, images and narratives acquired at an unconscious level by the individual, making them their own. This production process may be one that the individual may not be fully aware of. According to Luo (2024), originality is traditionally individual. However, today, originality is increasingly becoming a collaborative process with GenAI, and it is emphasized that a more detailed conceptualization of originality is needed. The well-known tools used in the production process are enriched by GenAI technology, and the user may not even be aware of the use of AI in the production process. A new conceptualization of originality may allow for a more nuanced understanding of originality by providing clarity on which aspects of the work are performed by students and which tasks are delegated to GenAI for which purposes. Bozkurt (2024) states that merely reporting GenAI usage is insufficient and that innovative strategies that include controlled usage of GenAI are needed. He states that it is time to start adapting more detailed strategies that specify where, when, in which sections and for what purposes it is used as an approach and to activate additional mechanisms. In particular, the expression of human approval declaration in works emphasizes the importance of defining the prompts in the collaboration processes with GenAI in order to protect academic honesty, transparency and ethics. In order to provide this in academic writing, the researcher proposes a framework that expects the author to detail the GenAI collaboration within the framework of "Direct Contribution, General Assistance, Specific Sections, Idea Development, Editing and Reviewing, Language Translation and Localization, Data Analysis, Data Visualization, Code or Algorithms" options, and emphasizes that GenAI will emerge as the new cornerstone of mastery, intellectual and creative expression.

Fenwick, & Jurcys (2023) reconsider the concepts of creativity and originality through a work made by French DJ David Guetta using GenAI, and argue that human contribution still plays a central role in works created with GenAI human collaboration. They emphasize that there is no content produced entirely by GenAI, that is, there is always a human/author in the creative process, namely "co-creation with GenAI". However, one of the uncertainties created by GenAI in terms of copyright law is whether the usage rights of the data used to train these systems will be included in the evaluation of the originality of the output created using these systems. The uncertainty in the working and decision-making processes of the systems questions the extent to which co-created content can be considered original and creative, and leads to serious debates about whether these contents are covered by copyright. The multi-layered structure of GenAI systems, namely the supply chain, which includes data collection, model training, infrastructure providers, software developers, and end users, complicates copyright issues. Copyright infringement can occur at various stages of the supply chain, including model training, distribution, and production, and can lead to liability (Dornis, 2025). Resolving legal uncertainties in this area is critical for both protecting the rights of creators and for the responsible development and use of GenAI technology (Lee, Cooper, & Grimmelmann, 2023). Dzuong, Wang, & Zhang, (2024) point out that, at the intersection of creativity and technology, current methods and techniques for protecting copyrighted works from GenAI models are not sufficiently emphasized. Researchers state that many GenAI models produce strongly similar text, image, and video outputs based on copyrighted works, and many companies that produce GenAI models have been sued. It is seen that some models transfer liability in the event of copyright infringement in their terms of service, i.e., they put it on the shoulders of users.

The ownership of the content produced by generative models is a separate topic of discussion. Bozkurt (2024) states that ownership can only be for human creations and that AI cannot undertake such a mission due to its nature. However, he also reports that the fact that GenAI generates content based on training data creates a gray area that can pose serious issues regarding ownership. The issue of ownership of content produced by GenAI requires inclusive and collaborative frameworks that must be addressed legally, economically, and ethically. This may be evolving from the traditional understanding of ownership into a landscape such as joint and collaborative ownership of the content produced. In co-creation, the rights holders can be (i) the owner of the training data, (ii) the person who created the dataset, (iii) the developer of the model, (iv) the end user who uses the model, (v) the model itself, or the content can be considered public domain (Malevé, 2024; Avrahami, & Tamir, 2021). Avrahami, & Tamir (2021) emphasize that GenAI will have broader impacts that go beyond the question of ownership, that it may threaten the roles of artists, that the datasets on which the models are trained may increase biases, that a few technology giants will have great power to influence societies, and that automated creation processes may be independent of state control mechanisms, and that these risks will have economic, cultural, and social impacts beyond the question of ownership.

5. CONCLUSION

Studies on the use of creative GenAI in education are still in their infancy. The idea that technical advances will transform education in a way that encourages human creativity seems very valuable for the future. It seems that all stakeholders, from policy makers to educational institutions, technology experts, researchers, educators and students, should share this vision, adopt an interdisciplinary dialogue process and focus on principles, strategies and practices that integrate GenAI in a way that supports human creativity.

GenAI technology is rapidly being integrated into today's workplace applications and it is important to provide it to future employees and today's students as a lifelong learning skill. The question of "What should the content of effective GenAI education be?" has not been fully clarified. In addition, GenAI literacy, ethical and sustainable use and critical thinking skills are promoted as priorities in the literature. Integrating courses in this direction into curricula, updating curricula and developing and implementing multidisciplinary educational programs are priorities, especially at the higher education level.

It is important that GenAI is positioned in learning environments in a way that will develop students' creativity and innovation skills. This requires an inclusive and innovative GenAI integration where students can express their own feelings, thoughts and ideas in an effective and innovative way. Curricula should be updated to encourage this, and teachers should take on the role of facilitator and guide of the process. Prioritizing ethical values and the central role of the teacher in preparing students for lifelong learning are critical. Professional training opportunities are important for teachers to adapt to these new technologies and develop creative teaching strategies. Providing development opportunities customized to the individual needs of teachers for their professional development, providing educational practices that will allow them to develop innovative teaching methods, and creating platforms that will enable national or international collaboration to share and develop these experiences will contribute to the process.

In today's educational environments, GenAI integration should support students both cognitively and emotionally. Studies examining the effects of GenAI use on motivation are new in the literature and can contribute to a more positive approach to the learning process by providing students with various conveniences in terms of rapid access to information, facilitating task completion processes, verifying information, and evaluating results. In addition, structures that allow for interaction and feedback can trigger students' curiosity and increase their motivation. However, it should not be forgotten that excessive use of these tools can create addiction, blunt innovative ideas, and lead to laziness. Again, the hallucinations and false information production of these tools bring about reliability problems. Therefore, it is recommended that GenAI's motivational effects may be different and that educators should carefully integrate these tools in line with pedagogical goals. GenAI can take on the role of a collaborator that supports students' knowledge/field or expertise. Especially in the process of generating creative solutions to a problem or task, it may become possible to original and new solutions with human-directed creative questioning. It can respond to students' demands such as text, code, graphics and problem solving according to their cognitive development or education level, and allow them to recognize and complete their deficiencies. GenAI, which can accelerate students' process of completing their deficiencies in their field skills, can pave the way for problems such as excessive dependency, problem solving and dulling of thinking skills. A student who structures his/her interaction with GenAI as asking questions and getting answers may increasingly become superficial in his/her learning. It is critical that the student is not a passive receiver of information in interactions with GenAI, but an active questioner. Fleischmann (2024) has proposed a structure for GenAI to become a potential partner in today's learning environments. This structure includes 4 main modules: (i) General history of GenAI and how it works, introducing major language models, (ii) Ethical issues such as copyright violations, intellectual property, stereotyping and inequality, defining institutional policies regarding the use of GenAI, (iii) Introducing domain-specific GenAI platforms and providing examples, taking sample lessons from professionals, (iv) Prompt engineering training, discussion about the benefits and disadvantages of GenAI, creating a project involving GenAI, reflective practice, discussion and critiquing the results in groups.

GenAI has the potential to provide equal opportunities in education, interactive and creative learning environments. Personalized learning experiences, automatic assessments, instant feedback can create more accessible and effective learning environments with more creative and effective educational materials. Thus, increased student participation, academic success and motivation, and more qualified learning outcomes emerge. Using GenAI for repetitive tasks can lighten teachers' workload, allowing them to focus on more important tasks such as making individual interactions with students more meaningful, providing guidance according to individual needs, and monitoring learning processes more closely. All these processes require the ethical and sustainable use of GenAI technology and the internalization of ethical principles by teachers, students, and educational institutions.

REFERENCES

Amabile, T. M. (1983). *The social psychology of creativity: A componential conceptualization*. Springer-Verlag. DOI: 10.1007/978-1-4612-5533-8

Amabile, T. M. (1988). A model of creativity and innovation in organizations. *Research in Organizational Behavior, 10*(1), 123–167.

Amabile, T. M. (1993). Motivational synergy: Toward new conceptualizations of intrinsic and extrinsic motivation in the workplace. *Human Resource Management Review, 3*(3), 185–201. DOI: 10.1016/1053-4822(93)90012-S

Amabile, T. M. (1996). *Creativity in context: Update to the social psychology of creativity*. Westview Press.

Amabile, T. M., & Pratt, M. G. (2016). The dynamic componential model of creativity and innovation in organizations: Making progress, making meaning. *Research in Organizational Behavior, 36*, 157–183. DOI: 10.1016/j.riob.2016.10.001

Anantrasirichai, N., & Bull, D. (2022). Artificial intelligence in the creative industries: A review. *Artificial Intelligence Review, 55*(1), 589–656. DOI: 10.1007/s10462-021-10039-7

Anantrasirichai, N., & Bull, D. (2022). Artificial intelligence in the creative industries: A review. *Artificial Intelligence Review, 55*(1), 589–656. DOI: 10.1007/s10462-021-10039-7

Avrahami, O., & Tamir, B. (2021). Ownership and creativity in generative models. *arXiv preprint arXiv:2112.01516.*

Beghetto, R. A., & Zamana, F. (2025). A Principled Approach to Human Creativity x AI in Education. In *The Cyber-Creativity Process: How Humans Co-Create with Artificial Intelligence* (pp. 71–97). Springer Nature Switzerland. DOI: 10.1007/978-3-031-84535-2_3

Bereczki, E. O., & Kárpáti, A. (2021). Technology-enhanced creativity: A multiple case study of digital technology-integration expert teachers' beliefs and practices. *Thinking Skills and Creativity, 39*, 100791. DOI: 10.1016/j.tsc.2021.100791

Bittle, K., & El-Gayar, O. (2025). Generative AI and Academic Integrity in Higher Education: A Systematic Review and Research Agenda. *Information (Basel), 16*(4), 296. DOI: 10.3390/info16040296

Boussioux, L., Lane, J. N., Zhang, M., Jacimovic, V., & Lakhani, K. R. (2024). The crowdless future? Generative AI and creative problem-solving. *Organization Science*, *35*(5), 1589–1607. DOI: 10.1287/orsc.2023.18430

Bozkurt, A. (2023). Generative artificial intelligence (AI) powered conversational educational agents: The inevitable paradigm shift. *Asian Journal of Distance Education*, *18*(1), 198–204. DOI: 10.5281/zenodo.7716416

Bozkurt, A. (2024). GenAI et al.: Cocreation, Authorship, Ownership, Academic Ethics and Integrity in a Time of Generative AI. *Open Praxis*, *16*(1), 1–10. https://doi.org/. DOI: 10.55982/openpraxis.16.1.654

Bozkurt, A., Xiao, J., Farrow, R., Bai, J. Y., Nerantzi, C., Moore, S., Dron, J., Stracke, C. M., Singh, L., Crompton, H., Koutropoulos, A., Terentev, E., Pazurek, A., Nichols, M., Sidorkin, A. M., Costello, E., Watson, S., Mulligan, D., Honeychurch, S., & Asino, T. I. (2024). The manifesto for teaching and learning in a time of generative AI: A critical collective stance to better navigate the future. *Open Praxis*, *16*(4), 487–513. DOI: 10.55982/openpraxis.16.4.777

Candelon, F., Krayer, L., Rajendran, S., & Martinez, D. Z. (2023). How people Can create–and destroy–value with generative AI. *BCG Global, 21.*

Cheng, X. & Zhang S. (2024). Tool, Teammate, Superintelligence: Identification of ChatGPTEnabled Collaboration Patterns and their Benefits and Risks in Mutual Learning.

Creely, E., & Blannin, J. (2025). Creative partnerships with generative AI. Possibilities for education and beyond. *Thinking Skills and Creativity*, *56*, 101727. DOI: 10.1016/j.tsc.2024.101727

Creely, E., Henriksen, D., Henderson, M., & Mishra, P. (2024, October 18). The Staging of AI: Exploring Perspectives about Generative AI, Creativity and Education. *Creative Education.*

Cubillos, C., Mellado, R., Cabrera-Paniagua, D., & Urra, E. (2025). Generative Artificial Intelligence in Computer Programming: Does it enhance learning, motivation, and the learning environment? *IEEE Access : Practical Innovations, Open Solutions*, *13*, 40438–40455. DOI: 10.1109/ACCESS.2025.3532883

Divya, V., & Mirza, A. U. (2024). Transforming content creation: The influence of generative AI on a new frontier. *Exploring the frontiers of artificial intelligence and machine learning technologies, 143.*

Dornis, T. W. (2025). Generative AI, reproductions inside the model, and the making available to the public. *IIC-International Review of Intellectual Property and Competition Law*, 1-30.

Doshi, A. R., & Hauser, O. P. (2024). Generative AI enhances individual creativity but reduces the collective diversity of novel content. *Science Advances*, *10*(28), eadn5290. DOI: 10.1126/sciadv.adn5290 PMID: 38996021

Duran, G. ve Alejandro, A. (2024). Üretken Sanat ve Ortaöğretim: Yapay Zeka Araçlarının Öğrenci Yaratıcılığı Üzerindeki Etkisi. *Eğitimde Ortaya Çıkan Teknolojiler Dergisi*, *2*(6), 420–433.

Dzuong, J., Wang, Z., & Zhang, W. (2024). Uncertain boundaries: multidisciplinary approaches to copyright issues in generative AI. *arXiv preprint arXiv:2404.08221.*

Erickson, K. (2024). AI and work in the creative industries: Digital continuity or discontinuity? *Creative Industries Journal*, •••, 1–21. DOI: 10.1080/17510694.2024.2421135

Fenwick, M., & Jurcys, P. (2023). Originality and the Future of Copyright in an Age of Generative AI. *Computer Law & Security Review*, *51*, 105892. DOI: 10.1016/j.clsr.2023.105892

Figoli, F. A., Rampino, L., & Mattioli, F. (2022). AI in design idea development: A workshop on creativity and human-AI collaboration. In Lockton, D., Lloyd, P., & Lenzi, S. (Eds.), *DRS2022: Bilbao, 25 June - 3 July.*, DOI: 10.21606/drs.2022.414

Fleischmann, K. (2024). The commodification of creativity: Integrating Generative Artificial Intelligence in higher education design curriculum. *Innovations in Education and Teaching International*, •••, 1–15. DOI: 10.1080/14703297.2024.2427039

Fleischmann, K. (2024). The commodification of creativity: Integrating Generative Artificial Intelligence in higher education design curriculum. *Innovations in Education and Teaching International*, •••, 1–15. DOI: 10.1080/14703297.2024.2427039

Foung, D., Lin, L., & Chen, J. (2024). Reinventing assessments with ChatGPT and other online tools: Opportunities for GenAI-empowered assessment practices. *Computers and Education: Artificial Intelligence*, *6*, 100250. DOI: 10.1016/j.caeai.2024.100250

Furze, L., Perkins, M., Roe, J., & MacVaugh, J. (2024). The AI Assessment Scale (AIAS) in action: A pilot implementation of GenAI-supported assessment. *Australasian Journal of Educational Technology*, *40*(4), 38–55. DOI: 10.14742/ajet.9434

Geetha, M. P., Hariharan, S., Jeevanprasanth, T., & Sanjay, L. (2024, December). Multimodal Content Generation: A Project for AI Creativity. In *2024 International Conference on Emerging Research in Computational Science (ICERCS)* (pp. 1-5). IEEE.

Geyer, R., & Rosignoli, A. (2024). The Influence of Generative AI on Creativity in the Front End of Innovation. https://www.diva-portal.org/smash/get/diva2:1865236/FULLTEXT01.pdf

Glăveanu, V. P. (2020). A Sociocultural Theory of Creativity: Bridging the Social, the Material, and the Psychological. *Review of General Psychology*, *24*(4), 335–354. DOI: 10.1177/1089268020961763

Habib, S., Vogel, T., Anli, X., & Thorne, E. (2024). How does generative artificial intelligence impact student creativity? *Journal of Creativity*, *34*(1), 100072. DOI: 10.1016/j.yjoc.2023.100072

Hacohen, U. Y., & Elkin-Koren, N. (2024). Copyright Regenerated: Harnessing Genai To Measure Originality And Copyright Scope. *Harvard Journal of Law & Technology*, *37*(2).

Heigl, R. (2025). Generative artificial intelligence in creative contexts: a systematic review and future research agenda. *Management Review Quarterly,* 1-38.

Heigl, R. (2025). Generative artificial intelligence in creative contexts: a systematic review and future research agenda. Management Review Quarterly, 1-38.

Henriksen, D., Creely, E., Henderson, M., & Mishra, P. (2021). Creativity and technology in teaching and learning: A literature review of the uneasy space of implementation. *Educational Technology Research and Development*, *69*(4), 1–18. DOI: 10.1007/s11423-020-09912-z

Hmoud, M., Swaity, H., Hamad, N., Karram, O., & Daher, W. (2024). Higher education students' task motivation in the generative artificial intelligence context: The case of ChatGPT. *Information (Basel)*, *15*(1), 33. DOI: 10.3390/info15010033

Hosanagar, K., & Ahn, D. (2024). Designing Human and Generative AI Collaboration. *arXiv preprint arXiv:2412.14199.*

Hughes, R. T., Zhu, L., & Bednarz, T. (2021). Generative adversarial networks–enabled human–artificial intelligence collaborative applications for creative and design industries: A systematic review of current approaches and trends. *Frontiers in Artificial Intelligence*, *4*, 604234. DOI: 10.3389/frai.2021.604234 PMID: 33997773

Hughes, R. T., Zhu, L., & Bednarz, T. (2021). Generative adversarial networks–enabled human–artificial intelligence collaborative applications for creative and design industries: A systematic review of current approaches and trends. *Frontiers in Artificial Intelligence*, *4*, 604234. DOI: 10.3389/frai.2021.604234 PMID: 33997773

Jia, N., Luo, X., Fang, Z., & Liao, C. (2024). When and how artificial intelligence augments employee creativity. *Academy of Management Journal*, *67*(1), 5–32. DOI: 10.5465/amj.2022.0426

Kadel, R., Mishra, B. K., Shailendra, S., Abid, S., Rani, M., & Mahato, S. P. (2024, July). Crafting tomorrow's evaluations: assessment design strategies in the era of generative AI. In *2024 International Symposium on Educational Technology (ISET)* (pp. 13-17). IEEE. DOI: 10.1109/ISET61814.2024.00012

Kalpokienė, J. (2024). *Law, Human Creativity and Generative Artificial Intelligence: Regulatory Options*. Taylor & Francis. DOI: 10.4324/9781003464976

Kozbelt, A., Beghetto, R. A., & Runco, M. A. (2010). Theories of Creativity. In Kaufman, J. C., & Sternberg, R. J. (Eds.), *Cambridge Handbook of Creativity* (pp. 20–47). Cambridge University Press., DOI: 10.1017/CBO9780511763205.004

Kshetri, N., Dwivedi, Y. K., Davenport, T. H., & Panteli, N. (2024). Generative artificial intelligence in marketing: Applications, opportunities, challenges, and research agenda. *International Journal of Information Management*, *75*, 102716. DOI: 10.1016/j.ijinfomgt.2023.102716

Kshetri, N., Dwivedi, Y. K., Davenport, T. H., & Panteli, N. (2024). Generative artificial intelligence in marketing: Applications, opportunities, challenges, and research agenda. *International Journal of Information Management*, *75*, 102716. DOI: 10.1016/j.ijinfomgt.2023.102716

Lee, K., Cooper, A. F., & Grimmelmann, J. (2023). Talkin''Bout AI Generation: Copyright and the Generative-AI Supply Chain. *arXiv preprint arXiv:2309.08133*.

Lindqvist, G. (2003) Vygotsky's Theory of Creativity, Creativity Research, Journal, 15:2-3, 245-251, DOI: DOI: 10.1080/10400419.2003.9651416

Luo, J. (2024). A critical review of GenAI policies in higher education assessment: A call to reconsider the "originality" of students' work. *Assessment & Evaluation in Higher Education*, *49*(5), 651–664. DOI: 10.1080/02602938.2024.2309963

Malevé, N. (2024). Lost in Compression: Models of Authorship in Generative AI. *Media Theory*, *8*(1), 205–228. DOI: 10.70064/mt.v8i1.1074

Omran Zailuddin, M. F. N., Nik Harun, N. A., Abdul Rahim, H. A., Kamaruzaman, A. F., Berahim, M. H., Harun, M. H., & Ibrahim, Y. (2024). Redefining creative education: A case study analysis of AI in design courses. *Journal of Research in Innovative Teaching & Learning*, *17*(2), 282–296. DOI: 10.1108/JRIT-01-2024-0019

Pahi, K., Hawlader, S., Hicks, E., Zaman, A., & Phan, V. (2024). Enhancing active learning through collaboration between human teachers and generative AI. *Computers and Education Open*, *6*, 100183. DOI: 10.1016/j.caeo.2024.100183

Peng, S., Kalliamvakou, E., Cihon, P., & Demirer, M. (2023). The impact of ai on developer productivity: Evidence from github copilot. *arXiv preprint arXiv:2302.06590.*

Perkins, M., Furze, L., Roe, J., & MacVaugh, J. (2024). The Artificial Intelligence Assessment Scale (AIAS): A Framework for Ethical Integration ofGenerative AI in Educational Assessment. *Journal of University Teaching & Learning Practice*, *21*(6). Advance online publication. DOI: 10.53761/q3azde36

Peschl, M. F. (2024). Human innovation and the creative agency of the world in the age of generative AI. *Possibility Studies & Society*, *2*(1), 49–76. DOI: 10.1177/27538699241238049

Ryan, M., & Stahl, B. C. (2020). Artificial intelligence ethics guidelines for developers and users: Clarifying their content and normative implications. *Journal of Information. Communication and Ethics in Society*, *19*(1), 61–86. DOI: 10.1108/JICES-12-2019-0138

Sawyer, R. K., & Henriksen, D. (2024). *Explaining creativity: The science of human innovation.* Oxford university press.

Sengar, S. S., Hasan, A. B., Kumar, S., & Carroll, F. (2024). Generative artificial intelligence: A systematic review and applications. *Multimedia Tools and Applications*, *84*(21), 1–40. DOI: 10.1007/s11042-024-20016-1

Shahzad, M. F., Xu, S., & Zahid, H. (2024). Exploring the impact of generative AI-based technologies on learning performance through self-efficacy, fairness & ethics, creativity, and trust in higher education. *Education and Information Technologies*, •••, 1–26.

Singha, S., & Singha, R. (2024). Revolutionizing content creation and curriculum development through generative AI. In *Transforming Education With Generative AI: Prompt Engineering and Synthetic Content Creation* (pp. 261-280). IGI Global Scientific Publishing. DOI: 10.4018/979-8-3693-1351-0.ch013

Tanweer, M., & Ismail, A. (2024). Generative AI in curriculum development: A framework for adaptive, customized, and personalized learning. In *Impacts of Generative AI on Creativity in Higher Education* (pp. 193–226). IGI Global. DOI: 10.4018/979-8-3693-2418-9.ch008

Yan, L., Greiff, S., & Teuber, Z. ve Gašević, D. (2024). İnsan öğrenmesi için üretken yapay zekanın vaatleri ve zorlukları. *Doğa İnsan Davranışı*, *8*(10), 1839–1850.

Yao, F., Li, C., Nekipelov, D., Wang, H., & Xu, H. (2024). Human vs. generative AI in content creation competition: symbiosis or conflict? *arXiv preprint arXiv:2402.15467.*

Zhao, J., Chapman, E., & Sabet, P. G. (2024). Generative AI and Educational Assessments: A Systematic Review. *Education Research and Perspectives (Online)*, *51*, 124–155. DOI: 10.70953/ERPv51.2412006

Zhou, E., & Lee, D. (2024). Generative artificial intelligence, human creativity, and art. *PNAS Nexus*, *3*(3), pgae052. DOI: 10.1093/pnasnexus/pgae052 PMID: 38444602

KEY TERMS AND DEFINITIONS

Autonomy: What allows individuals' autonomy to be protected in decision-making processes is that individuals are not deceived, manipulated in user-system interactions, and to make their own decisions freely is protected and supported.

Beneficence: It is the inclusive design of artificial intelligence systems to serve the common good of individuals and societies, produce solutions to social problems, support the production of scientific knowledge and increase the level of welfare.

Dignity: It is the observation of the intrinsic value and dignity of humans by artificial intelligence systems and the meticulous consideration of this value in the development and use processes of the system.

Ethics: Morality philosophy that deals with what is right and wrong.

Freedom: The operation of artificial intelligence systems should be transparent, explainable and based on the protection of freedoms, and should be developed and used in a way that does not include processes and elements that limit or harm the fundamental rights and freedoms of individuals.

Justice: The development processes and outputs of an artificial intelligence system should be structured in a way that ensures equality and fairness among all individuals and is based on human well-being.

Non-Maleficence: It is the development and use of artificial intelligence systems in a way that does not cause economic, cultural, political, environmental, social and psychological harm, taking into account social health, security and human dignity.

Privacy: The development of artificial intelligence systems within the framework of an understanding that ensures the confidentiality of personal data, the protection of personal rights and privacy in the processes of collecting, processing, storing and sharing personal data, and the development of preventive, supervisory and limiting mechanisms against the risk of violation.

Responsibility: In the development of accountable AI systems, responsibility is distributed among developers, users, institutions and decision makers, and the roles and responsibilities are clear at all stages from the development of a safe, transparent and ethical system to its use, and the system itself cannot be held accountable.

Solidarity: The principle is that artificial intelligence systems should support the preservation and maintenance of social solidarity, protect cultural values and contribute to the strengthening of social ties.

Sustainability: Artificial intelligence systems should not harm the environment, should take into account not only today but also the future, should observe the ecological balance of the planet, should protect and use natural resources efficiently, should promote renewable technologies and should be environmentally friendly.

Transparency: Providing clear, understandable and accessible information about the design, operation, decisions, data and outputs of the artificial intelligence system.

Trust: It expresses the expectation of individuals that artificial intelligence systems operate in a consistent, reliable, predictable manner and will produce understandable responses in unexpected situations.

Chapter 6
The McFlai Model:
Back to the Future of Distance Education With AI

Sefa Emre Öncü
https://orcid.org/0009-0008-2314-4628
Anadolu University, Turkey

ABSTRACT

This book chapter introduces the McFlai Model, which aims to shape the future of distance education by integrating micro-credentials, flipped learning models, and artificial intelligence. The model proposes employing various language models for distinct purposes throughout the learning process, from enrolment to assessment stages. Consequently, it envisages designing highly personalised, flexible, and interactive learning experiences. The model is supported by dynamic content tailored to learners' individual needs and proficiency levels, learning analytics, and guidance systems powered by generative artificial intelligence. Furthermore, it recommends utilising large language models to convert instructional materials into micro-credential formats and to monitor learner progress, thereby supporting educators. Artificial intelligence systems, overseen by human experts at every step, aim to enhance learner success while enabling educators to subtly contribute to content design and guidance. McFlai offers a sustainable, practical, and scalable solution for distance education systems.

INTRODUCTION: FROM PAST TO THE FUTURE IN DISTANCE EDUCATION

In the Back to the Future film series, directed by Zemeckis (1985, 1989, 1990) and produced by Spielberg, Marty McFly realises he has reshaped the future by al-

DOI: 10.4018/979-8-3373-7579-3.ch006

ght © 2026, IGI Global Scientific Publishing. Copying or distributing in print or electronic forms without written permission of IGI Global Scientific Publishing is prohibited. Use of this chapter to generative artificial intelligence (AI) technologies is expressly prohibited. The publisher reserves all rights to license its use for generative AI training and machine learning model development.

tering events in the past during his journey with Doctor Emmett Brown's DeLorean. The clearest depiction of this phenomenon is the photograph in his pocket, which instantaneously changes according to his actions. Could science and technology allow us to metaphorically "travel in time"-learning from the past, informing the present, and envisioning the future of education? If we prompted Generative Artificial Intelligence (GenAI) to simulate such capabilities or requested predictive modelling from Agentic AI, could we reimagine our trajectory in educational innovation? For instance, would it not be fascinating to use a time machine to return to 1985 and witness the initial enthusiasm during the golden days of distance education (DE)? Alternatively, can we foresee what we will experience even a year from now-how artificial intelligence (AI) will evolve and where we will stand?

Setting aside dystopian scenarios, our primary focus should be on the potential of today's GenAI. Just as Marty's photograph dynamically adapts based on his actions, GenAI can similarly deliver personalised and dynamic experiences to learners, directly inspiring DE. At this juncture, two ironic discussions arise. Firstly, institutions unable to adapt to this new dynamism-that is, AI-may find their names engraved on gravestones, akin to those depicted in Marty's photograph. Secondly, institutions surrendering entirely and unconditionally to AI may inadvertently inscribe their own names on those same gravestones. One-size-fits-all approaches that fail to embrace the dynamism offered by AI may thus become destined for disappearance, mirroring the fading image in Marty's photo. GenAI and Large Language Models (LLMs) may serve as a modern-day "flux capacitor"-a catalyst that powers the entire educational journey, from personalised programme selection to adaptive content completion at the learner's own pace.

This chapter aims to position the learner as a navigator on their educational journey, considering all processes from selecting the most suitable programme/course/MC before even commencing the learning experience, to successfully completing all dynamic and interactive content. Additionally, predictions are discussed regarding how trained and structured GenAI tools, along with their underlying LLMs, might be effectively used under human supervision. Ultimately, machines bear neither ethical nor legal responsibility; hence, the accountability for GenAI tools lies squarely with the individuals and institutions that design, deploy, and supervise them. Pedagogical responsibility within DE rests with educators and institutional administrators. Consequently, the future of DE should be determined by experts, and the "Synchronise Your Watches" component (designing the learning process) should remain in the hands of specialists.

This chapter elaborates on the use of trained and structured AI tools that empower learners as navigators, providing detailed examples. While inventing a time machine may be impossible, we will explore the boundaries of what can indeed be achieved. We envision instructional materials tailored to specific micro-credentials that dynamically adapt to each learner's profile. Within this context, we aim to place the learner as the captain of their own journey, seeking to answer the question: "The McFlai Model: Back to the Future of Distance Education with AI."

BACKGROUND: UNDERSTAND THE CURRENT TRANSFORMATION

To what extent does the integration of technology in education diversify pedagogical approaches, and to what extent might it constrain learning within rigid structures? Do technology-enhanced environments genuinely promote learner agency, or do they risk relegating learners to passive recipients of information? Although the use of technology in education holds the potential to foster personalised learning experiences, has this potential always been fully realised? Regarding these and similar questions, there are differing perspectives about whether technology genuinely creates personalised learning experiences or instead promotes a more standardised, mass-produced, and homogenous approach to education (Selwyn, 2011). Some studies argue that although technology initially promised diversity and autonomy in education, it has evolved into a more standardised model due to economic and structural pressures (Cuban, 1986).

Although it is acknowledged that technology is not a panacea, there is an increasing imperative to shift from one-size-fits-all approaches to intentional, learner-centred, and diversity-oriented practices in DE (Anderson & Dron, 2011). Information and communication technologies (ICT), in particular, have historically manifested in various forms in DE, including correspondence courses, radio broadcasts, television programmes, computer-assisted learning, and mobile applications. Since the 2020s, research into how GenAI tools and LLMs can be utilised in education has accelerated (Bozkurt, 2023).

Regardless of the type of technology used, the essential issue remains the extent to which learners' genuine needs are met. Rapidly advancing technologies, such as GenAI, must be continuously assessed from a critical perspective. Responsible use lies not solely with learners but also with institutions and educators. The effectiveness of educational technologies should be evaluated not just by their innovativeness but also by their pedagogical impact. The convergence of technology and DE is establishing a new paradigm, transforming instructional design from a static to a dynamic and interactive structure, making learning an experience that transcends spatial and temporal boundaries. However, due to limited interdisciplinary research, the field of educational technology occasionally remains trapped in cyclical repetitions. Approaching education from only one disciplinary perspective can result in superficial analyses.

Against this evolving backdrop, this chapter explores the integration of Flipped Learning (FL) and Micro-Credentials (MC) with Generative AI (GenAI) to offer scalable, personalised solutions in distance education. FL initially prepares learners conceptually and subsequently engages them in higher-level inquiry-based learning experiences (Lo & Hew, 2017; O'Flaherty & Phillips, 2015). MC, described as "portable" certificates, institutionally validate learners' competencies in specific measurable areas, providing personalised learning opportunities despite their massive reach (Ralston, 2021). Institutions aiming to realise personalised learning concretely focus on AI-supported adaptive content systems. Such systems not only target examinations but also continuously support learners by establishing individualised feedback loops (Luckin, 2017; Popenici & Kerr, 2017).

In both traditional and MC learning experiences, learners should be supported effectively and precisely at the moment of need. Comprehensive learner support services are crucial, particularly in DE, to ensure sustained academic achievement and motivation (Simpson, 2008; Tait, 2000). Traditional definitions of support have evolved with advancements in ICT, especially with the increased application of AI technologies in DE. Learner support systems have transformed into structures capable of providing personalised and instantaneous responses (Bozkurt, 2024). AI-based learner support systems play a pivotal role in shaping individual learning experiences. Specifically, GenAI-based support systems analyse learners' individual needs and provide personalised guidance, ensuring motivational support by optimising learning processes continuously. These developments have elevated learner support to become an integral part of the learning experience.

In this context, for learners seeking brief and flexible educational experiences, the combined and integrated use of FL and MC approaches with advanced GenAI and sophisticated LLM integration offers significant potential for effective learning. This book chapter aims to propose a model that harnesses this potential learning experience.

MOVING FORWARD: THE NEED FOR NAVIGABLE PATHWAYS

DE is an educational approach through which learners can experience macro (long-term) or micro (goal-oriented and modular) learning in their desired fields, shaping their learning processes more freely compared to traditional educational methods. Historically, DE has consistently evolved through the effective use of technology (e.g., correspondence, radio, television, internet). Due to its adaptive nature, DE has successfully leveraged contemporary technologies to provide accessible environments for learners. Today, smart mobile devices enable learners to benefit from DE opportunities anytime and anywhere.

Open universities, which offer a learner-centred model at the institutional level, have played a pioneering role in the expansion of DE. Historically, DE systems have supported individualised learning experiences since their inception. For instance, individuals watching educational broadcasts while sipping coffee in front of their televisions after a day's work or after farming experienced distinctive learning opportunities, demonstrating that DE could be successfully implemented through open universities. The societal impact of open universities can be metaphorically compared to the introduction of mass-produced automobiles-initially met with scepticism (e.g., "Why buy cars when we have horses?") but eventually becoming indispensable to daily life. Similarly, open universities have facilitated access to knowledge, bringing a new dimension to learners' lives. Following the success of BBC Radio's educational broadcasts, the establishment of The Open University in 1969 demonstrated that DE could be implemented systematically and institutionally, attracting global interest (Tresman, 2002). Open universities have become particularly appealing alternatives for learners constrained by time, location, and financial factors. Furthermore, these institutions have remained relevant by continuously adapting to technological innovations. The primary objective of institutionalised DE models, established through open universities, is to empower learner autonomy, personalise learning, and enable learners to manage their own learning processes effectively (Koçdar et al., 2024). Realising the full transformative potential of emerging technologies such as GenAI requires a strategic emphasis on the intersection of pedagogy and technology within educational design (Bozkurt & Sharma, 2023). In this context, redefining educator and learner roles, revising knowledge access policies, and creating flexible curricula have become inevitable (Ashby, 2004).

The concept of social presence is used in DE to articulate whether learners are positioned as mere objects or as genuine subjects within the learning process. Social presence refers to learners' sense of being real, visible, and relatable subjects in distance learning environments. This concept was initially introduced by Garrison et al. (1999) within the Community of Inquiry (CoI) model, providing a theoretical foundation for the social dimension of online learning. Social presence is regarded not merely as an emotional state but as a crucial determinant of active participation, interactive bonds, and learner engagement within the learning process.

In GenAI-supported learning environments, the concept of social presence may play a pivotal role. Personalising communication between learners and GenAI-based systems, delivering meaningful feedback, and creating environments in which learners can discover their own learning identities are directly associated with social presence (Kozan & Richardson, 2014). When GenAI systems become more than mere knowledge delivery tools-transforming into structures that support social interaction and render the learner's presence visible-the learning experience can deepen and become more sustainable (Lowenthal & Snelson, 2017).

Bozkurt et al.'s (2024) manifesto on the use of Generative Artificial Intelligence (GenAI) in teaching and learning offers a concise and collective framework for integrating GenAI into education, emphasizing equity, human agency, ecological sustainability, and evidence-based practice. The fundamental principles of this manifesto directly shape the ethical safeguards of the McFlai Model, specifically fairness, sustained human oversight, and environmentally conscious innovation. In this context, the manifesto serves as a guiding framework for the vision of GenAI-enhanced distance learning articulated in this chapter.

In this context, the proposed McFlai model positions the concept of social presence at its core, aiming to establish learners not merely as recipients of information but as actively participating, meaning-making, and feedback-providing subjects. GenAI-supported interactive content delivery, personalised learning pathways, and multilingual discussion environments are designed to enhance learners' visibility and sense of belonging in their digital learning journeys.

THEORETICAL AND CONCEPTUAL FOUNDATIONS

The following section outlines the core concepts of FL and MCs, which underpin this book chapter.

Flipped Learning: The New Normal in Distance Education

Flipped learning (FL) is an approach that reverses the traditional teaching model by placing the learner at the centre of the educational process. This model was initially adapted for secondary education by Bergman & Sams (2012), who introduced it into academic literature. The FL approach aims to increase individual responsibility, encouraging learners to engage actively in their learning experiences (Bishop & Verleger, 2013). O'Flaherty & Phillips (2015) classified FL processes into three primary phases:

- Preparation Phase: Learners individually acquire fundamental concepts, using tools such as videos, articles, or interactive content to gain preliminary knowledge.
- Implementation Phase: Learners consolidate knowledge acquired during the preparation phase through active learning activities, such as problem-solving, discussions, and project-based learning, within classroom, lecture, or course environments.

- Evaluation Phase: Learning outcomes are assessed, activating feedback mechanisms focused on both process and outcomes.

In this three-stage structure, enabling learners to independently sustain individual learning processes in DE is essential for fostering continuous motivation towards lifelong learning. Following the COVID-19 pandemic, FL has effectively become the "new normal" in DE (Bond et al., 2021; Hew et al., 2020). Additionally, when AI-based adaptive learning systems are integrated into FL, it enhances opportunities for delivering learner-specific content, thereby facilitating personalisation of the learning process (López-Villanueva et al., 2024). Sein-Echaluce et al. (2024) demonstrated that the integration of AI-supported tools into FL within DE promotes a more learner-centred and collaborative approach. AI-supported FL enables learners to enhance their academic performance, as well as collaborative skills and competencies. In this context, the FL model is highly compatible with the use of AI technologies in DE, serving as an important resource for enriching learning experiences. The skilful involvement of human experts in pedagogically designing learning processes is crucial to effectively leveraging this resource. Once appropriate systems are designed, learners should be supported by AI tools trained and managed by human experts.

Micro-credentials: Towards Modular and Personalised Learning

The literature provides diverse definitions of Micro-credential (MC). Broadly, MCs are defined as short-term, modular, and verifiable certifications in specific areas of expertise. Hollands & Tirthali (2014) characterise MCs as accredited certificates within modern higher education, emphasising their significance as flexible, career-oriented learning alternatives compared to traditional, long-term programmes. UNESCO (2023) has proposed a classification for MC structures based on principles of "flexibility, transparency, and portability," positioning these structures as central components of lifelong learning strategies.

MCs can metaphorically be described as a form of "portable" learning-lightweight, easily transportable, ready to learn anytime and anywhere, occupying minimal space (Oliver, 2019; Ralston, 2021). Since the early 2010s, with the rise of massive open online courses (MOOCs), the MC concept has gained prominence in education. Particularly since 2012, when platforms such as Coursera, edX, and Udemy began offering large-scale online courses, individuals have gained measurable and verifiable skills and knowledge within shorter periods. This development has clarified the necessity of achieving learning outcomes.

In the context of DE, MC is critical for personalised and outcome-oriented learning designs. Traditional DE systems typically rely on broad, well-defined programmes, whereas MC provides smaller-scale, targeted, and learner-sensitive experiences. This structure allows learners to progress at their own pace in specific skills or knowledge areas, focusing on personal and professional development. Moreover, technologies such as digital badges, open certificates, and digital verification systems have enabled MCs acquired through DE to become reliable and internationally recognised (Hunt et al., 2020). These advancements transform DE from merely an access-oriented model into a dynamic system offering personalised, competency-based learning pathways. Consequently, MC has become integral to creating learner-centred ecosystems in DE, supporting individual learning trajectories (Peterson & Cox, 2025; Van de Laar et al., 2024).

Ward et al. (2024) highlighted that integrating skill profiling and badge systems into a universal MC framework within informatics education enriches interdisciplinary learning and assessment processes by supporting AI-enhanced personalised learning pathways. In this context, combining AI with MC enables learners to define their own learning paths and addresses industry needs by developing skilled professionals in specific sectors. Designing accessible, effective, and self-paced systems is therefore crucial (Barrera et al., 2024).

While MCs appear in diverse forms in the literature, they share core standard principles:

- Transparent Definition Document: Each MC must be publicly available through a "spec sheet," clearly detailing learning outcomes, level, workload, and assessment methods (Oliver, 2019).
- Transparent Metadata: Badges/certificates should be provided in machine-readable formats, preferably including European Qualification Framework (EQF) levels and European Credit Transfer System (ECTS) workload information (The European Commission, 2022).
- Stackability: MCs should be modular and designed to be stackable, contributing towards higher-level qualifications (UNESCO, 2023).
- Portability: Digital badges must comply with open badge standards, enabling verification within interoperable learner wallets (Ward et al., 2024).
- Quality Assurance: Programmes must undergo independent quality assessments, regularly publishing external evaluation reports (Oliver, 2019).
- Assessment: Multiple assessment methods should be employed (Miao et al., 2024).
- Access & Equity: Designs must adhere to equity and accessibility principles, providing transparent information accessible to all user profiles (UNESCO, 2023).

- Workload Declaration: Workload details must be explicitly stated in metadata, and associated with ECTS credits where applicable (The European Commission, 2022).
- Continuity: Programme catalogues should be regularly updated, incorporating labour market data and learner feedback in revision processes (Ward et al., 2024).
- Data Privacy: Learner data must be processed in compliance with the General Data Protection Regulation (GDPR) or equivalent, and sharing must be based on explicit learner consent (Miao et al., 2024).

Despite institutional variations in implementation, these ten principles constitute a foundational framework for ensuring that MCs function as transparent, learner-centred, and sustainable educational components.

The McFlai Model: A Model Of Micro-Credential, Flipped Learning, And Artificial Intelligence

This book chapter aims to model a learner-centred, flexible, and personalised AI-supported learning pathway by integrating the flipped learning (FL) approach with micro-credential (MC) structures. MC effectively develops learners' 21st-century skills, particularly critical thinking, problem-solving, and communication (Li & Ironsi, 2024). Since the 2019 pandemic, FL has been established as the "new normal," demonstrated to be fully implementable online not only theoretically but also practically, as learners have experienced and continue to experience in real-life settings (Hew et al., 2020). Although the combined use of FL and MC approaches is not entirely novel, there is limited research explicitly proposing this integration. One such work by Atas (2025) suggests that FL can be integrated into MC structures popularised by MOOCs through expert instructors.

The McFlai model (micro-credential, flipped learning with artificial intelligence) proposed in this chapter aims to offer learning pathways tailored to learners' individual needs through a GenAI-supported flipped MC approach. The fundamental stages of the model are presented in the infographic shown in Figure 1.

Figure 1. Infographic illustrating the role of Generative Artificial Intelligence in the McFlai Model

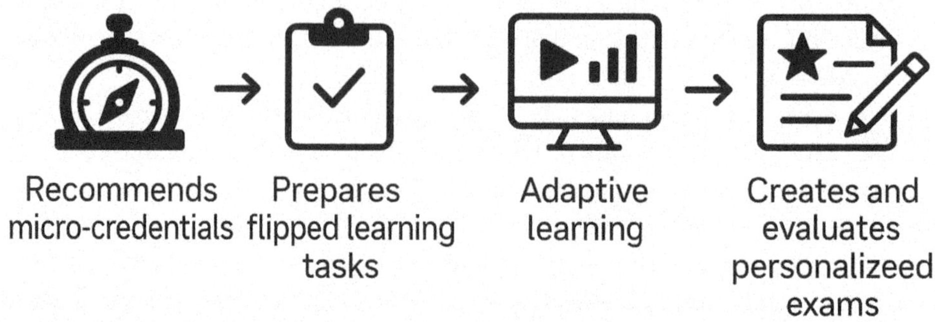

In Figure 1, the McFlai Model is designed to cover the entire process from enrolment to examination. Within this framework, the key stages of the model are listed below:

- Recommends micro-credentials: After human expert instructors design the learning process, GenAI (recommends the most suitable MCs for learners.
- Prepares flipped learning tasks: A critical stage of the model involves GenAI providing learners with preparatory tasks related to module content prior to each module, within the FL framework. At this stage, instructors must determine how the LLMs will be used. Based on the learner's performance in the FL tasks, module content will dynamically adapt to individual learner needs.
- Adaptive learning: Real-time learning analytics monitored by GenAI track the learner's progress in FL tasks, subsequently delivering dynamically personalised content tailored to their proficiency levels.
- Creates and evaluates personalised exams: Upon completion of all modules, personalised examinations aligned with evaluation criteria determined by human instructors are created by GenAI. These assessments are administered by GenAI but subsequently reviewed by human instructors.

Learner support in DE must be systematically provided, enabling learners to chart their own course independently. Distance learners without guidance risk becoming lost on open seas. The McFlai Model is designed to enable distance learners to reach their desired educational destinations through their own efforts. To this end, Figure 2 describes the steps of the model that use GenAI and LLMs as navigational tools.

Figure 2.The steps of the McFlai Model

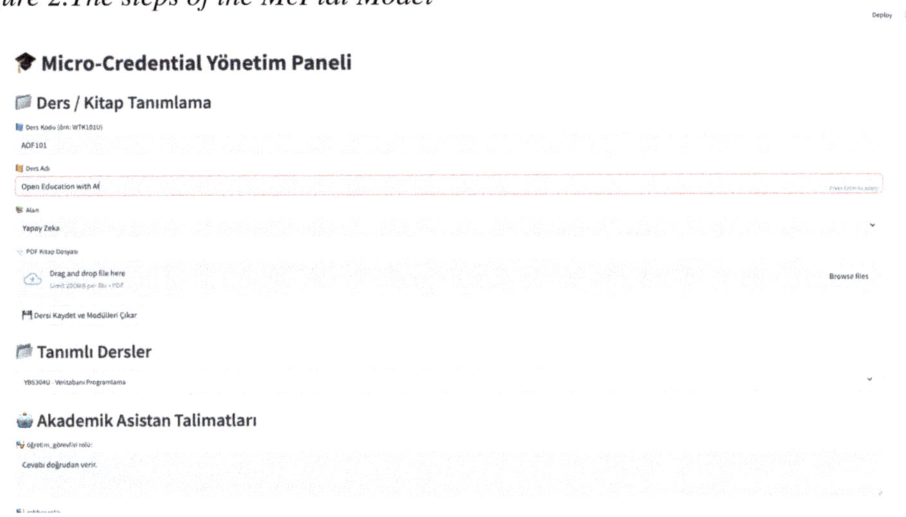

The McFlai Model, detailed in ten steps, has been meticulously aligned with the personalised structure of DE. Each step encourages active learner participation while simultaneously incorporating instructor guidance. The timing for learners to complete each module may vary depending on their prior knowledge, learning pace, and module complexity. However, thanks to the AI-supported system, instructors will design the learning process only once for each module. The specific steps of the model are presented below.

PHASE 1: PATHWAY DESIGN

Phase 1 establishes bespoke learning trajectories by sequentially generating GenAI-based content, transforming that material into flipped micro-credential packages and recommending the most appropriate credential pathway for each learner.

Step 1: Designing GenAI-Based Educational Content

"Understanding the Flux Capacitor": In this step, the instructor creates the initial educational content for the learning process. These materials will subsequently be transformed into the required formats by GenAI tools.

The integration of GenAI into learning systems represents a pivotal moment in the evolution of DE. Discussions around AI began with Alan Turing's (1950) question, "Can machines think?", and AI was formally established as a scientific field at the 1956 Dartmouth Conference (McCarthy et al., 1955). This ongoing evolution continues in higher education-and particularly in DE-through the development and deployment of LLMs. MCs, as a recent development within this trajectory, offer a new perspective on modular, AI-supported learning.

LLMs are increasingly used in learner-centred instructional design within DE due to their capacity for contextual analysis, content generation, and personalised recommendations. Educational programmes and content can be customised according to individual learner profiles. For instance, systems such as OpenAI's "MyGPT" allow even users with no programming experience to generate instructional materials tailored to their needs. Furthermore, LLMs can automatically convert learning content into MC formats, offering both time-saving and institutional standardisation benefits (Haase & Hanel, 2023; Öncü, 2025; Zawacki-Richter et al., 2020).

This technological transformation should not be understood merely as a change in tools and applications; it also marks a pedagogical and ethical paradigm shift. Mao et al. (2024) stress the importance of institutional frameworks concerning fairness, transparency, and data privacy in the use of GenAI. Likewise, Luckin (2017) highlights pedagogical and ethical responsibilities in AI-supported assessment systems. Popenici and Kerr (2017) assert that GenAI renders educational environments more dynamic, while Zawacki-Richter et al. (2020) point out that GenAI has the potential to redefine educators' roles and transform existing educational structures. Accordingly, the use of GenAI in the development of learning materials not only facilitates the construction of individualised and accessible educational pathways but also supports a sustainable digital infrastructure that simplifies the content design process for educators.

This initial stage of the McFlai Model focuses on the reconfiguration of MC materials into institutional formats by AI-based systems, ensuring alignment with programme outcomes and learning objectives. However, for this transformation to be effective, it is essential that instructions given to GenAI systems are clearly defined. Such clarity ensures the establishment of quality standards for MC content and enhances the efficiency of labour and institutional resources.

Step 2: Converting Material into Flipped Micro-Credential Format

"Hitting 88 MPH": In this stage, GenAI tools restructure static educational materials into modular content aligned with FL principles and MC standards.

AI technologies enhance MC processes by analysing learner data and offering personalised learning pathways and adaptive content, thereby making the learning experience more effective and efficient (Ali & Khan, 2023; Miao et al., 2024). In contrast to traditional learning methods and standard degree programmes, this approach enables learners to access the required knowledge swiftly and flexibly. Moreover, the ability to shape content according to learners' individual habits and needs represents a significant milestone in personalised education.

Although the effectiveness of this step within the McFlai Model may vary depending on the capabilities of the selected LLMs, institutions can, within their own quality standards, enable expert instructors to convert existing materials into the required formats. At this juncture, it is essential to establish well-defined standards and modular structures and to ensure that processes are carefully designed.

By "hitting 88 MPH"-a reference to the critical speed at which time travel is triggered in Back to the Future-this step symbolises the transformative point at which static content accelerates into dynamic, personalised, and recognisable MC pathways, enabling a truly learner-centred experience.

Step 3: Recommending the Best-Fit Micro-credential Path for Each Learner

"Your Future Isn't Written Yet": At this stage, GenAI analyses learners' interests, professions, and career goals to recommend the most suitable micro-credential pathway.

Research on automated, digital, rule-based AI academic advisors and personalised counselling systems has demonstrated their significance in supporting distance learners at the moment of need. These systems help ensure that learners can continue their educational journeys without losing motivation due to unanswered questions or lack of support (Almutawah, 2014; Kamarthi et al., 1992; Sutton & Sankar, 2011; Taha, 2012; Valtorta et al., 1984). Since the 2020s, advancements in LLMs have made it possible for GenAI tools to understand and guide learners more effectively, thereby enabling high-quality academic support (McKinney et al., 2024; Pangestu & Karnalim, 2023; Thottoli et al., 2024). However, studies focused on AI-based advisory systems prior to enrolment remain limited. Post-enrolment academic counselling has been shown to play a critical role in learners' academic success.

Academic advisors assist learners in developing responsibility, critical thinking, and decision-making skills (Saiyad & Mahajan, 2023). Human advisors, through interaction and analysis, help learners realise their true potential (Gong et al., 2024). In DE, however, the absence of academic counselling-or its limitation due to high learner numbers-often leads to the assumption that learners will conduct their own research independently. Furthermore, inadequate institutional websites, complex navigation, missing information, or the lack of clear guidance services can hinder learner retention (Bañeres et al., 2023; Gündüz & Karaman, 2020). In this context, GenAI tools powered by LLMs have substantial potential to recommend the most appropriate programme or course to each learner (Öncü et al., 2025).

The third step of the McFlai Model aims to match each learner with the most appropriate MC based on their individual profiles. This process aligns with the Self-Determination Theory (SDT), which emphasises the psychological needs of autonomy, competence, and relatedness. According to SDT, meeting these needs is essential for sustaining intrinsic motivation (Ryan & Deci, 2023). Therefore, designing personalised learning pathways that consider learners' interests, prior knowledge, and educational goals adds value to the learning process.

Within this model, learners receive course recommendations through LLMs before selecting an MC. GenAI analyses key terms related to their interests and career objectives to suggest the most appropriate MC. Learners may then enrol in the recommended MC or one of their own choosing.

PHASE 2: ADAPTIVE MODULE DELIVERY

Phase 2 integrates flipped-learning analytics with real-time content orchestration, creating adaptive modules, guiding personalised pathways through data-driven insights and presenting dynamic GenAI content to sustain learner engagement.

Step 4: Creating Adaptive Modules Based on Flipped Learning Performance

"Roads? Where We're Going, We Don't Need Fixed Roads": At this stage, adaptive modules are dynamically generated based on responses to FL tasks and real-time learner data.

Choosing the right programme or course is one of the most critical decisions in a learner's academic journey. Once this decision is made, the next pivotal step involves developing content tailored to the learner's needs. There is increasing focus on designing systems capable of understanding learners, continuously tracking their progress, and delivering personalised, interactive content. In this context, AI's role in curriculum personalisation has shown that adapting learning experiences to individual needs can enhance learners' motivation and positively influence academic success (Wang et al., 2024). Although AI-based support systems-through smart recommendations and automated feedback-are said to improve learners' independent learning abilities, concerns have also been raised about the potential for technological dependency and a weakening of critical thinking skills (du Plooy et al., 2024). To mitigate such negative effects, the integration of the FL approach is particularly valuable. Baig & Yadegaridehkordi (2023) emphasise that FL enhances learner engagement and supports academic achievement, while Villarica (2023) highlights the positive impact of FL experiences on improving learning processes.

In this step of the McFlai Model, LLMs are used to generate a MC content structure that can be dynamically adapted based on learners' performance in FL tasks. This pre-module preparation phase involves tasks that may vary depending on the specific MC and module. However, in order to ensure the effective operation of learning analytics and the delivery of dynamic, interactive content, it is essential to establish clear standards for the FL approach.

By avoiding rigid pathways-hence "no fixed roads"-the model embraces a flexible, responsive structure, ensuring that each learner's journey is uniquely aligned with their demonstrated learning behaviours and needs.

Step 5: Applying Learning Analytics to Guide Personalised Pathways

"Prepare for the Lightning Strike": Learning analytics involves the systematic collection, analysis, and reporting of data generated in digital learning environments to monitor learners and their learning contexts.

The aim of this process is to optimise learning experiences and adapt them to individual differences. The term was first introduced by Long & Siemens (2011), who associated it with "data-driven decision-making in education." It was given a theoretical framework at the inaugural Learning Analytics and Knowledge (LAK) conference held the same year. Unlike traditional assessment approaches, learning analytics enables dynamic monitoring of the learning process and the development of data-informed intervention strategies. Ferguson (2012) highlighted its paradigmatic impact on educational technologies, while Gašević et al. (2015) stressed the importance of its integration into learning design. Ifenthaler (2022) emphasised the use of visualisation techniques in developing learner models and examined AI integration. Alfredo et al. (2023) demonstrated how AI-supported learning analytics contribute to pedagogical decision support systems.

AI-powered learning analytics hold significant potential for improving learning processes by analysing learner data to adapt content dynamically. The combination of learning analytics and AI algorithms enables real-time tracking of learner progress. In summary, AI-supported learning analytics reinforce learner-centred approaches in education (Alfredo et al., 2023; Avcı et al., 2021; Sousa et al., 2021).

Assessing learners' prior knowledge before each module is critical for enabling personalisation within the McFlai Model. This stage involves an online learning process that begins with AI-supported tasks and instant feedback, progresses with content that dynamically adapts to the learner's task performance, includes a level-based mini-assessment and feedback at the end of each module, highlights challenging topics before the next module, and concludes with a comprehensive final evaluation once all modules are completed.

At this step, interaction data-such as content access frequency, exam performance, and participation in discussions-is analysed. The insights gained are used to provide timely and targeted feedback to learners. Moreover, learning analytics also offer valuable insights to instructional designers and educators, enabling them to evaluate and enhance the effectiveness of learning materials and instructional strategies.

Step 6: Presenting Dynamic Content through Generative Artificial Intelligence

"Watch the Photograph Change": At this stage, personalised, dynamic, and interactive content is presented by GenAI, tailored in real time according to the learner's level and previous performance.

The use of interactive learning methods is essential for helping learners apply theoretical knowledge in practice, develop cognitive skills, and enhance overall competencies. Marchenko et al. (2023) suggest that learner-centred education encourages educators to adopt innovative instructional methods. Jauhiainen & Garagorry Guerra (2024), in their examination of ChatGPT in educational practice, demonstrated that content can be adapted in real time according to learners' levels, thus enabling highly personalised learning materials. Personalised and adaptive learning approaches not only support the development of critical thinking but also contribute to increased academic performance and learning motivation by shaping the learning process around individual needs (Song & Cai, 2024). Zhou (2025) further notes that adaptive learning significantly boosts learner engagement, motivation, and learning outcomes. Within the McFlai Model, GenAI is employed not only for content generation but also for dynamically restructuring content in real time based on the learner's performance level. This adaptive structure transforms the learning experience into a truly personalised and sustainable process. The model's adaptivity functions not only at the content level but also in determining the configuration of subsequent steps based on the learner's performance in previous tasks. For example:

- For lower-performing learners, foundational content is supplemented with detailed explanations, illustrative examples, and conceptual scaffolding to support knowledge construction.
- For intermediate learners, the standard content is maintained, with selective examples provided to reinforce conceptual connections.
- For advanced learners, only essential content is delivered, enabling a streamlined and self-directed learning experience.

Throughout this step, learner performance is regularly monitored and analysed. The resulting data is used to deliver specific and timely feedback, allowing learners to reflect on and adjust their own learning trajectories.

In essence, just as the photograph in Back to the Future changes in response to Marty's actions, each learner can "change the photograph" of their learning future based on their past performance.

PHASE 3: ASSESSMENT & FEEDBACK LOOP

Phase 3 closes the instructional cycle by administering reflective, learning-outcome-aligned examinations and delivering immediate, AI-mediated formative feedback that informs subsequent learning decisions.

Step 7: Conducting Reflective Exams Aligned with Learning Outcomes

"Like Auto-Adjusting Jackets & Hoverboards": In this stage, assessment tools aligned with previously defined learning outcomes are generated and evaluated by AI, dynamically adapting to the learner's performance level-just as self-adjusting jackets and hoverboards adapt to the user in Back to the Future.

There are varying perspectives on the role of LLMs in the assessment processes within education. Wei et al. (2025) demonstrated that concept-based rubrics enhance the formative assessment capabilities of LLMs, enabling more accurate and explanatory evaluation of learners' responses to open-ended questions. Similarly, Cohn et al. (2024) found that GPT-4, when supported by chain-of-thought prompts, proved effective in automatically scoring short-answer responses and providing explanatory feedback. Moreover, Ye et al. (2022) reported that the integration of LLMs into the FL approach positively influences learners' cognitive development. Collectively, these studies suggest that incorporating LLMs into pedagogical approaches such as FL and MCs can make assessment processes more flexible, learner-centred, and effective.

Accordingly, in the McFlai Model, mini exams supported by LLMs are administered at the end of each module. These exams are tailored to the learner's current level, ensuring that the adaptive learning journey is sustained in a data-driven manner. Thanks to the capabilities of LLMs, each learner receives dynamically generated, interactive, and level-specific questions that reflect their real-time performance.

By aligning assessment closely with learning outcomes and using GenAI to personalise the format and content, this step ensures that evaluation becomes not a static endpoint, but a meaningful and responsive element of the learner's continuous development.

Step 8: Delivering Timely and Constructive Feedback via Artificial Intelligence

"It Requires Precise Timing": In this stage, feedback is provided in real time by AI systems, supporting learners' self-regulation skills, motivation, and metacognitive awareness.

AI-powered feedback systems possess the potential to make learning processes more effective and personalised. For instance, the LLM-based system developed by Uchiyama et al. (2023) delivers immediate feedback to learners during the preparatory phase of FL, increasing motivation and encouraging active participation. Similarly,, Zhang et al. (2025) proposed the SEFL (Synthetic Educational Feedback Loops) framework, which uses LLMs to offer instant and personalised feedback on learners' assignments, thereby enhancing the efficiency and effectiveness of learning processes. Moreover, Kuzminykh et al. (2024) introduced a personalised feedback framework that integrates LLMs into learning management systems (LMS), providing feedback tailored to individual learner needs.

These studies highlight the potential of integrating AI-driven feedback systems into pedagogical models such as FL and MCs making learning more flexible, learner-centred, and impactful. In the FL process, just as the alignment of pre-module tasks with module goals and content is crucial, the provision of timely, structured feedback during these tasks is equally vital for learning success.

In the McFlai Model, feedback provided at the end of each module plays a decisive role in reinforcing learners' knowledge and in helping them plan their next steps. Furthermore, at the beginning of a subsequent module, it is essential not only to offer general reminders about the previous one but also to highlight specific gaps and errors. Thanks to the AI-supported model, learners receive personalised reminders and warnings before each new module, which help to uncover and address weaknesses that may have gone unnoticed. This enables learners to engage in continuous self-improvement throughout the learning process.

Without being informed of their shortcomings, learners may fail to use their time effectively and fall short of the desired progress. Thus, AI-facilitated real-time feedback becomes a critical mechanism in ensuring that each learner's journey is both reflective and strategically aligned with their evolving needs.

PHASE 4: COLLABORATIVE REFLECTION & VALIDATION

Phase 4 promotes scholarly discourse via AI-supported online discussions while upholding academic integrity through human-supervised verification of AI-assessed final exams, thereby ensuring rigorous and trustworthy outcomes.

Step 9: Facilitating AI-Supported Online Discussion Experiences

"This Is Your DeLorean": In this step, AI-supported translation and discussion-structuring tools enable multilingual and asynchronous interactions, expanding access and inclusivity in online learning environments.

GenAI-supported discussion-based learning environments foster deeper learning experiences by enhancing learners' cognitive and social engagement. Wang et al. (2024) highlighted that GenAI-supported learner systems in asynchronous environments strengthen learners' cognitive and social presence, encouraging more active participation in the learning process. These systems simulate interactive learning settings by supporting learners' textual and visual communication. Similarly, Peng et al. (2025) developed the GLITTER platform, which supports material-based asynchronous discussions within the FL framework. It improves learners' conceptual coherence and reflective thinking skills by analysing their discussion contributions and providing personalised reflection reports, thereby better preparing them for in-class activities. Such studies demonstrate GenAI's substantial potential to enrich the learning experience within online discussion environments.

Within the McFlai Model, support is provided around the clock-starting from enrolment and course selection and continuing through the FL and module phases. One of the most critical components, however, is the GenAI-supported online class experience. In this setting, each learner's comments are opened for discussion, promoting interaction among peers. Through LLM-powered translation, learners can understand one another regardless of language, as the AI tool enables automatic multilingual communication.

Moreover, learners who are unable to attend live sessions can asynchronously watch the lecture videos and engage in the ongoing discussion beneath the video. This structure renders the learning experience more inclusive, interactive, and sustainable (Öncü & Süral, 2024).

In essence, this step equips every learner with their own metaphorical DeLorean-allowing them to travel through diverse languages, time zones, and interaction modes to engage meaningfully with the learning community.

Step 10: Validating AI-Assessed Final Exams through Human Supervision

"Your Future Is Whatever You Make It": In this final step, a comprehensive exam aligned with programme goals and learning outcomes is first assessed by AI, then reviewed and, if necessary, revised by a human instructor before results are confirmed and certification is granted.

AI can play a significant role in the assessment process, from generating exam questions to evaluating learner responses, thereby increasing efficiency and objectivity. Bennett (2024) highlights AI's potential to reduce human bias and improve consistency in assessment. However, the use of AI-based assessment systems also introduces certain challenges. Concerns remain around the transparency and explainability of AI-generated evaluation decisions. Khademi (2023) notes that the assessment consistency of LLMs, such as ChatGPT, can fall short when compared to human evaluators, raising issues of reliability. Similarly, Olivos et al. (2025) found inconsistencies in AI's evaluation of open-ended responses and stressed that AI should function as a support tool, not a replacement for human evaluators.

Historically, the integration of tools such as calculators and personal computers into educational assessment has facilitated the evaluation of higher-order thinking skills. Calculators eliminated time constraints associated with manual calculations, enabling more effective assessment of problem-solving skills. Likewise, personal computers and word processors have enhanced written expression by streamlining the writing and editing process. Today, LLMs and GenAI technologies represent a comparable shift in education, offering the potential for personalised learning and more diverse assessment strategies. However, integrating these tools into assessment requires educators to rethink their approach. Instructors must increasingly focus on teaching learners how to work effectively with AI, develop critical thinking skills, and internalise ethical values (Hao et al., 2024). Although GenAI may improve the surface quality of learners' work, determining whether such work meets educational standards still demands expert judgement (Bower et al., 2024). Thus, it is essential to foster learners' ability to assess not only the quality of AI outputs but also their interactions with these technologies. In this sense, GenAI can act as a collaborative partner in helping learners develop evaluative judgement (Bearman et al., 2024).

Ultimately, the integration of GenAI and LLMs in education allows for the measurement of higher-order thinking skills while simultaneously necessitating a reconfiguration of educator and learner roles in the assessment process. This shift may contribute to the development of fairer, more personalised, and more effective evaluation practices.

The McFlai Model proposes a structure in which each module concludes with a level-based mini-assessment conducted by AI. Upon completion of all modules, learners proceed to a comprehensive final exam aligned with the defined outcomes.

This final assessment is first evaluated by AI, then reviewed and validated by human instructors. Successful learners are then awarded certification. This hybrid approach combines the efficiency of AI with the reliability and discernment of human judgement, offering a more equitable and robust assessment system.

Bonus: Human–Machine Collaboration in Application Development

"You Have to Input the Destination Time": In this bonus section, a learner-centred, GenAI-supported flipped MC process is envisioned as a product of human–machine collaboration.

For early humans, fire; a few decades ago, radio-now largely overlooked; and today, AI applications, autonomous vehicles, and humanoids represent the technological signatures of their respective eras. Technology, in this regard, can be seen as a continuum of tools and applications developed within the scope of available capabilities to meet evolving societal needs, continuously renewing itself. The key challenge lies not in whether technology should be integrated into DE, but in deciding how, when, to what extent, for whom, and under what conditions such integration should occur.

While learner autonomy is a strength of DE, poorly designed programmes or courses can result in demotivation or dropout, especially when learners struggle to receive timely support or find answers to their questions. In this context, the idea of deploying machines that dictate what other machines should do-even machines training and being supervised by other machines-does not reduce the human role but rather reinforces the necessity of coexisting with them. Since the Industrial Revolution, machines-whether intelligent or not-have established a cooperative dynamic with humans. With the rise of GenAI in the early 2020s, humans began integrating LLMs-faster-learning, faster-thinking agents-into daily life for everyday queries like "What should I eat?", "What should I wear?", or "What will the match score be tonight?" This integration has positioned human–machine collaboration not as a future concept, but as a present reality-one that also holds powerful implications for researchers, educators, developers, and workers across various sectors (Haase & Hanel, 2023).

In today's world, even individuals without coding knowledge can develop basic applications using GenAI and LLMs. With Agent AI, even higher-level automation and autonomy in application development is becoming possible. Yet, removing the human element from educational processes entirely is neither viable nor desirable.

Rather, AI tools should function as assistants. In the proposed model, the process begins and ends with human involvement. While machines may now perform tasks that once consumed significant human time, a human expert-who understands the learning goals and outcomes-must still oversee the programme and evaluate learner performance. Even if machines achieve a 99% accuracy rate, the 1% margin of error could yield critical consequences for learners. Hence, in AI-based systems structured by human experts, full delegation to machines remains premature.

Accordingly, both the initial instructional design phase and the final assessment phase in the proposed model are entrusted to human agents. How GenAI interprets and implements this model, and how it codes its application, is a central point of interest for human–machine collaboration. A basic prototype of the envisioned system is presented in the Appendix.

As LLM capabilities advance and institutional implementation becomes more affordable, AI-supported learning analytics may enable the design of professional, scalable, and dynamic systems for large learner populations in the near future. This underscores the significance of responsible co-design, where machines function not as replacements, but as powerful partners in education.

Implications For Practice And Policy

The McFlai Model offers a structured framework to bridge pedagogical innovation with institutional policy reform in DE environments. Foremost, the transformation of existing course materials into MC structures marks a structural shift in instructional design. This transformation facilitates the creation of scalable, verifiable, and stackable learning experiences, while offering a modular framework directly aligned with learning outcomes. One of the model's most practical strengths lies in its capacity to provide real-time academic guidance during programme and course selection. AI-based academic advising systems analyse learners' individual profiles, career goals, and subject interests to support more informed decision-making. Furthermore, GenAI-powered virtual assistants offer continuous support in asynchronous learning environments, ensuring that learners are never left unsupported throughout their journey (Öncü, 2025).

Another key dimension of the model involves the assignment of tasks prior to each module, framed within the FL approach. Lo & Hew (2017) demonstrated that AI-enhanced FL environments foster deeper learning and increase learner engagement in digital settings. Alan & Yurt (2024) likewise showed that the personalisation and interactivity features offered by GenAI tools adapt learning materials to individual learner needs, thereby enhancing interest and participation. Moreover, the model's capacity to deliver learner-specific content that dynamically adjusts to the learner's level, and to structure mini-assessments based on progress, renders the learning experience both more effective and inclusive. The automatic adaptation of content and assessments based on learner performance also strengthens diagnostic feedback mechanisms.

This triadic integration of AI, Micro-Credentials, and Flipped Learning fosters a holistic educational model, positioning institutions to lead the transformation of DE systems. (Durak & Çankaya, 2024).

The opportunities, challenges, and risks of this study are detailed below.

Opportunities

"The Time Train Upgrade": Technology is not merely a tool but a process-capable of evolving over time and adapting to the conditions of its era.

The most promising opportunity of GenAI lies in its ability to transcend fixed frameworks, reshaping how knowledge is structured and delivered. However, it is essential to discuss both the benefits and limitations of using GenAI within The McFlai Model to maintain transparency. Key opportunities include:

- Enhancing Engagement: AI-supported systems can provide proactive learning experiences that foster higher learner engagement (Zawacki-Richter et al., 2020).
- Motivation: Customised feedback and goal-oriented content recommendations have the potential to significantly boost learner motivation (Bozkurt, 2024).
- Learning Outcomes: AI-supported learning systems can improve outcomes through personalised instructional strategies (Luckin, 2017).
- 24/7 Support: AI-based virtual assistants can ensure continuous learning by offering around-the-clock learner support (Popenici & Kerr, 2017).
- Personalisation: Large LLMs and adaptive learning systems can construct personalised pathways by tailoring content to individual learner needs (Knox, 2020).
- Gamification: AI-enhanced gamification applications can increase learner engagement by integrating game mechanics into educational experiences (Lo & Hew, 2017).
- The Evolving Role of Educators: The role of educators may shift from content delivery to guidance and mentorship, offering opportunities to enrich the learning experience (Selwyn, 2011).

Challenges and Risks

"Temporal Paradox": Despite the rapid advancement of AI-driven innovations, educational systems, policies, and human factors often lag behind, creating a temporal mismatch.

For The McFlai Model, the following challenges and risks are notable:

- Algorithmic Bias in Recommendations and Content: AI systems trained on biased datasets may provide inaccurate or unfair recommendations, compromising educational equity (Binns, 2018).
- Data Privacy and Surveillance: The collection and analysis of learner data raise serious ethical concerns around data security and personal privacy (Zuboff, 2023).
- Equity and Access: Unequal access to technology may deepen the digital divide, threatening equitable access to education (Van Hooft et al., 2021).
- Pricing: High costs associated with AI-powered educational technologies may restrict access for low-income learners (Selwyn, 2011).
- Measurement and Evaluation: Accurately and holistically assessing learning outcomes within AI-supported environments remains a significant challenge (Siemens, 2013).
- The Evolving Role of Educators: While the transformation of educators' roles can be empowering, it also carries risks-such as reduced pedagogical autonomy or the oversimplification of teaching into automated processes-thus representing both an opportunity and a threat (Knox, 2020).

CONCLUSION AND RECOMMENDATIONS

This book chapter presents the McFlai Model as a roadmap for designing a personalised, sustainable, and measurable learning structure in DE. The model is rooted in the integration of technological innovation with pedagogical design, aiming to meaningfully employ the affordances of GenAI and LLMs within educational contexts.

The model begins with converting educator-developed content into a modular MC format using GenAI, aligning content with institutional expectations and clearly defined learning outcomes (Öncü, 2025; Zawacki-Richter et al., 2020). Steps two and three involve learner profiling and matching appropriate courses to each profile, designing learning journeys that align with learners' interests and skill objectives (McKinney et al., 2024; Sutton & Sankar, 2011).

Step four highlights the model's dynamism, wherein GenAI adapts content in real time based on learners' performance in FL tasks. Content complexity is matched to the learner's current knowledge level, facilitating a personalised, interactive, and adaptive learning experience (Baig & Yadegaridehkordi, 2023; Villarica, 2023). The dynamic content structure ensures that learning is not just transmitted but constructed.

Steps five and six incorporate learning analytics and adaptive content strategies. Learner performance in tasks and mini-assessments directly informs the difficulty and structure of subsequent modules. Through real-time monitoring, AI continuously refines both content delivery and assessment strategies (Ifenthaler, 2022; Sousa et al., 2021).

In step seven, level-appropriate mini-assessments generated by LLMs offer formative feedback. Step eight builds on this by delivering timely, structured, and explanatory feedback-not just right/wrong evaluations, but insights that guide future learning actions (Cohn et al., 2024; Peng et al., 2025).

Step nine encourages social learning through AI-moderated, multilingual, and asynchronous online discussions. GenAI facilitates cross-linguistic accessibility, ensuring that all learners can contribute and benefit from peer interaction (Bañeres et al., 2023).

Finally, step ten implements a dual-layered final assessment process: GenAI evaluates learners' performance, which is then verified by human instructors. This approach balances the efficiency of automation with the reliability and accountability of human judgement (Bharathi et al., 2024; Mao et al., 2024).

McFlai thus offers a comprehensive design for learner-centred, flexible, and measurable education, synchronising AI's diverse functionalities across content development, learner tracking, diagnostic evaluation, and feedback. Each phase reflects pedagogical coherence, technological scalability, and ethical responsibility, making the model not only theoretically grounded but also practically implementable-whether embedded in a GenAI system or an LMS environment.

The model emerged from a critical need to unify fragmented approaches in DE into an integrated, functional whole. The integration of GenAI into learning processes compels a transformation of assessment systems. As LLM capabilities expand, assessment approaches that prioritise process, open-ended thinking, and critical analysis will become increasingly vital. For instance, learners might be asked to critique or reconstruct an AI-generated text to evaluate their critical thinking and adaptability.

As Einstein's attributed quote reminds us, "Not everything that counts can be counted, and not everything that can be counted counts." The goal is not to reduce learning to metrics, but to interpret what those metrics signify and embed them into meaningful learning design. Technology should enhance, not mechanise, the spirit of education. Data must not only serve as a tool for measurement, but as a foundation for enriching learning experiences.

Therefore, there is a pressing need for individuals who not only use AI but understand its limitations, uphold ethical responsibilities, and can intervene when necessary. "Thinking with AI, but not because of AI" may become one of the most crucial cognitive abilities of the new era. In the future, the integration of technology with human agency in learning environments will gain even more significance. Mental health, wellbeing, and mentorship-based support systems are likely to become central pillars of AI-mediated educational ecosystems. As technology becomes not only accessible but ubiquitous, institutions and practitioners must adapt or risk obsolescence-a reality not confined to DE but one that will shape traditional higher education as well.

MOOCs, short-term courses, and certification programmes must evolve in tandem with this transformation. The integration of GenAI and LLMs into next-generation learning technologies has the potential to redefine the scope and impact of DE. The full scale of this transformation will unfold more clearly in the years ahead. Today's essential question is no longer "What do you know?" but "What can you do with what you know?" Yet, current education systems often reduce assessment to performance on tests, failing to reflect this paradigm shift. Thus, it is imperative to foster holistic, discussion-driven models like McFlai.

Mishra et al. (2009), in The Song Remains the Same, caution against blind adherence to technological hype, reminding us that "even if the melody changes, the chorus remains the same." Enduring success lies not in novelty, but in learner-centred, pedagogically grounded design. Humans, inherently prone to cognitive disorientation, often attribute blame to external forces when they lose their way. Navigating complex knowledge systems-whether human- or machine-constructed-requires self-awareness. The potential of AI in education is not only technical but relational: how humans interact with it matters deeply. Learning is not just acquisition, but purposeful disorientation and reorientation.

Building upon the McFlai framework, an innovative extension could involve the integration of affective AI. By analysing emotional cues-such as motivation, stress, or engagement-content and support systems could be adapted not only cognitively but also emotionally. This would allow GenAI to become a more empathetic learning partner. Additionally, learners could be offered expressive, creative spaces-such as digital storytelling or interactions with virtual characters-to deepen reflection and personal connection. In this way, AI evolves from merely "understanding" learners to also "feeling with" them, fostering a more humanised and meaningful learning experience in digital education environments.

While GenAI has succeeded in simulating human-like capabilities, it also raises risks for core human skills-reading, understanding, and questioning. The threat lies not in AI's "hallucinations" but in learners' uncritical acceptance of them. Just as machines strive to understand human language, so too must humans develop a basic understanding of machine logic. The McFlai Model offers learners the opportunity to break from conventional patterns and grow through self-directed, self-aware learning journeys. But this requires instructors capable of authentic collaboration with machines.

McFlai demonstrates that GenAI can be orchestrated around pedagogical intent rather than confined by algorithmic boundaries, thereby granting learners greater agency over their educational futures while educators retain strategic oversight. By inviting DE learners to interrogate content and process alike, the model is well-positioned for adaptation within emerging micro-credential ecosystems committed to equitable and sustainable learning. Crucially, McFlai shows the potential to scale ethically to broad audiences without eroding academic integrity.

Finally, for McFlai to operate effectively, both learners and educators must possess ethical awareness and digital literacy. The aim is to cultivate individuals who do not merely consume AI outputs, but critique, reinterpret, and-when needed-resist them. Just as Asimov's (1950) Three Laws of Robotics provided a foundation for ethical machine behaviour, so too must we craft new ethical principles and social responsibility norms in educational contexts. Learners must be raised not only as users of AI-generated answers, but as critical thinkers capable of interrogating and reshaping them. As the film reminds us, "Your future is whatever you make it; so make it a good one." Educational innovation remains legitimate only when educators retain control of the camera's shutter echoing Bozkurt et al.'s (2024) insistence that technology must augment, not automate, the human work of teaching. Ultimately, learners themselves fill the photographic frame and determine its composition; the future, though technologically mediated, gains meaning from human intentionality rather than machine autonomy.

Future Research Directions

This book chapter has demonstrated the potential for machines to make meaningful contributions to education-provided that the processes initiated by humans are also guided by them. It has also included a creative appendix exploring the question "What if AI coded this chapter?", inspired by the unfinished bridge in Back to the Future that is expected to be completed in the future. From the perspective of tomorrow, what seems innovative today may appear simplistic. Yet in the context of the time this chapter was written, prompting GenAI to develop and run an educational application is itself a significant milestone. Perhaps twenty years from now, we may realise that even our boldest dreams have not surpassed the future itself. After all, no one will hand us an almanac from the future-we, as humans, must write that future ourselves.

In this context, the McFlai Model represents a GenAI-supported learning structure shaped by human insight-emphasising, much like completing an unfinished bridge, that the meaningful and sustainable use of technology is only possible through human foresight and design. The model offers not just a vision, but a blueprint for those who seek to build the future, not merely predict it.

To that end, several future research directions are proposed:

- Investigating the Impact of GenAI and LLMs on Diverse Learner Profiles: Future studies should explore how GenAI and LLMs influence learners from various age groups, cultural backgrounds, and educational contexts. By leveraging more advanced learning analytics, researchers can monitor and support individual learner development more comprehensively.
- Experimental Research on Fully AI-Driven Models Integrating FL and MC: Studies could examine the effectiveness of end-to-end AI-supported ecosystems that integrate FL and MC, particularly their impact on learner engagement, performance, and satisfaction.
- Ethics and Privacy in AI-Supported Learning Environments: As AI becomes more embedded in education, comprehensive studies are needed on how to structure ethical responsibilities and protect learner privacy, especially within adaptive and personalised learning frameworks.
- Reconceptualising Institutional and Educator Roles: Future research should not only focus on learner experiences but also address how the roles of institutions, policymakers, and educators are evolving within AI-mediated learning environments. Organisational readiness and policy implications must be critically examined.

As a footnote to this future-oriented vision, the Appendix of this chapter presents a prototype developed entirely through human–AI collaboration. In line with the spirit of the work, GenAI (ChatGPT-4o) was prompted to directly generate code for the application, and the entire development process was completed through this interaction. The resulting prototype, designed with different LLMs and tailored to meet specific instructional goals across various languages, illustrates the emerging capacity of AI to truly understand learners. The applications created for this chapter suggest that we are approaching an era in which GenAI and LLMs will enable the construction of deeply personalised DE models. These systems will not only analyse learner behaviour but also respond proactively to their evolving needs-echoing the speculative futures of Westworld, Black Mirror, or Her. Such a transformation reinforces the idea that education is more than just the transmission of information; it is a living, adaptive process.

The evolution of education can be likened to an endless journey through time in a metaphorical time machine. And as with all time travel tales, the next chapter of this story is just around the corner: "To be continued…"

Disclosure Statement

Generative artificial intelligence tools, specifically ChatGPT-4o, were utilized to literature review, refine English phrasing during the translation process and to review code snippets provided for illustrative purposes. Furthermore, generative artificial intelligence tools were employed in the development of the prototype application. Despite the use of these tools for specific tasks, the core arguments, critical analysis, framework design, and final written expression remain the original work and sole responsibility of the author.

ACKNOWLEDGEMENT

This book chapter stems from experiences gained in the inspiring graduate course, Current Approaches in Distance Education. The course instructor is gratefully acknowledged for the enlightening discussions that enabled the practical application of ideas conceived at the intersection of Distance Education and generative art, as presented in this chapter. Additionally, inspired by Spielberg's Back to the Future trilogy, quotes from the trilogy are utilized in the headings and content of this chapter.

REFERENCES

Alan, S., & Yurt, E. (2024). Flipped Learning: An Innovative Model for Enhancing Education Through ChatGPT. *International Journal of Modern Education Studies*, *8*(1), 124. DOI: 10.51383/ijonmes.2024.328

Alfredo, R., Echeverria, V., Jin, Y., Yan, L., Swiecki, Z., Gašević, D., & Martinez-Maldonado, R. (2023). Human-Centred Learning Analytics and AI in Education: A Systematic Literature Review. *Computers and Education: Artificial Intelligence*, *6*, 100215. Advance online publication. DOI: 10.1016/j.caeai.2024.100215

Ali, S. A., & Khan, R. (2023). *Harnessing the Digital Nature of Micro-Credentials in Higher Education*. DOI: 10.20944/preprints202303.0045.v1

Almutawah, K. A. (2014). A decision support system for academic advisors. *International Journal of Business Information Systems*, *16*(2), 177–195. DOI: 10.1504/IJBIS.2014.062837

Anderson, T., & Dron, J. (2011). Three generations of distance education pedagogy. *International Review of Research in Open and Distance Learning*, *12*(3), 80–97. DOI: 10.19173/irrodl.v12i3.890

Ashby, A. (2004). Monitoring student retention in the Open University: Definition, measurement, interpretation and action. *Open Learning*, *19*(1), 65–77. Advance online publication. DOI: 10.1080/0268051042000177854

Asimov, I. (1950). *I, Robot*. Gnome Press.

Atas, A. H. (2025). Flipped classroom approach to incorporate MOOCs as micro-credentials into higher education. In Durak, G., & Çankaya, S. (Eds.), *Integrating micro-credentials with AI in open education* (pp. 313–340). IGI Global., DOI: 10.4018/979-8-3693-5488-9.ch013

Avcı, Z. Y., Erguleç, F., Mısırlı, O., & Süral, I. (2021). *Flipped learning in information technology courses: benefits and challenges*. DOI: 10.1080/0309877X.2021.1986623

Baig, M. I., & Yadegaridehkordi, E. (2023). Flipped classroom in higher education: A systematic literature review and research challenges. *International Journal of Educational Technology in Higher Education*, *20*(1), 1–26. DOI: 10.1186/s41239-023-00430-5

Bañeres, D., Rodríguez-González, M. E., Guerrero-Roldán, A. E., & Cortadas, P. (2023). An early warning system to identify and intervene online dropout learners. *International Journal of Educational Technology in Higher Education*, *20*(1), 1–25. DOI: 10.1186/s41239-022-00371-5

Barrera, A. G., Heston, T. F., Sharma, D. M., & Jose, J. (2024). *The AI revolution in micro-credentialing: personalized learning paths*. DOI: 10.3389/feduc.2024.1445654

Bearman, M., Tai, J., Dawson, P., Boud, D., & Ajjawi, R. (2024). Developing evaluative judgement for a time of generative artificial intelligence. *Assessment & Evaluation in Higher Education*, *49*(6), 893–905. https://doi.org/https://doi.org/10.1080/02602938.2024.2335321. DOI: 10.1080/02602938.2024.2335321

Bergman, J., & Sams, A. (2012). *Flip Your Classroom: Reach Every Student in Every Class Every Day* (1st ed.). ISTE.

Bharathi, G. P., Chandra, I., Sanagana, D. P. R., Tummalachervu, C. K., Rao, V. S., & Neelima, S. (2024). AI-driven adaptive learning for enhancing business intelligence simulation games. *Entertainment Computing*, *50*, 100699. DOI: 10.1016/j.entcom.2024.100699

Binns, R. (2018). Fairness in Machine Learning: Lessons from Political Philosophy. In *Proceedings of Machine Learning Research* (Vol. 81, pp. 149–159). PMLR. https://proceedings.mlr.press/v81/binns18a.html

Bishop, J. L., & Verleger, M. A. (2013). The flipped classroom: A survey of the research. *ASEE Annual Conference and Exposition, Conference Proceedings*. DOI: 10.18260/1-2--22585

Bond, M., Bedenlier, S., Marín, V. I., & Händel, M. (2021). Emergency remote teaching in higher education: Mapping the first global online semester. *International Journal of Educational Technology in Higher Education*, *18*(1), 1–24. DOI: 10.1186/s41239-021-00282-x PMID: 34778537

Bower, M., Torrington, J., Lai, J. W. M., Petocz, P., & Alfano, M. (2024). How should we change teaching and assessment in response to increasingly powerful generative Artificial Intelligence? Outcomes of the ChatGPT teacher survey. *Education and Information Technologies, 29*(12), 15403–15439. DOI: 10.1007/s10639-023-12405-0

Bozkurt, A. (2023). Generative AI, Synthetic Contents, Open Educational Resources (OER), and Open Educational Practices (OEP): A New Front in the Openness Landscape. *Open Praxis, 15*(3), 178–184. DOI: 10.55982/openpraxis.15.3.579

Bozkurt, A. (2024). Tell me your prompts and I will make them true: The alchemy of prompt engineering and generative AI. *Open Praxis, 16*(2), 111–118. DOI: 10.55982/openpraxis.16.2.661

Bozkurt, A., & Sharma, R. C. (2023). Challenging the Status Quo and Exploring the New Boundaries in the Age of Algorithms: Reimagining the Role of Generative AI in Distance Education and Online Learning. *Asian Journal of Distance Education, 18*(1), 2023. https://asianjde.com/ojs/index.php/AsianJDE/article/view/714

Bozkurt, A., Xiao, J., Farrow, R., Bai, J. Y. H., Nerantzi, C., Moore, S., Dron, J., Stracke, C. M., Singh, L., Crompton, H., Koutropoulos, A., Terentev, E., Pazurek, A., Nichols, M., Sidorkin, A. M., Costello, E., Watson, S., Mulligan, D., Honeychurch, S., & Asino, T. I. (2024). The manifesto for teaching and learning in a time of Generative AI: A critical collective stance to better navigate the future. *Open Praxis, 16*(4), 487–513. DOI: 10.55982/openpraxis.16.4.777

Cohn, C., Hutchins, N., Le, T., & Biswas, G. (2024). A Chain-of-Thought Prompting Approach with LLMs for Evaluating Students' Formative Assessment Responses in Science. *Proceedings of the AAAI Conference on Artificial Intelligence, 38*(21), 23182–23190. DOI: 10.1609/aaai.v38i21.30364

Cuban, L. (1986). *Teachers and Machines: The Classroom of Technology Since 1920* (1st ed.). Teachers College Press.

de Sousa, E. B. G., Alexandre, B., Ferreira Mello, R., Pontual Falcão, T., Vesin, B., & Gašević, D. (2021). Applications of Learning Analytics in High Schools: A Systematic Literature Review. *Frontiers in Artificial Intelligence, 4*, 737891. DOI: 10.3389/frai.2021.737891 PMID: 34647016

du Plooy, E., Casteleijn, D., & Franzsen, D. (2024). Personalized adaptive learning in higher education: A scoping review of key characteristics and impact on academic performance and engagement. *Heliyon, 10*(21), e39630. DOI: 10.1016/j.heliyon.2024.e39630 PMID: 39524879

Durak, G., & Çankaya, S. (2024). *Integrating Micro-Credentials With AI in Open Education*. IGI Global. DOI: 10.4018/979-8-3693-5488-9

Ferguson, R. (2012). Learning analytics: Drivers, developments and challenges. *International Journal of Technology Enhanced Learning*, *4*(5–6), 304–317. DOI: 10.1504/IJTEL.2012.051816

Garrison, D. R., Anderson, T., & Archer, W. (1999). Critical inquiry in a text-based environment: Computer conferencing in higher education. *The Internet and Higher Education*, *2*(2–3), 87–105. DOI: 10.1016/S1096-7516(00)00016-6

Gašević, D., Dawson, S., & Siemens, G. (2015). Let's not forget: Learning analytics are about learning. *TechTrends*, *59*(1), 64–71. DOI: 10.1007/s11528-014-0822-x

Gong, T., Li, J., Yeung, J. Y., & Zhang, X. (2024). The association between course selection and academic performance: Exploring psychological interpretations. *Studies in Higher Education*, *49*(12), 2506–2519. Advance online publication. DOI: 10.1080/03075079.2024.2310151

Gündüz, M., & Karaman, S. (2020). Open Education Faculty and distance education students' dropout reasons: The case of a Turkish state university. *Open Praxis*, *12*(1), 7–25. DOI: 10.5944/openpraxis.12.1.970

Haase, J., & Hanel, P. H. P. (2023). Artificial muses: Generative artificial intelligence chatbots have risen to human-level creativity. *Journal of Creativity*, *33*(3), 100066. DOI: 10.1016/j.yjoc.2023.100066

Hao, J., von Davier, A. A., Yaneva, V., Lottridge, S., von Davier, M., & Harris, D. J. (2024). Transforming Assessment: The Impacts and Implications of Large Language Models and Generative AI. *Educational Measurement: Issues and Practice*, *43*(2), 16–29. DOI: 10.1111/emip.12602

Hew, K. F., Jia, C., Gonda, D. E., & Bai, S. (2020). Transitioning to the "new normal" of learning in unpredictable times: Pedagogical practices and learning performance in fully online flipped classrooms. *International Journal of Educational Technology in Higher Education*, *17*(1), 1–22. DOI: 10.1186/s41239-020-00234-x PMID: 34778516

Hollands, F., & Tirthali, D. (2014). *MOOCs: Expectations and Reality* (Issue 50). https://repository.upenn.edu/handle/20.500.14332/5727

Hunt, T., Carter, R., Zhang, L., & Yang, S. (2020). Micro-credentials: The potential of personalized professional development. *Development and Learning in Organizations*, *34*(2), 33–35. DOI: 10.1108/DLO-09-2019-0215

Ifenthaler, D. (2022). A systems perspective on data and analytics for distance education. *Distance Education*, *43*(2), 333–341. DOI: 10.1080/01587919.2022.2064828

Jauhiainen, J. S., & Garagorry Guerra, A. (2024). Generative AI and education: Dynamic personalization of pupils' school learning material with ChatGPT. *Frontiers in Education*, *9*, 1288723. Advance online publication. DOI: 10.3389/feduc.2024.1288723

Kamarthi, S. V., Al Valbuena, A., Velou, M., Kumara, S., & Enscore, E. (1992). ADVISOR - An expert system for the selection of courses. *Expert Systems with Applications*, *5*(1–2), 153–165. DOI: 10.1016/0957-4174(92)90104-Z

Knox, J. (2020). Artificial intelligence and education in China. *Learning, Media and Technology*, *45*(3), 298–311. DOI: 10.1080/17439884.2020.1754236

Koçdar, S., Hamutoğlu, N. B., Erdoğdu, E., & Uçar, H. (2024). Academic performance of learners with special needs in open and distance learning: A study in Anadolu University open education system. *European Journal of Special Needs Education*. Advance online publication. DOI: 10.1080/08856257.2024.2380594

Kozan, K., & Richardson, J. C. (2014). Interrelationships between and among social, teaching, and cognitive presence. *The Internet and Higher Education*, *21*, 68–73. DOI: 10.1016/j.iheduc.2013.10.007

Kuzminykh, I., Nawaz, T., Shenzhang, S., Ghita, B., Raphael, J., & Xiao, H. (2024). *Personalised Feedback Framework for Online Education Programmes Using Generative AI*. https://arxiv.org/pdf/2410.11904

Li, W., & Ironsi, C. S. (2024). Efficacy of micro credential learning spaces in developing students' twenty-first century skills: Towards graduate work readiness. *Education and Information Technologies*, *29*(1), 1201–1216. DOI: 10.1007/s10639-023-12294-3

Lo, C. K., & Hew, K. F. (2017). A critical review of flipped classroom challenges in K-12 education: Possible solutions and recommendations for future research. *Research and Practice in Technology Enhanced Learning*, *12*(1), 1–22. DOI: 10.1186/s41039-016-0044-2 PMID: 30613253

Long, P., & Siemens, G. (2011). Penetrating the Fog: Analytics in Learning and Education. *EDUCAUSE Review*. https://er.educause.edu/articles/2011/9/penetrating-the-fog-analytics-in-learning-and-education

López-Villanueva, D., Santiago, R., & Palau, R. (2024). Flipped Learning and Artificial Intelligence. *Electronics 2024, Vol. 13, Page 3424*, *13*(17), 3424. DOI: 10.3390/electronics13173424

Lowenthal, P. R., & Snelson, C. (2017). In search of a better understanding of social presence: An investigation into how researchers define social presence. *Distance Education, 38*(2), 141–159. DOI: 10.1080/01587919.2017.1324727

Luckin, R. (2017). Towards artificial intelligence-based assessment systems. *Nature Human Behaviour 2017 1:3, 1*(3), 1–3. DOI: 10.1038/s41562-016-0028

Mao, J., Chen, B., & Liu, J. C. (2024). Generative Artificial Intelligence in Education and Its Implications for Assessment. *TechTrends, 68*(1), 58–66. DOI: 10.1007/s11528-023-00911-4

Marchenko, N., Slipchuk, V., & Yuzkiv, H. (2023). INTERACTIVE LEARNING METHODS IN HIGHER EDUCATION INSTITUTIONS. *The Modern Higher Education Review, 8*(8), 146–156. DOI: 10.28925/2518-7635.2023.810

McCarthy, J., Minsky, M. L., Rochester, N., & Shannon, C. E. (1955). A proposal for the Dartmouth Summer Research Project on Artificial Intelligence, August 31, 1955. *AI Magazine, 27*(4), 12–12. DOI: 10.1609/AIMAG.V27I4.1904

McKinney, L., Bourdeau, G. V., Burridge, A. B., Lee, M., Miller-Waters, M., & Barnes, Y. M. (2024). "I Advise, You Decide": How Academic Advisors Shape Community College Students' Enrollment and Credit Load Decisions. *Review of Higher Education, 47*(4), 519–547. DOI: 10.1353/rhe.2024.a930108

Miao, M., Ahmed, M., Ahsan, N., & Qamar, B. (2024). Intention to use technology for micro-credential programs: Evidence from technology acceptance and self-determination model. *International Journal of Educational Management, 38*(4), 948–977. DOI: 10.1108/IJEM-02-2023-0066

Mishra, P., Koehler, M. J., & Kereluik, K. (2009). The song remains the same: Looking back to the future of educational technology. *TechTrends, 53*(5), 48–53. DOI: 10.1007/s11528-009-0325-3

O'Flaherty, J., & Phillips, C. (2015). The use of flipped classrooms in higher education: A scoping review. *The Internet and Higher Education, 25*, 85–95. DOI: 10.1016/j.iheduc.2015.02.002

Oliver, B. (2019). Making micro-credentials work for learners, employers and providers. In *Deakin University*.

Olivos, F., Kamelski, T., & Ascui-Gac, S. (2025). *Assessing instructor-AI cooperation for grading essay-type questions in an introductory sociology course*. https://arxiv.org/pdf/2501.06461

Öncü, S. E. (2025). Transforming open and distance learning with generative AI: Custom micro-credentials from existing curriculums. *Journal of Open, Distance, and Digital Education, 1*(2). Advance online publication. DOI: 10.25619/WERERA06

Öncü, S. E., Gevher, M., & Erdoğdu, E. (2025). Exploring the potential use of generative AI for learner support in ODL at scale. *Journal of Educational Technology and Online Learning, 8*(1), 80–99. DOI: 10.31681/jetol.1559442

Öncü, S. E., & Süral, İ. (2024). Examining Occupation Fields of Programs According to Artificial Intelligence: Anadolu University Open Education System Case. *Osmangazi Journal of Educational Research, 11*(1), 39–72. DOI: 10.59409/ojer.1407007

Pangestu, M. A., & Karnalim, O. (2023). Advisor-Oriented Course Recommendation System Using Student Grades. [Journal of Information Technology and Computer Engineering]. *JITCE, 7*(2), 63–72. DOI: 10.25077/jitce.7.2.63-72.2023

Peng, W., Yang, Y., Zhang, Z., & Li, T. J.-J. (2025). *GLITTER: An AI-assisted Platform for Material-Grounded Asynchronous Discussion in Flipped Learning.* https://arxiv.org/pdf/2504.14695

Peterson, P. L., & Cox, C. B. (2025). Adapting to the future: How microcredentials fuel self-directed learning in the evolving workplace. *Industrial and Organizational Psychology: Perspectives on Science and Practice, 18*(1), 139–142. DOI: 10.1017/iop.2024.72

Popenici, S. A. D., & Kerr, S. (2017). Exploring the impact of artificial intelligence on teaching and learning in higher education. *Research and Practice in Technology Enhanced Learning, 12*(1), 1–13. DOI: 10.1186/s41039-017-0062-8 PMID: 30595727

Ralston, S. J. (2021). Higher Education's Microcredentialing Craze: A Postdigital-Deweyan Critique. *Postdigital Science and Education, 3*(1), 83–101. DOI: 10.1007/s42438-020-00121-8 PMID: 40476912

Ryan, R. M., & Deci, E. L. (2023). Self-Determination Theory. *Encyclopedia of Quality of Life and Well-Being Research*, 6229–6235. DOI: 10.1007/978-3-031-17299-1_2630

Saiyad, S., & Mahajan, R. (2023). Revisiting Academic Advising: Potential Role and Implications in Undergraduate Medical Training in India. *International Journal of Applied & Basic Medical Research, 13*(4), 193–197. DOI: 10.4103/ijabmr.ijabmr_476_23 PMID: 38229727

Selwyn, N. (2011). *Education and Technology: Key Issues And Debates* (3rd ed.). Bloomsbury Publishing Plc.

Siemens, G. (2013). Learning Analytics. *The American Behavioral Scientist*, *57*(10), 1380–1400. DOI: 10.1177/0002764213498851

Simpson, O. (2008). Motivating learners in open and distance learning: Do we need a new theory of learner support? *Open Learning*, *23*(3), 159–170. DOI: 10.1080/02680510802419979

Song, H., & Cai, L. (2024). Interactive learning environment as a source of critical thinking skills for college students. *BMC Medical Education*, *24*(1), 1–9. DOI: 10.1186/s12909-024-05247-y PMID: 38475788

Sutton, K. L., & Sankar, C. S. (2011). Student Satisfaction with Information Provided by Academic Advisors. *Journal of STEM Education: Innovations and Research*, *12*(7), 71. https://www.jstem.org/jstem/index.php/JSTEM/article/view/1734

Taha, K. (2012). Automatic academic advisor. *CollaborateCom 2012 - Proceedings of the 8th International Conference on Collaborative Computing: Networking, Applications and Worksharing*, 262–268. https://doi.org/DOI: 10.4108/ICST

Tait, A. (2000). Planning student support for open and distance learning. *Open Learning*, *15*(3), 287–299. DOI: 10.1080/713688410

The European Commission. (2022). *European project MICROBOL Micro-credentials linked to the Bologna Key Commitments*. https://microbol.microcredentials.eu/microbol-framework-published/

Thottoli, M. M., Alruqaishi, B. H., & Soosaimanickam, A. (2024). Robo academic advisor: Can chatbots and artificial intelligence replace human interaction? *Contemporary Educational Technology*, *16*(1), ep485. DOI: 10.30935/cedtech/13948

Tresman, S. (2002). Towards a strategy for improved student retention in programmes of open, distance education: A case study from the Open University UK. *International Review of Research in Open and Distance Learning*, *3*(1), 1–11. https://eric.ed.gov/?id=EJ646665. DOI: 10.19173/irrodl.v3i1.75

Turing, A. M. (1950). Computing Machinery and Intelligence. *Mind*, *LIX*(236), 433–460. DOI: 10.1093/mind/LIX.236.433

Uchiyama, S., Umemura, K., & Morita, Y. (2023). *Large Language Model-based System to Provide Immediate Feedback to Students in Flipped Classroom Preparation Learning*. https://arxiv.org/pdf/2307.11388

UNESCO. (2023). *Guidance for generative AI in education and research | UNESCO*. https://www.unesco.org/en/articles/guidance-generative-ai-education-and-research

Valtorta, M. G., Smith, B. T., & Loveland, D. W. (1984). The Graduate Course Advisor: A Multi-Phase Rule-Based Expert System. *IEEE Workshop on Principles of Knowledge-Based Systems.* https://cse.sc.edu/~mgv/papers/ieeePKBS84.pdf

Van de Laar, M., West, R. E., Cosma, P., Katwal, D., & Mancigotti, C. (2024). The value of educational microcredentials in open access online education: A doctoral education case. *Open Learning, 39*(4), 373–386. Advance online publication. DOI: 10.1080/02680513.2022.2072721

Van Hooft, E. A. J., Kammeyer-Mueller, J. D., Wanberg, C. R., Kanfer, R., Basbug, G., & Wan, C. R. (2021). *Job Search and Employment Success: A Quantitative Review and Future Research Agenda. 106*(5), 674–713. DOI: 10.1037/apl0000675.supp

Villarica, M. (2023). The Effectiveness of Flipped Classrooms in Distance Education During the Covid-19 Pandemic. *International Journal of Computing Sciences Research, 7*, 2296–2314. DOI: 10.25147/ijcsr.2017.001.1.160

Wang, T., Wu, T., Liu, H., Brown, C., & Chen, Y. (2024). *Generative Co-Learners: Enhancing Cognitive and Social Presence of Students in Asynchronous Learning with Generative AI.* https://arxiv.org/pdf/2410.04365

Ward, R., Grant, S., Larsen, M. W., & Giovacchini, K. (2024). The Universal Micro-Credential Framework: The Role of Badges, Micro-Credentials, Skills Profiling, and Design Patterns in Developing Interdisciplinary Learning and Assessment Paths for Computing Education. *IEEE Transactions on Education, 67*(6), 897–906. Advance online publication. DOI: 10.1109/TE.2024.3486016

Wei, Y., Pearl, D., Beckman, M., & Passonneau, R. J. (2025). *Concept-based Rubrics Improve LLM Formative Assessment and Data Synthesis.* https://arxiv.org/pdf/2504.03877

Ye, S., Kim, D., Jang, J., Shin, J., & Seo, M. (2022). Guess the Instruction! Flipped Learning Makes Language Models Stronger Zero-Shot Learners. *11th International Conference on Learning Representations, ICLR 2023.* https://arxiv.org/pdf/2210.02969

Zawacki-Richter, O., Conrad, D., Bozkurt, A., Aydin, C. H., Bedenlier, S., Jung, I., Stöter, J., Veletsianos, G., Blaschke, L. M., Bond, M., Broens, A., Bruhn, E., Dolch, C., Kalz, M., Kerres, M., Kondakci, Y., Marin, V., Mayrberger, K., Müskens, W., & Xiao, J. (2020). Elements of open education: An invitation to future research. *International Review of Research in Open and Distance Learning, 21*(3), 319–334. DOI: 10.19173/irrodl.v21i3.4659

Zemeckis, R. (1985). *Back to the Future* [Film]. Universal Pictures.

Zemeckis, R. (1989). *Back to the Future Part II* [Film Universal Pictures. Zemeckis, R. (1990). *Back to the Future Part III* [Film]. Universal Pictures.

Zhang, M., Dilling, A. P., Gondelman, L., Erik, N., Lyngdorf, R., Lindsay, E. D., & Bjerva, J. (2025). *SEFL: Harnessing Large Language Model Agents to Improve Educational Feedback Systems*. https://arxiv.org/pdf/2502.12927

Zhou, H. (2025). Exploring the dynamic teaching-learning relationship in interactive learning environments. *Interactive Learning Environments*, *33*(7), 4363–4393. Advance online publication. DOI: 10.1080/10494820.2025.2462149

Zuboff, S. (2023). The Age of Surveillance Capitalism. In Koch, D. J., & Will, C. H. (Eds.), *Social Theory Re-Wired* (pp. 203–213). Routledge., DOI: 10.4324/9781003320609-27

KEY TERMS AND DEFINITIONS

Adaptive Learning: A learning approach where content difficulty, feedback, and assessment criteria are adjusted in real-time to adapt to each learner's learning process.

Flipped Learning (FL): An instructional approach where foundational content is studied independently before class.

Generative Artificial Intelligence (GenAI): Machine learning systems that create novel text, images, audio, or code based on human prompts, capable of augmenting static data with creative elements.

Large Language Model (LLM): A probabilistic language engine trained on extensive text-based data, usable for learning or teaching purposes, and possessing the ability to predict and generate fluent, context-aware sentences for summarization and content transformation.

Learner Support: An AI-based virtual assistant that provides 24/7 support by assisting learners with problems experienced during the educational process or by answering their questions.

Learning Analytics: A system that collects and interprets learner interaction data, enabling the identification of gaps and facilitating timely interventions.

Micro-Credential (MC): A compact and stackable certificate that systematically evidences expertise in a skill set within a specific domain.

APPENDIX

The interface designs and prototype logic were generated by prompting ChatGPT-4o to code each individual component. The screenshots and functional mockups, developed in collaboration with various large language models (LLMs), are presented below.

Appendix 1: Micro-Credential Content Creation Panel for Instructors

Figure 3. Admin Panel

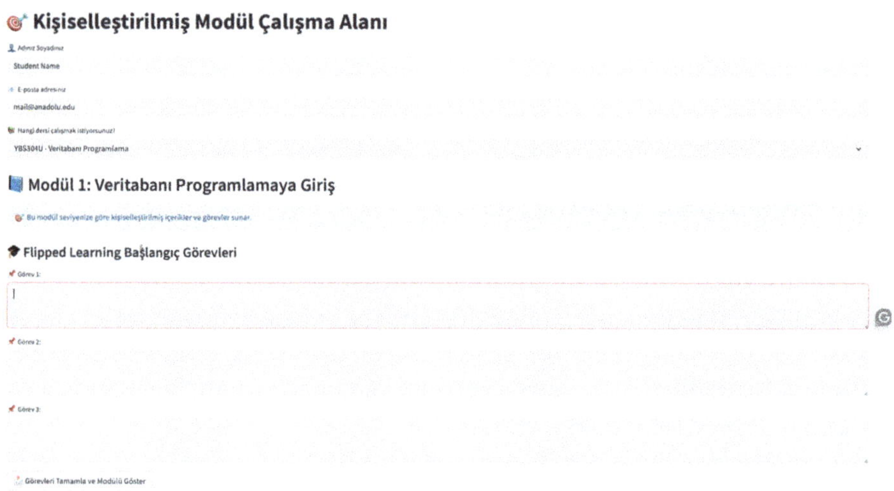

A visual interface that allows instructors and system administrators to manage course structures, assign MCs (MCs), and monitor learner progress. The panel includes tools for setting learning outcomes, defining modular content, and configuring GenAI support for each module.

Appendix 2: Generative AI-Powered Micro-Credential Recommendation Panel for Learners

Figure 4. MC Recommendation and Selection Panel for Learners

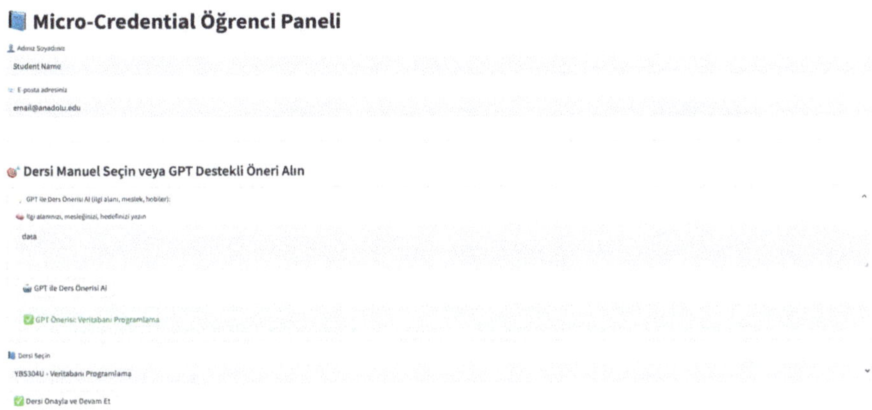

This panel enables learners to receive AI-generated MC recommendations based on their interests, prior knowledge, and career goals. It also allows them to manually select or refine course options, with real-time guidance from a virtual academic advisor.

Appendix 3: Flipped Learning Task Panel

Figure 5. FL Task Interface

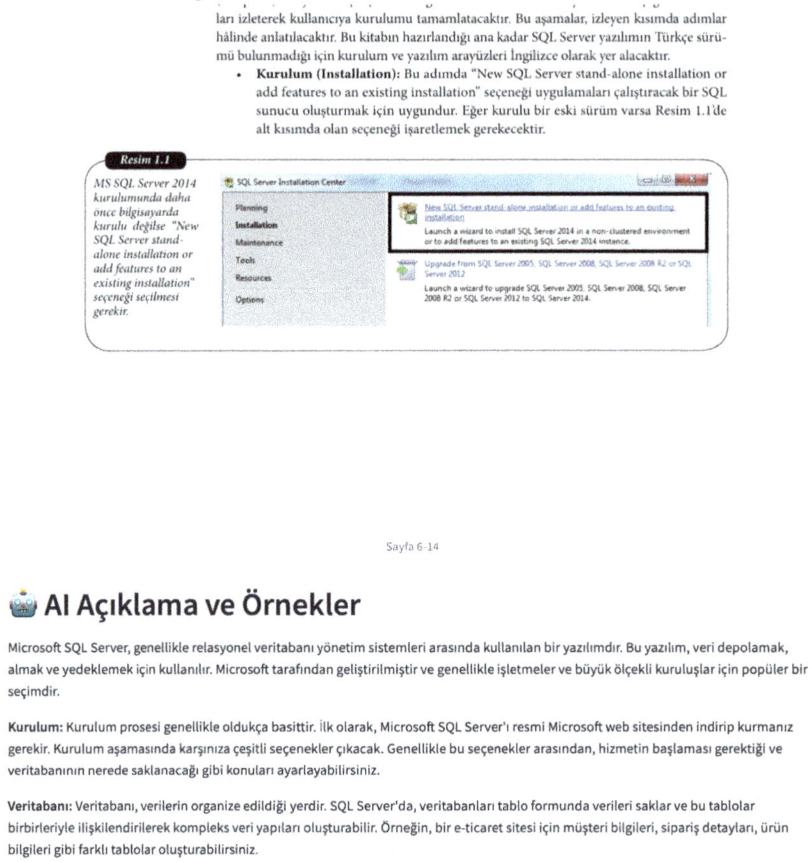

Learners access their pre-module tasks here. Tasks are dynamically generated by GenAI based on the selected MC and learner profile. This screen supports multimedia content, reflective prompts, and interactive submissions with immediate AI feedback.

Appendix 4: Dynamic Content Interface Adapted by AI Based on Learner Proficiency

Figure 6. Module Content Display

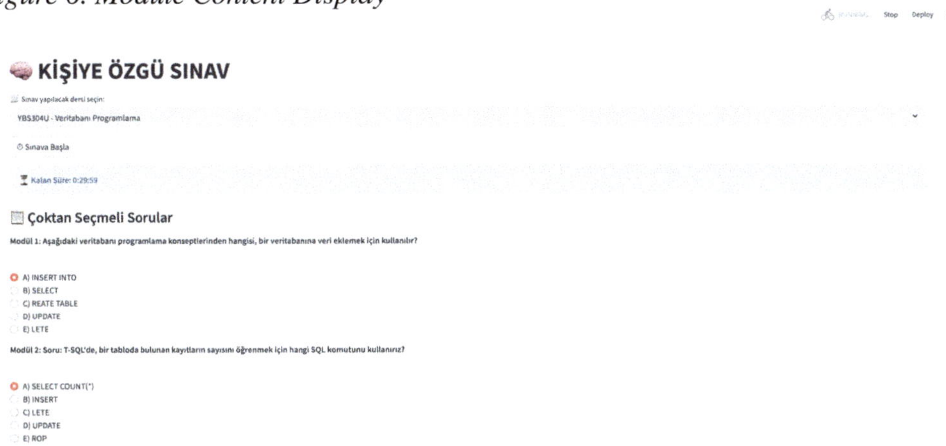

This panel delivers adaptive module content that evolves according to the learner's progress and performance. The GenAI system adjusts complexity and interactivity in real-time, offering varied pathways for different proficiency levels.

Appendix 5: Personalised Assessment Interface Generated by AI

Figure 7. Personalised Examination Interface

At the end of each module, learners complete a dynamically generated, level-appropriate assessment. This interface delivers AI-generated questions and formative feedback. Final exams are also administered here, with results validated by human instructors.

Chapter 7
Integration of Generative AI Into Higher Education:
Challenges, Opportunities, and Regulations

Dana Volosevici
https://orcid.org/0009-0000-9109-4679
Petroleum-Gas University of Ploiesti, Romania

Simona Eftimie
Petroleum-Gas University of Ploiesti, Romania

Iulia Adelina Ghita
Petroleum-Gas University of Ploiesti, Romania

ABSTRACT

The integration of generative AI into higher education is reshaping traditional teaching, learning, and assessment practices. This paper examines the opportunities AI offers for personalized learning, engagement, and administrative efficiency, while also addressing critical challenges, such as ethical risks, digital literacy gaps, and legal implications, including data protection and copyright issues. It highlights the evolving student profile shaped by digital technologies and the need for balanced educational strategies that integrate AI tools without compromising critical thinking and social interaction. Emphasizing a middle-path approach, the study advocates for legally compliant, pedagogically sound, and socially just AI use in universities, calling for enhanced teacher training, updated academic policies, and the promotion of AI literacy among students to ensure responsible and equitable technological integration.

DOI: 10.4018/979-8-3373-7579-3.ch007

ght © 2026, IGI Global Scientific Publishing. Copying or distributing in print or electronic forms without written permission of IGI Global Scientific Publishing is prohibited. Use of this chapter to
generative artificial intelligence (AI) technologies is expressly prohibited. The publisher reserves all rights to license its use for generative AI training and machine learning model development.

INTRODUCTION: AI AND (HIGHER) EDUCATION

The rapid advancement of digital technologies has transformed various sectors, with education being no exception. AI tools, in particular, have revolutionized the learning environment, offering significant benefits such as time efficiency, personalized learning, and improved engagement and motivation. While the initial use of AI tools can be exciting and enjoyable, if not carefully managed, it can adversely affect behavior and learning outcomes. A close examination of the recent academic performance of our university's graduating class reveals a noteworthy shift in their approach to semester work assignments and final projects. This shift is believed to be influenced by the increasing adoption of AI tools. Consequently, there was a necessity to examine the circumstances under which these shifts transpired, accentuating the expanding disparity between conventional pedagogical approaches and students' capacity to access and utilize alternative, AI-aided resources in the development of assignments. In this regard, it is evident that there is a discrepancy between pedagogical expectations and student practices. Moreover, there is a concerning trend of excessive and indiscriminate use of AI tools, in the absence of adequate evaluation or processing of the generated content. An analysis of portfolios, reports, and other assessment work reveals a decrease in the creative component and an increased reliance on automated solutions. This phenomenon raises essential questions about the role of the teacher, students' digital competences, and the adaptation of the educational process to new technological realities. Consequently, it is imperative to explore potential solutions by examining research conducted on this subject in Romania and other nations.

NEW GENERATION CHALLENGES

The conceptual foundations of artificial intelligence in education, as noted by Delello et al. (2025), were established over 30 years ago and are rooted in Alan Turing's work in 1950 on machine thinking. John McCarthy et al. (2006) formally introduced the concept of artificial intelligence, highlighting the possibility that machines could be designed to simulate aspects of human intelligence. Recently, we have noticed the high interest of researchers in GenAI, and specialists consider that this "is anticipated to accelerate and transform scientific knowledge" (Benbya et al., 2024; apud Andresen et al., 2025).

The extension of using digital technology has become natural for today's generations. Pupils / students' profiles become more different from previous generations, and as a consequence are relational difficulties in the educational field. Romanian specialty literature (see Bonchi , 2021) describes the evolution of generations after the 1900s. So, we could identify:

- *builders generation* described as conservators and conformists,
- *baby boomers generation* was guided by "living for working" in order to obtain material welfare and professional status,
- *X generation* whose motto was "working for living", characterized as versatile, entrepreneurial, competitional,
- and *Y generation (me generation)* guided by those who emphasize prolonging the period of education, are ambitious, have high self-esteem, self-oriented to the point of individualism.

The generation whose representatives are still in the field of education and who represent a challenge for both university and pre-university teachers are the *Z generation (hic et nunc generation)*; and also, the most recent generations, alpha and beta, generations whose characteristics are unknown to specialists and still in the process of research.

Z generation is described in the literature (Haidt, 2024) as the anxious generation, being affected by the Great Remodeling of Childhood, a smart phone-based childhood (instead of play-based childhood), which affected their emotions, physical activity, and even sleep patterns, and social relationships (feeling lonely and missing friends at school).

Another significant issue about Z generation is about the effects of the expansion of access to social networks. Citing a research conducted by Boyd & Richardson, J. Haidt (2024) draws attention to two possible effects of the accessibility and extension of social network for young people: *the conformity bias* (social networks are the most effective engines of conformity ever invented so that valuing membership in social groups determine individuals to align their perceptions and behaviors with group norms - see also Khalil et al., 2025; Li et al., 2025; Wang & Wang, 2024; Zhang & Gläscher, 2020;) and *the prestige bias* (social network platforms have decoupled excellence and prestige, people becoming "prestigious" through these networks without real foundations based on role models, their fame being artificially maintained - see researches of Brady et al., 2023; Kraft & Lyon, 2024; Kunst & Mesoudi, 2025; Niitsuma et al., 2025).

The intersection in the education field of generations with different characteristics determines consequences in education relationships (communication, interests, reaction to stimulus, etc). This is the reason for educators to maintain a balance between integrating AI technologies and using traditional teaching methods that foster critical thinking and social interaction (Bozkurt et al., 2024).

That's why we have to be aware that AI could be harmful for children (because of the unrestricted access to inappropriate information for certain ages - sex, violence, suicide promotion, or because of the amount of information that keeps children so many hours away from the real world and real interactions, etc.) as J. Haidt (2024) demonstrates with meta-analysis and statistics. Social reactions to his theory are mentioned in a post by J. Haidt (2025) - in which he relates that mothers from the U.S. and UK have reacted and started support groups for delaying the access to smartphones for children: parents' reaction was incredible; so, in the first week from creating the group (to the beginning of the 21st century) 10.000 parents joined the initiative and after a year, 300.000 parents have joined. Also, legislative initiatives are mentioned in the U.S. and Australia about raising the age for accessing social media to 16. These reactions could be proof that parents of recent generations have become more and more aware of the damage that the excess of digital device use and the replacement of children's natural/free play with social networks could cause to their children.

Still, when it comes to students (after 16), we have to agree that learning to properly use AI is crucial, considering their need to prepare for professional life, as challenges of contemporary society. So, it is obvious that the profile of the younger generations opting for university studies is significantly different from that of previous generations. The specialized Romanian literature – studies, translations, or literature reviews (for example, Ceobanu et al. (eds.), 2020; Bonchi (ed.), 2021; Bonchi , 2022) offers a new perspective on this profile and can empower/inspire educators in developing useful tools for working with these students. It may be seen as a challenging but stimulating process, yet it is absolutely necessary to (re) design academic discourse and interaction with students based on a new type of communication, adapted to the specific characteristics of this generation.

The integration of AI tools is a necessary process in the context that the main purpose of the educational system is to prepare graduates for social and professional integration. As literature reveals (see Hertz, 2023), the work field is deeply connected with AI from sending a CV, to applying to a job interview, to performing jobs' tasks and supervising and measuring / evaluating employees' productivity.

INTEGRATING AI IN EDUCATION

According to the Report on the State of Higher Education in Romania, conducted by the Ministry of Education, 54.8% of university professors are in the 40-54 age group, which shows a significant concentration of academic staff in this age group. Also, the evolution of the gender distribution shows an increase in female staff, representing 52.3% of the total, compared to 47.7% for male staff (Ministerul

Educației, 2023) In terms of teaching load, the report notes that the average number of students per teacher is significantly higher in private university education - 21.7 students/teacher, compared to 14.8 students/teacher in the state education system, with a difference of about 7 students in favor of private institutions. Therefore, in the educational field in the Romanian university environment, professors belonging to generation X and Z, in the person of those who were trained in the communist period or with basic training in the communist period, most often meet young people who fall into generation Z. The socio-demographic characteristics of students, according to the EUROSTUDENT VII report, show an average age of 25.2 years for students in Romania, which is close to the European average of 25.5 years. This increase in the average age is influenced by the increasing age of entry to higher education, a phenomenon observed at both national and European level. As regards the gender distribution, there is a predominance of female students, a trend observed at European level. However, in Romania, the proportion of female students is slightly lower than the average in the other countries participating in the EUROSTUDENT study. We have chosen to talk about Romania even though we are part of the European Union, taking into account some significant differences in the characteristics of the actors in the field of education in Romania and other European countries. Given the constant accumulation of professional responsibilities, a plausible hypothesis emerges that the attitudinal reactions of university teachers are the expression of an adaptation to institutional and academic stress.

Teaching appears to be an inherently stressful profession, which may contribute to a higher risk of job burnout (Marković et al., 2025). In the current academic context, university teachers are subject to an increased level of stress, caused by a combination of technological factors. Among the sources of overload is the intense information flow in the scientific field, along with the pressure of continuous adaptation to new educational technologies, sometimes insufficiently mastered by teachers. These challenges can generate attitudinal reactions of withdrawal, manifested by the maintenance of rigid behavioral patterns, which limit the dialogue with students and negatively affect both the quality of the educational act and the performance of the direct beneficiaries of the system, the students.

Data from various analyses point to a high overload of teaching staff due to the dual professional role of teaching and research imposed by current university standards. According to Eurostat, the steady increase in student numbers has implicitly contributed to a greater workload for teachers, leading to increasingly formal and limiting educational relationships. This reality has been accentuated in the post-pandemic period by the multiplication of communication channels between students and teachers, e-mails, phone messages, digital platforms, multiple WhatsApp groups, which have increased the pressure on teachers, significantly reducing the time available for reflection and professional development. At the same time, the lack of professional psychotherapy courses in the curricula for initial and in-service teacher training exacerbates teachers' vulnerability to stress and emotional exhaustion. The obligation to meet the research standard in the area of specialization leads to frequent neglect of training in the sphere of psycho-pedagogical methodology, which leads to an imbalance between scientific and pedagogical competencies. In addition, the results of a survey of students in the classroom indicate a widespread perception that teachers make insufficient use of technological resources in teaching. There is also a selective attitude on the part of teachers in terms of interaction with students, which may reflect a self-protective strategy in relation to the pressure generated by the system. All these elements outline a complex framework, in which the university teacher is under simultaneous pressure on several levels, without sufficient psycho-pedagogical and institutional support resources. In this respect, it becomes imperative to rethink university educational policies, by rebalancing research and teaching requirements and by introducing mental health support components and adapting to the new demands of the educational process.

Integrating AI in education can significantly enhance the learning process in several key areas. For instance, AI tools are used for the *evaluation process* (Delello et al., 2024), providing immediate feedback to students. Additionally, AI-driven platforms can support retention by delivering personalized content that aligns with *individual learning* styles (Zawacki-Richter et al., 2019). Furthermore, AI technologies have been shown to increase student engagement and motivation by offering adaptive learning experiences (Kamalov et al., 2023).

In the academic environment, GenAI could be perceived as a potentially harmful tool, and solid, well-founded arguments rarely accompany its rejection. The main objections include general allegations regarding copyright infringement, the possibility of educational fraud, and reduced direct student involvement in the learning process. These concerns are legitimate, but punitive approaches or outright rejection ignore the complexity and transformative potential of GenAI. A meta-analysis of researchers from the University of Valencia (Altamura et al., 2023) has concluded that paper reading raises the capacity of understanding in comparison with digital content reading. But another conclusion of that study was that, when it comes to adolescents from high schools and universities, the relationship between recreational reading and text comprehension becomes positive. We could conclude that using paper text support for learning or digital content could determine significant differences in terms of efficiency of learning and this is an important conclusion for researchers, teachers, and policymakers.

On the other hand, the academic environment, with its profoundly traditional infrastructures and mindsets, seems not to have had the necessary time to understand and adapt GenAI for educational purposes. The main teaching methods remain traditional, such as direct lectures, and reading - and discussion-based seminars, while assessments are also in classic forms, such as written tests or oral examinations. These methods, although valuable, are designed for an educational model centered on unidirectional teaching, where the professor is the central figure, and students play a predominantly receptive role.

Professors' limited engagement in online teaching has significantly contributed to high dropout rates in virtual learning environments. This is largely due to lack of digital competencies and insufficient experience with online platforms. Moreover, many teachers failed to adapt their pedagogical approaches, often replicating traditional face-to-face methods rather than developing strategies suited to online education (Csorba & Dabija, 2024) High dropout rates in online education are not only due to students' struggle to balance work and learning, but also to professors' limited involvement and lack of digital competencies. Many instructors failed to adapt their teaching methods to the online environment, often replicating traditional approaches. While student perceptions of online education remain mixed, the pandemic experience has increased acceptance, suggesting a potential shift towards hybrid models through challenges in engagement and adaptability persist (Frolova et al., 2021).

A study conducted by Csorba and Dabija (2024) examined student perceptions of online teaching and learning during the pandemic period, identifying a correlation between online courses satisfaction and generational differences. Based on a sample of 187 Millennials (also named Generation Y) and 610 members of Generation Z, the study found that, despite prior exposure to digital technologies, students generally do not favor online courses as a long-term solution. This reluctance is primarily attributed to the lack of engaging and socially responsive pedagogical strategies (Frolova et al., 2021). During the pandemic, universities were compelled to transition rapidly to online education (Csorba & Dabija, 2024; Msalimova et al., 2022), a shift that exposed significant gaps in instructional design and delivery. Despite the acknowledged role of online pedagogical strategies in influencing student engagement (Amir et al., 2020; apud Csorba & Dabija, 2024) a significant sample of students remain reluctant to adopt online learning as a permanent model of education.

Other education systems / academic institutions are more open to GenAI use as; for example, a research indicated: 'a survey at a large U.S. research university revealed mixed attitudes among faculty and students towards GenAI, with a general openness to training despite current usage and comfort levels, particularly in research contexts' (Andresen et al., 2025; Petricini et al., 2024).

The process of teachers' professionalization is a difficult one and is defined mostly through developing specific competencies for the education field as a professional domain (Păun, 2017). There is an intense analysis around the concept of competence - the process of competencies development is dependent on professional and vocational contexts that could be closed contexts (quasi-algorithmic and standardizable) and open contexts (with new situations, uncertain). This is why a teacher has to develop *transversal competencies* - because their professional context is an action space with a large spectrum of *unpredictability* that requires reflective attitudes and permanent education to keep up with state-of-the-art knowledge tools that could be successfully integrated in an educational relationship. For that we have identified several AI tools that could serve both for teachers and students and their communication.

AI TOOLS FOR PERSONALIZED LEARNING

One of the critical elements for ensuring successful formative assessment is providing *formative feedback* (Hattie & Timperley, 2007). Feedback serves as a mechanism to inform students about the quality of their work during the learning process and offers guidance on how to improve to meet specific standards (Black & Wiliam, 1998). Recent research revealed that AI technologies can enhance the quality and personalization of feedback provided to students. For instance, Burner et al. (2025) emphasize that AI tools enable more tailored feedback, addressing individual students' needs in real time.

A study conducted by Lee (2023) involving the assessment of 2500 essays revealed that *AI-generated feedback* significantly improves the effectiveness of assessments. Students also reported finding the feedback meaningful and actionable. Similarly, Albadarin et al. (2024) found that students who utilized ChatGPT for immediate feedback demonstrated enhanced abilities to explain complex topics, develop their writing skills, and effectively translate or summarize texts. Additionally, these tools are beneficial for teachers, supporting them in lesson planning and quiz creation. By streamlining routine tasks, AI saves educators time and creates more interactive lessons. However, the overuse of tools like ChatGPT can negatively impact student creativity and collaboration, raising concerns about their long-term educational implications. Farrokhnia et al. (2024) mentioned both opportunities and challenges associated with AI tools in education. On the positive side, ChatGPT facilitates access to information and promotes complex learning by encouraging students to develop critical arguments. On the other hand, the study also points out significant limitations, such as the lack of understanding of educational contexts, risks to data security, and the potential for academic dishonesty.

Writing assistants, text generators and smart content creation

AI-powered tools designed to improve the quality of written texts play a significant role in modern education and professional communication. These tools analyze the inserted text to detect grammatical errors and typographical mistakes while providing suggestions for appropriate modifications. For instance, applications like Grammarly are widely used by educators, students, and professionals seeking to refine their language and adjust their writing style based on situational contexts, such as preparing for interviews, drafting articles, or practicing a foreign language.

In the literature review, the most commonly used tools in educational and professional settings include *ProWritingAid, Writing Mentor, and Grammarly* (Alharbi, 2023). Other tools, such as Lingofy and Linguix, focus primarily on grammar checking but are limited to identifying basic errors. Meanwhile, PerfectIt emphasizes consistency in usage, including punctuation and formatting, and WordRake specializes in editing for clarity (Dale & Viethen, 2021). Additionally, models designed to correct or transform text, such as *Ginger, Gramara, Outwrite Pro, and Wordtune*, are also widely referenced in academic and professional contexts (Dale & Viethen, 2021).

Text generation tools, such as *WriteSonic, Copy.AI, and Content Bot*, are designed to generate text based on user input. *Gemini* is a friendly AI tool that has transformed the way students access information by delivering more advanced responses in various fields for digital content, future technology integration, educators, and for researchers. In contrast, Gemini AI has broader multimodal capabilities, allowing it to generate images, audio, text, and video, while *ChatGPT* primarily focuses on text-based interactions, with some image capabilities (Imran & Almusharraf, 2024). *Scalenut, ContentBot, Copy.AI, Jasper, and Writesonic* applications provide extensive training resources (Delcker et al., 2024).

Certain applications can enhance knowledge acquisition by providing a structured conceptual *map of key concepts*. Encouraging students to adopt effective methods and techniques for systematically organizing their lessons is essential, as it enables them to identify the most relevant information for their future careers. Mind mapping is a valuable tool in this process, as it prompts students to focus on a central concept and establish meaningful connections with related terms. One such application that facilitates this approach is *MindMap*. For instance, by using the MindMap application, students can create a genosociogram to identify recurring patterns across generations, from great-grandparents to children or grandchildren.

The genosociogram serves as an important tool for analyzing psychological, medical, and sociological factors that may contribute to an individual's challenges. Unlike a traditional genealogical tree, which typically represents males with squares, circles for females, and marital relationships with parallel lines, the genosociogram provides a more comprehensive framework for examining intergenerational influences and patterns.

Additionally, *Magic School AI* revolutionizes lesson planning, empowers students to design assessments, enhances contemporary learning, and optimizes instructional strategies. According to Rojas Lozano et al. (2024), this application fosters student-centered learning by allowing teachers to tailor content to their available resources and vocabulary while incorporating grammar practice. Furthermore, it upholds ethical standards and ensures data privacy, making it a valuable tool for English Language Teaching (ELT) educators in creating engaging and dynamic classrooms.

Chatbot and Personalized Learning

Chatbots, as described by Jürgen et al. (2023), are conversational tools derived from the terms "chat" and "bot", the latter being an abbreviation of the term "robot". The concept of a robot originates from the Czech word "robota" (meaning labor) and was introduced in 1920 by Karel Čapel. Chatbots simulate intelligent discussions and have become increasingly relevant in both business and education by facilitating automated interactions.

In educational contexts, chatbots are particularly useful for generating presentations, texts, or images and providing instant feedback to learners. *ChatGPT*, for instance, is an AI model made widely available in March 2023 (Aydin & Karaarslan, 2025; OpenAI, 2023). It grants access to a vast repositioning of knowledge across various subjects and can perform a wide range of tasks, from answering questions and explaining complex concepts to providing feedback on students' work. For example, a student aiming to refine an essay can use ChatGPT to generate an outline, improve specific sections, correct grammar, and even receive suggestions on vocabulary or structure based on defined criteria. Similarly, teachers can use ChatGPT to input keywords such as learning, methods, or efficiency and generate targeted feedback for specific sections of a student's work (Burner et al., 2025).

ChatGPT provides continuous formative feedback by generating new insights or suggestions with every revision, enabling students to enhance the coherence and quality of their writing over time. Vukojičić and Krstić (2023) demonstrated that such tools also improve coding proficiency, while students in their study reported high levels of satisfaction with the personalized and real-time feedback provided, particularly during periods of heavy workloads (Brooks et al., 2019). From a teacher's perspective, AI tools like ChatGPT can significantly reduce the time spent preparing for lessons by automating tasks such as *feedback generation and content customization*. Despite these advantages, many educators remain hesitant to adopt AI tools due to concerns about ethics and professional integrity.

Beyond ChatGPT, other advanced chatbots, such as *Bard and BingChat*, provide similar functionalities, offering immediate support and assistance outside classroom hours and promoting independent learning.

Personalized learning is one of the main principles of education, where the student is at the center of the teacher's preoccupation, making learning more effective and engaging. For example, there are tools designed to personalize learning plans, allowing students to progress at their own pace through structured modules, ensuring comprehensive mastery before advancing to the next level. *Duolingo* users can advance to the next level after completing all the required skills in the previous task. This tool can be utilized to develop new language skills, enhance linguistic expression, and refine grammar for those seeking to learn a new language. Learning is structured through a series of exercises, collectively known as a session. Additionally, if a user wishes to focus on a specific skill, they can navigate to the menu and complete the corresponding session.

According to Sampurno (2024), Wolfram Alpha was made publicly accessible in May 2009. This AI-powered tool utilizes licensed databases licensed by experts. The system, driven by artificial intelligence, presents information in the form of lists to provide users precise answers to their queries. Wolfram Alpha's objective is rooted in the accomplishments of science and systematic knowledge, aiming to serve as a single authoritative source for users seeking definitive answers to factual questions. Sampurno (2024) also emphasized the tool's ability to accurately assist human tasks. However, it is noted that this convenience may come at the cost of human creativity. From this perspective, the role of educators is gradually being overshadowed by AI, which draws from its vast databases and sources from the internet.

A study conducted by Petr Nečesal and Jan Pospíšil (2012) explored the integration of *Wolfram Alpha* into mathematics courses for engineering students. This study demonstrated its effectiveness in solving simple equations, analyzing matrix properties, and enhancing computational learning. Furthermore, Wolfram Alpha is accessible not only from computers but also from various mobile devices, making it a versatile tool for students. Wolfram Alpha illustrates real-world applications of various theories, helping students grasp the interconnectedness of multiple fields of study.

Labster provides virtual laboratory simulations that allow students to safely explore and experiment with scientific concepts in an interactive and controlled environment, fostering a deeper understanding of key terms (Elmesalawy et al., 2021). Additionally, Labster enhances student motivation (Tsirulnikov et al., 2023).

Ahmet Rizwan (2021) conducted a study on the use of a vocabulary-building application, highlighting its effectiveness in enhancing vocabulary acquisition and retention among graduate students. The findings suggest that digital flashcards and mobile applications, such as *MAVL*, can facilitate vocabulary learning by improving retention rates. Additionally, multimedia models can register learners' progress in real-time time is a math AI tool that offers a real-time experience based on individual students' needs, emphasizing young learners' insights into early education and engagement strategy (Palakurti, 2025). A study on Digital Innovation and Transformation, published on the Harvard website and conducted on 10,000 students, found that Knewton, an AI-powered tool, demonstrated a direct correlation between mastering subjects through its program's assignments and improved academic performance in courses.

Some AI tools, like *Dysolve AI*, are useful for individuals diagnosing children with dyslexia by adapting to their individual learning needs and enhancing cognitive engagement.

CHALLENGES AND OPPORTUNITIES OF AI INTEGRATION IN THE EDUCATIONAL SYSTEM

Despite its benefits, for a country like Romania, the challenge is not merely whether teachers, students, and, in certain cases, parents will adapt to AI technologies, but rather how effectively these stakeholders can integrate such tools into the educational process to improve learning, particularly for those lacking access to basic resources.

The pandemic context underscored the pivotal role of technology in education, with mathematics instructors exemplifying this shift by employing graphic tablets to facilitate virtual learning. These tools enabled educators to illustrate complex concepts such as matrices or formulas, generating and sharing notes instantaneously during platforms like Zoom or Google Meet. As noted by Pantelimon et al. (2021) in their statistical work, the pandemic context catalyzed the integration of AI-driven tools within the educational system, transforming traditional pedagogical practices. Romania ranks among the EU countries with the lowest levels of administrative digitalization, as noted by Tinholt et al. (2019). Their findings suggest that Romania should prioritize investments and improvements in educational software licenses, technological infrastructure and digital libraries and how they can access the relevant resources.

According to Xianli et al. (2020), AI algorithms were also employed in experimental projects and for detecting plagiarism, further demonstrating the versatility and potential of AI in addressing diverse educational challenges.

A key challenge, according to Botnariuc et al. (2020) lies in outdated pedagogical methods and curricula that do not adequately address the demands of the digital era. Online lessons present significant challenges for students with special educational needs, as the virtual format often lacks the adaptability required. In a traditional classroom setting, teachers can adapt the complexity of the material to align with the specific needs and abilities of these students, providing more personalized support.

Ai tools present significant opportunities for enhancing efficiency, innovation, and analytical capacity across diverse domains. As AI becomes increasingly integrated into educational and professional contexts, its potential to transform traditional practices continues to expand. In the context of education, Pantelimon et al.

(2021) identifies a key advantage of transitioning to an online educational model: it empowers students by granting them greater autonomy over their learning process. Students take responsibility for gathering, analyzing, and assimilating information, while teachers focus on offering guidance and support.

Reconfiguring Evaluative Practices in the Digital Era

Specialty and methodological competencies, communication, counseling, and orientation for students, class management, organization, and personal development are key areas of competencies for teachers (Păun, 2017). From these, evaluation and communication competencies have rapid and direct effects on the teacher-student relationship; every human action needs feedback, and delayed feedback in the teacher-student relationship could be a source of Z-generation student dissatisfaction.

Describing digital natives, H. Støle (2018) considers that "... they are used to receiving information really fast. They like to parallel processes and multi-tasking. They prefer their graphics before their text rather than the opposite. They prefer random access (like hypertext). They function best when networked. They thrive on instant gratification and frequent rewards. They prefer games to 'serios' work."

But, despite recent generations' preference for digital tools, it has been demonstrated (Altamura et al., 2023) that paper text reading has superior effectiveness considering comprehension, so teachers have to, with diplomacy, make decisions based on research evidence. Both teachers and students have to make efforts - teachers have the duty to persuade students to do what is best for them in the long term, even if this means effort and opposition to effort.

The assessment tools used in digital evaluation are often limited and may impose constraints on students. The reconfiguration of the educational system to integrate digital assessment methods faces resistance from educators (Apostolache, 2022).

Nevertheless, digital assessment practices offer significant *advantages*, including immediate feedback, which facilitates the diagnosis of errors. Likewise, the proposed solutions are adaptable and personalized, aspects that support self-regulated learning. Alternative digital tools can identify and measure complex skills such as decision-making, selecting the most effective strategies, and domain-specific competencies. Through applications, students can monitor their progress while also benefiting from the flexibility to choose the form and method of assessment.

The reconfiguration of evaluative practices in the digital era extends beyond the mere adoption of technological tools, requiring a fundamental shift toward more learner-centered and motivationally responsive assessment strategies. Within this framework, gamification presents itself as a promising pedagogical approach, offering dynamic and interactive assessment formats that foster engagement, autonomy, and sustained academic growth. This aligns with the understanding that, from birth, children are naturally encouraged to explore their environment through active interaction, highlighting the importance of incorporating interactive elements into learning and assessment. This *innate drive for exploration* is fundamental to human development. It forms the basis for how children engage with the world around them and is essential for their cognitive, emotional, and social growth. In this context, both Montessori and Waldorf pedagogy promote free exploration of the environment. These pedagogical approaches allow children the possibility to have an authentic experience, fostering a sense of independence and self-discovery. In Montessori and Waldorf classrooms, children are not simply recipients of information, but active participants in the learning process. Play, therefore, becomes the first form of real learning and is recognized as one of the most fundamental means through which the child develops cognitive, emotional, and social skills. Through play, children learn through a trial-and-error process, which allows them to experiment with ideas and concepts. This experiential learning helps them to form a functional understanding of the world around them. Furthermore, play is inherently social, providing opportunities for emotional and social development as children engage with their peers.

This natural inclination towards learning through play underpins the modern principles of gamification. Gamification refers to the use of game-like elements within non-game contexts, such as education, to enhance engagement and motivate learning. One of the most significant advancements in modern education has been the integration of gamification with artificial intelligence (AI). In this way, AI has the potential to create interactive, adaptive, and safe learning environments that reflect the individual needs, learning style, and interests of students, contributing to a more personalized learning experience.

As for the concept of gamification, Karl Kapp defines it as the process of applying elements and techniques characteristic of video games to stimulate engagement, motivate action, and facilitate problem solving. This approach not only transforms learning but also makes it more interactive and engaging. On the other hand, Emil Stan (2021) emphasizes a crucial dimension of gamification, namely that it entails significant changes in how students perceive educational reality. Gamification is not limited to enjoyable experiences but also aims to stimulate students' engagement, responsibility, and motivation. In this regard, one of the biggest challenges for educators remains the identification of effective strategies to foster active student engagement, especially when it comes to reward management.

In terms of the educational preferences of the new generation, Gai ă (2021) observes a clear tendency of IGen students to turn to digital tools at the expense of traditional ones. She draws a parallel between activity workbooks and PlayStation-type video games, noting that both offer the possibility of advancement to a higher level following the accumulation of scores or points. However, in contrast to activity books, video games are much more effective in keeping students motivated due to their interactivity and freedom of choice of strategies. In this respect, Mihály Csíkszentmihályi (2011) describes the phenomenon of flow, a state of intense concentration and complete involvement, in which the student is absorbed in the activity and learns genuinely.

Also, in teaching activities, the teacher can integrate elements of play to stimulate curiosity and facilitate the assimilation of knowledge. In this way, learning becomes an interactive process and the teacher assumes the role of 'learning architect', creating an educational game with clear gamification rules. These rules may include tasks involving the use of digital devices or artificial intelligence-based tools, but it is important to note that gamification does not depend exclusively on AI technology. This can also be implemented through traditional methods of reward, such as badges, diplomas, points, or bonuses awarded throughout the semester. Referring to Game-Based Learning (GBL), Gu u (2023) emphasizes the use of educational games with a clearly defined purpose to support the learning process. "Serious" games are selected according to the skills they develop. For example, action games such as *Mirror's Edge, Re-Mission, Mario Galaxy*, or *Asteroids* contribute to the development of spatial thinking and resource planning, while games such as *Fable, The Elder Scrolls*, or *Neverwinter Nights* are designed to promote strategic thinking and problem solving. Strategy games such as *Civilization, StarCraft, or Dune II* are recognized for their educational potential in the field of complex strategies. Simulation games such as *Sim City, Angry Birds, Theme Hospital*, or *Flight Simulator,* on the other hand, help to develop systematic thinking, while sports or fighting games (e.g., FIFA Soccer, NBA Live) are excellent for fostering team coordination and collaboration.

However, according to Cu ulab (2024), the key difference between Game-Based Learning and gamification is that GBL involves the use of complete, already developed games for educational purposes, whereas gamification refers to the integration of specific game elements into an existing educational setting, transforming learning into a game-like experience.

Dan Pink (2011) argues that gamification is based on stimulating internal motivation, built around three fundamental pillars: autonomy, competence, and purpose. This approach does not focus on immediate external rewards but encourages genuine emotional engagement of the learner. Effectiveness occurs when the learner can manage their own pace of learning and when progress is recognized, thus reinforcing a sense of competence.

An eloquent example of the use of gamification in education is provided by the Khan Academy platform presented by Burke (2014). It uses a reward system based on merit badges awarded to students who answer correctly within a predetermined time. After correctly solving a set of ten questions, users are recognized as "experts" and can move to the next level, and their progress is visualized through a knowledge map. The reward system, which includes badges and points, is designed to maintain motivation and support students' continued engagement.

Emil Stan (2021) lists some of the specific elements of gamification that contribute to the success of this process, including praise, awarding points, badges, extending the game, performances, ways of self-expression, and access to additional powers. These tools are essential for creating a dynamic educational experience that stimulates the motivation and active engagement of students.

A topic of continuing interest in educational literature is the impact of external rewards on *intrinsic motivation*. In this context, studies show that external rewards, particularly when used frequently and unjustified, can erode students' internal motivation in the medium and long term. Thus, modern education, underpinned by the principles of gamification, tends to focus on fostering intrinsic motivation and promoting learner autonomy.

Moreover, in terms of the use of digital technologies in education, Codreanu (2021) argues that gamification is an effective tool for educators, being a challenging means to make learning more engaging and interactive. However, it is essential to note that the difference between games and gamification lies in the purpose of these two concepts. While games are often intended to create an engaging and engaging experience for the player, gamification refers to the integration of game-specific design elements into an educational context to enhance the attractiveness and effectiveness of the learning process (Stan, 2021).

Beyond the challenges and opportunities, a less explored and clarified sphere of recent interest (especially in Romanian academic research) is that of the ethical and legislative dimensions, which is why we have chosen to analyze some issues considering these aspects. A clear normativity considering the use and opportunity of AI use in (higher) education could help teachers / managers to establish healthy limits and anticipate / become aware of possible risks.

Exploring Some Legal Dimensions of AI Literacy in Higher Education

Universities today face a dual imperative, both ethical and legal, to proactively engage with the technological transformations reshaping education and society. As institutions entrusted with the formation of future professionals, they bear the responsibility of ensuring that their teaching and research practices remain socially relevant and legally compliant. This is especially critical in the context of emerging technologies such as generative artificial intelligence, which are no longer peripheral but central to the academic, economic, and social structures in which students will participate.

Generative AI, including tools such as large language models, is rapidly entering university environments-through learning platforms, writing support tools, automated feedback systems, and even content creation in teaching and research. These developments compel institutions to reconsider the foundational principles that guide their mission, particularly those of learner-centered education and relevance. The student-centered approach, for example, must now be understood as encompassing the digital empowerment of learners: equipping them not only with technical fluency but also with the critical capacity to understand, question, and responsibly use AI systems (Bearman et al., 2023).

This shift requires re-evaluating what constitutes the "best interests" of the student in a digital age. Protecting students from AI tools entirely, out of fear of academic dishonesty or dehumanization, may ultimately undermine their right to a future-oriented education. Conversely, uncritical adoption of generative AI without legal safeguards or pedagogical reflection may expose students to risks such as data misuse, algorithmic bias, or dependency on automated outputs. The legal and educational challenge, therefore, is to navigate a middle path: integrating generative AI in ways that are pedagogically sound, legally compliant, and socially just.

The principle of Educational Relevance

The principle of educational relevance reinforces this necessity. As higher education institutions respond to socio-economic demands and prepare graduates for a digital labor market, curricula must evolve to include not only technical knowledge of AI systems but also legal frameworks, ethical principles, and governance models for their responsible use (Thurzo et al., 2023). This includes competencies in data protection, intellectual property, algorithmic transparency, and human oversight-all of which are particularly urgent in the context of generative AI, where content creation may blur the boundaries between originality and automation.

A recent case that illustrates the real-world implications of AI governance is the €32 million fine imposed by the French data protection authority (CNIL) on Amazon France Logistique (CNIL, 2024). The company was penalized for its use of AI-powered monitoring systems that tracked employee productivity and idle time in ways deemed excessively intrusive (Volosevici, 2024). Although the setting was a warehouse, not a university, the implications for higher education are clear: students must be taught not only how AI works, but also when and how its deployment crosses legal or ethical lines. This is particularly important given that generative AI, like other forms of AI, often operates in opaque ways, raising concerns about informed consent, surveillance, and the erosion of academic autonomy.

In the academic context, similar risks arise when generative AI is used for automated grading, plagiarism detection, or behavioral analytics. These systems may unintentionally replicate bias, operate with limited transparency, or collect sensitive student data without adequate justification or oversight. Universities must ensure that the deployment of such tools adheres to the principles of necessity, proportionality, and transparency, as required by the General Data Protection Regulation and other relevant legal instruments. Moreover, under the EU Artificial Intelligence Act, educational applications of high-risk AI systems will be subject to stricter obligations related to risk management, documentation, and human oversight.

Beyond compliance, there is a deeper institutional responsibility to foster what Smuha (2021) describes as AI literacy with integrity, an approach that empowers students to become not only competent users of AI tools but also critical agents in shaping their use. For this reason, legal and ethical education must be embedded into all disciplines where generative AI is likely to be used, ranging from humanities and social sciences to business, computer science, and teacher training.

In failing to do so, universities risk abdicating their role as civic institutions and knowledge custodians. A strict traditionalist stance that excludes generative AI from the educational environment is not only impractical, it risks producing graduates who are ill-equipped to navigate the realities of the digital economy, either as employees subjected to AI-driven decision-making or as professionals responsible for deploying these systems themselves. Likewise, an uncritical embrace of generative AI, without regulatory or pedagogical safeguards, may lead to infringements on student rights, academic standards, and public trust in higher education.

In this context, universities are not merely adapting to technological change, they are shaping its trajectory. Their legal and ethical obligations are not limited to protecting students from harm but include actively contributing to the democratic governance of digital technologies. By educating students about the social, legal, and epistemic conditions under which generative AI operates, higher education institutions fulfil not only their pedagogical mission but also their legal mandate to support an informed, critical, and rights-conscious citizenry.

The legal obligations of universities in this context are increasingly delineated in both national and international education law. In parallel, European education policies promote adaptability and innovation in higher education, with an emphasis on the recognition of competencies acquired in non-formal learning environments and the integration of advanced educational technologies. Within the *Digital Education Action Plan 2021–2027: Resetting education and training for the digital age* (European Commission, 2020), a comprehensive rethinking of education and training systems is proposed to ensure alignment with the demands of the digital era. The plan outlines two fundamental strategic directions: the development of a high-performing digital education ecosystem and the enhancement of digital skills and competencies necessary for a fair and sustainable digital transformation. Both priorities necessitate significant structural transformations within educational institutions, particularly universities, which are expected to play a leading role in cultivating a culture of pedagogical and technological innovation.

This expectation entails not only the digitization of learning materials and infrastructure but also the reconfiguration of teaching, assessment, and academic governance practices through the use of advanced technologies, including AI-based solutions. These developments reflect a broader shift toward learner-centered, data-informed, and flexible education systems, supported by adaptive, analytical, and predictive tools (Zawacki-Richter et al., 2019). In this regard, digital literacy and critical engagement with technology are not peripheral skills but central components of democratic participation, social inclusion, and academic integrity (Redecker, 2017).

Universities, as central actors in the knowledge economy, are therefore not merely transmitters of disciplinary content but strategic institutions tasked with producing scientifically rigorous and socially meaningful knowledge. Their mission includes fostering critical reflection on technological change and equipping students to live and act responsibly in a world shaped by rapid innovation, ethical ambiguity, and systemic transformation. As Barnett (2000) contends, university must be a space where individuals are prepared not just for employability but for critical agency in a complex, uncertain world.

This role is further reinforced by legal and policy instruments at both international and European levels. The *UNESCO Recommendation on the Role of Higher Education in the 21st Century* asserts that universities have a duty to respond to the evolving needs of society through the creation and dissemination of relevant and inclusive knowledge (UNESCO, 1998). At the European level, Article 165 of the *Treaty on the Functioning of the European Union* (European Union, 2012) explicitly calls for the development of education systems that foster innovation, employment, and active citizenship, thereby linking the public mission of universities to legal obligations to support sustainable development, democratic values, and social progress.

In light of these frameworks, the integration of generative AI into the academic environment cannot be treated as a mere technological upgrade or discretionary pedagogical tool. It raises foundational questions not only about academic responsibility and equity but also about the legally mandated role of universities in upholding the principles of learner-centered education and educational relevance.

Preparing Students for AI: The Role of Legal Literacy

AI is increasingly embedded in the fabric of modern society, impacting domains ranging from healthcare and law to education, finance, and the arts. In medicine, AI systems assist in early disease detection, such as using machine learning algorithms to identify cancerous cells in radiological scans (Esteva et al., 2017). The financial sector relies on AI for fraud detection and algorithmic trading (Berg et al., 2020), while legal professionals are adopting AI tools for contract review and predictive analytics in litigation. In education, AI enables adaptive learning platforms and automated assessment, reshaping pedagogical models (Holmes et al., 2019). Even creative disciplines are being transformed, with AI systems generating original music, text, and art (McCormack et al., 2019).

Given this pervasive influence, basic AI literacy should be considered essential for all university students, irrespective of their field of study. As Holmes et al. (2019) argue, AI literacy encompasses not only technical understanding but also awareness of the ethical, social, and legal implications of AI use. This foundational knowledge enables students to critically assess and responsibly engage with AI technologies in both personal and professional contexts. Teaching AI literacy is not about training all students as developers, but about cultivating informed users who can understand and challenge the societal impact of these systems (Long & Magerko, 2020). As AI continues to shape employment, governance, communication, and creativity, it represents a core component of what it means to be educated in the 21st century. Preparing students to navigate this landscape is not merely an academic preference, it is an educational imperative.

We will refer to three key aspects that should be critically examined within the educational context. First, the use of artificial intelligence inherently involves *the use of data.* These data are collected from a wide range of sources, with a significant portion voluntarily shared by data subjects themselves in the public domain. This includes not only social media platforms but also various e-commerce websites and digital services. Notably, many of these platforms are headquartered outside the European Union and therefore fall outside the protective scope of the EU's data protection regulations, such as GDPR.

Consequently, educational institutions should develop and promote a set of best practices to guide students in the secure management of both their own personal data and the data they routinely process, often unknowingly, in digital environments. In everyday online interactions, individuals may unintentionally disclose a wide range of sensitive information, such as their location, personal preferences, names, educational background, and data concerning third parties. This often occurs through the use of digital tools, mobile applications, and online platforms without a full understanding of the implications. Every minute of the day nowadays, AI tools such as Google's Gemini receive over 8,500 visits, TikTok users upload 16,000 videos, Netflix streams nearly 363,000 hours of content, Google processes 5.9 million searches, and Siri answers over a million questions. Simultaneously, users send 18.8 million text messages, view 3.5 million YouTube videos, play 138.9 million reels on Facebook and Instagram, and dispatch 251.1 million emails (Domo, 2024). These figures underscore the extent to which individuals continuously generate, share, and interact with vast amounts of data—often unconsciously and without fully grasping the implications. In this context, schools and universities have a critical role in fostering digital literacy. They must equip students with the competencies to recognize, evaluate, and mitigate the risks associated with the collection and dissemination of personal information in virtual spaces. The ability to navigate this data-saturated environment responsibly is now a core component of modern education.

Students are not only at risk of becoming victims of excessive personal data exposure but may also be held accountable for the harm caused by the unauthorized disclosure of others' personal information. This responsibility extends beyond peer interactions and includes instances where data belonging to fellow students, research participants, or individuals involved in university-based experiments are mishandled. For example, in academic projects involving surveys, interviews, or digital trace analysis, students may inadvertently reveal identifiable information without proper anonymization or consent protocols. Similarly, sharing screenshots, recordings, or documents containing sensitive information on social media or collaborative platforms can lead to data breaches or reputational harm. These scenarios highlight the dual role of students as both data subjects and data controllers, underscoring the urgent need for formal education on data ethics, legal compliance, and responsible digital conduct within academic settings.

A second aspect that merits critical analysis is the emergence of a new contractual reality shaped by the growing applicability of smart contracts. As generative AI continues to reshape higher education and the broader knowledge economy, it also contributes to a shift in how agreements and legal obligations are understood, created, and executed. One notable development in this regard is the emergence of *smart contracts*, a concept rooted in blockchain technology and increasingly relevant across sectors influenced by automation and algorithmic decision-making. A smart contract is a self-executing digital agreement, expressed in code and stored on a decentralized blockchain. It automatically performs actions when specified conditions are met, without requiring human oversight or intermediaries (Christidis & Devetsikiotis, 2016).

The growing deployment of smart contracts—particularly in domains such as finance, intellectual property licensing, decentralized education platforms, and digital credentials, signals a broader transformation in how legal relationships are conceptualized in digitally mediated environments. For students in any discipline engaging with generative AI, this transformation is especially relevant. Smart contracts exemplify the convergence of AI, automation, and law, raising questions around legal enforceability, algorithmic interpretation of contractual terms, and the risks of coding errors or exploitation (Werbach & Cornell, 2017).

Universities have a critical role to play in preparing students for this new landscape. Integrating courses that explore smart contracts, legal automation, and AI-assisted legal reasoning equips future professionals with both the technical literacy to understand these tools and the critical awareness to question their limitations and ethical implications. Such education is essential not only for students in law, business, or computer science, but for anyone who will interact with digital infrastructures, particularly as AI systems increasingly govern access, compliance, and transactions in both public and private sectors.

Moreover, in the context of generative AI, where content, services, and even decisions may be produced and delivered autonomously, understanding the logic of smart contracts becomes a foundational component of digital citizenship. From verifying authorship and ownership of AI-generated content to managing intellectual property rights in collaborative research projects, the implications of automated contractual systems are deeply intertwined with the ethical and legal challenges posed by AI in education.

A third critical dimension of integrating generative AI into higher education concerns the ongoing *redefinition of copyright law* in the context of machine-generated content. As AI systems become increasingly capable of autonomously producing images, texts, music, and other creative works, legal systems around the world are being challenged to determine the ownership, originality, and protectability of such outputs. This is particularly relevant in educational and research environments, where students and scholars frequently employ generative AI tools in the creation of essays, artworks, data visualizations, and academic publications.

In a landmark decision, the Beijing Internet Court ruled in November 2023 that an AI-generated image, created using the tool "Stable Diffusion", could be protected by copyright under Chinese law, on the grounds that the human user exercised sufficient creative control over the process and the result met the threshold of originality. The court emphasized the user's intellectual input in prompting and selecting the final output, thus affirming a form of "human-machine co-authorship" (Beijing Internet Court, 2023). This decision reflects a growing trend in certain jurisdictions to recognize hybrid forms of creativity where AI acts as a tool, rather than as an independent author.

Conversely, courts in the United States have taken a stricter stance. On August 18, 2023, the U.S. District Court for the District of Columbia ruled that AI-generated works are not eligible for copyright protection if there is no human authorship involved (*Thaler v. Perlmutter*, 2023). The court reaffirmed the U.S. Copyright Office's (2023) long-standing position that authorship must be attributable to a natural person, thus excluding works created entirely by AI systems without substantial human creative input. This highlights the legal fragmentation that complicates the use of AI tools in cross-border academic projects and content creation.

Another pressing issue is whether the use of copyrighted materials as training data for AI systems constitutes an infringement of intellectual property rights. Large language models and generative AI tools are frequently trained on a vast corpus of copyrighted texts scraped from the internet, raising concerns among authors, publishers, and educators. If AI systems generate content that is derivative of, or replicates, protected works, the entities that develop, deploy, or use those systems may be exposed to legal liability for copyright infringement (Samuelson, 2023). While some developers argue that such training qualifies as "fair use" under U.S. law or as legitimate text and data mining under European exceptions, courts have yet to reach a consensus on the matter.

For universities, these developments carry both pedagogical and compliance implications. Institutions must educate students on the evolving rules of authorship, attribution, and fair use in the context of AI-assisted creation. Academic integrity policies should be updated to address co-authorship with AI and the proper citation of AI-generated content. Furthermore, students should be encouraged to critically assess the legal and ethical boundaries of using generative AI, particularly when such tools draw upon protected cultural and intellectual materials.

In an era defined by rapid technological transformation, universities carry a fundamental obligation to provide relevant, future-oriented education that prepares students to thrive in digitally mediated societies. This responsibility extends beyond disciplinary knowledge to include equipping learners with the competencies necessary to navigate, interpret, and shape the evolving technological landscape. As artificial intelligence becomes a pervasive feature of daily life, from data-driven decisions and algorithmic interactions to automated contracts and content creation, higher education institutions must take a proactive role in both integrating AI tools and fostering critical engagement with their implications.

This dual role requires not only the implementation of AI in teaching, research, and administration, but also the systematic development of AI literacy across disciplines. AI literacy involves understanding how AI systems function, recognizing their societal and legal impacts, and developing the ability to use them ethically and responsibly. As examined in this section, this includes awareness of data protection principles, familiarity with smart contract technologies, and knowledge of intellectual property frameworks that are being redefined in the context of generative AI.

Such competencies are no longer optional but essential. Students must be prepared to engage with intelligent systems not merely as users, but as informed citizens and professionals capable of addressing the legal, ethical, and social challenges these technologies pose. By prioritizing AI and legal literacy, universities can ensure that graduates are equipped not only to benefit from AI's capabilities, but also to contribute to its responsible and equitable development in society.

CONCLUSIONS, LIMITS AND FUTURE RESEARCH DIRECTIONS

The advent of AI tools has precipitated a paradigm shift in the realm of education, encompassing every facet of the educational process, from its planning and implementation to its evaluation. The impact of these changes is observable across a variety of dimensions, including the learning environment, time management, personalization of educational resources, student engagement, and motivation. This rapid change is placing considerable pressure on educational professionals to balance traditional teaching-learning-assessment methods with the new AI tools. The challenge is compounded by the coexistence and collaboration of two generations with disparate relationships to technology within the same educational space. The majority of the teachers are from Generation X, who are accustomed to traditional teaching methods such as blackboard, chalk, or, in the most advanced cases, PowerPoint presentations. In contrast, the students of Generation Z, often referred to as digital natives, are familiar with contemporary tools for exploration, learning, and interaction. This methodological discrepancy underscores the challenges encountered by the university system in attempting to harmonize fundamentally opposed educational styles.

In this context, we endeavor to collaborate with our colleagues from other universities to examine exemplary practices and formulate recommendations for adapting teaching-learning-assessment strategies during the annual conferences. It is imperative to acknowledge that our experience does not define the overarching framework of Romanian universities; however, we must substantiate the perspectives from other universities, recognizing that our experience cannot be universally applied.

AI tools evolution determined a revolution inside education - from planning to implementing and evaluation. The effects (both positive and negative) are visible both on the learning environment, time management, personalizing learning tools, engagement and motivation. Students' behavior towards learning is a challenge for educators that have to balance between AI tools and traditional teaching / learning / evaluation methods.

The integration of artificial intelligence tools into educational settings marks a significant evolution in how teachers approach the learning process. By incorporating the principles of gamification, AI enables a more dynamic, personalized learning experience that caters to the diverse needs of students. This synergy between gamification and AI tools offers the potential to not only enhance student motivation but also engagement, foster deeper and more meaningful learning. The successful implementation of such technologies requires a balanced approach. New generations are a challenge for the education field (policy, strategies for teaching / evaluation / teachers' training, etc.). Digital technology is a reality in the contemporary world, and, in spite of all the research that demonstrates the negative effects that the excessive use of technology could have, the future seems to belong to those who know how to use and master technology.

There are a multitude of applications that can facilitate the teaching process - from exploring and creating digital content to navigating in time and space, assessment, practicing/developing practical skills in virtual space with applicability in various professions. Rapid feedback, writing assistance, text generation, chat, and personalized learning are opportunities offered by AI tools in education. Both teachers and students need to cooperate and explore digital technology and find the middle path between classical strategies and digital ones.

Intersection of generation in the same space - education field - is also a challenge that involves cooperation between people that have been raised in different manners and have to learn from each other to communicate using a similar language. Z generation's childhood has been deeply influenced by the presence / large access to smart technology for early ages. This has affected both their emotions, physical activity, and social relationships and parents, teachers and policy makers have to pay attention to those alarming studies and statistics. Still, present challenges request the integration of technology in education so as to enable new generations for optimal social and professional integration.

Studies indicate the opportunity of using technology not only as tools for facilitating the process of learning (writing assistance, text generation, Chatbots, MindMap, or other instrument that facilitate learning for disabled children or study in different areas - like Duolingo, Wolfram Alpha etc.) but also for evaluation (offering prompt feedback and also various instruments for collecting data and creating statistics as base for decisions considering efficient teaching and learning strategies).

Optimizing AI tools integration in education depends both on students' characteristics (age, specific / individual needs, motivation etc.) and teachers' expertise and openness to develop transversal competences that allows them to cope with a large spectrum of unpredictability specific to the education field. Also, legal issues are determined by AI integration in education and teachers and students have to become aware and learn about ethical and legal limitations (data use, smart contracts, redefining copyright laws etc.).

The legal and educational challenge, therefore, is to navigate a middle path: integrating generative AI in ways that are pedagogically sound, legally compliant, and socially just. So, limiting access to children of an inappropriate age for social networks is an imperative. To give childhood back to childhood, but also to take into account the context of the contemporary world in which we need to learn how to explore technology without allowing it to dominate/lead us at the expense of the life skills specific to a human being, of a social nature.

Researchers could analyze these issues concerning directions for teachers' training as promoters of change in the education system, the optimal combination between digital and classic tools/strategies for learning (considering studies' findings) and efficiency of AI tools depending on the differences between the (psychological) characteristics of students of different ages.

The effects of training programs for teachers on efficiency of planning activities (including personal and professional development), using applications that facilitate and personalize learning, monitoring students' progress etc. should be analyzed by studies. Also, legal and ethical implications of AI use in education should be analyzed and monitored; more, we believe that training programs considering these issues should be included as distinctive disciplines in schools and universities curricula.

REFERENCES

Albadarin, Y., Saqr, M., Pope, N., & Tukiainen, M. (2024). A systematic literature review of empirical research on ChatGPT in education. *Discover Education*, *3*(1), 60. DOI: 10.1007/s44217-024-00138-2

Alharbi, W. (2023). AI in the foreign language classroom: A pedagogical overview of automated writing assistance tools. *Education Research International*, *1*, 4253331. DOI: 10.1155/2023/4253331

Altamura, L., Vargas, C., & Salmerón, L. (2023). Do New Forms of Reading Pay Off? A Meta-Analysis on the Relationship Between Leisure Digital Reading Habits and Text Comprehension. *Review of Educational Research, 95*(1), 53-88. https://doi .org/ (Original work published 2025)DOI: 10.3102/00346543231216463

Amir, L. R., Tanti, I., Maharani, D. A., Wimardhari, Y. S., Julia, V., Sulijaya, B., & Puspitawati, R. (2020). Student perspective of classroom and distance Learning during Covid-19 pandemic in the undergraduate dental study program Universitas Indonesia. *BMC Medical Education*, *20*(1), 1–8. DOI: 10.1186/s12909-020-02312-0 PMID: 33121488

Andresen, J. P., Degn, L., Fishberg, R., Graversen, E. K., Horbach, S. P. J. M., Schmidt, E. K., Schneider, J. W., & Sørensen, M. P. (2025). Generative Artificial Intelligence (GenAI) in the research process – a survey of researchers' practices and perceptions. *Technology in Society*, *81*, 102813. DOI: 10.1016/j.techsoc.2025.102813

Apostolache, R. (2022). *Competen a pedagogică digitală* [Digital pedagogical competence]. Polirom.

Aydin, O., & Karaarslan, E. (2025). OpenAI ChatGPT interprets Radiological Images: GPT-4 as a Medical Doctor for a Fast Check-Up. *Computer Vision and Pattern Recognition. arXiv preprint* arXiv:2501.06269

Barnett, R. (2000). University knowledge in an age of supercomplexity. *Higher Education*, *40*(4), 409–422. DOI: 10.1023/A:1004159513741

Bearman, M., Ryan, J., & Ajjawi, R. (2023). Discourses of artificial intelligence in higher education: A critical literature review. *Higher Education*, *86*(2), 369–385. DOI: 10.1007/s10734-022-00937-2

Beijing Internet Court. (2023, November). Decision on copyright protection for AI-generated images using Stable Diffusion.

Benbya, H., Strich, F., & Tamm, T. (2024). Navigating Generative Artificial Intelligence Promises and Perils for Knowledge and Creative Work. *Journal of the Association for Information Systems*, *25*(1), 23–36. DOI: 10.17705/1jais.00861

Berg, T., Burg, V., Gombović, A., & Puri, M. (2020). On the rise of FinTechs: Credit scoring using digital footprints. *Review of Financial Studies*, *33*(7), 2845–2897. DOI: 10.1093/rfs/hhz099

Black, P., & Wiliam, D. (1998). Assessment and classroom learning. *Assessment in Education: Principles, Policy & Practice*, *5*(1), 7–74. DOI: 10.1080/0969595980050102

Bonchi , E. (Ed.). (2021). *Genera ia Z* [Generation Z]. Polirom.

Bonchi , E. (2022). *Plictiseala la copii i adolescen i: O perspectivă psihosociologică* [Boredom in children and adolescents: A psychosociological perspective]. Polirom.

Botnariuc, P., Cuco , C., Glava, C., Ilie, M. D., Istrate, O., Labăr, A. V., Pâni oară, I. O., tefănescu, D., & Velea, S. (2020). *coala online – elemente pentru inovarea educa iei* [Online school: Elements for innovating education]. University of Bucharest Publishing House. https://unibuc.ro/wp-content/uploads/2020/05/Scoala_Online_Raport_aprilie_2020.pdf

Bozkurt, A., Xiao, J., Farrow, R., Bai, J. Y. H., Nerantzi, C., Moore, S., Dron, J., Stracke, C. M., Singh, L., Crompton, H., Koutropoulos, A., Terentev, E., Pazurek, A., Nichols, M., Sidorkin, A. M., Costello, E., Watson, S., Mulligan, D., Honeychurch, S., & Asino, T. I. (2024). The Manifesto for Teaching and Learning in a Time of Generative AI: A Critical Collective Stance to Better Navigate the Future. *Open Praxis*, *16*(4), 487–513. DOI: 10.55982/openpraxis.16.4.777

Brady, W. J., Jackson, J. C., Lindström, B., & Crockett, M. J. (2023). Algorithm-mediated social learning in online social networks. *Trends in Cognitive Sciences*, *27*(10), 947–960. DOI: 10.1016/j.tics.2023.06.008 PMID: 37543440

Brooks, C., Carroll, A., Gilles, R. M., & Hattie, J. (2019). A matrix of feedback for learning. [Online]. *The Australian Journal of Teacher Education*, *44*(4), 14–32. DOI: 10.14221/ajte.2018v44n4.2

Burke, B. (2014). Gamify: How gamification motivates people to do extraordinary things. *Bibliomotion: Inc.*, (Apr). Advance online publication. DOI: 10.4324/9781315230344

Burner, T., Lindvig, Y., & Wærness, J. I. (2025). "We Should Not Be Like a Dinosaur"—Using AI Technologies to Provide Formative Feedback to Students. *Education Sciences*, *15*(1), 58. DOI: 10.3390/educsci15010058

Čapel, K. (1920). R.U.R. (Rossum's Universal Robots). Translate by Paul Selver and Nigel Playfair (1923). Project Gutenberg. The Project Gutenberg eBook of R. U. R. (Rossum's Universal Robots), by Karel Capek.

Ceobanu, C., Cuco , C., Istrate, O., & Pâni oară, I. O. (Eds.). (2020). *Educa ia digitală* [Digital education]. Polirom.

Christidis, K., & Devetsikiotis, M. (2016). Blockchains and smart contracts for the Internet of Things. *IEEE Access : Practical Innovations, Open Solutions*, *4*, 2292–2303. DOI: 10.1109/ACCESS.2016.2566339

CNIL. (2024). *La CNIL sanctionne AMAZON FRANCE LOGISTIQUE à hauteur de 32 millions d'euros pour un système de surveillance jugé excessif.* Retrieved from https://www.cnil.fr

Codreanu, A. D. (2021). Gamificarea ca strategie de stimulare a motiva iei [Gamification as a strategy for stimulating motivation]. In *Conferin a „Dezvoltarea personală i integrarea socială a actorilor educa ionali"* [Conference "Personal development and social integration of educational actors"] (pp. 169–173). Chi inău, Moldova.

Csíkszentmihályi, M. (2011). *Fluir: una psicología de la felicidad.* Debolsillo.

Csorba, L. M., & Dabija, D. C. (2024). The impact of the Covid-19 pandemic on students' future on online education behavior. *Heliyon*, *10*(20), e39560. DOI: 10.1016/j.heliyon.2024.e39560 PMID: 39502205

Cu ulab, A. (2024). Învă area prin joc didactic reflectat în gamificare – un nou domeniu motiva ional [Learning through didactic play reflected in gamification – a new motivational field]. In *Instruire prin cercetare pentru o societate prosperă* [Proceedings of the Conference "Learning through research for a prosperous society"] (pp. 221–227).

Dale, R., & Viethen, J. (2021). The automated writing assistance landscape in 2021. *Natural Language Engineering*, *27*(4), 511–518. DOI: 10.1017/S1351324921000164

Delcker, J., Heil, J., Seufert, S., & Spirgi, L. (2024). First-year students AI-competence as a predictor for intended and de facto use of AI-tools for supporting learning processes in higher education. *International Journal of Educational Technology in Higher Education*, *21*(18), 18. Advance online publication. DOI: 10.1186/s41239-024-00452-7

Delello, J., Sung, W., Mokhtari, K., & De Giuseppe, T. (2024). Are K-16 educators prepared to address the educational and ethical ramifications of artificial intelligence software? In Arai, K. (Ed.), *Future of information and communication conference* (pp. 406–432). Springer Nature Switzerland., DOI: 10.1007/978-3-031-54053-0_28

Delello, J. A., Sung, W., Mokhtari, K., Hebert, J., Bronson, A., & De Giuseppe, T. (2025). AI in the Classroom: Insights from Educators on Usage, Challenges, and Mental Health. *Education Sciences*, *15*(2), 113. DOI: 10.3390/educsci15020113

Domo. (2024). *Data never sleeps 12.0* [Infographic]. https://www.domo.com/data-never-sleeps

Elmesalawy, M. M., Atia, A., Yousef, A. M. F., El-Haleem, A. M. A., Anany, M. G., Elmosilhy, N. A., Salama, A. I., Hamdy, A., Zoghby, H. M. E., & Din, E. S. E. (2021). *AI-based Flexible Online Laboratory Learning System for Post-COVID-19 Era: Requirements and Design. In: 2021 International Mobile, Intelligent, and Ubiquitous Computing Conference (MIUCC), 1-7.* IEEE., DOI: 10.1109/MIUCC52538.2021.9447601

Esteva, A., Kuprel, B., Novoa, R. A., Ko, J., Swetter, S. M., Blau, H. M., & Thrun, S. (2017). Dermatologist-level classification of skin cancer with deep neural networks. *Nature*, *542*(7639), 115–118. DOI: 10.1038/nature21056 PMID: 28117445

European Commission. (2020). *Digital Education Action Plan 2021–2027: Resetting education and training for the digital age*. COM (2020) 624 final. Brussels.

European Union. (2012). *Treaty on the Functioning of the European Union* (consolidated version 2012), Article 165.

Farrokhnia, M., Banihashem, S. K., Noroozi, O., & Wals, A. (2024). A SWOT analysis of ChatGPT: Implications for educational practice and research. *Innovations in Education and Teaching International*, *61*(3), 460–474. DOI: 10.1080/14703297.2023.2195846

Frolova, E. V., Rogach, O. V., Tyurikov, A. G., & Razov, P. V. (2021). Online student education in a pandemic: New challenges and risks. *European Journal Contemporary Education*, *10*(1), 43–52. DOI: 10.13187/ejced.2021.1.43

Gai ă, R. (2021). Gamificarea în educa ie. Defini ie, elemente, mituri, tipuri de jucători i limite [Gamification in education: Definition, elements, myths, player types, and limits]. *Philologica Banatica*, *2021*(II), 66–81.

Gu u, V. (2023). Explorarea jocurilor video: resursă actuală în procesul de transformare a paradigmei de predare–învă are [Exploring video games: A current resource in the process of transforming the teaching–learning paradigm]. In *Educa ia i învă ământul extra colar: configurări i experien e* [Proceedings of the Conference "Education and extracurricular teaching: Configurations and experiences"] (pp. 234–239). Chi inău, Moldova. https://ibn.idsi.md/gu u

Haidt, J. (2024). *The anxious generation: How the great rewiring of childhood is causing an epidemic of mental illness*. Penguin Press.

Haidt, J. (2025). *Taking Back Childhood From Phones - Finally*. https://www.afterbabel.com/p/taking-back-childhood?utm_source=substack&publication_id=1221094&post_id=159917172&utm_medium=email&utm_content=share&utm_campaign=email-share&triggerShare=true&isFreemail=true&r=58nple&triedRedirect=true, accessed in 5th of April 2025

Hattie, J., & Timperley, H. (2007). The Power of Feedback. *Review of Educational Research*, *77*(1), 81–112. DOI: 10.3102/003465430298487

Hertz, N. (2023). Secolul singurătă ii [The Lonely Century]. *Humanitas.*

Holmes, W., Bialik, M., & Fadel, C. (2019). *Artificial intelligence in education: Promises and implications for teaching and learning* (1st ed.). Center for Curriculum Redesign.

Imran, M., & Almusharraf, N. (2024). Google Gemini as a next generation AI educational tool: A review of emerging educational technology. *Smart Learning Environments*, *11*(1), 22. Advance online publication. DOI: 10.1186/s40561-024-00310-z

Jürgen, R., Tan, S., & Tan, S. (2023). War of the Chatsbots: Bard, Bing Chat, ChatGPT, Ernie and beyond. The new AI gold rush and its impact on higher education. *Journal of Applied Learning & Teaching*, *6*(1). Advance online publication. DOI: 10.37074/jalt.2023.6.1.23

Kamalov, F., Santandreu Calonge, D., & Gurrib, I. (2023). New era of artificial intelligence in education: Towards a sustainable multifaceted revolution. *Sustainability (Basel)*, *15*(16), 12451. DOI: 10.3390/su151612451

Khalil, A., Abdallah, S., Hijazi, R., & Sheikh, K. (2025). Trust but verify: The effect of religiosity and social conformity on verification of content shared via social media. *Information Technology & People*, *38*(1), 70–86. DOI: 10.1108/ITP-11-2022-0827

Kraft, M. A., & Lyon, M. A. (2024). The rise and fall of the teaching profession: Prestige, interest, preparation, and satisfaction over the last half century. *American Educational Research Journal*, *61*(6), 1192–1236. DOI: 10.3102/00028312241276856

Kunst, J. R., & Mesoudi, A. (2025). Decoding the dynamics of cultural change: A cultural evolution approach to the psychology of acculturation. *Personality and Social Psychology Review*, *29*(2), 111–144. DOI: 10.1177/10888683241258406 PMID: 39056551

Lee, A. V. Y. (2023). Supporting students' generation of feedback in large-scale online course with artificial intelligence-enabled evaluation. *Studies in Educational Evaluation*, *77*, 101250. DOI: 10.1016/j.stueduc.2023.101250

Li, Y., Pan, Y., & Zhao, D. (2025). Understanding the neurobiology and computational mechanisms of social conformity: Implications for psychiatric disorders. *Biological Psychiatry*. Advance online publication. DOI: 10.1016/j.biopsych.2025.05.011 PMID: 40409524

Long, D., & Magerko, B. (2020). What is AI literacy? Competencies and design considerations. In *Proceedings of the 2020 CHI Conference on Human Factors in Computing Systems* (pp. 1–16). Association for Computing Machinery. https://doi .org/DOI: 10.1145/3313831.3376727

Marković, M., Jeremić, I., & Vujović, M. (2025). Experience of implementing online teaching at the beginning of the Covid-19 pandemic - The mediating role of teaching style, stress resilience of teachers, and other individual variables. *Journal of Educational Sciences & Psychology*, *XV*(LXXVII), 108–120. DOI: 10.51865/ JESP.2025.1.10

McCarthy, J., Minsky, M. L., Rochester, N., & Shannon, C. E. (2006). A proposal for the Dartmouth Summer Research Project on Artificial Intelligence, August 31, 1955. *AI Magazine*, *27*(4), 12. DOI: 10.1609/aimag.v27i4.1904

McCormack, J., Gifford, T., & Hutchings, P. (2019). Autonomy, authenticity, authorship and intention in computer-generated art. In Ekárt, A., Liapis, A., & Castro Pena, M. L. (Eds.), Vol. 11261, pp. 35–50). Lecture Notes in Computer Science. Springer., DOI: 10.1007/978-3-030-16667-0_3

Ministerul Educa iei. (2023). *Raport privind starea învă ământului superior din România 2022–2023* [Report on the state of higher education in Romania 2022–2023]. Raport-Starea-invatamantului-superior-2022-2023.pdf

Nečesal, P., & Pospíšil, J. (2012). Experience with teaching mathematics for engineers with the aid of Wolfram Alpha. In *Proceedings of the World Congress on Engineering and Computer Science* (Vol. 1, pp. 271-274). https://web.archive.org/web/pdf

Niitsuma, T., Yoshida, M., Tamori, H., & Nakawake, Y. (2025). Prestige bias drives the viral spread of content reposted by influencers in online communities. *Scientific Reports*, *15*(1), 15282. DOI: 10.1038/s41598-025-98955-4 PMID: 40312546

Open, A. I. (2023). *ChatGPT*. Retrieved from https://openai.com

Palakurti, N. R. (2025). Comparative Study of Adaptive Learning Platforms: A Machine Learning Perspective. *International Journal of Advanced Researchin Education and Technology, 12*(1). Advance online publication. DOI: 10.15680/IJARETY.2025.1201002

Pantelimon, F.-V., Bologa, R., Toma, A., & Posedaru, B.-S. (2021). The Evolution of AI-Driven Educational Systems during the COVID-19 Pandemic. *Sustainability (Basel), 13*(23), 13501. DOI: 10.3390/su132313501

Păun, E. (2017). *Pedagogie. provocări i dileme privind coala i profesia didactică.* Polirom.

Petricini, T., Wu, C., & Zipf, S. (2024). Perceptions About Artificial Intelligence and ChatGPT Use by Faculty and Students. *Transformative Dialogues: Teaching and Learning Journal, 17*(2) 63-87. https://doi.org/DOI: 10.26209/td2024vol17iss21825

Pink, D. H. (2011). *Drive: The surprising truth about what motivates us.* Penguin.

Redecker, C. (2017). *European framework for the digital competence of educators: DigCompEdu* (Y. Punie, Ed.; EUR 28775 EN; JRC107466). Publications Office of the European Union. https://doi.org/DOI: 10.2760/159770

Rizwan, A. (2021). Effect of digital flashcards on low-frequency vocabulary retention by graduate students. *International Journal of Infrastructure Research and Management, 9*(1), 7–18. ISSN 2811-3705.https://klust.edu.my//Ahmed-Rizwan

Rojas Lozano, J. R., Ramos, Y., Tecnologia, E., & Cruz, C. E. C. (2024). *Enhancing English Language Teaching Through AI: The Case of Magic School AI.* (available at https://www.researchgate.net/profile/Jean-Paul-Rojas-2/publication/388757322_Enhancing_English_Language_Teaching_Through_AI_The_Case_of_Magic_School_AI/links/67a4eb53461fb56424cc7bbc/Enhancing-English-Language-Teaching-Through-AI-The-Case-of-Magic-School-AI.pdf)

Sampurno, M. T. (2024). Wolfram Alpha (AI): Between technological transformation and ethical ideas in education. *Proceedings of the International Conference on Religion. Science and Education, 3*, 377–384.

Samuelson, P. (2023). Generative AI meets copyright. *Science, 381*(6654), 158–161. DOI: 10.1126/science.adi0656 PMID: 37440639

Smuha, N. A. (2021). Beyond the individual: Governing AI's societal harm. *Internet Policy Review, 10*(3). Advance online publication. DOI: 10.14763/2021.3.1574

Stan, E. (2021). *Managementul clasei i nativii digitali: Fundamentări din perspectiva neuro tiin elor* [Classroom management and digital natives: Foundations from a neuroscientific perspective]. Institutul European.

Støle, H. (2018). Why digital natives need books: The myth of the digital native. *First Monday*. Advance online publication. DOI: 10.5210/fm.v23i10.9422

Thaler v. Perlmutter. (2023). No. 1:22-cv-01564 (D. D. C. Aug. 18, 2023). U.S. District Court for the District of Columbia.

Thurzo, A., Strunga, M., Urban, R., Surovková, J., & Afrashtehfar, K. I. (2023). Impact of artificial intelligence on dental education: A review and guide for curriculum update. *Education Sciences*, *13*(2), 150. DOI: 10.3390/educsci13020150

Tinholt, D., van der Linden, N., Enzerink, S., Geilleit, A., Cattaneo, G., Aguyyi, S., Pallaro, F., Noci, G., Benedetti, M., Tangi, L., & Alfano Saverio, A. (2019). *eGovernment benchmark 2019: Empowering Europeans through trusted digital public services*. Publications Office of the European Union. https://op.europa.eu/en/publication-detail/-/publication/c896937b-f554-11e9-8c1f-01aa75ed71a1/language-en

Tsirulnikov, D., Suart, C., Abdullah, R., Vulcu, F., & Mullarkey, C. E. (2023). Game on: Immersive virtual laboratory simulation improves student learning outcomes & motivation. *FEBS Open Bio*, *13*(3), 396–407. DOI: 10.1002/2211-5463.13567 PMID: 36723273

Turing, A. (1950). Computing Machinery and Intelligence. *Mind*, *LIX*(236), 433–460. DOI: 10.1093/mind/LIX.236.433

UNESCO. (1998). *World Declaration on Higher Education for the Twenty-First Century: Vision and Action*.

U.S. Copyright Office. (2023). *Copyright Registration Guidance: Works Containing Material Generated by Artificial Intelligence*. https://www.copyright.gov/ai/

Volosevici, D. (2024). AI use in the workplace: Some legal risks and challenges. *Analele tiin ifice ale Universităţii Alexandru Ioan Cuza din Ia i, seria Ştiinţe Juridice*, *LXX*(2), 65–77. DOI: 10.47743/jss-2024-70-2-5

Vukojičić, M., & Krstić, J. (2023). ChatGPT in programming education: ChatGPT as a programming assistant. *Inspired Teachers'. Voice*, *2023*(1), 7–13.

Wang, X.-J., & Wang, L.-L. (2024). Co-evolution of opinions and behaviors based on conformity in social networks. *Physics Letters. [Part A]*, *522*, 129753. DOI: 10.1016/j.physleta.2024.129753

Werbach, K., & Cornell, N. (2017). Contracts ex machina. *Duke Law Journal*, *67*(2), 313–382. DOI: 10.5040/9781509937059.ch-001

Xianli, W. U., Huchang, L. I. A. O., Tang, M., Ruxandra, G., & Smeureanu, I. (2020). Global trends and characteristics of the publications in economic computation and economic cybernetics studies and research from 1969 to 2020 based on bibliometric analysis. *Economic Computation and Economic Cybernetics Studies and Research*, *54*(4), 23–42. Advance online publication. DOI: 10.24818/18423264/54.4.20.02

Zawacki-Richter, O., Marín, V. I., Bond, M., & Gouverneur, F. (2019). Systematic review of research on artificial intelligence applications in higher education - where are the educators? *International Journal of Educational Technology in Higher Education*, *16*(1), 39. Advance online publication. DOI: 10.1186/s41239-019-0171-0

Zhang, L., & Gläscher, J. (2020). A brain network supporting social influences in human decision-making. *Science Advances*, *6*(34), eabb4159. Advance online publication. DOI: 10.1126/sciadv.abb4159 PMID: 32875112

KEY TERMS AND DEFINITIONS

AI literacy of students: refers to their ability to understand, use, and critically assess artificial intelligence technologies and their implications. It includes foundational knowledge of how AI systems work, awareness of their capabilities and limitations, and the ability to evaluate the ethical, legal, and social impacts of AI in academic, professional, and everyday contexts. AI-literate students can interact responsibly with AI tools, make informed decisions about their use, and recognize potential biases, risks, and accountability issues.

AI tools for personalized learning: are designed to tailor educational experience to individual students. By analyzing data such as learning progress, performance, and preference, these tools adapt content and feedback in real-time, making learning more efficient, engaging, student-centered, while helping students to improve their skills.

Generation Z: is a demographic group born approximately between 1997 and 2012. In general, specialists in the field are paying close attention to this generation because it is the first to grow up with smartphones, use social media, and have widespread internet access from a young age. Known for being tech-savvy and socially conscious, Gen Z presents a real challenge for educators, who must adapt their teaching methods to meet the unique characteristics of the so-called IGen.

Integrating AI in education: refers to the use of artificial intelligence technologies to enhance learning, teaching, and administrative processes. This includes AI tools such as adaptive learning platforms, personalized learning experiences, automated feedback systems which is designed to improve educational outcomes and efficiency.

Legal literacy of students: refers to their ability to understand, interpret, and apply basic legal concepts, rights, and responsibilities relevant to their personal, academic, and future professional lives. It includes knowledge of fundamental laws (such as constitutional rights, data protection, and contract law), awareness of legal procedures, and the capacity to critically engage with legal information in a responsible and informed manner.

Principle of educational relevance: refers to the idea that educational content, methods, and objectives should be closely aligned with the real-world needs, interests, and future roles of learners. This principle ensures that what is taught in educational settings is meaningful, applicable, and beneficial for students' personal development, societal participation, and professional success. It emphasizes the importance of adapting curricula to current social, technological, economic, and cultural contexts, fostering critical thinking, practical skills, and lifelong learning.

Reconfiguring evaluative practices in the digital era: refers to the process of transforming traditional assessment methods to align with the demands, tools, efficiency, and opportunities of modern digital education. This shift moves away from static, standardized testing toward more flexible, technology-enhanced, and learner-centered approaches that emphasize continuous feedback and personalized learning pathways.

Chapter 8

Assessment in Higher Education in the Era of Generative AI:

A Mediator for New Opportunities and Unique Challenges

Hayri Eren Suna
https://orcid.org/0000-0002-6874-7472
Ministry of National Education, Turkey

Mahmut Özer
Turkish Grand National Assembly Commission of National Education, Culture, Youth, and Sports, Turkey

ABSTRACT

A wide range of traditional approaches to education continue to be challenged by the development of generative artificial intelligence (Gen AI). These developments and emerging technologies has the potential to provide alternative solutions to assessment problems that have not been adequately addressed in the past. Gen AI has the potential to increase efficiency in diverse areas, which have annually been performed with intensive human labor. Could this "hype" concerning the strengths and potential of Gen AI be concealing its weaknesses? The development of Gen AI is already causing significant problems concerning academic integrity. Second, Gen AI tools are prone to incorporating the biases, since they incorporate almost all human made data. Furthermore, recent studies show that Gen AI algorithms can "hallucinate" or "fabricate". The purpose of this study is to review the opportunities

DOI: 10.4018/979-8-3373-7579-3.ch008

ght © 2026, IGI Global Scientific Publishing. Copying or distributing in print or electronic forms without written permission of IGI Global Scientific Publishing is prohibited. Use of this chapter to generative artificial intelligence (AI) technologies is expressly prohibited. The publisher reserves all rights to license its use for generative AI training and machine learning model development.

and challenges of Gen AI-based assessments in higher education, as well as make recommendations regarding its effective and fair use within the context of recent studies and policy guidelines.

INTRODUCTION

The use of GenAI technologies has only been widespread for a few years, but they continue to play a significant role in transforming education (Chiu, 2024; Sharma & Bozkurt, 2024). After the publication of ChapGPT, one of the most widely used Gen AI tools, in late 2022, the spread of these technologies gained great momentum, and their potential has generated considerable interest among users and researchers (Chakraborty, Roy & Kumar, 2023; Strzelecki, 2024). ChapGPT has indeed achieved historical popularity according to this criterion, as it reached more than 100 million users within two months of publication. This indicates people's interest in AI technologies that stand out for their innovative and creative characteristics. The development of large language models (LLM) and natural language processing (NLP) tools, which have been enhanced by recent improvements, have become the focal point of debates concerning AI technologies which have intensified since 2010 (Laakso, 2023; Ungless et al., 2025).

In addition to the widespread use of Gen AI across virtually all sectors and fields, education is one of the areas most affected by the current discussion and development surrounding the technology (The Open Innovation Team and Department for Education, 2024). Indeed, Gen AI technologies have rapidly climbed to the top of the agenda of many education systems due to their capability of resolving chronic problems in education, including providing personalized learning opportunities, providing rapid feedback, and increasing accessibility (Capano, He & McMinn, 2025; Francis, Jones & Smith, 2025; Sousa & Cardoso, 2025). Researchers in education have also characterized the capabilities of Gen AI tools as "revolutionary" and predict that the digitalization process that began after the Covid-19 outbreak is likely to reach its peak with the advent of Gen AI. It is for the first time that humanity is experiencing technological advancements that can be used to assist teachers and school administrators autonomously, as well as provide students with completely new opportunities.

The higher education sector has began immediately to adopt Gen AI technologies into its own processes (Capano, He & McMinn, 2025; Lee et al., 2024). A higher education system which seeks to provide students with a high level of cognitive, social-emotional, and professional skills, as well as prepare students for employment, cannot be free from digital technologies providing creative outputs. It is estimated that 88% of students in higher education will benefit from Gen AI technologies in some manner by 2025, which is an important indicator of this technology's prevalence at the higher education level (Freeman, 2025). While students use Gen AI tools extensively, the approach of higher education systems is to wait and see, since they are not used to such rapid and large changes (Wang et al., 2023).

This transformation primarily affects assessment, which stands out as one of the areas where Gen AI technologies create new opportunities, but also cause new bottlenecks (Awadallah Alkouk & Khalif, 2024; Ogunleye et al., 2024; Özer, 2025a, 2025b; Weng et al., 2024). As AI technologies are shaking the throne of classical assessments at the higher education level, concerns about the validity and security of these assessments have reached a fever pitch with the advent of modern Gen AI technologies (Broadfoot & Rockey, 2025; Wachira, Liu & Koç, 2024). In fact, a number of advanced Gen AI tools –particularly most advanced tolls such as ChatGPT 4.0– are capable of receiving passing grades without the need for human intervention in many assessments that have been implemented and trusted for many years (Eulerich et al., 2023). As a consequence, higher education institutions are faced with the challenge of defining assessment approaches that, on the one hand, enable the potential of Gen AI tools to be realized and, on the other hand, prevent their misuse.

A critical collective stance to better navigate the future is outlined in the comprehensive study titled "The manifesto for teaching and learning in a time of generative AI: A critical collective stance to better navigate the future" (Bozkurt et al., 2024). The purpose of this study is to analyze the benefits and limitations of Gen AI technologies when applied to higher education assessments in detail with reference to current studies. Our examination covers the advantages, challenges, and policy implications to overcome Gen AI challenges in educational assessments.

METHOD

DESIGN

In our study, we used a systematic literature review (SLR), which is one of the qualitative research approaches. SLRs provide an opportunity for detailed exploration of the focused topic or phenomenon (Xiao & Watson, 2017). In order to use the SLR design, we require a clear protocol as to how the focused topic or phenomenon is examined by the author(s), how the methods are employed, and how selected studies are included or excluded from the study (Bandara & Syed, 2023). Specifically, we reviewed the findings of studies in the education literature regarding the benefits of

Gen AI algorithms in higher education assessments, as well as the challenges and bottlenecks they cause, as well as policies and implications for overcoming them.

DATA COLLECTION AND ANALYSIS

As part of the SLR, the PRISMA approach (Agrawal et al., 2024) was used to determine the criteria for inclusion in the study. As a prerequisite of this approach, we used the following keywords to include in the study: "Gen AI in/and higher education / tertiary education assessments", "Gen AI and higher education/tertiary education assessments", "Gen AI and assessments/educational assessments", "Gen AI and measurements/assessments/evaluations in higher education", "student assessment and Gen AI in higher education / tertiary education", "student performance/outputs and Gen AI in higher education/tertiary education". A search of Web of Science, Scopus, EBSCO Education Source and Google Scholar was performed using the determined keywords, and studies that were accessible in full text and addressed the benefits and challenges of Gen AI tools were included in this study.

FINDINGS

Advantages/Benefits of Gen AI in Higher Education Assessment

Assessment and Feedback for Personal Learning Needs

The most important advantage of Gen AI technologies in terms of assessment is their ability to offer numerous opportunities for personalized assessment (Arslan et al., 2024; Kizilcec et al., 2024). Gen AI tools are capable of creating personalized assessment opportunities that are relevant to students' learning needs by utilizing large data sets and complex algorithms. Gen AI stands out as the most flexible, high-capacity technology that humanity has ever developed to assess learning, which is a very individual process. Utilizing this opportunity effectively will allow for the creation of assessment tools that are aligned with students' learning needs, available at the right time, and possess a high degree of psychometric properties.

Enhancing personal assessment opportunities can result in increased learning aspects when they are accompanied by personalized feedback, one of the most important elements of assessment (Cheng et al., 2024; Wei et al., 2024). As a matter of fact, one of the most significant criticisms of today's assessment processes is the inability to provide students with adequate personal feedback (Hankins & Harrington,

2022). Education systems may adopt improved policies, but the challenge of providing feedback to each student in the most appropriate and personalized manner remains – such as feedback consistency, effectiveness and timeliness (Hankins & Harrington, 2022; Williams, 2024). In contrast, it has been demonstrated in numerous studies that providing students with timely and meaningful feedback in a way they can fully understand is extremely valuable in enhancing their learning (Williams, 2024; Wisniewski, Zierer & Hattie, 2020). The quality of the feedback provided to the student after the assessment is generally regarded as the most important determinant of the quality of the assessment process (Australian Institute for Teaching and School Leadership, 2017; Morris, Perry & Wardle, 2021). At this point, Gen AI technologies are capable of identifying each student's learning deficiencies through assessment and of providing rapid, diverse, and sufficient feedback to eliminate these deficiencies.

Developing Test Items, Tasks and Assessment Tools

Developing reliable and valid assessment tools is an important step in evaluating student behaviors at the higher education level, as well as at all other levels of education. An increase in the number of assessment tools that are psychometrically determined to provide valid and reliable results will contribute to greater accuracy in assessing a wide range of student characteristics (Rust, 2006). Meanwhile, traditional assessment tool development processes include a multi-stakeholder group with test development experts and field experts and require a considerable amount of labor. It is the creative nature of Gen AI technologies that offers new opportunities for the development of new test items and their transformation into holistic assessment tools (Chan et al., 2025; Circi, Hicks & Sikali, 2023). It is becoming increasingly prevalent and commonly used to create new multiple-choice test items with the help of GenAI tools (Circi, Hicks & Sikali, 2023; Nwafor & Onyenwe, 2021). Furthermore, the items that are developed through the application of Gen AI technologies are not limited to multiple-choice type; according to the psychometrics literature, an increasing number of assessment tools are being developed with the help of Gen AI for other types of items (Avidov et al., 2024; Li et al., 2024).

The use of scenario-based assessments and situational judgment tests is another important potential of Gen AI technologies (Avidov et al., 2024; Li et al., 2024; Nurul et al., 2024). A growing number of assessment designs are utilizing algorithms to generate new items based on students' responses to test items and to continue this process in a conversational manner. By using "adaptive assessment", and Gen AI, it is possible to develop many new approaches to assessment, including combining the predictive power of assessment with students' preferred learning methods (Khlaif, Odeh & Bsharat, 2024) and incorporating the content and variables students prefer more often in the assessment process. By utilizing innovative item types and assessment designs, teachers can increase students' interest in assessment and change traditional perceptions of the assessment process.

Improvement in Automated Scoring and Use of Open-Ended Items

Another field of innovation where Gen AI technology opens up new opportunities for assessment in higher education is the automatic scoring of student responses (Floden, 2024; Pack, Barrett & Escalante, 2024). It is well known that for the development of an assessment tool, the results need to provide adequate psychometric evidence, and scoring is essential to this process. In order to ensure sufficient reliability and consistency, the raters must possess the necessary qualifications and experience (Gerritsen-van Leeuwenkamp, Brinke & Kester, 2017). Since higher order skills such as analytical thinking and critical thinking are particularly focused at the higher education level (Hague, 2024), open-ended items used to assess these skills, as well as items that students are expected to structure their own responses, are particularly important. There are several reasons why such items may not be potentially reach their full potential, including the fact that scoring is quite time-consuming, subjectivity problems encountered in scoring, and possible issues of reliability between raters (Gobrecht et al., 2024; Jauhiainen & Garagorry Guerra, 2024; Leiva, Montoro Rios & Luque Martinez, 2006).

A significant advantage of Gen AI algorithms is that they provide a window of opportunity for assessing high order cognitive skills. Several automatic scoring algorithms have been developed over the course of the years, supported by the potential of Gen AI tools, and today their outcomes are significantly correlated to that of human raters (Geçkin, Kızıltaş & Çınar, 2023; Kim et al., 2024). A leading feature of Gen AI tools is the ability to score open-ended items and written tasks where students can structure their answers so they can be completed in a short period of time, even in large groups. This indicates that Gen AI offers a very important opportunity to assess the high order skills of large groups of students in a very short amount of time. The use of automatic scoring algorithms are now considered in national and international large-scale assessments (Jung, Tyack & von Davier, 2025; Vo et al., 2023)

CHALLENGES OF GEN AI IN HIGHER EDUCATION ASSESSMENTS

Academic Integrity

In addition to their benefits, the creative nature and openness to innovation of GenAI technologies also bring with them significant limitations and bottlenecks in terms of assessment (Francis et al., 2025; Gruenhagen et al., 2024; Ogunleye et al., 2024; Weng et al., 2024). These technologies pose the greatest threat to academic integrity, as has been repeatedly emphasized in the literature (Francis et al., 2025; Gruenhagen et al., 2024). In the global higher education system, one of the greatest challenges is the suspicion of academic integrity that occurs when students misuse these powerful tools to generate answers. In fact, higher education systems put to a great emphasis on whether the answers are generated by students, especially in traditional assessment approaches that tend to focus on students' lower and middle order cognitive skills. There is evidence in academic studies that answers generated with the use of Gen AI tools can achieve passing grades in many advanced assessment systems in use today (Chau et al., 2024; Fuentes-Martin et al., 2023). A recent study showed that %94 of AI-generated successfully submitted to the examination system of well-respected university from UK and scored significantly higher than students (Scarfe et al., 2024).

Higher education institutions use a variety of strategies to ascertain whether students use Gen AI tools as part of their assessments. In many cases, this strategy involves the use of teacher competencies and digital technologies in order to detect whether responses were generated by Gen AI tools (Ardito, 2024; Fleckenstein et al., 2024). In spite of the fact that these technologies may appear to provide substantial benefits to educators on paper, scientific studies have shown that they can often lead to incorrect conclusions (Ardito, 2024; Elkhatat, Elsaid & Almeer, 2023; Perkins et al., 2024). As a matter of fact, the majority of digital platforms that provide this service calculate the probability that responses are generated by AI platforms and use the responses patterns generated by AI platforms in this calculation (Ardito, 2024). Even though this approach seems reasonable, recent research indicates that many human-made artifacts (including those written before Gen AI technologies) can be regarded as Gen AI productions, and many artifacts produced by Gen AI tools can be regarded as human-made (Ardito, 2024; Weber-Wulff et al., 2023). To summarize, solutions aimed at digital platforms that attempt to detect the productions of Gen AI technologies in their entirety lead to incorrect conclusions. As Ardito (2024) noted, the interaction between Gen AI technologies and those that attempt to detect their products is akin to a "cat-and-mouse game" in which Gen AI technologies always prevail.

As a further measure to protect academic integrity, some higher education institutions have banned the use of generation AI tools in assessment processes entirely (Chan, 2023) or conducted assessments within a completely controlled physical environment that limits students' access to these technologies (Gooch et al., 2024; Gonsalves, 2025). These approaches eliminate the threats to academic integrity posed by Gen AI technologies, but they also prevent students from reaping the benefits of Gen AI technologies. Several researchers contend that Gen AI tools have become irreversibly embedded in the educational system, and that practices that completely restrict these technologies are unsustainable (An, Yu & James, 2025; Lodge et al., 2023). As part of the recommendations presented in this context to ensure academic integrity without banning Gen AI tools entirely, it is recommended that assessment be designed to require students to demonstrate higher order skills using the outputs obtained from these tools (Borge, Smith & Aldemir, 2024; Khlaif et al., 2025; Yatani, Sramek & Yang, 2024).

Algorithmic Bias and Rising Inequalities

As Gen AI technologies become more prevalent in educational assessments, there is also an increasing concern about algorithm bias and social inequalities (Ferrara, 2023; OECD, 2023; Özer, 2024b, 2024d; Suna & Özer, 2025). AI algorithms are structured to achieve the desired outputs with the highest degree of accuracy, and while they often achieve this goal, they fail to consider important values such as "harmlessness", "equality" that are crucial for humanity (Ngo, Chan & Mindermann, 2025; Suna & Özer, 2024c, 2025). Due to their structural characteristics, AI algorithms have led to many different types of biased results today (Baker & Hawn, 2022; Idowu, 2024; Suna & Özer, 2025). Several factors, including the type of data used in AI algorithms, the prediction methods, and the distribution of student groups using the algorithms, have been shown to result in bias (Baker & Hawn, 2022; Idowu, 2024).

Social negativities associated with bias, which is a statistical and systematic issue, are clear indicators for the need to use Gen AI technologies very sensibly and to constantly monitor the results produced by the algorithms. Several recent studies have revealed that AI tools disadvantage individuals with an immigrant background (Creely & Henderson, 2025; Tomasev, Maynard & Gabriel, 2025), minorities and marginalized groups in society (Ferrara, 2023; Hofmann et al., 2024; Yang, 2025), and people whose native language is not English (Liang et al., 2023). In this way, bias has evolved from being a statistical problem to one with a social dimension. Particularly when Gen AI applications are used to make important decisions about individuals, the results of the algorithm provide systematic advantages to certain groups while disadvantages to others.

A continuous evaluation of algorithm bias is necessary due to the fact that bias is a degree issue rather than a black-and-white debate. As the results of current studies demonstrate, there are factors that can lead to bias at every stage of algorithm development (Baker & Hawn, 2022; Idowu, 2024; Suna & Özer, 2025). Even if an algorithm provides relatively unbiased results until it is used, it is likely that it will begin to produce biased results as a result of the unequal socioeconomic distribution of users (Baker & Hawn, 2022; Idowu, 2024; Suna & Özer, 2025). It is for this reason that methods for detecting and dealing with biases fall under the headings of pre-processing, in-processing, and post-processing. In order to make AI algorithms more reliable and fair for all social groups, these methods are extremely important.

Synthetization and Dissemination of Error Loops

As AI technologies have become increasingly prevalent, especially Gen AI, the weight of the outputs produced by these technologies is increasing in the literature. Since Gen AI algorithms use their own outputs as well as the outputs of other AI algorithms in their subsequent production, the use of data produced by Gen AI applications by other Gen AI applications has significant implications. In the first instance, it should be noted that Gen AI technologies require a substantial amount of data to function (Graux et al., 2024). As well, it is important to note that the data that is required to create successful Gen AI algorithms should not be defined only by its volume, but it must also have the following four characteristics: value, volume, variety, and veracity (Geerts & O'Leary, 2022). According to predictions, if AI continues to use human-generated data at the current rate, all human-written texts will be exhausted by 2026 or 2032 (Villalobos et al., 2024).

So, will the technology of Gen AI come to an end when the amount of human-generated data runs out? Here, "synthetic data" comes into play and enables AI algorithms to work more effectively (Goyal & Mahmoud, 2024; Resnik et al., 2025). Synthetic data does not only replace human-generated data, it may also function as a facilitator for Gen AI algorithms, since it is not always possible to provide all the information required by Gen AI technologies from humans. Thus, Gen AI technologies must be able to produce adequate and relevant data in a manner similar to how humans would do so in order to make accurate predictions. Therefore, Gen AI technologies produce data on required subjects by taking into account various characteristics of humans (Resnik et al., 2025). Consequently, synthetic data has increased exponentially following the advent of Gen AI technologies due to their superior computational and creative capabilities (Karkera et al., 2024). Based on particular predictions, majority of Gen AI tools will use synthetic data in 2030 (Karkera et al., 2024; Majeed & Hwang, 2025). However, recent studies have demonstrated that the excessive use of synthetic data significantly differentiates the distribution of synthetic data from human-generated data and ultimately results in the collapse of established models (Goyal & Mahmoud, 2024; Hao et al., 2024; United Nations University, 2024).

Furthermore, the widespread use of Gen AI technology coupled with an increase in synthetic data has led to algorithm errors becoming chronic as a consequence of becoming part of cycles. As a result, the prediction errors of the algorithms begin to consume more space in the data set, and their quality of predictions gradually begins to diverge from reality (Shumailov et al., 2024). Due to the fact that prediction errors are incorrect information, this indicates that the place of "disinformation" in the literature will continue to increase with time. Additionally, it can be expected that the dividing line between truth and error will diminish in the long run as Gen AI produces a greater degree of similarity to human products.

Homogenization and the Undermining of Creativity

In synthetic data production, data with a structure similar to human production is produced in areas where the algorithm requires data, but there is not enough of it available in human production (Joshi et al., 2024). The use of synthetic data plays an important role in the development of Gen AI algorithms, as well as in the replacement of human production data. Due to the constant use of outputs from other algorithms, synthetic data tends to become repetitive, and with continued use, the data becomes homogenous. Essentially, synthetic data does not possess the diversity and richness of human production data as a result of repetitive processes (Alemohammed et al., 2023; Apellaniz, Parras & Zazo, 2025). In fact, homogenization is the cause for the similarity in patterns and structures between Gen AI productions.

Having a homogenized data set as a result of the proliferation of synthetic data has the effect of reducing creative energy in the data set. Limiting "creativity", one of humanity's most valuable and revolutionary skills, through Gen AI algorithms could have significant consequences. Increasing the use of Gen AI algorithms in higher education, which aims to increase students' cognitive and social-emotional skills, may limit students' ability to use their creativity skills, which requires significant dedication and effort.

Challenges in Assessing High Order Cognitive Skills

The use of Gen AI technologies in assessments of high order cognitive skills is one of the biggest threats to assessment at the higher education level (Kizilcec et al., 2024; Lubbe, Marais & Kruger, 2025). In view of the increasing capabilities of Gen AI technologies in the areas of visual, written, and artistic production, it has been speculated that they will surpass human capabilities (Azoff, 2025). Would it be fair to expect students who have access to advanced Gen AI technologies to develop high order cognitive skills in any field by giving them just a few commands to develop creative products? Meanwhile, how will students' high order cognitive skills be evaluated when Gen AI tools are able to produce the expected products? Would it be reasonable to evaluate students' personal efforts under the same conditions with a technology that can generate an original product in a few minutes by examining thousands of sources using a few lines of code?

Among the most significant learning risks associated with the widespread use of Gen AI technologies is the resulting decrease in student effort (Ahmad et al., 2023; Fan et al., 2025). We are aware of the psychometric problems associated with low motivation and low engagement in low stake assessments (Akyol, Krishna & Wang, 2018; Shüttpelz-Brauns et al., 2020). Low levels of effort and engagement may negatively affect both the validity and reliability of even highly qualified assessment instruments and methods. Since students can easily access Gen AI tools, they may tend to use them frequently in developing products requiring relatively high order cognitive skills instead of using their own skills (Krullaars et al., 2023; Zhai, Wibowo & Li, 2024). Further, as previously stated, technologies that are intended to detect whether student outputs are the work of the students or generated by Gen AI technologies do not yet demonstrate sufficient performance, thus encouraging students to utilize Gen AI technologies.

The trend also poses a great risk for assessment in higher education, since assessments focusing on students' higher order cognitive skills require relatively more effort and the simultaneous use of many skills. A number of studies have shown that the widespread use of Gen AI will result in the development of metacognitive skills; however, it is also indicated that "laziness" is on the rise (Ahmad et al., 2023; Fan et al., 2025). Considering the impact of Gen AI on high order cognitive skills, Lubbe, Marais, and Kruger (2025) suggested that the Bloom Taxonomy, which is the most commonly used classification of educational outcomes, should be revised. To counteract the destructive nature of modern AI tools, Akbar (2025) developed a new digital tool and provided information on the level of tasks and assignments teachers develop for their students based on Bloom Taxonomy, as well as the extent to which they can be effectively completed by modern Gen AI tools.

Algorithmic Hallucinations or Fabrications

While AI algorithms are designed to achieve the most accurate results to the expected outputs by using learning data and appropriate estimation methods, the design process does not always guarantee that they will provide the best results. The term "AI hallucination" or "AI fabrication", which has been verified by numerous studies today, refers to algorithmic outputs that are either completely inadequate, illogical or don't exist at all (Maleki, Padmanabhan & Dutta, 2024; Özer, 2024a; Sun et al., 2024). In other words, Gen AI algorithms can produce outputs that are not found in the learning data, are illogical, are unrelated to human-generated data, or could even be the opposite. There is a great deal of controversy surrounding the cause of algorithm hallucinations, and a number of factors can lead to these hallucinations, including distortions and errors in the learning data, poor estimation models, and utilizing AI models for other purposes than their reason for development. Additionally, experts in the field of AI have pointed out that hallucinations are an essential feature of today's algorithms that utilize large data sets and complex estimation methods (Xu, Jain & Kankanhalli, 2024; Zhao et al., 2024). Therefore, although there are methods to reduce AI hallucinations, it is not possible to eliminate them completely (Xu, Jain & Kankanhalli, 2024; Zhao et al., 2024).

The potential spread of false and inaccuracy information resulting from AI hallucinations, combined with society's overdependence tendency to AI algorithms as absolute truths, constitute a serious problem that needs to be addressed. A failure to approach the results of Gen AI algorithms with suspicion, considering them as "all-knowing" digital tools, may result in the rapid adoption of the erroneous information produced by these algorithms. Users and test developers should be aware of the possibility that this situation might lead to negative assessment scenarios. Furthermore, it must be noted that Gen AI algorithms can render incorrect suggestions to students as a result of the hallucinatory effect of their fast and instantaneous feedback capabilities. In the context of automated test item and measurement tool development processes using Gen AI tools, algorithm hallucinations may also be reflected in the content of the tests.

Digital Hegemony, Technological Oligarchy and the Domination of Western Values

In light of the proliferation of Gen AI algorithms, there is even more controversy surrounding the role of states and institutions in shaping these technologies. The leading positions played by the USA and China in the development of AI algorithms provide significant opportunities for these countries to incorporate their own norms and values into their products (Dakakni, 2025; Varoufakis, 2024). At the institutional level, it is well known that large-scale organizations, such as Google, Amazon, Meta, etc. (GAFAM and BAT are used as terms for USA-based and China-based Big Techs [Kaplan & Haenlein, 2020]), have pioneered AI technologies by utilizing global data derived from their users (Kaplan & Haenlein, 2020, Verdegem, 2022).

Therefore, the countries and companies have the potential to spread the social norms on their agendas through the use of Gen AI technologies.

A concern is expressed when focusing on the Gen AI technologies, that the risk of digital hegemony and technological oligarchy could be greater. A production and creation-oriented structure of Gen AI algorithms and the fact that Western values and norms are primarily represented in the large data sets they use may lead these technologies to produce results that are more reflective of cultural codes and norms (Johnson et al., 2022; Tao et al., 2024). A few examples could be the use of male characters in executive visual productions, and higher accuracy in defining white faces as reflections of such cultural norms in Gen AI productions (AlDahoul, Rahwan & Zaki, 2025; Yang, 2025). Furthermore, Gen AI technologies can be used to protect users by imposing restrictions on the production of content. For example, Stephanie Dinkins and Minne Atairu pointed out that some Gen AI tools do not respond to the terms "slave" or "slavery," even though past eras are historically real, demonstrating that such blocking may fail to recognize historical realities that go beyond their protective functions.

We can expect to see the reflection of Western norms and social codes in the measurement tools provided to students at higher education levels, as well as in the AI models used to assess students' responses and essays, particularly to open-ended questions. The fact that the foundation of Generation AI technologies is mostly comprised of English resources further disadvantages students with other native languages (Liang et al., 2023). The Gen AI algorithms do not have the adequate capability to incorporate the diversity of responses to facts in different languages, nor are they able to incorporate norms other than Western norms and response patterns in communities speaking other native languages. Further, it is possible that content that is prohibited by Gen AI tools for the purpose of protecting users will be ignored and remain in the background.

Black Box Functioning and Lack of Accountability

Using large data sets and highly complex prediction methods, Gen AI algorithms are programmed to respond to commands with the highest level of accuracy. Due to the design and structure of the algorithms, they are able to provide very detailed and accurate responses. However, the complexity of AI algorithms does not always provide users with sufficient information about how they reached the results they present (Hassija et al., 2024; Hayes, 2023). To put it another way, many participants remain unclear as to how AI algorithms reach the outputs they present to users. Research into how AI applications achieve the results they produce has shown that it is sometimes practically impossible to determine the reasons behind the results and the background of the process. As a result of their complex structures and difficult-to-understand designs, AI algorithms are often referred to as "black boxes" (Hassija et al., 2024; Hayes, 2023).

The fact that AI algorithms work as a black box brings with them discussions regarding many ethical and equal issues, even though many users of AI do not care much about the principles of the algorithms as long as they receive appropriate responses to their commands. The structure described here is completely contrary to the principle of "accountability", which requires that the processes used to make important decisions about individuals are explainable and transparent (Rudin & Radin, 2019). Meanwhile, institutions that develop AI algorithms may avoid making accountability and transparency a priority in order to increase competitiveness, accuracy (Nussberger et al., 2022) and avoid criticism resulting from the disclosure of potential problems.

As we consider an assessment process based on Gen AI algorithms, it is necessary to discuss the issue of the inability to provide sufficient details about the content presented to test takers, the scoring performed, and the "how" and "why" of any information that may be inferred by test takers. Furthermore, the more complex the design of advanced and more complex AI technologies such as Gen AI, the more difficult it is for students to comprehend the background of the content presented to them and their assessment outcomes. Additionally, the lack of justification provided by Gen AI tools for important decisions about students may lead to legal bottlenecks (Gryz & Rojszczak, 2021).

Data Privacy Problems and Intellectual Property Rights Violations

As AI algorithms have become more prevalent, discussions have arisen concerning the rights to use large data sets for training and optimizing algorithms (OECD, 2024). It is well known that users have been monitored by digital technologies since the earliest days of the internet, when AI algorithms were not yet widely used but the internet was widely available. To fulfill their intended purpose, AI algorithms, including GenAI tools, require large data sets, and synthetic data production methods are utilized when the data sets are insufficient (Goyal & Mahmoud, 2024; Resnik et al., 2025). On the other hand, the data used by AI algorithms ultimately belongs to individuals as a reflection of their opinions and a result of their personal production. It will be easier to understand the risks posed by AI algorithms that use this data if it is taken into account that all content created by individuals in the digital world is their property.

As the large datasets used by these algorithms are more likely to contain personal and demographic information, data privacy risks are further exacerbated within the context of Gen AI technologies, which may further increase existing security risks by the possibility that these variables will be used to achieve expected results. Since AI technologies function as a "black box," users are unable to obtain adequate information about the nature, content, or nature of the datasets used (Hassija et al., 2024; Hayes, 2023; Rudin & Radin, 2019). Thus, the sharing policies of data may potentially allow the use of data in latent context and purposes. As a consequence, educational and pedagogical issues may be pushed to the background over time as Gen AI tools prioritize commercial concerns.

At the higher education level, it is clear that the nature of the personal and educational information collected from students during the assessment process presents a significant risk. In addition to all other contextual data, information concerning students' academic performance is personal information belonging to students. However, it has been shown in a number of studies that many LLM programs do not fully comply with generally accepted data protection regulations (Nolte, Finck & Meding, 2025). This violation may give rise to a legal offense, for example, uploading the outcomes of a student's assessments to a Gen AI tool for interpretation.

Digital Divide

It is essential that all stakeholders in education have sufficient physical infrastructure and appropriate digital skills in order to benefit from the advantages of AI technologies, including Gen AI technologies, as described in the first section. Today's increasing socioeconomic gaps, however, suggest that there are significant differences in physical infrastructure and digital skills between social groups and between countries and regions (Lythreatis, Singh & El-Kassar, 2022; OECD, 2021). The current statistics for 2025 indicate that more than 2.5 billion people still lack access to the internet (World Economic Forum, 2025), and these deficiencies are distributed unevenly across countries and between rural and urban areas. Even in the United States, a country with a high level of technological advancement, nearly 24 million people do not have access to high-speed internet (McKinsey & Company, 2022).

Apart from the lack of infrastructure, knowledge and skills required to use these technologies also vary significantly across countries and social groups at different socioeconomic status (Heinz, 2016; van de Werfhorts, Kessenich & Geven, 2022). Recent assessments by the International Labor Organization have shown that high-income countries that pioneer AI algorithms benefit the most from AI and invest the most in increasing AI literacy (UN & ILO, 2024). Furthermore, this may result in an even greater disparity in digital skills across socioeconomic levels. In consequence, AI literacy gaps in higher education, which prepares students for the workplace, are likely to exacerbate socioeconomic disparities in their use of these technologies.

In the context of assessment, the differences in access to Gen AI tools among social groups have important implications. First, it prevents students with lower socioeconomic status from taking advantage of the advantages offered by Gen AI tools and discussed in the first section. Additionally, recent studies on algorithm bias suggest that AI algorithms can be shaped according to the characteristics of particular user groups (Baker & Hawn, 2022; Idowu, 2024; Suna & Özer, 2025). Specifically, the fact that students from higher socioeconomic backgrounds are more likely to utilize Gen AI algorithms may increase the weight of the data that these students provide in the entire data set, leading to AI algorithms reflecting the norms of this group and creating bias. Consequently, the Gen AI tools may become biased due to the unequal use of AI algorithms by students from a variety of socioeconomic backgrounds.

POLICY IMPLICATIONS

Explainable AI Approach

As we have seen so far, the biggest challenge and most significant risk for higher education is the fact that these tools operate as black boxes (Hassija et al., 2024; Hayes, 2023; Rudin & Radin, 2019). The fact that students have easy access to these tools and the difficulty in identifying whether the products are generated by Gen AI tools may lead them to over rely on these tools. The probability of overdependence to Gen AI tools, which can lead to overlooking the realities that they have the problems described so far.

As Gen AI tools, especially those used in assessment processes, provide important inferences about individuals, particularly students, it is essential to reveal the reasoning behind these inferences. Additionally, as noted in previous sections, it is known that Gen AI algorithms may produce biased results and even cause hallucinations (Maleki, Padmanabhan & Dutta, 2024; Sun et al., 2024; Xu, Jain & Kankanhalli, 2024; Zhao et al., 2024). In this context, it becomes increasingly important to employ an “Explainable AI” approach that aims to determine how and in what way the generated results from Gen AI tools will be achieved (Cheong, 2024; Rane, Choudhary & Rane, 2023). A system that allows users to understand the feedback provided to students and the reasons behind the assessment outputs can improve student understanding. A further benefit of Explainable AI systems is their ability to provide a clear structure to determine whether or not the results are biased and the reasons for potential bias in outcomes.

Participatory Management Model

A participatory management model (PMM) is also often recommended to increase inclusiveness in tools using AI algorithms, including Gen AI tools, to ensure that AI algorithms act in accordance with human values and produce as unbiased outputs as possible (Özer, Perc & Suna, 2024; Parthasarathy et al., 2024). PMM involves ensuring that all social groups, likely to use the algorithm or be affected by its results, are represented in the algorithm development process. As a result of this approach, a potential bias can be avoided by strengthening social representation during the algorithm design and development process and by incorporating the views of a variety of stakeholders (Delgado et al., 2023). Despite the fact that Gen AI algorithms are powerful by design, it is important to remember that they have the potential to reflect imbalances and distortions in the learning data in their results and to propagate biases already present. Through the PMM model, the possible sources of bias are identified at the design stage, decision processes are conducted in collaboration with experts representing various groups, and the algorithm processes are evaluated jointly.

The adoption of the PMM model has many advantages for assessment in higher education. As a first advantage, the inclusion of both higher education institutions and student groups studying in higher education institutions in the development of Gen AI algorithms increases awareness of AI algorithms among higher education stakeholders; furthermore, it has the potential to contribute significantly to the development of legal regulations, which will be discussed in detail in the last article. Due to the highly heterogeneous student population of higher education, the PMM model allows for the reduction of possible biases towards different student groups during the design process. Accordingly, PMM is considered to be an important approach in the context of increasing familiarity with assessment processes in higher education and developing more valid and fair assessment tools as well.

Transformation in Assessment Methods

A holistic examination of the impact of Gen AI on higher education assessment and future suggestions implies that a revision of traditional assessment approaches is inevitable. A traditional assessment typically consists of tasks and test items requiring low and medium levels of cognitive abilities, and such assessments can be successfully completed by Gen AI technologies (Akbar, 2025). It is recommended that current assessment approaches be revised in light of the ineffectiveness of current methods for determining whether student responses are generated by Gen AI tools and their tendency to produce incorrect results. Lye and Lim (2024) suggested Against, Avoid and Adopt (AAA) method to group the assessments in these groups and allow the use of Gen AI algorithms based on the context and purpose of assessments (Against=no Gen AI, Avoid= Assessments That Generative AI Does Not Cope Well with Yet, and Adopt= Integrating Generative AI in Assessments).

Is there a way to create an assessment approach that will prevent the misuse of the great potential of Gen AI tools in higher education? In order to address this issue, one of the most recent suggestions is to conduct project-based assessments which prioritize students' physical and psychological production (Kadel et al., 2024; Plessis, 2025). As stated, tasks requiring the use of social and emotional skills, for which Gen AI tools lack high proficiency, and those requiring the coordination of work within a common goal and the production of a common product are more protected from the risks of current Gen AI technologies. Furthermore, such assessments provide students with the opportunity to contribute to the 21st century skills and social-emotional skills expected to be acquired at the higher education level. It also provides an opportunity to assess social and emotional skills, as well as the ability to collaborate on products.

The second prominent suggestion for transforming assessment processes in higher education is to plan assessments hierarchically, allowing students to use Gen AI tools up to the permitted level, and expecting them to contribute fully at the subsequent levels (Lye & Lim, 2024). The purpose of this approach is to enable students to take advantage of this potential without prohibiting the use of Gen AI tools, while at the same time allowing their own contributions. It is the view of this approach that Gen AI tools are now irreversibly embedded in higher education, and that it would be unrealistic to have them banned completely.

Setting Regulations and Providing Training Opportunities for the Effective Use of AI

It has been observed so far that Gen AI technologies bring significant advantages and bottlenecks in all aspects of higher education assessment. This dichotomous structure creates reservations in the minds of all stakeholders, particularly educators and administrators (Roe et al., 2025). Furthermore, current studies indicate that education stakeholders, while many acknowledge that Gen AI tools have a revolutionary role to play in education and assessment, they may the need for more awareness and improved skills to utilize this great potential effectively (Chan, 2023; Pelletier et al., 2022). Education and administration may even be responsible for legal mistakes due to a lack of understanding of the subject, as discussed in previous sections.

On a global level, higher education institutions are expected to prepare legal guidelines that outline how Gen AI tools should be used, prohibitions (if any), recommendations, and examples of best practice. Since the use of Gen AI tools varies across academic fields, these guidelines should be helpful in assisting educational personnel and administrators in gaining a common understanding of the technology. While the preparation of these guidelines is important for all educators and administrative personnel in order to obtain a basic understanding and awareness of Gen AI tools and to adhere to the rules, they are not sufficient on their own. To be able to effectively use Gen AI technologies, which are among the most advanced AI algorithms, structured training beyond the guidelines is required (European Union, 2023; UNESCO, 2023). Higher education institutions are encouraged to offer skill development opportunities that will enable stakeholders to effectively utilize Gen AI technologies. Building the AI skills of higher education stakeholders will also contribute to the development of student assessments in a way that is safer and minimizes the risks associated with Gen AI.

DISCUSSION AND CONCLUSION

Gen AI tools have created a great deal of excitement and enthusiasm among stakeholders in education and have reinforced the idea that they can provide solutions to chronic educational problems. A number of factors explain this great motivation, including the fact that humanity has developed technology that is capable of producing high order cognitive skills independently, making use of large amounts of information resources, and being readily accessible. As a result of this motivation, which has emerged because of the advantages of Gen AI technology, Gen AI technology has become increasingly prevalent in higher education and assessment has become one of the most intense uses of Gen AI technology.

A reflection of this excitement for Gen AI technologies in higher education has given rise to a variety of responsibilities for all stakeholders. Through the use of advanced Gen AI technologies, many aspects of academic responsibilities expected of students in higher education can now be met through algorithms. The biggest problem regarding the aspect of assessment is the academic integrity, and it has been extensively studied in the literature, since it is among the most pressing challenges that higher education systems are expected to address. The bottlenecks introduced by Gen AI tools, however, extend beyond academic integrity and remain hidden behind the interest generated by these technologies.

Several issues are raised by the development of Gen AI tools, as highlighted in the study, including deepening social inequalities through biased results, chronic failures of algorithms, implicit impositions of Western values on users, unprecedented difficulties in measuring higher-level cognitive abilities, and commercial exploitation of assessment data. The extent of each of these issues is sufficient to warrant separate attention, however, the black-box nature of Gen AI algorithms as well as the socially attributed "perfection" of Gen AI tools restrict the scope of discussions on these subjects.

The use of Gen AI tools is necessary to monitor all of these problems and bottlenecks, particularly at the higher education level. Considering the risks associated with Gen AI algorithms, some institutions have completely prohibited the use of these technologies for assessment purposes. As of now, however, it appears that the approach of ignoring and banning these technologies will not be able to keep up with the spread of Gen AI tools. To begin with, a study by the 50 top universities in the world showed that Gen AI tools are increasingly accepted, and more efforts are being made to prevent their risks rather than ban them.

Despite the growing number of guides developed by higher education institutions and the acceptance of Gen AI technologies, it is evident that these guides do not provide a comprehensive solution to eliminate the risks identified in this study. However, the research has revealed that most reviews of these guides concentrate on students and instructors, and therefore do not provide sufficient feedback to researchers and administrative managers (An, Yu & James, 2025). Avoid addressing other issues while focusing on data privacy, only general information and risks regarding bias and equality issues are addressed, and practical recommendations provided to practitioners are insufficient (Nguyen et al., 2023; Gihimire & Edwards, 2024). Additionally, some studies indicate that the current guidelines do not provide the most comprehensive information regarding the risks posed by Gen AI tools since they were published before advanced Gen AI tools such as ChatGPT were developed (205) or do not address the general problems that arise with Gen AI tools and do not address higher education and assessment (206).

In conclusion, it is evident that there is a need for a comprehensive set of regulations and guidelines on what stakeholders can do in order to reduce some of the risks identified in this study in order for Gen AI tools to be effectively used in higher education. Also, it is important to develop applied training programs that take into account the innovations and challenges that Gen AI tools provide to higher education, as well as to ensure the involvement of all stakeholders in higher education.

REFERENCES

Agrawal, S., Oza, P., Kakkar, R., Tanwar, S., Jetani, V., Undhad, J., & Singh, A. (2024). Analysis and recommendation system-based on PRISMA checklist to write systematic review. *Assessing Writing*, *61*, 100866. DOI: 10.1016/j.asw.2024.100866

Ahmad, S. F., Han, H., Alam, M. M., Rehmat, M. K., Irshad, M., Arraño-Muñoz, M., & Ariza-Montes, A. (2023). Impact of artificial intelligence on human loss in decision making, laziness and safety in education. *Humanities & Social Sciences Communications*, *10*(1), 311. DOI: 10.1057/s41599-023-01787-8

Akbar, M. S. (2025). Beyond detection: Designing AI-resilient assessments with automated feedback tool to foster critical thinking. *arXiv*, 2503.23622. https://doi.org//arXiv.2503.23622DOI: 10.48550

Akyol, Ş. P., Krishna, K., & Wang, J. (2018). *Taking PISA seriously: How accurate are low stakes exams?* NBER Working Paper No. 24930.

AlDahoul, N., Rahwan, T., & Zaki, Y. (2025). AI-generated faces influence gender stereotypes and racial homogenization. *Scientific Reports*, *15*(1), 14449. DOI: 10.1038/s41598-025-99623-3

An, Y., Yu, J. H., & James, S. (2025). Investigating the higher education institutions' guidelines and policies regarding the use of generative AI in teaching, learning, research, and administration. *International Journal of Educational Technology in Higher Education*, *22*(1), 10. DOI: 10.1186/s41239-025-00507-3

Apellániz, P. A., Parras, J., & Zazo, S. (2025). Improving synthetic data generation through federated learning in scarce and heterogeneous data scenarios. *Big Data and Cognitive Computing*, *9*(2), 18. DOI: 10.3390/bdcc9020018

Ardito, C. G. (2024). Generative AI detection in higher education assessments. *New Directions for Teaching and Learning*, •••, 1–18. DOI: 10.1002/tl.20624

Arslan, B., Lehman, B., Tenison, C., Sparks, J. R., López, A. A., Gu, L., & Zapata-Rivera, D. (2024). Opportunities and challenges of using generative AI to personalize educational assessment. *Frontiers in Artificial Intelligence*, *7*, 1460651. DOI: 10.3389/frai.2024.1460651

Australian Institute for Teaching and School Leadership. (2017). *Spotlight: Reframing feedback to improve teaching and learning.* AITSL. Retrieved from https://www.aitsl.edu.au/docs/default-source/research-evidence/spotlight/feedback.pdf?sfvrsn=cb2eec3c_14

Avidov, D., Ezra, O., Cohen, A., & Bronshtein, A. (2024). Generative AI in the service of situational judgment tests (SJT) for self-regulation learning during problem solving (SRL-PS). *Ubiquity Proceedings*, *4*(1), 23. DOI: 10.5334/uproc.145

Awadallah Alkouk, W., & Khlaif, Z. N. (2024). AI-resistant assessments in higher education: Practical insights from faculty training workshops. *Frontiers in Education*, *9*, 1499495. DOI: 10.3389/feduc.2024.1499495

Azoff, E. M. (2025). *Toward human-level artificial intelligence: How neuroscience can inform the pursuit of artificial general intelligence or general AI*. CRC Press.

Baker, R. S., & Hawn, A. (2022). Algorithmic bias in education. *International Journal of Artificial Intelligence in Education*, *32*(4), 1052–1092. DOI: 10.1007/s40593-021-00285-9

Bandara, W., & Syed, R. (2023). The role of a protocol in a systematic literature review. *Journal of Decision Systems*, *33*(4), 583–600. DOI: 10.1080/12460125.2023.2217567

Borge, M., Smith, B. K., & Aldemir, T. (2024). Using generative ai as a simulation to support higher-order thinking. *International Journal of Computer-Supported Collaborative Learning*, *19*(4), 479–532. DOI: 10.1007/s11412-024-09437-0

Bozkurt, A., Xiao, J., Farrow, R., Bai, J. Y. H., Nerantzi, C., Moore, S., Dron, J., Stracke, C. M., Singh, L., Crompton, H., Koutropoulos, A., Terentev, E., Pazurek, A., Nichols, M., Sidorkin, A. M., Costello, E., Watson, S., Mulligan, D., Honeychurch, S., & Asino, T. I. (2024). The manifesto for teaching and learning in a time of generative AI: A critical collective stance to better navigate the future. *Open Praxis*, *16*(4), 487–513. DOI: 10.55982/openpraxis.16.4.777

Broadfoot, P., & Rockey, J. (2025). Generative AI and the social functions of educational assessment. *Oxford Review of Education*, *51*(2), 281–300. DOI: 10.1080/03054985.2025.2455549

Capano, G., He, A. J., & McMinn, S. (2025). Riding the tide of generative artificial intelligence in higher education policy: An Asian perspective. *Journal of Asian Public Policy*, *18*(2), 1–15. DOI: 10.1080/17516234.2025.2450571

Chakraborty, U., Roy, S., & Kumar, S. (2023). *Rise of Generative AI and ChatGPT: Understand how Generative AI and ChatGPT are transforming and reshaping the business world*. BPB Publications.

Chan, C. K. Y. (2023). A comprehensive AI policy education framework for university teaching and learning. *International Journal of Educational Technology in Higher Education*, *20*(1), 38. DOI: 10.1186/s41239-023-00408-3

Chan, K. W., Ali, F., Park, J., Sham, K. S. B., Tan, E. Y. T., Chong, F. W. C., Qian, K., & Sze, G. K. (2025). Automatic item generation in various STEM subjects using large language model prompting. *Computers and Education: Artificial Intelligence*, *8*, 100344. DOI: 10.1016/j.caeai.2024.100344

Cheng, L., Croteau, E., Baral, S., Heffernan, C., & Heffernan, N. (2024). Facilitating student learning with a chatbot in an online math learning platform. *Journal of Educational Computing Research*, *62*(4), 907–937. DOI: 10.1177/07356331241226592

Cheong, B. C. (2024). Transparency and accountability in AI systems: Safeguarding wellbeing in the age of algorithmic decision-making. *Front. Hum. Dyn.*, *6*, 1421273. DOI: 10.3389/fhumd.2024.1421273

Chiu, T. K. F. (2024). Future research recommendations for transforming higher education with generative AI. *Computers and Education: Artificial Intelligence*, *6*, 100197. DOI: 10.1016/j.caeai.2023.100197

Circi, R., Hicks, J., & Sikali, E. (2023). Automatic item generation: Foundations and machine learning-based approaches for assessments. *Frontiers in Education*, *8*, 858273. DOI: 10.3389/feduc.2023.858273

Creely, E., & Henderson, M. (2025). Artificial intelligence and the digital dis/empowerment of migrant and refugee learners. In E. Tour, E. Creely, P. Waterhouse, & M. Henderson (Eds.), *Digital empowerment for refugee and migrant learners: Applying strengths-based practice to adult education* (1st ed., pp. 47-63). Routledge. https://doi.org/DOI: 10.4324/9781003422891-5

Dakakni, D. (2025). Artificial intelligence as a tool for data, economic and political hegemony: Releasing the djinn. *Ethics in Science and Environmental Politics*, *25*, 1–10. DOI: 10.3354/esep00216

Delgado, F., Yang, S., Madaio, M., & Yang, Q. (2023). The participatory turn in AI design: theoretical foundations and the current state of practice. In *Equity and access in algorithms, mechanisms, and optimization*. ACM., DOI: 10.1145/3617694.3623261

Elkhatat, A. M., Elsaid, K., & Almeer, S. (2023). Evaluating the efficacy of AI content detection tools in differentiating between human and AI-generated text. *International Journal for Educational Integrity*, *19*(1), 17. DOI: 10.1007/s40979-023-00140-5

Eulerich, M., Sanatizadeh, A., Vakilzadeh, H., & Wood, D. A. (2023). Is it all hype? ChatGPT's performance and disruptive potential in the accounting and auditing industries. *SSRN,* http://dx.doi.org/DOI: 10.2139/ssrn.4452175

European Union (2023). *EU AI Act: first regulation on artificial intelligence*. European Union.

Fan, Y., Tang, L., Le, H., Shen, K., Tan, S., Zhao, Y., Shen, Y., Li, X., & Gašević, D. (2025). Beware of metacognitive laziness: Effects of generative artificial intelligence on learning motivation, processes, and performance. *British Journal of Educational Technology*, *56*(2), 489–530. DOI: 10.1111/bjet.13544

Ferrara, E. (2023). Fairness And bias in artificial intelligence: A brief survey of sources, ımpacts, and mitigation strategies. *Sci*, *6*(1), 3. DOI: 10.3390/sci6010003

Francis, N. J., Jones, S., & Smith, D. P. (2025). Generative AI in higher education: Balancing innovation and integrity. *British Journal of Biomedical Science*, *81*, 14048. DOI: 10.3389/bjbs.2024.14048

Freeman, J. (2025). *Student generative AI survey 2025*. Higher Education Policy Institute. HEPU Policy Note 61.

Fuentes-Martín, A., Cilleruelo-Ramos, A., Segura-Méndez, B., & Mayol, J. (2023). Can an artificial ıntelligence model pass an examination for medical specialists? *Archivos de Bronconeumología*, *59*(8), 534–536. DOI: 10.1016/j.arbres.2023.03.017

Geçkin, V., Kızıltaş, E., & Çınar, Ç. (2023). Assessing second-language academic writing: AI vs. Human raters. *Journal of Educational Technology & Online Learning*, *6*(4), 1096–1108. DOI: 10.31681/jetol.1336599

Geerts, G., & O'Leary, D. (2022). V-matrix: A wave theory of value creation for big data. *International Journal of Accounting Information Systems*, *47*, 100575. DOI: 10.1016/j.accinf.2022.100575

Gerritsen-van Leeuwenkamp, K. J., Brinke, D. J., & Kester, L. (2017). Assessment quality in tertiary education: An integrative literature review. *Studies in Educational Evaluation*, *55*, 94–116. DOI: 10.1016/j.stueduc.2017.08.001

Gobrecht, A., Tuma, F., Möller, M., ... (2024). Beyond human subjectivity and error: A novel AI grading system. *arXiv*, 2405.04323. https://doi.org//arXiv.2405.04323DOI: 10.48550

Gonsalves, C. (2025). Contextual assessment design in the age of generative AI. *Journal of Learning Development in Higher Education*, *34*(34). Advance online publication. DOI: 10.47408/jldhe.vi34.1307

Gooch, D., Waugh, K., Richards, M., Slaymaker, M., & Woodthorpe, J. (2024). Exploring the profile of university assessments flagged as containing aı-generated material. *ACM Inroads*, *15*(2), 39–47. DOI: 10.1145/3656478

Goyal, M., & Mahmoud, Q. H. (2024). A Systematic review of synthetic data generation techniques using generative AI. *Electronics (Basel), 13*(17), 3509. DOI: 10.3390/electronics13173509

Graux, H., Gryffroy, P., Gad-Nowak, M., & Boghaert, L. (2024). *The role of artificial intelligence in processing and generating new data*. Data.Europe.EU. European Commission.

Gruenhagen, J. H., Sinclair, P. M., Carroll, J. A., Baker, P. R. A., Wilson, A., & Demant, D. (2024). Computers and Education. *Artificial Intelligence*, *7*, 100273. DOI: 10.1016/j.caeai.2024.100273

Gryz, J., & Rojszczak, M. (2021). Black box algorithms and the rights of individuals: No easy solution to the "explainability" problem. *Internet Policy Review*, *10*(2). Advance online publication. DOI: 10.14763/2021.2.1564

Hague, C. (2024). *Fostering higher-order thinking skills online in higher education: A scoping review*. OECD Education Working Paper No 306. OECD Publishing. https://dx.doi.org/DOI: 10.1787/19939019

Hankins, A., & Harrington, C. (2022). Lack of high-quality, frequent feedback contributes to low success rates for community college students. *Impacting Education: Journal on Transforming Professional Practice*, *7*(4), 2–7. Advance online publication. DOI: 10.5195/ie.2022.201

Hao, S., Han, W., Jiang, T., Li, Y., Wu, H., Zhong, C., Zhou, Z., & Tang, H. (2024). Synthetic data in AI: Challenges, applications, and ethical implications. *ArXiv, abs/2401.01629*.

Hassija, V., Chamola, V., Mahapatra, A., Singal, A., Goel, D., Huang, K., Scardapane, S., Spinelli, I., Mahmud, M., & Hussain, A. (2024). Interpreting black-box models: A review on explainable artificial ıntelligence. *Cognitive Computation*, *16*(1), 45–74. DOI: 10.1007/s12559-023-10179-8

Hayes, C. M. (2023). Generative artificial intelligence and copyright: Both sides of the black box *SSRN*. http://dx.doi.org/DOI: 10.2139/ssrn.4517799

Heinz, J. (2016). Digital skills and the ınfluence of students' socio-economic background: An exploratory study in german elementary schools. *Italian Journal of Sociology of Education*, *8*(2), 186–212. DOI: 10.14658/pupj-ijse-2016-2-9

Hofmann, V., Kalluri, P. R., Jurafsky, D., & King, S. (2024). AI generates covertly racist decisions about people based on their dialect. *Nature*, *633*(8028), 147–154. DOI: 10.1038/s41586-024-07856-5

Idowu, J. A. (2024). Debiasing education algorithms. *International Journal of Artificial Intelligence in Education, 34*(4), 1510–1540. DOI: 10.1007/s40593-023-00389-4

Jauhiainen, J. S., & Garagorry Guerra, A. (2024). Evaluating students' open-ended written responses with LLMs: Using the RAG framework for GPT-3.5, GPT-4, Claude-3, and Mistral-Large. *arXiv,* 2405.05444. https://doi.org//arXiv.2405.05444DOI: 10.48550

Johnson, R. L., Pistilli, G., Menédez-González, N., ... (2022) The ghost in the machine has an American accent: value conflict in GPT-3. 2022. *arXiv*, 2203.07785. https://doi.org//arXiv.2203.07785DOI: 10.48550

Joshi, I., Grimmer, M., Rathgeb, C., Busch, C., Bremond, F., & Dantcheva, A. (2024). Synthetic data in human analysis: A survey. *IEEE Transactions on Pattern Analysis and Machine Intelligence*, *46*(7), 1–20. DOI: 10.1109/TPAMI.2024.3362821

Jung, J. Y., Tyack, L., & von Davier, M. (2025). Towards the implementation of automated scoring in international large-scale assessments: Scalability and quality control. *Computers and Education: Artificial Intelligence*, *8*, 100375. DOI: 10.1016/j.caeai.2025.100375

Kadel, R., Mishra, B. K., Shailendra, S., Abid, S., Rani, M., & Mahato, S. P. (2024). Crafting tomorrow's evaluations: Assessment design strategies in the era of generative AI. *arXiv,* 2405.01805. https://doi.org//arXiv.2405.01805DOI: 10.1109/ISET61814.2024.00012

Kaplan, A., & Haenlein, M. (2020). Rulers of the world, unite! The challenges and opportunities of artificial intelligence. *Business Horizons*, *63*(1), 37–50. DOI: 10.1016/j.bushor.2019.09.003

Karkera, A., Greene, M., Hall, A., Henderson, L., & Lewis, K. (2024). *Transformational impacts of generative AI on synthetic data generation*. Deloitte.

Khlaif, Z., Odeh, A., & Bsharat, T. R. K. (2024). Generative AI-powered adaptive assessment. In Sanmugam, M., Lim, D., & Barkhaya, N. M. M. (Eds.), *Power of persuasive educational technologies in enhancing learning*. IGI Global. DOI: 10.4018/979-8-3693-6397-3.ch007

Khlaif, Z. N., Alkouk, W. A., Salama, N., & Abu Eideh, B. (2025). Redesigning assessments for AI-enhanced learning: A framework for educators in the generative AI era. *Education Sciences*, *15*(2), 174. DOI: 10.3390/educsci15020174

Kim, J., Lee, T. H., Bae, Y., & Kim, M. K. (2024). A Comparison Between AI and Human Evaluation with a Focus on Generative AI. In Lindgren, R., Asino, T. I., Kyza, E. A., Looi, C. K., Keifert, D. T., & Suárez, E. (Eds.), *Proceedings of the 18th International Conference of the Learning Sciences - ICLS 2024* (1722-1725). International Society of the Learning Sciences. DOI: 10.22318/icls2024.930382

Kizilcec, R. F., Huber, E., Papanastasiou, E. C., Cram, A., Makridis, C. A., Smolansky, A., Zeivots, S., & Raduescu, C. (2024). Perceived impact of generative AI on assessments: Comparing educator and student perspectives in Australia, Cyprus, and the United States. *Computers and Education: Artificial Intelligence*, *7*, 100269. DOI: 10.1016/j.caeai.2024.100269

Krullaars, Z. H., Januardani, A., Zhou, L., & Jonkers, E. (2023). Exploring initial interactions: High school students and generative ai chatbots for relationship development. https://doi.org/DOI: 10.18420/muc2023-mci-src-415

Laakso, A. (2023). *Ethical challenges of large language models: A systematic literature review*. Master dissertation from the University of Helsinki.

Lee, D., Arnold, M., Srivastava, A., Plastow, K., Strelan, P., Ploeckl, F., Lekkas, D., & Palmer, E. (2024). The impact of generative AI on higher education learning and teaching: A study of educators' perspectives. *Computers and Education: Artificial Intelligence*, *6*, 100221. DOI: 10.1016/j.caeai.2024.100221

Leiva, F. M., Ríos, F. J. M., & Martínez, T. L. (2006). Assessment of ınterjudge reliability in the open-ended questions coding process. *Quality & Quantity*, *40*(4), 519–537. DOI: 10.1007/s11135-005-1093-6

Li, C. J., Zhang, J., Tang, Y., & Li, J. (2024). Automatic item generation for personality situational judgment tests with large language models. *arXiv,* 2412.12144. https://doi.org//arXiv.2412.12144DOI: 10.48550

Liang, W., Yuksekgonul, M., Mao, Y., Wu, E., & Zou, J. (2023). GPT detectors are biased against non-native English writers. [NY]. *Patterns (New York, N.Y.)*, *4*(7), 100779. DOI: 10.1016/j.patter.2023.100779

Lodge, J. M., Thompson, K., & Corrin, L. (2023). Mapping out a research agenda for generative artificial intelligence in tertiary education. *Australasian Journal of Educational Technology*, *39*(1), 1–8. DOI: 10.14742/ajet.8695

Lubbe, A., Marais, E., & Kruger, D. (2025). Cultivating independent thinkers: The triad of artificial intelligence, Bloom's taxonomy and critical thinking in assessment pedagogy. *Education and Information Technologies*, *30*(12), 17589–17622. Advance online publication. DOI: 10.1007/s10639-025-13476-x

Lye, C. Y., & Lim, L. (2024). Generative artificial intelligence in tertiary education: Assessment redesign principles and considerations. *Education Sciences*, *14*(6), 569. DOI: 10.3390/educsci14060569

Lythreatis, S., Singh, S. K., & El-Kassar, A. N. (2022). The digital divide: A review and future research agenda. *Technological Forecasting and Social Change*, *175*, 121359. DOI: 10.1016/j.techfore.2021.121359

Majeed, A., & Hwang, S. O. (2025). Synthetic data: A new frontier for democratizing artificial intelligence and data access. *Computer*, *58*(2), 106–114. Advance online publication. DOI: 10.1109/MC.2024.3515412

Maleki, N., Padmanabhan, B., & Dutta, K. (2024). AI hallucinations: A misnomer worth clarifying. *arXiv,* 2401.06796. https://doi.org//arXiv.2401.06796DOI: 10.1109/CAI59869.2024.00033

McKinsey & Company. (2022, June 1). *Are states ready to close the US digital divide?* Retrieved from https://www.mckinsey.com/industries/public-sector/our-insights/are-states-ready-to-close-the-us-digital-divide

Morris, R., Perry, T., & Wardle, L. (2021). Formative assessment and feedback for learning in higher education: A systematic review. *Review of Education*, *9*(3), e3292. DOI: 10.1002/rev3.3292

Ngo, R., Chan, L., & Mindermann, S. (2025). The alignment problem from a deep learning perspective. *arXiv*, 2209.00626. https://doi.org//arXiv.2209.00626DOI: 10.48550

Nguyen, A., Ngo, H. N., Hong, Y., Dang, B., & Nguyen, B. P. T. (2023). Ethical principles for artifcial intelligence in education. *Education and Information Technologies*, *28*(4), 4221–4241. DOI: 10.1007/s10639-022-11316-w

Nolte, H., Finck, M., & Meding, K. (2025). Machine learners should acknowledge the legal implications of large language models as personal data. *arXiv*, 2503.01630. https://doi.org//arXiv.2503.01630DOI: 10.48550

Nurul, A. Z., Syafiza, A. H., Noorsuhana, M. Y., & Ummi, K. I. (2024). Integrating Gen-AI in authentic scenario-based assessment for sustainable chemical engineering education. *Proceedings of the International Conference on Innovation & Entrepreneurship in Computing, Engineering & Science Education,* 209-218. https://doi.org/ DOI: 10.2991/978-94-6463-589-8_21

Nussberger, A. M., Luo, L., Celis, L. E., & Crockett, M. J. (2022). Public attitudes value interpretability but prioritize accuracy in Artificial Intelligence. *Nature Communications*, *13*(1), 5821. DOI: 10.1038/s41467-022-33417-3

Nwafor, C. A., & Onyenwe, I. E. (2021). An automated multiple-choice question generation using natural language processing techniques. *arXiv,* 2103.14757. https://doi.org/DOI: 10.5121/ijnlc.2021.10201

OECD. (2021). *Bridging digital divides in G20 countries: OECD report for the G20 infrastructure working group*. OECD Publishing.

OECD. (2023). *OECD digital education outlook 2023: Towards an effective digital education ecosystem*. OECD Publishing., DOI: 10.1787/c74f03de-

OECD. (2024). *AI, data governance and privacy: Synergies and areas of international co-operation. OECD Artificial Intelligence Papers, No. 22*. OECD Publishing., DOI: 10.1787/2476b1a4-

Özer, M. (2024a). Is artificial intelligence hallucinating? *Türk Psikiyatri Dergisi = Turkish Journal of Psychiatry, 35*(4), 333–335. DOI: 10.5080/u27587

Özer, M. (2024b). Dynamics of the meritocracy trap and artificial intelligence. *International Journal of Management Economics and Business, 20*(3), 845–869.

Özer, M. (2024c). Artificial intelligence bias and the amplification of inequalities in the labor market. *Journal of Economy. Cultura e Scuola, 69*(1), 159–168.

Özer, M. (2024d). Potential benefits and risks of artificial intelligence in education. *Bartın University Journal of Faculty of Education, 13*(2), 232–244. DOI: 10.14686/buefad.1416087

Özer, M. (2025a). Can mathematical models be weapons of mass destruction? *Reflektif Journal of Social Sciences, 6*(1), 259–268. DOI: 10.47613/reflektif.2025.212

Özer, M. (2025b). *Yapay zekâ ve toplum*. Nobel Publishing.

Özer, M., Perc, M., & Suna, H. E. (2024). Participatory management can help artificial intelligence ethics adhere to social consensus. *İstanbul Üniversitesi Sosyoloji Dergisi, 44*, 221-238. https://doi.org/DOI: 10.26650/SJ.2024.44.1.0001

Pack, A., Barrett, A., & Escalante, J. (2024). Large language models and automated essay scoring of English language learner writing: Insights into validity and reliability. *Computers and Education: Artificial Intelligence, 6*, 100234. DOI: 10.1016/j.caeai.2024.100234

Parthasarathy, A., Phalnikar, A., Jauhar, A., Somayajula, D., Krishnan, G. S., & Ravindran, B. (2024). Participatory approaches in aı development and governance: a principled approach. *arXiv,* 2407.13100. https://doi.org//arXiv.2407.13100DOI: 10.48550

Pelletier, K., McCormack, M., Reeves, J., Robert, J., Arbino, N., Al-Freih, M., Dickson-Deane, C., Guevara, C., Koster, L., Sánchez-Mendiola, M., Bessette, L. S., & Stine, J. (2022). *EDUCAUSE Horizon Report, teaching and learning edition.* EDUCAUSE.

Perkins, M., Roe, J., Vu, B. H., Postma, D., Hickerson, D., McGaughran, J., & Khuat, H. Q. (2024). Gen AI detection tools, adversarial techniques and implications for inclusivity in higher education. *ArXiv,* abs/2403.19148.

Plessis, E. (2025). Embracing project-based assessments in the age of AI in open distance e-learning. *International Journal of Information and Education Technology (IJIET), 15*(2), 372–381. DOI: 10.18178/ijiet.2025.15.2.2249

Rane, N., Choudhary, S., & Rane, J. (2023). Explainable artificial intelligence (XAI) approaches for transparency and accountability in financial decision-making. *SSRN.* http://dx.doi.org/DOI: 10.2139/ssrn.4640316

Resnik, D. B., Hosseini, M., Kim, J. J. H., Epiphaniou, G., & Maple, C. (2025). GenAI synthetic data create ethical challenges for scientists. Here's how to address them. *Proceedings of the National Academy of Sciences of the United States of America, 122*(9), e2409182122. DOI: 10.1073/pnas.2409182122

Roe, J., Perkins, M., Somoray, K., Miller, D., & Furze, L. (2025). To deepfake or not to deepfake: Higher education stakeholders' perceptions and intentions towards synthetic media. *arXiv*, 2502.18066. https://doi.org//arXiv.2502.18066DOI: 10.48550

Rudin, C., & Radin, J. (2019). Why are we using black box models in ai when we don't need to? A lesson from an explainable ai competition. *Harvard Data Science Review, 1*(2). Advance online publication. DOI: 10.1162/99608f92.5a8a3a3d

Rust, J. (2006). *Discussion piece: The psychometric principles of assessment.* Cambridge Assessment.

Scarfe, P., Watcham, K., Clarke, A., & Roesch, E. (2024). A real-world test of artificial intelligence infiltration of a university examinations system: A "Turing Test" case study. *PLoS One, 19*(6), e0305354. DOI: 10.1371/journal.pone.0305354

Schüttpelz-Brauns, K., Hecht, M., Hardt, K., Karay, Y., Zupanic, M., & Kämmer, J. E. (2020). Institutional strategies related to test-taking behavior in low stakes assessment. *Advances in Health Sciences Education : Theory and Practice, 25*(2), 321–335. DOI: 10.1007/s10459-019-09928-y

Sharma, R. C., & Bozkurt, A. (2024). *Transforming education with generative AI: Prompt engineering and synthetic content creation.* IGI Global., DOI: 10.4018/979-8-3693-1351-0

Shumailov, I., Shumaylov, Z., Zhao, Y., Papernot, N., Anderson, R., & Gal, Y. (2024). AI models collapse when trained on recursively generated data. *Nature*, *631*(8022), 755–759. DOI: 10.1038/s41586-024-07566-y

Sousa, A. E., & Cardoso, P. (2025). Use of generative AI by higher education students. *Electronics (Basel)*, *14*(7), 1258. DOI: 10.3390/electronics14071258

Strzelecki, A. (2024). Is ChatGPT-like technology going to replace commercial search engines? *Library Hi Tech News*, *41*(6), 18–21. DOI: 10.1108/LHTN-02-2024-0026

Sun, Y., Sheng, D., Zhou, Z., & Wu, Y. (2024). AI hallucination: Towards a comprehensive classification of distorted information in artificial intelligence-generated content. *Humanities & Social Sciences Communications*, *11*(1), 1278. DOI: 10.1057/s41599-024-03811-x

Suna, H. E., & Özer, M. (2025). The human complimentary usage of AI and ML for fair and unbiased educational assessments. *Chinese/English Journal of Educational Measurement and Evaluation*, *6*(1), 9. DOI: 10.59863/YPKL4338

Tao, Y., Viberg, O., Baker, R. S., & Kizilcec, R. F. (2024). Cultural bias and cultural alignment of large language models. *PNAS Nexus*, *3*(9), pgae346. Advance online publication. DOI: 10.1093/pnasnexus/pgae346

The Open Innovation Team & Department for Education. (2024). *Generative AI in education: Educator and expert views.* UK Department for Education. Retrieved from https://assets.publishing.service.gov.uk/media/65b8cd41b5cb6e000d8bb74e/DfE_GenAI_in_education_-_Educator_and_expert_views_report.pdf

Tomasev, N., Maynard, J. L., & Gabriel, I. (2025). Manifestations of xenophobia in AI systems. *AI & Society*, *40*(2), 741–763. DOI: 10.1007/s00146-024-01893-4

UN & ILO. (2024). *Mind the AI divide: Shaping a global perspective on the future of work.* United Nations.

UNESCO. (2023). Guidance for generative AI in education and research. [United Nations Educational, Scientific and Cultural Organization.]. *Education*, •••, 2030.

Ungless, E. L., Vitsakis, N., & Talat, Z., Garforth1, J., Ross, B., Onken, A., Kasirzadeh, A., & Birch, A. (2025). The only way is ethics: A guide to ethical research with large language models. *Proceedings of the 31st International Conference on Computational Linguistics*, 8992–9005.

United Nations University. (2024). *Recommendations on the use of synthetic data to train AI models.* Policy Guideline. Retrieved from https://collections.unu.edu/eserv/UNU:9480/Use-of-Synthetic-Data-to-Train-AI-Models.pdf

Varoufakis, Y. (2024). *Technofeudalism: what killed capitalism*. Melville House.

Verdegem, P. (2022). Dismantling AI capitalism: The commons as an alternative to the power concentration of Big Tech. *AI & Society*. Advance online publication. DOI: 10.1007/s00146-022-01437-8

Villalobos, P., Ho, A., Sevilla, J., Besiroglu, T., Heim, L., & Hobbhahn, M. (2024). Position: will we run out of data? Limits of LLM scaling based on human-generated data. In *Proceedings of the 41st International Conference on Machine Learning 235* (49523–49544).

Vo, Y., Rickels, H., Welch, C., & Dunbar, S. (2023). Human scoring versus automated scoring for english learners in a statewide evidence-based writing assessment. *Assessing Writing*, *56*, 100719. DOI: 10.1016/j.asw.2023.100719

Wachira, P. W., Liu, X., & Koc, S. (2024). *Educational assessments in the age of generative AI*. IGI Global Publishing.

Wang, H., Dang, A., Wu, Z., & Mac, S. 2023. Seeing chatgpt through universities' policies, resources and guidelines. *arXiv preprint arXiv:*2312.05235.

Weber-Wulff, D., Anohina-Naumeca, A., Bjelobaba, S., Foltýnek, T., Guerrero-Dib, J., Popoola, O., Šigut, P., & Waddington, L. (2023). Testing of detection tools for AI-generated text. *International Journal for Educational Integrity*, *19*(1), 26. DOI: 10.1007/s40979-023-00146-z

Wei, Y., Jiang, Y. H., Liu, J., Qi, C., & Jia, R. (2024). The advancement of personalized learning potentially accelerated by generative AI. *arXiv*, 2412.00691v1

Weng, X., Xia, Q., Gu, M., Rajaram, K., & Chiu, T. K. F. (2024). Assessment and learning outcomes for generative AI in higher education: A scoping review on current research status and trends. *Australasian Journal of Educational Technology*, *40*(6), 37–55. DOI: 10.14742/ajet.9540

Williams, A. (2024). Delivering effective student feedback in higher education: An evaluation of the challenges and best practice. *International Journal of Research in Education and Science*, *10*(2), 473–501. DOI: 10.46328/ijres.3404

Wisniewski, B., Zierer, K., & Hattie, J. (2020). The power of feedback revisited: A meta-analysis of educational feedback research. *Frontiers in Psychology*, *10*, 3087. Advance online publication. DOI: 10.3389/fpsyg.2019.03087

World Economic Forum. (2025, Jan 14). *How can we bring 2.6 billion people online to bridge the digital divide*? Retrieved from https://www.weforum.org/stories/2024/01/digital-divide-internet-access-online-fwa/

Xiao, Y., & Watson, M. (2017). Guidance on conducting a systematic literature review. *Journal of Planning Education and Research, 39*(1), 93–112. DOI: 10.1177/0739456X17723971

Xu, Z., Jain, S., & Kankanhalli, M. (2024). Hallucination is inevitable: An innate limitation of large language models. *arXiv*, 2401.11817. https://doi.org//arXiv.2401.11817DOI: 10.48550

Yang, Y. (2025). Racial bias in AI-generated images. *AI & Society*. Advance online publication. DOI: 10.1007/s00146-025-02282-1

Yatani, K., Sramek, Z., & Yang, C. L. (2024). AI as extraherics: Fostering higher-order thinking skills in human-AI interaction. *ArXiv*, 2409.09218. https://doi.org//arXiv.2409.09218DOI: 10.48550

Zhai, C., Wibowo, S., & Li, L. D. (2024). The effects of over-reliance on AI dialogue systems on students' cognitive abilities: A systematic review. *Smart Learn. Environ., 11*(1), 28. DOI: 10.1186/s40561-024-00316-7

Zhao, W., Goyal, T., Chiu, Y., Jiang, L., Newman, B., Ravichander, A., Chandu, K., Bras, R. L., Cardie, C., Deng, Y., & Choi, Y. (2024). WildHallucinations: Evaluating long-form factuality in LLMs with real-world entity queries. *arXiv, abs/2407.17468*. https://doi.org//arXiv.2407.17468DOI: 10.48550

Chapter 9
Challenges of Educational Evaluation in the Era of Generative Artificial Intelligence

Jésica Alhelí Cortés Ruiz
https://orcid.org/0000-0002-5459-4874
Instituto Politécnico Nacional, Mexico

María Elena Zepeda Hurtado
https://orcid.org/0000-0001-9764-5013
Instituto Politécnico Nacional, Mexico

Edgar Oliver Cardoso Espinosa
https://orcid.org/0000-0001-7588-9439
Instituto Politécnico Nacional, Mexico

ABSTRACT

The objective of the chapter is to determine the challenges of educational evaluation in the era of generative Artificial Intelligence to recognize its implications in the academic training of students. The influence of digital technologies on contemporary educational environments, as educational institutions opt for the use of generative AI tools, raises questions and actions that directly impact the conceptualization, methodologies, strategies, and evaluation of the teaching-learning process. Generative AI is transforming educational assessment in ways that offer both challenges and opportunities. However, technology dependence, learning authenticity, security, information bias, and algorithms are legitimate concerns. Therefore, maximizing

DOI: 10.4018/979-8-3373-7579-3.ch009

ght © 2026, IGI Global Scientific Publishing. Copying or distributing in print or electronic forms without written permission of IGI Global Scientific Publishing is prohibited. Use of this chapter to generative artificial intelligence (AI) technologies is expressly prohibited. The publisher reserves all rights to license its use for generative AI training and machine learning model development.

the positive impact of generative AI in education is of utmost importance, and it is crucial that educators, researchers, and policymakers work together to address these challenges and develop effective strategies.

INTRODUCTION[1]

Higher education in the 21st century has been transformed by scientific and technological advances, which have expanded both the coverage and impact on the development of human capital required by the workforce. This has led to expanding opportunities and challenges for higher education due to greater access to and positioning of technology. Similarly, generative artificial intelligence (AI) has revolutionized multiple sectors, and education is at the center of this transformation, in the use of its tools by students and teachers, supporting the planning and execution of the teaching-learning process, and creating new and adaptive content. This also has profound implications for the way learning is assessed.

Therefore, the influence of digital technologies on contemporary educational environments, as educational institutions opt for the use of generative AI tools, raises questions and actions that directly impact the conceptualization, methodologies, strategies, and evaluation of the teaching-learning process. Since generative AI has implications in the educational field, one of the immediate challenges is preparing students for the constant and advanced changes in technology that permeate everyday life, such as the use of mobile devices in the classroom; online platforms and distance education; and ethical challenges such as privacy, the digital divide, and equal access. Therefore, it is important to understand how the benefits and risks of AI work (Araujo et al., 2024).

Likewise, the use of AI in learning expresses that it fundamentally impacts the personalization of learning, since, instead of following a uniform educational model for all, it seeks to provide educational experiences that are relevant and meaningful for each student, using various strategies, technologies and methods to allow students to have greater control over their own learning process, thus promoting a deeper and more lasting understanding of the concepts (Cisneros Vásquez et al., 2024). Therefore, the use of AI as intelligent tutors, according to J. A. Romero (2024), intelligent tutoring systems, adaptive learning platforms and virtual assistants can provide continuous support to students, regardless of their geographical location.

Furthermore, AI can provide immersive learning experiences, such as virtual reality and augmented reality, which opened up possibilities for the creation of immersive learning environments and employs digital technologies to immerse students in virtual or augmented environments that represent real-world experiences (Alvarado & Cuzco, 2025). From Mora-Cruz et al.'s (2023) perspective, both augmented reality and virtual reality allowed students to virtually interact in three-dimensional spaces and experience simulations that were previously only possible in physical environments, such as laboratories or field trips. Furthermore, these support resources are varied, including videos, animations, games, interactive activities, and are tailored to each student's learning style. Generative AI not only transforms educational content but also redefines the roles of educators and students. In this context, it is essential to explore how these tools can be integrated into assessment processes and what implications they have for academic training.

In this regard, Porras (2024) considers that the strategy is produced through connections between people, ideas, technologies, and that the ability to establish and manage these connections is crucial, and proposes focusing on skills such as cognitive, knowledge acquisition, identification, communication, collaboration, creativity, exploration, analysis, application, development, evaluation and design referring specifically to the evaluation, the challenge is to comply with the characteristics of the evaluation: validity, equity and effectiveness of the evaluations. From this, emphasis is placed on the ability of AI to personalize learning and offer instant feedback that can radically change educational evaluation; however, it poses significant challenges that must be addressed. For this reason, the present research proposes to analyze the challenges and benefits of generative AI in educational evaluation, as well as the future lines of research that could emerge in this field.

Additionally, it is mentioned how the Government of Spain (2024) points out that the teaching strategy in artificial intelligence is structured on three fundamental pillars:

- Strengthening key technological capabilities, including significant investments in supercomputing, sustainable storage infrastructure, development of multilingual foundational models, and promotion of AI talent.
- Promoting the adoption of AI in the public sector and small and medium-sized enterprises (SMEs), fostering innovation and entrepreneurship ecosystems, and articulating specific cybersecurity measures to support the digital transformation process.
- Developing transparent, responsible, and humanistic AI through the creation of the Spanish Agency for the Supervision of Artificial Intelligence (AESIA), which will play a central role in validating, regulating, and promoting good practices in the ethical and reliable use of AI models, in accordance with European regulations. This implies that its strategies also emphasize sustainability as a cross-cutting principle, through the promotion of green data centers, green AI certification, and the implementation of environmental metrics in model training and its inclusive approach.

BACKGROUND

Education and its Assessment in Times of Generative AI

Historically in education, evaluation has been a structured practice that includes pedagogical, epistemic and ethical relationships focused on activities, processes and procedures that allow evaluation to be an important phase to establish performances, achievements, deficiencies in a given period and context, it is carried out with the purpose of making decisions, making changes in the areas or aspects necessary to expand and strengthen those that generate good results. On the other hand, in the case of the administrative or management process, evaluation is considered within the stages: planning, organization, direction, control and evaluation, this last stage, in addition to allowing to know what are the weak points of the process and its strengths, mainly allows to verify the fulfillment of the objectives and goals (United Nations Educational, Scientific and Cultural Organization [UNESCO], 2024).

It is true that, in the specific case of the educational field, according to Espinoza (2022), educational evaluation is considered a systematic process of collecting and analyzing information obtained through specific methods, procedures, and techniques to formulate value judgments on educational objects that guide decisions and support their improvement and through this, it seeks to determine criteria that allow guiding actions to contribute to raising the quality of education. In short, the evaluation within the teaching-learning process expresses that "it is essential to promote meaningful learning to provide clear and specific feedback, establish realistic goals, and allow adjustments in teaching strategies" (García, 2024, p.13).

It is worth mentioning that the Observatorio de Inteligencia Artificial en Educación Superior (OIAES, 2025) conducted an in-depth and structured reflection on the need to transform university curricula in the face of the rise of artificial intelligence (AI), both in its generative and general aspects. From a critical and prospective perspective, the document highlights that the integration of AI in higher education should not be limited to technical fields but should transversally encompass all disciplines of knowledge. One of the central axes is curricular adaptation, understood as an unavoidable process to ensure that graduates not only master technological tools but also possess an ethical and legal understanding of their use. In this context, the need to incorporate new specific subjects on AI, modify existing content, and promote a flexible and personalized learning structure through strategies such as micromodules is established.

Another essential component is the redefinition of the graduate profile, which must integrate classic competencies such as critical thinking and effective communication, along with emerging skills: responsible use of AI, critical evaluation of automated solutions, adaptation to technological change, and data management. An approach based on three competency levels is proposed: transformative (humanistic) competencies, general digital competencies, and specific AI competencies. Regarding assessment, the report advocates a transformation toward more competency-based, formative, and personalized models. AI can play a key role by generating immediate and evidence-based feedback, contributing to autonomous and continuous learning. The report emphasizes the importance of maintaining the integrity of the training process, regulating when, how, and for what purposes AI can be used in assessment contexts.

Likewise, the fundamental role of educational institutions as active agents of change is emphasized. They must lead the updating of curricula, train teachers in the pedagogical and critical use of AI and collaborate closely with industry and regulators to ensure relevant and up-to-date education. However, the document warns of the need for agile mechanisms to review qualifications and adapt learning outcomes based on technological advances. Finally, the importance of having a robust regulatory framework—such as that provided by the 2024 European legislation—to guide the incorporation of AI into education in an ethical, legal, and socially responsible manner is highlighted (European Parliament & Council of the European Union, 2024). The combination of technical, pedagogical, legal, and humanistic elements allows for a comprehensive vision of the future of universities in the era of artificial intelligence.

Furthermore, Heggart (2024) points out that AI will not replace teachers but will transform their functions because AI will not replace the role of humans in teaching, but will redefine it, since the teacher will be less a transmitter of content and more a designer of learning experiences and pedagogical mediator. In addition to the above, AI can reduce the administrative burden on teachers by supporting generative AI tools by taking care of repetitive tasks such as test writing, data analysis, and report writing, allowing teachers to focus on relational and didactic aspects of the educational process (Esterman, 2024; Heggart, 2024).

Consequently, according to the authors, evaluation is conceived as a process to assess whether a performance or evidence of learning meets pre-established attributes or parameters, through evidence and instruments that provide information for decision-making. This implies that evaluation must be continuous in order to detect training needs. Educational evaluation in the era of artificial intelligence and paradigm shifts shows what the technological resources generated by AI can achieve and how these can easily be used to promote learning or seek shortcuts (Flores Contrera, 2024).

According to Flores and Borges (2024), assessment is a daily and permanent exercise through which improvements in the construction of learning are sought, and both students and teachers are jointly responsible for carrying it out, since both are essential to achieve the established learning outcomes. Considering that the principle of assessment is learning and that learning at this time is associated with technology, Guárdia Ortiz et al. (2024) propose that special attention be paid to the effectiveness of interactions between AI, the student, and emotions, due to their repercussions on the learning process. As well as considering that AI's ability to support students in real time facilitates more dynamic and responsive learning, constantly adapting to the student's needs. (Piedra-Castro et al., 2024). Therefore, assessment is a solid basis for obtaining information on the acquisition of skills; information is essential for detecting difficulties and problems that may hinder learning, allowing teachers to identify areas of attention and design personalized interventions.

It is necessary to characterize the evaluation in a general way, to give a clear answer between the evaluation of learning and the skills developed in the use of technology: 1. What? (learning object); 2. For what? (diagnosis, certification, promotion, improvement of practice, feedback, etc.); 3. How? (qualitative, quantitative approach or a combination of both); 4. With what? (techniques and instruments); 5. When? (moments in which it is carried out: Initial or diagnostic, procedural or formative, final or summary); 6. Who? (self-assessment, peer-assessment, hetero-assessment), the intention is to comply with a systematic process that collects, analyzes and interprets information about student learning (Ordoñez et al., 2024).

Generative AI can influence each of these characteristics of educational assessment. For example, by enabling the creation of personalized questions and tasks, it can improve the validity and relevance of assessments. However, it also poses challenges in terms of reliability and fairness, since the quality of the assessments generated will depend on the data and algorithms used. Therefore, it is important to highlight the value and importance of using technologies in assessment. Authors such as K. Fernández (2024) value the advantages they offer in guaranteeing high-quality assessments, in synchronous and asynchronous contexts. He highlights the importance of continuous feedback throughout the process to strengthen confidence in the results, prioritizing the specific needs of each student, and emphasizes the importance of planning, developing, and implementing assessment techniques and instruments using technological tools.

Subsequently among other benefits of carrying out the evaluation using AI tools, is to improve the indeterminacy and ambiguity of the current world through educational processes with a pedagogical approach based on the use of AI applications and programs and enables the relationship with the pertinent strategies of transfer to social reality (Copado, 2024). Therefore, with the use of AI tools, not only theoretical knowledge is evaluated but also practical, deep knowledge and social skills. Consequently, Guárdia Ortiz et al. (2024) exemplifies these ideas about evaluation through intelligent virtual laboratories on the development: competencies such as critical thinking, problem-solving skills, collaborative work skills, communication, the promotion of innovation, the ability to learn and unlearn, creativity and entrepreneurship, arguing that they are at the basis of change and the introduction of AI in society.

As an example, An et al. (2025) offers a comprehensive review of the policies and guidelines issued by the top 50 universities in the United States regarding the use of generative artificial intelligence (GenAI) in higher education. The results revealed four major thematic areas: integration of GenAI into learning and assessment, use of GenAI in visual and multimodal media, ethical and security considerations, and preservation of academic integrity. All of these reflect a growing recognition of the pedagogical potential of these technologies, but also a persistent concern about their ethical implications, such as privacy, algorithmic bias, and plagiarism. Sentiment analysis showed a broadly positive attitude toward GenAI among institutions, especially in documents addressed to administrators and faculty, in contrast to a more cautious attitude in guidelines addressed to students and researchers. Smaller institutions were the most optimistic, while larger ones showed more nuanced positions.

On the other hand, another study conducted by Chan and Hu (2023) rigorously examines university students' perceptions, attitudes, expected benefits, and concerns regarding the use of GenAI, specifically tools such as ChatGPT, in higher education contexts and found a predominantly positive attitude toward these technologies, although tempered by ethical, pedagogical, and social concerns. Students identify as key benefits of GenAI its ability to provide personalized learning support, immediate feedback on academic writing, support for idea generation and information analysis, as well as for the creation of visual and administrative content. Its usefulness for self-learning and as an auxiliary tool in future professional and teaching scenarios is also highlighted.

Consequently, the incorporation of generative artificial intelligence (GenAI) into higher education has generated a turning point in the way we conceive teaching and learning processes. In this context, the "Manifesto for Teaching and Learning in Times of Generative AI" (Bozkurt et al., 2024) stands as an ethical, critical, and collective declaration in the face of the radical transformation that the emergence of these technologies represents in contemporary education. This reading seeks to explore the fundamental postulates of the manifesto, understand its implications within the framework of a humanistic and technologically informed pedagogy, and propose a comprehensive reflection from the philosophical, epistemic, and socio-educational horizons.

GenAI, in its rapid rise, promises to streamline tasks, personalize learning paths, and automate assessment. However, these technical promises are intertwined with complex ethical, epistemological, and cultural issues. The manifesto does not deny the virtues of these tools, but rather encourages their conscious and situated use, where technology does not replace but rather complements human agency. The position adopted by its authors is clear: constant epistemic and ethical vigilance is required to navigate the dilemmas that emerge from human-machine interaction in educational settings.

One of the first calls the manifesto makes is for the preservation of human agency. In a world where algorithms can suggest, decide, and even create content, what place is left for the educator's critical judgment? How is pedagogical authority redefined when students turn to intelligent systems to solve complex tasks? These questions, far from being merely technical, open a vein of analysis on the very meaning of education. Faced with this dilemma, the manifesto proposes strengthening teacher training in critical digital competencies, understood as the ability to understand, question, and transform the algorithmic logic that underlies our daily practices.

The text also warns against the temptation to fall into a technology of substitution. That is, a technology that replaces the educator, that completely automates assessment, that standardizes learning paths. In the face of this trend, the manifesto advocates for an augmentation technology, one that enhances human capabilities, that allows for new forms of expression, creativity, and collaboration. Learning, as an eminently human process, cannot be reduced to a series of computational inputs and outputs; it requires empathy, context, error, and intuition—elements that can hardly be codified by a machine.

Equity is another pillar of the manifesto. Digital divides are not only technical, but also social, economic, and geopolitical. Unequal access to GenAI can amplify existing inequalities in educational systems. In this sense, a technology policy committed to social justice is required, guaranteeing access, but also understanding and meaningful appropriation of these tools. Digital literacy should not be limited to instrumental use but should extend toward a critical and liberating literacy.

The manifesto is also a call to collective action. It is not enough for a few teachers, in isolation, to integrate GenAI into their classrooms. A systemic, institutional, and interdisciplinary transformation is required. Universities must rethink their curricula, their ethical frameworks, their assessment strategies, and their pedagogical methodologies. But this task cannot be accomplished without students, who must be recognized as active agents in building a more humane, more just, and more technologically aware education.

From a philosophical perspective, the manifesto invites us to rethink the relationship between technology and humanity. Heidegger already warned of the dangers of a technology that forgets its poetic roots, which becomes an end rather than a means for the unfolding of being. In this vein, GenAI cannot be understood solely as a tool, but as a form of existence that transforms our ways of thinking, knowing, and connecting. By emphasizing the need for a critical and collective stance, the manifesto aligns itself with a humanist tradition that neither fears technology nor surrenders to it.

In practical terms, the manifesto proposes concrete actions: forming ethics committees for the adoption of GenAI, including specific modules on AI in teacher training, establishing auditing mechanisms and algorithmic transparency, and promoting interdisciplinary research that crosses pedagogical, computer science, and sociocultural knowledge. These actions, far from being mere recommendations, constitute a roadmap for building a more resilient and reflective educational ecosystem.

Finally, the manifesto is also an act of hope. In times where automation seems unavoidable, where standardization threatens to stifle singularity, the manifesto reminds us that education is, above all, an act of human encounter. And that in this encounter, mediated by words, silence, and the gaze, there is also room for a technology that doesn't dominate, but accompanies; that doesn't dictate, but suggests; that doesn't impose, but engages in dialogue.

With this manifesto, Bozkurt et al. (2024) offer us an ethical map to navigate the uncertain times of GenAI. But more than a map, they provide us with a compass: a guide that reminds us that, even in the age of machines that write, calculate, and teach, the center of education remains human.

However, participants also express significant concerns, such as: the accuracy of the generated content and the lack of transparency in how the models operate; the potential for privacy violations and ethical dilemmas related to automated plagiarism or authorship; the risk of student overdependence, with negative effects on the development of critical thinking, creativity, and other holistic skills; the labor implications of automation, with fears of the replacement of certain professions and an increase in the demand for digital skills; and the need for clear and up-to-date institutional policies governing the responsible use of GenAI.

For their part, Perkins et al., (2024) present the AI Assessment Scale (AIAS), an innovative methodological proposal for integrating GenAI into educational assessments in an ethical, clear, and pedagogically sound manner. This framework arises in response to the growing use of tools such as ChatGPT in higher education and the debate about their impact on academic integrity, meaningful learning, and curriculum design. The AIAS builds on the need to avoid binary approaches (allowing or prohibiting the use of AI) and instead proposes a five-level scale of integration:

- Without AI: The student cannot use any GenAI tools.
- AI for ideas and structure: AI is allowed to generate ideas and outlines, but not in the final product.
- AI for editing: It allows for improving the language and structure of the text but does not allow for generating new content.
- AI for human-assessed assignments: AI may be used in parts of the assignment, but the student must critically analyze and evaluate its use.

- Full AI: GenAI is allowed to be used as a collaborator throughout the entire task, integrating its use creatively and ethically.

Each level is designed to align the use of AI with the expected learning outcomes and foster a critical and ethical understanding of the tools used in students. This approach recognizes the diversity of disciplines, teaching styles, and institutional needs, offering flexibility for adaptation. It also critically addresses the tendency to consider all use of AI as plagiarism and proposes redefining academic integrity in the digital age, shifting from punishment to ethical AI literacy, transparency in its use, and the development of professional-related skills. Finally, it emphasizes that the AIAS must be accompanied by clear institutional policies, complementary resources, and strategies to bridge the digital divide. The framework represents a pragmatic and ethical response to preparing students for the responsible use of AI, in line with the current and future challenges of higher education.

From another perspective, Jin et al. (2025) introduced the GLAT (Generative AI Literacy Assessment Test), an innovative, rigorous, and performance-based instrument designed to assess GenAI literacy in higher education contexts. Unlike previous instruments, which focus on subjective self-assessments, the GLAT focuses on measuring real competencies through objective tests that explore technical knowledge, practical skills, critical evaluation, and ethical awareness in the use of GenAI. It was designed based on a conceptual framework that integrates four fundamental dimensions:

Know and understand (key concepts such as foundational models, model alignment, or zero-shot learning).

Use and apply (multimodal content generation, token management, information synthesis).

Evaluate and create (authenticity, hallucinations, cross-checking, reliability of outputs).

Ethics (biases, black box, copyright and privacy).

The study emphasizes that adequately measuring GenAI literacy is essential in today's educational environment, given that students often overestimate their abilities and lack critical skills for interacting with tools such as ChatGPT, Gemini, or Claude. The GLAT represents a valuable diagnostic tool for designing personalized pedagogical interventions and fostering comprehensive AI literacy, encompassing technical, practical, and ethical aspects. The authors conclude that it not only assesses students' current proficiency level but also serves as a basis for improving higher education training programs, preparing them for a future driven by artificial intelligence. They also recommend its periodic updating to remain relevant in the face of the rapid advancement of generative technologies.

DISCUSSION

Challenges of Educational Assessment in the era of Generative AI (GenAI)

Throughout the text, the importance of assessment as an important component in the educational process is mentioned, however, Kadel et al. (2024) describes the contemporary challenges of assessment design in the face of the emergence of generative AI (GenAI), the integration of GenAI in educational contexts has profoundly disrupted traditional assessment methodologies. The main emerging challenges are maintaining academic integrity, ensuring meaningful learning, and developing competencies on the ethical and effective use of digital tools. And, two main categories are proposed:

1. Learning-based assessments: focused on conceptual understanding, problematization, and initial use of GenAI.
2. Action-based assessments: aimed at applying knowledge and skills in real-life scenarios, making strategic use of them.

Regarding the ethical and transparent use of GenAI in assessments, the need to explicitly declare the level of use (prohibited, assisted, or comprehensive), design activities that require critical discernment about the quality, reliability, and limits of AI-generated outputs, and ensure that students cannot complete the task using GenAI alone, without applying their own knowledge, is emphasized. Similarly, tailored assessment strategies propose a dual approach to assessment, such as traditional methods for learning-centered assessments and automated assessment (including formative feedback) in action-based contexts using specific or ad hoc AI tools.

Based on this, a comprehensive methodological proposal is made to redesign the evaluation and a five-step model for redesigning evaluations is established:

- Define the type of assessment (learning or action).
- Set the permitted use of GenAI.
- Apply authentic design principles.
- Validate assessments against GenAI to ensure their effectiveness and pedagogical relevance.
- Clearly communicate expectations to students and teachers.

This entails conceptualizing and rethinking assessment methods, instruments, tools, and criteria to ensure the validity and reliability of the assessment. While AI is a tool that facilitates tasks, problem-solving, and project development carried out by students, which could call into question learning, care must be taken to assess the acquired knowledge. The integration of AI, which requires reflection on the processes, competencies, and skills to be assessed, implies improving the training process and includes establishing criteria to avoid academic plagiarism. In this regard, Copado (2024) advises that, to avoid this practice, the sources of information consulted must be correctly detailed, demonstrating the quality and reliability of the information presented.

It is worth noting that AI-generated content poses ethical and quality challenges, as the proliferation of "slop" (low-quality synthetic content) in digital environments demands new critical and ethical skills from students to differentiate valid information from that which is not (Furze, 2024). For this reason, Liu et al. (2024) indicate that AI should be considered a pedagogical collaborator, not a mere technical resource, and therefore, a transformation of the teaching approach is recommended, moving from surveillance and prohibition to pedagogical design, integrating AI as a tool for co-creation, critique, feedback, and analysis. While the integration of AI requires clear regulatory and policy frameworks, the absence of coherent national policies around AI in education can accentuate inequalities and fragment the education system. The need for frameworks such as the Australian Framework for Generative AI in Schools is raised (Valeri, 2024).

Certainly, the humanistic approach must prevail in the educational digital transformation, since human connection, ethical judgment, empathy and social interaction remain irreplaceable, so AI must complement and not replace these essential aspects of learning (Callanan & Rangelov, 2024). Learning in the AI era requires new skills, among which critical digital literacy, self-regulation, collaboration with non-human agents and understanding, ethics of algorithmic systems (Esterman, 2024). This suggests that the challenges of generative AI in educational assessment are oriented towards technological dependence and implies the necessary use to carry out activities and tasks, which undermines the development of thinking skills, since AI, by facilitating instant responses and automating information processing, can decrease motivation, intellectual effort and autonomous exploration, the development of critical thinking and problem-solving skills (L. O. Fernández et al., 2023).

Regarding this idea, Puche (2024) states that technological dependence impacts self-directed learning, the development of analytical and reflective skills that are essential for the comprehensive training of students, and that is why AI must be implemented with caution, ensuring that its use does not compromise the development of fundamental competencies. In addition to impacting the development of critical thinking, it can also impact creativity, inclusion, and authenticity. According to Wexell Machado and Canese (2024), the aim is to promote inclusive and adaptive teaching that respects cultural and linguistic diversity, delving into the ethical implications of AI in education, with an emphasis on the authenticity and intellectual property of the content generated, as well as the promotion of equity in the creation of educational meaning.

Therefore, the incorporation of AI has implications for the authenticity of learning, S. C. Ordoñez et al. (2024) propose that the decrease in the effort to understand and critically analyze information represents a major challenge for education, which has sought to foster fundamental skills for meaningful learning and personal development. Some studies suggest that it can decrease students' participation in their education and limit the development of critical thinking and problem-solving skills. However, Alpizar Garrido and Martínez Ruiz (2024) suggest that when AI analyzes data and learning patterns, it identifies areas of strength and weakness, offers feedback and resources to maximize academic progress, which improves academic performance, intrinsic motivation, and engagement, hoping that it does not translate into excessive dependence on technology or a reduction of human interaction in the educational process (Aparicio-Gómez & Cortés Gallego, 2024).

Now, the use of technology is inevitable, and contrary to previous positions, Serrano and Moreno (2024) propose creating opportunities to think critically about the information obtained. Being creative or critical requires having knowledge based on validated information. Students will not be able to question the content generated by AI if they do not master it first. Among the challenges are security, privacy, and data use. It is known that AI works through the collection and analysis of data. This data can include personal information, study habits, online interactions, and academic performance. However, the handling of this data raises ethical questions about the privacy and protection of student information (Sánchez, 2025) so that it is used ethically.

However, AI systems must be subject to constant ethical oversight to avoid algorithmic biases and ensure that educational decisions are not influenced by irrelevant or discriminatory variables. It is essential to implement strategies to identify and correct these biases, thus ensuring fairness and impartiality in the application of algorithms (Aparicio-Gómez & Cortés Gallego, 2024). On the other hand, despite the challenges, generative AI also offers several significant benefits for educational assessment. Furthermore, AI can help teachers identify patterns and trends in student performance that might go unnoticed in traditional assessments. By analyzing student behavior, AI systems can alert educators to potential problems before they become significant barriers to learning. This allows for earlier and more effective intervention, improving educational outcomes (R. Romero, 2024).

As generative AI continues to evolve and become more firmly integrated into academic life, research will focus on key aspects. One of these is developing regulatory frameworks for the use of AI in education and the development of academic and research output, ensuring copyright, privacy, certainty, and transparency in the use of information. Regarding the use of AI in teaching, its use will be supported by an educational intent, theoretical and methodological foundations of didactics and pedagogy to generate activities, projects, and assessment tools. It is important to investigate how AI truly impacts learning, and not just the development of digital skills. It is also necessary to incorporate an assessment process that provides an opportunity to rethink assessment.

On the other hand, Yan et al. (2024) emphasizes the ethical challenges, highlighting three main aspects:

1. Transparency, as most studies are understandable only to AI specialists, without adequately involving teachers or students in the development or evaluation.
2. Privacy, due to the significant lack of informed consent and data protection when using student-generated texts to train or test models.
3. Equity and Beneficence shows that tools based on large-scale language models (LLMs) are often English-centric and require expensive infrastructure, which can widen regional gaps and limit access. Furthermore, there is a risk of algorithmic biases that perpetuate stereotypes and unfair decisions if not properly controlled.

From another perspective, Educ.ar S.E. (2024) presents a further challenge: empowering teachers in the conscious, ethical, and creative use of AI to enrich the teaching-learning process. It emphasizes that the incorporation of ChatGPT is not intended to replace teachers, but rather to enhance their role through the automation of administrative tasks, the personalization of learning, the creation of educational content, the design of differentiated activities, and the promotion of student creativity. AI is presented as a pedagogical resource that streamlines teaching practice, always under criteria of privacy, inclusion, and equity. On the pedagogical level, the document proposes multiple uses of ChatGPT in institutional management and school planning: from creating meeting agendas and writing performance reports to preparing support materials and communicating with families.

In addition, it shows how AI can assist in classroom management, monitoring student progress, and organizing teaching resources. All of this is exemplified through specific prompts, facilitating their replicability in different educational contexts. Another central focus is the didactic and disciplinary use of ChatGPT. The manual proposes concrete strategies for personalizing learning, adapting materials, conducting formative assessments, and designing interdisciplinary activities. In language teaching, for example, ChatGPT is suggested for generating dialogues, correcting essays, conducting role-playing games, or conducting listening comprehension activities. In arts and literature, students are encouraged to use AI to develop characters, create plots, write dialogues, and receive immediate feedback. Thus, the text dedicates a chapter to the development of socio-community projects, proposing ChatGPT as a tool for designing educational materials relevant to specific contexts, thus promoting inclusion and community participation.

And, on the ethical and normative level, Ferrarelli (2024) addresses in depth topics such as student data privacy, informed consent, algorithmic bias, and the need for critical literacy in AI. Good practices are proposed to ensure responsible use of technology, including data anonymization, ongoing teacher training, and the design of school policies that regulate its use. Finally, it is highlighted that the key to a successful incorporation of generative AI lies in the professional judgment of the teacher, who must discern when and how to use technology in a contextualized, student-centered, and comprehensive development-oriented manner (García, 2024).

AI-mediated Evaluation Models and Approaches

The evolution of educational assessment systems has found in generative artificial intelligence (GAI) an opportunity to reconceptualize assessment practices from an algorithmic, adaptive, and automated perspective. One of the most significant models is AI-based Adaptive Testing (ABAT), which dynamically adjusts item difficulty based on student performance in real time. This approach allows for personalized assessment experience, reducing bias and increasing diagnostic accuracy (Ifenthaler et al., 2024). Another emerging model is AI-based e-proctoring, which incorporates facial recognition techniques, eye tracking, and behavioral pattern analysis to ensure academic integrity during remote testing. However, its implementation has generated debates around privacy, surveillance, and algorithmic discrimination (Luckin et al., 2024).

On the other hand, the field of Learning Analytics has been integrated with formative assessment through the analysis of large volumes of data on student behavior and performance on digital platforms. These analyses allow for the generation of personalized reports, the identification of intervention points, and the design of differentiated learning paths. Spector and Yuen (2016) argue that these approaches contribute to the consolidation of assessment based on objective evidence, although he warns of the risks of overinterpreting data without considering the contextual, cultural, and affective variables of the student. In short, AI-mediated assessment models must be critically assessed in light of their effectiveness, but also their pedagogical and ethical legitimacy.

International Case Studies

Several higher education institutions have implemented innovative policies and strategies to integrate generative artificial intelligence into their assessment systems. The University of Sydney, Australia, has developed a regulatory framework that classifies AI uses in academic tasks according to their level of intervention and proposes authentic assessment strategies that minimize algorithmic plagiarism. In Canada, the University of British Columbia promotes academic authorship practices by designing reflective activities where students must justify their creative processes, including the use of tools such as ChatGPT. This aligns with broader Organisation for Economic Co-operation and Development (OECD) discussions on the governance of generative AI in education (OECD, 2023) and evolving skill demands in Canada (Green, 2024).

In Finland, one of the most recognized education systems worldwide, AI-based simulated scenario assessment environments have been piloted, especially in teacher training. These environments allow future educators to interact with virtual agents that simulate real-life classroom situations, assessing not only theoretical knowledge but also socio-emotional skills, such as conflict management or ethical decision-making (Green, 2024). These case studies highlight the diversity of institutional approaches and the need for contextualized adaptation of AI in assessment practices, avoiding universal or standardized solutions that may ignore cultural and educational specificities.

Proposal of Indicators for Evaluation with Generative AI

To establish control and improvement mechanisms for generative AI-mediated assessment, a framework of pedagogical and ethical indicators is proposed to assess the quality of these processes. First, transparency in generative processes must be a fundamental principle, ensuring that students understand how the data that feeds the algorithms is generated, stored, and used. Likewise, inclusiveness must be guaranteed in the access and design of assessment tools, avoiding technological, language, or cognitive barriers (Puche, 2024).

The indicators should also consider criteria for the validity and reliability of digital instruments, assessing their ability to measure what is intended and their stability across different application contexts. Furthermore, it is necessary to incorporate metrics on the fairness of the assessment, that is, ensuring that the results are not influenced by algorithmic biases related to gender, ethnicity, or socioeconomic status. Finally, it is proposed to evaluate the quality of interactions between the student and the AI, considering factors such as the relevance of feedback, the adaptability of tasks, and the system's ability to promote critical thinking and metacognitive reflection (UNESCO, 2024).

Implications for Teacher Training in Critical Digital Assessment

The transformation of assessment models in AI-mediated contexts requires a profound reconfiguration of teacher training. It is essential for teachers to develop digital assessment skills, understood as the ability to design, implement, and evaluate assessment practices with technological support. These skills include platform management, the design of automated rubrics, and the interpretation of data from AI systems (Green, 2024).

Another key aspect is ethical literacy in AI, which involves understanding the risks, dilemmas, and responsibilities associated with the use of algorithmic technologies in the classroom. Pedagogical self-regulation becomes an essential competence for discerning when, how, and for what purpose to use generative tools. In this sense, García (2024) proposes a teacher training model based on the integration of algorithmic ethics, adaptive instructional design, and interdisciplinary collaboration. This holistic vision of teacher training seeks to empower teachers as transformative agents, capable of leading critical, creative, and student-centered evaluation processes in the era of artificial intelligence.

FUTURE RESEARCH DIRECTIONS

Given the structural changes brought about by the integration of generative artificial intelligence into assessment processes, there is a growing need to establish a robust research agenda. Below, we outline several future lines of study that will allow us to deepen, validate, and expand current findings, with a view to consolidating ethical, methodological, and pedagogical frameworks that guarantee inclusive, equitable, and contextualized assessment:

- Ethics of automated assessment mediated by generative artificial intelligence (GAI).
- Validity and reliability of the assessments generated or provided by IAG.
- Design of hybrid formative and summative assessment models supported by AI.
- Transformations in authorship, academic integrity, and the assessment of critical competencies.
- Digital teaching skills for assessment with generative AI.

- Diagnosis and training of the necessary skills in teachers to assess in contexts mediated by IAG.
- Design of instruments to measure literacy in critical digital assessment.
- Public policies and regulatory frameworks for regulating AI assessment in educational systems.
- Assessment of socio-emotional and ethical competencies through generative environments.
- Exploring the potential of generative AI to model simulated scenarios that assess soft skills.
- Psychoeducational impact of the use of generative AI in evaluative contexts.
- Neuroeducational studies that analyze cognitive processing in tasks solved with and without IAG assistance.

Evaluation as a Sociotechnical Phenomenon in the Digital age

In the contemporary context, educational assessment cannot be understood solely as a technical tool for measuring learning, but as a sociotechnical phenomenon deeply influenced by power dynamics, institutional interests, and epistemic frameworks. From the perspective of the sociology of technology, the incorporation of algorithmic systems into school assessment constitutes a reconfiguration of the ways in which knowledge is produced, validated, and distributed.

Critical pedagogy, for its part, proposes the need to understand assessment as a cultural and political practice that contributes to the reproduction or transformation of social structures. McLaren (2023) argue that every form of assessment implies a vision of knowledge, of the learner, and of the educational ideal that is intended to be formed. In this sense, generative AI systems incorporate assumptions about what should be learned, how it should be measured, and what outcomes are considered legitimate, all of which require epistemological vigilance on the part of the educational community.

The concept of 'algorithmic assessment' has emerged in recent years to describe the use of automated systems in pedagogical decision-making. Williamson (2017) argues that these systems operate as black boxes, rendering assessment criteria invisible and hindering accountability. This can have negative effects on student agency, the pedagogical relationship, and trust in assessment processes. Therefore, a critical appropriation of AI is required, allowing for the development of fair, transparent, and pedagogically meaningful assessment processes. Assessment in the age of AI must not only be accurate and efficient, but also democratic, contextualized, and emancipatory.

AI evaluation from a Decolonial and Feminist Perspective

The emergence of artificial intelligence in educational and assessment systems has been accompanied by a technocratic enthusiasm that often ignores the epistemological, cultural, and ethical implications of these technologies. From a decolonial perspective, automated assessment using AI can reproduce logics of exclusion and subordination that have historically affected marginalized communities.

In the feminist field, studies have shown how AI systems reflect and amplify gender inequalities, there is a risk of homogenizing criteria, rendering situated educational experiences invisible, and reducing the complexity of learning to quantifiable metrics. From this perspective, a "feminist AI assessment" is proposed that recognizes the diversity of learning trajectories, values emotions, care, and collaboration, and opposes the technocratic rationalization of the educational act (Toupin, 2024).

Both perspectives agree that AI should not be an instrument of cultural domestication, but rather an opportunity to democratize knowledge, as long as its implementation is based on principles of epistemic justice, cognitive pluralism, and community participation. Assessment, as an educational practice, must be reimagined as an act of dialogue, reciprocity, and collective meaning-making. In this framework, AI is not the center of the process, but rather a means at the service of transformative, situated, and critical education.

Algorithmic Inequalities and Educational Justice: Emerging Tensions in AI Assessment

One of the main ethical and political challenges surrounding assessment mediated by generative artificial intelligence (GAI) is the risk of amplifying pre-existing structural inequalities. So-called "algorithmic inequalities" arise when automated systems reproduce, legitimize, or even exacerbate social, economic, linguistic, or cultural biases. These inequalities not only affect access to digital educational resources but also how learning trajectories and academic performance are assessed.

Recent research has shown how recommendation, categorization, or scoring algorithms tend to replicate patterns of discrimination present in the data they were trained on. In educational contexts, this can translate into assessment systems that penalize non-standard dialects, ignore diverse cognitive styles, or ignore the sociocultural specificities of students. Thus, an evaluative AI model that has not been audited according to equity criteria can operate as a technology of exclusion rather than inclusion.

The concept of educational justice in the digital age therefore demands a profound review of the frameworks for the design, implementation, and regulation of assessment technologies. Instead of perpetuating hegemonic learning models, compensatory policies must be developed to ensure the contextual adaptability of algorithms. This includes: 1) algorithmic audits with student participation; 2) model training with representative and pluralistic data; 3) transparency regarding automated assessment criteria and processes; and 4) the development of multilingual, accessible, and culturally sensitive platforms.

From a critical perspective, AI assessment must be understood as a field of dispute where economic, technical, educational, and political interests are at odds. To ensure that this assessment does not become a tool for reproducing privileges, systems must be designed with a clear ethical intention, oriented toward promoting equity, inclusion, and cognitive justice. We must move from a market logic to an ecology of knowledge.

Finally, the path toward fair assessment in AI-mediated contexts cannot depend exclusively on technological development. It is essential to strengthen the political, pedagogical, and social capacities of educational institutions to engage with technical advances from a critical and transformative perspective. This entails training teachers with a digital ethical awareness, empowering school communities in the responsible use of technology, and establishing regulatory frameworks that not only regulate but also guide toward expanded educational justice. In this context, AI will not be the end, but rather a means to democratize learning and expand educational opportunities in all their diversity.

CONCLUSION

Generative AI is transforming educational assessment in ways that offer both challenges and opportunities. However, technology dependence, learning authenticity, security, information bias, and algorithms are legitimate concerns. Therefore, maximizing the positive impact of generative AI in education is of utmost importance, and it is crucial that educators, researchers, and policymakers work together to address these challenges and develop effective strategies. Furthermore, students must be provided with useful and up-to-date information for their training, as students express satisfaction with using online learning platforms and perceive that they can complete their assignments and projects quickly and easily.

Just as happens in the everyday use of AI, so does the educational field. Students apparently already use AI to solve school tasks without teachers knowing the applications or being up to par in the use of technology. This currently leads us to ask several questions, such as: What is the teacher's role in the use of technology and AI? How do we know if only tasks are solved and how is learning guaranteed? What skills should be developed or strengthened in students when faced with AI? And what happens with the ethical aspects and under this approach to the use of

AI? On the other hand, it is important to consider that the student is not a passive processor of information; on the contrary, they are active and conscious processors of the mediated information presented to them. Their attitudes and cognitive abilities will determine the possible cognitive, effective, or psychomotor influence of the environment.

Although access to AI is closer than we can imagine, it is a complex task that requires a series of competencies, skills, values, and attitudes to consider it as a tool that will strengthen, not limit, other skills, values, and attitudes such as reasoning, research, learning, ethics, etc. Furthermore, it is important to consider the challenges associated with the use of artificial intelligence in the creation of immersive learning environments. These challenges include the need for adequate technological infrastructure, teacher training in the use of educational technology, and ethics. Additionally, it is essential to address the state of access to technology and education to ensure a fair and effective integration. It can be deduced that artificial intelligence has the potential to contribute to the evolution of higher education by offering more personalized, adaptive, and effective learning experiences. To maximize these benefits, it is crucial to address the challenges involved in implementing AI in education, ensuring adequate investment in infrastructure and training, as well as regulations that promote equity and protect data.

Thus, throughout the chapter, it was evident that the incorporation of AI-based technologies into assessment processes is neither a neutral nor linear phenomenon. Indeed, generative AI alters traditional dynamics between teachers and students, redefines the role of content, introduces new forms of pedagogical interaction, and raises substantive questions about authorship, academic integrity, and learning autonomy. In this regard, the analysis revealed that educational institutions are called upon not only to incorporate technological tools but also to generate critical learning ecosystems that problematize their use, stimulate ethical thinking, and promote subject-centered assessment practices. Thus, the urgent need to promote artificial intelligence literacy that transcends technical training to embrace an ethical, pedagogical, and critical understanding is recognized.

In a different vein, the chapter analyzes in particular detail the role of generative AI as a catalyst for the redesign of assessment models. Tools such as the AI Assessment Scale (AIAS) and the Generative AI Literacy Assessment Test (GLAT) are presented as innovative methodological proposals that allow for the ethical and gradual integration of AI into assessment contexts. These scales overcome binary approaches (permitted or prohibited use) and favor a critical and gradual transition toward AI-powered assessment, considering levels of complexity, pedagogical purposes, authenticity criteria, and expected competencies. This implies that assessment is not reduced to a final product, but rather encompasses the process, design, interaction, and critical reflection on the use of the technology itself.

In addition to the above, it is important to highlight that the analysis undertaken refers to an understanding of assessment as a social, political, and cultural construction. This implies recognizing the structural inequalities that can be exacerbated by the uncritical incorporation of technologies, such as the digital divide, lack of infrastructure, language barriers, algorithmic biases, and the exclusion of underrepresented voices. Thus, the text urges ensuring assessment with an inclusive approach, which considers the cultural, linguistic, cognitive, and territorial diversity of students. Generative AI cannot become a tool for reproducing privileges, but rather an instrument for democratizing knowledge, when its implementation is critical, contextualized, and regulated.

Likewise, the ethical dimension of AI-based assessment was strongly highlighted. Automated content generation, mass data collection, and the use of opaque models pose a series of dilemmas that cannot be ignored. The privacy of student data, informed consent, intellectual property, automated plagiarism, algorithmic transparency, and accountability are all aspects that require a rigorous regulatory approach. Therefore, it is considered essential to have robust, participatory, and up-to-date regulatory frameworks that guide the responsible, fair, and safe use of AI in assessment contexts. In this regard, European legislation, the Australian framework, and Ibero-American proposals offer valuable references for the design of comprehensive educational policies.

No less important is the consideration of the humanistic approach in educational assessment with AI. While technology can optimize processes, expand opportunities, and facilitate early interventions, it does not replace ethical judgment, empathy, affective mediation, and the relational dimension of the educational process. Therefore, AI assessment must serve the holistic development of students, promoting not only technical knowledge and skills, but also socioemotional, ethical, and civic competencies. This requires articulating AI with student-centered methodologies such as project-based learning, critical thinking, collaborative learning, and critical pedagogy, where assessment becomes an opportunity to develop autonomous, reflective individuals committed to their reality.

Throughout the chapter, future lines of research are outlined that open a promising horizon for the study of assessment in the era of generative AI. These lines include, among others: the analysis of the ethics of automated assessment; the design of hybrid assessment models; the validity and reliability of AI-generated instruments; the transformation of academic authorship; critical literacy in digital assessment; and the assessment of soft skills through simulated environments. In this way, a research itinerary is proposed that articulates the production of scientific knowledge with the resolution of specific educational problems, in tune with the values of equity, sustainability, inclusion, and social justice.

Therefore, it is concluded that educational assessment in the era of generative artificial intelligence cannot be approached from a technocratic or reductionist perspective. A paradigmatic transformation is required that begins with the recognition of the changing times, embraces the complexity of the phenomenon, and guides the design of relevant, ethical, and meaningful assessment practices. AI is not an end, but rather a means that, if properly managed, can contribute to a more equitable, contextualized, personalized, and transformative education. However, if implemented uncritically, it can reproduce inequalities, erode academic autonomy, and distort teaching-learning processes. Therefore, the call is to build a humanized assessment in the digital age, where artificial intelligence complements, enhances, and enriches, not replaces, pedagogical work.

It is worth noting that the incorporation of generative artificial intelligence (GAI) into educational assessment does not simply constitute a methodological shift, but a paradigmatic transformation that challenges the very essence of pedagogical work. Assessment, traditionally understood as an instrument for measuring results, must now be reimagined as a complex, dialogical, and ethical process, in which technological mediation, educational justice, and student agency converge. This new paradigm entails shifting from grading-centered assessment models to learning ecologies where feedback, critical reflection, and the personalization of the learning process take center stage. In this sense, assessment with generative AI cannot be separated from the principles of algorithmic justice. It is essential to ensure that systems are auditable, inclusive, and bias-free, and that their operation is understandable for teachers and students. This requires not only the technical design of ethical algorithms but also the construction of an educational culture where the use of AI is subject to analysis, discussion, and collective decision-making. Likewise, assessment should foster critical digital literacy and digital citizenship, preparing students not only to use technological tools but also to understand their ethical, social, and political implications.

In the future, a scenario is envisioned in which AI coexists with transformative pedagogical methodologies, such as project-based learning, design thinking, and critical pedagogy. In this context, assessment becomes an act of emancipation and co-responsibility, recognizing the student as an active subject in the construction of knowledge. AI, far from replacing teaching, can act as a catalyst for more humane, meaningful, and equitable learning experiences, provided it is guided by clear regulatory frameworks, solid teacher training, and the active participation of the entire educational community. It concludes that assessment with generative AI opens a horizon of possibilities, but also confronts us with ethical, pedagogical, and political challenges that must be addressed in depth. This chapter has sought to lay the foundations for a comprehensive and purposeful reflection on the topic, in the conviction that only a humanized, critical, and transformative assessment will rise to the challenges of the present and future of education.

ACKNOWLEDGMENT

This research was supported by the Instituto Politécnico Nacional, México [SIP number 20253702; 20253876; 20250531].

REFERENCES

Alpizar Garrido, L. O., & Martínez Ruiz, H. (2024). Perspectiva de estudiantes de nivel medio superior respecto al uso de la inteligencia artificial generativa en su aprendizaje. *RIDE Revista Iberoamericana para la Investigación y el Desarrollo Educativo*, *14*(28). Advance online publication. DOI: 10.23913/ride.v14i28.1830

Alvarado, J. E. M., & Cuzco, C. I. U. (2025). Inteligencia artificial en la creación de entornos de aprendizaje inmersivos en la educación superior. Revisión sistemática. *RECIMUNDO, 9*(1), 220-237. https://doi.org/.(1).ene.2024.348-356DOI: 10.26820/reciamuc/8

An, Y., Yu, J. H., & James, S. (2025). Investigating the higher education institutions' guidelines and policies regarding the use of generative AI in teaching, learning, research, and administration. *International Journal of Educational Technology in Higher Education*, *22*(10), 10. Advance online publication. DOI: 10.1186/s41239-025-00507-3

Aparicio-Gómez, O.-Y., & Cortés Gallego, M. A. (2024). Desafíos éticos de la Inteligencia Artificial en la personalización del aprendizaje. *Revista Interamericana de Investigación Educación y Pedagogía RIIEP*, *17*(2), 377–392. DOI: 10.15332/25005421.10000

Araujo, G. J., Guerra, L. R., Bastidas, V. G., Diaz, C. F., & Planta, J. P. (2024). *Educación y tecnología digital.* CID - Centro de Investigación y Desarrollo. DOI: 10.37811/cli_w1041

Bozkurt, A., Xiao, J., Farrow, R., Bai, J. Y. H., Nerantzi, C., Moore, S., Dron, J., Stracke, C. M., Singh, L., Crompton, H., Koutropoulos, A., Terentev, E., Pazurek, A., Nichols, M., Sidorkin, A. M., Costello, E., Watson, S., Mulligan, D., Honeychurch, S., & Asino, T. I. (2024). The Manifesto for Teaching and Learning in a Time of Generative AI: A Critical Collective Stance to Better Navigate the Future. *Open Praxis*, *16*(4), 487–513. DOI: 10.55982/openpraxis.16.4.777

Callanan, L., & Rangelov, M. (Eds.). (2024). AI in Education. *TLN Journal, 31*(2), Winter 2024. Teacher Learning Network. https://tln.org.au/Web/Web/TLN-Journals/TLN%20Journal-Back-Catalogue.aspx

Chan, C. K. Y., & Hu, W. (2023). Students' voices on generative AI: Perceptions, benefits, and challenges in higher education. *International Journal of Educational Technology in Higher Education*, *20*(43), 43. Advance online publication. DOI: 10.1186/s41239-023-00411-8

Cisneros Vásquez, E. D., Nevárez Loza, R. F., Farez Cherrez, A. M., & Torres Montes, R. E. (2024). Uso de la inteligencia artificial en la personalización del aprendizaje. *Conocimiento global, 9*(1), 75-83. https://doi.org/DOI: 10.70165/cglobal.v9i1.339

Copado, A. E. (2024). Inteligencia artificial en la prevención del plagio académico y evaluación del aprendizaje. *Revista Senderos Pedagógicos*, *15*(1), 139–151. DOI: 10.53995/rsp.v15i1.1372

Educ.ar. S. E. (2024). *Cómo incorporar IA generativa al aula: Una orientación en ChatGPT para docentes* (1.ª ed.). Ciudad Autónoma de Buenos Aires: Educ.ar, S.E.

Espinoza, E. E. (2022). La evaluación de los aprendizajes. *Conrado, 18*(85), 120-127. https://conrado.ucf.edu.cu/index.php/conrado/article/view/2267

Esterman, M. (2024). The robots have arrived – what's next? In L. Callanan & M. Rangelov (Eds.), *AI in Education,* TLN Journal, 31(2). Teacher Learning Network. https://tln.org.au/Web/Web/TLN-Journals/TLN%20Journal-Back-Catalogue.aspx

European Parliament & Council of the European Union. (2024). *Regulation (EU) 2024/2847 of the European Parliament and of the Council. Official Journal of the European Union.* https://eur-lex.europa.eu/legal-content/EN/TXT/?uri=CELEX:32024R2847

Fernández, K. (2024). *Docencia en la era de la inteligencia artificial: Enfoques prácticos para docentes.* Universidad de Burgos. https://raeia.org/books/258-2/

Fernández, L. O., de Solar, C. Q., Hinostroza, M. B., Rodríguez, A. C., Nakata, H. M., Gutiérrez, L. C., Cadillo, E. M., Lizarraga, M. E. N., de la Cruz, J. B., Gastelú, J. V., Baigorria, A. S., & Marquez, Z. Q. (2023). Estilos De Aprendizaje y Rendimiento Académico en Estudiantes Ingresantes de las Cinco Áreas de las Carreras Profesionales de una Universidad Pública Peruana. In *Ciencias humanas: Perspectivas teóricas y fundamentos epistemológicos* (pp. 11–26). Atena Editora., DOI: 10.22533/at.ed.1862321062

Ferrarelli, M. (2024). *Inteligencia artificial y educación: Insumos para su abordaje desde Iberoamérica.* Organización de Estados Iberoamericanos para la Educación, la Ciencia y la Cultura (OEI).

Flores, E. F., & Borges, G. C. (2024). Concepciones de evaluación del aprendizaje. Un análisis para la transformación de las prácticas evaluativas. *Revista Panamericana de Pedagogía*, (37), 10–24. DOI: 10.21555/rpp.vi37.2796

Flores Contrera, C. J. (2024). La evaluación educativa en la era de la inteligencia artificial; cambios de paradigmas. *LATAM: Revista latinoamericana de Ciencias Sociales y Humanidades, 5*(1), 1579-1591. https://doi.org/DOI: 10.56712/latam.v5i1.1694

Furze, L. (2024). Digital plastic in education: Understanding the implications of synthetic media. In L. Callanan & M. Rangelov (Eds.), *AI in Education,* TLN Journal, 31(2). Teacher Learning Network. https://tln.org.au/Web/Web/TLN-Journals/TLN%20Journal-Back-Catalogue.aspx

García, G. (2024). La evaluación como herramienta para mejorar los aprendizajes: La retroalimentación y la evaluación auténtica. *Revista Latinoamericana Ogmios, 4*(9), 17–32. DOI: 10.53595/rlo.v4.i9.091

Government of Spain. (2024). *Artificial Intelligence Strategy 2024.* Ministerio para la Transformación Digital y de la Función Pública. https://transparencia.gob.es/transparencia/transparencia_Home/index/MasInformacion/Informes-de-interes/Ciencia_y_tecnologia/EstrategiaIA24.html

Green, A. (2024). *Artificial intelligence and the changing demand for skills in Canada: The increasing importance of social skills. OECD Artificial Intelligence Papers, No. 17.* OECD Publishing., DOI: 10.1787/1b20cdb6-

Guárdia Ortiz, L., Bekerman, Z., Zapata Ros, M., Perkins, M., Furze, L., Roe, J., & MacVaugh, J. (2024). The AI Assessment Scale (AIAS): A framework for ethical integration of generative AI in educational assessment. *Journal of University Teaching & Learning Practice, 21*(6), 1–18. DOI: 10.53761/q3azde36

Heggart, K. (2024). Are the robots coming for our jobs? In L. Callanan & M. Rangelov (Eds.), *AI in Education,* TLN Journal, 31(2). Teacher Learning Network. https://tln.org.au/Web/Web/TLN-Journals/TLN%20Journal-Back-Catalogue.aspx

Ifenthaler, D., Majumdar, R., Gorissen, P., Judge, M., Mishra, S., Raffaghelli, J., & Shimada, A. (2024). Artificial intelligence in education: Implications for policymakers, researchers, and practitioners. Technology. *Knowledge and Learning, 29*(4), 1693–1710. DOI: 10.1007/s10758-024-09747-0

Jin, Y., Martinez-Maldonado, R., Gašević, D., & Yan, L. (2025). GLAT: The Generative AI Literacy Assessment Test. *Computers and Education: Artificial Intelligence, 9*, 100436. DOI: 10.1016/j.caeai.2025.100436

Kadel, R., Mishra, B. K., Shailendra, S., Abid, S., Rani, M., & Mahato, S. P. (2024). Crafting Tomorrow's Evaluations: Assessment Design Strategies in the Era of Generative AI. *2024 International Symposium on Educational Technology (ISET)*, (pp. 13-17). DOI: 10.1109/ISET61814.2024.00012

Liu, D. Y. T., Bassett, M. A., & Iacono, C. (2024). Engaging with generative AI in education: Four important mindset shifts. In L. Callanan & M. Rangelov (Eds.), *AI in Education,* TLN Journal, 31(2). Teacher Learning Network. https://tln.org.au/Web/Web/TLN-Journals/TLN%20Journal-Back-Catalogue.aspx

Luckin, R., Rudolph, J., Grünert, M., & Tan, S. (2024). Exploring the future of learning and the relationship between human intelligence and AI. An interview with Professor Rose Luckin. *Journal of Applied Learning and Teaching*, *7*(1), 346–363. DOI: 10.37074/jalt.2024.7.1.27

McLaren, P. (2023). Critical pedagogy: A look at the major concepts. In *The critical pedagogy reader* (pp. 75–97). Routledge. DOI: 10.4324/9781003286080-6

Mora-Cruz, A., Palos-Sánchez, P. R., & Murrell-Blanco, M. (2023). Plataformas de aprendizaje en línea y su impacto en la educación universitaria en el contexto del COVID-19. *Campus Virtuales*, *12*(1), 53. DOI: 10.54988/cv.2023.1.1005

Observatorio de Inteligencia Artificial en Educación Superior. (2025). *Informe OIAES#3: El impacto de la IA en planes de estudio y resultados de aprendizaje.* Observatorio de Inteligencia Artificial en Educación Superior.

Ordoñez, M. P. M., Medina, K. E. R., Morocho, M. J. G., & Paltán, E. M. P. (2024). La Evaluación como Herramienta en el Proceso Enseñanza Aprendizaje. *Ciencia Latina Revista Científica Multidisciplinar*, *8*(4), 9510–9529. DOI: 10.37811/cl_rcm.v8i4.13107

Ordoñez, S. C., Padilla, L. E., Buenaño, L. A., & Herrera, M. V. (2024). Impacto de la inteligencia artificial en la formación del docente para la educación superior. *RECIAMUC*, *8*(1), 189–195. DOI: 10.26820/reciamuc/8.(1).ene.2024.189-195

Organisation for Economic Co-operation and Development. (2023). *OECD digital education outlook 2023: Towards an effective digital education ecosystem.* OECD Publishing., DOI: 10.1787/c74f03de-

Piedra-Castro, W. I., Burbano-Buñay, E. S., Tamayo-Verdezoto, J. J., & Moreira-Alcívar, E. F. (2024). Inteligencia artificial y su incidencia en la estrategia metodológica de aprendizaje basado en investigación. *Journal of Economic and Social Science Research*, *4*(2), 178–196. DOI: 10.55813/gaea/jessr/v4/n2/106

Porras, V. D. C. A. (2024). Taxonomía de aprendizaje conectivo IA-Net: Propuesta para la enseñanza basada en inteligencia artificial y red. *Varela, 24*(67), 73–82. DOI: 10.5281/zenodo.10429359

Puche, D. J. (2024). Inteligencia Artificial como herramienta educativa: Ventajas y desventajas desde la perspectiva docente. *Areté, Revista Digital del Doctorado en Educación, 10*(especial), 85-100.

Romero, J. A. (2024). Algoritmos de IA que se utilizan para los profesores virtuales y tutores inteligentes, pasado, presente y futuro. In *Enseñanza y aprendizaje en la era digital desde la investigación y la innovación* (pp. 14–23). Octaedro.

Romero, R. (2024). *Inteligencia artificial y tutorías inteligentes: nuevas fronteras en la educación digital*. Ediciones Académicas Digitales.

Sánchez, M. (2025). ¿Autonomía en riesgo? Ética y la dependencia de la inteligencia artificial generativa en la formación médica. *Investigación en Educación Médica, 14*(53), 5–7. DOI: 10.22201/fm.20075057e.2025.53.24670

Serrano, J. L., & Moreno, J. (2024). Inteligencia artificial y personalización del aprendizaje: ¿innovación educativa o promesas recicladas? *Edutec. Revista Electrónica de Tecnología Educativa*, (89), 1–17. DOI: 10.21556/edutec.2024.89.3577

Spector, J. M., & Yuen, A. H. K. (2016). *Educational Technology Program and Project Evaluation*. Routledge., DOI: 10.4324/9781315724140

Toupin, S. (2024). Shaping feminist artificial intelligence. *New Media & Society, 26*(1), 580–595. DOI: 10.1177/14614448221150776

United Nations Educational, Scientific and Cultural Organization. (2024). *Guía para el uso de IA generativa en educación e investigación*. UNESCO. [UNESCO], DOI: 10.54675/EWZM9535

Valeri, J. (2024). The need for a national AI framework in Australian education. In L. Callanan & M. Rangelov (Eds.), AI in Action (TLN Journal, 31(2)). Teacher Learning Network.

Wexell Machado, L. E., & Canese, V. (2024). Métodos de apropiación de la inteligencia artificial en la enseñanza de idiomas y sus consideraciones éticas. *Lengua y Sociedad, 23*(2), 1021–1045. DOI: 10.15381/lengsoc.v23i2.29268

Williamson, B. (2017). Big Data in Education: The digital future of learning, policy and practice. https://doi.org/DOI: 10.4135/9781529714920

Yan, L., Sha, L., Zhao, L., Li, Y., Martinez-Maldonado, R., Chen, G., Li, X., Jin, Y., & Gašević, D. (2024). Practical and ethical challenges of large language models in education: A systematic scoping review. *British Journal of Educational Technology*, *55*(1), 90–112. DOI: 10.1111/bjet.13370

KEY TERMS AND DEFINITIONS

Artificial intelligence: A field of computer science that develops systems capable of performing tasks that, if performed by humans, would require intelligence, such as reasoning, decision-making, language comprehension, or learning (RAE, s. f.).

Assessment: A systemic process through which information about student learning and performance is collected, analyzed, and interpreted, with the aim of establishing parameters and providing feedback for decision-making processes (RAE, s. f.).

Education: A sociocultural practice aimed at the integral development of the human being through intentional teaching and learning processes that promote knowledge, autonomy, ethics, and participation in collective life (RAE, s. f.).

Ethics: A philosophical discipline and practical dimension that guides human action toward goodness, justice, and responsibility, especially relevant in technological contexts where automated decisions can affect rights, equity, and social values (RAE, s. f.).

Generative artificial intelligence: Characteristics of some artificial intelligence models that allow them to create or generate new textual, visual, audio, etc. content from large volumes of data by imitating human linguistic, semantic, or creative structures (RAE, s. f.).

Learning: A dynamic and constructive process through which individuals acquire, modify, or consolidate knowledge, skills, attitudes, and values, whether formally, informally, or non-formally (Real Academia Española [RAE], s. f.).

Skills: An integrated set of knowledge, competencies, attitudes, and values that a person mobilizes in a relevant and ethical manner to solve problems and perform effectively in diverse contexts, including the critical use of technology (RAE, s. f.).

Teaching: An intentional and structured process through which learning is facilitated, promoting the construction of knowledge, skills and values through pedagogical mediation (RAE, s. f.).

Technology: A set of knowledge, techniques, and tools designed by humans to transform their environment and facilitate tasks; in education, it involves digital media that mediate, enhance, or influence learning and assessment (RAE, s. f.).

ENDNOTE

1 This chapter is a research product funded by the Instituto Politécnico Nacional, México [SIP number 20253702; 20253876; 20250531].

Chapter 10
Enhancing Formative Assessment With AI:
Supporting Cognitive Development Through Adaptive Feedback

Wissal El Fougour
https://orcid.org/0009-0000-8637-1985
TIMS Laboratory, S2IPU, Higher Normal School of Tetouan (ENS), Abdelmalek Essaadi University (UAE), Morocco

Mohamed Erradi
TIMS Laboratory, S2IPU, Higher Normal School of Tetouan (ENS), Abdelmalek Essaadi University (UAE), Morocco

ABSTRACT

This chapter explores the integration of generative artificial intelligence (GenAI) into formative assessment and its transformative potential for personalized learning in education. It examines how AI-powered tools, particularly large language models (LLMs), can provide real-time feedback, generate adaptive assessments, and support diverse learner needs. The chapter also addresses critical challenges, including algorithmic bias, hallucination, and over-reliance on AI, which may compromise fairness, critical thinking, and higher-order skills. Drawing from recent research and practical frameworks, it proposes strategies for ethical and effective AI implementation in educational settings. Emphasizing the irreplaceable role of human teachers, the chapter advocates for a balanced partnership between educators and AI to enrich learning without diminishing human agency.

DOI: 10.4018/979-8-3373-7579-3.ch010

ht © 2026, IGI Global Scientific Publishing. Copying or distributing in print or electronic forms without written permission of IGI Global Scientific Publishing is prohibited. Use of this chapter to generative artificial intelligence (AI) technologies is expressly prohibited. The publisher reserves all rights to license its use for generative AI training and machine learning model development.

INTRODUCTION

The emphasis on grades has overshadowed genuine learning within the education system. Traditional grading frameworks, long regarded as a cornerstone of academia, reduce intricate intellectual exploration to a singular letter or numerical value. Grading may place more emphasis on student comparisons than on fostering deeper comprehension, creativity, or curiosity. As one student, Claire, testified about her experience, *"I remember the first time that a grading rubric was attached to a piece of my writing.... Suddenly all the joy was taken away. I was writing for a grade. I was no longer exploring for me. I want to get that back. Will I ever get that back?"* (Olson, 2006). Her testimony echoes a simple reality: when evaluations depend on judgment, they have a tendency to deprive learning of joy and purpose.

However, the formative assessment calls into question this idea. It switches the focus from judgment to growth and from results to processes. Every instant in the educational setting adds to a student's development through formative assessment, which collects evidence of learning and uses it to deliver practical feedback. According to Klenowski (2009), Assessment for Learning (AfL) is "a component of daily practice by students, teachers, and peers that seeks, reflects upon, and responds to information from dialogue, demonstration, and observation in ways that enhance ongoing learning." These methods are consistent with AfL. Formative assessment's ongoing feedback loops turn educational institutions into places where knowledge gaps are filled in real time, enabling both teachers and students to create progress together.

However, such assessments do not function independently. It frequently coexists with conventional tests that follow the Standard Assessment Paradigm (SAP). SAP activities, like essays and multiple-choice questions, offer consistent evaluation techniques but are naturally limited. These tests simply assess a student's performance at one particular point in time; they have no consideration for how learning is dynamic and iterative (Wiliam, 2011). Additionally, conventional tests frequently give preference to abilities like manual computations and grammatical checks that are becoming more and more automated by technology. This change highlights the necessity of developing higher-order abilities that are more applicable in today's world, such critical thinking and problem-solving (Shaffer & Kaput, 1998). According to Saltman (2020), standardized and transmission-based methods equip students to work in a neoliberal labor market that rewards efficiency, measurement of performance, and surveillance. In this system, pupils' learning is constantly monitored and controlled, in a manner that is akin to the incessant measurement of employee work in a business setup. Such a system is likely to socialize learners to conform to set standards, pursue concrete results, and obey orders.

Nonetheless, Saltman argues that such a method tends to disregard the nurturing of crucial competencies such as self-regulation, creativity, and critical thinking. One of the shortcomings of current systems of education is that they fail to cater to each learner in a personalized manner, especially in large classrooms. In such a setup, educators face challenges in varying their instructional methods to meet diverse comprehension levels in a learning setup, ending up in a failure to meet each learner's unique learning needs. Such a problem is compounded when one looks at applying the theory of the Zone of Proximal Development (ZPD) of Vygotsky (1978), in that it highlights the need for personalized learning that balances challenge and support in order to allow learning to take place. Logistically, challenges in managing large groups of learners often hinder teachers in providing support required for learning, resulting in disengagement or knowledge gaps among students who require differentiated support.

AI: The Solution to Overcoming the Limitations of Traditional Assessment Methods

Artificial Intelligence (AI), a computer science field, aims to replicate processes of thinking in developing programs with intelligence, problem-solving, and decision-making (Rainer et al., 2016). Underlying AI is machine learning, a technology that can allow for improvement and learning through enabling programs to learn and adapt through information processing in an unsupervised manner and enhancing performance over a duration (Acemoglu & Restrepo, 2018; Mohammad, 2020). AI comes in three forms: Artificial Narrow Intelligence (ANI), having a narrow field of operations expertise (e.g., language translation); Artificial General Intelligence (AGI), a theoretical form with capabilities for thinking in a human manner in any domain; and Artificial Super Intelligence (ASI), a theoretical development with capabilities in addition to, and even possibly exceeding, human capabilities. GPT-4 and similar big language models (LLMs) are sophisticated types of Artificial Narrow Intelligence (ANI), in that they're high-prioritized tools for a single task, such as generating an essay, answering a question, or translating language. Big language models (LLMs) have been trained over enormous datasets, and in doing so, can generate and make predictions for high accuracy and relevant background for produced text, under direction of patterns developed. Though capable of producing language that will sound thoughtful or smart, these programs don't "Understand" language in the same manner humans do. Artificial Intelligence plays a key role in supporting both students and lecturers in assessment by generating questions suited to particular learning needs, automating grading, and providing immediate feedback. Additionally, the assessment process may be made more individualized by using these tools to adapt questions' complexity and type according to each student's ability and phase of cognitive development. By doing so, AI improves assessment efficiency and accuracy, giving instructors a greater understanding of their students' development and creating a more dynamic learning environment.

Large Language Models (LLMs) have greatly improved in recent years, offering major advantages to a range of educational fields. With the development of multimodality, these models are now able to analyze and integrate visuals, sounds, and videos in addition to producing textual outputs and interpreting written input. According to Huang et al. (2020) ,this feature is especially helpful in educational tools and digital learning settings where a variety of media types are employed to provide more captivating interactions.

The ability to fine-tune is a crucial feature of large language models (LLMs), allowing general- purpose models to be tailored to specialist fields like law or medical. This procedure improves the models' vocabulary and domain-specific knowledge, which raises their accuracy and applicability in these domains (Howard & Ruder, 2018). Furthermore, LLMs are now more broadly applicable and may be customized to fit each student's particular academic requirements while also complementing their field of study.

A noteworthy aspect is that embeddings allow the creation of personalized models using proprietary data (Devlin et al., 2018). As such, an AI system learns from a student's work, such as essays, quizzes, or class notes. By processing such material, the model attains better knowledge of the student's learning style, areas of strength, and areas that need improvement. As a result, it is better equipped to provide personalized feedback, suggest particular practice material, or produce tailored questions for quizzes in line with the student's identified cognitive potential.

Moreover, plugins boost large language models (LLMs) by providing access to tools such as a computer or the internet, thus improving their capability to access up-to-date information or solve complex math problems (Vaswani et al., 2017). Also, system messages enable developers to personalize LLMs for various purposes, such as a personal tutor, coach, or evaluator, hence enabling role-specific interactions that support learning or assessment in line with set goals (Brown et al., 2020). In this regard, should a student be struggling in a course like English literature, the system would take on the role of a learning facilitator by providing in-depth analysis of literary themes, suggesting relevant readings, and posing guiding questions to foster deeper analysis. Also, it would provide timely formative assessments, such as quizzes to determine comprehension, providing instant, personalized feedback to help boost the student's analysis capability.

These innovations are revolutionizing LLM support across various industries, delivering increasingly personalized, interactive, and specialized advancements in healthcare, education, and law. They are also transforming the use of artificial intelligence in formative assessment, making it more efficient, adaptive, and responsive to individual learning needs.

In modern contexts, these assessments can be customized to align with each learner's unique needs, providing instant feedback that steers their learning process forward and facilitates effective progress tracking. This revolution equips educators to craft relevant learning experiences that enable learner advancement, Reinforcing the perspective that knowledge measurement constitutes only a minor aspect of assessments, which are fundamentally designed to support ongoing learning and continuous improvement.

Initially, machines were developed to simulate basic human capabilities, with initial systems using rule-based approaches. The next phase was characterized by the development of Natural Language Processing (NLP), which allowed machines to process and interpret human language based on set rules. In time, NLP evolved to use statistical methods and machine learning to enable machines to identify patterns in language using large datasets, thus making applications such as sentiment analysis, machine translation, and speech recognition possible. The next phase was defined by the emergence of Large Language Models (LLMs), including GPT and BERT, which are grounded in the principles of Natural Language Processing (NLP). The models use deep learning—a sub-field of machine learning—that allows human language to be processed and created on a scale never previously conceived, enabling the processing of increasingly complex challenges using more sophisticated approaches. Generative AI came next, a force to be reckoned with, going beyond mere interpretation to having the capability to produce new material in different formats such as text, pictures, audio, or video. With methods such as Generative Adversarial Networks (GANs), Generative AI produces realistic results relevant to given contexts, thus advancing artificial intelligence's creative capabilities in new ways. The progression of Natural Language Processing (NLP) to Large Language Models (LLMs) to Generative AI is in Figure 1.

Figure 1. The evolution from NLP to LLMs and Generative AI

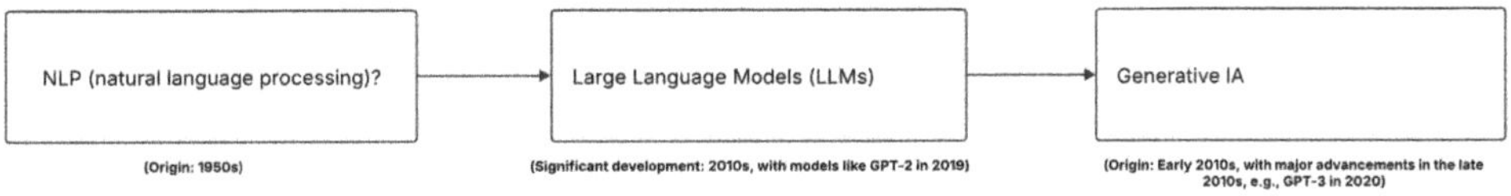

II. ADDRESSING CHALLENGES IN AI: BIAS, HALLUCINATION, AND OVERRELIANCE

1. Fairness in Every Byte: Exposing AI Bias

Educational institutions—from elementary and secondary schools to colleges and universities—must guard against hidden unfairness when integrating AI into formative assessment, even as it promises richer, more personalized insights into student learning. Because AI systems learn from vast—and inherently imperfect—datasets, they often inherit stereotypes that disadvantage students along socioeconomic, cultural, or gender lines. Zhai and Krajcik (2022) define such AI bias not as random error but as a systematic skew favoring certain outcomes; what many call "AI bias" may even be "pseudo-bias," born of misapplied technology or unrealistic expectations. To mitigate these risks—and unlock AI's pedagogical promise—tools must be built on data that truly reflects diverse learner populations. Equally important is a transparent governance process: stakeholders must agree on what constitutes unacceptable bias, establish evidence thresholds, and conduct regular fairness audits. As Guo et al. (2024) argue, embedding these practices into AI design can foster more inclusive, equitable learning experiences. Quarterly model updates, open transparency reports, and standing ethics committees will ensure that AI assessments evolve in step with our commitment to fairness.

The following table summarizes the five essential steps educational institutions should take to ensure fairness and transparency when using AI for student assessments.

Table 1. Key Strategies for Mitigating AI Bias in Formative Assessment

Step	What It Means	Why It Matters
Diverse Training Data	Include work from all cultures, languages, and learning levels	Prevents AI from learning only one "norm"
Clear Fairness Rules	Co-create a "Bias Charter" with teachers, students, experts	Everyone knows exactly what counts as unfair treatment
Regular Audits & Reports	Quarterly equity checks and simple public summaries	Detects and corrects drift before it harms students
Student Feedback Channels	Allow flags or annotations on AI-generated feedback	Empowers learners to catch mistakes and fosters trust
Continuous Retraining & Review	Feed error examples back into the model and listen to teachers	Ensures the AI evolves alongside real classroom needs

2. When AI Speaks Confidently—and Lies: Equipping Students to Spot Hallucinations

Imagine a student confidently citing an AI-generated explanation in their science homework—only to later discover that the information, while perfectly phrased and logical, is completely wrong. This alarming scenario highlights a critical issue in modern education: the phenomenon of "hallucination" in large language models like ChatGPT. These systems can produce content that sounds accurate but is, in fact, a blend of truths, half-truths, and fabrications. As Alkaissi and McFarlane (2023) point out, AI can deliver essays that seem scholarly yet are riddled with invented details. And as Bozkurt et al. (2024) caution in The Manifesto for Teaching and Learning in a Time of Generative AI, generative AI systems are prone to hallucinations—outputs that may appear plausible but are factually incorrect. The reason? These models don't actually understand the material; they predict words based on patterns in massive datasets, not on verified facts. That word-by-word prediction process can yield highly believable—but deeply flawed—responses, especially on topics like history or science where mismatched dates and names can slip in unnoticed. To fight back, educators must do more than just warn students about AI's limits. Schools should arm learners with practical tools—hands-on workshops where they fact-check AI outputs in real time, clear checklists and rubrics for vetting sources, low-stakes "myth-buster" exercises seeded with subtle errors, and classroom routines like teacher think-alouds that model healthy skepticism.

By weaving these strategies into everyday lessons, we build the critical-thinking muscles students need to harness AI's power without falling prey to its pitfalls.

3. Break the Over-Reliance Habit: Using AI Wisely

Artificial intelligence tools, such as GPT, function as useful tools in the learning process of students by providing support and responding to questions. However, there is a serious concern that students become over-reliant on such tools, especially in view of advances in Artificial Narrow Intelligence (ANI). As Bozkurt et al. (2024, p. 501) warn, "As GenAI provides instant solutions, students and educators may engage less deeply with the material, leading to passive learning and diminished development of essential skills like problem-solving and independent decision-making." In today's learning environments, it is easy for students to ask questions and receive elaborate answers. The problem lies when students just repeat the answers given by AI without going through careful comprehension, careful analysis, or careful reflection of the material. Instead of critically evaluating material, many students take results produced by artificial intelligence without ensuring their verifiability. Duhaylungsod and Chavez (2023) suggest that the easily accessible nature of AI tools can lead to a feeling of complacency, hence compromising students' cognitive processes regarding creativity and independent reasoning.While AI can certainly assist with tasks like writing and research, over-reliance on it can undermine students' critical thinking and problem-solving skills, which are essential for deeper learning and personal growth. Lecturers have also expressed concerns about academic dishonesty linked to students' growing dependence on AI. As one lecturer noted, "*Students no longer put effort into tasks. They forwarded the task to Chat GPT and copied what came from there. In most cases, we as lecturers fail to detect plagiarised work due to lack of expertise, and students get away with it*" (Mithi, Madzvamuse, Mbanje, & Lomahoza, 2024, p. 455).

Over-relying on AI in this way can also lead to a decline in cognitive abilities, making it harder for students to engage with the material on their own terms. Developing critical thinking skills allows students to generate more insightful ideas and solutions, which can greatly enhance their academic performance (Ruggiero, 2012). Therefore, it's crucial for students to use AI tools responsibly, ensuring that they complement, rather than replace, their independent learning efforts.

Relying on something implies placing trust in it, while over-relying suggests an excessive level of trust. Overtrust occurs when individuals place more trust in an AI system than its actual capabilities warrant (Lee & See, 2004).

The first step instructors can take is to help students understand how AI operates, including an explanation of the concept of "hallucination", where AI may provide inaccurate or incorrect responses. It is crucial for students to recognize that AI is not infallible, and there is a substantial chance it might generate wrong answers. By fostering this awareness, instructors can help break the perception of AI as a perfectly reliable source, which is essential for preventing over-reliance on technology.

Since it is not feasible to prevent students from using LLMs, particularly when they are studying remotely, the next best approach is to equip them with tools to critically analyze and evaluate AI- generated content. For example, instructors can design activities where students compare their own analysis with AI responses. This practice can help students develop independent thinking skills and encourage them to question and assess the information provided by AI, fostering a more discerning and thoughtful approach to using technology. Secondly, assessment reform—such as incorporating oral exams, project-based learning, or process-oriented tasks (e.g., drafts with revision logs)—can encourage students to document and explain the process behind their work. By requiring students to submit all drafts and provide an explanation of their approach, instructors can permit the use of AI for the purposes of guidance and brainstorming. This shift from a focus on the final product to one centered on cognitive development reduces the incentive for students to rely on copy-pasting and promotes more thoughtful engagement with the learning process.

Thirdly, licensed tools should be implemented within the institution to combat academic dishonesty and plagiarism. It is essential that lecturers remain well-informed about these tools to effectively utilize them (Mithi et al., 2024). Additionally, students should be made aware of these tools so that they are discouraged from resorting to copy-pasting out of fear or ego, ultimately fostering a culture of academic integrity.

III. STRATEGIES FOR EFFECTIVE AI IMPLEMENTATION

1. The Need for LLM Integration in Formative Assessment Systems

Large Language Models (LLMs), such as ChatGPT, can provide students with information, but merely offering this information is insufficient for facilitating genuine learning.

Learning is not a straightforward, linear process; rather, it is complex and multifaceted (Everwijn et al., 1993; Wittrock, 2000).From a neuroscience perspective, learning is not a simple, step-by-step process. The brain's neural networks do not always follow a direct path but are shaped by interactions between different regions, involving a process of reinforcement, error correction, and connection-making.

For example, when learners revisit concepts, make mistakes, or approach problems from various angles, they engage in the cognitive processes that strengthen synaptic connections, improving long-term retention and understanding. ChatGPT (and similar tools) might provide accurate information, but they do not facilitate the essential cognitive processes involved in learning, such as reflection, critical thinking, and making connections. Neuroscientific research suggests that learning involves complex neural changes, with active engagement leading to modifications in synaptic connections, particularly in areas like the hippocampus, which are crucial for memory formation (Kandel, 2001). These processes require learners to make mistakes, reflect on their understanding, and revise their knowledge, all of which contribute to synaptic plasticity and the formation of long-lasting neural connections. Without the opportunity for this deeper engagement, students may bypass critical stages of learning, such as integrating new knowledge with prior experiences, which can result in shallow learning rather than deep, meaningful understanding (Wittrock, 2000).

However, there's an exception: if a student gives a good prompt—one that asks for deeper engagement—then they might get a more thoughtful, step-by-step explanation. For example, instead of just asking for an answer, a student might ask: *'Help me understand this with step-by- step instructions, explaining each part so I can see how it fits together'*. In this case, ChatGPT could guide the student through the learning process in a more interactive and detailed way. But this kind of prompt is rare because most students usually just want a straight answer, rather than going through the thinking process step by step.

To address this, educational institutions should consider integrating a course into the curriculum that teaches students how to effectively interact with AI. This course would focus on how to craft thoughtful, specific prompts that encourage deeper engagement with the material. By training students to ask the right questions and utilize AI as a learning tool, they can gain a more comprehensive understanding and develop critical thinking skills that enhance their academic growth.

Therefore, integrating **Large Language Models (LLMs)** into formative adaptive assessment systems is essential. This integration empowers instructors to personalize and shape feedback according to each student's individual needs and progress. Rather than simply offering the correct answers, this approach nurtures three vital areas of learning: **cognition**, **metacognition**, and **motivation**. Students are no longer passive recipients of information, instead of just receiving feedback, they can actively engage in conversation with the system. If they encounter difficulties or struggle with understanding, they can ask questions, allowing for a more interactive and responsive learning experience.

2. Personalizing Feedback with LLMs

To answer this question, we can take **LEAP** as an example, a platform developed by Steinert et al. (2024). **LEAP (Learning with AI about Physics)** leverages **Large Language Models (LLMs)** to provide personalized formative feedback, adapting to each student's unique learning needs. The platform aims to enhance self-regulated learning (SRL) by offering feedback that stimulates students' cognitive, metacognitive, and motivational processes, thereby supporting deeper learning and reflection. Steinert et al. (2024) systematically designed the LLM prompts, dividing them into three segments: Condition, Consequence, and Refinement.

The Condition segment ensures that learning support is provided only when necessary, such as when a student's answer is incomplete or incorrect. This careful design is crucial, as research has shown that unnecessary adaptive learning support can be counterproductive, leading to the expertise reversal effect (Kalyuga, 2009). In such cases, repetitive or irrelevant feedback can overload the student's working memory, thus hindering performance.

The Consequence segment outlines the expected outcome when the condition is met, ensuring that the LLM provides personalized feedback rather than generic responses. This feedback is tailored to guide the student toward a deeper understanding of the material. The segment is divided into two elements: adaptable and adaptive. The adaptable element is determined by the teacher or researcher, who directs the LLM to encourage specific actions, such as prompting the student to reflect on misunderstood concepts or reconsider their approach. In contrast, the adaptive element is generated by the LLM itself, responding to the unique aspects of the student's answer. This allows the LLM to focus on particular areas the student may have misunderstood or missed, ensuring that the feedback is relevant and specific to their learning needs.

Finally, the Refinement segment aims to fine-tune the feedback to ensure that it is both effective and focused. As Steinert et al. (2024) explain, this segment includes the critical restriction of "without giving the correct answer". This is supported by studies from Kulhavy et al. (1985) and Phye & Bender (1989), which found that providing detailed feedback alongside the correct answer can lead to superficial learning. Such feedback prevents students from engaging deeply with the material or developing essential problem-solving skills, as it may lead them to simply accept the solution rather than work through the problem independently. By eliminating the direct solution, the LLM fosters a more active learning process, encouraging students to think critically and reflect on their understanding.

However, despite the potential of this system in enhancing personalized feedback, it may encounter the challenges discussed earlier (e.g., bias). As noted by Steinert et al. (2024), future research should focus on validating the effectiveness of AI-driven feedback and identifying strategies to minimize biases, ensuring its reliability and efficacy in educational contexts.

Another serious challenge we may face is a phenomenon known as emergent sensemaking, which suggests that using AI in formative assessments could increase unfairness because AI may not fully understand when students come up with unexpected or creative ways of thinking (Li et al., 2023). This issue often arises when students are operating at the higher levels of Bloom's Taxonomy, particularly in the Analysis and Synthesis (or Creating in the revised version) phases, where students are asked to evaluate, create, or solve complex problems (Bloom, 1956; Anderson & Krathwohl, 2001). In these stages, students might approach problems in novel and creative ways, yet the AI might overlook or undervalue these creative processes. As a result, students could receive feedback that fails to recognize the depth of their thinking, leading to potential biases or unfair assessments.

This can cause demotivation and misguidance, as students may feel their innovative solutions are not being properly recognized or valued, thus impacting their overall learning experience.

3. QuestionCraft: AI That Asks the Right Questions

Other advanced AI systems allow educators to effortlessly upload course materials in a range of formats, including Word documents, PowerPoint presentations, and

PDFs, and request the system to create questions based on the content they provide. For instance, Walton (2023) highlights the pedagogical potential of generative AI in personalized cognitive tutoring, with a focus on the dynamic creation and assessment of adaptive questions using the Davinci-003 API.

With the use of OpenAI's Davinci-003 API, this system can generate questions that are dynamically adjusted to a student's comprehension level and compare their answers to pre- generated solutions or predetermined standards.

The question that arises in one's mind is***: "To what extent are the questions generated by artificial intelligence both reliable and of high quality?"***

To answer this question, Jia, Zhou, Sun and Wu (2020) introduced an advanced, two-stage approach to improving the quality of artificially generated questions. Initially, they extract important textual information by employing an advanced Rough Answer and Key Sentence Tagging method to pinpoint sentences highly probable to generate important questions. The second step improves question accuracy and relevance by employing an Answer-guided Graph Convolutional Network (GCN); this network also considers sentence relationships within the text. However, the effectiveness of these AI methods is often contingent upon the availability of large and relevant datasets for model training. Educational texts, such as lecture transcripts or academic articles, often contain numerous sentences, but not all of them are suitable for generating insightful questions. Some sentences may present general information that does not lend itself well to meaningful inquiry. Therefore, identifying the most "question-worthy" sentences before feeding them into the AI model is essential. In this regard, Chen, Yang, and Gašević (2019) explored various strategies for selecting the best sentences from a text for question generation, finding that LexRank—a stochastic graph-based model—was the most effective across multiple datasets. LexRank highlights significant sentences by concentrating on those that contain important information within the text. It rates the significance of a sentence by comparing its similarity to the others in the document. The more alike a sentence is to others, the more it is a key element of the document content. Therefore, three crucial elements need to be given top priority in order for AI systems to provide insightful questions:

a. **Give careful consideration to the appropriate portions of the text**: An effective AI question generator should focus on the text's most pertinent and instructively useful passages.
b. **Choose the sentences that are most pertinent**: Only the most significant sentences must be recognized and used by the system in order to provide precise and perceptive questions.
c. **Work together with AI Don't depend blindly**: Without verification, instructors shouldn't put their trust in AI-generated questions. They must actively interact

with the AI system, revising the questions to check for bias, clarity, and purpose in order to make sure they support learning objectives.

Considering these factors, cooperation with AI is crucial as teachers must actively participate in improving the output rather than depending entirely on AI to manage every aspect of question generation.

4. AI in Predicting Student Performance:

Traditionally, educational institutions have mainly focused on evaluating learning outcomes using metrics such as grades, examination results, and attendance records that provide a limited view of a student's overall effectiveness. However, the emergence of artificial intelligence technology has dramatically opened up a wide range of new data to be gathered. In addition to traditional indicators of academic performance, AI systems can also capture a more varied range of information, such as aspects of student behavior. For example, AI is able to track the way in which students interact with learning material, such as time taken to complete assignments, engagement with the material, and active engagement in discussions. AI systems also have the capability to assess non-cognitive aspects such as motivation and cooperation that in the past presented challenges in measurement. In addition to that, biometric measurements boost this capability to include physical indicators such as facial expressions, eye movement, pitch of voice, and even heart rate, hence providing a more sophisticated view of students' emotional and cognitive status (Polonetsky & Jerome, 2014).

Extensive investigations in this field have shown that machine learning methods have the potential to predict educational achievements to a high extent of precision (Hellas et al., 2018). This allows not just the educational system but also educators to determine potential challenges, such as the chances of a student's dropout during a semester. In addition, it provides useful information in terms of particular parts of the curriculum that a student has yet to master appropriately. The identification of areas of challenges that a student faces is crucial, as it allows for intervention and support in a timely manner. In this respect, Hussain et al. (2019) focus their work towards predicting educational challenges encountered by learners undertaking a digital design course. The researchers analyze logs of data—including clickstream metrics, time elapsed on a task, and a set of performance indicators—derived from a Technology-Enhanced Learning (TEL) platform to determine patterns in learner behavior that can indicate learning challenges.

In order to forecast such challenges, different artificial intelligence (AI) models were utilized, namely:

Artificial Neural Networks (ANN): This model simulates how the human brain functions and may identify complex patterns in student assessment data, such response or improvement trends, to predict overall performance.

Support Vector Machines (SVM): This technique is highly effective when dealing with various factors or characteristics and is used to categorize and predict student outcomes in connection to numerous variables, such as attendance or quiz results.

Logistic Regression: Based on a student's prior performance, this statistical technique predicts binary exam results, such as the likelihood that the student will pass or fail a specific assignment.

Decision Trees: This modeling technique helps with test decision-making. Each node represents a distinct factor (e.g., study hours or quiz scores) that is used to predict a student's final grade.

Naïve Bayes: This probabilistic approach uses categorical factors, including the amount of right answers or participation in specific activities, to anticipate a student's likelihood of passing or failing a test.

Solis et al. (2018) posited that Random Forest method is the most accurate method of forecasting student retention rates. The robust artificial intelligence method is used to predict results using analysis of complex data sets. The Random Forest method is composed of predictive and classification modules that produce a large number of decision trees, each of which is programmed to pose a set of questions. An example of such questions is, "Does the student attend classes regularly?" or "Does the student produce satisfactory grades?" to assess a student's potential to continue in studies or withdraw. In making predictive results, the decision tree analyzes the response given to questions such as these. One of the defining aspects of Random Forest is that it is capable of making decisions without reliance on a particular tree. Instead, it combines a multitude of trees, each of which analyzes different aspects of the data. The compilation of results across these trees results in a prediction that is more accurate. The algorithmic structure of Random Forest is that it uses random samples of data to build each tree, hence incorporating randomness in the method. The method allows for variance in trees and reduces the impact of one particular point of data in making up a model. GritNet, a sophisticated deep learning system developed by Kim et al. (2018), addresses this problem in that it frames student performance prediction as a sequential forecasting problem of events. In contrast to most classic models that use fixed features, GritNet leverages genuine event data that is gathered over a student's learning period, such as viewing of video material, attempts at quizzes, and completion of assignments, that act as input to the model.

Bidirectional Long Short-Term Memory (BLSTM) networks are used to detect underlying patterns in student behavior, making them highly useful for forecasting future academic performance. In their work in 2018, Kim et al. compared GritNet, a sophisticated deep learning structure, to logistic regression, a widely used method of educational data mining. The results of their work showed that GritNet profoundly outperformed logistic regression, especially in the first few weeks of a course, a period when traditional methods often fail to provide accurate forecasts. By applying their system to Udacity Nanodegree courses, the researchers established that GritNet was capable of making dramatic improvements in predictive precision using just a few weeks of data. This aspect is highly beneficial in that it allows for interventions to be undertaken in a timely manner to help boost student success. Overall, their work highlights the revolution that deep learning can play in providing educators with more powerful tools for forecasting and responding to student results in today's highly dynamic online learning environment (Kim et al., 2018).

IV. BEYOND ANSWERS: AI AS YOUR SOCRATIC PARTNER IN CRITICAL THINKING

Rao (2005: 173) highlights an important distinction in education: the transmission of *what to think* versus *how to think*. According to Rao, education typically focuses on teaching students the content or subject matter of a course, which answers the question, "What should I know?" (i.e., the "what to think" aspect). However, Rao argues that we often fall short in teaching students how to engage with that content critically—how to analyze, evaluate, and understand it effectively. This involves teaching students cognitive skills to approach the subject matter with a critical mindset, enabling them to assess, question, and form their own conclusions, rather than simply absorbing information passively. As Bozkurt et al. (2024, p. 502) warn, "Easy access to answers might discourage analytical thinking and problem-solving... Over-use of GenAI may impede the development of synthesis, evaluation, and creation skills, and dependence on AI-generated solutions may reduce opportunities for original thought."

Rao suggests that while educational systems excel in imparting knowledge about specific fields (e.g., engineering or science), they frequently neglect the essential aspect of *critical thinking*— how to evaluate and make sense of that knowledge. This "how to think" element is crucial for fostering deeper learning, as it allows students not only to learn facts but also to develop the skills necessary to critically assess and apply those facts in various contexts.

Critical thinking can be defined as the ability to analyze facts, generate and organize ideas, defend opinions, make comparisons, draw inferences, evaluate arguments, and solve problems (Chance, 1986, p. 6). In 1956, Bloom and his colleagues proposed a framework that categorizes cognitive processes into six hierarchical levels: Knowledge, Comprehension, Application, Analysis, Synthesis, and Evaluation. Research over the past few decades has confirmed that the first four levels

(Knowledge, Comprehension, Application, and Analysis) form a clear hierarchy, where each level builds on the previous one. For instance, acquiring knowledge is considered less complex than comprehension, and comprehension serves as a foundation for analysis.

However, critical thinking is most closely associated with the higher-order levels of Bloom's taxonomy—Evaluation and Synthesis. Evaluation involves making judgments or assessments about the validity of propositions, which aligns with the process of critical thinking. It requires analyzing information and forming well-informed conclusions. On the other hand, Synthesis, often connected to creative thinking, requires combining various ideas (usually resulting from analysis) to create something new and original. While Evaluation focuses on critical judgment, Synthesis is more about creativity and innovation.

The key difference between critical thinking and creative thinking lies in their purpose and process. Critical thinking is analytical, structured, and focused on evaluating the validity and quality of ideas, often driven by logic and evidence. It typically involves using the left hemisphere of the brain, which is associated with analytical, logical, and objective thinking. In contrast, creative thinking is more holistic, divergent, and focused on producing new ideas and solutions. It often involves using the right hemisphere, which is associated with intuitive, emotional, and innovative thinking. Thus, while critical thinking emphasizes judgment and evaluation, creative thinking emphasizes originality and innovation. Both are essential cognitive skills, but they draw on different aspects of our cognitive processes.

However, In the age of AI, where vast amounts of information are generated by systems like GPT, it is essential to approach all AI outputs with a critical eye. This is especially important given the

limitations of tools like ChatGPT and other AI programs (Exintaris et al., 2023; Spector & Ma, 2019). Bjelland, Ludvigsen, and Mogelvang (2024) further emphasize this point, noting that students engaging with AI chatbots like ChatGPT use them cautiously, applying source criticism and critical thinking to the generated content. Instead of blindly trusting AI, students view the chatbot as a guide or sparring partner, maintaining an independent and thoughtful approach. Interestingly, many students use AI chatbots as discussion partners, highlighting a preference for individual, self-reflective engagement rather than collaborative interactions with peers or instructors.

Everything may appear straightforward until you consider the paradox: while attempting to critically evaluate ChatGPT, there is a genuine concern that the very act of relying on AI could erode the critical thinking skills one is trying to apply. Students have raised significant concerns about how AI chatbots may impact their learning, especially in the realm of critical thinking. There is an ongoing worry that relying too much on algorithmic outputs may prevent them from really engaging with the content, which would ultimately impair their ability to think independently and analyze information reflectively (Bjelland, Ludvigsen, & Mogelvang, 2024). Artificial intelligence (AI) technologies can therefore promote reflective inquiry by presenting open-ended questions or counterarguments, which will motivate students to think critically and actively interact with the material. This approach is similar to the philosopher Socrates' Socratic dialogue methodology, which uses probing questions to encourage self-discovery, challenge presumptions, and spark thought (Paul & Elder, 2006). The intention is to let students examine concepts independently and evaluate their logic critically, not to give them straight answers. Similar to this, AI encourages students to challenge their knowledge, consider their own thought processes, and consider alternative viewpoints when it presents open-ended questions or counterarguments. This fosters critical thinking and deeper learning. Furthermore, assessments ought to favor the process above the final output.

Instead of completely prohibiting AI, teachers may, for instance, ask students to check writings produced by ChatGPT for prejudice or logical errors. These kinds of activities fit within Bloom's updated taxonomy (Anderson & Krathwohl, 2001), which places an emphasis on higher-order abilities like evaluation and creation. This approach allows students to utilize AI as a tool for deeper engagement while simultaneously upholding the importance of critical thinking. By emphasizing the learning process and promoting critical thinking, instructors should make sure AI complements students' cognitive growth rather than take its place. In the end, this creates a well- rounded learning atmosphere where students can think critically, conduct their own independent analysis, and utilize AI sensibly as a tool for learning and development.

V. HUMAN TOUCH: WHY TEACHERS STILL MATTER IN AN AI-DRIVEN CLASSROOM

A silent but widespread fear has been raised by the development of artificial intelligence in education: *Will teachers eventually become obsolete?* This question remains relevant as adaptive platforms assess essays, personalize learning paths, and even use chatbots to mimic empathy, while AI systems like ChatGPT create lesson plans in seconds that are in line with Bloom's taxonomy (Ortega-Ochoa et al., 2024). These systems are transformational in addition to being effective.

According to recent research, for instance, AI-driven feedback can match conventional approaches in terms of academic results while also favorably boosting students' organizational and self- efficacy (Ortega-Ochoa et al., 2024).

Beneath these developments, however, is a more profound philosophical query: What role do educators still play if AI can provide 24/7 availability, emotional support, and individualized instruction—especially for students who find human connection intimidating? AI's judgment-free zone is revolutionary for students with social anxiety. There is just quick, individualized support— neither societal pressure to perform nor fear of humiliation.

AI presents both possibilities and difficulties for the educational field. On one hand, it helps schools spot students who might be falling behind early, gives teachers insights into how students learn (Fang, 2021), and offers quick answers and feedback anytime. But relying too much on AI could weaken the role of teachers, who do more than just teach—they mentor, inspire, and support students emotionally (Chen & Lin, 2023; Ghamrawi et al., 2024).

Teachers build trust and deep connections with students, which is crucial for learning (Shen et al., 2020). While AI can grade papers or plan lessons, it can't replace the empathy, creativity, or personal guidance teachers provide (Bertolin & Da Rin, 2020). For example, AI can't notice when a student feels lost or celebrate their "aha!" moment.

Some worry that AI might turn teachers into tech supervisors instead of leaders in the classroom (Ghamrawi et al., 2024). Others, though, believe AI could help teachers by handling boring tasks like grading, freeing them to focus on creative teaching, teamwork, and mentoring (Ghamrawi et al., 2024).However, Using AI tools in education isn't just about mastering a new app or clicking buttons—it demands that teachers deeply understand how these systems work to use them responsibly and guide students thoughtfully. As Ghamrawi et al. (2024) stress, educators need strong technological literacy: "It's not just about being tech-savvy; it's about understanding how AI works, analyzing data insights, and using technology as an enabler" (p. 8425). For example, data literacy abilities are necessary to analyze AI-generated data to customize classes, enabling educators to transform numerical data into practical strategies (Ghamrawi et al., 2024). With this knowledge, educators may go beyond passive usage of AI, addressing biases, critiquing its limits, and igniting important classroom debates about privacy, ethics, and the place of technology in society. Teachers who won't be "replaced by robots" must be prepared to handle the complexity of AI, not only its interface, as Akmal (2019) warns. Teaching is ultimately about making connections with people. AI is unable to instill compassion, settle disputes in the classroom, or encourage a pupil to enjoy studying. Teachers are now mentors and guides rather than only knowledge providers, as indicated by Halimatussa'diyah (2019). In the future of education, artificial intelligence (AI) will be used to assist teachers so they can continue to do what no computer can: care.

In practice, the synergy between AI's strengths and teachers' unique human qualities looks like this:

Figure 2. Synergy between AI Capabilities and Teacher Strengths for Enhanced Learning

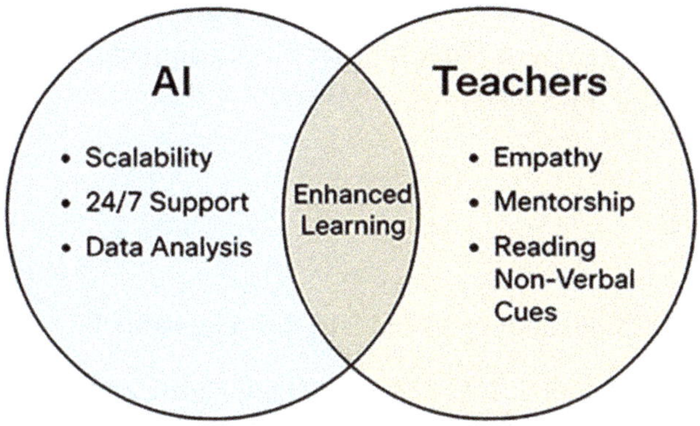

CONCLUSION

In conclusion, artificial intelligence has the ability to significantly improve formative assessment in educational settings by introducing novel strategies to individualized instruction and instantaneous, customized feedback. But as we enter this new era, we must not lose sight of the fact that human interaction in educational environments cannot be replaced by technology, no matter how sophisticated. The real promise of AI is not that it can take the role of teachers, but rather that it can help them create more in-depth, customized learning experiences. Teachers continue to play a significant role in helping students find connections, guide them through difficult cognitive processes, and promote critical reflection—tasks that technology cannot perform on its own. The rich, human-centered components of education must be enhanced rather than replaced by AI as we include it into formative assessment. If this balance is carefully managed, formative assessment may become an effective instrument for developing students' intellectual curiosity and academic success, which will benefit them even after they graduate.

ACKNOWLEDGMENTS

The authors extend their heartfelt gratitude to the National Center for Scientific and Technical Research (CNRST) for crucial support through the "PhD-Associate Scholarship – PASS" program. This support played a pivotal role in advancing the research and ensuring the successful completion of this study.

REFERENCES

Akmal. (2019). Lebih dekat dengan Industri 4.0. Deepublish.

Alkaissi, H., & McFarlane, S. I. (2023). Artificial Hallucinations in ChatGPT: Implications in Scientific Writing. *Cureus, 15*, e35179. DOI: 10.7759/cureus.35179 PMID: 36811129

Anderson, L. W., & Krathwohl, D. R. (2001). *A taxonomy for learning, teaching, and assessing: A revision of Bloom's taxonomy of educational objectives*. Longman.

Bertolin, M., & Da Rin, D. (2020). Chatbots for K-12 education: A review of recent advances, Opportunities, and Challenges. *Education Sciences, 10*(7), 181.

Bjelland, C., Ludvigsen, K., & Mogelvang, A. (2024). Unveiling the impact of AI chatbots on higher education: Insights from students. *Proceedings of the INTED2024 Conference*, 1458– 1465. https://www.researchgate.net/publication/378942626

Bloom, B. S. (1956). *Taxonomy of educational objectives: The classification of educational goals*. Handbook I: Cognitive Domain. David McKay Company.

Bozkurt, A., Xiao, J., Farrow, R., Bai, J. Y. H., Nerantzi, C., Moore, S., Dron, J., Stracke, C. M., Singh, L., Crompton, H., Koutropoulos, A., Terentev, E., Pazurek, A., Nichols, M., Sidorkin, A. M., Costello, E., Watson, S., Mulligan, D., Honeychurch, S., & Asino, T. I. (2024). The Manifesto for Teaching and Learning in a Time of Generative AI: A Critical Collective Stance to Better Navigate the Future. *Open Praxis, 16*(4), 487–513. DOI: 10.55982/openpraxis.16.4.777

Brown, T. B., Mann, B., Ryder, N., Subbiah, M., Kaplan, J., Dhariwal, P., Neelakantan, A., & Shinn, E.. (2020). Language models are few-shot learners. *Proceedings of the 34th International Conference on Neural Information Processing Systems*, 1877-1901.

Chance, P. (1986). *Thinking in the classroom: A survey of programs*. Teachers College, Columbia University.

Chen, J. J., & Lin, J. C. (2023). Artificial intelligence as a double-edged sword: Wielding the POWER principles to maximize its positive effects and minimize its negative effects. *Contemporary Issues in Early Childhood, 14639491231169813.* Advance online publication. DOI: 10.1177/14639491231169813

Devlin, J., Chang, M. W., Lee, K., & Toutanova, K. (2018). BERT: Pre-training of deep bidirectional transformers for language understanding. *Proceedings of NAACL-HLT*, 4171-4186

Duhaylungsod, A. V., & Chavez, J. V., (2023). Chatgpt and other ai users: Innovative and creative utilitarian value and mindset shift. *Journal of Namibian Studies: History Politics Culture*, *33*, 4367–4378. DOI: 10.59670/jns.v33i.2791

Everwijn, S. E. M., Bomers, G. B. J., & Knubben, J. A. (1993). Ability- or competence-based education: Bridging the gap between knowledge acquisition and ability to apply. *Higher Education*, *25*(4), 425–438. DOI: 10.1007/BF01383845

Exintaris, B., Karunaratne, N., & Yuriev, E. (2023). Metacognition and critical thinking: Using ChatGPT-generated responses as prompts for critique in a problem-solving workshop (SMARTCHEMPer). *Journal of Chemical Education*, *100*(8), 2972–2980. DOI: 10.1021/acs.jchemed.3c00481

Fang, Y. (2021). A systematic review of Natural Language Processing Applications in writing instruction. *Journal of Educational Computing Research*, *59*(3), 527–548.

Ghamrawi, N., Shal, T., & Ghamrawi, N. A. R. (2024). Exploring the impact of AI on teacher leadership: Regressing or expanding? *Education and Information Technologies*, *29*(7), 8415–8433. DOI: 10.1007/s10639-023-12174-w

Guo, H., Yi, W., & Liu, K. (2024). *Enhancing Constructivist Learning: The Role of Generative AI in Personalised Learning Experiences*. In *International Conference on Enterprise Information Systems*. https://doi.org/DOI: 10.5220/0012688700003690

Halimatussa'diyah. (2019). *Strategi Pembelajaran di Era Revolusi Industri 4.0.* Jakad Media Publishing.

Hellas, A., Ihantola, P., Petersen, A., Ajanovski, V. V., Gutica, M., Hynninen, T., Knutas, A., Leinonen, J., Messom, C., & Liao, S. N. (2018). Predicting academic performance: A systematic literature review. In Ro¨ßling, G., & Scharlau, B. (Eds.), *Proceedings Companion of the 23rd annual ACM Conference on Innovation and Technology in computer science education* (pp. 175–199). ACM. https://doi.org/DOI: 10.1145/3293881.3295783

Howard, J., & Ruder, S. (2018). Universal language model fine-tuning for text classification. *Proceedings of the 56th Annual Meeting of the Association for Computational Linguistics*, 328-339. DOI: 10.18653/v1/P18-1031

Huang, Y., Li, J., & Li, J. (2020). Multimodal learning with deep learning. *IEEE Transactions on Pattern Analysis and Machine Intelligence*, *42*(4), 910–927.

Hussain, M., Zhu, W., Zhang, W., Abidi, S. M. R., & Ali, S. (2019). Using machine learning to predict student difficulties from learning session data. *Artificial Intelligence Review*, *52*(1), 381–407. DOI: 10.1007/s10462-018-9620-8

Jia, Y., Zhou, Y., Sun, L., & Wu, Q. (2020). Improving the quality of generated questions via rough answer and key sentence tagging and graph convolutional networks. *Journal of Educational Technology & Society*, *23*(4), 118–129.

Kalyuga, S. (2009). The Expertise Reversal Effect. In Kalyuga, S. (Ed.), *Managing Cognitive Load in Adaptive Multimedia Learning* (pp. 58–80). IGI Global., DOI: 10.4018/978-1-60566-048-6.ch003

Kandel, E. R. (2001). The molecular biology of memory storage: A dialogue between genes and synapses. *Science*, *294*(5544), 1030–1038. DOI: 10.1126/science.1067020 PMID: 11691980

Kim, B.-H., Vizitei, E., & Ganapathi, V. (2018). GritNet: Student performance prediction with deep learning. arXiv preprint arXiv:1804.07405. https://doi.org//arXiv.1804.07405DOI: 10.48550

Klenowski, V. (2009). Assessment for learning revisited: An Asia-Pacific perspective. *Assessment in Education: Principles, Policy & Practice*, *16*(3), 263–268. DOI: 10.1080/09695940903319646

Kulhavy, R. W., White, M. T., Topp, B. W., Chan, A. L., & Adams, J. (1985). Feedback complexity and corrective efficiency. *Contemporary Educational Psychology*, *10*(3), 285–292. DOI: 10.1016/0361-476X(85)90025-6

Lee, J. D., & See, K. A. (2004). Trust in automation: Designing for appropriate reliance. *Human Factors*, *46*(1), 50–80. DOI: 10.1518/hfes.46.1.50.30392 PMID: 15151155

Li, T., Reigh, E., He, P., & Miller, E. (2023). Can we and should we use artificial intelligence for formative assessment in science? *Journal of Research in Science Teaching*, *60*(6), 1385–1389. DOI: 10.1002/tea.21867

Li, T., Reigh, E., He, P., & Miller, E. (2023). Can we and should we use artificial intelligence for formative assessment in science? *Journal of Research in Science Teaching*, *60*(6), 1385–1389. DOI: 10.1002/tea.21867

Mithi, J., Madzvamuse, S., Mbanje, S., & Lomahoza, S. (2024). *Generative Artificial Intelligence and Formative Assessment: Perspectives from Higher Education in South Africa. International Conference on Education Research.*

Mohammad, S. J., Hamad, A. K., Borgi, H., Thu, P. A., Sial, M. S., & Alhadidi, A. A. (2020). How artificial intelligence changes the future of the accounting industry. *International Journal of Economics and Business Administration*, *8*(3), 478–488. DOI: 10.35808/ijeba/538

Olson, K. (2006, November 8). The wounds of schooling. *Education Week*, •••, 28–29.

Ortega-Ochoa, J., Pardo, A., & Rodríguez, P. (2024). Empathic chatbot feedback in computer science education: A quasi-experimental study. *Computers and Education: Artificial Intelligence*, *5*, 100095. DOI: 10.1016/j.caeai.2024.100095

Paul, R., & Elder, L. (2006). *The Thinker's Guide to the Art of Socratic Questioning*. Foundation for Critical Thinking.

Phye, G. D., & Bender, T. (1989). Feedback complexity and practice: Response pattern analysis in retention and transfer. *Contemporary Educational Psychology*, *14*(1), 97–106. DOI: 10.1016/0361-476X(89)90028-3

Polonetsky, J., & Jerome, J. (2014). *Student data: Trust, transparency, and the role of consent*. SSRN Electronic Journal. https://doi.org/DOI: 10.2139/ssrn.2628877

Rainer, G., Nies, T., & Schmid, W. (2016). *Artificial Intelligence: Concepts and Applications*. Springer.

Rao, K. (2005). Infusing critical thinking into content of AI course. In *Proceedings of the 10th Annual SIGCSE Conference on Innovation and Technology in Computer Science Education* (pp. 173–177). ACM. https://doi.org/DOI: 10.1145/1067445.1067494

Ruggiero, V. R. (2012). *The art of thinking: A guide to critical and creative thought* (10th ed.). Pearson Learning Solutions.

Saltman, K. (2020). *AI in education and the future of standardized teaching*. Springer.

Shaffer, D. W., & Kaput, J. J. (1998). The role of computational media in reshaping how we think about assessment in education. *Journal of the Learning Sciences*, *7*(2), 183–212.

Shen, J., Wang, Y., & Zhang, L. (2020). Understanding the relationship between teacher leadership and teacher well-being: The mediating roles of trust in leaders and teacher efficacy. *Journal of Educational Administration*, *58*(6), 679–696. DOI: 10.1108/JEA-09-2022-0152

Solis, M., Moreira, T., Gonzalez, R., Fernandez, T., & Hernandez, M. (2018). Perspectives to predict dropout in university students with machine learning. In *2018 IEEE International Work Conference on Bioinspired Intelligence (IWOBI)* (pp. 1–6). IEEE. https://doi.org/DOI: 10.1109/IWOBI.2018.8464191

Spector, J. M., & Ma, S. (2019). Inquiry and critical thinking skills for the next generation: From artificial intelligence back to human intelligence. *Smart Learning Environments*, *6*(1), 8. DOI: 10.1186/s40561-019-0088-z

Steinert, S., Avila, K. E., Kuhn, J., & Küchemann, S. (2024). Harnessing large language models to develop research-based learning assistants for formative feedback. *Smart Learning Environments*, *11*(1), 62. DOI: 10.1186/s40561-024-00354-1

Steinert, S., Avila, K. E., Ruzika, S., Kuhn, J., & Küchemann, S. (2024). Harnessing large language models to develop research-based learning assistants for formative feedback. *Smart Learning Environments*, *11*(62), 62. Advance online publication. DOI: 10.1186/s40561-024-00354-1

Vaswani, A., Shazeer, N., Parmar, N., Uszkoreit, J., Jones, L., Gomez, A. A., Kaiser, Ł., & Polosukhin, I. (2017). Attention is all you need. *Advances in Neural Information Processing Systems*, •••, 30.

Vygotsky, L. S. (1978). *Mind in society: The development of higher psychological processes*. Harvard University Press.

Walton, D. (2023). *Personalized cognitive tutoring using Davinci-003 API for adaptive question generation and assessment*. CoRR. https://doi.org/DOI: 10.48550/ARXIV.2304.02772

Wiliam, D. (2011). What is assessment for learning? *Studies in Educational Evaluation*, *37*(1), 3–14. DOI: 10.1016/j.stueduc.2011.03.001

Wittrock, M. C. (2000). Learning as a generative process. In Segal, J. W., Chapman, S. F., & Glaser, R. (Eds.), *Educational psychology: A century of contributions* (pp. 277–294). Erlbaum.

Zhai, X., & Krajcik, J. (2022). Pseudo AI Bias. *SSRN*. DOI: 10.2139/ssrn.4368917

KEY TERMS AND DEFINITIONS

Adaptive Feedback: Tailored, real-time responses provided by AI tools based on student input, designed to guide individual learning paths more effectively.

AI Bias: A systematic and unfair pattern in AI results caused by imbalanced or non-representative data, potentially disadvantaging certain groups of learners.

Critical Thinking: The ability to thoughtfully analyze, evaluate, and synthesize information in order to make reasoned decisions and judgments.

Formative Assessment: A process of collecting and using feedback during learning to guide instructional decisions and help students improve before any final evaluation.

Generative AI: Artificial intelligence that can create new content—such as text, images, or audio—by identifying patterns in large datasets and predicting likely outcomes.

Hallucination (in AI): When an AI system produces a response that sounds correct but is actually factually wrong or entirely made up, due to predictive modeling rather than real understanding.

Higher-Order Thinking Skills: Advanced cognitive processes like analyzing, evaluating, and creating, which go beyond memorizing facts to include problem-solving and innovative thinking.

Large Language Model (LLM): A type of AI model trained on huge amounts of text data to understand and generate human-like responses across a variety of tasks.

Over-Reliance on AI: A situation where learners or educators depend too heavily on AI tools, leading to reduced critical thinking, creativity, or reflective engagement with the material.

Pseudo-AI Bias: A perceived bias in AI systems that actually results from misunderstanding how the technology works or misusing it, rather than from flaws in the model itself.

Chapter 11
AI-Supported Feedback for Writing:
A Multi-Dimensional Evaluation Framework

Seval Kemal
https://orcid.org/0009-0002-4286-2955
Dublin City University, Ireland

Dila Süzan
https://orcid.org/0009-0009-5372-695X
Gedik University, Turkey

Ali Öztüfekçi
https://orcid.org/0000-0002-4519-3796
Bahçeşehir University, Turkey

Sezin Eşfer
https://orcid.org/0000-0001-9095-6855
Bahçeşehir University, Turkey

ABSTRACT

This chapter takes a closer look at the use of AI-supported feedback in helping EFL students with their writing practices. Specifically, it focuses on how students engage with these tools and how feedback integrates into real classroom teaching. Drawing on current studies, classroom observations (e.g., students' essays), and reflections on practical use, the chapter proposes a framework with five areas to pay attention to: how detailed the feedback is, whether it feels tailored to the individual, how easy the tool is to use, how well it fits with teaching goals, and the ethical questions that arise along the way. Instead of viewing these tools as one-size-fits-all solutions, the

DOI: 10.4018/979-8-3373-7579-3.ch011

ght © 2026, IGI Global Scientific Publishing. Copying or distributing in print or electronic forms without written permission of IGI Global Scientific Publishing is prohibited. Use of this chapter to generative artificial intelligence (AI) technologies is expressly prohibited. The publisher reserves all rights to license its use for generative AI training and machine learning model development.

chapter explores both their potential benefits and their limitations, particularly in supporting meaningful learning. It also offers practical suggestions for how teachers might use them, while keeping the focus on what matters most: impactful teaching, trust in the classroom, and giving students space to develop their own voices.

INTRODUCTION

This chapter explores the role of Artificial Intelligence (AI)-supported feedback tools in enhancing English as a Foreign Language (EFL) writing skills. It specifically focuses on learner–AI interaction and proposes a comprehensive evaluation framework informed by theoretical perspectives and expert assessments of real student texts. The framework emphasizes the importance of context-sensitive feedback in fostering writing development. In an era in which AI is fundamentally reshaping educational paradigms, this work contributes to rethinking how EFL writing can evolve while maintaining learner agency and authenticity. Our framework specifically addresses how to transform the traditional feedback paradigm into a dynamic three-way interaction between learners, AI tools, and human mentors. Automated Writing Evaluation (AWE) systems and Large Language Models (LLMs) can offer prompt, adaptive feedback on grammar, vocabulary, and style (Yoon, 2021). However, there are ongoing concerns that these systems might fail to address critical rhetorical, cultural, and ethical aspects. These dimensions are particularly important in EFL writing, where learners often bring unique rhetorical traditions, audience expectations, linguistic identities that differ from mainstream norms, which, in turn, shapes their written work in meaningful ways (Warschauer, 2023). This tension between technological efficiency and learner autonomy demands a new approach to understanding and implementing AI-supported feedback tools. In response, this work proposes a five-pronged evaluation framework, encompassing *feedback depth, personalization, user experience, pedagogical alignment, and ethical considerations* to evaluate how three selected AI tools align with core teaching and learning needs. Given the accelerated adoption curve, LLMs are now embedded in MS 365, Google Workspace, and major LMS plugins, teachers must decide how (not whether) to integrate AI feedback. A robust evaluation therefore needs to:

1. Differentiate depth of feedback from mere error spotting.
2. Gauge personalization beyond template positivity.
3. Map UX frictions such as Gemini/Copilot task pauses.
4. Align with process-writing pedagogy, ensuring reflection cycles remain.
5. Audit ethics & privacy under current regional regulations and bias findings.

Informed by the learner-centered AI manifesto proposed by Bozkurt et al. (2024) and drawing on evaluations of selected tools that incorporated EFL learners' writing samples, this chapter outlines pedagogically grounded strategies for integrating AWE platforms and LLMs into EFL writing instruction. As such, emphasis is placed on ensuring context-sensitive, equitable, and ethically responsible use of these technologies. By highlighting each tool's strengths, limitations, and potential pitfalls, we aim to offer practical strategies for ensuring human mentorship and cultural sensitivity remain integral to the writing process. (Huawei & Aryadoust, 2022). Ultimately, our goal is to guide in bridging the efficiency of AI-driven feedback with the irreplaceable influence of human expertise (Escalante et al., 2023), thus fostering more holistic EFL writing development. While AI-supported writing tools have potential benefits for a variety of second language writers, they hold special relevance in higher education EFL contexts, where academic writing standards often demand both precision and rhetorical sophistication (Huawei & Aryadoust, 2022). To ensure responsible and meaningful integration of these tools into diverse writing scenarios, this chapter presents three main contributions:

- A practical guideline for effectively incorporating AI feedback into EFL writing practices in a way that balances machine-generated insights with essential human mentorship.
- A measurement framework that offers a set of evaluation criteria for AI-supported feedback provided by the selected tools.
- A brief review of widely used AI tools that examines their capabilities, user experience, and potential pitfalls in higher education contexts and self-directed study.

To this end, we underscore the importance of equitable and ethical practices in implementing AI, aligning with the principles outlined in the learner-centered AI manifesto (Bozkurt et al., 2024). The manifesto emphasizes *"prioritizing human agency, promoting transparency, and ensuring inclusivity"* in AI-enhanced learning environments, and these values directly inform our integration framework. By integrating these guiding tenets with our evaluation framework, we aim to harness the benefits of AI while safeguarding the integrity, equity, and authenticity of the writing process.

Table 1. Study Phase

Study Phase	Description
1.Problem Identification	Recognize the transformative role of AI in EFL writing and the need to balance efficiency with learner autonomy and authenticity.
2.Theoretical Foundation	Grounded in literature on AWE, LLMs, and the learner-centered AI Manifesto (Bozkurt et al., 2024). Emphasis on context-sensitive, ethical, and pedagogically aligned AI use.
3. Tool Selection	Systematic selection of 6 tools through literature review, usability testing, and expert validation based on accessibility and personalization.
4.Evaluation Framework Design	Design a five-pronged evaluation framework: feedback type & depth, personalization, UX, pedagogical alignment, and ethical/privacy concerns.
5. Tool Evaluation	Apply the framework to selected tools using EFL learner writing samples and expert judgments.
6.Thematic Synthesis	Analyze and compare tool outputs to identify strengths, limitations, and alignment with learner needs.
7.Integration Guidelines	Develop actionable, pedagogically grounded strategies for incorporating AI tools into EFL instruction with human mentorship.
8.Final Contributions and Alignment	Present three main contributions: guidelines, measurement framework, and critical review, aligned with the AI Manifesto principles.

PROBLEM IDENTIFICATION

Since the public release of ChatGPT in late 2022, LLMs have quickly shifted from experimental tools to everyday writing aids in EFL contexts. Emerging classroom studies report learners using ChatGPT to clarify thesis statements, explore genre conventions, and improve cohesion during the drafting process (Li et al., 2023), extending earlier research on AWE systems (Pack et al., 2024; Liew & Tan, 2024). However, unlike earlier parser-based tools, LLMs offer real-time, discourse-level feedback that significantly changes the dynamics of writing instruction. Despite this promise, recent empirical findings present a more complicated picture: while learners readily adopt surface-level suggestions, uptake of higher-order feedback remains limited without teacher mediation (Polakova & Ivenz, 2024; Huang & Teng, 2025). The effectiveness of AI-generated feedback remains inconsistent, with studies indicating that it does not necessarily lead to superior linguistic progress compared to traditional teacher feedback, highlighting the need for a blended approach that leverages the strengths of both methods (Tang, 2024). Methodological challenges also arise, including the complexities of designing effective instructional strategies and ensuring pedagogical alignment with AI tools (Gutai & Klimova, 2024). Furthermore, while AI tools like ChatGPT offer personalized guidance, they struggle with understanding specialized academic language and context-specific discussion, necessitating careful consideration of their limitations in educational contexts (Wu, 2024). These patterns raise urgent pedagogical questions about how feedback from generative AI should be integrated into EFL writing instruction, and what kinds of scaffolding are needed to ensure that such tools promote rather than replace meaningful language development (Mohammed & Khalid, 2025).

Human Feedback Quality

The literature consistently highlights that well-trained human evaluators tend to provide feedback of higher quality than AI across several critical dimensions (Steiss et al., 2024). Human feedback is often clearer in guiding improvement, more accurate in identifying core issues, and more adept at prioritizing essential writing features such as coherence, creativity, and logical reasoning. Instructors also offer a more supportive tone and demonstrate deeper contextual understanding of learners' needs, curriculum goals, and learning objectives (Steiss et al., 2024; Er et al., 2025). This enables them to generate feedback that is not only highly relevant but also pedagogically actionable. Moreover, human assessors excel in delivering personalized insights and constructive criticism, exhibiting greater sensitivity to elements such as originality, argument flow, and rhetorical nuance (Ramzan et al., 2025). Students often perceive human feedback as more useful, fair, developmental, and motivating compared to AI-generated comments (Er et al., 2025; Ramzan et al., 2025). This perception contributes positively to student engagement and motivation, encouraging deeper interaction with and response to feedback (Er et al., 2025). Despite its strengths, high-quality human feedback is inherently time-consuming and resource-intensive, particularly in large classes (Jukiewicz, 2024; Nazaretsky et al., 2024). The demands of grading multiple assignments often result in delays, which can affect students' ability to revise in a timely manner (Steiss et al., 2024). Furthermore, human evaluators may display inconsistency or bias, especially when evaluating subjective aspects of writing without clearly defined rubrics or across diverse student groups (Jukiewicz, 2024).

AI Feedback Quality

One of the most widely recognized advantages of AI-supported feedback is its ability to deliver rapid, large-scale responses, thereby reducing instructors' workload and offering students timely support (Steiss et al., 2024). Tools like ChatGPT can provide almost instantaneous feedback, which is particularly valuable in large classes or ongoing formative assessment contexts (Steiss et al., 2024). When properly calibrated with high-quality rubrics, prompts, and tone guidelines, AI can offer reliable criteria-based feedback and even outperform human raters in terms of consistency and objectivity (Awidi, 2024; Pahi et al., 2024). Moreover, AI is not subject to fatigue or emotional variation, ensuring a level of standardization in scoring (Jukiewicz, 2024). With access to extensive datasets and predefined evaluative formulas, AI systems can perform with notable precision, especially for tasks with clear-cut criteria (Biswas et al., 2024).

THEORETICAL FOUNDATION

A consistent theme emerging across recent studies is that AI-generated feedback is widely perceived as beneficial and, in certain contexts, even comparable to human feedback. However, user trust and perceptions of its quality are shaped significantly by factors such as disclosure, context, and interactional dynamics. For example, Nazaretsky et al. (2024) found that higher education students rated AI feedback on par with or superior to human feedback when unaware of its source. Yet, when the identity of the feedback provider was disclosed, participants rated human feedback significantly higher in terms of genuineness and credibility. This outcome reveals a persistent cognitive bias in favor of human input and underscores the critical role of perceived authenticity and trust in shaping the reception of feedback (Nazaretsky et al., 2024). Notably, GPT-4 performed more effectively on rejected papers, revealing its strength in identifying foundational flaws. However, it underperformed when assessing more nuanced dimensions, such as originality or methodological rigor. These limitations reinforce the conclusion that while AI can simulate aspects of expert evaluation, it lacks the depth required for fully autonomous scholarly critique (Liang et al., 2024).

The influence of user interaction, particularly in terms of prompt construction and engagement, is further highlighted in Tam's (2024) qualitative investigation. Her findings indicate that the effectiveness of AI feedback is closely linked to learners' language proficiency, self-regulation, and motivation. Advanced students who developed more refined prompts and engaged in reflective revision benefited more substantially from ChatGPT's feedback. In contrast, less proficient learners tended to accept responses at face value and sometimes misinterpreted the feedback's quality or relevance (Tam, 2024). These findings contrast with the broader patterns observed in Shi and Aryadoust's (2024) systematic review, which documents generally positive perceptions among students and teachers toward AWE systems such as Pigai and Grammarly. Nonetheless, the authors caution that such systems are predominantly focused on surface-level form and tend to fall short in providing feedback on content, organization, and argumentation, which are key elements of academic writing (Shi & Aryadoust, 2024).

Together, these studies reveal both the capabilities and limitations of AI-based feedback tools. While Liang et al. (2024) and Nazaretsky et al. (2024) emphasize the technical potential, and the perceptional barriers linked to feedback authenticity, Tam (2024) and Shi and Aryadoust (2024) highlight the learner's active role in shaping the efficacy of AI-mediated feedback. For instance, Tam stresses the importance of multilingual competence and metacognitive strategy use in effectively leveraging ChatGPT, while Shi and Aryadoust underscore the need for careful system design and contextual integration to optimize learner outcomes.

Variations in research design across these studies further enrich the discourse. Nazaretsky et al. (2024) employed an experimental methodology to investigate shifts in perception based on feedback source disclosure. Liang et al. (2024) relied on large-scale empirical analysis to measure content overlap between human and AI-generated reviews. Tam (2024) adopted a qualitative case study approach centered on learner AI interaction, and Shi and Aryadoust (2024) contributed a meta-analytic perspective through their comprehensive literature review. These diverse methodological approaches collectively offer a robust and multi-dimensional understanding of the opportunities and limitations of AI-supported feedback in academic writing contexts.

One of the most common themes across the articles is the potential for AI to improve both learning and teaching. For instance, Ji, Han, and Ko (2023) found that conversational AI-supported personalized learning in language education when used alongside human teachers. In a similar way, (Zapata et al., 2025) showed how AI speech evaluation programs can help EFL students by providing real-time feedback on their speaking. Both studies suggest that AI tools can encourage learner independence and engagement by offering timely, targeted input that helps students practice on their own. However, they also agree that AI should not replace human input. Ji et al. (2023) pointed out that AI works best with teacher guidance, and Zapata et al. emphasized that while AI is useful, it often lacks the subtle feedback and emotional nuance that teachers provide. This balance between AI support and human interaction shows up again in Tzirides' study (Zapata et al., 2025), which looked at generative AI feedback. While instructors liked the efficiency of AI-generated responses, they were also concerned that the feedback lacked empathy and the deeper understanding that only humans can offer.

Another big theme is how teachers perceive and feel about using AI. Wang et al. (2024) and Chai et al. (2024) looked at Chinese teachers' readiness to bring AI into their classrooms. In both cases, teachers' willingness to use AI was linked to their confidence, how useful they thought AI would be, and whether their schools supported it. Similarly, Kurshumova (2024) studied Bulgarian teachers and found that while many were curious about AI, they lacked experience or proper training. These studies show that teacher training and institutional support are essential for successful AI integration, but there are differences depending on national context.

For example, Chinese teachers seemed more open to AI, possibly because of stronger government support, while Bulgarian teachers were more hesitant due to fewer resources and less exposure. There is also the question of how well teachers actually understand what AI is. Antonenko and Abramowitz (2023) found that many science teachers had misconceptions, often imagining AI as futuristic robots rather than tools that could actually be useful in the classroom. Yau et al. (2023) built on this by showing that teachers had a range of understandings from seeing AI as just a technical tool to thinking of it more broadly as part of an educational system. These findings show that before we expect teachers to use AI effectively, we need to make sure they truly understand what it is and what it can do.

From the students' side, there is a similar mix of interest and caution. Peng and Wan (2024) found that students with social anxiety actually preferred using AI teaching assistants because they felt less pressure, especially for simple tasks. But when things got more complex, they preferred human help for better understanding and emotional support. This lines up with the concerns from Tzirides' study, where both students and teachers seemed unsure about relying too much on AI for deeper support. Another interesting angle comes from Dann et al. (2024), who explored how AI can be used not to teach, but to analyze student engagement and feedback. In this case, AI helped teachers understand how students were doing, showing that AI can be a powerful tool even behind the scenes, once again supporting rather than replacing human roles.

In conclusion, although AI-generated feedback is gaining traction across educational settings, its effectiveness remains highly dependent on contextual, cognitive, and pedagogical factors. Learners and instructors tend to value the immediacy, consistency, and accessibility of AI feedback, yet concerns persist regarding its capacity for depth, personalization, and credibility. The literature suggests that optimal use of AI in writing education requires not only continuous technological enhancement such as domain-specific training and discourse-level sensitivity but also user preparation through prompt engineering, metacognitive scaffolding, and critical engagement. A hybrid feedback model that combines the scalability of AI systems with the interpretive insight and contextual awareness of human instructors may offer the most pedagogically sound and ethically responsible pathway forward.

TOOL SELECTION

We followed a three-phase process (see Figure 1) designed to evaluate the nature and pedagogical value of feedback generated by AI-supported tools in the context of EFL writing instruction. Rather than conducting a tool comparison, our analysis centers on the quality, depth, and educational relevance of feedback, which employed an expert-driven thematic lens.

Figure 1. Study Process

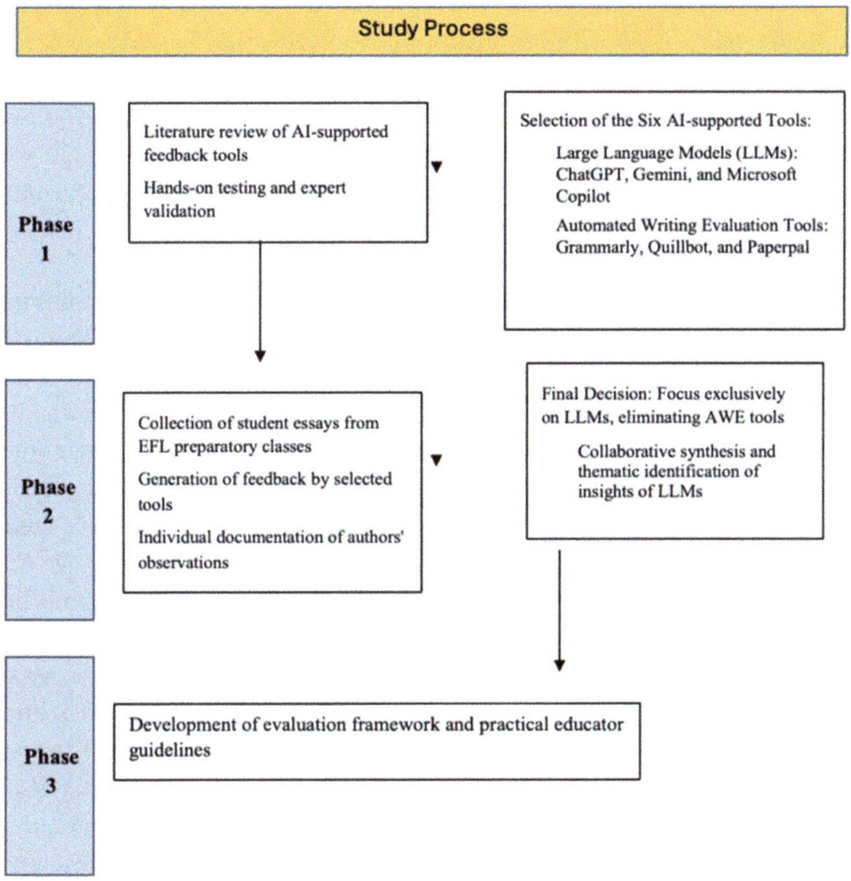

We began with a targeted literature review of AI-supported feedback technologies and as a result, two broad categories emerged:

1. AWE tools focused on mechanical accuracy and localized feedback such as grammar, syntax, vocabulary (Kenshinbay & Ghorbandordinejad, 2024; Koltovskaia, 2023).
2. LLM platforms that offer context-sensitive, dialogue-based guidance, supporting deeper discourse-level and communicative aspects of writing (Lingaiah et al., 2024)

We initially surveyed a range of AWE tools and LLM platforms, emphasizing accessibility, independence from institutional affiliations, and compatibility with personalized learning approaches. This examination allowed us to identify tools frequently highlighted for their potential in EFL writing contexts (Astutik et al., 2024). Simultaneously, we conducted preliminary exploratory testing of these platforms, focusing on usability and feedback sophistication (Stevenson & Phakiti, 2019). We then consulted experts in applied linguistics, educational technology, and language assessment to refine our shortlist of platforms. Using Lawshe's (1975) content validity method, experts rated each prospective tool as "essential," "useful," or "unnecessary" based on its relevance to the study's goals. Divergent opinions were addressed through structured discussion and consensus-building, allowing for a collective, well-rounded decision.

Initially, this screening produced a shortlist of six tools; three AWE tools (Grammarly, Quillbot, and PaperPal) and three LLM-supported platforms (ChatGPT, Copilot, and Gemini, as of their January 2025 versions). However, upon closer analysis, we identified several limitations of the AWE tools: their feedback was often limited to surface-level issues (e.g., grammar or mechanics), lacked meaningful contextual understanding, and offered minimal adaptability to individual learner needs. In contrast, LLMs provided more nuanced, dialogic, and context-sensitive feedback, better aligned with our pedagogical goals. Therefore, we decided to move forward exclusively with the three LLM platforms for the detailed investigation outlined in the following sections (see the right-hand box in Phase 1 of Figure 1).

We collected 15 representative student essays from English preparatory school students at a foundation university in Istanbul. These students, enrolled in an intensive English language program, were tasked with producing short essays in response to structured writing prompts. The prompts required them to compose at least 200 words, demonstrating coherence, lexical variety, grammatical accuracy, and adherence to academic writing conventions, including clear thesis statements, supporting details, logical organization, and appropriate transitions. Essays were anonymized and uploaded to every shortlisted tool. All machine-generated comments, scores, and revision suggestions were exported. We reviewed the feedback on every essay, recording observations in a shared Excel sheet under the five-pronged evaluative framework we co-created in advance. Figure 2 outlines this review workflow.

Figure 2. Analysis Process and Workflow

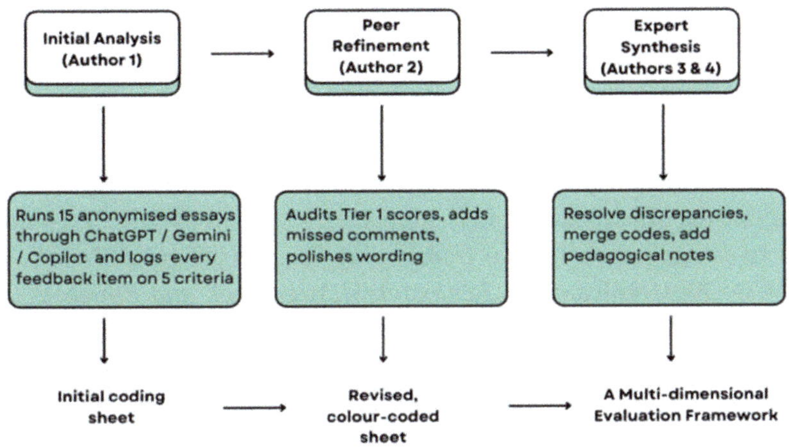

During this review, we observed that AWE outputs were largely limited to sentence-level mechanics and rarely addressed discourse organisation, rhetorical purpose, or cultural nuance. Conversely, LLMs provided interactive follow-up opportunities and richer discourse-level advice. Furthermore, the widespread adoption and accessibility of LLMs in both educational and informal writing spaces suggested a shift in the AI feedback landscape, rendering AWE tools increasingly outdated for higher-order writing development. As a result, continuing to evaluate both tool types equally risked skewing the study's focus toward features that no longer meet the demands of process-based writing pedagogy. Based on this evolving understanding, the authors unanimously decided to discontinue further analysis of the three AWE tools and narrow the focus to the LLM set (see the decision box in Phase 2 of Figure 1). All previously captured AWE data were archived but not included in the ensuing thematic synthesis.

In the last part of this process, we stepped back to look at everything we had gathered such as our notes, the feedback from each tool, and our own reflections to figure out what might actually be useful for teachers. To this end, the aim was not to rank the tools or come up with a one-size-fits-all answer. Instead, we focused on the kinds of things that matter in real classrooms: how helpful the feedback is, whether it fits the way students learn, and how easy it is for teachers to use without losing sight of what makes writing personal and meaningful. Out of these debriefing sessions, we developed a set of ideas. These are better understood as practical suggestions rather than strict rules, to help teachers reflect on when and how to use LLM-based feedback tools. What mattered to us most was making sure that these tools, if used, still leave room for student voice, teacher guidance, and cultural sensitivity. AI can be helpful, but it is only part of the picture. In the end, we sought to offer something grounded that teachers could actually work with, without giving up the parts of teaching that matter most.

EVALUATION FRAMEWORK DESIGN

To examine the effectiveness of AI-supported writing tools in EFL contexts, we propose a five-pronged evaluative framework: *Feedback Type & Depth, Personalization, User Experience (UX), Pedagogical Alignment, and Ethical & Privacy Concerns*. Below, each criterion integrates insights from EFL writing research, educational technology approaches, and practical insights from exploring AWE and LLM tools.

Feedback Type and Depth

When analyzing feedback type and depth in AI-based writing tools, it is useful to distinguish between surface-level corrections, such as spelling or punctuation, and higher-order concerns that address discourse structure, genre conventions, and rhetorical effectiveness (Ferris, 2003; Hyland & Hyland, 2006). Contemporary evaluations of LLM-based feedback confirm that learners still receive abundant sentence-level corrections yet gain far less guidance on argument structure unless the prompt demands it (Aylsworth & Castro, 2024). Like earlier parser studies, these findings underscore the need to separate surface fixes from discourse-level advice (Ferris, 2003; Hyland & Hyland, 2006). Moreover, the degree to which feedback successfully enhances a student's writing ability appears to vary based on proficiency, prompt type, and feedback (Thi & Nikolov, 2021). Traditional parser-based systems often emphasize local errors (grammar, mechanics) without providing metalinguistic explanations, leaving learners to guess *why* a given form is incorrect (Thi & Nikolov, 2021). In contrast, more in-depth feedback offers rule-based insights, e.g., "You need the third-person singular '-s' because your subject is he", and can even supply links to mini-lessons, thereby reinforcing noticing and prompting pushed output. Consequently, a tool that only provides superficial hints may underexploit learners' capacity to notice. Beyond sentence-level accuracy, discourse-oriented feedback can highlight issues like coherence, audience awareness, or pragmatic appropriateness, helping learners progress from "fixing errors *to* developing holistic communicative competence" (Choi, 2024). Ultimately, a robust evaluation of feedback type and depth should consider not only whether a system flags errors, but also how explicitly it explains those errors, how much contextual guidance it provides, and whether it encourages self-correction, factors known to significantly influence learner uptake and long-term writing development (Ferris, 2003; Bitchener & Knoch, 2010). In traditional L2 environments, input-output-interaction-feedback loops frequently arise during direct or peer interactions, wherein learners identify gaps in their interlanguage and negotiate meaning until mutual comprehension is attained (Bitchener & Knoch, 2010). AI-assisted writing tools can partially recreate these processes if the system (a) reacts to individual learner input, (b) recognizes the type of error, (c) offers a clear elucidation of the error, and (d) enables self-correction (Ghanham et al., 2025). In this context, "interaction" refers to learner-tool discourse rather than face-to-face negotiation: the AI identifies issues in written output, highlights linguistic discrepancies (e.g., erroneous verb forms, ambiguous referents), and frequently provides immediate ideas or rule-based clarifications. By directing learners to identify gaps between their output and target standards, and encouraging them to revise, the tool can replicate part of the negotiation typically found between human interlocutors. Although the system's immediate responses may seem to facilitate noticing (Choi, 2024) and encourage revisions, the lack of a genuine communicative partner raises doubts about whether learners are genuinely negotiating meaning or merely acquiescing to automated prompts. The extent to which AI feedback prompts self-correction and facilitates conceptual reorganization in learners, rather than superficial adjustments, ultimately dictates whether the intervention yields significant feedback that fosters authentic interlanguage growth. In conclusion, while AI-driven feedback shows potential for enhancing autonomous L2 writing practice, its effectiveness depends on creating interactions that transcend mere mechanical correction, fostering more profound input-output cycles and ongoing learner engagement. In light of this discussion, this chapter assesses the type and depth of feedback provided by the most favored AI-supported feedback tools concerning these three questions:

a. Does the tool offer rule-based or contextual explanations, including grammar clarifications or stylistic justifications?
b. Does it distinguish between surface-level errors, such as typographical and spelling mistakes, and higher-order concerns, including cohesion and argument structure?
c. What are the immediacy and interactivity of the feedback? Do learners receive prompts for self-correction, or are they simply given answers?

Personalization

Personalization in AI-based writing feedback systems revolves around the capacity of these tools to adapt their responses to each learner's distinctive needs, goals, and error patterns. A personalized AI tool may record repeated grammatical slips, like misplaced articles or incorrect subject-verb agreements, and then tailor future prompts or explanations to address those recurring issues (Woo & Choi, 2021). Over time, the system can dial back the amount of explicit detail if the learner shows progress or provide extra scaffolding if errors persist. Personalization also extends to style and content: some tools allow learners to specify a desired register or genre, such as academic essays or business communication, and consequently modify their suggestions (Nolan & Vang, 2023). Such targeted feedback not only sustains motivation but also fosters deeper engagement, since learners can see how revisions connect to actual linguistic growth (Nolan & Vang, 2023). Through the integration of mini-lessons, user notes, and adaptive analytics, a personalized AI platform can function like a virtual tutor, guiding learners towards progressively intricate writing assignments without causing them to feel overloaded. Ultimately, this individualized support may accelerate the internalization of language forms, encourage sustained drafting and revising, and create a more meaningful interplay between technology-mediated feedback and the learner's personal trajectory in second language acquisition (Lawrance et al., 2024). Given these considerations, this chapter evaluates the personalization features of popular AI-supported feedback tools in response to three key questions:

a. How effectively do they adapt feedback to individual learner profiles, goals, and error patterns?
b. To what extent do they offer scaffolding or mini lessons that resonate with each user's evolving proficiency level?
c. Do they track and display progress in a manner that fosters learner autonomy and sustained engagement?

User Experience

User experience implies the extent to which the interface and functionality of an AI-assisted writing tool facilitate learners' interaction with feedback in a fluid and captivating manner in AWE. Rooted in human-computer interaction principles, as emphasized by the Nielsen Norman Group, UX considerations underscore the significance of interface clarity, intuitive design, and minimal distraction. In an L2 writing situation, such characteristics are crucial since learners must digest linguistic feedback and systematically organize and revise their work. When the interface becomes cluttered or critical functionalities are obscured by ambiguous menus, users may experience frustration, thereby diminishing motivation and hindering revision attempts. In addition to removing interface obstacles, tools must also account for learner autonomy (Reeves & Hedberg, 2003). Allowing writers to choose when they receive feedback, either in real time during composition or after completing a draft, helps preserve their sense of autonomy. This flexibility corresponds with Krashen's concept of reducing emotive barriers: if the interface inundates learners by highlighting every minor inaccuracy immediately, they may experience anxiety or discouragement. Deterding et al. (2011) propose that minimal dosages of gamification, such as acknowledging error reductions or providing badges for persistent revision, can promote sustained engagement without devolving into trivial game mechanics. A well-designed and helpful user interface aids learners in concentrating on meaningful modifications while directing their cognitive efforts towards a more profound awareness and reconstruction of linguistic deficiencies. If the system's navigation presents continual difficulties, learners use more effort interpreting the feedback framework than enhancing their language production. From an SLA standpoint, minimizing the time a writer spends deciphering complex mistake markers maximizes the capacity available for producing precise and coherent text. Consequently, a tool's interface and feedback mechanism should focus learners' attention on substantive language tasks instead of diverting them with intricate design.

Accessibility is a critical component of the broader UX discourse, assuring that all learners, irrespective of their technological backgrounds, bandwidth constraints, or physical capabilities, can capitalize on AI-based writing feedback. In order to be genuinely user-friendly, systems must incorporate assistive technology features, including keyboard navigation, high-contrast layouts, and screen-reader compatibility, as emphasized by scholars in human-computer interaction (Nielsen Norman Group; Seale, 2006). In addition, the "digital divide" (Warschauer, 2003) remains a persistent challenge: learners in under-resourced settings, or those lacking steady internet access, can be excluded if a platform assumes broadband connections or frequent software updates. By embedding these accessibility measures into the interface design, rather than treating them as post-hoc add-ons, AI writing tools can support the diverse populations found in higher education contexts. Ultimately, weaving accessibility into UX ensures that an engaging, low-friction user experience is available to everyone, thereby aligning with inclusive educational goals rather than catering to a narrowly defined "typical" user. Given these considerations, this chapter evaluates the user experience of the mentioned AI-supported feedback tools in response to these questions:

a. Does the system's design effectively display error highlights and explanations, enabling learners to transition from feedback to correction without ambiguity?
b. Are users able to personalize the feedback presentation, for example by choosing real-time or post-draft modes, to align with their comfort levels and reduce anxiety?

c. Does the design incorporate motivating or progress-tracking features, such as badges or dashboards, that sustain interest without diminishing the significance of the revision process?
d. Does the interface alleviate cognitive burden by maintaining simplicity in pop-ups, menus, and icons, or does it potentially obscure writing duties with visual clutter?

Ethics and Privacy

Discussions about ethics in AI often revolve around data collection and privacy legislation, such as GDPR or FERPA. Yet, research by Hovy and Spruit (2016) reminds us of that natural language processing (NLP) carries broader social implications, especially when user text is more than just "neutral data" but reflects personal identity markers, regional dialects, or cultural practices. In their work, they draw attention to challenges like exclusion, overgeneralization, and topic overexposure, warning that NLP systems can inadvertently undermine the very populations they aim to serve if not designed with inclusivity and transparency in mind. This observation aligns with Blodgett et al. (2020), who argue that bias in NLP systems emerges not just from the data itself, but also from the broader sociopolitical context in which technologies operate. Bias, in other words, can become "baked in" to an AI-based writing tool when developers rely on corpora skewed toward particular dialects or demographics, and fail to correct for these imbalances.

Exclusion may occur when a platform's training data heavily skews toward certain demographics or language varieties, leaving speakers of less-represented dialects at a disadvantage. If a writing tool flags region-specific expressions or ethnolects as "incorrect," it perpetuates the bias that standard forms are inherently superior. This problem grows more acute when tools are deployed in multilingual or multicultural institutions, where large numbers of learners may have backgrounds only marginally reflected in the training sets. Over time, such systematic bias can reinforce digital hierarchies or discourage users from expressing their authentic linguistic identities.

A second pitfall, overgeneralization, emerges when models make sweeping inferences about user attributes based on limited text samples. While guessing a writer's approximate proficiency or topical interests might help deliver personalized suggestions, Hovy and Spruit's concerns become pressing once systems begin associating specific language cues with sensitive characteristics like religion or sexual orientation. False positives might be dismissed as harmless quirks in casual scenarios, thinking of receiving an email that misidentifies a user's gender. But the stakes rise sharply if the same misclassifications feed into higher-stakes contexts, such as scholarship applications or institutional evaluations. Oversimplified assumptions risk entrenching existing biases or reinforcing stereotypes, rather than supporting genuine writing improvement.

Overexposure further complicates matters. Certain cultural or demographic groups may be studied or tagged repeatedly leading to a perception that their language patterns are "unusual" or "problematic." This repeated spotlight can unintentionally validate prejudices and portray those groups as exceptions, regardless of actual language complexity or usage norms. By focusing too narrowly on certain "problematic" segments, an AI-based tool can end up ignoring other pressing issues or user populations. For large-scale writing platforms marketed globally, the risk of shaping broader perceptions about entire groups is nontrivial, especially when students across diverse cultural settings adopt these systems for academic or professional writing.

Finally, dual use emerges as an ongoing concern in NLP applications. While advanced text analysis may help detect plagiarism or generate valuable prompts, the same technologies might enable more intrusive surveillance or censorship. If a writing tool collects enough user data to improve its models, it may inadvertently facilitate third-party misuse. This can create scenarios in which institutional or governmental actors leverage the data for aims unrelated to language learning. Hovy and Spruit observe that responsibility for such outcomes often lies not just in the act of data collection, but in the broader ecosystem that repurposes these models for different aims.

In higher education, where students' work may include sensitive research topics or personal reflections, these concerns converge. Whether a writing tool identifies "at-risk" language or inadvertently accentuates differences in proficiency, it could shape how instructors and peers perceive learners. Consequently, ethical design requires more than simple compliance with data security laws. It involves deliberate efforts, such as thoughtful demographic representation in training sets, transparent disclaimers about data usage, and open channels for users to correct or contest model-driven judgments. Consequently, our objective is to conduct a critical analysis of these concerns in order to provide responses to the following questions:

a. Does the tool account for linguistic diversity in its training data, mitigating the risk of demographic exclusion?
b. How does it handle potential inferences about sensitive personal traits (religious views, orientation, etc.), and are there safeguards to prevent damaging overgeneralization?
c. Are certain communities or dialects repeatedly spotlighted as "problematic," potentially skewing how users or instructors perceive them?

TOOL EVALUATION

To systematically assess how AI-supported tools perform in EFL writing feedback, we designed a collaborative evaluation process grounded in our five-dimensional framework. After selecting six tools (three AWE platforms and three LLM-based systems), anonymized student essays were uploaded to each tool and the AI-generated feedback was carefully analyzed. This evaluation process involved all four authors, who independently reviewed the feedback using a shared spreadsheet. Each author coded the AI responses based on five key criteria: feedback type and depth, personalization, user experience, pedagogical alignment, and ethical and privacy concerns. Through this distributed and iterative review process, illustrated in Figure 2, we engaged in collective discussions to compare insights, resolve disagreements, and refine our interpretations of the feedback. As this process unfolded, it became clear that AWE tools, while effective at addressing surface-level issues, offered limited value for discourse-level guidance and rhetorical awareness. Therefore, we made a deliberate decision to focus the remainder of the analysis on LLM-supported tools, which demonstrated more potential for contextualized and pedagogically meaningful feedback.

Feedback Type and Depth

ChatGPT is clearly stronger in diagnostic feedback, while Gemini and Copilot need improvement in depth and actionable clarity. ChatGPT stood out for its *detailed and structured feedback*, providing both praise and suggestions: *"ChatGPT consistently provided detailed and structured feedback... rubric-aligned and tone-adjustable."*

Gemini and Copilot offered feedback of similar length (4–5 sentences) but lacked meaningful substance:

Gemini: *"Feedback felt mechanical and generic... lacked depth or personalization."*

Copilot: *"Provided 4–5 sentence feedback with praise but limited concrete examples or analysis."*

Personalized Feedback

Gemini lacked consistency, with personalization not evident across essays:
"Initially appeared to lack flexibility... personalization was inconsistent."
Copilot mirrored Gemini's limitations:
"Didn't demonstrate student-specific guidance or tone modulation."

ChatGPT excelled in generating feedback that feels tailored to individual students, a major pedagogical strength. ChatGPT demonstrated adaptive language and a supportive tone:

"Feels adaptive and personalized in its tone, mimicking a real teacher's feedback."

User Experience (UX):

ChatGPT leads in UX with smooth interface features; Gemini and Copilot present friction points for practical use at scale. ChatGPT offered a responsive and efficient workflow:

"Strong user experience... allows side-by-side viewing, quick copy/paste, and comment export."

Gemini lacked functionality that supports review efficiency:

"Interface was clean but not responsive... lacked export functionality."

Copilot experienced usability drops:

"Responded quickly at first, but it couldn't sustain fast processing with multiple essays."

Pedagogical Alignment

ChatGPT offers pedagogically aligned feedback that supports learning progression, while Gemini and Copilot are more assessment-oriented. All three tools showed some level of alignment, but with varied robustness:

Gemini: *"Shows a thoughtful structure aligned with the rubric."*

Copilot: *"Begins with direct scoring accompanied by a rationale."*

Gemini and Copilot sometimes over-relied on scoring without developmental feedback:

Copilot: *"Scoring system may lead to over-focus on grades rather than learning process."*

Ethical and Privacy Concerns

All tools are broadly ethical, but only Copilot foregrounds these concerns clearly. ChatGPT is safe for institutional use but would benefit from more visible privacy controls. Copilot explicitly highlights ethical standards:

"Demonstrates a clear commitment to ethical use and anonymization."

Gemini met basic standards but lacked transparency:

"Meets ethical expectations for a classroom tool, but gives no transparency in how it processes user data."

The comparative evaluation of Gemini, Microsoft Copilot and ChatGPT revealed distinct strengths and limitations across feedback quality, user interaction, and educational alignment. ChatGPT emerged as the most adaptable and pedagogically sound option, particularly when formative feedback and learner engagement are prioritized. Gemini offered structure and transparency but lacked personalization and adaptability. Copilot, while promising in certain technical aspects, proved inconsistent and less reliable for sustained educational use.

In sum, the effective use of generative AI tools in EFL writing assessment depends not only on the accuracy of feedback but also on the tool's ability to foster meaningful teacher-student dialogue, support revision cycles, and maintain ethical integrity in practice. As AI continues to evolve, teachers must critically assess both the capabilities and limitations of such tools to make informed decisions about their integration into teaching and learning.

THEMATIC SYNTHESIS

To evaluate the effectiveness of AI-supported feedback tools in EFL writing, our thematic synthesis aligns closely with a five-pronged evaluative framework grounded in SLA and educational technology literature. In terms of *Feedback Type and Depth*, ChatGPT was noted for its detailed and rubric-aligned comments, reflecting the call in prior research (Cotos & Pendar, 2015; Lee, 2020) for feedback that moves beyond surface-level corrections toward higher-order writing concerns. This contrasts with Gemini and CoPilot, whose mechanical and generic responses echo traditional AWE limitations in focusing on local errors (Ranalli et al., 2016) without fostering metalinguistic awareness or noticing (Leow, 2015).

Regarding *Personalized Feedback*, ChatGPT again demonstrated strength by simulating teacher-like scaffolding, which supports Kochmar et al. (2022) and Lim et al. (2020)'s emphasis on adaptive, dialogic feedback tailored to student proficiency. Conversely, Gemini and Copilot lacked dynamic responsiveness, falling short of effective adaptation for individual learning trajectories. From *UX perspective*, ChatGPT offered responsive features such as export options and side-by-side commenting, supporting Amershi et al. (2019)'s principles of effective human-computer interaction and Rahimi et al. (2024)'s call for accessible revision tools in multilingual classrooms. In contrast, Gemini's limited interface and Copilot's lag in batch processing revealed usability barriers that may further disadvantage learners with limited access, reinforcing digital divide concerns (UNESCO, 2023). In terms of *pedagogical alignment*, only ChatGPT encouraged process writing through structured, revision-oriented feedback consistent with the literature emphasizing iterative drafting and meaning focused output (Novia & Saptarina, 2020; Rahimi et al., 2024). In contrast,

Gemini and Copilot emphasized summative scoring without developmental cues, risking a reduction of writing to performance rather than process.

Finally, while all tools appeared ethically adequate, only Copilot made explicit efforts toward anonymization and transparency, aligning with Bozkurt et al. (2024)'s ethical imperatives in AI deployment. ChatGPT's institutional safety was noted, though greater transparency would enhance user trust, and Gemini's opaque data practices fall short of current expectations for fairness and accountability. Collectively, these findings reinforce the necessity of combining SLA principles with responsible EdTech design to optimize AI tool adoption in EFL writing contexts.

INTEGRATION GUIDELINES

The following guidelines and multi-dimensional evaluative framework are designed to assist teachers in making informed decisions when selecting and implementing AI-supported feedback tools in EFL writing contexts. Rather than offering prescriptive solutions, they reflect key insights drawn from our systematic evaluation of LLM-based feedback systems across multiple dimensions, including feedback depth, personalization, user experience, pedagogical alignment, and ethical considerations. These recommendations aim to balance the efficiency and scalability of AI-generated feedback with the critical need for human mediation, learner autonomy, and context-sensitive instructional practices. By highlighting important considerations from tool selection to classroom integration, the guidelines seek to support practitioners in leveraging AI tools in ways that enhance rather than replace teacher feedback, while also fostering meaningful, reflective learning experiences for students.

Actionable Guidelines for Human-AI Collaboration in EFL Writing

Based on the in-depth examination of AI-supported feedback in EFL writing, the following guidelines are proposed to inform the selection, implementation, and evaluation of LLMs in EFL writing instruction:

When selecting and combining LLMs:

1. Prioritize tools that demonstrate pedagogical alignment and revision-oriented feedback. ChatGPT encourages iterative drafting and structured feedback.
2. Choose systems offering adaptive feedback instead of static scoring. Personalized responses better support diverse learner needs and trajectories.

3. Evaluate UX carefully. Features like export options and efficient batch processing improve usability for both teachers and learners.

During feedback and revision:

4. Promote teacher mediation and student engagement with AI feedback. AI should complement, not replace, human input to foster reflective learning.
5. Integrate AI feedback within a broader feedback ecosystem, alongside peer review and teacher comments, to ensure meaningful support.
6. Combine tools strategically. While Gemini and Copilot address local errors, discourse-level feedback requires more context-sensitive models like ChatGPT.
7. Use exemplar seeding (e.g., pasting a model paragraph) to increase LLMs' depth of feedback.

For ethical and practical concerns:

8. Select tools with clear data privacy and ethical standards. Options like Copilot, which prioritize anonymization, can help protect user trust.
9. Monitor AI feedback for bias or formulaic tendencies. Teacher oversight is essential to maintain writing authenticity and cultural sensitivity.
10. Train learners to interpret AI suggestions critically, fostering autonomous decision-making during revision.

These guidelines not only emerged through our thematic evaluation but also directly informed the development of the *Framework for Integrating LLMs into Writing Assessment and Feedback Cycles* (see Table 2). The framework translates these key recommendations into a structured, step-by-step process that guides educators from the initial planning and prompt design stages through the practical application of LLM feedback and, ultimately, to fostering learner agency and ensuring ethical use. By aligning each phase and action with the evaluation dimensions highlighted earlier, such as feedback depth, pedagogical alignment, personalization, and ethical considerations, the framework offers a comprehensive roadmap for implementing AI-generated feedback meaningfully and responsibly in EFL writing contexts.

Table 2. Framework for Integrating LLMs into Writing Assessment and Feedback Cycles

Phase	Step	Action	Purpose	Evaluation Criteria
I. Planning & Design	1. Define the feedback goal	Identify the instructional focus and choose a specific writing skill or rubric dimension (e.g., organization, grammar, cohesion).	Targeted prompts lead to more focused, relevant, and rubric-aligned feedback.	Feedback Type & Depth · Pedagogical Alignment
	2. Design the prompt thoughtfully	Frame the prompt in clear and concise language. Avoid overloading the model with multiple requests.	Streamlined prompts help LLMs produce more accurate, coherent feedback.	Pedagogical Alignment · UX
II. First Pass with the LLM	3. Input drafts strategically	Process drafts in manageable batches (10–15 texts). Export results before editing or sharing.	Supports consistency and efficient data management while maintaining control.	UX · Feedback Type & Depth
	4. Apply the Keep–Adjust–Remove filter	Review LLM feedback: keep what is accurate, adjust tone/clarity, and remove generic or incorrect comments.	Enhances clarity and usefulness of feedback while preserving learner voice.	Personalization · Feedback Type & Depth
III. Enhancing for Learner Uptake	5. Add scaffolds: Tasks and examples	Convert feedback into specific revision actions. Provide model sentences where helpful.	Encourages meaningful revision through explicit instruction and modeling.	Pedagogical Alignment · Feedback Type & Depth
	6. Encourage student agency	Ask students to Accept, Modify, or Reject comments with brief justification.	Promotes critical thinking and student ownership of the revision process.	Personalization · Feedback Type & Depth
	7. Request clarification when needed	Use follow-up prompts to make vague feedback specific (e.g., "Point to the unclear sentence").	Improves clarity and helps students better understand the feedback.	Feedback Type & Depth · UX
	8. Integrate reflection	Conclude with a short reflective task (e.g., "Which LLM comment improved your draft most, and why?").	Deepens learning and supports transfer to future writing tasks.	Pedagogical Alignment · Personalization
IV. Ethical & Practical Considerations	9. Address privacy and consent	Anonymize student data, explain data storage procedures, and delete data post-analysis.	Builds trust and ensures compliance with privacy regulations.	Ethics & Privacy · UX
	10. Iterate and adapt	Review the impact of LLM integration regularly; revise prompts and workflows as needed.	Supports responsive instruction and continuous improvement.	Pedagogical Alignment · Ethics & Privacy

Revisiting the Framework: From Analytical Lens to Practical Model

The five-dimensional evaluation framework introduced in the early stages of this chapter was originally designed as a guiding heuristic to systematically examine the affordances and limitations of AI-supported feedback tools. Throughout the process of tool selection, thematic analysis, and guideline formulation, this framework proved to be not only analytically robust but also pedagogically generative. Each dimension (see Figure 3) was iteratively tested and substantiated through empirical engagement with the tools in authentic educational contexts. Consequently, rather than remaining a theoretical construct, the framework has evolved into a validated and context-sensitive model that underpins the practical recommendations presented in the preceding guidelines. In this regard, we conclude this chapter by reintroducing the finalized version of the framework, now reframed as a synthesized outcome of the study and as a scaffold for educators and researchers seeking principled integration of LLM-generated feedback into EFL writing pedagogy. In doing so, it reflects the AI Manifesto's emphasis on transparency, accountability, and learner protection, guiding the selection and implementation of AI tools based on pedagogical soundness and contextual relevance.

Figure 3. Five-Dimensional Framework for Evaluating AI-Supported Feedback Tools in EFL Contexts

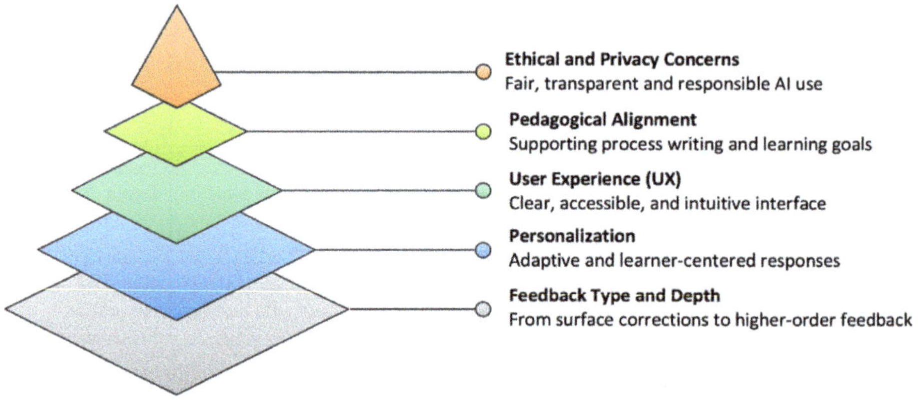

CONCLUSION

As AI tools for writing feedback become more common, their place in language education needs to be considered carefully, not just welcomed by default (Khuder, 2025). In this chapter, we looked at how LLMs, when paired with active teacher support, can play a role in helping EFL learners improve their writing. We zoomed onto three tools *Copilot, ChatGPT, and Gemini* and assessed them using five criteria: the depth of feedback, how well it is, if at all, personalized, the overall user experience, how closely it aligns with good teaching practices, and whether it meets ethical standards. While the tools were often helpful for grammar, structure, and clarity, they were observed to fall short when it came to more nuanced needs like cultural awareness or individualized advice. Rather than suggesting that one tool outperforms the others, what really matters is how and why they are used. These tools can certainly ease some of the pressure on teachers and give students more timely input, but they work best when they are part of a larger teaching approach: one that includes guidance, discussion, and reflection. In that sense, teachers are not optional; they are central. Their role is instrumental in interpreting the feedback, shaping how it is used, and keeping the focus on growth, not just correction.

Aligning the findings of this study with the learner-first principles set out in the AI Manifesto, this chapter is an attempt to contribute to a broader vision of educational AI that is not only functional per se, but also pedagogically responsive, ethically responsible, and socially inclusive. While the tools examined in this chapter show potential in helping EFL writing instruction, their effective use largely depends on how they are integrated into existing pedagogical practices. That is, critical questions remain: *How do learners engage with AI-generated feedback in practice? What forms of teacher mediation are most effective in guiding this engagement? And how can institutions establish policies that ensure responsible, transparent, and equitable implementation?* As such, we argue that AI feedback tools may expand the possibilities for language learning, but their value will ultimately depend on the ways teachers and learners choose to interact with them: consciously, critically, and with attention to context.

Suggestions and Implications

Based on the findings of this study, several recommendations can be made for the thoughtful integration of generative AI tools into EFL writing instruction. First, rather than viewing AI as a replacement for human evaluation, it should be embraced as a complementary support system that can enhance the feedback process. Platforms like ChatGPT can offer immediate, detailed, and language-focused responses that may benefit learners who need consistent practice and reinforcement, especially outside the classroom. However, the human element remains indispensable in offering nuanced, empathetic, and context-sensitive guidance.

These insights resonate with the principles outlined in the *AI Manifesto for Open and Digital Education* (Bozkurt et al., 2024), which emphasizes ethical, inclusive, and pedagogically sound uses of AI in education. The manifesto advocates for responsible integration of AI grounded in openness, transparency, and learner empowerment, values that should guide how feedback technologies are implemented in EFL writing contexts. In alignment with this vision, educators should be equipped to critically evaluate AI-generated feedback and help students develop reflective strategies to engage with it meaningfully.

Professional development programs can play a key role in supporting teachers to navigate the evolving AI landscape. Such programs should focus not only on technical use but also on ethical considerations and pedagogical adaptation. Students, in turn, should be encouraged to use AI tools as part of a broader metacognitive learning strategy, learning to revise and refine their writing based on feedback from both human and non-human sources.

Furthermore, curriculum designers and educational policymakers are urged to adopt an inclusive, student-centered approach to AI integration that reflects the manifesto's call for socially responsible and humanistic uses of technology. Considerations around data privacy, algorithmic bias, and equitable access must be at the forefront to ensure AI supports all learners effectively and fairly.

Future research should explore the long-term impact of AI-supported feedback on writing development, motivation, and learner autonomy. It would also be beneficial to examine how these tools can function in peer feedback environments, collaborative writing, and diverse assessment models. By grounding future developments in both empirical evidence and the ethical framework provided by the AI Manifesto, educators and researchers can work toward a more equitable and human-centered future for AI in language education.

REFERENCES

Amershi, S., Weld, D. S., Vorvoreanu, M., Fourney, A., Nushi, B., Collisson, P., Suh, J., Iqbal, S. T., Bennett, P. N., Quinn, K. I., Teevan, J., Kikin-Gil, R., & Horvitz, E. (2019).Guidelines for Human-AI Interaction. *Proceedings of the 2019 CHI Conference on Human Factors in Computing Systems.* DOI: 10.1145/3290605.3300233

Antonenko, P., & Abramowitz, B. (2023). In-service teachers' (mis)conceptions of artificial intelligence in K-12 science education. *Journal of Research on Technology in Education, 55*(1), 64–78. DOI: 10.1080/15391523.2022.2119450

Astutik, I., Widiati, U., Ratri, D., Jonathans, P., Nurkamilah, N., Devanti, Y., & Harfal, Z. (2024). Transformative practices: Integrating automated writing evaluation in higher education writing classrooms - A systematic review. [IJOLAE]. *Indonesian Journal on Learning and Advanced Education, 6*(3), 423–441. DOI: 10.23917/ijolae.v6i3.23675

Awidi, I. T. (2024). Comparing expert tutor evaluation of reflective essays with marking by generative artificial intelligence (AI) tool. *Computers and Education: Artificial Intelligence, 6*, 100226. DOI: 10.1016/j.caeai.2024.100226

Aylsworth, T., & Castro, C. (2024). *Kantian ethics and the attention economy.* Palgrave Macmillan., DOI: 10.1007/978-3-031-45638-1

Biswas, M. I., Talukder, M. S., & Khan, A. R. (2024). Who do you choose? Employees' perceptions of artificial intelligence versus humans in performance feedback. *China Accounting and Finance Review, 26*(4), 512–532. DOI: 10.1108/CAFR-08-2023-0095

Bitchener, J., & Knoch, U. (2010). Raising the linguistic accuracy level of advanced L2 writers with written corrective feedback. *Journal of Second Language Writing, 19*(4), 207–217. DOI: 10.1016/j.jslw.2010.10.002

Blodgett, S. L., Barocas, S., Daumé, H.III, & Wallach, H. (2020). Language (technology) is power: A critical survey of "bias" in NLP. In *Proceedings of the 58th Annual Meeting of the Association for Computational Linguistics* (pp. 5454–5476). ACL. https://doi.org/DOI: 10.18653/v1/2020.acl-main.485

Bozkurt, A., Xiao, J., Farrow, R., Bai, J. Y. H., Nerantzi, C., Moore, S., Dron, J., Stracke, C. M., Singh, L., Crompton, H., Koutropoulos, A., Terentev, E., Pazurek, A., Nichols, M., Sidorkin, A. M., Costello, E., Watson, S., Mulligan, D., Honeychurch, S., & Asino, T. I. (2024). The manifesto for teaching and learning in a time of generative AI: A critical collective stance to better navigate the future. *Open Praxis, 16*(4), 487–513. DOI: 10.55982/openpraxis.16.4.777

Chai, C. S., Liang, S., & Wang, X. (2024). A survey study of Chinese teachers' continuous intentions to teach artificial intelligence. *Education and Information Technologies*, *29*(11), 14015–14034. DOI: 10.1007/s10639-023-12430-z

Choi, J.-Y. (2024). *Generative AI-based writing feedback model development*. Korean Association for Literacy. DOI: 10.37736/KJLR.2024.10.15.5.01

Cotos, E., & Pendar, N. (2015). Discourse classification into rhetorical functions for AWE feedback. *CALICO Journal*, *33*(1), 92–116. Advance online publication. DOI: 10.1558/cj.v33i1.27047

Dann, C., Redmond, P., Fanshawe, M., Brown, A., Getenet, S., Shaik, T., Tao, X., Galligan, L., & Li, Y. (2024). Making sense of student feedback and engagement using artificial intelligence. *Australasian Journal of Educational Technology*, *40*(3), 58–76. DOI: 10.14742/ajet.8903

Deterding, S., Dixon, D., Khaled, R., & Nacke, L. (2011). From game design elements togamefulness: Defining "gamification." In *Proceedings of the 15th International Academic MindTrek Conference: Envisioning Future Media Environments* (pp. 9–15). ACM.

Er, E., Akçapınar, G., Bayazıt, A., Noroozi, O., & Banihashem, S. K. (2025). Assessing student perceptions and use of instructor versus AI-generated feedback. *British Journal of Educational Technology*, *56*(3), 1074–1091. DOI: 10.1111/bjet.13558

Escalante, J., Pack, A., & Barrett, A. (2023). AI-generated feedback on writing: Insights into efficacy and ENL student preference. *International Journal of Educational Technology in Higher Education*, *20*(1), 57. DOI: 10.1186/s41239-023-00425-2

Ferris, D. R. (2003). *Response to student writing: Implications for second language students*. Routledge., DOI: 10.4324/9781410607201

Greene Nolan, H., & Vang, M.C. (2023). Automated Essay Scoring in Middle School Writing: Understanding Key Predictors of Students' Growth and Comparing Artificial Intelligence- and Teacher-Generated Scores and Feedback.

Gutai, G., & Klímová, B. (2024). *Methodological challenges in teaching writing with ChatGPT*. Slavonic Pedagogical Studies Journal. DOI: 10.18355/PG.2024.13.2.14

Hovy, D., & Spruit, S. L. (2016). The social impact of natural language processing. *Annual Meeting of the Association for Computational Linguistics, 54,* 591–598. https://doi.org/DOI: 10.18653/v1/P16-2096

Huang, J., & Teng, M. (2025). *Peer feedback and ChatGPT-generated feedback on Japanese EFL students' engagement in a foreign language writing context*. Digital Applied Linguistics., DOI: 10.29140/dal.v2.102469

Huawei, S., & Aryadoust, V. (2022). A systematic review of automated writing evaluation systems. *Education and Information Technologies*, *28*(1), 771–795. Advance online publication. DOI: 10.1007/s10639-022-11200-7

Hyland, K., & Hyland, F. (2006). Feedback on second language students' writing. *Language Teaching*, *39*(2), 83–101. DOI: 10.1017/S0261444806003399

Ji, H., Han, I., & Ko, Y. (2023). A systematic review of conversational AI in language education: Focusing on the collaboration with human teachers. *Journal of Research on Technology in Education*, *55*(1), 48–63. DOI: 10.1080/15391523.2022.2142873

Jukiewicz, M. (2024). The future of grading programming assignments in education: The role of ChatGPT in automating the assessment and feedback process. *Thinking Skills and Creativity*, *52*, 101522. DOI: 10.1016/j.tsc.2024.101522

Kenshinbay, T., & Ghorbandordinejad, F. (2024). *Exploring AI-driven adaptive feedback in the second language writing skills prompt*. EIKI Journal of Effective Teaching Methods., DOI: 10.59652/jetm.v2i3.264

Khuder, B. (2025). Enhancing disciplinary voice through feedback-seeking in AI-assisted doctoral writing for publication. *Applied Linguistics*, •••, amaf022. DOI: 10.1093/applin/amaf022

Kochmar, E., Vu, D. D., Belfer, R., Gupta, V., Serban, I. V., & Pineau, J. (2022). Automated data-driven generation of personalized pedagogical interventions in intelligent tutoring systems. *International Journal of Artificial Intelligence in Education*, *32*(2), 323–349. DOI: 10.1007/s40593-021-00267-x

Koltovskaia, S. (2023). Postsecondary L2 writing teachers' use and perceptions of Grammarly as a complement to their feedback. *ReCALL*, *35*(3), 290–304. DOI: 10.1017/S0958344022000179

Kurshumova, D. A. (2024). A snapshot of Bulgarian school teachers' familiarity with, use of, and opinions on artificial intelligence at the threshold of its incorporation into the educational process. *Discover Education*, *3*(1), 138. DOI: 10.1007/s44217-024-00225-4

Lawshe, C. H. (1975). A quantitative approach to content validity. *Personnel Psychology*, *28*(4), 563–575. DOI: 10.1111/j.1744-6570.1975.tb01393.x

Lee, I. (2020). Utility of focused/comprehensive written corrective feedback research for authentic L2 writing classrooms. *Journal of Second Language Writing*, *49*, 100734. DOI: 10.1016/j.jslw.2020.100734

Leow, R. P. (2015). *Explicit learning in the L2 classroom: A student-centered approach*. Routledge., DOI: 10.4324/9781315887074

Li, W.-Y., Kau, K., & Shiung, Y.-J. (2023). Pedagogic Exploration Into Adapting Automated Writing Evaluation and Peer Review Integrated Feedback Into Large-Sized University Writing Classes. *SAGE Open*, *13*(4), 21582440231209087. Advance online publication. DOI: 10.1177/21582440231209087

Liang, W., Krasheninnikov, K., Kim, M., Zhang, Y., Guo, M., He, J., & Zou, J. (2024). *Can Large Language Models Provide Useful Feedback on Research Papers? A Large-Scale Empirical Analysis*. Stanford University. https://arxiv.org/abs/2310.01783

Liew, P. Y., & Tan, I. K. (2024). On automated essay grading using large language models. *Proceedings of the 2024 8th International Conference on Computer Science and Artificial Intelligence*.DOI: 10.1145/3709026.3709030

Lim, L.-A., Dawson, S., Gašević, D., Joksimović, S., Fudge, A., Pardo, A., & Gentili, S. (2020). Students' sense-making of personalised feedback based on learning analytics. *Australasian Journal of Educational Technology*, *36*(6), 15–33. DOI: 10.14742/ajet.6370

Lingaiah, J., Ishak, S. N., & Mishra, P. K. (2024). AI-driven chatbots as language tutors: Enhancing written proficiency in ESL. *International Journal of Humanities and Social Science*, *3*(5), 78–95. Advance online publication. DOI: 10.47941/ijhss.2410

Mohammed, S. J., & Khalid, M. W. (2025). Under the world of AI-generated feedback on writing: Mirroring motivation, foreign language peace of mind, trait emotional intelligence, and writing development. *Language Testing in Asia*, *15*(1), 7. DOI: 10.1186/s40468-025-00343-2

Nazaretsky, T., Mejia-Domenzain, P., Swamy, V., Frej, J., & Käser, T. (2024). AI or Human? Evaluating Student Feedback Perceptions in Higher Education. In Ferreira Mello, R., Rummel, N., Jivet, I., Pishtari, G., & Ruipérez Valiente, J. A. (Eds.), Lecture Notes in Computer Science: Vol. 15159. *Technology Enhanced Learning for Inclusive and Equitable Quality Education. EC-TEL 2024*. Springer., DOI: 10.1007/978-3-031-72315-5_20

Nielsen Norman Group. (n.d.). Usability and user experience research. [Online resource at https://www.nngroup.com/]

Novia, F., & Saptarina, E. (2020). Process Writing Approach (PWA): The Correlation between Students Writing Attitude and Writing Achievement. *Conference: 4th Sriwijaya University Learning and Education International Conference (SULE-IC 2020)* https://doi.org/DOI: 10.2991/assehr.k.201230.127

Pahi, K., Hawlader, S., Hicks, E., Zaman, A., & Phan, V. (2024). Enhancing active learning through collaboration between human teachers and generative AI. *Computers and Education Open*, *6*, 100183. DOI: 10.1016/j.caeo.2024.100183

Peng, Z., & Wan, Y. (2024). Human vs. AI: Exploring students' preferences between human and AI TA and the effect of social anxiety and problem complexity. *Education and Information Technologies*, *29*(1), 1217–1246. DOI: 10.1007/s10639-023-12374-4

Polakova, P., & Ivenz, P. (2024). The impact of ChatGPT feedback on the development of EFL students' writing skills. *Cogent Education*, *11*(1), 2410101. Advance online publication. DOI: 10.1080/2331186X.2024.2410101

Rahimi, M., Fathi, J., & Zou, D. (2024). Exploring the impact of automated written corrective feedback on the academic writing skills of EFL learners: An activity theory perspective. *Education and Information Technologies*. Advance online publication. DOI: 10.1007/s10639-024-12896-5

Ramzan, K., Batool, A., Arslan, M. F., & Fatima, H. (2025). Evaluating human vs AI feedback on students' performance; A comparative analysis of students at intermediate level. *Journal of Applied Linguistics and TESOL*, *8*(1).

Ranalli, J., Link, S., & Chukharev-Hudilainen, E. (2016). Automated writing evaluation for formative assessment of second language writing: Investigating the accuracy and usefulness of feedback as part of argument-based validation. *Educational Psychology*, *37*(1), 8–25. DOI: 10.1080/01443410.2015.1136407

Reeves, T. C., & Hedberg, J. G. (2003). *Interactive learning systems evaluation*. Educational Technology Publications.

Seale, J. (2006). *E-learning and disability in higher education: Accessibility research and practice*. Routledge. DOI: 10.4324/9780203969595

Shi, H., & Aryadoust, V. (2024). A systematic review of AI-based automated written feedback research. *ReCALL*, *36*(2), 187–209. Advance online publication. DOI: 10.1017/S0958344023000265

Steiss, J., Tate, T., Graham, S., Cruz, J., Hebert, M., Wang, J., Moon, Y., Tseng, W., Warschauer, M., & Olson, C. B. (2024). Comparing the quality of human and ChatGPT feedback of students' writing. *Learning and Instruction*, *91*, 101894. DOI: 10.1016/j.learninstruc.2024.101894

Stevenson, M., & Phakiti, A. (2019). Automated feedback and second language writing. In *The Cambridge Handbook of Language Learning*. https://doi.org/DOI: 10.1017/9781108635547.009

Tam, A. C. F. (2024). *Interacting with ChatGPT for Internal Feedback and Factors Affecting Feedback Quality*. The Hong Kong Polytechnic University., DOI: 10.1080/02602938.2024.2374485

Tang, X. (2024). An empirical study on the effects of AI-generated feedback on English writing. .DOI: 10.26789/ijest.v3i9.2010

Thi, N. K., & Nikolov, M. (2021). Feedback Treatments, Writing Tasks, and Accuracy Measures: A Critical Review of Research on Written Corrective Feedback. Tesl-Ej, 25(3), n3. Retrieved from https://files.eric.ed.gov/fulltext/EJ1332267.pdf

UNESCO. (2023). Global education monitoring report on technology in education. *United Nations Educational, Scientific and Cultural Organization.* https://unesdoc.unesco.org

Wang, K., Chai, C.-S., Liang, J.-C., & Sang, G. (2024). Exploring teachers' behavioural intentions to design artificial intelligence-assisted learning in Chinese K–12 education. *Technology, Pedagogy and Education*, *33*(5), 629–645. DOI: 10.1080/1475939X.2024.2369241

Warschauer, M. (2003). *Technology and social inclusion: Rethinking the digital divide*. MIT Press., DOI: 10.7551/mitpress/6699.001.0001

Warschauer, M., Tseng, W., Yim, S., Webster, T., Jacob, S., Du, Q., & Tate, T. (2023). The affordances and contradictions of AI-generated text for writers of English as a second or foreign language. *Journal of Second Language Writing*, *62*, 101071. DOI: 10.1016/j.jslw.2023.101071

Woo, J., & Choi, H. (2021). Systematic Review for AI-based Language Learning Tools. ArXiv, abs/2111.04455.https://doi.org//arXiv.2111.04455DOI: 10.48550

Wu, R., Zong, H., Wu, E., Peng, Z., Zhao, J., Yang, L., Xie, H., & Shen, B. (2024). Exploring the potential of artificial intelligence to enhance the writing of English academic papers by non-native English-speaking medical students - the educational application of ChatGPT. *BMC Medical Education*, *24*(1), 736. Advance online publication. DOI: 10.1186/s12909-024-05738-y

Yau, K. W., Chai, C. S., Chiu, T. K., Meng, H., King, I., & Yam, Y. (2023). A phenomenographic approach on teacher conceptions of teaching Artificial Intelligence (AI) in K-12 schools. *Education and Information Technologies*, *28*(1), 1041–1064. DOI: 10.1007/s10639-022-11161-x

Yoon, H. J. (2021). Interactions in EFL argumentative writing: Effects of topic, L1 background, and L2 proficiency on interactional metadiscourse. *Reading and Writing*, *34*(3), 705–725. DOI: 10.1007/s11145-020-10085-7

Zapata, G. C., Cope, B., Kalantzis, M., Tzirides, A. O., Saini, A. K., Searsmith, D., Whiting, J., Kastania, N. P., Castro, V., Kourkoulou, T., Jones, J. W., & Abrantes da Silva, R. (2025). AI and peer reviews in higher education: Students' multimodal views on benefits, differences and limitations. *Technology, Pedagogy and Education*, •••, 1–19. DOI: 10.1080/1475939X.2025.2480807

KEY TERMS AND DEFINITIONS

AI-Supported Feedback Tools: Digital platforms using AI algorithms to analyze learner writing and provide real-time, personalized suggestions for improvement.

Artificial Intelligence (AI): Computer systems designed to mimic human intelligence, performing tasks like language processing, pattern recognition, and decision-making, especially within educational feedback contexts.

Context-Sensitive Feedback: Feedback tailored to the learner's level, purpose, and specific writing context, rather than relying on generic language rules.

EFL (English as a Foreign Language): Learning and teaching English in a context where it is not the native language, typically for academic or professional use.

Evaluation Framework: A structured model combining theory and expert input to assess the relevance and quality of AI-generated feedback in educational settings.

Formative Feedback: Ongoing and constructive information aimed at guiding student improvement rather than judging final performance.

Human–AI Collaboration in Assessment: A cooperative model where both AI systems and human instructors contribute to evaluating student writing for more balanced and meaningful feedback.

Learner–AI Interaction: The process by which students engage with AI tools during writing tasks, interpreting and responding to automated feedback.

Compilation of References

Adiguzel, T., Kaya, M. H., & Cansu, F. K. (2023). Revolutionizing education with AI: Exploring the transformative potential of ChatGPT. *Contemporary Educational Technology*, *15*(3), ep429. DOI: 10.30935/cedtech/13152

Agarwal, N., & Tayal, D. K. (2022). FFT-based ensembled model to predict ranks of higher educational institutions. *Multimedia Tools and Applications*, *81*(23), 34129–34162. DOI: 10.1007/s11042-022-13180-9

Agrawal, S., Oza, P., Kakkar, R., Tanwar, S., Jetani, V., Undhad, J., & Singh, A. (2024). Analysis and recommendation system-based on PRISMA checklist to write systematic review. *Assessing Writing*, *61*, 100866. DOI: 10.1016/j.asw.2024.100866

Ahmad, S. F., Han, H., Alam, M. M., Rehmat, M. K., Irshad, M., Arraño-Muñoz, M., & Ariza-Montes, A. (2023). Impact of artificial intelligence on human loss in decision making, laziness and safety in education. *Humanities & Social Sciences Communications*, *10*(1), 311. DOI: 10.1057/s41599-023-01787-8

Akmal. (2019). Lebih dekat dengan Industri 4.0. Deepublish.

Akpan, I. J., Kobara, Y. M., Owolabi, J., Akpan, A. A., & Offodile, O. F. (2025). Conversational and generative artificial intelligence and human–chatbot interaction in education and research. *International Transactions in Operational Research*, *32*(3), 1251–1281. DOI: 10.1111/itor.13522

Akyol, Ş. P., Krishna, K., & Wang, J. (2018). *Taking PISA seriously: How accurate are low stakes exams?* NBER Working Paper No. 24930.

Alali, R., & Wardat, Y. (2024). Opportunities and Challenges of Integrating Generative Artificial Intelligence in Education. *International Journal of Religion*, *5*(7), 784–793. DOI: 10.61707/8y29gv34

Alan, S., & Yurt, E. (2024). Flipped Learning: An Innovative Model for Enhancing Education Through ChatGPT. *International Journal of Modern Education Studies*, *8*(1), 124. DOI: 10.51383/ijonmes.2024.328

Alasadi, E., & Baiz, C. (2023). Generative AI in education and research: Opportunities, concerns, and solutions. *Journal of Chemical Education*, *100*(8), 2965–2971. DOI: 10.1021/acs.jchemed.3c00323

Albadarin, Y., Saqr, M., Pope, N., & Tukiainen, M. (2024). A systematic literature review of empirical research on ChatGPT in education. *Discover Education*, *3*(1), 60. DOI: 10.1007/s44217-024-00138-2

AlDahoul, N., Rahwan, T., & Zaki, Y. (2025). AI-generated faces influence gender stereotypes and racial homogenization. *Scientific Reports*, *15*(1), 14449. DOI: 10.1038/s41598-025-99623-3

Alexander, W. R. J., & Belloni, R. (2024). Artificial Intelligence and the Sustainability of the Signaling and Human Capital Roles of Higher Education. *Sustainability (Basel)*, *16*(20), 8802. DOI: 10.3390/su16208802

Alfredo, R., Echeverria, V., Jin, Y., Yan, L., Swiecki, Z., Gašević, D., & Martinez-Maldonado, R. (2023). Human-Centred Learning Analytics and AI in Education: A Systematic Literature Review. *Computers and Education: Artificial Intelligence*, *6*, 100215. Advance online publication. DOI: 10.1016/j.caeai.2024.100215

Alharbi, W. (2023). AI in the foreign language classroom: A pedagogical overview of automated writing assistance tools. *Education Research International*, *1*, 4253331. DOI: 10.1155/2023/4253331

Ali, S. A., & Khan, R. (2023). *Harnessing the Digital Nature of Micro-Credentials in Higher Education*. DOI: 10.20944/preprints202303.0045.v1

Alkaissi, H., & McFarlane, S. I. (2023). Artificial Hallucinations in ChatGPT: Implications in Scientific Writing. *Cureus*, *15*, e35179. DOI: 10.7759/cureus.35179 PMID: 36811129

Allam, H., Khan, Z., Letsholo, K., Pandya, B., Shah, K., & Ahamed, J. (2023, 24-25 May). *A proposed AI method for tracking college students' academic progress* [Conference presentation]. *International Conference on Information Technology Trends (ITT)*, Dubai, United Arab Emirates, DOI: 10.1109/ITT59889.2023.10184256

Almutawah, K. A. (2014). A decision support system for academic advisors. *International Journal of Business Information Systems*, *16*(2), 177–195. DOI: 10.1504/IJBIS.2014.062837

Alpizar Garrido, L. O., & Martínez Ruiz, H. (2024). Perspectiva de estudiantes de nivel medio superior respecto al uso de la inteligencia artificial generativa en su aprendizaje. *RIDE Revista Iberoamericana para la Investigación y el Desarrollo Educativo, 14*(28). Advance online publication. DOI: 10.23913/ride.v14i28.1830

Al-Shaikh, R., Al-Malki, N., & Almasre, M. (2024). The implementation of the cognitive theory of multimedia learning in the design and evaluation of an AI educational video assistant utilizing large language models. *Heliyon*, 10. https://doi.org/10.1016/j.heliyon.2024.e25361 PMID: 38352730

Altamura, L., Vargas, C., & Salmerón, L. (2023). Do New Forms of Reading Pay Off? A Meta-Analysis on the Relationship Between Leisure Digital Reading Habits and Text Comprehension. *Review of Educational Research, 95*(1), 53-88. https://doi.org/ (Original work published 2025)DOI: 10.3102/00346543231216463

Alvarado, J. E. M., & Cuzco, C. I. U. (2025). Inteligencia artificial en la creación de entornos de aprendizaje inmersivos en la educación superior. Revisión sistemática. *RECIMUNDO, 9*(1), 220-237. https://doi.org/.(1).ene.2024.348-356DOI: 10.26820/reciamuc/8

Amabile, T. M. (1983). *The social psychology of creativity: A componential conceptualization*. Springer-Verlag. DOI: 10.1007/978-1-4612-5533-8

Amabile, T. M. (1988). A model of creativity and innovation in organizations. *Research in Organizational Behavior, 10*(1), 123–167.

Amabile, T. M. (1993). Motivational synergy: Toward new conceptualizations of intrinsic and extrinsic motivation in the workplace. *Human Resource Management Review, 3*(3), 185–201. DOI: 10.1016/1053-4822(93)90012-S

Amabile, T. M. (1996). *Creativity in context: Update to the social psychology of creativity*. Westview Press.

Amabile, T. M., & Pratt, M. G. (2016). The dynamic componential model of creativity and innovation in organizations: Making progress, making meaning. *Research in Organizational Behavior, 36*, 157–183. DOI: 10.1016/j.riob.2016.10.001

Amershi, S., Weld, D. S., Vorvoreanu, M., Fourney, A., Nushi, B., Collisson, P., Suh, J., Iqbal, S. T., Bennett, P. N., Quinn, K. I., Teevan, J., Kikin-Gil, R., & Horvitz, E. (2019).Guidelines for Human-AI Interaction. *Proceedings of the 2019 CHI Conference on Human Factors in Computing Systems*. DOI: 10.1145/3290605.3300233

Amir, L. R., Tanti, I., Maharani, D. A., Wimardhari, Y. S., Julia, V., Sulijaya, B., & Puspitawati, R. (2020). Student perspective of classroom and distance Learning during Covid-19 pandemic in the undergraduate dental study program Universitas Indonesia. *BMC Medical Education*, *20*(1), 1–8. DOI: 10.1186/s12909-020-02312-0 PMID: 33121488

Anantrasirichai, N., & Bull, D. (2022). Artificial intelligence in the creative industries: A review. *Artificial Intelligence Review*, *55*(1), 589–656. DOI: 10.1007/s10462-021-10039-7

Anderson, L. W., & Krathwohl, D. R. (2001). *A taxonomy for learning, teaching, and assessing: A revision of Bloom's taxonomy of educational objectives*. Longman.

Anderson, T., & Dron, J. (2011). Three generations of distance education pedagogy. *International Review of Research in Open and Distance Learning*, *12*(3), 80–97. DOI: 10.19173/irrodl.v12i3.890

Andresen, J. P., Degn, L., Fishberg, R., Graversen, E. K., Horbach, S. P. J. M., Schmidt, E. K., Schneider, J. W., & Sørensen, M. P. (2025). Generative Artificial Intelligence (GenAI) in the research process – a survey of researchers' practices and perceptions. *Technology in Society*, *81*, 102813. DOI: 10.1016/j.techsoc.2025.102813

Antoine, A.-N.-H., Mason, R., Mason, R., Palahicky, S., & De France, C. R. (2018). *Pulling Together: A Guide for Curriculum Developers*. BCcampus.

Antonenko, P., & Abramowitz, B. (2023). In-service teachers' (mis)conceptions of artificial intelligence in K-12 science education. *Journal of Research on Technology in Education*, *55*(1), 64–78. DOI: 10.1080/15391523.2022.2119450

An, Y., Yu, J. H., & James, S. (2025). Investigating the higher education institutions' guidelines and policies regarding the use of generative AI in teaching, learning, research, and administration. *International Journal of Educational Technology in Higher Education*, *22*(1), 10. DOI: 10.1186/s41239-025-00507-3

Aparicio-Gómez, O.-Y., & Cortés Gallego, M. A. (2024). Desafíos éticos de la Inteligencia Artificial en la personalización del aprendizaje. *Revista Interamericana de Investigación Educación y Pedagogía RIIEP*, *17*(2), 377–392. DOI: 10.15332/25005421.10000

Apellániz, P. A., Parras, J., & Zazo, S. (2025). Improving synthetic data generation through federated learning in scarce and heterogeneous data scenarios. *Big Data and Cognitive Computing*, *9*(2), 18. DOI: 10.3390/bdcc9020018

Apostolache, R. (2022). *Competen a pedagogică digitală* [Digital pedagogical competence]. Polirom.

Appiah-Twumasi, E. (2024). Scaffolding as a cognitive load reduction strategy for teaching atomic and nuclear physics. *Momentum: Physics Education Journal*, *8*(2), 194–209. DOI: 10.21067/mpej.v8i2.9580

Araújo, D., Brito, H., & Carrilho, D. (2023). Team decision-making behavior: An ecological dynamics approach. *Asian Journal of Sport and Exercise Psychology*, *3*(1), 24–29. DOI: 10.1016/j.ajsep.2022.09.005

Araujo, G. J., Guerra, L. R., Bastidas, V. G., Diaz, C. F., & Planta, J. P. (2024). *Educación y tecnología digital*. CID - Centro de Investigación y Desarrollo. DOI: 10.37811/cli_w1041

Ardimento, P., Bernardi, M. L., Cimitile, M., & Scalera, M. (2024, September). Enhancing Software Modeling Learning with AI-Powered Scaffolding. In *Proceedings of the ACM/IEEE 27th International Conference on Model Driven Engineering Languages and Systems* (pp. 103-106).https://doi.org/DOI: 10.1145/3652620.3687776

Ardito, C. G. (2024). Generative AI detection in higher education assessments. *New Directions for Teaching and Learning*, •••, 1–18. DOI: 10.1002/tl.20624

Arslan, B., Lehman, B., Tenison, C., Sparks, J. R., López, A. A., Gu, L., & Zapata-Rivera, D. (2024). Opportunities and challenges of using generative AI to personalize educational assessment. *Frontiers in Artificial Intelligence*, *7*, 1460651. DOI: 10.3389/frai.2024.1460651

Ascione, L. (2024, March 6). ASU, OpenAI look to AI's future in higher ed. *eCampus News*. https://www.ecampusnews.com/featured/2024/03/06/asu-openai-ai-future-higher-ed/

Ashby, A. (2004). Monitoring student retention in the Open University: Definition, measurement, interpretation and action. *Open Learning*, *19*(1), 65–77. Advance online publication. DOI: 10.1080/0268051042000177854

Asimov, I. (1950). *I, Robot*. Gnome Press.

Astutik, I., Widiati, U., Ratri, D., Jonathans, P., Nurkamilah, N., Devanti, Y., & Harfal, Z. (2024). Transformative practices: Integrating automated writing evaluation in higher education writing classrooms - A systematic review. [IJOLAE]. *Indonesian Journal on Learning and Advanced Education*, *6*(3), 423–441. DOI: 10.23917/ijolae.v6i3.23675

Atas, A. H. (2025). Flipped classroom approach to incorporate MOOCs as micro-credentials into higher education. In Durak, G., & Çankaya, S. (Eds.), *Integrating micro-credentials with AI in open education* (pp. 313–340). IGI Global., DOI: 10.4018/979-8-3693-5488-9.ch013

Attewell, S. (2025). *Student perceptions of AI 2025*. Joint Information Systems Committee (JISC). https://www.jisc.ac.uk/reports/student-perceptions-of-ai-2025

Australian Institute for Teaching and School Leadership. (2017). *Spotlight: Reframing feedback to improve teaching and learning*. AITSL. Retrieved from https://www.aitsl.edu.au/docs/default-source/research-evidence/spotlight/feedback.pdf?sfvrsn=cb2eec3c_14

Avcı, Z. Y., Erguleç, F., Mısırlı, O., & Süral, I. (2021). *Flipped learning in information technology courses: benefits and challenges*. DOI: 10.1080/0309877X.2021.1986623

Avidov, D., Ezra, O., Cohen, A., & Bronshtein, A. (2024). Generative AI in the service of situational judgment tests (SJT) for self-regulation learning during problem solving (SRL-PS). *Ubiquity Proceedings*, *4*(1), 23. DOI: 10.5334/uproc.145

Avrahami, O., & Tamir, B. (2021). Ownership and creativity in generative models. *arXiv preprint arXiv:2112.01516.*

Awadallah Alkouk, W., & Khlaif, Z. N. (2024). AI-resistant assessments in higher education: Practical insights from faculty training workshops. *Frontiers in Education*, *9*, 1499495. DOI: 10.3389/feduc.2024.1499495

Awidi, I. T. (2024). Comparing expert tutor evaluation of reflective essays with marking by generative artificial intelligence (AI) tool. *Computers and Education: Artificial Intelligence*, *6*, 100226. DOI: 10.1016/j.caeai.2024.100226

Aydin, O., & Karaarslan, E. (2025). OpenAI ChatGPT interprets Radiological Images: GPT-4 as a Medical Doctor for a Fast Check-Up. *Computer Vision and Pattern Recognition. arXiv preprint* arXiv:2501.06269

Aylsworth, T., & Castro, C. (2024). *Kantian ethics and the attention economy*. Palgrave Macmillan., DOI: 10.1007/978-3-031-45638-1

Azoff, E. M. (2025). *Toward human-level artificial intelligence: How neuroscience can inform the pursuit of artificial general ıntelligence or general AI*. CRC Press.

Baig, M. I., & Yadegaridehkordi, E. (2023). Flipped classroom in higher education: A systematic literature review and research challenges. *International Journal of Educational Technology in Higher Education*, *20*(1), 1–26. DOI: 10.1186/s41239-023-00430-5

Baker Stein, M., & Jones-Schenk, J. (2024). The Future of Nursing: Navigating the AI Revolution Through Education and Training. *Journal of Continuing Education in Nursing*, *55*(3), 108–109. DOI: 10.3928/00220124-20240221-03

Baker, R. S., & Hawn, A. (2022). Algorithmic bias in education. *International Journal of Artificial Intelligence in Education*, *32*(4), 1052–1092. DOI: 10.1007/s40593-021-00285-9

Bandara, W., & Syed, R. (2023). The role of a protocol in a systematic literature review. *Journal of Decision Systems*, *33*(4), 583–600. DOI: 10.1080/12460125.2023.2217567

Bañeres, D., Rodríguez-González, M. E., Guerrero-Roldán, A. E., & Cortadas, P. (2023). An early warning system to identify and intervene online dropout learners. *International Journal of Educational Technology in Higher Education*, *20*(1), 1–25. DOI: 10.1186/s41239-022-00371-5

Barnett, R. (2000). University knowledge in an age of supercomplexity. *Higher Education*, *40*(4), 409–422. DOI: 10.1023/A:1004159513741

Barrera, A. G., Heston, T. F., Sharma, D. M., & Jose, J. (2024). *The AI revolution in micro-credentialing: personalized learning paths*. DOI: 10.3389/feduc.2024.1445654

Bearman, M., & Ajjawi, R. (2023). Learning to work with the black box: Pedagogy for a world with artificial intelligence. *British Journal of Educational Technology*, *54*(5), 1160–1173. DOI: 10.1111/bjet.13337

Bearman, M., Ryan, J., & Ajjawi, R. (2023). Discourses of artificial intelligence in higher education: A critical literature review. *Higher Education*, *86*(2), 369–385. DOI: 10.1007/s10734-022-00937-2

Bearman, M., Tai, J., Dawson, P., Boud, D., & Ajjawi, R. (2024). Developing evaluative judgement for a time of generative artificial intelligence. *Assessment & Evaluation in Higher Education*, *49*(6), 893–905. https://doi.org/https://doi.org/10.1080/02602938.2024.2335321. DOI: 10.1080/02602938.2024.2335321

Beetham, H. (2024, March 28). How not to talk about AI in education—LSE Higher Education. *LSE Higher Education - Enabling Dialogue and Sharing Different Perspectives in a Changing HE Landscape*. https://blogs.lse.ac.uk/highereducation/2024/03/28/how-not-to-talk-about-ai-in-education/

Beghetto, R. A., & Zamana, F. (2025). A Principled Approach to Human Creativity x AI in Education. In *The Cyber-Creativity Process: How Humans Co-Create with Artificial Intelligence* (pp. 71–97). Springer Nature Switzerland. DOI: 10.1007/978-3-031-84535-2_3

Beijing Internet Court. (2023, November). Decision on copyright protection for AI-generated images using Stable Diffusion.

Belkina, M., Daniel, S., Nikolic, S., Haque, R., Lyden, S., Neal, P., Grundy, S., & Hassan, G. M. (2025). Implementing generative AI (GenAI) in higher education: A systematic review of case studies. *Computers and Education: Artificial Intelligence*, *8*, 100407. DOI: 10.1016/j.caeai.2025.100407

Benbya, H., Strich, F., & Tamm, T. (2024). Navigating Generative Artificial Intelligence Promises and Perils for Knowledge and Creative Work. *Journal of the Association for Information Systems*, *25*(1), 23–36. DOI: 10.17705/1jais.00861

Bereczki, E. O., & Kárpáti, A. (2021). Technology-enhanced creativity: A multiple case study of digital technology-integration expert teachers' beliefs and practices. *Thinking Skills and Creativity*, *39*, 100791. DOI: 10.1016/j.tsc.2021.100791

Bergman, J., & Sams, A. (2012). *Flip Your Classroom: Reach Every Student in Every Class Every Day* (1st ed.). ISTE.

Berg, T., Burg, V., Gombović, A., & Puri, M. (2020). On the rise of FinTechs: Credit scoring using digital footprints. *Review of Financial Studies*, *33*(7), 2845–2897. DOI: 10.1093/rfs/hhz099

Bertolin, M., & Da Rin, D. (2020). Chatbots for K-12 education: A review of recent advances, Opportunities, and Challenges. *Education Sciences*, *10*(7), 181.

Bharathi, G. P., Chandra, I., Sanagana, D. P. R., Tummalachervu, C. K., Rao, V. S., & Neelima, S. (2024). AI-driven adaptive learning for enhancing business intelligence simulation games. *Entertainment Computing*, *50*, 100699. DOI: 10.1016/j.entcom.2024.100699

Binns, R. (2018). Fairness in Machine Learning: Lessons from Political Philosophy. In *Proceedings of Machine Learning Research* (Vol. 81, pp. 149–159). PMLR. https://proceedings.mlr.press/v81/binns18a.html

Bishop, J. L., & Verleger, M. A. (2013). The flipped classroom: A survey of the research. *ASEE Annual Conference and Exposition, Conference Proceedings*. DOI: 10.18260/1-2--22585

Biswas, M. I., Talukder, M. S., & Khan, A. R. (2024). Who do you choose? Employees' perceptions of artificial intelligence versus humans in performance feedback. *China Accounting and Finance Review*, *26*(4), 512–532. DOI: 10.1108/CAFR-08-2023-0095

Bitchener, J., & Knoch, U. (2010). Raising the linguistic accuracy level of advanced L2 writers with written corrective feedback. *Journal of Second Language Writing*, *19*(4), 207–217. DOI: 10.1016/j.jslw.2010.10.002

Bittle, K., & El-Gayar, O. (2025). Generative AI and Academic Integrity in Higher Education: A Systematic Review and Research Agenda. *Information (Basel)*, *16*(4), 296. DOI: 10.3390/info16040296

Bjelland, C., Ludvigsen, K., & Mogelvang, A. (2024). Unveiling the impact of AI chatbots on higher education: Insights from students. *Proceedings of the INTED2024 Conference*, 1458– 1465. https://www.researchgate.net/publication/378942626

Black, P., & Wiliam, D. (1998). Assessment and classroom learning. *Assessment in Education: Principles, Policy & Practice*, *5*(1), 7–74. DOI: 10.1080/0969595980050102

Blodgett, S. L., Barocas, S., Daumé, H.III, & Wallach, H. (2020). Language (technology) is power: A critical survey of "bias" in NLP. In *Proceedings of the 58th Annual Meeting of the Association for Computational Linguistics* (pp. 5454–5476). ACL. https://doi.org/DOI: 10.18653/v1/2020.acl-main.485

Bloom, B. S. (1956). *Taxonomy of educational objectives: The classification of educational goals*. Handbook I: Cognitive Domain. David McKay Company.

Bonchi , E. (2022). *Plictiseala la copii i adolescen i: O perspectivă psihosociologică* [Boredom in children and adolescents: A psychosociological perspective]. Polirom.

Bonchi , E. (Ed.). (2021). *Genera ia Z* [Generation Z]. Polirom.

Bond, M., Bedenlier, S., Marín, V. I., & Händel, M. (2021). Emergency remote teaching in higher education: Mapping the first global online semester. *International Journal of Educational Technology in Higher Education*, *18*(1), 1–24. DOI: 10.1186/s41239-021-00282-x PMID: 34778537

Bone, T. (2022). *Key Components of Indigenous Pedagogies Literature Review*. Indspire.

Borge, M., Smith, B. K., & Aldemir, T. (2024). Using generative ai as a simulation to support higher-order thinking. *International Journal of Computer-Supported Collaborative Learning*, *19*(4), 479–532. DOI: 10.1007/s11412-024-09437-0

Botnariuc, P., Cuco , C., Glava, C., Ilie, M. D., Istrate, O., Labăr, A. V., Pâni oară, I. O., tefănescu, D., & Velea, S. (2020). *coala online – elemente pentru inovarea educa iei* [Online school: Elements for innovating education]. University of Bucharest Publishing House. https://unibuc.ro/wp-content/uploads/2020/05/Scoala_Online_Raport_aprilie_2020.pdf

Boussioux, L., Lane, J. N., Zhang, M., Jacimovic, V., & Lakhani, K. R. (2024). The crowdless future? Generative AI and creative problem-solving. *Organization Science*, *35*(5), 1589–1607. DOI: 10.1287/orsc.2023.18430

Bower, M., Torrington, J., Lai, J. W. M., Petocz, P., & Alfano, M. (2024). How should we change teaching and assessment in response to increasingly powerful generative Artificial Intelligence? Outcomes of the ChatGPT teacher survey. *Education and Information Technologies, 29*(12), 15403–15439. DOI: 10.1007/s10639-023-12405-0

Bozkurt, A. (2023). Generative AI, Synthetic Contents, Open Educational Resources (OER), and Open Educational Practices (OEP): A New Front in the Openness Landscape. *Open Praxis, 15*(3), 178–184. DOI: 10.55982/openpraxis.15.3.579

Bozkurt, A. (2023). Generative artificial intelligence (AI) powered conversational educational agents: The inevitable paradigm shift. *Asian Journal of Distance Education, 18*(1), 198–204. DOI: 10.5281/zenodo.7716416

Bozkurt, A. (2024). Tell me your prompts and I will make them true: The alchemy of prompt engineering and generative AI. *Open Praxis, 16*(2), 111–118. DOI: 10.55982/openpraxis.16.2.661

Bozkurt, A. (2024). Why generative AI literacy, why now and why it matters in the educational landscape? Kings, queens and GenAI dragons. *Open Praxis, 16*(3), 283–290. DOI: 10.55982/openpraxis.16.3.739

Bozkurt, A., & Sharma, R. C. (2023). Challenging the Status Quo and Exploring the New Boundaries in the Age of Algorithms: Reimagining the Role of Generative AI in Distance Education and Online Learning. *Asian Journal of Distance Education, 18*(1), 2023. https://asianjde.com/ojs/index.php/AsianJDE/article/view/714

Bozkurt, A., Xıao, J., Farrow, R., Baı, J. Y. H., Nerantzı, C., Moore, S., & Dron, J. (2024). The Manifesto for Teaching and Learning in a Time of Generative AI: A Critical Collective Stance to Better Navigate the Future. *Open Praxis, 16*(4), 1–27. DOI: 10.55982/openpraxis.16.1.654

Bozkurt, A., Xiao, J., Farrow, R., Bai, J. Y. H., Nerantzi, C., Moore, S., Dron, J., Stracke, C. M., Singh, L., Crompton, H., Koutropoulos, A., Terentev, E., Pazurek, A., Nichols, M., Sidorkin, A. M., Costello, E., Watson, S., Mulligan, D., Honeychurch, S., & Asino, T. I. (2024). The manifesto for teaching and learning in a time of generative AI: A critical collective stance to better navigate the future. *Open Praxis, 16*(4), 487–513. DOI: 10.55982/openpraxis.16.4.777

Brady, W. J., Jackson, J. C., Lindström, B., & Crockett, M. J. (2023). Algorithm-mediated social learning in online social networks. *Trends in Cognitive Sciences, 27*(10), 947–960. DOI: 10.1016/j.tics.2023.06.008 PMID: 37543440

Broadfoot, P., & Rockey, J. (2025). Generative AI and the social functions of educational assessment. *Oxford Review of Education, 51*(2), 281–300. DOI: 10.1080/03054985.2025.2455549

Brooks, C., Carroll, A., Gilles, R. M., & Hattie, J. (2019). A matrix of feedback for learning. [Online]. *The Australian Journal of Teacher Education, 44*(4), 14–32. DOI: 10.14221/ajte.2018v44n4.2

Brown, T. B., Mann, B., Ryder, N., Subbiah, M., Kaplan, J., Dhariwal, P., Neelakantan, A., & Shinn, E.. (2020). Language models are few-shot learners. *Proceedings of the 34th International Conference on Neural Information Processing Systems*, 1877-1901.

Bulathwela, S., Muse, H., & Yilmaz, E. (2023). Scalable Educational Question Generation with Pre-trained Language Models. In Wang, N., Rebolledo-Mendez, G., Matsuda, N., Santos, O. C., & Dimitrova, V. (Eds.), Lecture Notes in Computer Science: Vol. 13916. *Artificial Intelligence in Education. AIED 2023*. Springer., DOI: 10.1007/978-3-031-36272-9_27

Burke, B. (2014). Gamify: How gamification motivates people to do extraordinary things. *Bibliomotion: Inc.*, (Apr). Advance online publication. DOI: 10.4324/9781315230344

Burner, T., Lindvig, Y., & Wærness, J. I. (2025). "We Should Not Be Like a Dinosaur"—Using AI Technologies to Provide Formative Feedback to Students. *Education Sciences, 15*(1), 58. DOI: 10.3390/educsci15010058

Cain, W. (2024). Prompting Change: Exploring Prompt Engineering in Large Language Model AI and Its Potential to Transform Education. *TechTrends, 68*(1), 47–57. DOI: 10.1007/s11528-023-00896-0

Callanan, L., & Rangelov, M. (Eds.). (2024). AI in Education. *TLN Journal, 31*(2), Winter 2024. Teacher Learning Network. https://tln.org.au/Web/Web/TLN-Journals/TLN%20Journal-Back-Catalogue.aspx

Candelon, F., Krayer, L., Rajendran, S., & Martinez, D. Z. (2023). How people Can create–and destroy–value with generative AI. *BCG Global, 21.*

Capano, G., He, A. J., & McMinn, S. (2025). Riding the tide of generative artificial intelligence in higher education policy: An Asian perspective. *Journal of Asian Public Policy, 18*(2), 1–15. DOI: 10.1080/17516234.2025.2450571

Čapel, K. (1920). R.U.R. (Rossum's Universal Robots). Translate by Paul Selver and Nigel Playfair (1923). Project Gutenberg. The Project Gutenberg eBook of R. U. R. (Rossum's Universal Robots), by Karel Capek.

CAST. (2024). *Universal design for learning guidelines.* https://udlguidelines.cast.org/

Celik, I. (2023). Towards Intelligent-TPACK: An empirical study on teachers' professional knowledge to ethically integrate artificial intelligence (AI)-based tools into education. *Computers in Human Behavior, 138*, 107468. DOI: 10.1016/j.chb.2022.107468

Ceobanu, C., Cuco , C., Istrate, O., & Pâni oară, I. O. (Eds.). (2020). *Educa ia digitală* [Digital education]. Polirom.

Ch'ng, L. K. (2023). How AI makes its mark on instructional design. *Asian Journal of Distance Education, 18*(2), 32–41. DOI: 10.5281/zenodo.8188576

Chai, C. S., Liang, S., & Wang, X. (2024). A survey study of Chinese teachers' continuous intentions to teach artificial intelligence. *Education and Information Technologies, 29*(11), 14015–14034. DOI: 10.1007/s10639-023-12430-z

Chakraborty, U., Roy, S., & Kumar, S. (2023). *Rise of Generative AI and ChatGPT: Understand how Generative AI and ChatGPT are transforming and reshaping the business world.* BPB Publications.

Chan, C. K. Y. (2023). A comprehensive AI policy education framework for university teaching and learning. *International Journal of Educational Technology in Higher Education, 20*(1), 38. DOI: 10.1186/s41239-023-00408-3

Chan, C. K. Y., & Hu, W. (2023). Students' voices on generative AI: Perceptions, benefits, and challenges in higher education. *International Journal of Educational Technology in Higher Education, 20*(43), 43. Advance online publication. DOI: 10.1186/s41239-023-00411-8

Chance, P. (1986). *Thinking in the classroom: A survey of programs.* Teachers College, Columbia University.

Chan, K. W., Ali, F., Park, J., Sham, K. S. B., Tan, E. Y. T., Chong, F. W. C., Qian, K., & Sze, G. K. (2025). Automatic item generation in various STEM subjects using large language model prompting. *Computers and Education: Artificial Intelligence, 8*, 100344. DOI: 10.1016/j.caeai.2024.100344

Chen, C. H., & Chang, C. L. (2024). Effectiveness of AI-assisted game-based learning on science learning outcomes, intrinsic motivation, cognitive load, and learning behavior. *Education and Information Technologies, 29*(14), 18621-18642https://doi.org/DOI: 10.1007/s10639-024-12553-x

Chen, X., & Wu, D. (2024). Automatic generation of multimedia teaching materials based on generative AI: Taking Tang poetry as an example. *IEEE transactions on learning technologies*.https://ieeexplore.ieee.org/abstract/document/10474169

Cheng, X. & Zhang S. (2024). Tool, Teammate, Superintelligence: Identification of ChatGPTEnabled Collaboration Patterns and their Benefits and Risks in Mutual Learning.

Cheng, L., Croteau, E., Baral, S., Heffernan, C., & Heffernan, N. (2024). Facilitating student learning with a chatbot in an online math learning platform. *Journal of Educational Computing Research*, *62*(4), 907–937. DOI: 10.1177/07356331241226592

Chen, H., & Feng, Y. (2024). Breaking new ground or opening pandora's box? insights from the special issue on ai and social media advertising. *Journal of Interactive Advertising*, *24*(4), 424–427. DOI: 10.1080/15252019.2024.2428580

Chen, J. J., & Lin, J. C. (2023). Artificial intelligence as a double-edged sword: Wielding the POWER principles to maximize its positive effects and minimize its negative effects. *Contemporary Issues in Early Childhood, 14639491231169813*. Advance online publication. DOI: 10.1177/14639491231169813

Chen, M. F., Chen, Y. C., Zuo, P. Y., & Hou, H. T. (2023). Design and evaluation of a remote synchronous gamified mathematics teaching activity that integrates multi-representational scaffolding and a mind tool for gamified learning. *Education and Information Technologies*, *28*(10), 13207–13233. DOI: 10.1007/s10639-023-11708-6 PMID: 37361748

Cheong, B. C. (2024). Transparency and accountability in AI systems: Safeguarding wellbeing in the age of algorithmic decision-making. *Front. Hum. Dyn.*, *6*, 1421273. DOI: 10.3389/fhumd.2024.1421273

Chiu, T. K. F. (2023). The impact of Generative AI (GenAI) on practices, policies and research direction in education: A case of ChatGPT and Midjourney. *Interactive Learning Environments*, *32*(10), 6187–6203. DOI: 10.1080/10494820.2023.2253861

Chiu, T. K. F. (2024). Future research recommendations for transforming higher education with generative AI. *Computers and Education: Artificial Intelligence*, *6*, 100197. DOI: 10.1016/j.caeai.2023.100197

Choi, G. W., Kim, S. H., Lee, D., & Moon, J. (2024). Utilizing generative AI for instructional design: Exploring strengths, weaknesses, opportunities, and threats. *TechTrends*, *68*(4), 1–13. DOI: 10.1007/s11528-024-00967-w

Choi, J.-Y. (2024). *Generative AI-based writing feedback model development*. Korean Association for Literacy. DOI: 10.37736/KJLR.2024.10.15.5.01

Christidis, K., & Devetsikiotis, M. (2016). Blockchains and smart contracts for the Internet of Things. *IEEE Access : Practical Innovations, Open Solutions*, *4*, 2292–2303. DOI: 10.1109/ACCESS.2016.2566339

Chung, J., Henderson, M., Pepperell, N., Slade, C., & Liang, Y. (2024). *Student perspectives on AI in Higher Education: Student Survey.* Student Perspectives on AI in Higher Education Project. DOI: 10.26180/27915930

Circi, R., Hicks, J., & Sikali, E. (2023). Automatic item generation: Foundations and machine learning-based approaches for assessments. *Frontiers in Education*, *8*, 858273. DOI: 10.3389/feduc.2023.858273

Cisneros Vásquez, E. D., Nevárez Loza, R. F., Farez Cherrez, A. M., & Torres Montes, R. E. (2024). Uso de la inteligencia artificial en la personalización del aprendizaje. *Conocimiento global, 9*(1), 75-83. https://doi.org/DOI: 10.70165/cglobal.v9i1.339

CNIL. (2024). *La CNIL sanctionne AMAZON FRANCE LOGISTIQUE à hauteur de 32 millions d'euros pour un système de surveillance jugé excessif.* Retrieved from https://www.cnil.fr

Codreanu, A. D. (2021). Gamificarea ca strategie de stimulare a motiva iei [Gamification as a strategy for stimulating motivation]. In *Conferin a „Dezvoltarea personală i integrarea socială a actorilor educa ionali"* [Conference "Personal development and social integration of educational actors"] (pp. 169–173). Chi inău, Moldova.

Cohn, C., Hutchins, N., Le, T., & Biswas, G. (2024). A Chain-of-Thought Prompting Approach with LLMs for Evaluating Students' Formative Assessment Responses in Science. *Proceedings of the AAAI Conference on Artificial Intelligence*, *38*(21), 23182–23190. DOI: 10.1609/aaai.v38i21.30364

Cooper, G., & Tang, K. S. (2024). Pixels and Pedagogy: Examining Science Education Imagery by Generative Artificial Intelligence. *Journal of Science Education and Technology*, *33*(4), 556–568. DOI: 10.1007/s10956-024-10104-0

Copado, A. E. (2024). Inteligencia artificial en la prevención del plagio académico y evaluación del aprendizaje. *Revista Senderos Pedagógicos*, *15*(1), 139–151. DOI: 10.53995/rsp.v15i1.1372

Corbin, T., Dawson, P., Nicola-Richmond, K., & Partridge, H. (2025). 'Where's the line? It's an absurd line': Towards a framework for acceptable uses of AI in assessment. *Assessment & Evaluation in Higher Education*, *0*(0), 1–13. DOI: 10.1080/02602938.2025.2456207

Costa, K., Castranova, K., & Tumminia, M. (2021). Need to connect: How to build and sustain a faculty community of practice for online teaching. To Improve the Academy: *A Journal of Educational Development, 40*(1). DOI: 10.3998/tia.954

Cotos, E., & Pendar, N. (2015). Discourse classification into rhetorical functions for AWE feedback. *CALICO Journal, 33*(1), 92–116. Advance online publication. DOI: 10.1558/cj.v33i1.27047

Cotton, D. R. E., Cotton, P. A., & Shipway, J. R. (2024). Chatting and cheating: Ensuring academic integrity in the era of ChatGPT. *Innovations in Education and Teaching International, 61*(2), 228–239. DOI: 10.1080/14703297.2023.2190148

Cox, G., Willmers, M., Brown, R., & Held, M. (2024). Learning along the Way: A Case Study on a Pedagogically Innovative Approach to Engage Medical Students in the Creation of Open Educational Resources Using ChatGPT. *Mousaion: South African Journal of Information Studies, 42*(1), 1. Advance online publication. DOI: 10.25159/2663-659X/15331

Creely, E., & Henderson, M. (2025). Artificial intelligence and the digital dis/empowerment of migrant and refugee learners. In E. Tour, E. Creely, P. Waterhouse, & M. Henderson (Eds.), *Digital empowerment for refugee and migrant learners: Applying strengths-based practice to adult education* (1st ed., pp. 47-63). Routledge. https://doi.org/DOI: 10.4324/9781003422891-5

Creely, E., & Blannin, J. (2025). Creative partnerships with generative AI. Possibilities for education and beyond. *Thinking Skills and Creativity, 56*, 101727. DOI: 10.1016/j.tsc.2024.101727

Creely, E., Henriksen, D., Henderson, M., & Mishra, P. (2024, October 18). The Staging of AI: Exploring Perspectives about Generative AI, Creativity and Education. *Creative Education.*

Crompton, H., & Burke, D. (2022). Artificial intelligence in K-12 education. *SN Social Sciences, 2*(7), 1–14. DOI: 10.1007/s43545-022-00425-5

Csíkszentmihályi, M. (2011). *Fluir: una psicología de la felicidad.* Debolsillo.

Csorba, L. M., & Dabija, D. C. (2024). The impact of the Covid-19 pandemic on students' future on online education behavior. *Heliyon, 10*(20), e39560. DOI: 10.1016/j.heliyon.2024.e39560 PMID: 39502205

Cuban, L. (1986). *Teachers and Machines: The Classroom of Technology Since 1920* (1st ed.). Teachers College Press.

Cubillos, C., Mellado, R., Cabrera-Paniagua, D., & Urra, E. (2025). Generative Artificial Intelligence in Computer Programming: Does it enhance learning, motivation, and the learning environment? *IEEE Access : Practical Innovations, Open Solutions*, *13*, 40438–40455. DOI: 10.1109/ACCESS.2025.3532883

Curtis, G. J. (2025). The two-lane road to hell is paved with good intentions: Why an all-or-none approach to generative AI, integrity, and assessment is insupportable. *Higher Education Research & Development*, *0*(0), 1–8. DOI: 10.1080/07294360.2025.2476516

Cu ulab, A. (2024). Învă area prin joc didactic reflectat în gamificare – un nou domeniu motiva ional [Learning through didactic play reflected in gamification – a new motivational field]. In *Instruire prin cercetare pentru o societate prosperă* [Proceedings of the Conference "Learning through research for a prosperous society"] (pp. 221–227).

Czop Assaf, L., O'Donnell Lussier, K., Furness, S., & Hoff, M. (2019). Exploring How a Study Abroad and International Service-Learning Project Shaped Preservice Teachers' Understanding of Humanizing Pedagogy. *Teacher Educator*, *54*(2), 105–124. DOI: 10.1080/08878730.2018.1520376

da Silva, P. F., & Rockenbach Tarouco, L. M. (2022, September). A Scaffolding Strategy to Organize Collaborative Learning. In *International Conference on Interactive Collaborative Learning*(pp. 171-182). Cham: Springer International Publishing.https://doi.org/DOI: 10.1007/978-3-031-26876-2_16

Dakakni, D. (2025). Artificial intelligence as a tool for data, economic and political hegemony: Releasing the djinn. *Ethics in Science and Environmental Politics*, *25*, 1–10. DOI: 10.3354/esep00216

Dale, R., & Viethen, J. (2021). The automated writing assistance landscape in 2021. *Natural Language Engineering*, *27*(4), 511–518. DOI: 10.1017/S1351324921000164

Dann, C., Redmond, P., Fanshawe, M., Brown, A., Getenet, S., Shaik, T., Tao, X., Galligan, L., & Li, Y. (2024). Making sense of student feedback and engagement using artificial intelligence. *Australasian Journal of Educational Technology*, *40*(3), 58–76. DOI: 10.14742/ajet.8903

Darejeh, A., Marcus, N., & Sweller, J. (2021). The effect of narrative-based E-learning systems on novice users' cognitive load while learning software applications. *Educational Technology Research and Development*, *69*(5), 2451–2473. DOI: 10.1007/s11423-021-10024-5

Davidoff, M. (2024, November 11). How Broadening AI Access Can Help Bridge the Digital Divide. *EDUCAUSE Review*. https://er.educause.edu/articles/2024/11/how-broadening-ai-access-can-help-bridge-the-digital-divide

Davids, K., Rothwell, M., Hydes, S., Robinson, T., & Davids, C. (2023). Enriching Athlete—Environment Interactions in Youth Sport: The Role of a Department of Methodology. *Children (Basel, Switzerland)*, *10*(4), 4. Advance online publication. DOI: 10.3390/children10040752

Dawson, P., Bearman, M., Dollinger, M., & Boud, D. (2024a). Validity matters more than cheating. *Assessment & Evaluation in Higher Education*, *49*(7), 1005–1016. DOI: 10.1080/02602938.2024.2386662

de Fine Licht, K. (2024). Generative Artificial Intelligence in Higher Education: Why the 'Banning Approach' to Student use is Sometimes Morally Justified. *Philosophy & Technology*, *37*(3), 113. DOI: 10.1007/s13347-024-00799-9

de Sousa, E. B. G., Alexandre, B., Ferreira Mello, R., Pontual Falcão, T., Vesin, B., & Gašević, D. (2021). Applications of Learning Analytics in High Schools: A Systematic Literature Review. *Frontiers in Artificial Intelligence*, *4*, 737891. DOI: 10.3389/frai.2021.737891 PMID: 34647016

Del Carmen Salazar, M. (2013). A humanizing pedagogy: Reinventing the principles and practice of education as a journey toward liberation. *Review of Research in Education*, *37*(1), 121–148. DOI: 10.3102/0091732X12464032

Delcker, J., Heil, J., Seufert, S., & Spirgi, L. (2024). First-year students AI-competence as a predictor for intended and de facto use of AI-tools for supporting learning processes in higher education. *International Journal of Educational Technology in Higher Education*, *21*(18), 18. Advance online publication. DOI: 10.1186/s41239-024-00452-7

Delello, J. A., Sung, W., Mokhtari, K., Hebert, J., Bronson, A., & De Giuseppe, T. (2025). AI in the Classroom: Insights from Educators on Usage, Challenges, and Mental Health. *Education Sciences*, *15*(2), 113. DOI: 10.3390/educsci15020113

Delello, J., Sung, W., Mokhtari, K., & De Giuseppe, T. (2024). Are K-16 educators prepared to address the educational and ethical ramifications of artificial intelligence software? In Arai, K. (Ed.), *Future of information and communication conference* (pp. 406–432). Springer Nature Switzerland., DOI: 10.1007/978-3-031-54053-0_28

Delgado, F., Yang, S., Madaio, M., & Yang, Q. (2023). The participatory turn in AI design: theoretical foundations and the current state of practice. In *Equity and access in algorithms, mechanisms, and optimization*. ACM., DOI: 10.1145/3617694.3623261

Deterding, S., Dixon, D., Khaled, R., & Nacke, L. (2011). From game design elements togamefulness: Defining "gamification." In *Proceedings of the 15th International Academic MindTrek Conference: Envisioning Future Media Environments* (pp. 9–15). ACM.

Devlin, J., Chang, M. W., Lee, K., & Toutanova, K. (2018). BERT: Pre-training of deep bidirectional transformers for language understanding. *Proceedings of NAACL-HLT*, 4171-4186

Dhillon, P. S., Molaei, S., Li, J., Golub, M., Zheng, S., & Robert, L. P. (2024). Shaping Human-AI Collaboration: Varied Scaffolding Levels in Co-writing with Language Models. *Proceedings of the CHI Conference on Human Factors in Computing Systems.* https://doi.org/DOI: 10.1145/3613904.3642134

Dieker, L., & Zaugg, T. (2024). Artificial Intelligence and the Intersectionality of Disability. In Bennett, G., & Goodall, E. (Eds.), *The Palgrave Encyclopedia of Disability* (pp. 1–8). Springer Nature Switzerland., DOI: 10.1007/978-3-031-40858-8_121-1

Digital Education Council. (2024). *Digital Education Council Global AI Student Survey 2024*. Digital Education Council.

Digital Education Council. (2025). *DEC AI Literacy Framework*. The Digital Education Council.

Dillig, M., Böhmer, A., Mason, J., Bolaji, S., Isso, I., Stănescu, M. H., Sahin, H., & Kuraner, A. (2024). A segue from search to dialogue: leveraging GenAI for pre-service teacher training. In Sharma, R., & Bozkurt, A. (Eds.), *Transforming education with generative ai: prompt engineering and synthetic content creation* (pp. 1–34). IGI Global Scientific Publishing., DOI: 10.4018/979-8-3693-1351-0.ch002

Ding, M., Dong, S., & Grewal, R. (2024). Generative AI and usage in marketing classroom. *Customer Needs and Solutions*, *11*(5), 1–15. DOI: 10.1007/s40547-024-00145-2

Divya, V., & Mirza, A. U. (2024). Transforming content creation: The influence of generative AI on a new frontier. *Exploring the frontiers of artificial intelligence and machine learning technologies, 143*.

Diwan, C., Srinivasa, S., Suri, G., Agarwal, S., & Ram, P. (2023). AI- based learning content generation and learning pathway augmentation to increase learner engagement. *Computers & Education*, *4*, 100110. DOI: 10.1016/j.caeai.2022.100110

Domo. (2024). *Data never sleeps 12.0* [Infographic]. https://www.domo.com/data-never-sleeps

Dornis, T. W. (2025). Generative AI, reproductions inside the model, and the making available to the public. *IIC-International Review of Intellectual Property and Competition Law*, 1-30.

Doshi, A. R., & Hauser, O. P. (2024). Generative AI enhances individual creativity but reduces the collective diversity of novel content. *Science Advances, 10*(28), eadn5290. DOI: 10.1126/sciadv.adn5290 PMID: 38996021

Doughty, J., Wan, Z., Bompelli, A., Qayum, J., Wang, T., Zhang, J., Zheng, Y., Doyle, A., Sridhar, P., Agarwal, A., Bogart, C., Keylor, E., Kultur, C., Savelka, J., & Sakr, M. (2024). *A comparative study of AI-generated (GPT-4) and human-crafted MCQs in programming education*. In *Proceedings of the 26th Australasian Computing Education Conference* (pp. 114–123). Association for Computing Machinery. https://doi.org/DOI: 10.1145/3636243.3636256

Dowling, M., & Lucey, B. (2023). ChatGPT for (finance) research: The Bananarama conjecture. *Finance Research Letters*, *53*, 103662. DOI: 10.1016/j.frl.2023.103662

Drew, C. (2022). 18 scaffolding examples in education. Helpful Professor. Retrieved from https://helpfulprofessor.com/scaffolding-examples-in-education

du Plooy, E., Casteleijn, D., & Franzsen, D. (2024). Personalized adaptive learning in higher education: A scoping review of key characteristics and impact on academic performance and engagement. *Heliyon, 10*(21), e39630. DOI: 10.1016/j.heliyon.2024.e39630 PMID: 39524879

Duhaylungsod, A. V., & Chavez, J. V., (2023). Chatgpt and other ai users: Innovative and creative utilitarian value and mindset shift. *Journal of Namibian Studies: History Politics Culture, 33*, 4367–4378. DOI: 10.59670/jns.v33i.2791

Durak, G., & Çankaya, S. (2024). *Integrating Micro-Credentials With AI in Open Education*. IGI Global. DOI: 10.4018/979-8-3693-5488-9

Duran, G. ve Alejandro, A. (2024). Üretken Sanat ve Ortaöğretim: Yapay Zeka Araçlarının Öğrenci Yaratıcılığı Üzerindeki Etkisi. *Eğitimde Ortaya Çıkan Teknolojiler Dergisi*, *2*(6), 420–433.

Du, X., Dai, M., Tang, H., Hung, J. L., Li, H., & Zheng, J. (2023). A multimodal analysis of college students' collaborative problem solving in virtual experimentation activities: A perspective of cognitive load. *Journal of Computing in Higher Education, 35*(2), 272–295. DOI: 10.1007/s12528-022-09311-8 PMID: 35370382

Dzuong, J., Wang, Z., & Zhang, W. (2024). Uncertain boundaries: multidisciplinary approaches to copyright issues in generative AI. *arXiv preprint arXiv:2404.08221*.

Eaton, L. (2024, April 17). On Building a AI Policy for Teaching & Learning [Substack newsletter]. *AI + Education = Simplified*. https://aiedusimplified.substack.com/p/on-building-a-ai-policy-for-teaching?utm_campaign=post&triedRedirect=true

Eaton, S. E. (2023, February 25). 6 Tenets of Postplagiarism: Writing in the Age of Artificial Intelligence | Learning, Teaching and Leadership. *Learning, Teaching, and Leadership*. https://drsaraheaton.com/2023/02/25/6-tenets-of-postplagiarism-writing-in-the-age-of-artificial-intelligence/

Eduaide.Ai. (2024). *About us: created by teachers, for teachers* https://www.eduaide.ai/about

Educ.ar. S. E. (2024). *Cómo incorporar IA generativa al aula: Una orientación en ChatGPT para docentes* (1.ª ed.). Ciudad Autónoma de Buenos Aires: Educ.ar, S.E.

Ejjami, R. (2024). The Adaptive Personalization Theory of Learning: Revolutionizing Education with AI. *Journal of Next-Generation Research 5.0*. https://doi.org/ DOI: 10.70792/jngr5.0.v1i1.8

El Fathi, T., Saad, A., Larhzil, H., Lamri, D., & Al Ibrahmi, E. M. (2025). Integrating generative AI into STEM education: Enhancing conceptual understanding, addressing misconceptions, and assessing student acceptance. *Disciplinary and Interdisciplinary Science Education Research*, *7*(1), 6. DOI: 10.1186/s43031-025-00125-z

Elkhatat, A. M., Elsaid, K., & Almeer, S. (2023). Evaluating the efficacy of AI content detection tools in differentiating between human and AI-generated text. *International Journal for Educational Integrity*, *19*(1), 17. DOI: 10.1007/s40979-023-00140-5

Elkins, S., Kochmar, E., Cheung, J. C. K., & Serban, I. (2024). How Teachers Can Use Large Language Models and Bloom's Taxonomy to Create Educational Quizzes. *Proceedings of the AAAI Conference on Artificial Intelligence*, *38*(21), 23084–23091. DOI: 10.1609/aaai.v38i21.30353

Elmesalawy, M. M., Atia, A., Yousef, A. M. F., El-Haleem, A. M. A., Anany, M. G., Elmosilhy, N. A., Salama, A. I., Hamdy, A., Zoghby, H. M. E., & Din, E. S. E. (2021). *AI-based Flexible Online Laboratory Learning System for Post-COVID-19 Era: Requirements and Design. In: 2021 International Mobile, Intelligent, and Ubiquitous Computing Conference (MIUCC), 1-7*. IEEE., DOI: 10.1109/MIUCC52538.2021.9447601

Er, E., Akçapınar, G., Bayazıt, A., Noroozi, O., & Banihashem, S. K. (2025). Assessing student perceptions and use of instructor versus AI-generated feedback. *British Journal of Educational Technology*, *56*(3), 1074–1091. DOI: 10.1111/bjet.13558

Erickson, K. (2024). AI and work in the creative industries: Digital continuity or discontinuity? *Creative Industries Journal*, •••, 1–21. DOI: 10.1080/17510694.2024.2421135

Escalante, J., Pack, A., & Barrett, A. (2023). AI-generated feedback on writing: Insights into efficacy and ENL student preference. *International Journal of Educational Technology in Higher Education*, *20*(1), 57. DOI: 10.1186/s41239-023-00425-2

Espinoza, E. E. (2022). La evaluación de los aprendizajes. *Conrado, 18*(85), 120-127. https://conrado.ucf.edu.cu/index.php/conrado/article/view/2267

Esterman, M. (2024). The robots have arrived – what's next? In L. Callanan & M. Rangelov (Eds.), *AI in Education,* TLN Journal, 31(2). Teacher Learning Network. https://tln.org.au/Web/Web/TLN-Journals/TLN%20Journal-Back-Catalogue.aspx

Esteva, A., Kuprel, B., Novoa, R. A., Ko, J., Swetter, S. M., Blau, H. M., & Thrun, S. (2017). Dermatologist-level classification of skin cancer with deep neural networks. *Nature*, *542*(7639), 115–118. DOI: 10.1038/nature21056 PMID: 28117445

Eulerich, M., Sanatizadeh, A., Vakilzadeh, H., & Wood, D. A. (2023). Is it all hype? ChatGPT's performance and disruptive potential in the accounting and auditing industries. *SSRN,* http://dx.doi.org/DOI: 10.2139/ssrn.4452175

European Commission. (2020). *Digital Education Action Plan 2021–2027: Resetting education and training for the digital age*. COM (2020) 624 final. Brussels.

European Parliament & Council of the European Union. (2024). *Regulation (EU) 2024/2847 of the European Parliament and of the Council. Official Journal of the European Union*. https://eur-lex.europa.eu/legal-content/EN/TXT/?uri=CELEX:32024R2847

European Union (2023). *EU AI Act: first regulation on artificial intelligence*. European Union.

European Union. (2012). *Treaty on the Functioning of the European Union* (consolidated version 2012), Article 165.

Everwijn, S. E. M., Bomers, G. B. J., & Knubben, J. A. (1993). Ability- or competence-based education: Bridging the gap between knowledge acquisition and ability to apply. *Higher Education*, *25*(4), 425–438. DOI: 10.1007/BF01383845

Exintaris, B., Karunaratne, N., & Yuriev, E. (2023). Metacognition and critical thinking: Using ChatGPT-generated responses as prompts for critique in a problem-solving workshop (SMARTCHEMPer). *Journal of Chemical Education*, *100*(8), 2972–2980. DOI: 10.1021/acs.jchemed.3c00481

Falloon, G. (2011). Making the connection: Moore's theory of transactional distance and its relevance to the use of a virtual classroom in postgraduate online teacher education. *Journal of Research on Technology in Education*, *43*(3), 187–209. DOI: 10.1080/15391523.2011.10782569

Fang, Y. (2021). A systematic review of Natural Language Processing Applications in writing instruction. *Journal of Educational Computing Research*, *59*(3), 527–548.

Fan, Y., Tang, L., Le, H., Shen, K., Tan, S., Zhao, Y., Shen, Y., Li, X., & Gašević, D. (2025). Beware of metacognitive laziness: Effects of generative artificial intelligence on learning motivation, processes, and performance. *British Journal of Educational Technology*, *56*(2), 489–530. DOI: 10.1111/bjet.13544

Farrelly, T., & Baker, N. (2023). Generative artificial intelligence: Implications and considerations for higher education practice. *Education Sciences*, *13*(11), 1–14. DOI: 10.3390/educsci13111109

Farrokhnia, M., Banihashem, S. K., Noroozi, O., & Wals, A. (2024). A SWOT analysis of ChatGPT: Implications for educational practice and research. *Innovations in Education and Teaching International*, *61*(3), 460–474. DOI: 10.1080/14703297.2023.2195846

Fatima, S. S., Sheikh, N. A., & Osama, A. (2024). Authentic assessment in medical education: Exploring AI integration and student-as-partners collaboration. *Postgraduate Medical Journal*, *100*(1190), 959–967. DOI: 10.1093/postmj/qgae088

Fawns, T. (2024). *Discursive principles for human-technology collectives*. First International Symposium on Educating for Collective Intelligence, University of Technology, Sydney. https://cic.uts.edu.au/wp-content/uploads/2024/06/Fawns_CI.edu2024.pdf

Fenwick, M., & Jurcys, P. (2023). Originality and the Future of Copyright in an Age of Generative AI. *Computer Law & Security Review*, *51*, 105892. DOI: 10.1016/j.clsr.2023.105892

Ferguson, R. (2012). Learning analytics: Drivers, developments and challenges. *International Journal of Technology Enhanced Learning*, *4*(5–6), 304–317. DOI: 10.1504/IJTEL.2012.051816

Fernández, K. (2024). *Docencia en la era de la inteligencia artificial: Enfoques prácticos para docentes*. Universidad de Burgos. https://raeia.org/books/258-2/

Fernández, L. O., de Solar, C. Q., Hinostroza, M. B., Rodríguez, A. C., Nakata, H. M., Gutiérrez, L. C., Cadillo, E. M., Lizarraga, M. E. N., de la Cruz, J. B., Gastelú, J. V., Baigorria, A. S., & Marquez, Z. Q. (2023). Estilos De Aprendizaje y Rendimiento Académico en Estudiantes Ingresantes de las Cinco Áreas de las Carreras Profesionales de una Universidad Pública Peruana. In *Ciencias humanas: Perspectivas teóricas y fundamentos epistemológicos* (pp. 11–26). Atena Editora., DOI: 10.22533/at.ed.1862321062

Ferrara, E. (2023). Fairness And bias in artificial intelligence: A brief survey of sources, ımpacts, and mitigation strategies. *Sci*, *6*(1), 3. DOI: 10.3390/sci6010003

Ferrarelli, M. (2024). *Inteligencia artificial y educación: Insumos para su abordaje desde Iberoamérica*. Organización de Estados Iberoamericanos para la Educación, la Ciencia y la Cultura (OEI).

Ferris, D. R. (2003). *Response to student writing: Implications for second language students*. Routledge., DOI: 10.4324/9781410607201

Figoli, F. A., Rampino, L., & Mattioli, F. (2022). AI in design idea development: A workshop on creativity and human-AI collaboration. In Lockton, D., Lloyd, P., & Lenzi, S. (Eds.), *DRS2022: Bilbao, 25 June - 3 July*., DOI: 10.21606/drs.2022.414

Fırat, M. (2023). Integrating AI applications into learning management systems to enhance e-learning. *Instructional Technology and Lifelong Learning*, *4*(1), 1–14. DOI: 10.52911/itall.1244453

Fleischmann, K. (2024). The commodification of creativity: Integrating Generative Artificial Intelligence in higher education design curriculum. *Innovations in Education and Teaching International*, •••, 1–15. DOI: 10.1080/14703297.2024.2427039

Flores Contrera, C. J. (2024). La evaluación educativa en la era de la inteligencia artificial; cambios de paradigmas. *LATAM: Revista latinoamericana de Ciencias Sociales y Humanidades*, *5*(1), 1579-1591. https://doi.org/DOI: 10.56712/latam.v5i1.1694

Flores, E. F., & Borges, G. C. (2024). Concepciones de evaluación del aprendizaje. Un análisis para la transformación de las prácticas evaluativas. *Revista Panamericana de Pedagogía*, (37), 10–24. DOI: 10.21555/rpp.vi37.2796

Foltynek, T., Bjelobaba, S., Glendinning, I., Khan, Z. R., Santos, R., Pavletic, P., & Kravjar, J. (2023). ENAI Recommendations on the ethical use of Artificial Intelligence in Education. *International Journal for Educational Integrity*, *19*(1), 12, s40979-023-00133–00134. DOI: 10.1007/s40979-023-00133-4

Foung, D., Lin, L., & Chen, J. (2024). Reinventing assessments with ChatGPT and other online tools: Opportunities for GenAI-empowered assessment practices. *Computers and Education: Artificial Intelligence*, *6*, 100250. DOI: 10.1016/j.caeai.2024.100250

Fox, S., & Vitor, F. R. (2024). A cognitive load theory (CLT) analysis of machine learning explainability, transparency, interpretability, and shared interpretability. *Machine Learning and Knowledge Extraction*, *6*(3), 1494–1509. DOI: 10.3390/make6030071

Francis, N. J., Jones, S., & Smith, D. P. (2025). Generative AI in higher education: Balancing innovation and integrity. *British Journal of Biomedical Science*, *81*, 14048. DOI: 10.3389/bjbs.2024.14048

Freeman, J. (2025). *Student generative AI survey 2025.* Higher Education Policy Institute. HEPU Policy Note 61.

Freire, P. (2020). *Pedagogy of the oppressed.* Bloomsbury publishing. DOI: 10.4324/9781003060635-5

Frolova, E. V., Rogach, O. V., Tyurikov, A. G., & Razov, P. V. (2021). Online student education in a pandemic: New challenges and risks. *European Journal Contemporary Education*, *10*(1), 43–52. DOI: 10.13187/ejced.2021.1.43

Fu, B., Hadid, A., & Damer, N. (2025). Generative AI in the context of assistive technologies: Trends, limitations and future directions. *Image and Vision Computing*, *154*, 1–15. DOI: 10.1016/j.imavis.2024.105347

Fuentes-Martín, A., Cilleruelo-Ramos, A., Segura-Méndez, B., & Mayol, J. (2023). Can an artificial ıntelligence model pass an examination for medical specialists? *Archivos de Bronconeumología*, *59*(8), 534–536. DOI: 10.1016/j.arbres.2023.03.017

Furze, L. (2024). Digital plastic in education: Understanding the implications of synthetic media. In L. Callanan & M. Rangelov (Eds.), *AI in Education,* TLN Journal, 31(2). Teacher Learning Network. https://tln.org.au/Web/Web/TLN-Journals/TLN%20Journal-Back-Catalogue.aspx

Furze, L. (2024a, August 18). Design Refine Create: A Framework for GenAI Curriculum Design. *Leon Furze*. https://leonfurze.com/2024/08/19/design-refine-create-a-framework-for-genai-curriculum-design/

Furze, L. (2024b, August 28). Updating the AI Assessment Scale. *Leon Furze.Com*. https://leonfurze.com/2024/08/28/updating-the-ai-assessment-scale/

Furze, L., Perkins, M., Roe, J., & MacVaugh, J. (2024). The AI Assessment Scale (AIAS) in action: A pilot implementation of GenAI-supported assessment. *Australasian Journal of Educational Technology*, *40*(4), 4. Advance online publication. DOI: 10.14742/ajet.9434

Gai ă, R. (2021). Gamificarea în educa ie. Defini ie, elemente, mituri, tipuri de jucători i limite [Gamification in education: Definition, elements, myths, player types, and limits]. *Philologica Banatica*, *2021*(II), 66–81.

Garcia, M. B., Rosak-Szyrocka, J., Yilmaz, R., Metwally, A. H. S., Acut, D. P., Ofosu-Ampong, K., Erdoğdu, F., Fung, C. Y., & Bozkurt, A. (2025). *Rethinking educational assessment in the age of generative AI: Actionable strategies to mitigate academic dishonesty*. In *Pitfalls of AI Integration in Education: Skill Obsolescence, Misuse, and Bias* (pp. 1–24). IGI Global. https://doi.org/DOI: 10.4018/979-8-3373-0122-8.ch001

García, G. (2024). La evaluación como herramienta para mejorar los aprendizajes: La retroalimentación y la evaluación auténtica. *Revista Latinoamericana Ogmios*, *4*(9), 17–32. DOI: 10.53595/rlo.v4.i9.091

Garrison, D. R. (2017). *E-learning in the 21st century: A community of inquiry framework for research and practice* (3rd ed.). Routledge.

Garrison, D. R., Anderson, T., & Archer, W. (1999). Critical inquiry in a text-based environment: Computer conferencing in higher education. *The Internet and Higher Education*, *2*(2–3), 87–105. DOI: 10.1016/S1096-7516(00)00016-6

Gašević, D., Dawson, S., & Siemens, G. (2015). Let's not forget: Learning analytics are about learning. *TechTrends*, *59*(1), 64–71. DOI: 10.1007/s11528-014-0822-x

Geçkin, V., Kızıltaş, E., & Çınar, Ç. (2023). Assessing second-language academic writing: AI vs. Human raters. *Journal of Educational Technology & Online Learning*, *6*(4), 1096–1108. DOI: 10.31681/jetol.1336599

Geerts, G., & O'Leary, D. (2022). V-matrix: A wave theory of value creation for big data. *International Journal of Accounting Information Systems*, *47*, 100575. DOI: 10.1016/j.accinf.2022.100575

Geetha, M. P., Hariharan, S., Jeevanprasanth, T., & Sanjay, L. (2024, December). Multimodal Content Generation: A Project for AI Creativity. In *2024 International Conference on Emerging Research in Computational Science (ICERCS)* (pp. 1-5). IEEE.

George, A. S. (2023). Preparing Students for an AI-Driven World: Rethinking Curriculum and Pedagogy in the Age of Artificial Intelligence. *Partners Universal Innovative Research Publication, 1*(2), 2. Advance online publication. DOI: 10.5281/zenodo.10245675

Ge, R., Lu, J., & Hao, X. (2025). Exploring the impact of generative artificial intelligence scaffolding on university students' collaborative knowledge building. *Journal of Higher Education Research, 5*(6), 570–578. https://en.front-sci.com/index.php/jher/article/view/3391/3685. DOI: 10.32629/jher.v5i6.3391

Gerritsen-van Leeuwenkamp, K. J., Brinke, D. J., & Kester, L. (2017). Assessment quality in tertiary education: An integrative literature review. *Studies in Educational Evaluation, 55*, 94–116. DOI: 10.1016/j.stueduc.2017.08.001

Geyer, R., & Rosignoli, A. (2024). The Influence of Generative AI on Creativity in the Front End of Innovation. https://www.diva-portal.org/smash/get/diva2:1865236/FULLTEXT01.pdf

Ghamrawi, N., Shal, T., & Ghamrawi, N. A. R. (2024). Exploring the impact of AI on teacher leadership: Regressing or expanding? *Education and Information Technologies, 29*(7), 8415–8433. DOI: 10.1007/s10639-023-12174-w

Gibson, R. (2023, August 14). *10 ways artificial intelligence is transforming instructional design.* https://er.educause.edu/articles/2023/8/10-ways-artificial-intelligence-is-transforming-instructional-design#fn4

Gibson, R. (2024, September 10). The Impact of AI in Advancing Accessibility for Learners with Disabilities. *EDUCAUSE Review.* https://er.educause.edu/articles/2024/9/the-impact-of-ai-in-advancing-accessibility-for-learners-with-disabilities

Gkintoni, E., Antonopoulou, H., Sortwell, A., & Halkiopoulos, C. (2025). Challenging Cognitive Load Theory: The Role of Educational Neuroscience and Artificial Intelligence in Redefining Learning Efficacy. *Brain Sciences, 15*(2), 203. DOI: 10.3390/brainsci15020203 PMID: 40002535

Glăveanu, V. P. (2020). A Sociocultural Theory of Creativity: Bridging the Social, the Material, and the Psychological. *Review of General Psychology, 24*(4), 335–354. DOI: 10.1177/1089268020961763

Gleason, B. (2021). Expanding interaction in online courses: Integrating critical humanizing pedagogy for learner success. *Educational Technology Research and Development, 69*(1), 51–54. DOI: 10.1007/s11423-020-09888-w

Goddard, Y., Goddard, R., & Kim, M. (2015). School instructional climate and student achievement: An examination of group norms for differentiated instruction. *American Journal of Education*, *122*(1), 111–131. DOI: 10.1086/683293

Gong, T., Li, J., Yeung, J. Y., & Zhang, X. (2024). The association between course selection and academic performance: Exploring psychological interpretations. *Studies in Higher Education*, *49*(12), 2506–2519. Advance online publication. DOI: 10.1080/03075079.2024.2310151

Gonsalves, C. (2025). Contextual assessment design in the age of generative AI. *Journal of Learning Development in Higher Education*, *34*(34). Advance online publication. DOI: 10.47408/jldhe.vi34.1307

Gooch, D., Waugh, K., Richards, M., Slaymaker, M., & Woodthorpe, J. (2024). Exploring the profile of university assessments flagged as containing aı-generated material. *ACM Inroads*, *15*(2), 39–47. DOI: 10.1145/3656478

Government of Spain. (2024). *Artificial Intelligence Strategy 2024*. Ministerio para la Transformación Digital y de la Función Pública._https://transparencia.gob.es/transparencia/transparencia_Home/index/MasInformacion/Informes-de-interes/Ciencia_y_tecnologia/EstrategiaIA24.html

Goyal, M., & Mahmoud, Q. H. (2024). A Systematic review of synthetic data generation techniques using generative AI. *Electronics (Basel)*, *13*(17), 3509. DOI: 10.3390/electronics13173509

Graux, H., Gryffroy, P., Gad-Nowak, M., & Boghaert, L. (2024). *The role of artificial intelligence in processing and generating new data*. Data.Europe.EU. European Commission.

Green, A. (2024). *Artificial intelligence and the changing demand for skills in Canada: The increasing importance of social skills. OECD Artificial Intelligence Papers, No. 17*. OECD Publishing., DOI: 10.1787/1b20cdb6-

Greene Nolan, H., & Vang, M.C. (2023). Automated Essay Scoring in Middle School Writing: Understanding Key Predictors of Students' Growth and Comparing Artificial Intelligence- and Teacher-Generated Scores and Feedback.

Grévisse, C. (2024). LLM-based automatic short answer grading in undergraduate medical education. *BMC Medical Education*, *24*(1), 1–16. DOI: 10.1186/s12909-024-06026-5

Gruenhagen, J. H., Sinclair, P. M., Carroll, J. A., Baker, P. R. A., Wilson, A., & Demant, D. (2024). Computers and Education. *Artificial Intelligence*, *7*, 100273. DOI: 10.1016/j.caeai.2024.100273

Gryz, J., & Rojszczak, M. (2021). Black box algorithms and the rights of individuals: No easy solution to the "explainability" problem. *Internet Policy Review, 10*(2). Advance online publication. DOI: 10.14763/2021.2.1564

Gündüz, M., & Karaman, S. (2020). Open Education Faculty and distance education students' dropout reasons: The case of a Turkish state university. *Open Praxis, 12*(1), 7–25. DOI: 10.5944/openpraxis.12.1.970

Guo, H., Yi, W., & Liu, K. (2024). *Enhancing Constructivist Learning: The Role of Generative AI in Personalised Learning Experiences*. In *International Conference on Enterprise Information Systems*. https://doi.org/DOI: 10.5220/0012688700003690

Gupta, T. (2024). Adaptive learning systems: Harnessing AI to personalize educational outcomes. *International Journal for Research in Applied Science and Engineering Technology, 12*(11), 458–464. DOI: 10.22214/ijraset.2024.65088

Gutai, G., & Klímová, B. (2024). *Methodological challenges in teaching writing with ChatGPT*. Slavonic Pedagogical Studies Journal. DOI: 10.18355/PG.2024.13.2.14

Gu u, V. (2023). Explorarea jocurilor video: resursă actuală în procesul de transformare a paradigmei de predare–învă are [Exploring video games: A current resource in the process of transforming the teaching–learning paradigm]. In *Educa ia i învă ământul extra colar: configurări i experien e* [Proceedings of the Conference "Education and extracurricular teaching: Configurations and experiences"] (pp. 234–239). Chi inău, Moldova. https://ibn.idsi.md/gu u

Haase, J., & Hanel, P. H. P. (2023). Artificial muses: Generative artificial intelligence chatbots have risen to human-level creativity. *Journal of Creativity, 33*(3), 100066. DOI: 10.1016/j.yjoc.2023.100066

Habib, S., Vogel, T., Anli, X., & Thorne, E. (2024). How does generative artificial intelligence impact student creativity? *Journal of Creativity, 34*(1), 100072. DOI: 10.1016/j.yjoc.2023.100072

Hacohen, U. Y., & Elkin-Koren, N. (2024). Copyright Regenerated: Harnessing Genai To Measure Originality And Copyright Scope. *Harvard Journal of Law & Technology, 37*(2).

Hague, C. (2024). *Fostering higher-order thinking skills online in higher education: A scoping review*. OECD Education Working Paper No 306. OECD Publishing. https://dx.doi.org/DOI: 10.1787/19939019

Haidt, J. (2025). *Taking Back Childhood From Phones - Finally*. https://www.afterbabel.com/p/taking-back-childhood?utm_source=substack&publication_id=1221094&post_id=159917172&utm_medium=email&utm_content=share&utm_campaign=email-share&triggerShare=true&isFreemail=true&r=58nple&triedRedirect=true, accessed in 5th of April 2025

Haidt, J. (2024). *The anxious generation: How the great rewiring of childhood is causing an epidemic of mental illness*. Penguin Press.

Halimatussa'diyah. (2019). *Strategi Pembelajaran di Era Revolusi Industri 4.0*. Jakad Media Publishing.

Halkiopoulos, C., & Gkintoni, E. (2024). Leveraging AI in e-learning: Personalized learning and adaptive assessment through cognitive neuropsychology—A systematic analysis. *Electronics (Basel)*, *13*(18), 3762. DOI: 10.3390/electronics13183762

Hamerman, E. J., Aggarwal, A., & Martins, C. (2024). An investigation of generative AI in the classroom and its implications for university policy. *Quality Assurance in Education*. Advance online publication. DOI: 10.1108/QAE-08-2024-0149

Hamilton, A. (2024). Artificial Intelligence and Healthcare Simulation: The Shifting Landscape of Medical Education. *Cureus*, *16*(5). Advance online publication. DOI: 10.7759/cureus.59747

Hanke, M. (2022). Living the spiral curriculum: Using the Swanwick/Tillman sequence of musical development to support music in primary schools in the 1980s. *British Journal of Music Education*, *39*(1), 115–119. DOI: 10.1017/S0265051721000267

Hankins, A., & Harrington, C. (2022). Lack of high-quality, frequent feedback contributes to low success rates for community college students. *Impacting Education: Journal on Transforming Professional Practice*, *7*(4), 2–7. Advance online publication. DOI: 10.5195/ie.2022.201

Hao, S., Han, W., Jiang, T., Li, Y., Wu, H., Zhong, C., Zhou, Z., & Tang, H. (2024). Synthetic data in AI: Challenges, applications, and ethical implications. *ArXiv, abs/2401.01629.*

Hao, J., von Davier, A. A., Yaneva, V., Lottridge, S., von Davier, M., & Harris, D. J. (2024). Transforming Assessment: The Impacts and Implications of Large Language Models and Generative AI. *Educational Measurement: Issues and Practice*, *43*(2), 16–29. DOI: 10.1111/emip.12602

Harden, R. M. (1999). What is a spiral curriculum? *Medical Teacher*, *21*(2), 141–143. DOI: 10.1080/01421599979752

Hassija, V., Chamola, V., Mahapatra, A., Singal, A., Goel, D., Huang, K., Scardapane, S., Spinelli, I., Mahmud, M., & Hussain, A. (2024). Interpreting Black-Box Models: A Review on Explainable Artificial Intelligence. *Cognitive Computation, 16*(1), 45–74. DOI: 10.1007/s12559-023-10179-8

Hattie, J., & Timperley, H. (2007). The Power of Feedback. *Review of Educational Research, 77*(1), 81–112. DOI: 10.3102/003465430298487

Hayes, C. M. (2023). Generative artificial intelligence and copyright: Both sides of the black box *SSRN*. http://dx.doi.org/DOI: 10.2139/ssrn.4517799

Healy, V. (2024, October 17). *Gen AI and VR – Changing the way we learn soft skills*. https://virtualspeech.com/blog/chatgpt-vr-learning

Heggart, K. (2024). Are the robots coming for our jobs? In L. Callanan & M. Rangelov (Eds.), *AI in Education,* TLN Journal, 31(2). Teacher Learning Network. https://tln.org.au/Web/Web/TLN-Journals/TLN%20Journal-Back-Catalogue.aspx

Heigl, R. (2025). Generative artificial intelligence in creative contexts: a systematic review and future research agenda. *Management Review Quarterly,* 1-38.

Heinz, J. (2016). Digital skills and the ınfluence of students' socio-economic background: An exploratory study in german elementary schools. *Italian Journal of Sociology of Education, 8*(2), 186–212. DOI: 10.14658/pupj-ijse-2016-2-9

Hellas, A., Ihantola, P., Petersen, A., Ajanovski, V. V., Gutica, M., Hynninen, T., Knutas, A., Leinonen, J., Messom, C., & Liao, S. N. (2018). Predicting academic performance: A systematic literature review. In Ro¨ßling, G., & Scharlau, B. (Eds.), *Proceedings Companion of the 23rd annual ACM Conference on Innovation and Technology in computer science education* (pp. 175–199). ACM. https://doi.org/ DOI: 10.1145/3293881.3295783

Henriksen, D., Creely, E., Henderson, M., & Mishra, P. (2021). Creativity and technology in teaching and learning: A literature review of the uneasy space of implementation. *Educational Technology Research and Development, 69*(4), 1–18. DOI: 10.1007/s11423-020-09912-z

Hertz, N. (2023). Secolul singurătă ii [The Lonely Century]. *Humanitas*.

Heston, T. F., & Khun, C. (2023). Prompt Engineering in Medical Education. *International Medical Education, 2*(3), 198–205. DOI: 10.3390/ime2030019

Hew, K. F., Jia, C., Gonda, D. E., & Bai, S. (2020). Transitioning to the "new normal" of learning in unpredictable times: Pedagogical practices and learning performance in fully online flipped classrooms. *International Journal of Educational Technology in Higher Education, 17*(1), 1–22. DOI: 10.1186/s41239-020-00234-x PMID: 34778516

Hillier, M. (2023, March 30). A proposed AI literacy framework. *TECHE.* https://teche.mq.edu.au/2023/03/a-proposed-ai-literacy-framework/

Hmoud, M., Swaity, H., Hamad, N., Karram, O., & Daher, W. (2024). Higher education students' task motivation in the generative artificial intelligence context: The case of ChatGPT. *Information (Basel), 15*(1), 33. DOI: 10.3390/info15010033

Hocky, G. M., & White, A. D. (2022). Natural language processing models that automate programming will transform chemistry research and teaching. *Digital Discovery, 1*(2), 79–83. DOI: 10.1039/D1DD00009H PMID: 35515080

Hofmann, V., Kalluri, P. R., Jurafsky, D., & King, S. (2024). AI generates covertly racist decisions about people based on their dialect. *Nature, 633*(8028), 147–154. DOI: 10.1038/s41586-024-07856-5

Hollands, F., & Tirthali, D. (2014). *MOOCs: Expectations and Reality* (Issue 50). https://repository.upenn.edu/handle/20.500.14332/5727

Holmes, W., Bialik, M. and Fadel, C. (2023) Artificial Intelligence in Education. Globethics Publications, 621-653. https://doi.org/DOI: 10.58863/20.500.12424/4276068

Holmes, W. (2024). AIED—Coming of Age? | International Journal of Artificial Intelligence in Education. *International Journal of Artificial Intelligence in Education, 34*(1), 1–11. DOI: 10.1007/s40593-023-00352-3

Holmes, W., Bialik, M., & Fadel, C. (2019). *Artificial intelligence in education: Promises and implications for teaching and learning* (1st ed.). Center for Curriculum Redesign.

Hong, X., & Guo, L. (2025). Effects of AI-enhanced multi-display language teaching systems on learning motivation, cognitive load management, and learner autonomy. *Education and Information Technologies, 30*(12), 17155–17189. Advance online publication. DOI: 10.1007/s10639-025-13472-1

Hosanagar, K., & Ahn, D. (2024). Designing Human and Generative AI Collaboration. *arXiv preprint arXiv:2412.14199.*

Hovy, D., & Spruit, S. L. (2016). The social impact of natural language processing. *Annual Meeting of the Association for Computational Linguistics, 54,* 591–598. https://doi.org/DOI: 10.18653/v1/P16-2096

Howard, J., & Ruder, S. (2018). Universal language model fine-tuning for text classification. *Proceedings of the 56th Annual Meeting of the Association for Computational Linguistics*, 328-339. DOI: 10.18653/v1/P18-1031

Hsu, Y. C., & Ching, Y. H. (2023). Generative artificial intelligence in education, part one: The dynamic frontier. *TechTrends*, *67*(4), 603–607. DOI: 10.1007/s11528-023-00863-9

Huang, J., & Teng, M. (2025). *Peer feedback and ChatGPT-generated feedback on Japanese EFL students' engagement in a foreign language writing context.* Digital Applied Linguistics., DOI: 10.29140/dal.v2.102469

Huang, Y., Li, J., & Li, J. (2020). Multimodal learning with deep learning. *IEEE Transactions on Pattern Analysis and Machine Intelligence*, *42*(4), 910–927.

Huawei, S., & Aryadoust, V. (2022). A systematic review of automated writing evaluation systems. *Education and Information Technologies*, *28*(1), 771–795. Advance online publication. DOI: 10.1007/s10639-022-11200-7

Hughes, R. T., Zhu, L., & Bednarz, T. (2021). Generative adversarial networks–enabled human–artificial intelligence collaborative applications for creative and design industries: A systematic review of current approaches and trends. *Frontiers in Artificial Intelligence*, *4*, 604234. DOI: 10.3389/frai.2021.604234 PMID: 33997773

Hunt, T., Carter, R., Zhang, L., & Yang, S. (2020). Micro-credentials: The potential of personalized professional development. *Development and Learning in Organizations*, *34*(2), 33–35. DOI: 10.1108/DLO-09-2019-0215

Hussain, M., Zhu, W., Zhang, W., Abidi, S. M. R., & Ali, S. (2019). Using machine learning to predict student difficulties from learning session data. *Artificial Intelligence Review*, *52*(1), 381–407. DOI: 10.1007/s10462-018-9620-8

Hutson, J., & Plate, D. (2023). *Human-AI Collaboration for Smart Education: Reframing Applied Learning to Support Metacognition.* IntechOpen., DOI: 10.5772/intechopen.1001832

Hwang, J., Hong, S., Eom, T., & Lim, C. (2024, June 10-14). *Enhancing pre-service teachers' competence with a generative artificial intelligence-enhanced virtual reality simulation* [Conference presentation]. International Society of the Learning Sciences, Buffalo, New York, USA.

Hyland, K., & Hyland, F. (2006). Feedback on second language students' writing. *Language Teaching*, *39*(2), 83–101. DOI: 10.1017/S0261444806003399

Idowu, J. A. (2024). Debiasing education algorithms. *International Journal of Artificial Intelligence in Education*, *34*(4), 1510–1540. DOI: 10.1007/s40593-023-00389-4

Ifenthaler, D. (2022). A systems perspective on data and analytics for distance education. *Distance Education*, *43*(2), 333–341. DOI: 10.1080/01587919.2022.2064828

Ifenthaler, D., Majumdar, R., Gorissen, P., Judge, M., Mishra, S., Raffaghelli, J., & Shimada, A. (2024). Artificial intelligence in education: Implications for policymakers, researchers, and practitioners. Technology. *Knowledge and Learning*, *29*(4), 1693–1710. DOI: 10.1007/s10758-024-09747-0

Ilkou, E., Linzbach, S., & Wallat, J. (2024). *Hybrid Evaluation of Socratic Questioning for Teaching*. In *Proceedings of the 23rd International Semantic Web Conference (ISWC'24)*, Baltimore, USA. Retrieved fromhttps://www.researchgate.net/publication/385516268

Impact Research. (2024). *AI chatbots in schools: Findings from a poll of K–12 teachers, students, parents, and college undergraduates*. https://8ce82b94a8c4fdc3ea6d-b1d233e3bc3cb10858bea65ff05e18f2.ssl.cf2.rackcdn.com/bf/24/cd3646584af89e7c668c7705a006/deck-impact-analysis-national-schools-tech-tracker-may-2024-1.pdf

Imran, M., & Almusharraf, N. (2024). Google Gemini as a next generation AI educational tool: A review of emerging educational technology. *Smart Learning Environments*, *11*(1), 22. Advance online publication. DOI: 10.1186/s40561-024-00310-z

Ireland, J., & Mouthaan, M. (2020). Perspectives on curriculum design: Comparing the spiral and the network models. *Research Matters*, *30*, 7–12. DOI: 10.17863/CAM.100405

Irwin, V., Wang, K., Tezil, T., Zhang, J., Filbey, A., Jung, J., & Parker, S. (2023). Report on the condition of education 2023. NCES 2023- 144 (Tech. Rep.). National Center for Education Statistics. https://nces.ed.gov/use-work/resource-library/report/compendium/condition-education-2023?pubid=2023144

Israni, S. (2025, January 24). Nigeria's AI University: A Revolution for Africa. *CIO Africa*. https://cioafrica.co/nigerias-ai-university-a-revolution-for-africa/

Ita Olszewska, A., Bondy, E., Hagler, N., & Jinna Kim, H. (2023). A humanizing pedagogy of engagement: Beliefs and practices of award-winning instructors at a U.S. university. *Teaching in Higher Education*, *28*(7), 1671–1687. DOI: 10.1080/13562517.2021.1920575

Ivanović, I. (2025). Cognitive load in AI-assisted vs traditional foreign language classroom: Mixed methods research. Disputatio Philosophica. *International Journal for Philosophy of Religion*, *6*, 361–380. DOI: 10.18485/dpls_plucast.2025.6.ch22

Jack, E., Alexander, C., & Jones, E. M. (2024). Levelling up learning: Exploring the impact of gamification in flipped classrooms. *University of Glasgow.* https://arxiv.org/html/2402.18313v1

Jamieson, S. (2022). The AI "Crisis" and A (Re)turn To Pedagogy. *Composition Studies*, *50*(3), 153–157.

Jauhiainen, J. S., & Garagorry Guerra, A. (2024). Generative AI and education: Dynamic personalization of pupils' school learning material with ChatGPT. *Frontiers in Education*, *9*, 1288723. Advance online publication. DOI: 10.3389/feduc.2024.1288723

Jauhiainen, J. S., & Garagorry Guerra, A. (2024a). Generative AI in education: ChatGPT-4 in evaluating students' written responses. *Innovations in Education and Teaching International*, •••, 1–18. DOI: 10.1080/14703297.2024.2422337

Jauhiainen, J. S., & Garagorry Guerra, A. (2024b). Evaluating students' open-ended written responses with LLMS: Using the RAG Framework for GPT-3.5, GPT-4, Claude-3, and Mistral-Large. *Advances in Artificial Intelligence and Machine Learning.*, *4*(4), 3097–3113. DOI: 10.54364/AAIML.2024.44177

Jensen, C. G., Dau, S., & Gade, P. (2024). *The role of AI chatbots in scaffolding: Linking learning outcomes with assessment.* Learning Tech – Tidsskrift for læremidler, didaktik og teknologi, (14), 73–97. https://tidsskrift.dk/learningtech/article/view/141213

Jerusha, J. A., & Rajakumari, R. (2024). *Longitudinal analysis of student progress in AI-integrated English language courses* [Conference presentation]. International Conference on Knowledge Engineering and Communication Systems (ICKECS), Chikkaballapur, India. DOI: 10.1109/ICKECS61492.2024.10616489

Jia, N., Luo, X., Fang, Z., & Liao, C. (2024). When and how artificial intelligence augments employee creativity. *Academy of Management Journal*, *67*(1), 5–32. DOI: 10.5465/amj.2022.0426

Jia, Y., Zhou, Y., Sun, L., & Wu, Q. (2020). Improving the quality of generated questions via rough answer and key sentence tagging and graph convolutional networks. *Journal of Educational Technology & Society*, *23*(4), 118–129.

Ji, H., Han, I., & Ko, Y. (2023). A systematic review of conversational AI in language education: Focusing on the collaboration with human teachers. *Journal of Research on Technology in Education*, *55*(1), 48–63. DOI: 10.1080/15391523.2022.2142873

Jin, L., Lin, B., Hong, M., Zhang, K., & So, H.-J. (2025). *Exploring the impact of an LLM-powered teachable agent on learning gains and cognitive load in music education*. arXiv. https://arxiv.org/abs/2504.00636

Jin, Y., Martinez-Maldonado, R., Gašević, D., & Yan, L. (2025). GLAT: The Generative AI Literacy Assessment Test. *Computers and Education: Artificial Intelligence*, *9*, 100436. DOI: 10.1016/j.caeai.2025.100436

Joshi, I., Grimmer, M., Rathgeb, C., Busch, C., Bremond, F., & Dantcheva, A. (2024). Synthetic data in human analysis: A survey. *IEEE Transactions on Pattern Analysis and Machine Intelligence*, *46*(7), 1–20. DOI: 10.1109/TPAMI.2024.3362821

Jukiewicz, M. (2024). The future of grading programming assignments in education: The role of ChatGPT in automating the assessment and feedback process. *Thinking Skills and Creativity*, *52*, 101522. DOI: 10.1016/j.tsc.2024.101522

Jung, J. Y., Tyack, L., & von Davier, M. (2025). Towards the implementation of automated scoring in international large-scale assessments: Scalability and quality control. *Computers and Education: Artificial Intelligence*, *8*, 100375. DOI: 10.1016/j.caeai.2025.100375

Jürgen, R., Tan, S., & Tan, S. (2023). War of the Chatsbots: Bard, Bing Chat, ChatGPT, Ernie and beyond. The new AI gold rush and its impact on higher education. *Journal of Applied Learning & Teaching*, *6*(1). Advance online publication. DOI: 10.37074/jalt.2023.6.1.23

Jury, B., Lorusso, A., Leinonen, J., & Denny, P., & Luxton- Reilly, A. (2024). Evaluating LLM- generated worked examples in an introductory programming course. In *Proceedings of the 26th Australasian Computing Education Conference* (pp. 77–86). Association for Computing Machinery. . DOI: 10.1145/3636243.3636252

Kadel, R., Mishra, B. K., Shailendra, S., Abid, S., Rani, M., & Mahato, S. P. (2024, July). Crafting tomorrow's evaluations: assessment design strategies in the era of generative AI. In *2024 International Symposium on Educational Technology (ISET)* (pp. 13-17). IEEE. DOI: 10.1109/ISET61814.2024.00012

Kalpokienė, J. (2024). *Law, Human Creativity and Generative Artificial Intelligence: Regulatory Options*. Taylor & Francis. DOI: 10.4324/9781003464976

Kalyuga, S. (2009). The expertise reversal effect. In *Managing cognitive load in adaptive multimedia learning* (pp. 58–80). IGI Global., DOI: 10.4018/978-1-60566-048-6.ch003

Kalyuga, S., Chandler, P., & Sweller, J. (1998). Levels of Expertise and Instructional Design. *Human Factors*, *40*(1), 1–17. DOI: 10.1518/001872098779480587

Kamali, J., Alpat, M. F., & Bozkurt, A. (2024). AI ethics as a complex and multifaceted challenge: Decoding educators' AI ethics alignment through the lens of activity theory. *International Journal of Educational Technology in Higher Education*, *21*(1), 62. DOI: 10.1186/s41239-024-00496-9

Kamalov, F., Santandreu Calonge, D., & Gurrib, I. (2023). New era of artificial intelligence in education: Towards a sustainable multifaceted revolution. *Sustainability (Basel)*, *15*(16), 12451. DOI: 10.3390/su151612451

Kamarthi, S. V., Al Valbuena, A., Velou, M., Kumara, S., & Enscore, E. (1992). ADVISOR - An expert system for the selection of courses. *Expert Systems with Applications*, *5*(1–2), 153–165. DOI: 10.1016/0957-4174(92)90104-Z

Kanbach, D. K., Heiduk, L., Blueher, G., Schreiter, M., & Lahmann, A. (2024). The GenAI is out of the bottle: Generative artificial intelligence from a business model innovation perspective. *Review of Managerial Science*, *18*(1), 1189–1220. DOI: 10.1007/s11846-023-00696-z

Kandel, E. R. (2001). The molecular biology of memory storage: A dialogue between genes and synapses. *Science*, *294*(5544), 1030–1038. DOI: 10.1126/science.1067020 PMID: 11691980

Kanık, M. (2024). The use of ChatGPT in assessment. *International Journal of Assessment Tools in Education*, *11*(3), 608–621. DOI: 10.21449/ijate.1379647

Kaplan, A., & Haenlein, M. (2020). Rulers of the world, unite! The challenges and opportunities of artificial intelligence. *Business Horizons*, *63*(1), 37–50. DOI: 10.1016/j.bushor.2019.09.003

Karataş, F., & Ataç, B. A. (2024). When TPACK meets artificial intelligence: Analyzing TPACK and AI-TPACK components through structural equation modelling. *Education and Information Technologies*. Advance online publication. DOI: 10.1007/s10639-024-13164-2

Karkera, A., Greene, M., Hall, A., Henderson, L., & Lewis, K. (2024). *Transformational impacts of generative AI on synthetic data generation*. Deloitte.

Kaswan, K. S., Dhatterwal, J. S., & Ojha, R. P. (2024). AI in personalized learning. In *Advances in technological innovations in higher education* (pp. 103–117). CRC Press. DOI: 10.1201/9781003376699-9

Kearney, K., & Hyle, A. (2003). The Grief Cycle and Educational Change: The Kubler-Ross Contribution. *Planning and Changing, 34*(1 and 2), 32–57.

Kenshinbay, T., & Ghorbandordinejad, F. (2024). *Exploring AI-driven adaptive feedback in the second language writing skills prompt.* EIKI Journal of Effective Teaching Methods., DOI: 10.59652/jetm.v2i3.264

Khalil, M., & Er, E. (2023). Will ChatGPT get you caught? rethinking of plagiarism detection. In: Zaphiris, P., Ioannou, A. (eds) *Learning and Collaboration Technologies.* HCII 2023. Lecture Notes in Computer Science, *14040*. https://doi.org/DOI: 10.1007/978-3-031-34411-4_32

Khalil, A., Abdallah, S., Hijazi, R., & Sheikh, K. (2025). Trust but verify: The effect of religiosity and social conformity on verification of content shared via social media. *Information Technology & People*, *38*(1), 70–86. DOI: 10.1108/ITP-11-2022-0827

Khasawneh, Y. J. A., & Khasawneh, M. A. S. (2024). Cognitive load analysis of adaptive learning technologies in special education classrooms: A quantitative approach. *International Journal of Advanced and Applied Sciences*, *11*(12), 34–41. https://www.science-gate.com/IJAAS/2024/V11I12/1021833ijaas202412004.html. DOI: 10.21833/ijaas.2024.12.004

Khlaif, Z. N., Alkouk, W. A., Salama, N., & Abu Eideh, B. (2025). Redesigning assessments for AI-enhanced learning: A framework for educators in the generative AI era. *Education Sciences*, *15*(2), 174. DOI: 10.3390/educsci15020174

Khlaif, Z., Odeh, A., & Bsharat, T. R. K. (2024). Generative AI-powered adaptive assessment. In Sanmugam, M., Lim, D., & Barkhaya, N. M. M. (Eds.), *Power of persuasive educational technologies in enhancing learning*. IGI Global. DOI: 10.4018/979-8-3693-6397-3.ch007

Khosrawi-Rad, B., Rinn, H., Schlimbach, R., Gebbing, P., Yang, X., Lattemann, C., ... & Robra-Bissantz, S. (2022). Conversational agents in education–a systematic literature review. https://www.researchgate.net/publication/361039365_Conversational_Agents_in_Education_-_A_Systematic_Literature_Review

Khuder, B. (2025). Enhancing disciplinary voice through feedback-seeking in AI-assisted doctoral writing for publication. *Applied Linguistics*, •••, amaf022. DOI: 10.1093/applin/amaf022

Kim, H. J., Kong, Y., Hernandez, C., & Soban, M. (2023). Student Emotions and Engagement: Enacting Humanizing Pedagogy in Higher Education. *IAFOR Journal of Education, 11*(3), 185–206. DOI: 10.22492/ije.11.3.09

Kim, J., Lee, T. H., Bae, Y., & Kim, M. K. (2024). A Comparison Between AI and Human Evaluation with a Focus on Generative AI. In Lindgren, R., Asino, T. I., Kyza, E. A., Looi, C. K., Keifert, D. T., & Suárez, E. (Eds.), *Proceedings of the 18th International Conference of the Learning Sciences - ICLS 2024* (1722-1725). International Society of the Learning Sciences. DOI: 10.22318/icls2024.930382

Kim, J., Yu, S., Detrick, R., & Li, N. (2024). Exploring students' perspectives on generative AI-assisted academic writing. *Education and Information Technologies, 30*(1), 1265–1300. DOI: 10.1007/s10639-024-12878-7

Kim, P. W. (2024). Fog Computing for Artificial Intelligence Digital Textbooks: Educational Scaffolding and Security and Privacy Challenges. *Expert Systems: International Journal of Knowledge Engineering and Neural Networks, 13801.* Advance online publication. DOI: 10.1111/exsy.13801

Kirkham, H. (2023). *The rise of AI in education? research report on teacher usage, teacher wishes and teacher concerns. education intelligence AI in education,* Oriel Square, https://www.orielsquare.co.uk/wp-content/uploads/2023/10/education-intelligence_report_summer-2023_digital-1.pdf

Kirschenbaum, M. (2023, March 8). *Prepare for the Textpocalypse.* The Atlantic, https://www.theatlantic.com/technology/archive/2023/03/ai-chatgpt-writing-language-models/673318/

Kirschner, P., Sweller, J., & Clark, R. (2006). Why minimal guidance during instruction does not work: An analysis of the failure of constructivist, discovery, problem-based, experiential and inquiry based teaching. *Educational Psychologist, 41*(2), 75–86. DOI: 10.1207/s15326985ep4102_1

Kizilcec, R. F., Huber, E., Papanastasiou, E. C., Cram, A., Makridis, C. A., Smolansky, A., Zeivots, S., & Raduescu, C. (2024). Perceived impact of generative AI on assessments: Comparing educator and student perspectives in Australia, Cyprus, and the United States. *Computers and Education: Artificial Intelligence, 7,* 100269. DOI: 10.1016/j.caeai.2024.100269

Klenowski, V. (2009). Assessment for learning revisited: An Asia-Pacific perspective. *Assessment in Education: Principles, Policy & Practice, 16*(3), 263–268. DOI: 10.1080/09695940903319646

Klepsch, M., Schmitz, F., & Seufert, T. (2017). Development and Validation of Two Instruments Measuring Intrinsic, Extraneous, and Germane Cognitive Load. *Frontiers in Psychology*, *8*, 1997. DOI: 10.3389/fpsyg.2017.01997 PMID: 29201011

Knox, J. (2020). Artificial intelligence and education in China. *Learning, Media and Technology*, *45*(3), 298–311. DOI: 10.1080/17439884.2020.1754236

Ko'c-Januchta, M. M., Schonborn, ¨. K. J., Roehrig, C., Chaudhri, V. K., Tibell, L. A., & Heller, H. C. (2022). "Connecting concepts helps put main ideas together": Cognitive load and usability in learning biology with an AI-enriched textbook. *International Journal of Educational Technology in Higher Education*, *19*(1), 11. DOI: 10.1186/s41239-021-00317-3

Koçdar, S., Hamutoğlu, N. B., Erdoğdu, E., & Uçar, H. (2024). Academic performance of learners with special needs in open and distance learning: A study in Anadolu University open education system. *European Journal of Special Needs Education*. Advance online publication. DOI: 10.1080/08856257.2024.2380594

Kochmar, E., Vu, D. D., Belfer, R., Gupta, V., Serban, I. V., & Pineau, J. (2022). Automated data-driven generation of personalized pedagogical interventions in intelligent tutoring systems. *International Journal of Artificial Intelligence in Education*, *32*(2), 323–349. DOI: 10.1007/s40593-021-00267-x

Koehler, M. J., & Mishra, P. (2005). What Happens When Teachers Design Educational Technology? The Development of Technological Pedagogical Content Knowledge. *Journal of Educational Computing Research*, *32*(2), 131–152. DOI: 10.2190/0EW7-01WB-BKHL-QDYV

Kohnke, L. (2024). *How GenAI impacts technostress among secondary school English teachers* [Conference presentation]. International CALL Research Conference, Waseda University, Tokyo, Japan. https://doi.org/DOI: 10.29140/9780648184485-17

Koltovskaia, S. (2023). Postsecondary L2 writing teachers' use and perceptions of Grammarly as a complement to their feedback. *ReCALL*, *35*(3), 290–304. DOI: 10.1017/S0958344022000179

Korbach, A., Brünken, R., & Park, B. (2018). Differentiating different types of cognitive load: A comparison of different measures. *Educational Psychology Review*, *30*(2), 503–529. DOI: 10.1007/s10648-017-9404-8

Koumpouros, Y. (2024). Revealing the true potential and prospects of augmented reality in education. *Smart Learn. Environ.*, *11*(2), 1–62. DOI: 10.1186/s40561-023-00288-0

Kozan, K., & Richardson, J. C. (2014). Interrelationships between and among social, teaching, and cognitive presence. *The Internet and Higher Education*, *21*, 68–73. DOI: 10.1016/j.iheduc.2013.10.007

Kozbelt, A., Beghetto, R. A., & Runco, M. A. (2010). Theories of Creativity. In Kaufman, J. C., & Sternberg, R. J. (Eds.), *Cambridge Handbook of Creativity* (pp. 20–47). Cambridge University Press., DOI: 10.1017/CBO9780511763205.004

Kraft, M. A., & Lyon, M. A. (2024). The rise and fall of the teaching profession: Prestige, interest, preparation, and satisfaction over the last half century. *American Educational Research Journal*, *61*(6), 1192–1236. DOI: 10.3102/00028312241276856

Krishna, L., Prasad, J., & Anjali, S. (2024). The Impact of Artificial Intelligence in Reshaping Education: An Analysis Based on Learning Theories. In *ITM Web of Conferences* (Vol. 68, p. 01008). EDP Sciences.DOI: 10.1051/itmconf/20246801008

Krullaars, Z. H., Januardani, A., Zhou, L., & Jonkers, E. (2023). Exploring initial interactions: High school students and generative ai chatbots for relationship development. https://doi.org/DOI: 10.18420/muc2023-mci-src-415

Kshetri, N., Dwivedi, Y. K., Davenport, T. H., & Panteli, N. (2024). Generative artificial intelligence in marketing: Applications, opportunities, challenges, and research agenda. *International Journal of Information Management*, *75*, 102716. DOI: 10.1016/j.ijinfomgt.2023.102716

Kulhavy, R. W., White, M. T., Topp, B. W., Chan, A. L., & Adams, J. (1985). Feedback complexity and corrective efficiency. *Contemporary Educational Psychology*, *10*(3), 285–292. DOI: 10.1016/0361-476X(85)90025-6

Kunst, J. R., & Mesoudi, A. (2025). Decoding the dynamics of cultural change: A cultural evolution approach to the psychology of acculturation. *Personality and Social Psychology Review*, *29*(2), 111–144. DOI: 10.1177/10888683241258406 PMID: 39056551

Kurshumova, D. A. (2024). A snapshot of Bulgarian school teachers' familiarity with, use of, and opinions on artificial intelligence at the threshold of its incorporation into the educational process. *Discover Education*, *3*(1), 138. DOI: 10.1007/s44217-024-00225-4

Kurtz, G., Salmon, G., Watkins, R., Kalz, M., & Buchem, I. (2024). Special Issue: The integration of generative AI in teaching and learning. *European Journal of Open. Distance and E-Learning*, *26*(1), 1–4. DOI: 10.2478/eurodl-2024-0010

Kuzminykh, I., Nawaz, T., Shenzhang, S., Ghita, B., Raphael, J., & Xiao, H. (2024). *Personalised Feedback Framework for Online Education Programmes Using Generative AI*. https://arxiv.org/pdf/2410.11904

Laakso, A. (2023). *Ethical challenges of large language models: A systematic literature review*. Master dissertation from the University of Helsinki.

Lademann, J., Henze, J., & Becker-Genschow, S. (2025). Augmenting learning environments using AI custom chatbots: Effects on learning performance, cognitive load, and affective variables. *Physical Review. Physics Education Research*, *21*(1), 010147. DOI: 10.1103/PhysRevPhysEducRes.21.010147

Lawshe, C. H. (1975). A quantitative approach to content validity. *Personnel Psychology*, *28*(4), 563–575. DOI: 10.1111/j.1744-6570.1975.tb01393.x

Le Lagadec, D., Jackson, D., & Cleary, M. (2024). Artificial intelligence in nursing education: Prospects and pitfalls. *Journal of Advanced Nursing*, *80*(10), 3883–3885. DOI: 10.1111/jan.16276

Leaton Gray, S., Edsall, D., & Parapadakis, D. (2025). AI-Based Digital Cheating At University, and the Case for New Ethical Pedagogies. *Journal of Academic Ethics*, *23*(4), 2069–2086. Advance online publication. DOI: 10.1007/s10805-025-09642-y

Lee, C. S., & Hughes, J. H. (2019). Refocusing on cognitive load design through a meta-analysis on learnability, goal-based intentions and extensibility: towards personalized cognitive-social-affective engagement among seniors. In *Advancing Technology Industrialization Through Intelligent Software Methodologies, Tools and Techniques* (pp. 456-469). IOS Press.

Lee, J., & Kim, D. (2025). Levelling up learning in higher education: Gamification of in-video components to supercharge student learning and achievement in video-based learning. *British Journal of Educational Technology*. Advance online publication. https://bera-journals.onlinelibrary.wiley.com/doi/abs/10.1111/bjet.13564

Lee, K., Cooper, A. F., & Grimmelmann, J. (2023). Talkin''Bout AI Generation: Copyright and the Generative-AI Supply Chain. *arXiv preprint arXiv:2309.08133*.

Lee, A. V. Y. (2023). Supporting students' generation of feedback in large-scale online course with artificial intelligence-enabled evaluation. *Studies in Educational Evaluation*, *77*, 101250. DOI: 10.1016/j.stueduc.2023.101250

Lee, D., Arnold, M., Srivastava, A., Plastow, K., Strelan, P., Ploeckl, F., Lekkas, D., & Palmer, E. (2024). The impact of generative AI on higher education learning and teaching: A study of educators' perspectives. *Computers and Education: Artificial Intelligence*, *6*, 100221. DOI: 10.1016/j.caeai.2024.100221

Lee, I. (2020). Utility of focused/comprehensive written corrective feedback research for authentic L2 writing classrooms. *Journal of Second Language Writing*, *49*, 100734. DOI: 10.1016/j.jslw.2020.100734

Lee, J. D., & See, K. A. (2004). Trust in automation: Designing for appropriate reliance. *Human Factors*, *46*(1), 50–80. DOI: 10.1518/hfes.46.1.50.30392 PMID: 15151155

Leiker, D., Finnigan, S., Gyllen, A. R., & Cukurova, M. (2023). Prototyping the use of Large Language Models (LLMs) for adult learning content creation at scale. arXiv preprint. https://arxiv.org/abs/2306.01815

Leiva, F. M., Ríos, F. J. M., & Martínez, T. L. (2006). Assessment of ınterjudge reliability in the open-ended questions coding process. *Quality & Quantity*, *40*(4), 519–537. DOI: 10.1007/s11135-005-1093-6

Leow, R. P. (2015). *Explicit learning in the L2 classroom: A student-centered approach*. Routledge., DOI: 10.4324/9781315887074

Li, C., Liang, L., Fryer, L. K., & Shum, A. (2024). The use of leaderboards in education: A systematic review of empirical evidence in higher education. *Journal of Computer Assisted Learning*. Advance online publication. https://onlinelibrary.wiley.com/doi/abs/10.1111/jcal.13077

Li, H., Xu, T., Zhang, C., Chen, E., Liang, J., Fan, X., . . . Wen, Q. (2024). Bringing generative AI to adaptive learning in education. *arXiv:2402.14601*. https://doi.org/arXiv.2402.14601DOI: 10.48550

Liang, W., Krasheninnikov, K., Kim, M., Zhang, Y., Guo, M., He, J., & Zou, J. (2024). *Can Large Language Models Provide Useful Feedback on Research Papers? A Large-Scale Empirical Analysis*. Stanford University. https://arxiv.org/abs/2310.01783

Liang, W., Yuksekgonul, M., Mao, Y., Wu, E., & Zou, J. (2023). GPT detectors are biased against non-native English writers. [NY]. *Patterns (New York, N.Y.)*, *4*(7), 100779. DOI: 10.1016/j.patter.2023.100779

Liao, J., Zhong, L., Zhe, L., Xu, H., Liu, M., & Xie, T. (2024). Scaffolding computational thinking with ChatGPT. *IEEE Transactions on Learning Technologies*, *17*, 1628–1642. DOI: 10.1109/TLT.2024.3392896

Liew, P. Y., & Tan, I. K. (2024). On automated essay grading using large language models. *Proceedings of the 2024 8th International Conference on Computer Science and Artificial Intelligence*.DOI: 10.1145/3709026.3709030

Lim, L.-A., Dawson, S., Gašević, D., Joksimović, S., Fudge, A., Pardo, A., & Gentili, S. (2020). Students' sense-making of personalised feedback based on learning analytics. *Australasian Journal of Educational Technology*, *36*(6), 15–33. DOI: 10.14742/ajet.6370

Limo, F. A. F., Tiza, D. R. H., Roque, M. M., Herrera, E. E., Murillo, J. P. M., Huallpa, J. J., Flores, V. A. A., Castillo, A. G. R., Peña, P. F. P., Carranza, C. P. M., & Gonzáles, J. L. A. (2023). Personalized tutoring: ChatGPT as a virtual tutor for personalized learning experiences. *Przestrzen Spoleczna*, *23*(1), 292–312.

Lindqvist, G. (2003) Vygotsky's Theory of Creativity, Creativity Research, Journal, 15:2-3, 245-251, DOI: DOI: 10.1080/10400419.2003.9651416

Lingaiah, J., Ishak, S. N., & Mishra, P. K. (2024). AI-driven chatbots as language tutors: Enhancing written proficiency in ESL. *International Journal of Humanities and Social Science*, *3*(5), 78–95. Advance online publication. DOI: 10.47941/ijhss.2410

Lin, L., Ginns, P., Wang, T., & Zhang, P. (2020). Using a pedagogical agent to deliver conversational style instruction: What benefits can you obtain? *Computers & Education*, *143*, 103658. DOI: 10.1016/j.compedu.2019.103658

Li, Q., Bañuelos, M., Liu, Y., & Xu, D. (2022). Online instruction for a humanized learning experience: Techniques used by college instructors. *Computers & Education*, *189*, 104595. Advance online publication. DOI: 10.1016/j.compedu.2022.104595

Li, T., Reigh, E., He, P., & Miller, E. (2023). Can we and should we use artificial intelligence for formative assessment in science? *Journal of Research in Science Teaching*, *60*(6), 1385–1389. DOI: 10.1002/tea.21867

Liu, D. Y. T., & Bates, S. (2025). *Generative AI in Higher Education: Current Practices and Ways Forward.* The Association of Pacific Rim Universities. https://www.apru.org/resources_report/whitepaper-generative-ai-in-higher-education-current-practices-and-ways-forward/

Liu, D. Y. T., Bassett, M. A., & Iacono, C. (2024). Engaging with generative AI in education: Four important mindset shifts. In L. Callanan & M. Rangelov (Eds.), *AI in Education,* TLN Journal, 31(2). Teacher Learning Network. https://tln.org.au/Web/Web/TLN-Journals/TLN%20Journal-Back-Catalogue.aspx

Liu, L. (2024). Impact of AI gamification on EFL learning outcomes and nonlinear dynamic motivation: Comparing adaptive learning paths, conversational agents, and storytelling. *Education and Information Technologies*. Advance online publication. DOI: 10.1007/s10639-024-13296-5

Li, W., & Ironsi, C. S. (2024). Efficacy of micro credential learning spaces in developing students' twenty-first century skills: Towards graduate work readiness. *Education and Information Technologies*, *29*(1), 1201–1216. DOI: 10.1007/s10639-023-12294-3

Li, W.-Y., Kau, K., & Shiung, Y.-J. (2023). Pedagogic Exploration Into Adapting Automated Writing Evaluation and Peer Review Integrated Feedback Into Large-Sized University Writing Classes. *SAGE Open*, *13*(4), 21582440231209087. Advance online publication. DOI: 10.1177/21582440231209087

Li, Y., Pan, Y., & Zhao, D. (2025). Understanding the neurobiology and computational mechanisms of social conformity: Implications for psychiatric disorders. *Biological Psychiatry*. Advance online publication. DOI: 10.1016/j.biopsych.2025.05.011 PMID: 40409524

Li, Y., Sha, L., Yan, L., Lin, J., Raković, M., Galbraith, K., Lyons, K., Gašević, D., & Chen, G. (2023). Can large language models write reflectively. *Computers and Education: Artificial Intelligence*, *4*, 100140. DOI: 10.1016/j.caeai.2023.100140

Lo, C. K., & Hew, K. F. (2017). A critical review of flipped classroom challenges in K-12 education: Possible solutions and recommendations for future research. *Research and Practice in Technology Enhanced Learning*, *12*(1), 1–22. DOI: 10.1186/s41039-016-0044-2 PMID: 30613253

Lodge, J., Howard, S., & Bearman, M. (2023). *Assessment reform for the age of artificial intelligence*. Tertiary Education Quality and Standards Agency. https://www.teqsa.gov.au/sites/default/files/2023-09/assessment-reform-age-artificial-intelligence-discussion-paper.pdf

Lodge, J. M., de Barba, P., & Broadbent, J. (2023). Learning with Generative Artificial Intelligence Within a Network of Co-Regulation. *Journal of University Teaching & Learning Practice*, *20*(7), 7. Advance online publication. DOI: 10.53761/1.20.7.02

Lodge, J. M., Thompson, K., & Corrin, L. (2023). Mapping out a research agenda for generative artificial intelligence in tertiary education. *Australasian Journal of Educational Technology*, *39*(1), 1–8. DOI: 10.14742/ajet.8695

Long, P., & Siemens, G. (2011). Penetrating the Fog: Analytics in Learning and Education. *EDUCAUSE Review*. https://er.educause.edu/articles/2011/9/penetrating-the-fog-analytics-in-learning-and-education

Long, D., & Magerko, B. (2020). What is AI Literacy? Competencies and Design Considerations. *Proceedings of the 2020 CHI Conference on Human Factors in Computing Systems*, 1–16. DOI: 10.1145/3313831.3376727

Lopez, S. (2024). The Impact of Cognitive Load Theory on the Effectiveness of Microlearning Modules. *European Journal of Education and Pedagogy*, *5*(2), 29–35. DOI: 10.24018/ejedu.2024.5.2.799

López-Villanueva, D., Santiago, R., & Palau, R. (2024). Flipped Learning and Artificial Intelligence. *Electronics 2024, Vol. 13, Page 3424, 13*(17), 3424. DOI: 10.3390/electronics13173424

Lorenz, U., & Romeike, R. (2023). What Is AI-PACK? – Outline of AI Competencies for Teaching with DPACK. In J.-P. Pellet & G. Parriaux (Eds.), *Informatics in Schools. Beyond Bits and Bytes: Nurturing Informatics Intelligence in Education* (pp. 13–25). Springer Nature Switzerland. DOI: 10.1007/978-3-031-44900-0_2

Lowenthal, P. R., & Snelson, C. (2017). In search of a better understanding of social presence: An investigation into how researchers define social presence. *Distance Education*, *38*(2), 141–159. DOI: 10.1080/01587919.2017.1324727

Lubbe, A., Marais, E., & Kruger, D. (2025). Cultivating independent thinkers: The triad of artificial intelligence, Bloom's taxonomy and critical thinking in assessment pedagogy. *Education and Information Technologies*, *30*(12), 17589–17622. Advance online publication. DOI: 10.1007/s10639-025-13476-x

Luckin, R. (2017). Towards artificial intelligence-based assessment systems. *Nature Human Behaviour 2017 1:3, 1*(3), 1–3. DOI: 10.1038/s41562-016-0028

Luckin, R., Rudolph, J., Grünert, M., & Tan, S. (2024). Exploring the future of learning and the relationship between human intelligence and AI. An interview with Professor Rose Luckin. *Journal of Applied Learning and Teaching*, *7*(1), 346–363. DOI: 10.37074/jalt.2024.7.1.27

Luo, J. (2024). A critical review of GenAI policies in higher education assessment: A call to reconsider the "originality" of students' work. *Assessment & Evaluation in Higher Education*, *49*(5), 651–664. DOI: 10.1080/02602938.2024.2309963

Lye, C. Y., & Lim, L. (2024). Generative artificial intelligence in tertiary education: Assessment redesign principles and considerations. *Education Sciences*, *14*(6), 569. DOI: 10.3390/educsci14060569

Lythreatis, S., Singh, S. K., & El-Kassar, A. N. (2022). The digital divide: A review and future research agenda. *Technological Forecasting and Social Change*, *175*, 121359. DOI: 10.1016/j.techfore.2021.121359

MagicSchool. (2025). *Mainpage.* https://app.magicschool.ai/tools

Majeed, A., & Hwang, S. O. (2025). Synthetic data: A new frontier for democratizing artificial intelligence and data access. *Computer*, *58*(2), 106–114. Advance online publication. DOI: 10.1109/MC.2024.3515412

Maleki, N., Padmanabhan, B., & Dutta, K. (2024). AI hallucinations: A misnomer worth clarifying. *arXiv*, 2401.06796. https://doi.org//arXiv.2401.06796DOI: 10.1109/CAI59869.2024.00033

Malevé, N. (2024). Lost in Compression: Models of Authorship in Generative AI. *Media Theory*, *8*(1), 205–228. DOI: 10.70064/mt.v8i1.1074

Malik, R., Abdi, D., Wang, R., & Demszky, D. (2025). Scaffolding middle school mathematics curricula with large language models. *British Journal of Educational Technology*, *56*(3), 999–1027. Advance online publication. DOI: 10.1111/bjet.13571

Maltagliati, A. J., Paree, J. H., McIntosh, K. L., Moynahan, K. F., & Vanderah, T. W. (2023). Development and evaluation of a pre-clerkship spiral curriculum: Data from three medical school classes. *Medical Education Online*, *28*(1), 2167258. Advance online publication. DOI: 10.1080/10872981.2023.2167258

Mao, J., Chen, B., & Liu, J. C. (2024). Generative Artificial Intelligence in Education and Its Implications for Assessment. *TechTrends*, *68*(1), 58–66. DOI: 10.1007/s11528-023-00911-4

Marchenko, N., Slipchuk, V., & Yuzkiv, H. (2023). INTERACTIVE LEARNING METHODS IN HIGHER EDUCATION INSTITUTIONS. *The Modern Higher Education Review*, *8*(8), 146–156. DOI: 10.28925/2518-7635.2023.810

Marković, M., Jeremić, I., & Vujović, M. (2025). Experience of implementing online teaching at the beginning of the Covid-19 pandemic - The mediating role of teaching style, stress resilience of teachers, and other individual variables. *Journal of Educational Sciences & Psychology*, *XV*(LXXVII), 108–120. DOI: 10.51865/JESP.2025.1.10

Maslej, N., Fattorini, L., Perrault, R., Parli, V., Reuel, A., Brynjolfsson, E., Etchemendy, J., Ligett, K., Lyons, T., Manyika, J., Niebles, J. C., Shoham, Y., Wald, R., & Clark, J. (2024). *AI Index Report 2024 – Artificial Intelligence Index*. Stanford University Institute for Human-Centred Artificial Intelligence. https://aiindex.stanford.edu/report/

Mayer, R. E. (2008). Applying the science of learning: Evidence-based principles for the design of multimedia instruction. *The American Psychologist*, *63*(8), 760–769. DOI: 10.1037/0003-066X.63.8.760 PMID: 19014238

Mayer, R. E. (2009). *Multimedia Learning* (2nd ed.). Cambridge University Press. DOI: 10.1017/CBO9780511811678

Mayer, R. E. (2010). Applying the Science of Learning to Medical Education. *Medical Education, 39*(6), 169–175. DOI: 10.1111/j.1365-2923.2010.03624.x PMID: 20604850

Mayer, R. E. (2017). Using multimedia for e-learning. *Journal of Computer Assisted Learning, 33*(5), 403–423. DOI: 10.1111/jcal.12197

Mayer, R. E. (2021). *Multimedia learning* (3rd ed.). Cambridge University Press.

Mayer, R. E. (2024). Increasing the Effectiveness of Digital Learning. In Gegenfurtner, A., & Kollar, I. (Eds.), *Designing Effective Digital Learning Environments* (pp. 279–288). Routledge. DOI: 10.4324/9781003386131-26

Mayer, R. E. (Ed.). (2005). *The Cambridge handbook of multimedia learning*. Cambridge University Press., DOI: 10.1017/CBO9780511816819

McCarthy, J., Minsky, M. L., Rochester, N., & Shannon, C. E. (1955). A proposal for the Dartmouth Summer Research Project on Artificial Intelligence, August 31, 1955. *AI Magazine, 27*(4), 12–12. DOI: 10.1609/AIMAG.V27I4.1904

McCormack, J., Gifford, T., & Hutchings, P. (2019). Autonomy, authenticity, authorship and intention in computer-generated art. In Ekárt, A., Liapis, A., & Castro Pena, M. L. (Eds.), Vol. 11261, pp. 35–50). Lecture Notes in Computer Science. Springer., DOI: 10.1007/978-3-030-16667-0_3

McKinney, L., Bourdeau, G. V., Burridge, A. B., Lee, M., Miller-Waters, M., & Barnes, Y. M. (2024). "I Advise, You Decide": How Academic Advisors Shape Community College Students' Enrollment and Credit Load Decisions. *Review of Higher Education, 47*(4), 519–547. DOI: 10.1353/rhe.2024.a930108

McKinsey & Company. (2022, June 1). *Are states ready to close the US digital divide?* Retrieved from https://www.mckinsey.com/industries/public-sector/our-insights/are-states-ready-to-close-the-us-digital-divide

McLaren, P. (2023). Critical pedagogy: A look at the major concepts. In *The critical pedagogy reader* (pp. 75–97). Routledge. DOI: 10.4324/9781003286080-6

Mhlanga, D. (2023). Open AI in education, the responsible and ethical use of ChatGPT: Towards lifelong learning. https://doi.org/DOI: 10.1007/978-3-031-37776-1_17

Miao, F., Holmes, W., Huang, R., & Zhang, H. (2021). *AI and education: guidance for policy-makers.* UNESCO, https://unesdoc.unesco.org/ark:/48223/pf0000376709

Miao, M., Ahmed, M., Ahsan, N., & Qamar, B. (2024). Intention to use technology for micro-credential programs: Evidence from technology acceptance and self-determination model. *International Journal of Educational Management*, *38*(4), 948–977. DOI: 10.1108/IJEM-02-2023-0066

Milner, H. R. (2013, February 28). *Policy reforms and de-professionalization of teaching*. National Education Policy Center. https://nepc.colorado.edu/publication/policy-reforms-deprofessionalization

Ministerul Educa iei. (2023). *Raport privind starea învă ământului superior din România 2022–2023* [Report on the state of higher education in Romania 2022–2023]. Raport-Starea-invatamantului-superior-2022-2023.pdf

Mishra, P., Koehler, M. J., & Kereluik, K. (2009). The song remains the same: Looking back to the future of educational technology. *TechTrends*, *53*(5), 48–53. DOI: 10.1007/s11528-009-0325-3

Mishra, P., Warr, M., & Islam, R. (2023). TPACK in the age of ChatGPT and Generative AI. *Journal of Digital Learning in Teacher Education*, *39*(4), 235–251. DOI: 10.1080/21532974.2023.2247480

Mithi, J., Madzvamuse, S., Mbanje, S., & Lomahoza, S. (2024). *Generative Artificial Intelligence and Formative Assessment: Perspectives from Higher Education in South Africa. International Conference on Education Research.*

Mohammad, S. J., Hamad, A. K., Borgi, H., Thu, P. A., Sial, M. S., & Alhadidi, A. A. (2020). How artificial intelligence changes the future of the accounting industry. *International Journal of Economics and Business Administration*, *8*(3), 478–488. DOI: 10.35808/ijeba/538

Mohammed, S. A. A. Q., Osman, Y. M. M., Ibrahim, A. M., & Shaban, M. (2025). Ethical and regulatory considerations in the use of AI and machine learning in nursing: A systematic review. *International Nursing Review*, *72*(1), e70010. DOI: 10.1111/inr.70010

Mohammed, S. J., & Khalid, M. W. (2025). Under the world of AI-generated feedback on writing: Mirroring motivation, foreign language peace of mind, trait emotional intelligence, and writing development. *Language Testing in Asia*, *15*(1), 7. DOI: 10.1186/s40468-025-00343-2

Mollick, E. (2024). *Co-Intelligence: Living and working with AI*. Portfolio Penguin.

Moodle. (2024, February 15). *Personalised Study Guide format*. https://moodle.org/plugins/format_psg

Moore, M. G. (2019). The theory of transactional distance. In Moore, M. G., & Diehl, W. C. (Eds.), *Handbook of distance education* (4th ed., pp. 22–38). Routledge.

Moorhouse, B. L., Yeo, M. A., & Wan, Y. (2023). Generative AI tools and assessment: Guidelines of the world's top-ranking universities. *Computers and Education Open*, *5*, 1–10. DOI: 10.1016/j.caeo.2023.100151

Mora-Cruz, A., Palos-Sánchez, P. R., & Murrell-Blanco, M. (2023). Plataformas de aprendizaje en línea y su impacto en la educación universitaria en el contexto del COVID-19. *Campus Virtuales*, *12*(1), 53. DOI: 10.54988/cv.2023.1.1005

Morris, R., Perry, T., & Wardle, L. (2021). Formative assessment and feedback for learning in higher education: A systematic review. *Review of Education*, *9*(3), e3292. DOI: 10.1002/rev3.3292

Moya, B., Eaton, S., Pethrick, H., Hayden, K., Brennan, R., Wiens, J., Mcdermott, B., & Lesage, J. (2023). Academic integrity and artificial intelligence in higher education contexts: A rapid scoping review protocol. *Canadian Perspectives on Academic Integrity*, *5*(2), 59–75. https://doi.org/DOI: 10.11575/cpai.75990

Naseer, F., Khan, M. N., Addas, A., Awais, Q., & Ayub, N. (2025). Game Mechanics and Artificial Intelligence Personalization: A Framework for Adaptive Learning Systems. *Education Sciences*, *15*(3), 301. DOI: 10.3390/educsci15030301

Nazaretsky, T., Mejia-Domenzain, P., Swamy, V., Frej, J., & Käser, T. (2024). AI or Human? Evaluating Student Feedback Perceptions in Higher Education. In Ferreira Mello, R., Rummel, N., Jivet, I., Pishtari, G., & Ruipérez Valiente, J. A. (Eds.), Lecture Notes in Computer Science: Vol. 15159. *Technology Enhanced Learning for Inclusive and Equitable Quality Education. EC-TEL 2024*. Springer., DOI: 10.1007/978-3-031-72315-5_20

Naznin, K., Al Mahmud, A., Nguyen, M. T., & Chua, C. (2025). ChatGPT Integration in Higher Education for Personalized Learning, Academic Writing, and Coding Tasks: A Systematic Review. *Computers*, *14*(2), 53. DOI: 10.3390/computers14020053

Nečesal, P., & Pospíšil, J. (2012). Experience with teaching mathematics for engineers with the aid of Wolfram Alpha. In *Proceedings of the World Congress on Engineering and Computer Science* (Vol. 1, pp. 271-274). https://web.archive.org/web/pdf

Newell, K. M. (1986). Constraints on the Development of Coordination. In Wade, M. G., & Whiting, H. T. A. (Eds.), *Motor Skill Acquisition in Children: Aspects of Coordination and Control* (pp. 314–360). Martinus Nijhoff. DOI: 10.1007/978-94-009-4460-2_19

Ng, D. T. K., Leung, J. K. L., Chu, S. K. W., & Qiao, M. S. (2021). Conceptualizing AI literacy: An exploratory review. *Computers and Education: Artificial Intelligence, 2*, 100041. DOI: 10.1016/j.caeai.2021.100041

Ng, L.-K., & Lo, C.-K. (2022). Online Flipped and Gamification Classroom: Risks and Opportunities for the Academic Achievement of Adult Sustainable Learning during COVID-19 Pandemic. *Sustainability (Basel), 14*(19), 12396. DOI: 10.3390/su141912396

Nguyen, A., Ngo, H. N., Hong, Y., Dang, B., & Nguyen, B. P. T. (2023). Ethical principles for artifcial intelligence in education. *Education and Information Technologies, 28*(4), 4221–4241. DOI: 10.1007/s10639-022-11316-w

Nielsen Norman Group. (n.d.). Usability and user experience research. [Online resource at https://www.nngroup.com/]

Niitsuma, T., Yoshida, M., Tamori, H., & Nakawake, Y. (2025). Prestige bias drives the viral spread of content reposted by influencers in online communities. *Scientific Reports, 15*(1), 15282. DOI: 10.1038/s41598-025-98955-4 PMID: 40312546

Nikolic, S., Sandison, C., Haque, R., Daniel, S., Grundy, S., Belkina, M., Lyden, S., Hassan, G. M., & Neal, P. (2024). ChatGPT, Copilot, Gemini, SciSpace and Wolfram versus higher education assessments: An updated multi-institutional study of the academic integrity impacts of Generative Artificial Intelligence (GenAI) on assessment, teaching and learning in engineering. *Australasian Journal of Engineering Education, 29*(2), 126–153. DOI: 10.1080/22054952.2024.2372154

Ning, Y., Zhang, C., Xu, B., Zhou, Y., & Wijaya, T. T. (2024). Teachers' AI-TPACK: Exploring the Relationship between Knowledge Elements. *Sustainability (Basel), 16*(3), 3. Advance online publication. DOI: 10.3390/su16030978

Novia, F., & Saptarina, E. (2020). Process Writing Approach (PWA): The Correlation between Students Writing Attitude and Writing Achievement. *Conference: 4th Sriwijaya University Learning and Education International Conference (SULE-IC 2020)* https://doi.org/DOI: 10.2991/assehr.k.201230.127

Nurul, A. Z., Syafiza, A. H., Noorsuhana, M. Y., & Ummi, K. I. (2024). Integrating Gen-AI in authentic scenario-based assessment for sustainable chemical engineering education. *Proceedings of the International Conference on Innovation & Entrepreneurship in Computing, Engineering & Science Education,* 209-218. https://doi.org/DOI: 10.2991/978-94-6463-589-8_21

Nussberger, A. M., Luo, L., Celis, L. E., & Crockett, M. J. (2022). Public attitudes value interpretability but prioritize accuracy in Artificial Intelligence. *Nature Communications, 13*(1), 5821. DOI: 10.1038/s41467-022-33417-3

Nwafor, C. A., & Onyenwe, I. E. (2021). An automated multiple-choice question generation using natural language processing techniques. *arXiv,* 2103.14757. https://doi.org/DOI: 10.5121/ijnlc.2021.10201

O'Flaherty, J., & Phillips, C. (2015). The use of flipped classrooms in higher education: A scoping review. *The Internet and Higher Education, 25*, 85–95. DOI: 10.1016/j.iheduc.2015.02.002

Observatorio de Inteligencia Artificial en Educación Superior. (2025). *Informe OIAES#3: El impacto de la IA en planes de estudio y resultados de aprendizaje.* Observatorio de Inteligencia Artificial en Educación Superior.

OECD. (2021). *Bridging digital divides in G20 countries: OECD report for the G20 infrastructure working group.* OECD Publishing.

OECD. (2023). *OECD digital education outlook 2023: Towards an effective digital education ecosystem.* OECD Publishing., DOI: 10.1787/c74f03de-

OECD. (2024). *AI, data governance and privacy: Synergies and areas of international co-operation. OECD Artificial Intelligence Papers, No. 22.* OECD Publishing., DOI: 10.1787/2476b1a4-

Oliva, P. F., & Gordon, W. R. (2012). *Developing the curriculum* (8th ed.). Pearson.

Oliveira, W., Hamari, J., Shi, L., Toda, A. M., Rodrigues, L., Palomino, P. T., & Isotani, S. (2023). Tailored gamification in education: A literature review and future agenda. *Education and Information Technologies, 28*(1), 373–406. DOI: 10.1007/s10639-022-11122-4

Oliver, B. (2019). Making micro-credentials work for learners, employers and providers. In *Deakin University.*

Olivos, F., Kamelski, T., & Ascui-Gac, S. (2025). *Assessing instructor-AI cooperation for grading essay-type questions in an introductory sociology course.* https://arxiv.org/pdf/2501.06461

Olson, K. (2006, November 8). The wounds of schooling. *Education Week,* •••, 28–29.

Olugbade, D., Edwards, B. I., & Ojo, O. A. (2024). Facilitating cognitive load management and improved learning outcomes and attitudes in middle school technology and vocational education through AI chatbot. *Journal of Technical Education and Training*, *16*(3), 114–131. https://doibet.org/10.30880/jtet.2024.16.03.009. DOI: 10.30880/jtet.2024.16.03.009

Omran Zailuddin, M. F. N., Nik Harun, N. A., Abdul Rahim, H. A., Kamaruzaman, A. F., Berahim, M. H., Harun, M. H., & Ibrahim, Y. (2024). Redefining creative education: A case study analysis of AI in design courses. *Journal of Research in Innovative Teaching & Learning*, *17*(2), 282–296. DOI: 10.1108/JRIT-01-2024-0019

Öncü, S. E. (2025). Transforming open and distance learning with generative AI: Custom micro-credentials from existing curriculums. *Journal of Open, Distance, and Digital Education*, *1*(2). Advance online publication. DOI: 10.25619/WERERA06

Öncü, S. E., Gevher, M., & Erdoğdu, E. (2025). Exploring the potential use of generative AI for learner support in ODL at scale. *Journal of Educational Technology and Online Learning*, *8*(1), 80–99. DOI: 10.31681/jetol.1559442

Öncü, S. E., & Süral, İ. (2024). Examining Occupation Fields of Programs According to Artificial Intelligence: Anadolu University Open Education System Case. *Osmangazi Journal of Educational Research*, *11*(1), 39–72. DOI: 10.59409/ojer.1407007

Open, A. I. (2025, February 2). Introducing deep research. *OpenAI News*. https://openai.com/index/introducing-deep-research/

Open, A. I. (2025, January). *What is the canvas feature in ChatGPT and how do I use it?* https://help.openai.com/en/articles/9930697-what-is-the-canvas-feature-in-chatgpt-and-how-do-i-use-it

Open, A. I. (2023). *ChatGPT*. Retrieved from https://openai.com

Ordoñez, M. P. M., Medina, K. E. R., Morocho, M. J. G., & Paltán, E. M. P. (2024). La Evaluación como Herramienta en el Proceso Enseñanza Aprendizaje. *Ciencia Latina Revista Científica Multidisciplinar*, *8*(4), 9510–9529. DOI: 10.37811/cl_rcm.v8i4.13107

Ordoñez, S. C., Padilla, L. E., Buenaño, L. A., & Herrera, M. V. (2024). Impacto de la inteligencia artificial en la formación del docente para la educación superior. *RECIAMUC*, *8*(1), 189–195. DOI: 10.26820/reciamuc/8.(1).ene.2024.189-195

Ornstein, A. C., & Hunkins, F. P. (2018). *Curriculum: Foundations, principles, and issues*. Pearson.

Ortega-Ochoa, J., Pardo, A., & Rodríguez, P. (2024). Empathic chatbot feedback in computer science education: A quasi-experimental study. *Computers and Education: Artificial Intelligence*, *5*, 100095. DOI: 10.1016/j.caeai.2024.100095

Orth, D., van der Kamp, J., & Button, C. (2019). Learning to be adaptive as a distributed process across the coach–athlete system: Situating the coach in the constraints-led approach. *Physical Education and Sport Pedagogy*, *24*(2), 146–161. DOI: 10.1080/17408989.2018.1557132

Ovsyannikova, D., de Mello, V. O., & Inzlicht, M. (2025). Third-party evaluators perceive AI as more compassionate than expert humans. *Communications Psychology*, *3*(1), 1–11. DOI: 10.1038/s44271-024-00182-6

Oyekan, K., Ayorinde, A., & Adenuga, O. (2023). The problem of out-of-school children in Nigeria. *RISE Insights*, *58*(1). Advance online publication. DOI: 10.35489/BSG-RISE-RI_2023/058

Özer, M., Perc, M., & Suna, H. E. (2024). Participatory management can help artificial intelligence ethics adhere to social consensus. *İstanbul Üniversitesi Sosyoloji Dergisi, 44*, 221-238. https://doi.org/DOI: 10.26650/SJ.2024.44.1.0001

Özer, M. (2024a). Is artificial intelligence hallucinating? *Türk Psikiyatri Dergisi = Turkish Journal of Psychiatry*, *35*(4), 333–335. DOI: 10.5080/u27587

Özer, M. (2024b). Dynamics of the meritocracy trap and artificial intelligence. *International Journal of Management Economics and Business*, *20*(3), 845–869.

Özer, M. (2024c). Artificial intelligence bias and the amplification of inequalities in the labor market. *Journal of Economy. Cultura e Scuola*, *69*(1), 159–168.

Özer, M. (2024d). Potential benefits and risks of artificial intelligence in education. *Bartın University Journal of Faculty of Education*, *13*(2), 232–244. DOI: 10.14686/buefad.1416087

Özer, M. (2025a). Can mathematical models be weapons of mass destruction? *Reflektif Journal of Social Sciences*, *6*(1), 259–268. DOI: 10.47613/reflektif.2025.212

Özer, M. (2025b). *Yapay zekâ ve toplum*. Nobel Publishing.

Paas, F., Renkl, A., & Sweller, J. (2004). Cognitive Load Theory: Instructional Implications of the Interaction between Information Structures and Cognitive Architecture. *Instructional Science*, *32*(1/2), 1–8. http://www.jstor.org/stable/41953634. DOI: 10.1023/B:TRUC.0000021806.17516.d0

Pacansky-Brock, M. (2020). How to humanize your online class, version 2.0. Retrieved from https://humanizeol.org/infographic/

Pacansky-Brock, M., Smedshammer, M., & Vincent-Layton, K. (2020). Humanizing online teaching to equitably engage students. *Current Issues in Education (Tempe, Ariz.), 21*(2), 1–20. https://cie.asu.edu/ojs/index.php/cieatasu/article/view/1905

Pacansky-Brock, M., Smedshammer, M., & Vincent-Layton, K. (2023). In search of belonging online: Achieving equity through transformative professional development. *Journal of Educational Research and Practice, 12*(0), 39–64. DOI: 10.5590/JERAP.2022.12.0.04

Pack, A., Barrett, A., & Escalante, J. (2024). Large language models and automated essay scoring of English language learner writing: Insights into validity and reliability. *Computers and Education: Artificial Intelligence, 6*, 100234. DOI: 10.1016/j.caeai.2024.100234

Paguyo, C. H., Sponsler, L. E., & Iturbe-LaGrave, V. (2022). Centering theories of learning to design humanizing pedagogies and inclusive assessments. *New Directions for Student Services, 2022*(178-179), 175–183. DOI: 10.1002/ss.20438

Pahi, K., Hawlader, S., Hicks, E., Zaman, A., & Phan, V. (2024). Enhancing active learning through collaboration between human teachers and generative AI. *Computers and Education Open, 6*, 100183. DOI: 10.1016/j.caeo.2024.100183

Paivio, A. (1986). *Mental representations: A dual coding approach*. Oxford University Press.

Palakurti, N. R. (2025). Comparative Study of Adaptive Learning Platforms: A Machine Learning Perspective. *International Journal of Advanced Researchin Education and Technology, 12*(1). Advance online publication. DOI: 10.15680/IJARETY.2025.1201002

Palaniappan, K., Lin, E. Y. T., & Vogel, S. (2024). Global Regulatory Frameworks for the Use of Artificial Intelligence (AI) in the Healthcare Services Sector. *Healthcare (Basel), 12*(5), 5. Advance online publication. DOI: 10.3390/healthcare12050562

Pangestu, M. A., & Karnalim, O. (2023). Advisor-Oriented Course Recommendation System Using Student Grades. [Journal of Information Technology and Computer Engineering]. *JITCE, 7*(2), 63–72. DOI: 10.25077/jitce.7.2.63-72.2023

Pantelimon, F.-V., Bologa, R., Toma, A., & Posedaru, B.-S. (2021). The Evolution of AI-Driven Educational Systems during the COVID-19 Pandemic. *Sustainability (Basel), 13*(23), 13501. DOI: 10.3390/su132313501

Park, B., Knörzer, L., Plass, J. L., & Brünken, R. (2015). Emotional design and positive emotions in multimedia learning: An eyetracking study on the use of anthropomorphisms. *Computers & Education, 86*, 30–42. DOI: 10.1016/j.compedu.2015.02.016

Parker, M.J., Anderson, C., & Stone, C., & YeaRim, O. (. (2024). A large language model approach to educational survey feedback analysis. *International Journal of Artificial Intelligence in Education*. Advance online publication. DOI: 10.1007/s40593-024-00414-0

Parsons, B., & Curry, J. H. (2024). Can ChatGPT pass graduate-level instructional design assignments? potential implications of artificial intelligence in education and a call to action. *TechTrends*, *68*(1), 67–78. DOI: 10.1007/s11528-023-00912-3

Patac, L. P., & Patac, A. V.Jr. (2025). Using ChatGPT for academic support: Managing cognitive load and enhancing learning efficiency – A phenomenological approach. *Social Sciences & Humanities Open*, *11*, 101301. DOI: 10.1016/j.ssaho.2025.101301

Paul, R., & Elder, L. (2006). *The Thinker's Guide to the Art of Socratic Questioning*. Foundation for Critical Thinking.

Păun, E. (2017). *Pedagogie. provocări i dileme privind coala i profesia didactică*. Polirom.

Peercy, M. M., Tigert, J., Fredricks, D., Kidwell, T., Feagin, K., Hall, W., & Lawyer, M. D. (2022). From humanizing principles to humanizing practices: Exploring core practices as a bridge to enacting humanizing pedagogy with multilingual students. *Teaching and Teacher Education*, *113*, 103653. Advance online publication. DOI: 10.1016/j.tate.2022.103653

Pelletier, K., McCormack, M., Reeves, J., Robert, J., Arbino, N., Al-Freih, M., Dickson-Deane, C., Guevara, C., Koster, L., Sánchez-Mendiola, M., Bessette, L. S., & Stine, J. (2022). *EDUCAUSE Horizon Report, teaching and learning edition*. EDUCAUSE.

Peng, S., Kalliamvakou, E., Cihon, P., & Demirer, M. (2023). The impact of ai on developer productivity: Evidence from github copilot. *arXiv preprint arXiv:2302.06590.*

Peng, W., Yang, Y., Zhang, Z., & Li, T. J.-J. (2025). *GLITTER: An AI-assisted Platform for Material-Grounded Asynchronous Discussion in Flipped Learning*. https://arxiv.org/pdf/2504.14695

Peng, Z., & Wan, Y. (2024). Human vs. AI: Exploring students' preferences between human and AI TA and the effect of social anxiety and problem complexity. *Education and Information Technologies*, *29*(1), 1217–1246. DOI: 10.1007/s10639-023-12374-4

Perkins, M., Roe, J., Vu, B. H., Postma, D., Hickerson, D., McGaughran, J., & Khuat, H. Q. (2024). Gen AI detection tools, adversarial techniques and implications for inclusivity in higher education. *ArXiv,* abs/2403.19148.

Perkins, M., Furze, L., Roe, J., & MacVaugh, J. (2024). The Artificial Intelligence Assessment Scale (AIAS): A Framework for Ethical Integration of Generative AI in Educational Assessment. *Journal of University Teaching & Learning Practice, 21*(06), 06. Advance online publication. DOI: 10.53761/q3azde36

Perkins, M., Roe, J., Vu, B., Postma, D., Hickerson, D., McGaughran, J., & Khuat, H. Q. (2024). Simple techniques to bypass GenAI text detectors: Implications for inclusive education. *International Journal of Educational Technology in Higher Education, 21*(53), 1–25. DOI: 10.1186/s41239-024-00487-w

Perplexity Team. (2025, February 14). Introducing Perplexity Deep Research. *Perplexity Blog*. https://www.perplexity.ai/hub/blog/introducing-perplexity-deep-research

Peschl, M. F. (2024). Human innovation and the creative agency of the world in the age of generative AI. *Possibility Studies & Society*, *2*(1), 49–76. DOI: 10.1177/27538699241238049

Peterson, P. L., & Cox, C. B. (2025). Adapting to the future: How microcredentials fuel self-directed learning in the evolving workplace. *Industrial and Organizational Psychology: Perspectives on Science and Practice*, *18*(1), 139–142. DOI: 10.1017/iop.2024.72

Petricini, T., Wu, C., & Zipf, S. (2024). Perceptions About Artificial Intelligence and ChatGPT Use by Faculty and Students. *Transformative Dialogues: Teaching and Learning Journal, 17*(2) 63-87. https://doi.org/DOI: 10.26209/td2024vol17iss21825

Phye, G. D., & Bender, T. (1989). Feedback complexity and practice: Response pattern analysis in retention and transfer. *Contemporary Educational Psychology, 14*(1), 97–106. DOI: 10.1016/0361-476X(89)90028-3

Piedra-Castro, W. I., Burbano-Buñay, E. S., Tamayo-Verdezoto, J. J., & Moreira-Alcívar, E. F. (2024). Inteligencia artificial y su incidencia en la estrategia metodológica de aprendizaje basado en investigación. *Journal of Economic and Social Science Research*, *4*(2), 178–196. DOI: 10.55813/gaea/jessr/v4/n2/106

Pink, D. H. (2011). *Drive: The surprising truth about what motivates us*. Penguin.

Plessis, E. (2025). Embracing project-based assessments in the age of AI in open distance e-learning. *International Journal of Information and Education Technology (IJIET), 15*(2), 372–381. DOI: 10.18178/ijiet.2025.15.2.2249

Polakova, P., & Ivenz, P. (2024). The impact of ChatGPT feedback on the development of EFL students' writing skills. *Cogent Education, 11*(1), 2410101. Advance online publication. DOI: 10.1080/2331186X.2024.2410101

Polonetsky, J., & Jerome, J. (2014). *Student data: Trust, transparency, and the role of consent*. SSRN Electronic Journal. https://doi.org/DOI: 10.2139/ssrn.2628877

Popenici, S. A. D., & Kerr, S. (2017). Exploring the impact of artificial intelligence on teaching and learning in higher education. *Research and Practice in Technology Enhanced Learning*, *12*(1), 1–13. DOI: 10.1186/s41039-017-0062-8 PMID: 30595727

Porras, V. D. C. A. (2024). Taxonomía de aprendizaje conectivo IA-Net: Propuesta para la enseñanza basada en inteligencia artificial y red. *Varela*, *24*(67), 73–82. DOI: 10.5281/zenodo.10429359

Pratschke, B. M. (2024). *Generative AI and Education: Digital Pedagogies, Teaching Innovation and Learning Design*. Springer Nature Switzerland., DOI: 10.1007/978-3-031-67991-9

Prihar, E., Lee, M., Hopman, M., Kalai, A. T., Vempala, S., Wang, A., & Heffernan, N. (2023). Comparing different approaches to generating mathematics explanations using large language models. In N. Wang, G. Rebolledo- Mendez, V. Dimitrova, N. Matsuda, & O. C. Santos (Eds.), *Artificial intelligence in education. Posters and late breaking results, workshops and tutorials, industry and innovation tracks, practitioners, doctoral consortium and blue sky* (pp. 290–295). Springer Nature Switzerland DOI: 10.1007/978-3-031-36336-8_45

Puche, D. J. (2024). Inteligencia Artificial como herramienta educativa: Ventajas y desventajas desde la perspectiva docente. *Areté, Revista Digital del Doctorado en Educación, 10*(especial), 85-100.

Qadir, J. (2022). Engineering education in the era of ChatGPT: Promise and pitfalls of generative AI for education. *TechRxiv*. Preprint. https://doi.org/DOI: 10.36227/techrxiv.21789434.v1

Rahimi, M., Fathi, J., & Zou, D. (2024). Exploring the impact of automated written corrective feedback on the academic writing skills of EFL learners: An activity theory perspective. *Education and Information Technologies*. Advance online publication. DOI: 10.1007/s10639-024-12896-5

Rainer, G., Nies, T., & Schmid, W. (2016). *Artificial Intelligence: Concepts and Applications*. Springer.

Ralston, S. J. (2021). Higher Education's Microcredentialing Craze: A Postdigital-Deweyan Critique. *Postdigital Science and Education*, *3*(1), 83–101. DOI: 10.1007/s42438-020-00121-8 PMID: 40476912

Ramzan, K., Batool, A., Arslan, M. F., & Fatima, H. (2025). Evaluating human vs AI feedback on students' performance; A comparative analysis of students at intermediate level. *Journal of Applied Linguistics and TESOL, 8*(1).

Ranalli, J., Link, S., & Chukharev-Hudilainen, E. (2016). Automated writing evaluation for formative assessment of second language writing: Investigating the accuracy and usefulness of feedback as part of argument-based validation. *Educational Psychology, 37*(1), 8–25. DOI: 10.1080/01443410.2015.1136407

Rane, N., Choudhary, S., & Rane, J. (2023). Explainable artificial intelligence (XAI) approaches for transparency and accountability in financial decision-making. *SSRN*. http://dx.doi.org/DOI: 10.2139/ssrn.4640316

Rao, K. (2005). Infusing critical thinking into content of AI course. In *Proceedings of the 10th Annual SIGCSE Conference on Innovation and Technology in Computer Science Education* (pp. 173–177). ACM. https://doi.org/DOI: 10.1145/1067445.1067494

Razak, N. A., Zulkifli, C. Z., Abdullah, Y., Khairuddin, A. Z., Misron, A., Somasundram, P., & Shakirdjanovna, A. G. (2025). Bridging technology and humanity: Humanizing online pedagogy in digital environments. *International Journal of Evaluation and Research in Education, 14*(3), 2207–2223. DOI: 10.11591/ijere.v14i3.31937

Redecker, C. (2017). *European framework for the digital competence of educators: DigCompEdu* (Y. Punie, Ed.; EUR 28775 EN; JRC107466). Publications Office of the European Union. https://doi.org/DOI: 10.2760/159770

Reeves, T. C., & Hedberg, J. G. (2003). *Interactive learning systems evaluation*. Educational Technology Publications.

Rehman, A., Mehfooz, Q., Saleem, Q., Ikram, N., Sadiq, M. S., Javaid, N., & Tahir, F. N. (2024). Artificial intelligence-assisted learning in medical education: A randomized study on its effectiveness. *African Journal of Biological Sciences, 6*(2), 4209–4215. DOI: 10.48047/AFJBS.6.16.2024.4209-4215

Renden, P. G., & Dikken, J. (2023). Introducing the constraints-led approach in nurse education: An innovative perspective on skill acquisition. *Nurse Education Today, 121*, 105672. DOI: 10.1016/j.nedt.2022.105672

Renshaw, I., Chow, J. Y., Davids, K., & Hammond, J. (2010). A constraints-led perspective to understanding skill acquisition and game play: A basis for integration of motor learning theory and physical education praxis? *Physical Education and Sport Pedagogy, 15*(2), 117–137. DOI: 10.1080/17408980902791586

Renshaw, I., & Chow, J.-Y. (2019). A constraint-led approach to sport and physical education pedagogy. *Physical Education and Sport Pedagogy*, *24*(2), 103–116. DOI: 10.1080/17408989.2018.1552676

Renshaw, I., Davids, K., Newcombe, D., & Roberts, W. (2019). *The Constraints-Led Approach: Principles for Sports Coaching and Practice Design*. Routledge., DOI: 10.4324/9781315102351

Rentier, E. S. (2024). To use or not to use: Exploring the ethical implications of using generative AI in academic writing. *AI and Ethics*. Advance online publication. DOI: 10.1007/s43681-024-00649-6

Research, I. F. F. (2023). *School and college panel* https://assets.publishing.service.gov.uk/media/652ea669d86b1b000d3a513e/School_and_college_panel_April_2023.pdf UK Department for Education.

Resnik, D. B., Hosseini, M., Kim, J. J. H., Epiphaniou, G., & Maple, C. (2025). GenAI synthetic data create ethical challenges for scientists. Here's how to address them. *Proceedings of the National Academy of Sciences of the United States of America*, *122*(9), e2409182122. DOI: 10.1073/pnas.2409182122

Rettberg, J. (2022, December 6). *ChatGPT is multilingual but monocultural, and it's learning your values.* https://jilltxt.net/right-now-chatgpt-is-multilingual-but-monocultural-but-its-learning-your-values/

Rizwan, A. (2021). Effect of digital flashcards on low-frequency vocabulary retention by graduate students. *International Journal of Infrastructure Research and Management, 9*(1), 7–18. ISSN 2811-3705.https://klust.edu.my//Ahmed-Rizwan

Rodriguez- Torrealba, R., Garcia- Lopez, E., & Garcia- Cabot, A. (2022). End- to-end generation of multiple- choice questions using text- to- text transfer transformer models. *Expert Systems with Applications*, *208*(118), 258. https://www.sciencedirect.com/science/article/pii/S0957417422014014?via%3Dihub

Rojas Lozano, J. R., Ramos, Y., Tecnologia, E., & Cruz, C. E. C. (2024). *Enhancing English Language Teaching Through AI: The Case of Magic School AI.* (available at https://www.researchgate.net/profile/Jean-Paul-Rojas-2/publication/388757322_Enhancing_English_Language_Teaching_Through_AI_The_Case_of_Magic_School_AI/links/67a4eb53461fb56424cc7bbc/Enhancing-English-Language-Teaching-Through-AI-The-Case-of-Magic-School-AI.pdf)

Romadona, M. R., & Setiawan, S. (2021). Researchers' View on R&D Organizational Change Using the Grief Cycle. *Journal of STI Policy and Management*, *6*(2), 157–171. DOI: 10.14203/STIPM.2021.313

Romero, J. A. (2024). Algoritmos de IA que se utilizan para los profesores virtuales y tutores inteligentes, pasado, presente y futuro. In *Enseñanza y aprendizaje en la era digital desde la investigación y la innovación* (pp. 14–23). Octaedro.

Romero, R. (2024). *Inteligencia artificial y tutorías inteligentes: nuevas fronteras en la educación digital.* Ediciones Académicas Digitales.

Roose, K. (2025, February 1). How Helpful Is Operator, OpenAI's New A.I. Agent? *The New York Times.* https://www.nytimes.com/2025/02/01/technology/openai-operator-agent.html

Rudin, C., & Radin, J. (2019). Why are we using black box models in aı when we don't need to? A lesson from an explainable aı competition. *Harvard Data Science Review, 1*(2). Advance online publication. DOI: 10.1162/99608f92.5a8a3a3d

Ruggiero, V. R. (2012). *The art of thinking: A guide to critical and creative thought* (10th ed.). Pearson Learning Solutions.

Rust, J. (2006). *Discussion piece: The psychometric principles of assessment.* Cambridge Assessment.

Ryan, R. M., & Deci, E. L. (2023). Self-Determination Theory. *Encyclopedia of Quality of Life and Well-Being Research*, 6229–6235. DOI: 10.1007/978-3-031-17299-1_2630

Ryan, M., & Stahl, B. C. (2020). Artificial intelligence ethics guidelines for developers and users: Clarifying their content and normative implications. *Journal of Information. Communication and Ethics in Society, 19*(1), 61–86. DOI: 10.1108/JICES-12-2019-0138

Sætra, H. S. (2022). Scaffolding human champions: AI as a more competent other. *Human Arenas*, 1-23.https://hdl.handle.net/11250/3015827

Şahin Kölemen, C., & Yıldızhan Bora, B. (2025). Oyunlaştırılmış eğitim platformlarının bilişsel yükü azaltmadaki rolü [The role of gamified educational platforms in reducing cognitive load]. *15th International Congress on Social, Humanities, Administrative, and Educational Sciences in a Changing World Full Text Proceedings Book.* Akademik Platform Yayınları. https://doi.org/DOI: 10.30546/19023.978-9952-8545-8-9.2025.601

Saiyad, S., & Mahajan, R. (2023). Revisiting Academic Advising: Potential Role and Implications in Undergraduate Medical Training in India. *International Journal of Applied & Basic Medical Research, 13*(4), 193–197. DOI: 10.4103/ijabmr.ijabmr_476_23 PMID: 38229727

Saltman, K. (2020). *AI in education and the future of standardized teaching*. Springer.

Salvaggio, E. (2024, August 29). Challenging The Myths of Generative AI | Tech-Policy.Press. *Tech Policy Press*. https://www.techpolicy.press/challenging-the-myths-of-generative-ai

Sampurno, M. T. (2024). Wolfram Alpha (AI): Between technological transformation and ethical ideas in education. *Proceedings of the International Conference on Religion. Science and Education*, *3*, 377–384.

Samuelson, P. (2023). Generative AI meets copyright. *Science*, *381*(6654), 158–161. DOI: 10.1126/science.adi0656 PMID: 37440639

Sánchez, M. (2025). ¿Autonomía en riesgo? Ética y la dependencia de la inteligencia artificial generativa en la formación médica. *Investigación en Educación Médica*, *14*(53), 5–7. DOI: 10.22201/fm.20075057e.2025.53.24670

Sawyer, R. K., & Henriksen, D. (2024). *Explaining creativity: The science of human innovation*. Oxford university press.

Sayma, S. R. (2023). *Creating effective multimedia learning material with AI for K12*. https://edtechbooks.s3.us-west-2.amazonaws.com/pdfs/713/13501.pdf

Scarfe, P., Watcham, K., Clarke, A., & Roesch, E. (2024). A real-world test of artificial intelligence infiltration of a university examinations system: A "Turing Test" case study. *PLoS One*, *19*(6), e0305354. DOI: 10.1371/journal.pone.0305354

Schmidt, D. A., Baran, E., Thompson, A. D., Mishra, P., Koehler, M. J., & Shin, T. S. (2009). Technological pedagogical content knowledge (TPACK): The development and validation of an assessment instrument for preservice teachers. *Journal of Research on Technology in Education*, *42*(2), 123–149. DOI: 10.1080/15391523.2009.10782544

Schüttpelz-Brauns, K., Hecht, M., Hardt, K., Karay, Y., Zupanic, M., & Kämmer, J. E. (2020). Institutional strategies related to test-taking behavior in low stakes assessment. *Advances in Health Sciences Education : Theory and Practice*, *25*(2), 321–335. DOI: 10.1007/s10459-019-09928-y

Seale, J. (2006). *E-learning and disability in higher education: Accessibility research and practice*. Routledge. DOI: 10.4324/9780203969595

Seifert, L., Papet, V., Strafford, B. W., Coughlan, E. K., & Davids, K. (2018). Skill transfer, expertise and talent development: An ecological dynamics perspective. *Movement & Sport Sciences - Science & Motricité, 102*, Article 102. DOI: 10.1051/sm/2019010

Selwyn, N. (2011). *Education and Technology: Key Issues And Debates* (3rd ed.). Bloomsbury Publishing Plc.

Selwyn, N. (2022). The future of AI and education: Some cautionary notes. *European Journal of Education*, *57*(4), 620–631. DOI: 10.1111/ejed.12532

Selwyn, N. (2024a). Constructive Criticism? Working with (Rather than Against) the AIED Back-Lash. *International Journal of Artificial Intelligence in Education*, *34*(1), 84–91. DOI: 10.1007/s40593-023-00344-3

Selwyn, N. (2024b). On the Limits of Artificial Intelligence (AI) in Education. *Nordisk Tidsskrift for Pedagogikk Og Kritikk*, *10*(1), 1. Advance online publication. DOI: 10.23865/ntpk.v10.6062

Sengar, S. S., Hasan, A. B., Kumar, S., & Carroll, F. (2024). Generative artificial intelligence: A systematic review and applications. *Multimedia Tools and Applications*, *84*(21), 1–40. DOI: 10.1007/s11042-024-20016-1

Serrano, J. L., & Moreno, J. (2024). Inteligencia artificial y personalización del aprendizaje: ¿innovación educativa o promesas recicladas? *Edutec. Revista Electrónica de Tecnología Educativa*, (89), 1–17. DOI: 10.21556/edutec.2024.89.3577

Shaffer, D. W., & Kaput, J. J. (1998). The role of computational media in reshaping how we think about assessment in education. *Journal of the Learning Sciences*, *7*(2), 183–212.

Shahzad, M. F., Xu, S., & Zahid, H. (2024). Exploring the impact of generative AI-based technologies on learning performance through self-efficacy, fairness & ethics, creativity, and trust in higher education. *Education and Information Technologies*, •••, 1–26.

Shangguan, C., Gong, S., Guo, Y., Wang, X., & Lu, J. (2020). The effects of emotional design on middle school students' multimedia learning: The role of learners' prior knowledge. *Educational Psychology*, *40*(9), 1076–1093. DOI: 10.1080/01443410.2020.1714548

Sharma, R. C., & Bozkurt, A. (2024). *Transforming education with generative AI: Prompt engineering and synthetic content creation*. IGI Global., DOI: 10.4018/979-8-3693-1351-0

Shen, J., Wang, Y., & Zhang, L. (2020). Understanding the relationship between teacher leadership and teacher well-being: The mediating roles of trust in leaders and teacher efficacy. *Journal of Educational Administration*, *58*(6), 679–696. DOI: 10.1108/JEA-09-2022-0152

Shi, H., & Aryadoust, V. (2024). A systematic review of AI-based automated written feedback research. *ReCALL*, *36*(2), 187–209. Advance online publication. DOI: 10.1017/S0958344023000265

Shimmei, M., Bier, N., & Matsuda, N. (2023). Machine- generated questions attract instructors when acquainted with learning objectives. In N. Wang, G. Rebolledo-Mendez, N. Matsuda, O. C. Santos, & V. Dimitrova (Eds.), *Artificial intelligence in education* (pp. 3–15). Springer Nature Switzerland. https://doi.org/10.1007/978-3-031-36272-9_1

Shoaib, M. R., Wang, Z., Ahvanooey, M. T., & Zhao, J. (2023, November 28-30). *Deepfakes, misinformation, and disinformation in the era of frontier AI, generative AI, and large AI models* [Conference presentation]. International Conference on Computer and Applications (ICCA) Cairo, Egypt. DOI: 10.1109/ICCA59364.2023.10401723

Shokoohifar, M. (2024). *Artificial Intelligence-Assisted Translation: A Study of Cognitive Load and Time Through EEG*(Doctoral dissertation, Allameh Tabataba'i University).

Shumailov, I., Shumaylov, Z., Zhao, Y., Papernot, N., Anderson, R., & Gal, Y. (2024). AI models collapse when trained on recursively generated data. *Nature*, *631*(8022), 755–759. DOI: 10.1038/s41586-024-07566-y

Siemens, G. (2013). Learning Analytics. *The American Behavioral Scientist*, *57*(10), 1380–1400. DOI: 10.1177/0002764213498851

Simpson, O. (2008). Motivating learners in open and distance learning: Do we need a new theory of learner support? *Open Learning*, *23*(3), 159–170. DOI: 10.1080/02680510802419979

Singha, S., & Singha, R. (2024). Revolutionizing content creation and curriculum development through generative AI. In *Transforming Education With Generative AI: Prompt Engineering and Synthetic Content Creation* (pp. 261-280). IGI Global Scientific Publishing. DOI: 10.4018/979-8-3693-1351-0.ch013

Singh, S. V. (2023, January). *The prospects for advancing adaptive learning technology through AI methods. In 2023 Future of Educational Innovation-Workshop Series Data in Action.*, DOI: 10.1109/IEEECONF56852.2023.10105111

Skulmowski, A., & Xu, K. M. (2022). Understanding cognitive load in digital and online learning: A new perspective on extraneous cognitive load. *Educational Psychology Review*, *34*(1), 171–196. DOI: 10.1007/s10648-021-09624-7

Sluijs, J. P., Gilissen, H. K., & van Look, K. C. J. (2023). Training law students like athletes: Experimenting with the constraints-led approach in law clinics. *The Law Teacher*, *57*(4), 458–477. DOI: 10.1080/03069400.2023.2275495

Smith, C. S. (2025, March 8). *China's Autonomous Agent, Manus, Changes Everything*. https://www.forbes.com/sites/craigsmith/2025/03/08/chinas-autonomous-agent-manus-changes-everything/

Smith, R. F. (2025, January 20). Closing the digital divide as we enter the Intelligent Age. *World Economic Forum*. https://www.weforum.org/stories/2025/01/digital-divide-intelligent-age-how-everyone-can-benefit-ai/

Smuha, N. A. (2021). Beyond the individual: Governing AI's societal harm. *Internet Policy Review*, *10*(3). Advance online publication. DOI: 10.14763/2021.3.1574

Smyth, G., & Kum, H. (2010). 'When they don't use it they will lose it': professionals, deprofessionalization and reprofessionalization: the case of refugee teachers in Scotland. *Journal of Refugee Studies*, *23*(4), 503–522. DOI: 10.1093/jrs/feq041

Solis, M., Moreira, T., Gonzalez, R., Fernandez, T., & Hernandez, M. (2018). Perspectives to predict dropout in university students with machine learning. In *2018 IEEE International Work Conference on Bioinspired Intelligence (IWOBI)* (pp. 1–6). IEEE. https://doi.org/DOI: 10.1109/IWOBI.2018.8464191

Song, H., & Cai, L. (2024). Interactive learning environment as a source of critical thinking skills for college students. *BMC Medical Education*, *24*(1), 1–9. DOI: 10.1186/s12909-024-05247-y PMID: 38475788

Sorden, S. D. (2013). The cognitive theory of multimedia learning. In B. J. Irby, G. Brown, R. Lara-Alecio, & S. Jackson (Eds.), *The handbook of educational theories* (pp. 155–167). IAP Information Age Publishing.

Souchet, A. D., Philippe, S., Lourdeaux, D., & Leroy, L. (2022). Measuring visual fatigue and cognitive load via eye tracking while learning with virtual reality head-mounted displays: A review. *International Journal of Human-Computer Interaction*, *38*(9), 801–824. DOI: 10.1080/10447318.2021.1976509

Sousa, A. E., & Cardoso, P. (2025). Use of generative AI by higher education students. *Electronics (Basel)*, *14*(7), 1258. DOI: 10.3390/electronics14071258

Spector, J. M., & Ma, S. (2019). Inquiry and critical thinking skills for the next generation: From artificial intelligence back to human intelligence. *Smart Learning Environments*, *6*(1), 8. DOI: 10.1186/s40561-019-0088-z

Spector, J. M., & Yuen, A. H. K. (2016). *Educational Technology Program and Project Evaluation*. Routledge., DOI: 10.4324/9781315724140

Stan, E. (2021). *Managementul clasei i nativii digitali: Fundamentări din perspectiva neuro tiin elor* [Classroom management and digital natives: Foundations from a neuroscientific perspective]. Institutul European.

Stanislaw, P. (2024). Solving the global STEM educational crisis using Cognitive Load Optimization and Artificial Intelligence–A preliminary comparative analysis. *Eurasia Journal of Mathematics, Science and Technology Education*, *20*(5), em2436. Advance online publication. DOI: 10.29333/ejmste/14448

Steinert, S., Avila, K. E., Ruzika, S., Kuhn, J., & Küchemann, S. (2024). Harnessing large language models to develop research-based learning assistants for formative feedback. *Smart Learning Environments*, *11*(1), 62. DOI: 10.1186/s40561-024-00354-1

Steiss, J., Tate, T., Graham, S., Cruz, J., Hebert, M., Wang, J., Moon, Y., Tseng, W., Warschauer, M., & Olson, C. B. (2024). Comparing the quality of human and ChatGPT feedback of students' writing. *Learning and Instruction*, *91*, 101894. DOI: 10.1016/j.learninstruc.2024.101894

Stevenson, M., & Phakiti, A. (2019). Automated feedback and second language writing. In *The Cambridge Handbook of Language Learning*. https://doi.org/DOI: 10.1017/9781108635547.009

Stewart, O. G. (2023). Understanding what works in humanizing higher education online courses: Connecting through videos, feedback, multimodal assignments, and social media. *Issues and Trends in Learning Technologies.*, *11*(2), 2–26. DOI: 10.2458/itlt.5566

Støle, H. (2018). Why digital natives need books: The myth of the digital native. *First Monday*. Advance online publication. DOI: 10.5210/fm.v23i10.9422

Strzelecki, A. (2024). Is ChatGPT-like technology going to replace commercial search engines? *Library Hi Tech News*, *41*(6), 18–21. DOI: 10.1108/LHTN-02-2024-0026

Suna, H. E., & Özer, M. (2025). The human complimentary usage of AI and ML for fair and unbiased educational assessments. *Chinese/English Journal of Educational Measurement and Evaluation*, *6*(1), 9. DOI: 10.59863/YPKL4338

Sun, Y., Sheng, D., Zhou, Z., & Wu, Y. (2024). AI hallucination: Towards a comprehensive classification of distorted information in artificial intelligence-generated content. *Humanities & Social Sciences Communications*, *11*(1), 1278. DOI: 10.1057/s41599-024-03811-x

Suresh Babu, S., & Dhakshina Moorthy, A. (2024). Application of artificial intelligence in adaptation of gamification in education: A literature review. *Computer Applications in Engineering Education*, *32*(1), e22683. DOI: 10.1002/cae.22683

Susilana, R., Dewi, L., Rullyana, G., Hadiapurwa, A., & Khaerunnisa, N. (2022). Can microlearning strategy assist students' online learning? *Jurnal Cakrawala Pendidikan*, *41*(2), 437–451. DOI: 10.21831/cp.v41i2.43387

Sutton, K. L., & Sankar, C. S. (2011). Student Satisfaction with Information Provided by Academic Advisors. *Journal of STEM Education: Innovations and Research*, *12*(7), 71. https://www.jstem.org/jstem/index.php/JSTEM/article/view/1734

Sweller, J. (2010). Cognitive Load Theory: Recent Theoretical Advances. In J. L. Plass, R. Moreno, & R. Brünken (Eds.), *Cognitive Load Theory* (pp. 29–47). chapter, Cambridge: Cambridge University Press.

Sweller, J. (2023). The development of cognitive load theory: Replication crises and incorporation of other theories can lead to theory expansion. *Educational Psychology Review*, *35*(4), 95. Advance online publication. DOI: 10.1007/s10648-023-09817-2

Sweller, J., Kirschner, P., & Clark, R. E. (2007). Why minimally guided teaching techniques do not work: A reply to commentaries. *Educational Psychologist*, *42*(2), 115–121. DOI: 10.1080/00461520701263426

Sweller, J., van Merriënboer, J. J. G., & Paas, F. (2019). Cognitive architecture and instructional design: 20 years later. *Educational Psychology Review*, *31*(2), 261–292. DOI: 10.1007/s10648-019-09465-5

Sweller, J., Van Merrienboer, J. J. G., & Paas, F. G. W. C. (1998). Cognitive architecture and instructional design. *Educational Psychology Review*, *10*(3), 251–29. DOI: 10.1023/A:1022193728205

Synthesia. (2025). *Turn text the video in minutes*. https://www.synthesia.io/

Taba, H. (1962). *Curriculum development: Theory and practice*. Harcourt, Brace & World.

Taha, K. (2012). Automatic academic advisor. *CollaborateCom 2012 - Proceedings of the 8th International Conference on Collaborative Computing: Networking, Applications and Worksharing*, 262–268. https://doi.org/DOI: 10.4108/ICST

Tait, A. (2000). Planning student support for open and distance learning. *Open Learning*, *15*(3), 287–299. DOI: 10.1080/713688410

Tam, A. C. F. (2024). *Interacting with ChatGPT for Internal Feedback and Factors Affecting Feedback Quality*. The Hong Kong Polytechnic University., DOI: 10.1080/02602938.2024.2374485

Tang, X. (2024). An empirical study on the effects of AI-generated feedback on English writing. .DOI: 10.26789/ijest.v3i9.2010

Tanweer, M., & Ismail, A. (2024). Generative AI in curriculum development: A framework for adaptive, customized, and personalized learning. In *Impacts of Generative AI on Creativity in Higher Education* (pp. 193–226). IGI Global. DOI: 10.4018/979-8-3693-2418-9.ch008

Tao, Y., Viberg, O., Baker, R. S., & Kizilcec, R. F. (2024). Cultural bias and cultural alignment of large language models. *PNAS Nexus*, *3*(9), pgae346. Advance online publication. DOI: 10.1093/pnasnexus/pgae346

Tapalova, O., & Zhiyenbayeva, N. (2022). Artificial Intelligence in Education: AIEd for Personalised Learning Pathways. *Electronic Journal of e-Learning*, *20*(5), 639–653. DOI: 10.34190/ejel.20.5.2597

Tarafdar, M., Stich, J.-F., Maier, C., & Laumer, S. (2024). Techno-eustress creators: Conceptualization and empirical validation. *Information Systems Journal*, *34*(6), 2097–2131. DOI: 10.1111/isj.12515

Taraporewalla, K., Barach, P., Lipman, J., & Van Zundert, A. (2024). The Effectiveness of the Constraint-Led Approach in Developing Medical Procedural Skills. *Universal Library of Medical and Health Sciences*, *02*(02), 11–18. DOI: 10.70315/uloap.ulmhs.2024.0202003

Taub, M., & Azevedo, R. (2023). Teachers as self-regulated learners: The role of multimodal data analytics for instructional decision making. *New Directions for Teaching and Learning*, *2023*(174), 25–32. DOI: 10.1002/tl.20545

Teacher Tapp. (2023, November 28). *How to improve behaviour and wellbeing, and how you're using AI in schools* https://teachertapp.com/uk/articles/how-to-improve-behaviour-wellbeing-and-how-youre-using-ai-in-schools/

Tertiary Education Quality and Standards Agency (TEQSA). (2024). *GenAI strategies for Australian higher education: Emerging practice*. TEQSA, Australian Government. https://www.teqsa.gov.au/guides-resources/resources/corporate-publications/gen-ai-strategies-australian-higher-education-emerging-practice

Thaler v. Perlmutter. (2023). No. 1:22-cv-01564 (D. D. C. Aug. 18, 2023). U.S. District Court for the District of Columbia.

The European Commission. (2022). *European project MICROBOL Micro-credentials linked to the Bologna Key Commitments.* https://microbol.microcredentials.eu/microbol-framework-published/

The Open Innovation Team & Department for Education. (2024). *Generative AI in education, educator and expert views.* https://assets.publishing.service.gov.uk/media/65b8cd41b5cb6e000d8bb74e/dfe_genai_in_education_-_educator_and_expert_views_report.pdf

The Open Innovation Team & Department for Education. (2024). *Generative AI in education: Educator and expert views.* UK Department for Education. Retrieved from https://assets.publishing.service.gov.uk/media/65b8cd41b5cb6e000d8bb74e/DfE_GenAI_in_education_-_Educator_and_expert_views_report.pdf

Thi, N. K., & Nikolov, M. (2021). Feedback Treatments, Writing Tasks, and Accuracy Measures: A Critical Review of Research on Written Corrective Feedback. Tesl-Ej, 25(3), n3. Retrieved from https://files.eric.ed.gov/fulltext/EJ1332267.pdf

Thompson, A. D. (2007). Editor's Remarks: TPCK: A New Direction for Technology in Teacher Education Programs. *Journal of Computing in Teacher Education, 23*(3), 78–104. DOI: 10.1080/10402454.2007.10784564

Thottoli, M. M., Alruqaishi, B. H., & Soosaimanickam, A. (2024). Robo academic advisor: Can chatbots and artificial intelligence replace human interaction? *Contemporary Educational Technology, 16*(1), ep485. DOI: 10.30935/cedtech/13948

Thurzo, A., Strunga, M., Urban, R., Surovková, J., & Afrashtehfar, K. I. (2023). Impact of artificial intelligence on dental education: A review and guide for curriculum update. *Education Sciences, 13*(2), 150. DOI: 10.3390/educsci13020150

Tinholt, D., van der Linden, N., Enzerink, S., Geilleit, A., Cattaneo, G., Aguyyi, S., Pallaro, F., Noci, G., Benedetti, M., Tangi, L., & Alfano Saverio, A. (2019). *eGovernment benchmark 2019: Empowering Europeans through trusted digital public services.* Publications Office of the European Union. https://op.europa.eu/en/publication-detail/-/publication/c896937b-f554-11e9-8c1f-01aa75ed71a1/language-en

Tomasev, N., Maynard, J. L., & Gabriel, I. (2025). Manifestations of xenophobia in AI systems. *AI & Society, 40*(2), 741–763. DOI: 10.1007/s00146-024-01893-4

Topu, F. B. (2023). Effects of Cognitive Load Level on Students' Attitude towards the Gamified Course. *Journal of Learning and Teaching in Digital Age, 8*(1), 93–112. DOI: 10.53850/joltida.1147246

Toupin, S. (2024). Shaping feminist artificial intelligence. *New Media & Society*, *26*(1), 580–595. DOI: 10.1177/14614448221150776

Trabelsi, Z., Alnajjar, F., Parambil, M. M. A., Gochoo, M., & Ali, L. (2023). Real-time attention monitoring system for classroom: A deep learning approach for student's behavior recognition. *Big Data and Cognitive Computing*, *7*(1), 1–17. DOI: 10.3390/bdcc7010048

Tresman, S. (2002). Towards a strategy for improved student retention in programmes of open, distance education: A case study from the Open University UK. *International Review of Research in Open and Distance Learning*, *3*(1), 1–11. https://eric.ed.gov/?id=EJ646665. DOI: 10.19173/irrodl.v3i1.75

Tsirulnikov, D., Suart, C., Abdullah, R., Vulcu, F., & Mullarkey, C. E. (2023). Game on: Immersive virtual laboratory simulation improves student learning outcomes & motivation. *FEBS Open Bio*, *13*(3), 396–407. DOI: 10.1002/2211-5463.13567 PMID: 36723273

Turing, A. M. (1950). Computing Machinery and Intelligence. *Mind*, *LIX*(236), 433–460. DOI: 10.1093/mind/LIX.236.433

Tyler, R. W. (1949). *Basic principles of curriculum and instruction*. University of Chicago Press.

U.S. Copyright Office. (2023). *Copyright Registration Guidance: Works Containing Material Generated by Artificial Intelligence*. https://www.copyright.gov/ai/

Uchiyama, S., Umemura, K., & Morita, Y. (2023). *Large Language Model-based System to Provide Immediate Feedback to Students in Flipped Classroom Preparation Learning*. https://arxiv.org/pdf/2307.11388

UN & ILO. (2024). *Mind the AI divide: Shaping a global perspective on the future of work*. United Nations.

UNESCO. (1998). *World Declaration on Higher Education for the Twenty-First Century: Vision and Action*.

UNESCO. (2019). *Artificial intelligence in education: challenges and opportunities for sustainable development.* UNESCO, https://unesdoc.unesco.org/ark:/48223/pf0000366994

UNESCO. (2023). Global education monitoring report on technology in education. *United Nations Educational, Scientific and Cultural Organization*. https://unesdoc.unesco.org

UNESCO. (2023). *Guidance for generative AI in education and research | UNESCO*. https://www.unesco.org/en/articles/guidance-generative-ai-education-and-research

UNESCO. (2023). Guidance for generative AI in education and research. [United Nations Educational, Scientific and Cultural Organization.]. *Education*, •••, 2030.

UNESCO. (2024a). *AI competency framework for teachers* https://unesdoc.unesco.org/ark:/48223/pf0000391104

UNESCO. (2024b). *Guidance for generative AI in education and research* https://unesdoc.unesco.org/ark:/48223/pf0000386693

Ungless, E. L., Vitsakis, N., & Talat, Z., Garforth1, J., Ross, B., Onken, A., Kasirzadeh, A., & Birch, A. (2025). The only way is ethics: A guide to ethical research with large language models. *Proceedings of the 31st International Conference on Computational Linguistics*, 8992–9005.

United Nations Educational, Scientific and Cultural Organization. (2024). *Guía para el uso de IA generativa en educación e investigación*. UNESCO. [UNESCO], DOI: 10.54675/EWZM9535

United Nations University. (2024). *Recommendations on the use of synthetic data to train AI models.* Policy Guideline. Retrieved from https://collections.unu.edu/eserv/UNU:9480/Use-of-Synthetic-Data-to-Train-AI-Models.pdf

Valeri, J. (2024). The need for a national AI framework in Australian education. In L. Callanan & M. Rangelov (Eds.), AI in Action (TLN Journal, 31(2)). Teacher Learning Network.

Vallor, S. (2024). *The AI Mirror: How to reclaim our humanity in an age of machine thinking*. Oxford University Press. DOI: 10.1093/oso/9780197759066.001.0001

Valtorta, M. G., Smith, B. T., & Loveland, D. W. (1984). The Graduate Course Advisor: A Multi-Phase Rule-Based Expert System. *IEEE Workshop on Principles of Knowledge-Based Systems*. https://cse.sc.edu/~mgv/papers/ieeePKBS84.pdf

Van de Laar, M., West, R. E., Cosma, P., Katwal, D., & Mancigotti, C. (2024). The value of educational microcredentials in open access online education: A doctoral education case. *Open Learning*, *39*(4), 373–386. Advance online publication. DOI: 10.1080/02680513.2022.2072721

Van Hooft, E. A. J., Kammeyer-Mueller, J. D., Wanberg, C. R., Kanfer, R., Basbug, G., & Wan, C. R. (2021). *Job Search and Employment Success: A Quantitative Review and Future Research Agenda. 106*(5), 674–713. DOI: 10.1037/apl0000675.supp

Varoufakis, Y. (2024). *Technofeudalism: what killed capitalism*. Melville House.

Vaswani, A., Shazeer, N., Parmar, N., Uszkoreit, J., Jones, L., Gomez, A. A., Kaiser, Ł., & Polosukhin, I. (2017). Attention is all you need. *Advances in Neural Information Processing Systems*, ●●●, 30.

Verdegem, P. (2022). Dismantling AI capitalism: The commons as an alternative to the power concentration of Big Tech. *AI & Society*. Advance online publication. DOI: 10.1007/s00146-022-01437-8

Vergara, D., Lampropoulos, G., Antón-Sancho, Á., & Fernández-Arias, P. (2024). Impact of artificial intelligence on learning management systems: A bibliometric review. *Multimodal Technologies and Interaction*, *8*(9), 75. DOI: 10.3390/mti8090075

Villalobos, P., Ho, A., Sevilla, J., Besiroglu, T., Heim, L., & Hobbhahn, M. (2024). Position: will we run out of data? Limits of LLM scaling based on human-generated data. In *Proceedings of the 41st International Conference on Machine Learning 235* (49523–49544).

Villarica, M. (2023). The Effectiveness of Flipped Classrooms in Distance Education During the Covid-19 Pandemic. *International Journal of Computing Sciences Research*, *7*, 2296–2314. DOI: 10.25147/ijcsr.2017.001.1.160

Volosevici, D. (2024). AI use in the workplace: Some legal risks and challenges. *Analele tiin ifice ale Universităţii Alexandru Ioan Cuza din Ia i, seria Ştiinţe Juridice, LXX*(2), 65–77. DOI: 10.47743/jss-2024-70-2-5

Vo, Y., Rickels, H., Welch, C., & Dunbar, S. (2023). Human scoring versus automated scoring for english learners in a statewide evidence-based writing assessment. *Assessing Writing*, *56*, 100719. DOI: 10.1016/j.asw.2023.100719

Vukojičić, M., & Krstić, J. (2023). ChatGPT in programming education: ChatGPT as a programming assistant. *Inspired Teachers'. Voice*, *2023*(1), 7–13.

Vygotsky, L. S. (1978). *Mind in society: The development of higher psychological processes*. Harvard University Press.

Vygotsky, L. S. (1978). *Mind in Society: The Development of Higher Psychological Processes*. Harvard University Press.

Wachira, P. W., Liu, X., & Koc, S. (2024). *Educational assessments in the age of generative AI*. IGI Global Publishing.

Walter, Y. (2024). Embracing the future of Artificial Intelligence in the classroom: The relevance of AI literacy, prompt engineering, and critical thinking in modern education. *International Journal of Educational Technology in Higher Education*, *21*(1), 15. DOI: 10.1186/s41239-024-00448-3

Walther, C. (2024, October 9). *Are we unleashing a treasure chest or pandora's box onto humanity?* https://www.forbes.com/sites/corneliawalther/2024/10/09/are-we-unleashing-a-treasure-chest-or-pandoras-box-onto-humanity/

Walton, D. (2023). *Personalized cognitive tutoring using Davinci-003 API for adaptive question generation and assessment.* CoRR. https://doi.org/DOI: 10.48550/ARXIV.2304.02772

Wang, H., Dang, A., Wu, Z., & Mac, S. 2023. Seeing chatgpt through universities' policies, resources and guidelines. *arXiv preprint arXiv:*2312.05235.

Wang, T., Wu, T., Liu, H., Brown, C., & Chen, Y. (2024). *Generative Co-Learners: Enhancing Cognitive and Social Presence of Students in Asynchronous Learning with Generative AI.* https://arxiv.org/pdf/2410.04365

Wang, K., Chai, C.-S., Liang, J.-C., & Sang, G. (2024). Exploring teachers' behavioural intentions to design artificial intelligence-assisted learning in Chinese K–12 education. *Technology, Pedagogy and Education*, *33*(5), 629–645. DOI: 10.1080/1475939X.2024.2369241

Wang, T., Lund, B. D., Marengo, A., Pagano, A., Mannuru, N. R., Teel, Z. A., & Pange, J. (2023). Exploring the Potential Impact of Artificial Intelligence (AI) on International Students in Higher Education: Generative AI, Chatbots, Analytics, and International Student Success. *Applied Sciences (Basel, Switzerland)*, *13*(11), 6716. DOI: 10.3390/app13116716

Wang, X.-J., & Wang, L.-L. (2024). Co-evolution of opinions and behaviors based on conformity in social networks. *Physics Letters. [Part A]*, *522*, 129753. DOI: 10.1016/j.physleta.2024.129753

Ward, R., Grant, S., Larsen, M. W., & Giovacchini, K. (2024). The Universal Micro-Credential Framework: The Role of Badges, Micro-Credentials, Skills Profiling, and Design Patterns in Developing Interdisciplinary Learning and Assessment Paths for Computing Education. *IEEE Transactions on Education*, *67*(6), 897–906. Advance online publication. DOI: 10.1109/TE.2024.3486016

Warschauer, M. (2003). *Technology and social inclusion: Rethinking the digital divide.* MIT Press., DOI: 10.7551/mitpress/6699.001.0001

Warschauer, M., Tseng, W., Yim, S., Webster, T., Jacob, S., Du, Q., & Tate, T. (2023). The affordances and contradictions of AI-generated text for writers of English as a second or foreign language. *Journal of Second Language Writing*, *62*, 101071. DOI: 10.1016/j.jslw.2023.101071

Weber-Wulff, D., Anohina-Naumeca, A., Bjelobaba, S., Foltýnek, T., Guerrero-Dib, J., Popoola, O., Šigut, P., & Waddington, L. (2023). Testing of detection tools for AI-generated text. *International Journal for Educational Integrity*, *19*(1), 26. DOI: 10.1007/s40979-023-00146-z

Wei, Y., Jiang, Y. H., Liu, J., Qi, C., & Jia, R. (2024). The advancement of personalized learning potentially accelerated by generative AI. *arXiv*, 2412.00691v1

Wei, Y., Pearl, D., Beckman, M., & Passonneau, R. J. (2025). *Concept-based Rubrics Improve LLM Formative Assessment and Data Synthesis*. https://arxiv.org/pdf/2504.03877

Wells, R. (2024, November 5). 71% Of Employers Prefer AI Skills Above Experience In 2024. *Forbes*. https://www.forbes.com/sites/rachelwells/2024/11/05/71-of-employers-prefer-ai-skills-above-experience-in-2024/

Weng, X., Xia, Q., Gu, M., Rajaram, K., & Chiu, T. K. F. (2024). Assessment and learning outcomes for generative AI in higher education: A scoping review on current research status and trends. *Australasian Journal of Educational Technology*, *40*(6), 37–55. DOI: 10.14742/ajet.9540

Werbach, K., & Cornell, N. (2017). Contracts ex machina. *Duke Law Journal*, *67*(2), 313–382. DOI: 10.5040/9781509937059.ch-001

Westfall, C. (2023, January 28). Educators Battle Plagiarism As 89% Of Students Admit To Using OpenAI's ChatGPT For Homework. *Forbes*. https://www.forbes.com/sites/chriswestfall/2023/01/28/educators-battle-plagiarism-as-89-of-students-admit-to-using-open-ais-chatgpt-for-homework/?sh=221930a3750d

Wexell Machado, L. E., & Canese, V. (2024). Métodos de apropiación de la inteligencia artificial en la enseñanza de idiomas y sus consideraciones éticas. *Lengua y Sociedad*, *23*(2), 1021–1045. DOI: 10.15381/lengsoc.v23i2.29268

Whalen, J., Grube, W., Xu, C., & Trust, T. (2024). K-12 educators' reactions and responses to ChatGPT and GenAI during the 2022–2023 school year. *TechTrends*, •••, 1–13. DOI: 10.1007/s11528-024-01028-y

Wiggers, K. (2025, May 22). A safety institute advised against releasing an early version of Anthropic's Claude Opus 4 AI model. *TechCrunch*. https://techcrunch.com/2025/05/22/a-safety-institute-advised-against-releasing-an-early-version-of-anthropics-claude-opus-4-ai-model/

Wiliam, D. (2011). What is assessment for learning? *Studies in Educational Evaluation*, *37*(1), 3–14. DOI: 10.1016/j.stueduc.2011.03.001

Wilkins, A. (2024, July 25). DeepMind AI gets silver medal at International Mathematical Olympiad. *New Scientist*. https://www.newscientist.com/article/2441450-deepmind-ai-gets-silver-medal-at-international-mathematical-olympiad/

William, C. (2022). The constraints-led approach in nursing education is being introduced as a novel viewpoint on skill acquisition. *Journal of Nursing Research and Practice*, *6*(12), 192–193. https://doi.org/DOI. DOI: 10.37532/ Puljnrp. 22.6(12).192-193

Williams, A. (2024). Delivering effective student feedback in higher education: An evaluation of the challenges and best practice. *International Journal of Research in Education and Science*, *10*(2), 473–501. DOI: 10.46328/ijres.3404

Williams, A., & Ingle, E. (2025). Assessment design through co-creation: Student-staff partnership in evaluating the impact of artificial intelligence. *International Journal for Students as Partners*, *9*(1), 1. Advance online publication. DOI: 10.15173/ijsap.v9i1.5802

Williamson, B. (2017). Big Data in Education: The digital future of learning, policy and practice. https://doi.org/DOI: 10.4135/9781529714920

Wisniewski, B., Zierer, K., & Hattie, J. (2020). The power of feedback revisited: A meta-analysis of educational feedback research. *Frontiers in Psychology*, *10*, 3087. Advance online publication. DOI: 10.3389/fpsyg.2019.03087

Wittrock, M. C. (2000). Learning as a generative process. In Segal, J. W., Chapman, S. F., & Glaser, R. (Eds.), *Educational psychology: A century of contributions* (pp. 277–294). Erlbaum.

Wood, D. J., Bruner, J. S., & Ross, G. (1976). The Role of Tutoring in Problem Solving. *Journal of Child Psychology and Psychiatry, and Allied Disciplines*, *17*(2), 89–100. DOI: 10.1111/j.1469-7610.1976.tb00381.x PMID: 932126

Woodley, X., Hernandez, C., Parra, J., & Negash, B. (2017). Celebrating difference: Best practices in culturally responsive teaching online. *TechTrends*, *61*(5), 470–478. DOI: 10.1007/s11528-017-0207-z

Wood, M. A., Mellalieu, S. D., Araújo, D., Woods, C. T., & Davids, K. (2023). Learning to coach: An ecological dynamics perspective. *International Journal of Sports Science & Coaching*, *18*(2), 609–620. DOI: 10.1177/17479541221138680

World Economic Forum. (2025, Jan 14). *How can we bring 2.6 billion people online to bridge the digital divide*? Retrieved from https://www.weforum.org/stories/2024/01/digital-divide-internet-access-online-fwa/

Wu, R., Zong, H., Wu, E., Peng, Z., Zhao, J., Yang, L., Xie, H., & Shen, B. (2024). Exploring the potential of artificial intelligence to enhance the writing of English academic papers by non-native English-speaking medical students - the educational application of ChatGPT. *BMC Medical Education*, *24*(1), 736. Advance online publication. DOI: 10.1186/s12909-024-05738-y

Xianli, W. U., Huchang, L. I. A. O., Tang, M., Ruxandra, G., & Smeureanu, I. (2020). Global trends and characteristics of the publications in economic computation and economic cybernetics studies and research from 1969 to 2020 based on bibliometric analysis. *Economic Computation and Economic Cybernetics Studies and Research*, *54*(4), 23–42. Advance online publication. DOI: 10.24818/18423264/54.4.20.02

Xiao, Y., & Watson, M. (2017). Guidance on conducting a systematic literature review. *Journal of Planning Education and Research*, *39*(1), 93–112. DOI: 10.1177/0739456X17723971

Xu, T., Liu, Y., Jin, Y., Qu, Y., Bai, J., Zhang, W., & Zhou, Y. (2024). From recorded to AI-generated instructional videos: A comparison of learning performance and experience. *British Journal of Educational Technology*, *00*, 1–25. DOI: 10.1111/bjet.13530

Yan, L., Martinez-Maldonado, R., Jin, Y., Echeverria, V., Milesi, M., Fan, J., . . . Gašević, D. (2024). From Data Stories to Dialogues: A Randomised Controlled Trial of Generative AI Agents and Data Storytelling in Enhancing Data Visualisation Comprehension. *arXiv preprint arXiv:2409.11645*. https://arxiv.org/abs/2409.11645

Yang, E., & Beil, C. (2024). Ensuring data privacy in AI/ML implementation. *New Directions for Higher Education*, *2024*(207), 63–78. DOI: 10.1002/he.20509

Yang, Y. (2025). Racial bias in AI-generated images. *AI & Society*. Advance online publication. DOI: 10.1007/s00146-025-02282-1

Yan, L., Greiff, S., & Teuber, Z. ve Gašević, D. (2024). İnsan öğrenmesi için üretken yapay zekanın vaatleri ve zorlukları. *Doğa İnsan Davranışı*, *8*(10), 1839–1850.

Yan, L., Sha, L., Zhao, L., Li, Y., Martinez-Maldonado, R., Chen, G., Li, X., Jin, Y., & Gašević, D. (2024). Practical and ethical challenges of large language models in education: A systematic scoping review. *British Journal of Educational Technology*, *55*(1), 90–112. DOI: 10.1111/bjet.13370

Yao, F., Li, C., Nekipelov, D., Wang, H., & Xu, H. (2024). Human vs. generative AI in content creation competition: symbiosis or conflict? *arXiv preprint arXiv:2402.15467.*

Yaseen, H., Mohammad, A. S., Ashal, N., Abusaimeh, H., Ali, A., & Sharabati, A.-A. A. (2025). The Impact of Adaptive Learning Technologies, Personalized Feedback, and Interactive AI Tools on Student Engagement: The Moderating Role of Digital Literacy. *Sustainability (Basel)*, *17*(3), 1133. DOI: 10.3390/su17031133

Yau, K. W., Chai, C. S., Chiu, T. K., Meng, H., King, I., & Yam, Y. (2023). A phenomenographic approach on teacher conceptions of teaching Artificial Intelligence (AI) in K-12 schools. *Education and Information Technologies*, *28*(1), 1041–1064. DOI: 10.1007/s10639-022-11161-x

Ye, S., Kim, D., Jang, J., Shin, J., & Seo, M. (2022). Guess the Instruction! Flipped Learning Makes Language Models Stronger Zero-Shot Learners. *11th International Conference on Learning Representations, ICLR 2023*. https://arxiv.org/pdf/2210.02969

Yıldızhan-Bora, B. (2024). *Alfa kuşağına atfedilen dört becerinin erken çocukluk dönemi kapsamında araştırılması: Dijital okuryazarlık, problem çözme ve eleştirel düşünme, yaratıcılık, iş birliği* [*An investigation of four skills attributed to Generation Alpha in early childhood: Digital literacy, problem-solving and critical thinking, creativity, collaboration*] (Doctoral dissertation, Bahçeşehir Üniversitesi, Eğitim Bilimleri Enstitüsü). Council of Higher Education Thesis Center. https://tez.yok.gov.tr

Yılmaz Soylu, M., & Akkoyunlu, B. (2020). Bilişötesi Düşünme. D*ijital Teknoloji Aracılı Düşünme Öğretimi Düşünme - Akıl Yürütme Dijital Teknoloji Öğretim Teknolojisi* .DOI: 10.14527/9786257880992.15

Yi, Y. (2021). Establishing the concept of AI literacy. *Jahr – European. Journal of Bioethics*, *12*(2), 2.

Yoon, H. J. (2021). Interactions in EFL argumentative writing: Effects of topic, L1 background, and L2 proficiency on interactional metadiscourse. *Reading and Writing*, *34*(3), 705–725. DOI: 10.1007/s11145-020-10085-7

Yousef, M., Mohamed, K., Medhat, W., Muhammed, E. H., Khoriba, G., & Arafa, T. (2024). BeGrading: large language models for enhanced feedback in programming education. *Neural Comput & Applic.*, 1-14. https://doi.org/DOI: 10.1007/s00521-024-10449-y

Zapata, G. C., Cope, B., Kalantzis, M., Tzirides, A. O., Saini, A. K., Searsmith, D., Whiting, J., Kastania, N. P., Castro, V., Kourkoulou, T., Jones, J. W., & Abrantes da Silva, R. (2025). AI and peer reviews in higher education: Students' multimodal views on benefits, differences and limitations. *Technology, Pedagogy and Education*, •••, 1–19. DOI: 10.1080/1475939X.2025.2480807

Zawacki-Richter, O., Conrad, D., Bozkurt, A., Aydin, C. H., Bedenlier, S., Jung, I., Stöter, J., Veletsianos, G., Blaschke, L. M., Bond, M., Broens, A., Bruhn, E., Dolch, C., Kalz, M., Kerres, M., Kondakci, Y., Marin, V., Mayrberger, K., Müskens, W., & Xiao, J. (2020). Elements of open education: An invitation to future research. *International Review of Research in Open and Distance Learning*, *21*(3), 319–334. DOI: 10.19173/irrodl.v21i3.4659

Zawacki-Richter, O., Marín, V. I., Bond, M., & Gouverneur, F. (2019). Systematic review of research on artificial intelligence applications in higher education – where are the educators? *International Journal of Educational Technology in Higher Education*, *16*(1), 2–27. DOI: 10.1186/s41239-019-0171-0

Zemeckis, R. (1985). *Back to the Future* [Film]. Universal Pictures.

Zemeckis, R. (1989). *Back to the Future Part II* [Film Universal Pictures. Zemeckis, R. (1990). *Back to the Future Part III* [Film]. Universal Pictures.

Zhai, C., Wibowo, S., & Li, L. D. (2024). The effects of over-reliance on AI dialogue systems on students' cognitive abilities: A systematic review. *Smart Learn. Environ.*, *11*(1), 28. DOI: 10.1186/s40561-024-00316-7

Zhai, X. (2024). Transforming teachers' roles and agencies in the era of generative AI: Perceptions, acceptance, knowledge, and practices. *Journal of Science Education and Technology*, 1–11. DOI: 10.1007/s10956-024-10174-0

Zhai, X., & Krajcik, J. (2022). Pseudo AI Bias. *SSRN*. DOI: 10.2139/ssrn.4368917

Zhai, X., & Nehm, R. H. (2023). AI and formative assessment: The train has left the station. *Journal of Research in Science Teaching*, *60*(6), 1390–1398. DOI: 10.1002/tea.21885

Zhang, M., Dilling, A. P., Gondelman, L., Erik, N., Lyngdorf, R., Lindsay, E. D., & Bjerva, J. (2025). *SEFL: Harnessing Large Language Model Agents to Improve Educational Feedback Systems*. https://arxiv.org/pdf/2502.12927

Zhang, L., & Gläscher, J. (2020). A brain network supporting social influences in human decision-making. *Science Advances*, *6*(34), eabb4159. Advance online publication. DOI: 10.1126/sciadv.abb4159 PMID: 32875112

Zhang, Y., Lucas, M., Bem-haja, P., & Pedro, L. (2024). The effect of student acceptance on learning outcomes: AI-generated short videos versus paper materials. *Computers and Education: Artificial Intelligence*, *7*, 100286. DOI: 10.1016/j.caeai.2024.100286

Zhao, J., Chapman, E., & Sabet, P. G. (2024). Generative AI and Educational Assessments: A Systematic Review. *Education Research and Perspectives (Online)*, *51*, 124–155. DOI: 10.70953/ERPv51.2412006

Zhou, E., & Lee, D. (2024). Generative artificial intelligence, human creativity, and art. *PNAS Nexus*, *3*(3), pgae052. DOI: 10.1093/pnasnexus/pgae052 PMID: 38444602

Zhou, H. (2025). Exploring the dynamic teaching-learning relationship in interactive learning environments. *Interactive Learning Environments*, *33*(7), 4363–4393. Advance online publication. DOI: 10.1080/10494820.2025.2462149

Zichermann, G., & Cunningham, C. (2011). *Gamification by Design: Implementing Game Mechanics in Web and Mobile Apps*. O'Reilly Media.

Zuboff, S. (2023). The Age of Surveillance Capitalism. In Koch, D. J., & Will, C. H. (Eds.), *Social Theory Re-Wired* (pp. 203–213). Routledge., DOI: 10.4324/9781003320609-27

Zuo, M., Kong, S., Ma, Y., Hu, Y., & Xiao, M. (2023). The Effects of Using Scaffolding in Online Learning: A Meta-Analysis. *Education Sciences*, *13*(7), 705. DOI: 10.3390/educsci13070705

About the Contributors

Aras Bozkurt is a researcher and faculty member at Anadolu University, Türkiye. With MA and PhD degrees in distance education, Dr. Bozkurt's work focuses on empirical studies in areas such as distance education, online learning, networked learning, and educational technology. He applies critical theories like connectivism, rhizomatic learning, and heutagogy to his research. Dr. Bozkurt is also interested in emerging research paradigms, including social network analysis, sentiment analysis, and data mining. Dr. Bozkurt's studies also cover the integration of artificial intelligence technologies into educational processes in the axis of human-machine interaction. His dedication to advancing the field is reflected in his editorial roles as the Editor-in-Chief of Open Praxis and Asian Journal of Distance Education, as well as his roles as an associate editor for prestigious journals like Higher Education Research and Development, Online Learning, eLearn Magazine, and Computer Applications in Engineering Education.

***

Barış Avcı holds a Ph.D. in Curriculum and Instruction from Anadolu University, Türkiye. His research encompasses curriculum development, teacher education, online education and innovative applications of technology in learning environments, with a particular focus on artificial intelligence in education. Currently, he explores the transformative potential of generative artificial intelligence and its capacity to revolutionize teaching and learning practices.

Nick Baker is currently the Institutional Advisor on AI and a Digital Learning Specialist in the Centre for Teaching and Learning at the University of Windsor, Canada where he has been a faculty member and educational developer since 2009 and spent 12 years as the Director of the Office of Open Learning. An award-winning educator and leader, Nick's research and writing broadly focuses on AI, educational technologies, accessibility, Open Educational Practices, online and digital learning, and educational development. Nick holds undergraduate degrees in Journalism and Geography, Biology (Ecology and conservation), Honours First Class in Wildlife Ecology, and a Graduate Certificate in Tertiary Education from the University of Southern Queensland, Australia. He is pursuing a PhD in Education from the University of Windsor, Canada, where he also teaches courses on educational technologies.

Edgar O. Cardoso, PhD is Professor - Researcher since 2009 on Division of Postgraduate Studies and Research of the Superior School of Commerce and Administration (ESCA) of the National Polytechnic Institute (IPN), Mexico City. In his position conducts research projects focused on the management and development of education in educational programs at senior level. He teaches courses Methodological Seminar I, II, III and Statistics for Educational Research to Master's and Research Seminars I, II and III as well as Research Visits I, II, III and IV to PhD level. Dr. Cardoso earned his doctorate at the IPN. He has a master of science in management and development of education in the ESCA-IPN. His research includes evaluation of educational programs and executive education. He belongs to the National System of Researchers with the level I distinction in the CONACyT of Mexico. He has directed several research projects in the area of educational management. He has conducted thesis addresses at the master's and doctoral level in the educational area.

Simona Eftimie is Associate Professor PhD at the Teacher Training Department from Petroleum-Gas University of Ploiesti. She had received Ph.D in Educational Sciences at University of Bucharest, Romania. She teaches courses at Pedagogy, Curriculum theory and methodology, Online Counselling. She was teacher in national project "Developing new key competences for teachers from Braila and Prahova Counties, expert in international project "Training of teaching staff in scientific and technological field by means of a master program" (countries involved – Romania and Netherlands), researcher in international project Daphne III "Preventing submerged violence" (countries involved – Italy, Romania and Spain).

Wissal El Fougour is a second-year PhD student in the Computer Science and University Educational Engineering research team at the Higher Normal School of Tetouan, Abdelmalek Essaadi University, Morocco. Her research focuses on adaptive formative assessment, exploring how technology and AI-driven feedback can enhance learning outcomes. She is deeply passionate about education, eLearning, and the intersection of technology with pedagogy, aiming to innovate and improve digital learning environments. With an ambitious vision for the future of education, she is dedicated to advancing research in formative assessment, cognitive development, and adaptive learning technologies to empower students and educators alike.

Mohamed Erradi is a higher education teacher, researcher, and trainer specializing in educational engineering, teaching, learning modeling, digital e learning, and lifelong learning. He has extensive experience in engineering training and teaching techniques and works as a resource designer for education and training. Additionally, he serves as the Director of the "Information Sciences and University Educational Engineering" research team. Currently, he is the Head of the Department of Mathematics, Physical Sciences, and Computer Science at the Higher Normal School in Tetouan, Morocco.

Sezin Eşfer is a passionate educator and researcher specialising in Computer Education and Instructional Technology. She holds a Ph.D. from Middle East Technical University (METU) and currently serves on the faculty of the CEIT department at Bahçeşehir University (BAU). Dr. Eşfer's research interests lie in Human Computer Interaction, Open Educational Resources (OER), Artificial Intelligence (AI) in Education, lifelong learning, MOOCs and professional development. She has a prolific research record, contributing over 30 publications, including book chapters, articles, and conference papers. Her deep understanding of educational technology is further bolstered by active participation in MOOC projects and Erasmus initiatives, giving her a global perspective on its application in various learning environments.

William Evans is a lecturer in the Department of Nursing and Health Care Sciences in the Munster Technological University (MTU) Tralee Campus Co Kerry. He graduated with First Class Honours from the Royal College of Surgeons in Ireland (RCSI) holding a Bachelors in Nursing Studies and also holds a Higher Diploma in Sick Children's Nursing from University College Dublin (UCD), a Postgraduate Diploma in Education and a Master's of Science in Advanced Nursing from The University of Ulster. In 2013 he completed a Doctorate in Education in the University of Sheffield. The focus of his research was on how dyslexic identities are socially constructed in nurse education. William is registered as a General Nurse, Sick Children's Nurse and Nurse Tutor with the Nursing and Midwifery Board of Ireland (NMBI). William worked previously in clinical nursing practice in neurosurgery (Beaumont Hospital) and paediatric intensive care (Our Lady's Hospital for Sick Children Crumlin). William is a First Aid, Basic Life Support and Manual and Handling instructor and delivers courses across a number of programs in MTU. He lectures in both undergraduate and post graduate nursing programs specifically on research modules where he coordinates and leads large teams of research supervisors involved in supporting students on their research journey. In addition, he supervises students completing undergraduate and post graduate research dissertations thesis. He has previously been the lead supervisor on successful Masters by Research projects undertaken in MTU. His research interests include systematic review and discourse analysis methodologies, the social construction of disability in health care, professional identity construction, and finally on how artificial intelligence will shape the future of healthcare education. He has published widely in a diverse number of academic journals. In 2023 William was awarded a Senior Fellow in Higher Education from Advanced HE.

Tom Farrelly is a social science lecturer and academic developer with Munster Technological University in Ireland's southwest. His research focuses on Social Research Approaches and Digital Education, with expertise in technology-enhanced learning, VLE usage by lifelong learners, and supporting non-traditional students, including Irish Traveller communities. He's an open access advocate and co-chairs MTU's Human Research Ethics Committee.

Iulia Adelina Ghi ă studied Pedagogy and holds a Ph.D. in Science Education at the University of Bucharest. The thesis is based on the fundamental phenomenon of Nonverbal communication. A means of regaining the state of authenticity. She is an Assistant professor at the Educational Sciences Department within the Faculty of Letters and Sciences of Petroleum-Gas University of Ploiesti, Romania. She trains the students to become professionals in science education. Since 2019, she has held seminars in the following disciplines: Psychology of education, Fundamentals of pedagogy, Psychopedagogy of play, Class management, Class/group management, Intercultural education, Curriculum theory and methodology, Educational Management, History of pedagogy, Project management, Assistance and protection of children's rights, Pedagogy I, Pedagogy II, Time and stress management. Among the published works, we mention: The Dilema of teaching in the Digital Era: Artificial Intelligence - Risks and Challenges for Education, Student Perspective on Teaching and Learning in Real Science and Humanities: A comparative study, The Paradigm of the exam session, a Bermuda Triangle for students, Nonverbal communication. A means of regaining the state of authenticity, Perspectives on Human Nature.

Seval Kemal is a Microsoft-funded doctoral researcher at the Centre for Assessment Research, Policy and Practice in Education (CARPE) at the Institute of Education, Dublin City University. Her work focuses on educational technology, AI in education, assessment, self-assessment, and self-regulated learning. With a strong foundation in English Language Teaching and a passion for innovation in higher education, she is currently exploring how artificial intelligence (AI) can support and enhance student self-assessment practices. Her mixed-methods research investigates the cognitive and emotional dimensions of learner engagement with both traditional and AI-assisted feedback tools. In addition, Seval is studying learners' emotional and physiological responses, such as stress and confidence, through eye-tracking and electrodermal activity. This line of research aims to better understand how these affective states influence students' cognitive engagement and attentional focus during learning. She is dedicated to promoting ethical and evidence-informed approaches to AI integration in education, bridging research and practice to support meaningful, human-centered learning experiences.

Yeşim Nalkesen Akın specialises in educational technologies, teacher education, and language teaching. She currently works as an Instructional Design Consultant and First-Year Experience Programme Coordinator at Özyeğin University. Her academic interests include the integration of artificial intelligence into learning environments, instructional design, multimedia design, and educational psychology. She has worked on the design of professional development programmes, the pedagogical use of educational technologies, and the enhancement of teachers' digital literacy skills. Dr Akın has taught courses on educational technologies and instructional methods at several universities and has built a solid background in teacher training, AI applications in education, and digital material design.

Sefa Emre Öncü has been working at the Open Education Faculty of Anadolu University, Türkiye, since 2011. He completed his master's degree in Higher Education Administration at Eskişehir Osmangazi University and is currently pursuing a PhD in Distance Education. His work focuses on open and distance learning, particularly in learner support and the educational use of generative artificial intelligence. He is actively involved in national and international research projects related to these fields.

Ali Öztüfekçi is an Assistant Professor in the Department of English Language Teaching at Bahçeşehir University (BAU). He has authored articles, book chapters, and a monograph on Bilingualism, Translanguaging, and pre-service teacher training. His ongoing research is centred around multilingual teacher education and multilingual instruction.

Dila Süzan is an English lecturer at the School of Foreign Languages at Gedik University, Istanbul, where she also serves as the Associate Director. She teaches academic and vocational English courses and has extensive experience in curriculum design, educational assessment, and teacher professional development. She is currently pursuing a PhD in Educational Technology at Bahçeşehir University, focusing on the integration of artificial intelligence in language education and instructional feedback processes. Her research interests include AI-supported feedback systems, instructional design for digital environments, AI literacy, gamification in language learning, and assessment practices in higher education. She has been involved in various national and international academic projects and has presented at conferences on topics related to educational technology, language teaching, and AI integration in learning environments. In addition to her academic work, she actively contributes to institutional development through accreditation projects and the design of teacher training frameworks. Her recent research explores the pedagogical and ethical implications of AI-assisted learning tools in English as a Foreign Language (EFL) contexts.

Hasan Ucar is a researcher in the Learning Technologies Research and Development Unit at Faculty of Open Education, Anadolu University. Ucar received his Ph.D. and master's degree in Distance Education from Anadolu University, Turkey. His research focuses on designing and integrating motivational strategies to improve learner motivation in online learning environments. Additional areas of research include distance learning and teaching, online learning, instructional design/ technology, and online academic procrastination.

Dana Volosevici is a lawyer and professor at the Petroleum-Gas University of Ploie ti. Her research focuses on achieving a balance between organizations and their employees by promoting the values of equality and sustainability. Within this framework, Dana has published extensively on combating discrimination and harassment and fostering an organizational environment that champions equal opportunities. In the field of industrial relations, she has examined the actions and negotiated agreements through which organizations—whether acting independently or under the influence of social partners and collective bargaining—work to create balanced and sustainable working environments. Her research also focuses on the protection of personal data and the safeguarding of privacy rights, both in traditional employment settings and in emerging forms of work. In addition, Dana is deeply engaged in exploring the impact of artificial intelligence on employment relationships, organizational decision-making, and education, particularly the legal and ethical challenges AI raises in academic environments. She highlights the growing need to integrate data protection principles and critical AI literacy into educational systems, ensuring that future professionals are equipped to navigate a digitally transformed society.

Betül Yıldızhan Bora holds a PhD in educational technologies. She completed her undergraduate and postgraduate studies in the field of educational sciences. She is currently a faculty member in the Child Care and Youth Services Programme at the Vocational School of Health Services at Bingöl University. During the 2025–2026 academic year, she is serving as a visiting faculty member in the Department of Educational Sciences, Division of Educational Technologies, at the Dicle University. Her academic interests include instructional design, artificial intelligence applications, early childhood education, digital literacy, and learning theories. Her research focuses on the integration of educational technologies into learning processes and the development of digital literacy in early childhood. Dr Yıldızhan Bora has held academic positions at several universities over the years. Throughout her career, she has delivered training to university staff on integrating AI into educational processes. She has also taken on a number of administrative roles, including department and programme head, and has participated actively in both national and international academic events.

Index

A

B

C

D

E

F

G

H

I

L

M

O

P

R

S

T

W

Z

www.ingramcontent.com/pod-product-compliance
Ingram Content Group UK Ltd.
Pitfield, Milton Keynes, MK11 3LW, UK
UKHW050843101026
15624UKWH00018B/480

9 798337 375793